Reflections on Anthropology

A Four-Field Reader

Reflections on Anthropology
A FOUR-FIELD READER

edited by

Katherine A. Dettwyler
Vaughn M. Bryant
Texas A&M University

Boston   Burr Ridge, IL   Dubuque, IA   Madison, WI   New York   San Francisco   St. Louis
Bangkok   Bogotá   Caracas   Kuala Lumpur   Lisbon   London   Madrid   Mexico City
Milan   Montreal   New Delhi   Santiago   Seoul   Singapore   Sydney   Taipei   Toronto

Higher Education

REFLECTIONS ON ANTHROPOLOGY: A FOUR-FIELD READER

Published by McGraw-Hill, a business unit of The McGraw-Hill Companies, Inc., 1221 Avenue of the Americas, New York, NY, 10020.

Some ancillaries, including electronic and print components, may not be available to customers outside the United States.

This book is printed on acid-free paper.

1 2 3 4 5 6 7 8 9 0 FGR/FGR 0 9 8 7 6 5 4 3

ISBN 0-07-248598-1

Publisher: *Phillip A. Butcher*
Sponsoring editor: *Kevin Witt*
Developmental editor: *Pamela Gordon*
Senior marketing manager: *Daniel M. Loch*
Media producer: *Shannon Gattens*
Lead project manager: *Susan Trentacosti*
Production supervisor: *Carol A. Bielski*
Designer: *Mary E. Kazak*
Supplement producer: *Kathleen Boylan*
Permissions: *Marty Granahan*
Cover design: *Mary E. Kazak*
Cover photo: *Sanandan Sudhi*
Typeface: *10.5/12 Times Roman*
Compositor: *Carlisle Communications, Ltd.*
Printer: *Quebecor World Fairfield Inc.*

Library of Congress Cataloging-in-Publication Data

Reflections on anthropology : a four-field reader / edited by Katherine A. Dettwyler and
    Vaughn M. Bryant.
    p. cm.
    ISBN 0-07-248598-1 (softcover : alk. paper)
    1. Anthropology. 2. Physical anthropology. 3. Anthropological ethics. I. Dettwyler,
Katherine A. II. Bryant, Vaughn M.
GN25.R44 2004
301—dc22

                                                                2003059271

www.mhhe.com

Dedication

For my children: Miranda Hillary Dettwyler, Peter Hunter Dettwyler, and Alexander Logan Wolfgang Dettwyler, and for my all-time favorite students: Kristal Cain, Robbin Dearman, Kimery Duda, Sumati Ganeshan, Bowie Hogg, Elizabeth Miller, Edgar Nunnelly, Elaine Peacock, Joe Powell, Traci Stephens, and Cassady Yoder

–KAD

For Carol, my loving wife, and for my faithful companions, Angus and Heather

–VMB

Dedication

Contents

CHAPTER 9
HUMAN DIVERSITY AND "RACE" 114

CHAPTER 10
THE FIRST FARMERS 129

CHAPTER 11
THE FIRST CITIES AND STATES 147

CHAPTER 12
ETHICS AND METHODS IN CULTURAL ANTHROPOLOGY 166

CHAPTER 13
CULTURE 180

CHAPTER 20
GENDER   269

CHAPTER 21
RELIGION   289

CHAPTER 22
THE ARTS   308

CHAPTER 23
THE MODERN WORLD SYSTEM   316

CHAPTER 24
COLONIALISM AND DEVELOPMENT   322

CHAPTER 25
CULTURAL EXCHANGE AND SURVIVAL   331

Preface

THE STORY OF THE BOOK

Years ago, when we each began teaching introductory, four-field anthropology, we often made copies of interesting and important articles related to the factual materials presented in our chosen textbooks. We would hand these readings out in small classes or put copies on library reserve for the larger classes. Occasionally, we even placed copies in folders on a chair outside our office where students could sit and read them. These techniques don't seem to work as well today as they did back then.

So one of us (Vaughn Bryant) began working with McGraw-Hill publishers more than a decade ago in an effort to produce a useful four-field reader that would complement the chapters in Conrad Kottak's textbook, *Anthropology.* That first reader was called *Through the Looking Glass: Readings in General Anthropology,* and it was co-edited first by David Carlson and later by Lee Cronk. *Through the Looking Glass* emphasized the four-field approach and used a pattern of matching selected readings to the chapters in Kottak's textbook. After the printing of the second edition in that series, we noticed that a growing list of professors were using the reader because of its broad-based approach to all four major fields within anthropology, even though they were not necessarily using the Kottak textbook.

When we came to revise *Through the Looking Glass* for a new edition, we realized that the broader list of adopters was leading us to make significant changes to the text, changes that went beyond the bounds of a regular revision. We decided instead to review the entire book plan and create the new first edition reader, which you have in front of you, *Reflections on Anthropology: A Four-Field Reader.*

THE OBJECTIVE AND APPROACH

Reflections on Anthropology maintains many of the strengths that were in *Through the Looking Glass* but it has added many new and exciting features. First and foremost, *Reflections on Anthropology* continues with the goal of providing a balanced presentation of the four fields of anthropology. While there are many readers that cover one or two of the fields well, our text is one of the very few that is constructed with coverage of all four fields of anthropology as its goal.

Second, we designed this reader to be used as a complement to any standard introductory textbook in general four-field anthropology. Since many of the standard texts in the field follow a similar organization, we have continued with the original organizational plan of matching articles with the chapters in the latest edition of Kottak's textbook, *Anthropology*. However, with the understanding that many professors might wish to use this reader to complement other main texts, we have included a correlation chart at the front of the text, which suggests ways that articles in our reader can be assigned to students who are using one of the other textbooks.

Reflections on Anthropology contains many varied and exciting articles. We have found that professors want to use a supplemental collection of readings that will take introductory students on interesting journeys, beyond the factual data and jargon found in most basic textbooks. Thus, we have chosen articles that focus on topics not usually covered in depth in general textbooks. We strove to include interesting selections that will motivate and capture a student's interest in anthropology. To show students the up-to-date and relevant nature of the field, more than one-half of the articles are very current and reflect sources that were published between 2000 and 2003. As well, we have included many interesting articles on controversial topics to help students see familiar topics from new and different perspectives. Basic textbooks can rarely achieve this goal, but brief articles collected in a supplemental reader often can.

We have worked diligently to select the present collection of articles because they are very readable and should be easy for freshman students to understand. By intent, we have avoided articles that contain the types of scientific jargon often found in scholarly articles printed in major anthropological journals.

Above all, through our selected articles, we have tried to emphasize the important ways that anthropology can help each person understand his/her heritage, the importance of being a member of a human culture, and how each human culture is unique and yet similar to all others. Most importantly, we hope that through reading these articles each student will learn to appreciate his or her own uniqueness, understand how others see us, and gain new perspectives about other cultures that will promote compassion and understanding.

Some of our chapters contain only one reading, while others have as many as three selections. Our choices are based on several criteria. In some cases, we felt that a single but somewhat longer reading was sufficient. For other chapters, we have included two or three shorter readings that cover several topics in less detail. Overall, we have limited the total number of readings to 43, from which professors may wish to select some or all as assigned readings.

THE PEDAGOGY

Reflections on Anthropology offers students and professors a number of useful tools for understanding and exploring the articles. Each chapter opens with an introductory summary that ties the articles to the main text chapter and offers background and context for understanding the articles. Discussion questions follow the reading. Students can look at these ahead of time if they wish, or wait until after reading the article to look at them. These questions can be used by professors as lead-ins to discussion sections or as guidelines for group projects or writing assignments. Additional Resources can be found at the end of each of the chapters for students who are interested in further research.

THE SUPPLEMENTS

As a full-service publisher of quality educational products, McGraw-Hill does much more than just sell textbooks. They create and publish an extensive array of supplements for students and instructors. *Reflections on Anthropology* includes a comprehensive supplements package. Orders of new (versus used) textbooks help to defray the cost of developing such supplements, which is substantial. Please consult your local McGraw-Hill representative for more information on any of the supplements.

The Instructor's Resource CD-ROM—To assist the instructor and facilitate using *Reflections on Anthropology* as a supplementary reader, we have prepared an Instructor's Resource CD-ROM containing a guide to using the reader and a test bank. We have created a variety of multiple-choice and essay questions that cover each of the selections in the reader.

The Student Website—The website for the book is available at www.mhhe.com/dettwyler and contains updated links to additional resources for each topic.

ACKNOWLEDGMENTS

Both of us wish to thank the reviewers who helped with this project. Some of them reviewed the second edition of *Through the Looking Glass* and made suggestions, while others reviewed the proposed table of contents for *Reflections on Anthropology* and made suggestions. We appreciate their time and efforts, even if we did not always take their advice. The reviewers were:

Amber Bennett (*Virginia Commonwealth University*)

Philip de Barros (*Palomar College*)

Thomas Collins (*University of Memphis*)

Nancy Gonlin (*Bellevue Community College*)

Mathew Kapell (*University of Michigan, Dearborn*)

Adrian Rapp (*North Harris College*)

Alison Rautman (*Michigan State University*)

Eugenia Shanklin (*The College of New Jersey*)

Kathy Dettwyler also wishes to thank the following people for recommending articles: Steven Dettwyler, Luke Eric Lassiter, Karen Rosenberg, and Lori Wright. I want to thank all of the authors and publishers who gave us permission to reprint their articles, especially David Brooks, for his brilliant essay "Patio Man." In addition, I want to thank my family and friends, and my co-workers at the American Philosophical Association for their help and understanding during my work on this project.

Vaughn Bryant wishes to thank particularly his former co-editors, David L. Carlson and Lee Cronk, and the Anthropology Department at Texas A&M University.

In closing, both of us want to thank you for considering this reader. We also ask for your help. We welcome your comments and recommendations—please email us with your feedback.

Katherine A. Dettwyler (kadettwyler@hotmail.com)

Vaughn M. Bryant (vbryant@neo.tamu.edu)

About the Editors

KATHERINE A. DETTWYLER is a biocultural anthropologist. She earned her MA (1981) and Ph.D. (1985) in Anthropology from Indiana University, Bloomington. She taught for two years at the University of Southern Mississippi in Hattiesburg (1985–1987) and for 13 years at Texas A&M University in College Station (1987–2000). She is currently an Adjunct Associate Professor at Texas A&M. Her research focuses on breastfeeding and weaning from cross-cultural and evolutionary perspectives and includes field research in Mali. Her book *Dancing Skeletons: Life and Death in West Africa* was awarded the 1995 Margaret Mead Award from the American Anthropological Association and the Society for Applied Anthropology. Her co-edited volume *Breastfeeding: Biocultural Perspectives* is a best-seller among lactation consultants. She is a frequent speaker at lactation/breastfeeding conferences and universities around the country. Her current research focuses on women and children in the United States who breastfeed longer than three years. She has always enjoyed teaching four-field introductory anthropology to college freshmen. She currently lives in Delaware with her husband, three children, two dogs, and three cats and divides her time between research, publishing, lecturing, and working for the American Philosophical Association.

VAUGHN M. BRYANT is a Professor of Anthropology and Director of the Center for Ecological Archaeology at Texas A&M University. After receiving his doctorate from the University of Texas at Austin in 1969, he taught at Washington State University before joining the newly created Department of Sociology and Anthropology at Texas A&M University in 1971. As the first anthropologist at Texas A&M, he was the first chairperson and helped build a separate doctoral-granting department of anthropology. He enjoys teaching and consistently teaches both introductory four-field anthropology and graduate courses each semester. Dr. Bryant is a trained anthropologist and botanist who is known for his research in paleoethnobotany (the study of how ancient humans used plants), pollen analysis, and prehistoric diet analysis. During the 1980s and 1990s, Dr. Bryant edited a book on fossil pollen research in North America, completed the editing of the first and second editions of *Through the Looking Glass,* joint-authored an atlas of the modern pollen flora of the Southeastern United States, and finished editing a book on techniques used in pollen sampling and analysis. Dr. Bryant is a frequent guest on television programs and has appeared on network programs including "The Today Show," "1-2-3 Contact" (produced by the Children's Television Workshop in New York City), CNN, BBC, Discovery Channel, FOX-Network News, and the quiz program "To Tell the Truth." Dr. Bryant also writes for the popular press and his own articles, or articles about his research, have appeared in many U.S. magazines, including *People, Reader's Digest, Popular Science, Biblical Archaeology, Dig, Science Digest, Scientific American, Seventeen, Forbes, The National Geographic Magazine,* and *National Geographic World.* International magazines featuring his research include *Colours, Der Spiegel, The World and I,* and *Geowissen Nahrung & Gesundheit.* Dr. Bryant lives in College Station, Texas, where he teaches, continues his research, and spends time with his wife, three children, six grandchildren, and two Yorkshire Terriers.

Correlation with Major Textbooks

Reflections on Anthropology: A Four-Field Reader is designed so that it can be used to accompany any introductory anthropology text. The chapter arrangement correlates directly with Kottak's *Anthropology,* tenth edition (McGraw-Hill, 2004). The table below suggests appropriate readings for the chapters in Kottak and other major textbooks. The textbooks we considered are:

Ember, *Anthropology,* tenth edition (PH, 2002)

Ember, *Anthropology: A Brief Introduction,* fifth edition (PH, 2002)

Haviland, *Anthropology,* tenth edition (Wadsworth, 2003)

Kottak, *Anthropology,* tenth edition (MH 2003)

Park, *Introducing Anthropology,* second edition (MH 2003)

Schultz, *Anthropology,* third edition (MH, 2001)

Scupin, *Anthropology: A Global Perspective,* fourth edition (PH, 2001)

Reflections	Ember	Ember—BI	Haviland	Kottak	Park	Schultz	Scupin
Chapter 1							
Article 1	1	1	1	1	0	1	1
Chapter 2							
Article 2	14	2	16	2	10	24	24
Article 3	14	16	20	2	2	21	24
Chapter 3							
Article 4	2	2	2	3	10	7	2
Article 5	2	2	2	3	10	7	2
Chapter 4							
Article 6	3	3	3	4	3	3	3
Article 7	3	3	3	4	3	2	3

Reflections	Ember	Ember—BI	Haviland	Kottak	Park	Schultz	Scupin
Chapter 5							
Article 8	4	4	4	5	4	4	4
Article 9	4	4	4	5	4	4	4
Chapter 6							
Article 10	5	4	5	6	4	5	4
Chapter 7							
Article 11	6	5	6	7	5	6	5
Article 12	6	5	8	7	5	6	5
Chapter 8							
Article 13	7	6	7	8	6	5	7
Article 14	8	7	9	8	5	5	7
Chapter 9							
Article 15	12	9	13	9	14	12	6
Article 16	12	9	13	9	14	12	6
Chapter 10							
Article 17	10	8	11	10	8	8	8
Article 18	10	8	11	10	8	8	8
Article 19	10	8	10	10	8	8	8
Chapter 11							
Article 20	11	8	12	11	13	9	9
Chapter 12							
Article 21	16	12	20	12	2	10	14
Article 22	22	18	18	12	2	14	14
Chapter 13							
Article 23	13	10	14	13	15	15	12
Article 24	13	10	14	13	13	10	12
Chapter 14							
Article 25	18	14	16	14	15	22	21
Article 26	18	14	17	14	15	18	22
Chapter 15							
Article 27	15	11	15	15	11	13	12
Article 28	15	11	15	15	11	13	12
Chapter 16							
Article 29	17	13	17	16	8	18	17
Article 30	17	13	17	16	8	18	15

Reflections on Anthropology

A Four-Field Reader

CHAPTER 1

What Is Anthropology?

 1. TRANSFORMING THE CULTURE OF INTOLERANCE, by Mark
Nathan Cohen, *Culture of Intolerance: Chauvinism, Class, and Racism in the United
States.* New Haven, CT: Yale University Press, 1998, pp. 293–312.

The Bell Curve, *a book by Richard J. Herrnstein and Charles Murray, was published in 1994. This book claimed that human "races" are distinct entities, and that
members of different "races" have different, genetically based capacities for cognitive thought (intelligence) and accomplishments. The book was deservedly controversial, and sparked a number of scholarly replies aimed at countering its lies,
misstatements, and faulty conclusions.*

The first reading in this collection is the final chapter from one of these books,
Culture of Intolerance, *by Mark Nathan Cohen. Dr. Cohen is a professor of anthropology at the State University of New York in Plattsburgh. In this chapter, Cohen
sums up the current state of cultural intolerance and social stratification in the
United States, explains the cultural roots (and uses) of in-group/out-group thinking,
and discusses ways in which people can transform the culture of intolerance that
they were taught as part of their cultural heritage.*

*One of the main goals of an introductory anthropology course is to help students
understand the major role that learned cultural beliefs play in shaping the student's
world, and how other people's cultural beliefs shape their worlds, in turn. Another major goal is to help students understand the basics of human biological variation.
"Races" of different humans do not exist, and yet the idea of distinct races, with different talents and abilities, is a powerful one in U.S. culture. Likewise, the United States
is a long way from being a meritocracy—a system in which people are judged solely on
their talents and abilities—yet the idea of meritocracy is a powerful one in U.S. culture.
The idea is so powerful that those who benefit in our current culture from the automatic
advantages that come with being of European ancestry, male, able-bodied, and rich,*

often believe that it is their own talents and abilities that are responsible for their good fortune. As you read this selection, pay attention to your reactions. Does it ring true? Does it make you frustrated? Does it make you angry? Why?

It has become commonplace for some politicians and even some scholars to express concern that the United States is heading toward a future of extreme social stratification. They foresee increasing class distinctions involving a growing economic, social, and political gap between the rich and the poor and more poverty and hardship for those at the bottom of the social ladder, inevitably accompanied by increasing tension between groups and between "races." But much of that stratification has already occurred. As I have pointed out, the wealthiest Americans already enjoy property and incomes that are thousands of times larger than even those with moderate salaries can earn or amass and millions of times what the poor can earn or save. This disparity is a major factor in contemporary social strains. In particular, tensions between the lower and middle classes result from the fact that they are fighting for shares of a very small portion of the economic pie.

More important, these gloomy predictions of the future misstate the causes of the trend toward increasing stratification. In *The Bell Curve,* Richard J. Herrnstein and Charles Murray suggest that it will happen because natural, genetic superiority (primarily within the European "race" and the Asian "race") will rise inexorably to the top now that we have supposedly removed the barriers to the recognition of natural merit. More liberal scenarios bemoan the discrimination that still exists, the effects of growing up in poverty, and the weaknesses in our educational system, including the lack of high-tech education for American workers—all of which are real enough.

But both explanations miss the point badly. **The trend will occur—has occurred—because our arbitrary and very narrow system of economic, social, and political assumptions makes it inevitable.** It will happen also because too many people are happy to have others excluded from the pursuit of success. It will happen because, despite professed ideals, there is too little commitment to equal opportunity and racial justice and the well-being of all of our residents. Too few people are willing to sacrifice even a little personal freedom and privilege to help bring about change for the better. The reality and the ideal in American culture are very far apart.

It will happen because society does not demand that wealth be shared or used for collective purposes, even though society itself generates, protects, and preserves that wealth. No private individual, no matter how "intelligent," could generate or preserve such wealth without society's massive assistance. The prediction will come true also because society, led by the wealthy and the money managers, has decided that only an extremely narrow range of human skills, those producing immediate profits in dollars in private hands, are worthy of reward. It will come true as a result of all the contemporary cost cutting and downsizing, outsourcing, contracting in, contracting out to people who will work for less and without benefits or job security—all to increase "efficiency" in the midst of large profits and enormous salaries for top executives. We are rapidly and purposely building the lower class. It will happen as a result of "getting government off our backs"—reducing government services, eliminating funding for the arts, schools, and social services, and so forth, all of which employ real people in addition to enriching our lives. Eliminating those services not only reduces the quality of life for all, it eliminates middle-level skilled jobs. It forces people who have chosen to serve human needs other than profit into menial jobs or unemployment. Other socially productive career choices become impossible. There is a great deal of talk about merit and meritocracy without the realization that ever narrower, increasingly arbitrary limits are being set on the kinds of merit that are rewarded (not to mention that most of us have only limited ability to judge actual merit as opposed to a candidate's preexisting ties or membership in a favored group). At the moment, the definition of rewardable merit leaves out an enormous number of skills and ignores an enormous number of tasks that need to be done in order to improve the quality of our lives—tasks that involve caring for and educating people, generating knowledge, promoting beauty, caring for the environment, ensuring the health and welfare of others, and improving the state of our communities. Many of those tasks are not being carried out now, and increasingly they will not be carried out in the future. But it will not be because "they can't be done" or because "there is no money for that," but because the society, despite its wealth, chooses not to see the needs, pay the costs, or reward the skills.

"It can't be done" in modern parlance usually means that no private company will undertake it because it provides no immediate, private, dollar profit. Or it means that no politician can see an angle of personal advantage, as if those things were synonymous with real need and real potential. "There is no money for that" usually means that there is no money in a particular narrow and arbitrarily defined budget category. Health, education, human needs, and the environment must compete for funds, but for the most part military spending does not (even "defense" spending grotesquely in excess of any conceivable need). Projections for the future suggest that the balance between the military and nonmilitary budgets will get worse.

To say that there is no money for a project also carries with it the unspoken assumption that it is not possible to reevaluate our tax strategy to tap the enormous private wealth—more than the rest of us have put together—that is in the hands of a relative few. Our society has great natural and capital resources; it has a near-infinite range of human and environmental needs, and it has a huge number of people who are capable of addressing at least some of those needs. Jobs that need doing have people waiting in vain to do them. If the society can't use its wealth to employ people to take care of those needs, something is wrong with our assumptions, not our capabilities. Societies with far fewer resources (societies that we dismiss as "primitive") have managed to provide meaningful roles and economic support for all their people and managed to keep them housed and reasonably well-nourished without destroying the environment. If they can, why can't we?

If members of minority groups are left behind, now and in the future, it will not be because they lack capabilities or intelligence; it will be because too many people with wealth and power are determined to leave them out. It will be because their very real skills (except in narrow channels like sports or music) are not recognized or cultivated and they are not provided with genuinely equal access to education, training, and employment or allowed to live in circumstances that encourage participation rather than withdrawal. At the moment minorities are being left behind as a matter of fairly deliberate policy, not inferiority. They are being left behind as a matter of age-old hatreds but also as a matter of ongoing affirmative action for white male Americans who fear that others will take their jobs. White males fear that they will be left out of what they perceive to be an ever decreasing economic pie unless they maintain their social advantage. It is assumed that any gain minorities make must come from fragile gains of lower-class and lower-middle-class white men and that any assistance given to minorities must come from those who are their most immediate competition.

The whites are right to fear that they, too, may soon be left out, and they are right to resent the assumption that benefits for minorities must come primarily at the expense of their jobs. But the minorities are not their enemies, and the danger of being left out is not because of minority competition. Nor is the pie really shrinking—the only thing that is shrinking is the portion of the pie shared by the bottom 90 percent of the population. Blacks do not need to be pitted against whites, and welfare recipients need not be pitted against the working poor, unless we assume that there must be very narrow artificial limits on opportunities and the wealth available to all.

If the gap between our society and the Third World continues to widen, it will not be because the people in those areas are naturally inferior or because their cultural systems are inferior or natural resources are in short supply. To a large extent it will reflect those countries' own political and economic inequalities that divert wealth from human needs. But, too often, it will be because of a colonial legacy and a postcolonial structure that continue to siphon off wealth while demanding the repayment of debts—incurred largely to remake those countries in the image demanded by the colonizers. When the colonial powers gave those areas back their "independence," they too often gave them back their social problems, exacerbated rather than solved by economic distortions and other problems resulting from colonialism; but they forgot to return their natural resources or sources of productive wealth, or they left such a burden of debt or permitted the wealth to be concentrated in so few hands (while proclaiming democracy) that the wealth cannot be used for social purposes. Too often independence was given to small cadres of people willing to play along with colonial desires in order to enhance their own wealth rather than finding solutions to their country's problems. Such willingness to accede to the West, far more than any theoretical commitment to freedom or democracy, is the reason for the American government's continuing approval and support of some regimes rather than others.

Sources of Intolerance

People of different cultures face somewhat different problems and, having their own values, they sometimes find different solutions to common problems. No culture has a monopoly on good solutions. The cultures of the world exhibit enormous behavioral variation, which has the capacity to enrich our lives, protect our common future, and increase the range of possible solutions to the vast array of human problems. In the long run, cultural variation, like genetic variation, is a major guarantee of the future success of the species. We should celebrate it and reinforce it, not denigrate it.

Intolerance and racism don't result from the genetic inadequacy of some people or even from biological differences between groups of people, except that the few visible differences provide an easy target for human tensions. Nor do they stem from other people's cultural inadequacy. They do, however, stem in large part from the nature of cultural systems and the cultural filters through which human beings view the world and one another. Much of the tension we see between populations attempting to live together results from misunderstanding of cultural differences and misinterpretation of their significance. People seem unable to comprehend other peoples' behavior—or even to perceive and measure it accurately when it violates the standard categories and expectations of their own culture. We fail to recognize that most problems can be approached in more than one way. People on all sides are unable to recognize what is arbitrary and conventional in their own behaviors and beliefs. Cultures not only blind their members to alternatives but also actively foster chauvinism and intolerance as a way of reinforcing group identity. In the ancient world, in which each group was economically independent and relatively homogeneous—when societies and cultures had the same boundaries, faced only a limited number of neighbors, and had only limited weapons— such chauvinism may have been valuable. In the modern world of multicultural states, interdependence, rapid transportation, international communication, and weapons of mass destruction, such chauvinism is extremely dangerous.

American culture (like most) makes it difficult to recognize the value of others. There is a "natural" but irrational tendency to assume that our own culture is superior, not just in particular areas or for particular purposes where it may actually, if temporarily, excel, but in any and all ways. Intolerance is reinforced by a lack of positive exposure to, or education about, other people and their cultures, a lack that in turn reflects the very narrow limits of our system of education. "World" and American history are too often taught without regard for the successes and contributions of others, including minorities, and with a blinding disregard for the errors and shortcomings among our own very real successes.

Intolerance also results from the fact that many Americans, like members of other cultures, have a dangerous and anachronistic need to distinguish themselves from others as the chosen people with a manifest destiny. Our intolerance results from failure to perceive that there are alternative ways of doing things, alternative valid sets of beliefs and goals, and from the assumption that our culture is naturally superior to all others.

Intolerance results from the strong need felt by people subject to discrimination to define themselves as different and to defend themselves against the loss of identity that threatens all colonized peoples. Many of the distinctive behaviors of American minorities, particularly those that are "captives" or involuntary minorities, represent reactions to intolerance and hatred. Similarly, the nativist cultural revitalization movements—revolutions against modernization and Westernization which are often explicitly anti-American—occurring in recent years in many countries, including Iran and Turkey, are in part a reaction to American intolerance vis-à-vis other world cultures. These movements reject the idea that people must become Westernized or even Americanized in order to share the fruits of the modern world—or even if they don't care to share them. They resent the fact that so much of the space and wealth of their own countries is structured to serve Western needs. The movements also reflect the realization of a significant portion of the populations of those countries that no matter how "Western" they become, Western powers are not going to allow them full and equal access to the world's riches or even to world citizenship. The policy of the United States—to counter such resistance with coercion—confuses cause and effect and makes the problems worse. Reducing intolerance and permitting people the freedom to enjoy their own culture along with real access to the benefits of the world system will reduce the resistance.

Of course, intolerance and resistance are reciprocal. To some extent minorities would be more accepted into the mainstream if they expressed less hostility or were less determined to be separate and different. Similarly, it would be easier for many Americans to tolerate and appreciate Third World populations if these peoples expressed less hostility toward the United States. Resistance, hostility, and intolerance feed each other. But we can't reasonably expect the poor of the world who possess the least and have the greatest cause for fear and anger to initiate better relations; those in power have to start the trend. They have to "prime the pump"—and allow a reasonable period of time, perhaps several **generations,** for the priming to produce results.

Intolerance grows out of the need to find scapegoats. No cognitive system, no system of values, including our own, produces all the gratification everyone might wish. But culture demands that we not lose faith in the rules or the system itself. So we find reasons why the rules didn't work in a particular case, places to put the blame—on luck or witches, or, often, on other people, women or blacks or homosexuals or Jews, or, more recently, on Iraqis or Iranians. Scapegoats are safety valves for the cultural system against the pressure of disappointment. And, of course, leaders who have a particular stake in maintaining the status quo and avoiding an explosion of discontent have a particular interest in deflecting blame, so they encourage the pursuit of scapegoats or identify scapegoats to justify their own initiatives. Going to war helps relieve social tensions at home. (We have reached the stage in the United States where radio and television commentators can discuss—in matter-of-fact-tones—the possibility or even probability that a certain war was started at least in part to get a particular president reelected, to boost his popularity, or to prop up his administration.)

Intolerance increases because our leaders exploit narrow self-interests to play groups off against each other rather than taking the lead in promoting mutual understanding. In the United States leaders have played off whites against Native Americans, African Americans, Chinese, Japanese, Irish, Jews, and Hispanics; north versus south; rural versus urban. They have played off immigrants against those already here; men against women; the middle class against the lower class; and, most recently, the working poor against the welfare poor. They have even discouraged these groups' efforts to coexist and work out their differences.

Racism and the resistance of minorities in the United States stem from the fact that our culture and law set arbitrary, legalistic definitions of correct conduct and make interpretations of the law that are often skewed to benefit the powerful, as a substitute for common sense, human decency, good judgment, and good will. The government then enforces the laws unevenly in a manner heavily slanted to serve upper-class interests. The resistance and occasional lawlessness of minorities stems in large part from their accurate perception that the laws do not serve them.

Intolerance also grows out of setting arbitrarily narrow hurdles to full participation in society such as IQ tests and white, male styles of performance and referring to them, very unscientifically, as tests of innate ability and as measures of inherent quality. At the same time, the conduct of white males too often is permitted to fall far below the stated standards and far below what the standards would be if there were open competition for jobs. Members of minority groups accurately perceive the distinction between stated rules and standards and the application of those standards, and, not surprisingly, they resent it.

Intolerance comes from employment practices that favor the in-group, the rich, and the powerful, creating the inequality in performance which is then measured to justify the status quo. Intolerance thrives because it acts as affirmative action for the group in power; limiting competition and promoting the educational and career chances of people in the mainstream. The need for government-sanctioned affirmative action results not primarily from the legacy of slavery or past discrimination, but from the narrow monopoly of opportunity that these conditions created and still maintain.

Intolerance also grows out of guilt, as Albert Memmi has said. If one believes that enslaving other human beings or treating them unfairly is intolerable, but slaves or poor people are needed to work plantations or menial jobs, one finds people who can be defined as not quite human to be enslaved or demeaned—and then one proceeds to make them appear (and even become) as inhuman as possible. If one is a European (or any other) colonizer in Africa or elsewhere and has absorbed democratic principles from a European education or any other, how does one explain one's automatic privilege as a European in the colony except by defining the natives as inherently inferior or even subhuman? And if one is a white American man whose success has been built on such exploitation (or merely on the exclusion of women and minorities), how does one justify one's privilege except by racism, sexism, and the results of IQ tests, which appear to prove what people "know in their hearts" must be true—that other people really are inferior?

Intolerance results from the fact that every "interracial" encounter in American society carries with it the fear and tension of previous encounters, real and imagined. It's hard to find a member of the "other" group ready to meet you as an individual and potential friend, so the problem is self-perpetuating. Part of the solution is to put people in positions where they can get to know each other as people.

All societies, and particularly all civilizations—very large, complex organizations of heterogeneous groups of people, divided into social classes and held together by power—generate or have generated many of these same tensions. But certain American cultural beliefs compound the problem. Intolerance resides not just in individuals or political pressures but in the fabric of American culture, that structure that is instilled in us so early in our lives. Intolerance results from adhering to an arbitrary cultural code we are unwilling even to think about, much less to question. We live in a society whose conventional cultural rules actively create intolerance. Conventional racial beliefs are obviously part of the problem, but I am specifically referring to cultural ways of thinking that lie at the very core of our society—which few people associate with "race." For example, we insist that things and people must be ranked in a linear order. There has to be a top and a bottom, a winner and a loser, even though most human processes do not have such zero-sum outcomes. We have to act and be measured as individuals, although that is not really the way most human processes operate, either. We insist that it is our manifest destiny to race ahead toward some goal which no one can define. Intolerance results from the fashionable emphasis on being "number one" without regard for others or the community. We want to be number one, even if often it is not clear what being number one means. We want to "grow" economically, although it is not clear what growth accomplishes, either. We want to identify "losers" and dominate them.

Most Americans are taught arbitrary and often extreme values and rules about things like freedom and property and the profit motive which get in the way of finding solutions to human problems. These rules produce economic pressures that undermine job security and wage scales for large segments of the population, leading to intolerance and racism. These values and rules often are presented as if they are beyond examination, reevaluation, or adjustment.

And, there is the principle of limited good, which says that there is a fixed and limited supply of good things in the world, whether land, water, wealth, success, health, or even happiness. So, if you get more, I have to get less. I have to resent your success for fear that you are somehow getting what should be mine. This way of thinking characterizes many Americans' outlooks, despite the realities of economic growth, just as it does "primitive" peasants', and it contributes to our intolerance. The idea that affirmative action for minorities and women must take jobs from white males is a good example of the image of limited good in action. So are the resentments toward blacks or Irish or Chinese immigrants who appeared to be taking "our" jobs—a pattern as old as American history.

But, particularly in the context of economic growth, the good doesn't have to be limited (at least in the relatively short period that concerns us), and educated people are supposed to have advanced beyond that point in their thinking. The whole point of economic growth, presumably, is so that there are more goods to go around. And our wealth is growing rapidly, yet the division of the spoils makes "limited good" a reality for most of our population even as we are bombarded with images of affluence and consumerism. But, of course, it is intolerance of one another which keeps those who are not rich from pursuing our common goals through unity in democratic processes, such as voting for changes in the economic rules that affect us. And therein lies much of the latent power of our intolerance—it is a major weapon in defense of the excessive privilege of the upper class.

Finally, problems are generated or maintained by our limited perceptions and narrow assumptions as citizens. As in any culture, it is hard to contemplate or even recognize solutions that fall outside the closed circle of preexisting thought. Part of the problem is that portions of the American public seem unable or at least unwilling to think about issues of any complexity, to explore new ideas, or to move out of areas of thought that are comfortably familiar. Supporters of intelligence testing would undoubtedly say that this proves that those people are of inherently inferior intelligence. I don't think so. It is true that many people don't learn as children to deal with the subtleties and complexities of issues in the mainstream culture or to explore new ideas. They don't learn to deal with such issues at least partly because their parents never did. It's a matter of learning where and how to focus one's intelligence and a matter of practicing, beginning in childhood. Ignorance and insensitivity perpetuate themselves in families, but not primarily (if at all) for genetic reasons. (This is one of the ways in which affirmative action for parents would help improve the skills of their children, producing benefits in the next generation.)

But the ideas that the mainstream culture offers to families tend to make the problems worse, not better. The media bombard people with messages about being number one, as if nothing else mattered. The popular media—movies, television, advertising, music, magazines—teach us that violence is the path to glamour and success. They teach that money, profit, and material goods are all that matter: basketball shoes, not the ideas in people's heads, the cultural or natural beauty around them, not even the other people in their lives. And it teaches them that the ways to get ahead are magical or simpleminded, or associated with the use of a particular product; or they teach that getting ahead involves the one-in-a-million shot of the lottery or stardom, not the far more common pathway of productive diligence.

Our culture also teaches children that school is a waste of time. Over and over, in movies and television shows and popular music, school is portrayed as a distraction from real life in which fools purvey ritual knowledge that no one needs to know. The idea that school provides practice in mental skills that can be recombined for later use is completely lost. But that message is also conveyed more widely through the disdain with which many Americans collectively hold teachers and schools. Our system of allocating resources tells students that the wisdom we learn through schooling is not valued by the society. From the condition of school buildings, it is clear that what goes on there is not as important as selling stocks and bonds or even selling shoes or cosmetics. And the message is conveyed by allowing so much of the curriculum to be taught so poorly. If the size of the classroom makes no difference, if one teacher can teach (or baby-sit) any number of students, that is a clear signal that what happens in the classroom doesn't count. The fact that the unionized seniority rights or "academic freedom" of teachers appear to outweigh issues of competence or concern for students sends a similar message.

Many Americans have also learned disdain for scholarly inquiry. Conveying the real value of scholarship and knowledge itself also requires some education of the citizenry. The public, and politicians, too, need patience and imagination to appreciate the potential value of research and scholarship. Scholarship is like the antennae of a society, always needing to extend in all directions beyond the main body of the society for exploration and protection, even if not every scholar is reporting essential information at any given moment. But scholars, in turn, have to be far more willing than they often are to relate their studies to human needs and to communicate their significance clearly.

The people also learn their ignorance directly from the media, which actually undermine intelligent thought. They hear celebrities, politicians, and even some scholars using words that are meaningless, illogical, and obviously inaccurate (in a large sense, not in the sense of minor grammatical errors) in the context in which they are used. They hear words deliberately misused or stretched beyond their meaning in order to mislead. They hear their leaders constantly making statements in "sound bites" designed to activate emotional "hot buttons" in an audience rather than to stimulate thought. They hear politicians debate ethics in such a partisan manner that ethical principles are entirely lost in a sea of political chatter. It is hard not to come away with the impression that "unethical" means "whatever the other guys do." The news comes in short clips that lack intellectual content; they are often rote recitals that are both patriotic and chauvinistic instead of being critical, thoughtful, or insightful. Television fails to stretch the minds of even the least thoughtful viewers and teaches such a simplified version of human experience that it dulls perception and sensitivity. Viewers learn an oversimplified, self-centered morality and an idea of logic and of human issues that are utterly lacking in depth or subtlety. They then become impatient with real-life problems that don't have quick and simple solutions.

Improving the System from Within

It does not have to take a revolution to change our cultural assumptions and our sociocultural system. Mindlessly defying or rejecting the old system, as many protesters have done in recent decades, isn't the way to improve it. Revolutions are rarely very selective or accurate in identifying what to fix. The point is not that other lifestyles are "good" and ours is "bad." We can continue to revere our existing values—in fact, most of what I have written here is in defense of American values that need more of our honest attention. We need only to look more carefully at the balance among these values and to put more effort into some, like justice, equality, and even some important measures of real freedom that are getting only lip service now. We need to undertake thoughtful, selective reexamination of the ways we apply some of those values. We do not have to abandon belief in the right to individual initiative, profit, or private property. We don't have to live in a society so egalitarian that there is no incentive for people to be clever or creative. We don't have to embrace communism, although we ought to be able to examine it or any other social theory honestly to see what valuable lessons we might learn. We don't have to abandon the advantages of capitalism. We simply have to recognize the enormous debt capitalism owes to the social order in which it operates. We can soften capitalism by seeking a wiser, gentler form that pays attention to the needs of the community as it seeks its profits. We can allow profits but still limit or tax them to meet social needs. Capitalism has thrived in other times and places while providing more fully for the needs of the populace and without creating such a gap between rich and poor and such indifference to the poor. In fact, no other country in the industrial, capitalist world (including some with economies which have done as well as or better than ours in recent decades) has as great a gulf between rich and poor as we have come to consider natural and necessary. We certainly don't have to abandon our pride or our patriotism. What better way to be "number one" than to take world leadership as a society that is truly just and at peace and has a true balance of individual freedoms with community needs?

But if we ask those without wealth and power to be patient, thoughtful, and selective in their demands for change, we must first ask those with the wealth and power to be forthcoming in their offers of real reform. When one percent of the population controls nearly 40 percent of the wealth, there is enormous potential to bring wealth to bear on society's problems without forcing people into unemployment and poverty, without exploiting the Third World, without advancing the poor on the backs of the lower middle class, and without "soaking" the rich very severely. On the other hand, pretending that such wealth doesn't exist when discussing our social and financial problems simply generates cynicism and rage, as it should.

We can achieve a society with more freedom, equality of opportunity, and justice without cultural separation and also without cultural homogenization. We can be more varied, more multicultural, **and** more united, more efficient, and better educated if we comprehend the arbitrary nature of many of our cultural assumptions and if we tolerate the self-determination of others (within the limits of conformity and order that are truly necessary, not just conventions). We can learn to appreciate and perhaps adopt each other's wisdom as we have learned to appreciate and perhaps adopt each other's food. We also need to provide genuine (not just legalistic) fairness of opportunity, making equal participation possible.

Ideally, individual choices about how and where to contribute to the society and earn a living would be based on skills and inclination. Given free choice, people could choose their employment. Ethnic differences in patterns of participation might or might not emerge. We may find that members of certain groups gravitate toward certain professions, as Mohawk Indians in New York once gravitated toward high-rise construction, because those professions match experiences in their own culture and upbringing or reinforce their values. But individuals would be free not to follow the trend, and the patterns that emerge would reflect genuine choice, not options limited and funneled by lack of education or social pressures. They would emerge with less resentment and inhibition (perhaps none).

If the mainstream became more varied and more multicultural, people would be free to choose a style or to alternate between being mainstream Americans and enjoying their own ethnic patterns as well as those of other people. Many of us, particularly men who are white but with ethnic backgrounds, have become comfortable in the mainstream. We feel that the mainstream includes not only us but some of our heritage and some of the features of our ethnic cultures. We feel free either to practice or to ignore the traditions of our individual heritage and to share portions of that heritage with family and with friends (including friends who have different roots but who enjoy learning about ours).

We also feel free to express our ethnic heritage on the job. Our colleagues are familiar enough with each other's heritage that we can do this without endangering communication or team work. Our colleagues enjoy and benefit from our distinctive perceptions on the job. But they don't force us to play ethnic roles that we do not wish to adopt or to be ethnic at times we chose to focus on the common culture. We contribute to the quality of job performance and to the cultural and economic mainstream in our various individual ways, often enriched by our varied cultural heritage but without being constrained by it, and, most important, without being required by others to play the part. If we can maintain such tolerance (which is once again being threatened) and extend it to people who aren't "white" or who are female or gay, we will have a society in which everyone is more productive. Far more important, everyone can be assured of respect, dignity, and greater comfort.

Skin color and sex are, of course, more visible distinctions than ethnic heritage. However, many whites, myself included, have names that are almost as immediate a basis for stereotyping as color or sex and our names must be presented to others almost as immediately as our color; but, for the moment at least, we don't suffer the constant effects of stereotypes. The point is not that differences should be invisible or that people should be anonymous—quite the contrary; the point is to have friends and neighbors, members of one's community and one's nation, willing to accept one as a person even though they can see from your skin or your name that your roots are different from theirs. The same freedom that many white male "ethnics" now share should be extended to female, gay, and non-white individuals, people with disabilities—in fact, to all. But I know that we aren't there yet. People in other countries—and their traditional systems of values and behavior—should also be extended the same respect and the same basic rights and freedoms we extend ourselves. But I know we aren't there yet, either. It will require taking a good hard look at our values; and some of us, mostly those who have by far the most, will have to give up a little.

Greater tolerance and fairness have to come through learning and education. We can use our ability to understand the meaning of culture and society to tease apart the complex interrelationships among their various facets. We can separate the essential qualities and functions of our institutions from their cultural trimmings and from the myths and assumptions that surround them. We can learn how the pieces of a socio-cultural system are related to one another and anticipate what will change or will have to be changed if we change one thing. In short, we no longer need to be blindly bound by the complex interrelationships among facets of culture that resist change or produce unanticipated results. We can begin to separate benefits from costs.

In a democracy, we count on an educated electorate to direct the views and actions of their elected representatives. We have to organize as voters to demand that politicians address the needs of the citizens and residents of the country as their first priority before the needs of special interests or their own wealth and reelection. We have to demand the reform of policies like lobbying laws that give enormous advantage to the rich. Each of us has to be willing to vote for something beyond his or her own individual immediate self-interest, recognizing common goals as well as the legitimate needs of others.

The solution to the problems is not merely to change the laws or government policies or the behavior of corporations—even if some of that is obviously necessary. We must also change how we look at and react to one another. Citizens, not just governments, have to change some of their ways. So education is a key—but not just formal education and certainly not just higher education. The education has to come through all our schools, textbooks, families, media, leaders, celebrities, each other.

To begin with, Americans have to stop **teaching** prejudice and hatred. Whatever "natural" or even cultural tendency people may have to prefer their own kind and fear "others" can clearly be redirected by formal and especially informal education. We do it all the time. Hated "others" become friends and allies when they are traded to our basketball team, move to our school, play different roles, become known as individuals, or become allies in fighting a particular battle or war. So the notion that our particular patterns of hatred are "natural" is just absurd, as well as being dangerous.

We have to construct situations in which people will be exposed to one another under conditions that make positive interaction possible and permit them to build mutual respect. We have to teach all Americans about other people's humanity, their successes, their real and potential contributions, and their rights and needs. We have to teach about the impact of poverty and racism on the human spirit. We have to celebrate real biological and cultural diversity to the full depth and meaning of "culture." And we have to be willing to think and teach about the imperfections of the mainstream culture, as well as about its great strengths and contributions. We have to be willing to teach the realities, not just the glories, of American history. We have to remember why it is important that we teach about people, their needs, their artistic creations, their environment, their history, and the working of their societies—not just about jobs—so we can remember the other purposes and pleasures in our lives and understand the larger consequence of our actions.

Americans have to teach one another to be committed to our society and all our neighbors, not just to our flag. We have to teach ourselves that community is as important a value as freedom is. We have to remind ourselves of the wide range of things societies must do and of the fact that the profit motive is not sufficient to get some of them done. We have to remind ourselves that there are other values besides profit; that people of other colors in other places have made substantial contributions to our contemporary success; that commitment to excellence not the privilege of our white, male American skins (or IQs) will get us ahead.

We have to teach the rich and powerful to recognize that luck, affirmative action, and enormous contributions from the society that nurtured them (often, but not always, accompanied by hard work and ability) got them where they are. We have to teach them that they have an obligation to society, an obligation that, like the wealth and the services society renders them, is greater than that of poorer people. And we have to demand, by law, that they honor that obligation far more than they do. It is the discrepancy between rich and poor, not the number of out-of-wedlock births, that is our biggest social problem. The assertion that possessing property entails no obligations to community (and the failure of the community to demand what it is owed) are the most dangerous kinds of extremism that we now face. We have to use our power as consumers, investors, and voters to direct the market in favor of corporations that meet standards of social responsibility. Capitalism can be driven by socially conscious consumers, the power of opinion, the investment choices people make, and the social and political education of investors. By boycotting Nestle, consumers managed at least temporarily to put a halt to the harmful dissemination of infant formula in the Third World. (But that experience suggests that vigilance has to be maintained.)

Education is a primary road to resolving many of these problems, and that education has to extend beyond the elite. If only the elite understand how things work, our solutions will always continue to serve their narrow interests. The current movement to devalue or eliminate public higher education will have exactly that result, whether or not it is part of the intended purpose of the movement.

But education is a more complex and difficult process than most people seem to understand. One cannot educate by throwing facts or even ideas in the general direction of lecture halls of six hundred people or television audiences or even captive groups of twenty-five of any age who are permitted to receive but not to react. "Efficiency" in money saved by forcing students to learn in ever larger groups is not efficiency in education.

Education is not about providing "truth," particularly since we cannot agree what truth is. Education involves students reacting to real problems and real options (appropriate to their age) and learning how to get along in groups. Students must see that most problems are not solved in a simple way (as they are on IQ tests), that knowledge usually comes in graded shades of "truth" that must be evaluated, not memorized, and that real-life problems have complicated solutions that take time to work out, require balancing many things, and demand wisdom and judgment. This is one reason why multicultural education is necessary: it supplies the context for discussing the kind of problems that can help shape productive, thinking citizens, not cheerleaders for Western civilization and the American way.

Education also means students realizing that they must be actors in determining solutions and truths. As I emphasized at the outset, it also means encouraging students constantly to probe "knowledge" for unspoken and perhaps unwarranted assumptions—which is what really makes people free. All of this demands interaction between teachers and students and among students, in small classes, with teachers who themselves are able to think about complex issues and who will tolerate their students' explorations. Technology can facilitate these processes if it is subservient to teaching and learning; but high-tech teaching designed to serve ever larger, passive audiences without creating challenging problems and interactive paths to solutions isn't education at all. Simply putting a lecture on tape or disk or television and letting a student push an "on" button at his or her leisure isn't education. It fosters convenience, not thought.

But the schools can't do the job alone. Proper education also requires a home and a nation that will invest in learning not only with their financial resources but with their expectations. Parents and citizens should demand genuine education from teachers but also prepare students to accept their responsibilities. Most students don't know what they are supposed to contribute to the process, and we don't tell them until they are sitting in a college classroom, if ever.

We also need to communicate a sense of mutual interdependence and community responsibility in our homes, our churches, our political events, and our media. Our politicians and our media could be helping parents and teachers to raise standards of thought and tolerance. We can teach better values through television and radio by molding the choice and content of programming. We can use the power of advertising to suggest that high-quality teachers, clean streets, decent housing, health and nutrition, beautiful parks, dedicated care for children and the elderly, and many other values are as important and as worthy a "purchase" as the latest basketball shoes. But we seem unwilling to invest in the quality of our lives, because it doesn't provide any "profit" in the narrow sense—or perhaps because our leaders fear the power of an educated, thinking electorate.

A massive effort has to be made to feed, clothe, educate, and provide medical care for the poor. The effort will involve a commitment by government, which is the only institution that can undertake it on the scale and for the length of time (perhaps two generations) that is needed. The solution may well mean revising welfare "as we know it," but the revision cannot be one that begins and ends with a desire to "cut costs" and take even more money away, that denies social responsibility, or that sneers at the recipients of its own assistance. The costs do not have to be borne by the middle class. They can be paid by levying a reasonable tax on the very wealthy individuals who control the great bulk of our resources. We might begin simply by rescinding the Reagan tax breaks to the rich and more recent tax breaks.

The most important thing about a democratic society or state is that it represents the interests of its people, rather than the government having an agenda of its own which is at odds with their welfare. (The latter has been the norm throughout most of human history.) We have to insist that "growth" and "efficiency" be used to serve people. The purpose of money is to lubricate social and economic interactions among people, to buffer them against shortage, and to enable them to lead decent lives. We have lost track of this goal to the point where our notion of economic efficiency is directly opposed to preserving the quality of American lives. When are Americans going to realize that the people who lose their jobs as companies are downsized to produce tiny increments of efficiency and savings are their friends, relatives, neighbors, the people they depend on, and ultimately themselves. When are they going to realize that those people who look a little different are biologically as similar to them as they are to one another and—more important—could be their friends and allies?

By various estimates one-fifth to one-quarter of all American children are born into poverty, while a tiny fraction of the population controls the vast majority of the wealth; racism and hatred of other people are rampant; more Americans proportionally are in jail than are people in any other Western industrial country; more wealth is devoted to militarism than in any other Western country; schools are decaying, colleges and hospitals closing, while prisons are being built. Is our system, then, so perfect (or so brittle?) that it does not dare to examine its conventional assumptions? The slogan does not have to be "America—love it or leave it," as bumper stickers sneered a few years ago. The slogan can be instead: "America—love it and improve it." We have to help our country live up to its own high ideals.

Discussion Questions

1. Why does Cohen say that social and economic stratification in the United States is inevitable? Do you agree or disagree with his explanations?
2. Cohen writes, "In the long run, cultural variation, like genetic variation, is a major guarantee of the future success of the species." In what way does cultural variation contribute to the future success of the species?
3. Is there one right way to do things, or are there many right ways to do things? Do different cultural systems have different advantages and disadvantages?
4. What are the sources of intolerance in the United States?
5. Why do we actively teach children to be intolerant of others? Why do we teach prejudice and hatred?
6. Think of ways in which U.S. culture might be changed—in small, incremental steps, to reduce intolerance, prejudice, and hatred. How would one individual go about effecting such changes?
7. Discuss examples of how affirmative action for those who are of European ancestry, male, able-bodied, and rich is built into our cultural systems in the United States. If you design programs to take away these advantages, is this reverse discrimination? Is there any way to create equal opportunities for everyone without those in power protesting at the loss of their former privileged positions?

Additional Resources

For Internet links related to this chapter, please visit our website at www.mhhe.com/dettwyler

COHEN, MARK NATHAN. *Culture of Intolerance: Chauvinism, Class, and Racism in the United States.* New Haven, CT: Yale University Press, 1998.
EHRENREICH, BARBARA. *Nickel and Dimed.* New York: Owl Books, 2002.
KAPFERER, BRUCE. *Legends of People, Myths of State: Violence, Intolerance and Political Culture in Sri Lanka and Australia* (Smithsonian Series in Ethnographic Inquiry). Washington, DC: Smithsonian Institution Press, 1998.
QUINN, DANIEL. *Ishmael.* New York: Bantam Books, 1995.

Applying Anthropology

2. "The Archaeology of Grief," by Sylvia Grider, *Discovering Archaeology* 2, no. 3 (August 2000), pp. 68–74.

3. "Breastfeeding and Culture," by Katherine A. Dettwyler (2003).

The term "applied anthropology" often refers to anthropologists who work outside of academia and apply their cross-cultural and evolutionary perspectives to real-world social problems. Applied anthropologists may work for government agencies, nonprofit organizations, corporations, or school districts, or they may have their own consulting firms; however, there is more to applied anthropology than a career strategy. The two readings in this section show how anthropological perspectives and methods can be applied to understanding many aspects of our own lives. Learning how profoundly cultural beliefs influence and shape our behavior is illuminating and often surprising. Learning about different cultural solutions to common human problems, like child-rearing and coping with death, likewise can give us insights into our own beliefs and practices, as well as offering alternatives.

 ## 2. THE ARCHAEOLOGY OF GRIEF

In "The Archaeology of Grief," Sylvia Grider describes how standard archaeological techniques for recording material cultural remains of human activity were applied to the artifacts left at the site of the Texas A&M Bonfire collapse in the fall of 1999. The mementos themselves reflect the outpouring of grief and sympathy felt by members of the community at the deaths of 12 students, and the demise of an important tradition for the university. Spontaneous shrines like this were created in Germany in the 1960s for people killed trying to cross the Berlin Wall, and in the United States along roadsides for individuals killed in car accidents. Massive public shrines were created after the death of Princess Diana, and for the Murrah Federal Building bombing in Oklahoma City, the World Trade Center collapse in New

York, the disintegration of the space shuttle Columbia, and on a smaller scale for many other local tragedies. In addition, people often leave personal objects, flowers, letters, and religious items at permanent memorial sites such as the Vietnam Veterans Memorial Wall in Washington, D.C. As you read the article, think about the function such shrines serve, both for those who leave things, and for those who come to view what others have left.

The fatal collapse of the Texas A&M Bonfire—a four-story stack of logs being raised for a student football rally—spread shock and grief like an icy rain throughout this tightly knit campus that reveres the traditions of its military heritage. The site became an instant shrine. Students by the thousands came to stand before it. So did many others—faculty, graduates, townspeople, strangers. They wept and prayed. And many gently placed mementos on the now-hallowed ground, sad offerings to the memory of the 12 Aggies who were killed.

To save this remarkable outpouring, we turned to the techniques of archaeology to collect, document, and conserve these artifacts of modern grief. The collection will offer a rare research tool for understanding this increasingly common mass-mourning ritual. And it is our legacy to future scholars, evidence of how Americans handled tragedy as they began the twenty-first century.

Especially since the death of Princess Diana in 1997, the news media have showcased the way people express their grief by leaving memorabilia at the site of a tragedy or disaster. In the United States, these spontaneous shrines are now an expected part of the public grieving process. From the Vietnam Veterans Memorial in Washington, D.C., to the terrorist-bombed Murrah Building in Oklahoma City to the killings at Columbine High School to Nantucket Island where John F. Kennedy Jr. and his wife were killed, and at practically every other disaster site, we see these sad collections of flowers, poems, teddy bears, T-shirts, letters, and children's drawings.

The defining tradition of Texas A&M University, a school steeped in tradition, is building the huge Aggie Bonfire prior to the football game with arch-rival University of Texas (UT). With only rare exceptions, A&M students—known as Aggies—have built a bonfire each year since 1909. But last fall, in the pre-dawn hours of November 18, the unthinkable happened. The great stack of logs collapsed, crushing to death 12 of the more than 70 students who were working on it and injuring more than 25 others. Grief was palpable on the campus as Texas A&M University was plunged into perhaps the greatest crisis of its 124-year history.

Fallen Logs and Tears

Television trucks and news helicopters converged on the site in the kind of ritualized wake that has become all too familiar. Within hours after the last bodies were pulled from the tumbled chaos of the fallen and shattered bonfire logs, students and others began leaving mementos along the security fence erected around the site. The accumulated memorabilia developed into an almost-continuous shrine as a steady stream of the grief-stricken and the curious visited the site. A smaller shrine appeared at the base of the flagpole at the nearby Administration Building.

Making pilgrimages to the site to read the messages and weep or pray over the memorabilia became an integral part of the campus grieving process.

The items at the fence (and elsewhere on campus) reflect the unique student culture and traditions of A&M, as well as the deeply religious culture of its central Texas location. Christian iconography was prominent: Two large, 3.6-meter (12-foot) wooden crosses were erected at the site, as well as a tableau of 12 smaller crosses, one for each student killed. Memorabilia unique to each victim were placed around the small crosses, each inscribed with a student's name. They took on the appearance of graves.

Students left caps, T-shirts, and other personal items, as well as uniquely A&M artifacts, such as "Twelfth Man" towels, which the students wave at football games to signify their willingness to join the players on the field. They left ticket stubs from the UT football game, framed photographs, drawings, architectural models, and poems.

Most stunning of all were the more than 30 Aggie class rings, made of gold and encrusted with diamonds. Votive candles were placed around them, and the sight of the rings glittering in the candlelight moved visitors to tears. The rings were later collected and returned to their owners, with the understanding that they might be part of a future memorial.

Bibles and Hard Hats

Other students left their caps and gowns after graduation, while community members and former students brought military medals and insignia, Eagle Scout pins, photographs, Bibles, stuffed animals, rosaries, and many other personal possessions. Members of the Corps of Cadets, the military heart of the university, and other students left their pots (hard hats and helmets) and their grodes (the dirty clothes they were wearing when the stack fell), along with axes and other tools used in building the bonfire. In the month following the accident, the spontaneous shrines were constantly changing as people brought new offerings and others took away items for whatever personal reasons.

As a folklorist in A&M's Department of Anthropology, I have for several years been studying the phenomenon of spontaneous shrines at disaster sites. Thus, systematically collecting and preserving the artifacts left at the bonfire site is a natural extension of my research. The expertise of archaeologist colleagues helped us create an appropriate methodology, which we modified as the project proceeded.

Pilgrimages to the bonfire site almost certainly will continue for the foreseeable future, particularly on the date of the accident, the UT/A&M football game, and Muster—April 21, Texas Independence Day, when Aggies the world over pay homage to classmates who have died in the preceding year. More memorabilia are inevitable, and they also should be systematically collected and integrated into the core collection. Our model is the National Park Service's regular collection of memorabilia left at the Vietnam Veterans Memorial in Washington, D.C.

The immediate project had a certain urgency. The winter rain and winds whipped and flayed the fragile, wet artifacts. Furthermore, the semester was almost over, meaning our pool of student volunteers would soon disappear. We undertook the Bonfire Memorabilia Collection Project with the assistance of colleagues from the Center for Ecological Archaeology and the Department of Anthropology, as well as student leaders. The effort was supported by the vast infrastructure of the university—including trucks, supplies, equipment, and personnel—as well as more than 100 volunteers from throughout the university community, ranging from graduate students to undergraduates to faculty, staff, and administrators. Besides the depressing weather, we faced the emotional stress of handling the memorabilia and the constant presence of the jumbled bonfire logs.

We marked the security fence into 10-meter (32.8-foot) sections, each numbered with a tag, to maintain inventory control over the artifacts. The university Utilities Department created a precise, computer-generated map of the bonfire fence, matched to our lot numbers, to exactly document the location of each item. We used standard archaeological methodology but adapted it to fit collections from the vertical fence.

All artifacts in each lot were individually tagged and inventoried for entry into a database. Each box of tagged artifacts was assigned a separate number, and the inventory sheet was put directly into each box, with larger articles tagged and put into labeled garbage bags. The countless flowers were roughly inventoried by lot and placed in unlabeled garbage bags to be composted for use on university flower beds.

Our primary goal was to gather everything and conserve it. Most of the flowers, however, were beyond saving, although we did collect and press some well-preserved blossoms as botanical samples.

A Dozen Crosses

About 75 volunteers collected the bulk of the memorabilia from the bonfire fence on December 1–2. We left one active shrine area—the twelve individual crosses and associated memorabilia—as well as the flagpole area to give mourners as much time as possible before the mementos were removed and a more permanent security fence could be erected. People kept leaving items even as we were collecting artifacts from the fence. We collected the final artifacts on December 20.

The collection now comprises about 200 storage boxes and some oversized containers and bags of artifacts. Several boxes of wet paper items have been sorted, dried, and temporarily filed until further preservation can be undertaken. The remaining paper materials are in an archival freezer. The other memorabilia have been field-inventoried and stored in a university warehouse. We will undertake a more detailed inventory and create a computerized database soon.

The bonfire shrine is an outstanding example of the widespread custom of expressing grief through material culture. Many cultures throughout history have practiced some form of ritual pilgrimage to sacred sites, where they leave mementos. The official practice of placing wreaths at the Tomb of the Unknown Soldier is a modern manifestation of this ritual.

In our modern, technological society, the site of tragic death often becomes hallowed, and we mark these sites with material expressions of our losses. The custom of marking the sites of fatal car wrecks with small roadside crosses, which apparently originated as a Hispanic custom in the southwestern United States, is now widespread across all ethnic groups and regions of the country. The practice, in fact, is so common that some states have enacted legislation to limit the size of these roadside memorials lest they become distracting hazards to drivers. Many communities are grappling with the question of how to handle the memorabilia of these spontaneous shrines.

There is little precedent for the total and systematic collection of memorabilia of this type, especially under such emotional conditions. Nonetheless, the adapted archaeological methodology enabled us control of the assemblage through the collection process.

Our collection, and others like it, offers rich research opportunities. Analyses may shed light on the nature of grief and memory in contemporary society, as well as the role of news media in spreading the practice to other communities.

The ritual aspect of the shrines holds promise for understanding not only contemporary grief, but that of past societies as well. Comparative material from archaeological sites should enhance our understanding of this modern phenomenon—and perhaps vice versa. Our goal is a comparative study with other sites, such as Oklahoma City, the Princess Diana shrines, and the Vietnam Veterans Memorial.

But before such research can begin, we must develop an accurate and complete ethnographic description of the data we have collected and also gather as much information as possible about the cultural context of the shrines. Once this data-description phase is completed, we will be in a much better position to explore the deeper cultural meanings of spontaneous shrines.

The Nature of Grief

This much is clear: By creating spontaneous shrines at disaster sites, modern people are participating in an ageless ritual of grieving and anguish. Archaeologists routinely excavate burial or other sacred sites, but they seldom have such close contact with the human emotions that shape these sites.

All spontaneous shrines deserve respect and some, especially those which involve entire communities, can be collected and preserved for display at future memorials to the event. The artifacts are left to express our communal urge to make peace in a tactile and loving way with the tragic loss of loved ones in sudden and dramatic circumstances.

Discussion Questions

1. Why do people create these shrines?
2. How much can we infer about belief systems from the specific material objects that people leave behind?
3. In the case of the Texas A&M Bonfire, all the objects were carefully removed, conserved, catalogued, and stored. If they had been left to the elements, what would have remained to be recovered by archaeologists of the future—after one year, after 10 years, after 100 years, after 1,000 years?
4. How might archaeologists of the future interpret these remains, and the behaviors and beliefs they imply?
5. Since all the logs from the Bonfire itself were removed, even if the shrine had been left intact, would there have been any way to reconstruct what had happened at the site? What does this tell us about the limits of archaeological knowledge and interpretation?
6. List other instances where archaeological techniques for recovering and recording material remains might be used for contemporary situations.
7. List instances where the material remains left behind by human activity might be misleading, so that archaeologists would have a difficult time figuring out how they got there and what they meant.
8. How do spontaneous shrines differ from formal, designed memorials, such as the wall itself at the Vietnam Veterans Memorial in Washington, D.C., or the formal memorial planned for the World Trade Center site in New York City?

Breastfeeding is an excellent example of a physiological process that is greatly shaped by a wide variety of cultural beliefs and practices around the world. Identifying and understanding your own cultural beliefs about breasts, breastfeeding, children, and health can help you see what sorts of impact culture can have on human biology. Culture also influences other aspects of biology, such as diet, growth and development, health, reproduction, and aging. Before reading this selection, take a few minutes to write down your personal beliefs about breasts and breastfeeding. How much do you know about these topics, and where did you learn it? What do you think are the prevailing attitudes about breasts and breastfeeding in the United States among your peers? How often should newborns be breastfed, and what is the ideal duration of breastfeeding? As you read the article, think about how the comparative biological and cultural anthropological perspectives on this topic agree or conflict with your cultural beliefs.

In a perfect world—one where child health and cognitive development were optimal—all children would be breastfed for as long as they wanted. As large-bodied, highly intelligent primates, that would be for a minimum of 2.5 years and as long as 6 or 7 years, or longer. In a perfect world, all mothers would know how to breastfeed and be supported in their efforts to do so by health care providers, spouses, friends, neighbors, co-workers, and the general beliefs of their culture.

Breastfeeding is, first and foremost, a way to provide protective immunities and health-promoting factors to children. Breast milk should be the primary source of nutrition for the first two years of life, complemented by appropriate solid foods around six months of age. Breast milk provides important immunities and nutrients, especially for growing brains, for as long as the child is breastfed. It is a source of physical and emotional comfort to a child, and for the mother it is the wellspring of the important mothering hormones, prolactin and oxytocin.

Ordinarily, childbirth is followed by breastfeeding, with its flood of prolactin, the "mothering hormone," and oxytocin, "the hormone of love." Both hormones elicit caretaking, affective, and protective behaviors by the mother towards her child. If the mother does not breastfeed, her body interprets this as "the baby died," and enters a state of hormonal grieving, preparing for a new attempt at reproduction. The mother, however, still has to cope with a newborn, and later a toddler, without the calming and nurturing influence of prolactin and oxytocin.

Like childbirth, however, breastfeeding is influenced by a variety of cultural beliefs, some directly related to breastfeeding itself, and others pertaining to a woman's role in society, to the proper relationship between mother and child, to the proper relationship between mother and father, and even to beliefs about breasts themselves.

One way of thinking about cultural influences on breastfeeding initiation and duration is based on the Demographic Transition, in which societies move from a pre-transition state of high birth and death rates, through a transitional stage of high birth but low death rates (resulting in rapid population growth), and eventually into a post-transition stage of low birth and death rates. Margaret Mead was the first to recognize an "Infant Feeding Transition." A culture begins in a pre-transition state of almost everyone breastfeeding for several years, then moves through a transitional stage of bottle-feeding. Three main forces conspire to move women away from breastfeeding: (1) the separation of their productive labor and their reproductive labor, as societies shift from subsistence-based economies to wage labor-based economies, and/or women are taken away from both productive and reproductive work to be their husband's social partners; (2) increasing confidence in the power of science to provide "better living through chemistry" coupled with decreasing confidence in the ability of women's bodies to function normally, and (3) the rise of commercial interests intent on making a profit by convincing women that breastfeeding is less healthy, difficult, primitive, and/or shameful. The transition is initiated by women with more education and higher incomes turning to shorter and shorter durations of breastfeeding, and eventually only wet-nursing (in previous centuries) or bottle-feeding (in the 20th and 21st centuries) from birth.

As time goes by, women with less education and lower income levels emulate their social superiors and adopt bottle-feeding as well. By the time the last of the lower classes have adopted bottle-feeding as being "modern and scientific," the well-educated upper-class women are returning to breastfeeding, first for short periods, and then for increasing durations. They have moved on to the post-transition stage. The return to breastfeeding by well-educated upper-class women is fueled by several factors, including research during the last few decades clearly documenting the superiority of breastfeeding over formula in terms of maternal and child health and child cognitive development, feminism's insistence that women's reproductive powers are of great value, and a general backlash against the infant formula companies for promoting their products in unethical ways. Primarily, in the United States it has been well-educated middle- and upper-class women who have fought for legislation to protect the rights of mothers to breastfeed in public, and for better maternity care and on-site child care facilities.

In the late 1950s, anthropologist Margaret Mead urged researchers to: "Find out how we can get from the working class mothers who breastfeed to the upper middle class women who also breastfeed, without a generation of bottle feeders in between" (Raphael 1979). We still haven't figured out how to do this.

There are still a number of "pre-transition" cultures in the world, in which all women breastfeed each child for several years, but Western influence—particularly in the form of aggressive infant formula marketing strategies and the export of Western cultural beliefs about breasts as sex objects—is affecting even the remotest regions of the world. Korea, for example, is in the early stages of the transition from universal long-term breastfeeding to the adoption of bottles. Survey data reveal a decline in breastfeeding incidence and duration from the 1960s to the 1990s, led by upper-class, well-educated urban Korean women. China, likewise, has begun the transition to bottle-feeding, experiencing a rapid decline in the prevalence of breastfeeding in urban and periurban areas. Not surprisingly, China has been targeted by the infant formula companies as the next great market for their products.

Cuba is at the beginning of the infant feeding transition, with mothers of higher educational levels having the shortest duration of breastfeeding. Cuba seems to be well ahead of the United States in meeting established goals for maternal and child health through breastfeeding, with national strategies for supporting and promoting breastfeeding, including having all government hospitals participate in the World Health Organization's Baby-Friendly Hospital Initiative, and developing educational programs for day care centers and elementary and secondary schools to try to create a breastfeeding-friendly culture among both males and females from an early age. Cuba may be able to avoid a complete switch to bottle-feeding.

The Arabian Gulf countries (Bahrain, Kuwait, Oman, Qatar, Saudi Arabia, and the United Arab Emirates) are fully into the transitional phase, with middle- and upper-class women seldom breastfeeding, or only for a few weeks, and older women nursing longer than younger women. The influence of oil revenues on the lifestyles of these women, including the common employment of foreign housemaids and nannies, who bottle-feed the children, is fascinating and disturbing. The transition from full breastfeeding to almost full bottle-feeding has been particularly swift in this part of the world. "Westernized" hospital practices have been especially harmful, with hospital personnel and private clinics being used to promote the use of formula.

Australia, Canada, and the United States represent societies farthest along this "Infant Feeding Transition," with women of higher incomes and more education initiating breastfeeding in great numbers, and with increasing durations as well. This trend began in the 1970s, but was helped by the 1997 statement by the American Academy of Pediatrics that all children in the United States should be nursed for a minimum of one year (and thereafter as long as both mother and child wish), as well as by recent research showing that formula-fed children have lower IQs than their breastfed counterparts. In the United States, breastfeeding to the age of three years or beyond is becoming more and more common, as is breastfeeding siblings of different ages, known as "tandem nursing" (Dettwyler 2001). In the last decades, the biggest leaps in initiating breastfeeding in the United States have been among WIC clients (women, infants, and children), who tend to be poor and less well-educated, indicating a trickle-down effect of breastfeeding from the upper classes, as well as the success of WIC Peer Counselor training programs.

Exactly how a particular region responds to influence from the Western industrialized nations and from the multinational infant formula companies depends on many different social, political, and economic factors. This makes it difficult to predict how the infant feeding transition will look in a specific region, or how long the bottle-feeding stage will last.

Cultural beliefs affect breastfeeding in other ways as well. Among the Bambara of Mali, people believe that because breast milk is made from a woman's blood, the process of breastfeeding creates a special relationship between a child and the woman who breastfeeds that child, whether or not she is the child's biological mother. In addition, breastfeeding creates a bond among all of the children who nurse from the same woman, whether or not they are biological siblings.

Having milk-siblings expands one's kinship network, providing more people one can call on for help in times of need. However, these kinship ties also prohibit marriage between the related children. In order to reduce the impact on potential marriage partners, women try to breastfeed other women's children only if they would already be excluded as marriage partners. Thus, a woman might wet-nurse the children of her co-wives, the children of her husband's brothers, or her grandchildren, while avoiding breastfeeding the children of her best friend, who she hopes will grow up to marry her own children. Similar beliefs about the "milk tie" are found among people in Haiti, Papua New Guinea, the Balkans, Burma, and among the Badawin of Kuwait and Saudi Arabia. In cultures where everyone is breastfed, or where everyone is bottle-fed, one's identity does not hinge on how one was fed.

But in cultures entering or leaving the transition, feeding practices can be very important to one's identity. In a culture just entering the transition, to be bottle-fed is to have high status and be wealthy and modern. In a culture entering the final stage, to be breastfed is to have high status and be wealthy and modern.

In a wide variety of cultures, males are breastfed longer than females, sometimes much longer. These practices are supported by a variety of cultural beliefs, including the ideas that earlier weaning for girls insures a much-desired earlier menopause (Taiwan), that boys must be nursed longer so they will be willing to take care of their aged parents (Ireland), and that breast milk is the conduit for machismo, something boys need, but girls do not (Ecuador). Additionally, a number of societies have noted that males are physiologically weaker than females, more prone to illness and early death, so mothers nurse their sons longer to help ensure their survival.

Cultural beliefs about birth can have a profound influence on the success or failure of breastfeeding. Breastfeeding works best when the mother and baby are undrugged at delivery, when they are kept together after birth, when the baby is not washed, when the baby is fed at the first cue (long before crying), when breastfeeding occurs early and often, when free formula samples and other gifts are not given to the mother, and when all those who surround the mother are knowledgeable and supportive of breastfeeding. Where the culture of birthing meets most or all of these criteria, we find higher rates of breastfeeding as well as longer durations. The World Health Organization's Baby-Friendly Hospital Initiative provides both a blueprint for optimal breastfeeding conditions and references to support their recommendations.

Cultural beliefs about how often children should breastfeed can help or hinder the process. The composition of human milk, as well as studies of human populations where children are allowed to breastfeed on demand, suggests that the natural frequency of breastfeeding is several times an hour for a few minutes each time, rather than according to a schedule, with longer feedings separated by several hours. Infrequent feeding in the early days and weeks of breastfeeding can permanently affect a mother's milk supply. As control of breast milk production gradually shifts from primarily endocrine (prolactin) to primarily autocrine (based on breast fullness) during the first few months postpartum, women who have been nursing on a three- to four-hour schedule may find that they no longer have sufficient milk to meet their babies' needs. A simple strategy of unrestricted breastfeeding from birth onwards would prevent this supply problem.

Perhaps the most pernicious cultural belief affecting breastfeeding is the one found in the United States and a small number of other (mostly Western) cultures— the belief that women's breasts are naturally erotic. American culture is obsessed with the sexual nature of women's breasts and their role in attracting and keeping male attention, as well as their role in providing sexual pleasure. This is reflected by the "normal" circumstances under which breasts are exposed in the United States (*Playboy* centerfolds, low-cut evening gowns, bikinis), by the phenomenon of breast augmentation surgery, by the association of breasts with sexual pleasure, and by the reactions of some people when they see women breastfeeding (embarrassment, horror, disgust, disapproval). In fact, the cultural belief that breasts are intrinsically erotic is just that, a cultural belief of limited distribution—one that has devastating consequences for women who want to breastfeed their children.

The mammary glands play no role in sexual behavior in any species other than humans. Among humans, the cross-cultural evidence clearly shows that most cultures do not define the breasts as sex objects. Extensive cross-cultural research in the 1940s and 1950s, published by Ford and Beach, found that, of 190 cultures surveyed, only 13 viewed women's breasts as sexually attractive. Likewise, 13 cultures out of 190 involved women's breasts in sexual activity. Of these latter 13, only three are also listed among the 13 where breasts are considered sexually attractive.

In most cultures, breasts are viewed solely as functional body parts, used to feed children—similar to how the typical American male views women's elbows, as devices to bend arms. Thus, in most cultures, it doesn't matter whether they are covered or not, or how big they are; husbands do not feel jealous of their nursing children, and women are never accused of breastfeeding for their own sexual pleasure. In the United States, and increasingly where Western ideas about breasts as sex objects are taking hold, women find that they must be extremely discreet about where and how they breastfeed. They may get little support for breastfeeding, or even active resistance from jealous husbands; they may receive dirty looks or rude comments or be asked to go elsewhere (often the bathroom) to nurse. Still others are accused of sexually abusing their children for breastfeeding them longer than a year (Dettwyler 2001).

The evolution of cultural beliefs about breasts is difficult to pin down. Carolyn Latteier and Marilyn Yalom provide the most thorough research on the history of Western culture's obsession with breasts. The rise of both the infant formula industry and commercial pornography following World War II contributed to modern views of breasts as sex objects, rather than glands for producing milk for children.

Among health care providers themselves, a culture of denial about the health risks of formula contributes to the persistence of bottle-feeding. Many physicians view bottle-feeding as "almost as good" in spite of overwhelming research to the contrary. It is estimated that for every 1,000 deaths of infants in the United States, four of those deaths can be directly attributed to the use of infant formula. Additionally, children who are formula-fed have higher rates of many illnesses during childhood including diabetes, ear infections, gastrointestinal and upper respiratory infections, lymphoma, Sudden Infant Death Syndrome, and allergies. They continue to have higher rates of illnesses throughout life, including heart disease, some types of cancer, and multiple sclerosis. Children who are formula-fed likewise have lower average scores on intelligence tests and lower grades in school. Mothers who breastfeed their children, especially for longer durations, have lower rates of reproductive cancers (especially breast cancer), and lower rates of osteoporosis.

Unfortunately, obstetricians often view infant nutrition as the responsibility of the pediatrician, while the pediatrician claims that by the time the child is born, the mother has long since made up her mind about how she will feed her child. Many health care professionals say that they hesitate to discuss the dangers of formula for fear of "making women feel guilty." This is patronizing of parents and robs them of their chance to make an informed decision about this important area of child care.

In a perfect world, all cultural beliefs would support breastfeeding. The World Health Organization's Baby-Friendly Hospital Initiative and the Coalition for Improving Maternity Services' Mother-Friendly Childbirth Initiative are two attempts to clarify the best cultural practices for initiating breastfeeding. The Internet has also had a major impact on the culture of breastfeeding support. LactNet is an e-mail list for professionals who work in the lactation field. Kathleen Bruce and Kathleen Auerbach, both lactation consultants in the United States, began the list in March of

1995. It has grown to include more than 3,000 individuals from 38 countries who share ideas, beliefs, research studies, and clinical experience. Documents such as the Baby-Friendly Hospital Initiative and the Mother-Friendly Childbirth Initiative, and resources such as LactNet, are creating and sustaining a global culture of breast-feeding support.

Discussion Questions

1. Does it surprise you to learn that according to our heritage as large-bodied, intelligent, socially complex primates, modern human children are born expecting to be breastfed for at least 2.5 years, and as long as 6 or 7 years?

2. Do you know if you were breastfed, and if you were, for how long? What about your siblings, friends, and neighbors?

3. What impact does the lack of prolactin and oxytocin have on a mother's feelings towards her children, at the individual level and at the population level? In other words, think about the different experiences of women who mother in a culture where everyone breastfeeds, compared to the experiences of women who mother in a culture where everyone bottle-feeds. What impact might this have on general cultural ideas about the experience of being a mother? What about cultures, such as the U.S. culture, where some women breastfeed for a long time, others for a short time, and others not at all?

4. Create a chart with the following column headings: (1) Advantages of Breastfeeding for the Mother, (2) Advantages of Breastfeeding for the Child, (3) Advantages of Bottle-Feeding for the Mother, and (4) Advantages of Bottle-Feeding for the Child. Fill in the columns as indicated. Note that column 4 is empty—there are **no advantages** of bottle-feeding for the child. Why then are so many children in the United States bottle-fed from birth, or breastfed for only a few weeks or months?

5. What cultural beliefs serve to support the choice to bottle-feed children with formula in the United States? What cultural beliefs serve to make breastfeeding difficult in the United States?

6. What are the laws in your state concerning the rights of women to breastfeed in public? What are the laws in your state concerning the rights of women to have time off (paid or unpaid) to breastfeed or pump at work?

7. Does it surprise you to learn that viewing breasts as sex objects (and learning to get sexual pleasure from one's breasts) is a purely cultural phenomenon, one that is learned through enculturation rather than being part of our biological heritage? Can you think of other circumstances in which cultural beliefs acquired during childhood can lead to learned physical responses to stimuli? Think about different cultural beliefs about which foods are considered edible. For example, how would a vegetarian Hindu react differently to the smell of beef cooking on the barbecue than an omnivorous Baptist might? How would you react to the idea of eating grubs, termites, bush rat, goat kidneys, or sheep's eyes (all considered delicacies in some parts of the world)? If you were raised to think that seeing a black cat, walking under a ladder, breaking a mirror, or opening an umbrella in the house can lead to bad luck, how do you react when one of these occurs?

8. How might U.S. cultural beliefs about breasts, breastfeeding, and children be changed to be more supportive of breastfeeding? What long-term impact might that have on the health and well-being of the population as a whole?

9. Do you think that learning about the anthropological (cross-cultural and evolutionary) perspectives on this—or any—subject might lead you to make different choices about your beliefs and behaviors in the future? Does this prospect seem scary or liberating?

Additional Resources

For Internet links related to this chapter, please visit our website at www.mhhe.com/dettwyler

FORD, C. S.; and F. A. BEACH. *Patterns of Sexual Behavior.* New York: Harper & Row, 1951.

GIULIANI, RUDOLPH W. (Introduction) and the editors of LIFE Magazine. *One Nation: America Remembers September 11, 2001.* New York: Little Brown & Company, 2001.

KEAR, ADRIAN, and DEBORAH LYNN STEINBERG, eds. *Mourning Diana: Nation, Culture and the Performance of Grief.* New York: Routledge, 1999.

LATTEIER, C. *Breasts: The Women's Perspective on an American Obsession.* Binghamton, NY: Haworth Press, 1998.

PODOLEFSKY, AARON, and PETER J. BROWN, eds. *Applying Anthropology: An Introductory Reader.* 7th ed. New York: McGraw-Hill Higher Education, 2002.

RAPHAEL, D. "Margaret Mead—A Tribute." *The Lactation Review* 4, no. 1 (1979), pp. 1–3.

SIMOPOULOS, A. P., J. E. DUTRA DE OLIVEIRA, and I. D. DESAI, eds. *Behavioral and Metabolic Aspects of Breastfeeding: International Trends. World Review of Nutrition and Dietetics, Volume 78.* Basel, Switzerland: S. Karger, 1995.

STUART-MACADAM, PATRICIA, and KATHERINE A. DETTWYLER, eds. *Breastfeeding: Biocultural Perspectives.* New York: Aldine de Gruyter Publishers, 1995.

WALKER, M. "A Fresh Look at the Hazards of Artificial Infant Feeding, II." 1998. Available from the International Lactation Consultants Association.

YALOM, M. *A History of the Breast.* New York: Random House, Inc., 1997.

CHAPTER 3

Ethics and Methods in Physical Anthropology and Archaeology

4. "They Died With Custer: Preface/Prelude," by Douglas D. Scott, P. Willey, and Melissa A. Connor, from *They Died With Custer: Soldiers' Bones from the Battle of the Little Bighorn.* Norman, OK: University of Oklahoma Press, 1998, pp. xvii–xviii, 3–11.

5. "The Case of the Purloined Pots," by Kent Black, *Smithsonian* 32, no. 6. (September, 2001), pp. 34–44.

Archaeologists and physical anthropologists who study human skeletal remains (variously called bioarchaeologists, human osteologists, or skeletal biologists) are faced with two problems. First, where do the data leave off and the interpretations of and inferences from the data begin? It can be difficult to avoid letting the cultural beliefs of the modern anthropologist influence his or her interpretations of the data. Can we "tell a good story" from the relatively meager artifacts and osteological remains available to us and still remain true to the data themselves? What other sorts of information might help us make sense of our data? Second, what is to be done when the cultural beliefs of different sets of stakeholders are in conflict? Who "owns" the past and its remains? Should anyone be allowed to disturb the dead, and, if so, under what circumstances and for what purposes?

 ## 4. THEY DIED WITH CUSTER: PREFACE/PRELUDE

This selection includes the preface and the first chapter of a book describing the excavation and analysis of bones and artifacts from the site of the Battle of the Little

Bighorn, where George Armstrong Custer and his men from the U.S. Seventh Cavalry were defeated in battle by Sioux and Cheyenne warriors in June of 1876. The authors combine anthropological and historical data and analytical techniques to try to learn as much as possible about the men who died with Custer. The Native American Graves Protection and Repatriation Act (NAGPRA) was passed by Congress in 1990 to help protect Native American graves and to repatriate (return to the original owners) skeletal remains and cultural artifacts belonging to Native American tribes and housed in various U.S. museums and anthropology departments. Excavations and analyses of the remains of people of European ancestry in the United States are much rarer. As you read this selection, think about the conflicting rights of the dead to remain undisturbed, the rights of modern-day scientists to do research on the remains, and the rights of the descendants of these men to have a say in what happens to their bones.

Living bone supports the body. It protects the brain, creates the shapes in the human body. After death, bone and teeth are the last remaining tissues. When the muscles and skin are dust, the bone remains. Bones of the dead tell stories about the body and person they represent. To the osteologist, they tell a softly spoken tale of a person's dietary habits, diseases suffered, injuries endured, and sometimes something of the manner of death and what happened after death.

In these pages, we have set down how we listened to the tales whispered by a particular set of bones, the bones of the dead soldiers from the Battle of the Little Bighorn. Through unique circumstances we were able to conduct archeological investigations at the Little Bighorn Battlefield National Monument. Using dental picks, spoons, and chopsticks, we excavated. And then we took the bones back to the lab and listened. . .

We listened to the story the bones told us about the soldiers whose lives had been cut short in the action at the Little Bighorn. But we have not relied exclusively on the bones to tell their story, because unlike the prehistorian, who has only the artifacts and the bones to aid research, we who study history through archeological techniques have a myriad of other data to aid us—and at times confound us.

Our story is about those men who died with George Armstrong Custer, the soldiers and the scouts. We do not ignore the Native American combatants, the Sioux and Cheyenne, but all historical and oral history accounts tell us that these peoples removed their dead from the field of battle. The Indian dead were buried in villages and elsewhere away from the battlefield, leaving only the Seventh Cavalry dead on the field. Those were the bones we found and those are the remains we have studied.

In building the osteo-biography of the men with Custer we utilized historical documents to establish a background and set the stage where the archeological evidence could be placed in proper perspective. Those historic documents contain the oft-repeated details of the reason for the battle, the fight itself, and the aftermath. They tell the tale of the gruesome task of burying the dead, and they contain statistics on the ages, heights, birthplaces, and other details from the lives of the men themselves. Photographs exist of all of the officers and about 10 percent of the other men who served in the Seventh Cavalry on that fated day, and they give us a feel of how the men looked and how they dressed.

But the photographs and documents do not contain all the information on the men who rode and died with Custer. The archeological and physical anthropological data allow us now to expand our knowledge of the men's true ages, heights, state of health, and how they actually died. History can tell much about the past, but when it is coupled with the osteological evidence, a much more complete version of the men's lives and deaths emerges, forming a poignant picture of the past.

In 1983, a careless smoker threw a cigarette from a car while passing by Little Bighorn Battlefield National Monument, igniting a range fire that swept over the battlefield. At first, the fire seemed to spell disaster. Through quick action, however, fire fighters managed to save the visitor center and other buildings at the park. The white marble markers dotting the battlefield, marking where Custer's men had fallen in battle, were blackened by the smoke but otherwise undamaged.

What fared the worst, not surprisingly, was the vegetation. Because the area had been set aside as a memorial almost since the battle, the land had neither burned nor been grazed for decades. Before the fire, the sagebrush, prickly pear, and grasses were incredibly thick. Now all that was gone, and the soil lay bare.

But thick vegetation was not what brought visitors to the Little Bighorn battlefield and people still came to view the area where so many died. Families still trod the paths, less worried about rattlesnakes now that they were more easily seen. Walking down the Deep Ravine Trail, one sharp-eyed visitor spotted something white glinting in the sun. When he bent to investigate, he found an adult human tooth, which he promptly turned in to the park staff.

The dead from the battle were never well buried and, for years, the thick vegetation hid the remains of the fight. Now, without the sagebrush and prickly pear, cartridges, bullets, and bones were found strewn over the hills. Archeologist Richard A. Fox, Jr., spent ten days during the summer of 1983 wandering the battlefield and documenting the artifacts exposed by the fire.

Fox's report on his work was sent into the stream of bureaucratic paperwork that flows through the National Park Service. In the normal stream flow, a copy ended up on the desk of the Chief Division of Rocky Mountain Research at the Midwest Archeological Center. At the time, it was an empty desk.

The Midwest Archeological Center is an entity of the National Park Service responsible for assisting park units by planning, execution, and/or overseeing of the archeology done in the national parks in the Midwest and assists parks and other agencies elsewhere. These are professional archeologists who provide information to the parks for their displays and lectures. They also conduct archeological investigations necessary for the parks to comply with state and federal legislation regarding the preservation and protection of our nation's cultural heritage.

The center has a manager who oversees several divisions. In 1983, the then Rocky Mountain Research Division got a new chief. Dr. Douglas D. Scott reported to work there on December 5. Sitting at his desk, looking through the pile of material that had accumulated, he thought it an ironic coincidence that Fox's report was one of the first things he saw: as December 5 is the birthday of George Armstrong Custer.

During the winter of 1983, a spring dig was organized. First, building upon the ideas presented in Fox's report, a research design was developed and presented to Park Service management. Although the service could not fund the project, the Custer Battlefield Historical and Museum Association had a limited amount of money to fund archeological work. They could pay Fox a stipend and put some money toward the expenses of workers. The Midwest Center's manager, then Dr. F. A. Calabrese, assigned Scott to head the work. The workers would have to be volunteers, and there was no money to pay them.

The dig was planned in two parts. First, the archeologists and volunteers would cover the surface of the battlefield and record and collect all the artifacts they could find. This would be done by arranging five to ten people in a straight line and having them walk forward and put a pinflag into the ground whenever they spotted an artifact. People with metal detectors would be spaced throughout the line to see if the detectors could find material that could not be spotted otherwise. The position of each artifact located would then be recorded with a transit.

Second, the archeologists and volunteers would excavate around the markers placed on the battlefield. Supposedly, the markers were placed where men fell in battle, but there are more markers on the field than men who died. Some markers are obviously spurious. The excavations were based on the assumption that had a person ever been buried there, small bones and fragments, buttons, bullets, or other small items should remain.

The Custer Battlefield Historical and Museum Association placed in its newsletter a call for volunteers: no pay, lots of work, crowded living conditions. Such discouragements notwithstanding, 250 people wrote and asked if they could help with the archeological work—nearly the number of soldiers who died there. Only a few could be accommodated, and the difficult task of selecting the volunteers fell to Scott. He chose people with different interests and skills to meet the needs of the project. Some were lawyers, neurosurgeons, electricians, engineers, pathologists, and even professional archeologists, but all were interested in archeology and the story of the Little Bighorn.

The weekend before the dig was to start in early May, Scott moved into the old stone house that overlooks the National Cemetery at the battlefield and that once served as the superintendent's residence. This was to be his living quarters and dig headquarters for the next two summer expeditions. Scott, Fox, and the volunteers gathered in the living room of the stone house the first morning. Scott and Fox explained the procedures they expected to use. When they left, all participants knew what they were to do. Scott and Fox took the volunteers to the southern portion of the main battlefield. Everyone lined up, almost in skirmish order. When they started walking forward, almost immediately, someone found a sardine can. Before the excitement from the find had ebbed, someone else found another artifact. Then the metal detectors began to sing. Pinflags began to appear all over the hill. By the end of the first day, more than one hundred artifacts had been located, recorded, and collected, including the backstrap to a soldier's Colt revolver.

Scott and Fox were astounded, and exhausted. The sheer quantity of artifacts was many times what they had expected. The enthusiasm of the volunteers was remarkable. Despite the cold, and later the heat, they were ready to start before eight in the morning, ate only a quick lunch, and did not want to stop at quitting time.

By the end of the first week, Scott realized that the dig required a third archeologist to help with the artifacts and with supervising the volunteers. Eventually, Melissa Connor, one of the Midwest Archeological Center's staff archeologists, was sent to help. When human remains were found an osteologist, Dr. Clyde Snow, was added to the team.

That was the cast for the first field season. Three archeologists, an osteologist, and sixty-six volunteers. The volunteers stayed variously for the full five weeks or in a few cases only a day. The dig was an unmitigated success and plans were made to continue the work the next year. Over the winter, Scott and Fox put together a report on the findings of the first year (Scott and Fox 1987), and Scott, Fox, Connor, and firearms specialist Dick Harmon planned what would happen during the dig of 1985. The Reno-Benteen defense site would be metal detected just as the Custer field had been, and a sample of the Custer battlefield markers was selected for excavation to aid in determining why there were at least forty-two extra markers on the field.

Over the winter, another expert was added to the team. Dr. C. Vance Haynes, a well-known geoarcheologist and an authority on Indian Wars army firearms, contributed his expertise. He was to determine what geomorphological changes could have occurred in Deep Ravine to hide some twenty men believed to be buried there.

Scott asked Dr. Clyde Snow if he would continue the work of examining the bones. Snow had been employed for years as a forensic anthropologist for the Federal Aviation Administration, identifying the dead from airplane crashes. Then, when he retired, he really went to work. He acts as a consultant to the State of Oklahoma, to Cook County in Illinois, and to international human rights groups. He has worked for organizations in Argentina, identifying those who disappeared under a former regime and training Argentinians in this work, as well as in many more recent human rights abuse cases in the international arena.

The field season of 1985 started as poorly as the 1984 season had started well. Due to incomplete paperwork, federal and state agencies delayed the excavations for several days. Connor, who had taken over the excavations, was forced to fill in two units before the digging was complete. When Snow came to visit the battlefield in the second week of the dig, he had almost no bones to examine.

By the end of the second week, the dig was behind schedule but back on track. Excavation units were reopened and hard work by the volunteers and archeologists enabled them to complete the work planned for the field season in the shorter time available.

The spring of 1989 brought another opportunity to conduct archeological investigations at the battlefield, this time at the site of the Reno-Benteen equipment disposal dump. The dump was threatened by vandals and the park management team determined that excavations were the most appropriate means to preserve the information. A fortuitous find of a partial human skeleton on adjacent private land, uncovered by four of the volunteers, brought Dr. P. Willey onto the team. Dr. Willey is a professor of physical anthropology at California State University, Chico, and a diplomate of the American Board of Forensic Anthropology.

The months after the fieldwork were consumed by laboratory work and writing reports. The artifacts and bones were catalogued, cleaned, and analyzed. Some were sent to specialists for examination. Then, when all the information possible had been gleaned from the pieces and their associated context, the reports of investigation were written. As with any scientific endeavor, one line of evidence leads to a new set of questions. Not every question could be completely explored in the initial reports. On these pages we explore and discuss those questions relating to the men with Custer that we could not address in the government compliance reports, given the available time and budgets.

During the course of the 1984 and 1985 archeological investigations, partial remains from thirty-four individuals were studied, remains either excavated or found in the park's museum collection. All were soldiers from Custer's battalion. After our study all the remains were reburied, with appropriate ceremonies, in graves in the Custer National Cemetery. Before the reburial, the bones were measured, examined, photographed, chemically analyzed, and x-rayed. With the help of Gregory Brown at the Nebraska State Museum, molds and casts were made of bones with unique characteristics. Since then bones from seven more of Custer's men have turned up in museum collections. In another case, a partial skeleton was found eroding from the bank of the Little Bighorn River, and finally, the unidentified remains of ten more Little Bighorn soldiers were exhumed from the Custer National Cemetery and studied.

This synopsis of the Little Bighorn battlefield archeology projects shows clearly the multidisciplinary studies necessary in today's archeology. The field archeologists, the forensic specialists, the facial reconstructionist, and the geomorphologist were just a few of the specialists necessary for this archeological study to be successful. At historical sites, the ability to research and use historical documents is also essential. The context of the archeological material includes not only where it came from in the ground but all of the relevant historical documentation. From these sources of information, in archeological and historic context, we are able to create detailed pictures of the men of the Seventh Cavalry and their last moments. In five cases, we were able to identify individuals from the physical remains.

In some earlier works the joining of history and archeology has frequently been more in the nature of a poor splice than a good marriage. Historians claim that archeologists are not adequately trained in the techniques of historical research. Also, they argue that archeology is unnecessary as the historic record gives them all the information they need to know. Prehistoric archeologists claim that historic archeologists are not doing true "anthropology" (the discipline of which archeology is a subdiscipline). Historic archeologists are frequently made to feel like unwanted stepchildren, useful to neither discipline. Much the same thing can be said about forensic anthropologists. They are chastised by some anthropologists as not being true scientific anthropologists and are ignored by medical examiners, who believe a one-week course in the study of human bones and forensic anthropology teaches all they need to know.

History and anthropology have very different goals, different theoretical orientations, a fact often forgotten in the polemic of the dialogue regarding which discipline has the most to offer. The goal of history is to trace major events of the past, to focus on understanding the important players in decisions, and to understand the how and why of today's world. Anthropology, in contrast, studies people's day-to-day lives. It focuses on ordinary people and how they live, rather than leaders or major events.

These parallel, but equally valid, goals are reached using different data sets. Historians use written records as their data. This limits their investigations to cultures that have written records and biases their data to what people write about, but it allows detail in their investigations that archeologists can rarely match. Archeologists in the United States are actually trained as anthropologists. Anthropologists study culture. Cultural anthropologists (like the well-known Margaret Mead) study the culture of living peoples. Physical anthropologists (like Snow and Willey) study people through their biology. Linguistic anthropologists study people through their language. Archeologists study people through their material culture. Each specialty adds a different facet to the gem of our knowledge.

In this volume we summarize the historic data, the archeological data, and the physical anthropological data relating to the men who comprised the Seventh Cavalry. We compare the different data sets and find that none is complete or totally accurate. Beyond the differences, we are able to blend the disparate sources of data to produce greater insight into the men who rode with Custer than any of the disciplines can provide individually. Further, we have delved into the scientific literature analyzing the slowly growing mass of human skeletal remains from the period of westward expansion. We, in turn, compared these data, derived from the bones, to the historical record to go beyond mere bones and to reach an understanding of these people as a part of the population of the advancing frontier. From these osteobiological accounts we gain a picture of the life, health, and death of non-Indian settlers of the West. With this information we compare and contrast the data gained from the Seventh Cavalry Little Bighorn battlefield series. We develop for the ubiquitous westerner and the soldier of the Seventh a verbal portrait that sheds new light on details of their lives rarely recorded in historical documents.

We also go beyond the individual in history and look at the treatment of the dead and their monuments at the Little Bighorn battlefield. We seek to define how our cultural views have changed regarding what is the appropriate treatment for our war dead. Custer Battlefield National Monument, now Little Bighorn Battlefield National Monument, has always reflected the spirit of the times in the marble markers and monuments, in the story presented first by the army caretakers and then by the National Park Service, and most recently by the name change itself and the erection of a memorial to the American Indians who fought against the Seventh Cavalry.

The work that follows in this volume combines history, archeology, and physical anthropology. Each discipline provided information relevant to its unique data set. We hope to show that the goals of history and anthropology are not only compatible but, when combined, present a stronger interpretation of the past than any discipline alone—that in fact historical archeology and forensic anthropology, rather than being unwanted stepchildren, can represent the best of the disciplines.

Discussion Questions

1. What sorts of data can the bones and artifacts provide that cannot be garnered from historical records? What are the likely sources of bias or incompleteness in the archaeological remains?
2. What sorts of data can historical records provide that cannot be garnered from analyses of the bones and artifacts? What are the likely sources of bias or incompleteness in the historical records?
3. What circumstances led to the discovery and recovery of the bones and artifacts of the men of the Seventh Cavalry? Do you think it was fortunate that the battle site was not excavated in the 1880s, or even the 1950s? Does this suggest that preserving all or part of an archaeological site (leaving it protected, but undisturbed) for future advances in archaeological techniques and analyses is a good idea?
4. List and discuss all the different techniques that were used to find and recover the remains from the battlefield. Discuss the specialized knowledge of the different scientists involved in the analysis of the remains.
5. Why do you suppose the bodies of the men of the Seventh Cavalry were left lying on the battlefield, while the Sioux and Cheyenne casualties were recovered and taken away for burial?
6. Concerning the rights of the dead to remain undisturbed, do you think it matters if the people you want to dig up were intentionally buried according to the cultural customs of their times, compared to skeletons that are simply being recovered from the place where the people died? Think of the discovery of King Tut's tomb in Egypt, or the excavation of

a Native American burial mound in Illinois or Ohio, or of an 18th century African-American cemetery in Manhattan, on the one hand, versus the recovery of the skeletons of the Seventh Cavalry at the Little Bighorn Battlefield, or the recovery of the remains of people killed in the World Trade Center bombings and collapse in 2001, on the other hand. Should any of these remains be excavated? What about situations where the remains of people who have been killed are being recovered so they can be identified and returned to their families for burials (such as the mass graves in Guatemala and Bosnia)?

7. Should the cultural beliefs and ethnic origins of the people being excavated and analyzed make a difference—in terms of being destroyed or excavated, analyzed or not, stored or reburied? For example, suppose a U.S. highway is being widened and the bull-dozers expose a cemetery. Should the remains be treated differently depending on whether they are prehistoric, historic from the 17th or 18th century, or historic from the 20th century? Should the remains be treated differently depending on whether they are from prehistoric Native Americans or historic African Americans or historic British Americans or are of Christian versus non-Christian origins? Should "war dead" be given any special consideration?

8. What sorts of questions can only be answered by analysis of artifacts and skeletal remains of prehistoric and historic peoples? Will the questions we might want answered change over time?

5. THE CASE OF THE PURLOINED POTS

In "The Case of the Purloined Pots," Kent Black describes a specific case involving the trial of two pothunters accused of damaging federal lands and illegally digging up Mimbres pottery. Like the excavation of prehistoric human skeletal remains, the excavation of prehistoric artifacts is a controversial issue. A number of different per-spectives are put forth in the article. First is the view of the pothunters that what they are doing is simply recreation, a harmless hobby that doesn't hurt anyone and that has the potential to make them a lot of easy money. Second is the view of the park rangers and state and federal officials that archaeological remains constitute every-one's cultural heritage and must be rigorously protected. Third is the view of the ar-chaeologists that without context the pots are relatively meaningless, and that pothunting destroys any potential for learning about the past through careful ar-chaeological excavation of prehistoric sites. Fourth is the view of the art historians that the beautiful pots are valuable in themselves as art objects and should be re-covered for private collectors or museum goers to appreciate. Finally, we have the view of the serious amateurs who collect sherds and painstakingly glue them back together to experience a sort of mystic kinship with the distant past. As you read the article, think about what you would do if you found evidence of prehistoric activity. Think about how U.S. laws on this issue are structured to protect the sanctity of pri-vate land ownership so important in American culture.

Cathy Van Camp's beat is about average for a USDA Forest Service cop in New Mexico: a million and a half acres. In February 2000, she took advantage of some unusually warm weather to check on a couple of prehistoric ruins along the remote East Fork of the Gila River. Even in the deeply shadowed arroyos at 5,000 feet, the snow from earlier storms was thinning. It had been a year since Van Camp had vis-ited the sites, so she figured she was about due.

She first came to the Diamond Creek site. Located on a small rise about 80 feet above the river, the site was a thriving Mimbres village some 800 years ago. The Mimbres branch of the Mogollon culture, together with the Anasazi and Hohokam, flourished in the Southwest between approximately the 3rd and 13th centuries. They left behind tantalizing evidence of an advanced and artistic people. Their settlements, such as "Old Town" and "Swarts Ruin" on the Mimbres River, were important trading centers supporting several thousand people.

With its black-and-white geometric designs and complex interplay of animals, humans and mythical creatures, Mimbres pottery is among the most coveted of North American prehistoric artifacts. Because of the value of these antiquities, Van Camp was dismayed, but not particularly surprised, when she saw the condition of the sites. "There were fresh holes, dirt mounds and some blurred footprints," she recalled later. "There hadn't been a storm since January, so I knew the dig was recent."

After photographing the scene, Van Camp rode two miles along the Mimbres to another ruin known as the East Fork site. Here, too, a half-dozen fresh holes and other signs testified to a recent visit by a team of pothunters. "It looked to me like they hadn't found what they were after," Van Camp said later. "If they were coming back, we had a chance to catch them." Van Camp and fellow officer Mike Skinner set up seismic sensors on access roads leading to the wilderness. If a truck rumbled down the road, the sensor would send a signal back to the ranger station and alert the officers.

They didn't have to wait long. A little over two weeks later, at 7 A.M. on February 23, Van Camp was notified by the station dispatcher that the sensor had sounded. In short order, the two officers had rendezvoused and found a late-model truck parked near one of the trailheads. They followed tracks to the Diamond Creek site, but found no one. Pushing on, they reached the East Fork site, where, approaching, they could hear a clang of shovels and picks. Crawling on their hands and knees, they closed within a couple of hundred yards and saw three men.

Finally, after half an hour, Van Camp and Skinner, a muscular law enforcement veteran, inched across the open ground to where James Quarrell, 62, and his nephew, Aaron Sera, 31, were working in a trench. After determining that the men didn't seem to be armed, the officers made their move. Cathy Van Camp used cover as best she could to creep up on Mike Quarrell, 66, James' brother, who was a short distance away from his companions. "They were completely taken by surprise," Van Camp said later at the trial. "I don't think they had the slightest concern they'd be caught. Mike [Quarrell] said to me, 'I'm going to take my licks this time and be a lot more careful next time.' "

Ten years ago, Mike Quarrell's bravado would have made more sense. In those days, very few federal prosecutors pursued cases of archaeological theft, and most judges did little more than administer hand slaps, if they didn't throw the case out altogether.

Law enforcement's job is difficult because most looters don't believe that pothunting is wrong. In many parts of the country, digging for pots and hunting for arrowheads have been time-honored, multigenerational pastimes, as essential a part of the picnic experience as fried chicken and lemonade. Many regard it as a way to supplement their income, an avocation that rewards those with initiative. I have a friend, whom I will call Ted, who was a pothunter for two decades, amassing and selling a huge collection. "If you're about to lose your home or have your truck repossessed and you know where a Mimbres site is with a potential for ten pots worth $75,000, are you going to consider it?" he asked me one day at his New Mexico home. "Of course. You don't think of it as criminal. It's not like robbing a bank. It's just lying in the ground. No one's using it, no one sees it and no one's going to miss it when it's gone. So why not?"

Why not, indeed. Sarah Vogel, the assistant U.S. attorney prosecuting the Quarrell case, addressed that question in her opening statement to the jury. "This isn't about pottery sherds lying on the ground," she emphasized. "There's no difference between what these men did at the East Fork site and if they'd broken into a display at the Maxwell Museum of Anthropology. These sites are part of New Mexico's open-air museum."

The Quarrell case, which went to federal court in Las Cruces, New Mexico, in October 2000, was an important case not just for federal authorities but for state, local and Native American agencies attempting to control their own lands. A conviction here would signal that legal and public sentiment had changed toward the crime of stealing ancient artifacts. An acquittal would mean the law was still no more than a joke.

Even so, the proceedings were so low-key they might have been in family court. The only spectators were either relatives on the Quarrells' side or a half-dozen Forest Service personnel and prosecution witnesses across the aisle. There was no local press coverage. The Quarrells themselves didn't look particularly worried. Perhaps they were thinking about all the other looting cases that have been dismissed over the years. Though their nephew, Aaron Sera, had pleaded out to a misdemeanor, Mike and James were facing felony charges. Both were dressed in casual Southwest business chic: Mike was turned out in a safari jacket, jeans, and a cowboy shirt. James sported black jeans, a black western coat, and a cowboy shirt with a bola tie. Both wore cowboy boots and aviator sunglasses.

As presented by Vogel, a young woman who took a stern, brusque approach to the case, the prosecution was detailed and to the point. The defendants, she said, were caught in the act of digging. By federal law, damage to a historic site on public land in excess of $500 is a felony. The government would demonstrate that at least $12,000 would be required to restore the site.

The defense strategy was not to dispute that the defendants had been digging on public land but that they had only just arrived at the site and had barely scratched the earth. In fact, the defense insisted, most of the destruction had been perpetrated years before by parties unknown.

On the surface, the Quarrell case appeared to be not much more than a trespass on public lands. Yet as any archaeologist will tell you, it's a practice that has reached epidemic proportions.

Illegal trade in antiquities ranks as the world's fourth most lucrative illicit business after drugs, guns and money laundering. In 1998 the U.S. Information Agency reported that such trade was a $4.5 billion-a-year business. From back alleys to the most reputable auction houses, dealers, collectors, grave robbers and thieves buy and sell everything from Roman coins to Incan pottery to Sioux warbonnets. Some of these artifacts have been legally acquired, some have not. The dark side of antiquities trading often involves goods illegally excavated from historic sites. In the Old World, such commerce in plundered relics can involve material from an ancient sunken boat off a Greek island or a buried Celtic village on the English coast. In the Americas, the trade usually involves locating and looting graves.

In many countries there's not much gray area. On public or private land, all antiquities in the ground or lying around on top of it belong unequivocally to the state or to those with the most obvious cultural entitlement to them. Dig them up to decorate the mantel and you're going to jail. In the United States, however, private land ownership is one of the most time-honored principles. For the most part, if an object is found on your land, it's yours.

Nevertheless, federal and state authorities have strengthened laws and intensified prosecutions, especially in the past decade, to discourage looting. In passing the Antiquities Act of 1906, Congress made it illegal to excavate or destroy any "historic ruin" on federal lands. But it took the passage of the 1979 Archaeological Resources Protection Act to give it teeth. In 1990, NAGPRA, the Native American Graves Protection and Repatriation Act, provided for the protection of grave sites and for the repatriation to the appropriate tribe of human remains and artifacts held by institutions that receive federal funds. Many states passed similar laws, in some cases to regulate excavations on private land. For instance, in New Mexico it is against the law to dig a known grave site or hire someone to excavate a historic site with heavy equipment without a permit from the state.

One of the prosecution's first expert witnesses in the Quarrell trial was J. J. Brody, former director of the Maxwell Museum, at the University of New Mexico, and author of several seminal works on the art of the prehistoric Southwest. "The market was very low for this pottery until the '60s," he testified. "Up until the late '50s you could get prehistoric pottery, Anasazi or Mimbres, for about $25 a pot. All that changed in the '60s," he went on. "Suddenly, international collectors were interested and auction houses were interested. Mimbres pottery shot up to $5,000 to $6,000 per pot. Now, it's not unusual to hear about some of this pottery going for $40,000 to $60,000 per pot." Several years ago, in fact, a Mimbres "story bowl" sold at auction for $100,000.

Of course, pothunting is hardly confined to the Southwest. Every part of the country has been affected. Ancient totems from the Pacific Northwest have been cut up and sold for lawn ornaments, and Caddoan sites in the Mississippi River Valley have been bulldozed and re-bulldozed. Some experts believe that as much as 95 percent of the Eastern Seaboard's important indigenous sites have been disturbed by looters, many of them destroyed. But the Southwest does offer special attractions for looters. The area is sparsely populated and, as was the case with the Quarrells, detection is often a matter of luck.

Near where I live in the mountains of northern New Mexico, it's tough to kick up a clod of dirt without uncovering a prehistoric site. This area—the Galisteo Basin 20 miles southeast of Santa Fe—contains evidence of humanity's earliest habitation in the Southwest. A couple of years ago, a young woman managing a ranch west of Highway 14 asked me out to her place for dinner. I wandered around her casita, noticing small piles of sherds, many with ornate geometric designs. She told me she usually found a handful every time she walked her dog. Later, she showed me her workroom, where she had recently glued together the sherds of a large bowl. Except for a couple of small holes and chips on the rim, the bowl was nearly complete. Narrow at the base, it flared out to nearly 14 or 15 inches in diameter. Its opening was about half that. The bowl was polychromatic, deep reddish browns, some almost rust, crisscrossed with half-inch black lines. It was extraordinarily beautiful.

She described finding the sherds sticking out of a fallen embankment and the painstaking care she had taken in excavating the pieces. She regarded the artifact with something approaching reverence. She wasn't a greedy, insensitive looter. She wasn't motivated by avarice. She told me that while digging out the sherds, she felt moved by something deep in her, a curiosity and a desire to touch something ancient that had occupied this land before her.

That evening came back to me last spring when I visited Forrest Fenn at a site a few miles from my friend's house. I'd heard about Fenn for years but became interested in making his acquaintance when his name kept popping up in casual conversation at the Quarrell trial. Some regarded Fenn as one of the best practitioners of private archaeological conservation in the state; he was a man who hunted pots *within* the law. Others felt he was nothing more than a looter with good lawyers and deep pockets. Fenn is a gruff, plainspoken man, the edges of his West Texas drawl scarcely dulled by 30 years in Santa Fe. His manner may be partly due to his military background. He enlisted as a private in the Air Force at age 18 and rose to the rank of major, flying 328 combat missions over Vietnam before retiring in 1970. He opened Fenn Galleries in Santa Fe in 1972 and for the next 16 years was one of the Southwest's premier dealers and collectors.

On a tour of his house in Santa Fe, Fenn showed me a long table with more than a dozen extraordinary polychrome pots from the pueblo San Lazaro, part of an ancient city that had once supported nearly 1,800 people. The Tewa lived there for centuries before abandoning it sometime after the Pueblo Revolt of 1680 when the Spanish were driven briefly out of New Mexico. Thirteen years ago, Fenn acquired 160 acres of the former Cash Ranch, 73 of which contain the San Lazaro ruins. They are listed in the National Register of Historic Places.

He led me to a room adjacent to his four-car garage where he kept his neatly organized documentation of the story of San Lazaro. There were boxes of various metals, from nails to musket balls from the Spanish colonial period and even bits of Chinese porcelain (which came from Spanish traders from the Philippines), and countless boxes of various animal bones, stone tools and sherds. The San Lazaro collection is important to Fenn. It is his defense against those who claim he's nothing more than a wealthy looter exploiting a legal loophole.

Joe Watkins, an archaeologist with the Bureau of Indian Affairs who waged a well-publicized feud with Fenn over the ethical dilemma faced by archaeologists attending a Clovis symposium produced by Fenn, charged that "if you don't have contextural data, you don't have anything, just a meaningless, pretty artifact . . . a collector who does not provide provenance does not add to the research."

Eric Blinman, an archaeologist at the Museum of New Mexico, in Santa Fe, who has observed Fenn's work at San Lazaro, hasn't always agreed with his methods, but says he doesn't believe that Fenn is a complete villain. He says Fenn "possesses the most inexhaustible curiosity, and the main difference between Fenn and most archaeologists is that for him, it is a classic fight between archaeology and art history. He believes that the most important thing to come out of the earth is the artifact."

Of course, Fenn's excavations have not been illegal. Furthermore, considering the horrific damage done on private lands in the past, where acres and acres of important sites were bulldozed into oblivion, it is hard to fault Fenn's methods. Of the estimated 4,500 rooms in San Lazaro's complex, Fenn has excavated only 34, or 0.7 percent by his estimation. He has done no digging at all in two and a half years. At some point in the future, he plans to donate the site to a conservancy that will preserve it for archaeological study.

It would appear, then, that the issue at the Quarrell trial was black-and-white. Following certain strictures, it is legal to dig for mammoth bones or a new route to China if you're on private land. Otherwise, you've broken the law; hence, the Quarrells are guilty.

Except that there were several gray areas. Robert Kinney, the public defender, was skillful in disposing of several key federal allegations and pieces of evidence. The gun the Quarrells carried was excluded. Large boxes of sherds seized at both brothers' residences were excluded. Allegations that the Quarrells and Aaron Sera had dug at Diamond Creek were not mentioned to the jury, since none of the defendants were actually caught digging there. Kinney hammered away at the government's witnesses: J. J. Brody, Cathy Van Camp, and Bob Schiowitz, the Forest Service's archaeologist. Kinney's tactic was simple but potentially damaging to the government's case: Given that the expert witnesses have testified that thousands of prehistoric sites in New Mexico have already been looted, how can you prove the damage claimed if you haven't witnessed the accused actually dig every single hole? Kinney was marginalizing the eyewitness accounts of the officers to circumstantial evidence. Suddenly, the government's case looked vulnerable.

"There is so little forensic evidence," says Robin Poague, a Forest Service special agent stationed in New Mexico who was also the lead investigator on the Quarrell case. "Unless you catch somebody in the act of digging, it's tricky to make a case. You could stop a truck on Forest Service land, and there might be tools in the back and pots on the front seat and, a few hundred yards away, a couple of freshly dug holes. But you have to prove that this guy actually dug those pots out of the ground."

On the second day of the trial, Vogel, seemingly unshaken by Kinney's tactic, asked Mike and James Quarrell under cross-examination to recount the events of the previous February. Both men were polite and soft-spoken, though adamant that they had committed no crime, nor damaged the sites. Vogel was not interested in their denials. What she wanted to show the jury was that no one who packed in the kind of equipment found with the Quarrells and Aaron Sera could possibly be out for a little leisurely surface collecting. The Quarrells had brought an arsenal of digging tools to the site: picks, collapsible shovels and a—some might say telltale—thin piece of metal with a T-handle called a probe.

According to Ted, the former pothunter, this steel probe is the most specialized piece of equipment a grave robber can own. A typical probe is three-eighths of an inch in diameter, three to four feet long and has a 16-inch handle perpendicular to the shaft. The shaft is flexible steel and comes from the "X" rod that lines the trunk lid of a car. It is narrow and strong, so it creates less resistance going into the earth. "Diggers always concentrate on locating the walls of dwellings first," says Ted. "Then they locate the burial earth with their probes and start digging cross channels and sifting the dirt. Most successful diggers have become so adept with their probes that they rarely damage pots. That's a lot of trial and error, probably digging a hundred test holes, leaving your probe in place and digging down to find out what you've hit."

From his own testimony, it was established that James Quarrell had long been fascinated with Mimbres pottery, though not in any nefarious way. A talented potter, he had retired from a job with the city of Deming and devoted himself to making replicas of Mimbres pottery, one of which was on permanent display in a museum in nearby Silver City. But to my mind the most important question was never asked. What would the Quarrells and Sera do with a trove of Mimbres pottery if they uncovered it?

Usually, pothunters will contract with dealers, middlemen and collectors ahead of time. "There are probably 5,000 to 6,000 collectors of this type of material," said Joshua Baer, one of the few Santa Fe dealers who buys and sells prehistoric items. "And maybe 1,000 or less who are actively trading. However, there are a lot less than there were 20 years ago. With the laws these days, you'd be crazy to trade a pot without proper documentation; they [the authorities] could come and take your whole collection."

One factor not brought up in the trial is a new proactivism on the part of Native American groups. "There has been a tremendous amount of pressure on government agencies by Native Americans in the Southwest to enforce these laws," says Ted. "Parallel to the rise in political consciousness in the '60s and '70s in other parts of American society, Native Americans began a new kind of activism. One aspect was the realization that these sites were not only an important part of their cultural heritage but part of their natural resource. There is now a new generation of Native American lawyers, historians, anthropologists, archaeologists and social scientists who have the sophistication to fight on a state and federal level to protect their interests."

Says Dan Simplicio, a Zuni tribal councilman who has worked in the Navajo Nation Archaeological Department as well as spent several years as a Zuni cultural resource specialist, "It is not a matter of legal or illegal, public or private land when it comes to grave robbing. It doesn't matter if it is scientific or for profit. For indigenous peoples, these are living things. But museums and collectors take them and objectify them, like trophies."

Unfortunately, a cultural misunderstanding continues between many European Americans and Native Americans over the sanctity of grave sites and the funerary objects found in them. "One of the reasons Zuni and other tribes have so much difficulty with repatriation," says Simplicio, "is that we are not equipped for the implications. Through eons of our religious practices, we had no instance of looting or grave robbing. It simply didn't exist. The religion made no provision for what to do with remains that had been interrupted and disturbed in the middle of this very important cycle. Their life cycle has been damaged. We have nothing in our religion that allows us to exorcise or rebaptize them. That is why the whole idea of grave robbing is so incredibly painful to us. We simply cannot conceive of this crime. Slowly, we are learning ways to deal with repatriation and reburial, but you cannot expect people with a religion perhaps thousands of years old to change their belief structure overnight."

By the end of the second day of the trial, the momentum had once again swung back to the prosecution. Vogel was not easily distracted by Kinney's attempt to impeach the credibility of her witnesses and obfuscate the issue at hand. She was helped considerably in her case by the defendants themselves. During one notable exchange, Mike Quarrell damaged his position before the jury. Under cross-examination, he claimed that the only other time he and his brother had ever dug for pottery was 30 years before when a man paid them to dig on private land "and then wouldn't let us keep any of the sherds we found." Sarah Vogel raised an eyebrow. "Then where did you get those bags and bags of sherds police found in the closet of your home?" she asked. Quarrell did not respond. Vogel did not need to press the point.

The next morning it was announced that the jury had reached a verdict. There were even fewer spectators than there had been at the trial's beginning. Brody and several interested parties from the various state and federal agencies had departed the night before, and even the defendants' supporters on the other side of the aisle had thinned considerably. The defendants themselves seemed relaxed and unconcerned. They reclined in their chairs, legs crossed, and exchanged small talk with their lawyers and each other. At the prosecution's table, Sarah Vogel and Special Agent Robin Poague seemed nervous, intently discussing an array of documents spread out before them.

The jury filed in, a cross section of southern New Mexico society that included ranchers, small business owners, retirees and a housewife. I was told later that they'd reached their decision relatively quickly the night before. This foretold nothing. They could have rejected the government's evidence out of hand. After all, this is southern New Mexico, where individual rights and freedoms are not just an abstract theory. I wondered if Vogel had perhaps been a little overbearing. What if they weren't convinced that the Quarrells' offense was actually a crime?

The judge, who'd only spoken up a half-dozen times during the trial, read the verdict: guilty on all counts.

The Quarrells looked shocked, and then confused. Vogel took it in stride, but Poague was genuinely relieved. "You can have the best evidence possible in a trial like this, but you never know. This is really encouraging. It's making me think the tide's turning."

I still think back to the time in Colombia when a Tayrona Indian sold me an ancient stone effigy, or to the clandestine excavation I witnessed in southern Peru when one of the grave robbers gave me the hair comb from a 2,000-year-old corpse. Interestingly, I find myself torn in three directions: a sense of respect for the dead, a belief that both the art and detritus of past civilizations should be held in public trust, and a desire to touch something from the past. On one hand, I feel shame that after the decimation of this continent's indigenous peoples, European Americans are still out souvenir hunting. On the other, I feel kinship with my woman friend who laboriously reassembled the sherds and came up with a beautiful object hundreds of years old. To reach that far back in time and touch something real and material is, to me, a feeling like no other.

Ted, though retired from pothunting for more than a decade, says that in this day of advanced technology, digging up graves is less and less important to our knowledge of the past. "I go to a place like Antelope Mesa and look around. I know there are literally thousands and thousands of pots and other amazing artifacts in the ground there. But really, how many more pots do we need? Do museums even display half the pots they own? Will a hundred or a thousand more pots tell us that much more about the art and culture? These days, it gives me a great feeling just to go to the mesa and know that incredible art is lying in the ground, maybe forever."

Discussion Questions

1. Why is it difficult to catch pothunters in the act?
2. Is illegal trade in antiquities a big problem worldwide, or is it relatively rare and not particularly lucrative?

3. What is the main difference between antiquities laws in most of the world and antiquities laws in the United States? Why do U.S. laws allow the digging of antiquities on private land?

4. Why would anyone pay $100,000 to own a prehistoric Mimbres bowl? Why do art collectors spend so much money acquiring unique art objects? What makes something worth that much money?

5. Why did archaeologists face an ethical dilemma concerning whether or not to attend a Clovis symposium produced by collector Forrest Fenn? Do you think professional archaeologists should boycott any activity sponsored by pothunters?

6. Dan Simplicio, a Zuni tribal councilman, says, "It is not a matter of legal or illegal, public or private land when it comes to grave robbing. It doesn't matter if it is scientific or for profit. For indigenous peoples, these are living things. But museums and collectors take them and objectify them, like trophies." First, discuss what Simplicio might mean by saying that these (the pots and other grave goods) are living things. Are there any material objects in U.S. culture that have such special status that we don't allow people to desecrate them? Second, discuss Simplicio's equating of pothunting with scientific archaeological investigation. Is pothunting worse than archaeological excavation? Why? Is the quest for knowledge of the past more legitimate than the quest for monetary profit, or the quest to make a personal connection to people who lived long ago?

7. The article ends with Ted's perspective that no one should dig up the artifacts of the past. He says, "Will a hundred or a thousand more pots tell us that much more about the art and culture?" How important do you think it is to understand the past?

8. Should archaeologists be allowed to excavate sites on public and private lands, in order to learn more about the past? Should pothunters be allowed to excavate sites on private lands in order to find pots for collecting or resale?

9. How might one balance the different perspectives on these issues?

Additional Resources

For Internet links related to this chapter, please visit our website at www.mhhe.com/dettwyler

FINE-DARE, KATHLEEN S. *Grave Injustice: The American Indian Repatriation Movement and NAGPRA (Fourth World Rising).* Nebraska: University of Nebraska Press, 2002.

FLUEHR-LOBBAN, CAROLYN, and ROBYN RHUDY, eds. *Ethics and the Profession of Anthropology: A Dialogue for Ethically Conscious Practice.* 2nd edition. New York: Rowman & Littlefield, 2003.

LARSEN, CLARK SPENCER. *Skeletons in Our Closet: Revealing Our Past through Bioarchaeology.* Princeton, NJ: Princeton University Press, 2002.

RENFREW, COLIN. *Loot, Legitimacy and Ownership: The Ethical Crisis in Archaeology* (Duckworth Debates in Archaeology). London: Duckworth Publishers, 2001.

SCOTT, DOUGLAS D., P. WILLEY, and MELISSA A. CONNOR. *They Died With Custer: Soldiers' Bones from the Battle of the Little Bighorn.* Norman, OK: University of Oklahoma Press, 1998.

THOMAS, DAVID HURST. *Skull Wars: Kennewick Man, Archaeology, and the Battle for Native American Identity.* New York: Basic Books, 2001.

CHAPTER 4

Evolution and Genetics

6. "Reading the Language of Our Ancestors," by Jeff Wheelwright, *Discover* 23, no. 2 (February 2002), pp. 70–77.

7. "15 Answers to Creationist Nonsense," by John Rennie, *Scientific American,* July, 2002 (from website www.sciam.com/article.cfm?articleID=000D4FEC-7D5B-1D07-8E49809EC588EEDF).

People have long debated the different effects of "nature" and "nurture" on human existence. Are we mostly the products of the genes (nature) we inherited from our distant and recent ancestors? Or is what happens to us as we grow and develop (nurture—the environment and culture) more important in determining what kinds of lives we lead? The answer, of course, is that human existence is the complex result of an intricate and ongoing dance between our genetic heritage and our environmental and cultural experiences. Research into the human genome is proceeding at a rapid pace. Most of you have faced or will face a variety of issues in your lives concerning your genes and how they affect your life. It is important to understand what is known about human genetics and how much is still unknown. Understanding that humans have evolved (and continue to evolve) through the many different processes of evolution will help you make sense of who we are as biological creatures.

 ## 6. READING THE LANGUAGE OF OUR ANCESTORS

This article discusses the life work of Dr. Victor A. McKusick, who began a quest years ago to figure out how human genetic variation was expressed in the forms of disease or physical impairment. Dr. McKusick's work has included studies of people with Marfan's syndrome, a dominant allelic variation, and Ellis–van Creveld syndrome, a recessive disorder common among some groups of Amish people. His work was the motivating force behind the international Human Genome Organization (HUGO). Along with the public company, Celera, HUGO has worked over the

past two decades to map the entire human genome in broad outline. To date, only four chromosomes have been completely mapped, but detailed maps of all 23 human chromosomes are expected to be complete by 2030, if not before. Understanding the DNA sequences of specific genes linked to disease may help in the development of treatments or even cures for some conditions.

On the wall of Victor A. McKusick's office in Baltimore hangs a portrait of a sad-faced woman holding a six-fingered infant. The photograph, which he calls the Amish Madonna, was taken during McKusick's pioneering studies of the Old Order Amish of Pennsylvania 40 years ago. McKusick described genetic diseases in these and other patients long before there were tools to pinpoint the mistakes in their DNA.

McKusick is a white-haired, dark-suited figure, still vigorous and straight but, at 80 years old, slightly tremulous. Near the Amish Madonna portrait, he keeps a row of books holding the fruits of his patient and relentless efforts to place genetics in the mainstream of clinical medicine. First published in 1966 and now in its 12th edition, *Mendelian Inheritance in Man* is an ever-expanding catalog of human genes and the medical disorders associated with them. McKusick still oversees the compilation of the catalog that has earned him the honorific "father of medical genetics." His office is at the eponymous McKusick-Nathans Institute of Genetic Medicine, which is part of the Johns Hopkins School of Medicine, where McKusick has worked since World War II.

McKusick became famous for linking genes to disease; but the slim single volume of the original *Mendelian Inheritance in Man* recorded no actual genes, although it described hundreds of genetic disorders. Their locations were unknown. The third edition reflects medical genetics in the early 1970s. "It recorded all the genes that had been mapped at that time," McKusick says with a smile. "It filled one page." During those early years, McKusick collected genetic disorders one by one, working alone at first and later assisted by staff and other associates. He culled the journals for rare conditions and wrote up his own observations. He watched as medical genetics grew from a research backwater into a hot spot of medical inquiry.

In recent years improvements in genomics—the detailed study of genes' structure and function—have greatly speeded his task. With automated sequencing machines and supercomputers, researchers have assembled electronic banks of genetic code and begun analyzing them for possible links to disease. In June 2000 their efforts yielded the first rough draft of the human genome sequence—a close reading of the 3.2 billion chemical letters that define our species and drive our cells. "Victor McKusick started this whole thing in motion," says Francis Collins, director of the government's National Human Genome Research Institute. "He's the guy who led us here."

In the meantime gene sequences have poured into the catalog, and the print editions of McKusick's opus have multiplied. Since 1987 there has been an online version, *Online Mendelian Inheritance in Man,* accessible at no cost through a government Web site; at last count it contained more than 13,000 entries.

As the constellation of genomics has ascended, promising a skyful of medical benefits, the field has so far generated much more dazzle than useful applications. In that sense, little has changed. While he diagnosed and cataloged his patients' unfortunate ailments, Victor McKusick had no cures to offer. On the wall above his computer, the Madonna, her white cap imparting a sort of halo, looks down gravely. The doctor once used her photo for a Christmas card.

McKusick has always been aware that his interest in unusual genetic disorders could be considered "stamp collecting." "From the beginning," he writes in the preface of the latest *Mendelian Inheritance in Man,* "I have thought of these catalogs . . . as a photographic negative from which a positive picture of the human genetic constitution can be made." A history buff, McKusick likes to quote from a letter written by William Harvey in 1657: "Nature is no where accustomed more openly to display her secret mysteries than in cases where she shows traces of her workings apart from the beaten path."

The term *disease gene* bothers many scientists. They don't like promoting the idea, says Francis Collins, that "a gene's only reason for being in the genome is to create havoc." People are accustomed to reading about a newly discovered gene "for" this condition or that, even genes for behavioral characteristics such as those "for" homosexuality, manic depression, or risk taking. Almost always what is meant by the reports is that a gene with a different spelling than usual has been statistically linked to a certain trait. In comparison people who are not sick or who don't exhibit the trait carry the normal, or usual, form of the gene. Often the gene itself isn't identified, only its area on a chromosome.

Genes are both matter and message, structure as well as information. The structural component is the double-stranded DNA molecule, consisting of the nucleotides adenine (A), thymine (T), cytosine (C), and guanine (G). The information component lies in the order of those As, Ts, Cs, and Gs. That sequence, called the genetic code, tells the cell to assemble amino acids in order to make particular proteins.

A single gene may be hundreds or thousands of letters long, and if a mutation misspells some part of the sequence, disease may ensue. "I prefer the term 'allelic variation' to 'mutation,' " says McKusick, a stickler in his choice of words. He defines a disease gene as one having "disease-related alleles." An allele is simply a variant, a version with a different spelling, which may be inherited from a parent or arise at random.

The first disease gene to be mapped (traced to a chromosome) was for a type of red-green color blindness found mostly in males, in 1911. Researchers knew that the disease was passed down in families from mothers to sons. That pointed to a problem with the X and Y chromosomes, which are the sex-determining chromosomes. Girls have two X chromosomes, one inherited from each parent. If one of the X chromosomes is faulty, usually the other one will keep the girl healthy. But boys inherit a male-making Y chromosome from their father and an X chromosome from their mother, and so a bad X chromosome in them has no backup. All the early mapping of genetic disorders was to the X chromosome because researchers were studying disorders that affected only males. Another reason was that the X and Y was the only chromosomal pair that scientists could distinguish with their crude microscopes.

When McKusick joined the faculty of Johns Hopkins School of Medicine in 1946, gene mapping had hardly moved beyond the X chromosome. Genes were still abstractions, mysterious particles of inheritance. The problems caused by genetic errors were strikingly real, though. Odd and rare deformities often cropped up within inbred populations in recognizable patterns—patterns that conformed to rules laid down by Gregor Mendel, the 19th-century monk and botanist. In his breeding experiments, Mendel observed predictable patterns of inheritance. Geneticists call these patterns dominant or recessive, and they now recognize that many inherited disorders in humans, if they are not X-linked, are inherited as Mendel predicted.

Genes, as noted, are handed down in pairs, one from each parent. In dominant disorders, only one defective copy of a gene is required to cause disease. So a child will become ill if a sick parent passes along the faulty copy of the gene. The chance of this occurring is one in two. In recessive disorders, a child will become ill only if both copies of the gene are flawed. But the parents show no sign of disease because each usually has a second, healthy copy of the gene that can compensate for the problem. If both parents carry a gene for a recessive disease, the chance of having an afflicted child is one in four.

In the mid-20th century, tracking the pedigrees of Mendelian illnesses made genetics exciting to academics, but the field was discouraging for physicians. The difference was between medical genetics, a research interest, and genetic medicine, a clinical need. "When I went into it, people thought I was committing professional suicide," recalls McKusick, who had initially specialized in cardiology. Physicians would rather tackle infectious disease, using newly discovered antibiotics such as penicillin and sulfa drugs. Infections then were the big killers of humankind.

As scientists unraveled the structure and workings of DNA, they learned that genes make proteins and that proteins make the body run. A genetic disorder occurs when a misspelling, or allelic variation, in the DNA cripples or knocks out the corresponding protein. Diagnoses can be made on the basis of the missing or mutated protein. In a few cases, if the protein is an enzyme, the disease can be treated with dietary measures. An early success story was phenylketonuria, or PKU, a recessive disorder. Infants who lacked the enzyme for breaking down phenylalanine became mentally retarded. Eliminating foods containing phenylalanine can prevent the disease.

McKusick's first book, *Heritable Disorders of Connective Tissue,* published in 1956, included a description of Marfan's syndrome, a dominant genetic disorder. People with Marfan's have skeletal abnormalities. They tend to be tall, with long limbs, curved spines, and misshapen chests. Their eyeballs elongate, and they are prone to dislocated lenses and detached retinas. Their feet flatten beneath the weight of their bodies. The worst sign is an enlarged aorta, the artery bearing blood from the heart. It can fatally burst when the person is as young as 30. According to the National Marfan Foundation, "it is estimated that at least 200,000 people in the United States have the Marfan syndrome or a related connective tissue disorder." McKusick became a leading diagnostician of the disorder and traced its Mendelian pedigree in scores of families.

In the 1960s he brought the same skills to the Old Order Amish in the farm country of Pennsylvania. Centuries of intermarriage among members in this small community have reduced the variation in their gene pool, making them more likely to exchange defective DNA. One genetic disease, called Ellis–van Creveld syndrome, intrigued McKusick. These patients have an extra finger on each hand, heart murmurs, and short stature. Although the Amish are notoriously suspicious of outsiders, the direct manner of this former New England farm boy eventually won them over. By studying their genealogical records, McKusick tracked the disorder's origin back to an immigrant who arrived in the United States in the 1800s. Either this man or his wife was the "founder" of this recessive disorder among the American sect.

McKusick had arrived at his calling. He researched the histories of hemophilia in colonial New England, familial Mediterranean fever among Armenians who had immigrated to California, and various recessive disorders in Finland. He scoured scientific journals—and asked his Hopkins students to do the same—for reports about medical genetics. The first edition of *Mendelian Inheritance in Man,* in 1966, formalized the collections. "It was on a mainframe, making huge printouts, before it was even in print form," McKusick says proudly.

McKusick soon realized that a piecemeal, descriptive catalog of Mendelian-type illnesses would never be comprehensive. The basic data about genes was missing. Moreover, for the more common illnesses that tend to run in families, like breast cancer and high blood pressure, multiple genes appeared to be involved, intersecting in unpredictable patterns. So in 1969 he proposed a "complete mapping" of all human genes, an idea that was 20 years ahead of its time because the technology to realize it did not yet exist.

Slowly, researchers began to map genes to particular locations on a chromosome. To map a gene is not the same thing as identifying it. As an analogy, think of rows of brick houses along an urban street. Each house represents a gene. A map can take you to the street (chromosome) and then to the exact address. But you have no sense of what is going on inside each house (gene). The inhabitants—the sequence of the gene—need to be identified.

The original technique of mapping genes involved identifying a disease-related protein and working backward with a variety of probes to locate the gene that made it. This approach was not only slow and cumbersome but also required knowing exactly what protein was causing the inherited disease. In the 1980s scientists devised a more powerful technique to close in on mutated genes for which the dysfunctional protein was unknown. Researchers sampled the DNA of afflicted family members and looked for a distinctive marker, a stretch of DNA they all possessed. The marker was like a lamppost at the head of a street, illuminating the likely location of the gene. By the end of the decade, they'd mapped enough markers to begin decoding the entire genetic landscape—the genome.

In 1988 McKusick was named the founder-president of HUGO, the international Human Genome Organization, which promoted the launch of the public consortium, in 1990. He also became a champion of J. Craig Venter, who had developed a way to capture genes en masse. When Venter split from the public venture in 1998 to found Celera, a private genomics company, McKusick cheered on both efforts and kept above the fray.

Meanwhile, with genetic information mushrooming, McKusick and his helpers struggled to stay abreast of the field. In 1995, the National Center for Biotechnology Information took over the maintenance of the online version of *Mendelian Inheritance in Man.* Today McKusick, a staff of nine, and several freelancers comb the literature; they update the archives nearly every day. McKusick has broadened the criteria for entry so that a Mendelian scheme of disease is no longer required. Disease itself is no longer required. In these archives the number of genes described (genotypes) has now outpaced the number of disease descriptions, or phenotypes. For researchers and physicians the archive is the only bridge between the raw As, Ts, Cs, and Gs of genetic sequences and the human conditions presented in textbooks and examination rooms. "If you need functional information about the gene," says McKusick, "you need *Mendelian Inheritance in Man.*" The staff doesn't even know the number of entries in each category of the online catalog. They're too busy gathering new information.

What makes Victor McKusick a giant? He is only an M.D. and admits to being unskilled in the laboratory—"not very able manually," as he puts it. When he was elected to the National Academy of Sciences in 1973, a few questioned whether he was a scientist or merely a "natural historian." McKusick replies: "There's a distinction, I've always thought, between the scientist, who knows more and more about less and less, and the scholar, who knows the background of his field."

His strength, like an oarsman's, is applied while looking backward. When he was promoted to physician in chief of the Johns Hopkins Hospital in 1973, McKusick attained a position held at the turn of the 20th century by the great diagnostician Sir William Osler. McKusick likes to show visitors the space under the golden dome of the central building where Osler wrote his famous medical manual. He compares his own catalog to Osler's work and to other intensively researched classics: the encyclopedia by Diderot et al. of the 18th century and Murray's *Oxford English Dictionary* of the 19th.

Mendelian Inheritance in Man takes about three-quarters of his time, he estimates. Most of his updating is done at his home computer, medical journals spread in front of him, but several days of the week he appears at his Hopkins office. There are conferences to plan, calls to return. McKusick has the telling accent of a Mainer and sometimes, too, the Maine abruptness. Look away and he is gone, departing the room in midthought or midconversation, not because his mind has wandered but because it has made a forceful, 90-degree turn to a more urgent matter.

"Medical genetics as a clinical discipline was instituted with me," McKusick declares, returning to his career. "I fostered the development of people in the field. In the 1970s medical genetics was a bit like nutrition, in that there weren't freestanding practitioners in the community. But in the 1990s, with the coming of chromosome and DNA tests, the development of reproductive and prenatal genetics, and the fact that there was so much more we could do in this field, we had the need for regulation and for the board certification of practice." In short, "I consider myself a teacher, a researcher, a physician."

Is there a deliberate order to the list?

"I'd prefer not to weigh them," McKusick replies.

Still, with human gene therapy far from being effective, what does the gene doctor do for the patient?

"I don't feel I've left clinical medicine," he says. "I pride myself on the fact that I still see patients. When I was department head, three times a week I made rounds with students."

McKusick stepped down from his medical school post in 1985, but he still serves as an unpaid professor and consultant at the hospital's genetics clinic. Today he will see a patient named Roy M. for his annual appointment. Roy M. has Marfan's syndrome, the condition McKusick investigated almost 50 years ago, when he was starting to compile the connective-tissue disorders caused by disease genes.

Rapping briefly on an examination room door, McKusick enters and finds a patient sitting in consultation with a young doctor. The patient, an African American, has long arms, which reach nearly to the floor. He has Marfan's syndrome, but he is not Roy M.

McKusick withdraws, and shortly his own charge arrives. Surprisingly this man also is African American. His body appears normal, save for a surgical scar down the middle of his chest. The scar is proof of the value of a proper genetic diagnosis. Years ago Roy M.'s distended aorta and a faulty heart valve were replaced with plastic parts.

The patient's father had suffered a burst aorta in 1981, which revealed the Marfan's syndrome postmortem. Doctors examined the young Roy and found he had inherited his father's illness. Preventive surgery may have saved his life, but his disease continued. He couldn't go all out when playing sports. Now 30, he has been a heart patient for almost 20 years; he wonders whether he should have children. In the exam room he seems to move carefully and talk softly, as if he might strain himself.

After a brief exam, McKusick reviews the patient's medication and latest test results. He pronounces himself satisfied.

"So it sounds OK?" asks Roy M., meaning both his heart and his future.

"It sounds as though you're doing well," McKusick says firmly. "I wouldn't do anything differently. Good to see you as always, Roy."

This patient knew what was wrong with him. He was not in distress, unlike certain families who show up at the Hopkins clinic from small communities in distant states, wondering why their daughter is sick, why their son is not normal. McKusick and his colleagues diagnose the patient and treat symptoms as best they can. The doctor has admitted that his eyes light up when he comes across a phenotype that is new, another entry for the catalog. It's fair to say that Victor McKusick embodies both interpretations of the word *clinical,* one having to do with the medical clinic, the other indicating a coolness or coldness of vision.

"It's a great comfort to families who come to me to have a label," he says, "even though there's not much we can do. Then they can find other families, join support groups. . . ."

He pauses, turns his head to the side, and defends his approach: "The intellectual challenge of genetic disorders, yes. There's the fascination of the problem of the definition. But please don't label me as lacking in empathy for the patients and their families. It doesn't help them for me to be scared off by the pain of their situation. You have to put up with that. If I were undone by one patient, well, I've had dozens of such."

He pauses again, framing his reply. "Osler's most famous essay was titled 'Aequanimitas.' He meant that in order to do your best for your patients, you have to maintain a certain equanimity."

That the two Marfan's patients in the clinic were African American raises another ticklish question. No, says McKusick, Marfan's isn't more common among African Americans than among other groups. It is just chance that the two were here. Nor do genes tell us much about race. Racial characteristics are due to relatively few genetic variants. Compare any two human beings in the world, an African with a European, say, and their DNA will be on average 99.9 percent alike. But the human genome contains so much DNA that it accommodates all their innate individual differences in health.

That holds true for the two men at the clinic. Within the 0.1 percent of their differences were allelic variations of Marfan's syndrome. Different spellings of the disease gene resulted in different phenotypes—their dissimilar physical appearances.

The medical conditions that interest genomics researchers and drug companies are not Marfan's or Ellis–van Creveld syndromes. They are cancer, heart disease, arthritis, and diabetes: complex disorders involving multiple genes. The permutations in DNA that contribute to heart disease or high blood pressure are almost endless. Although the genes you inherit play a part, that part is neither decisive nor quantifiable. A family history indicates a risk, but an individual's genetic susceptibilities are so tangled that Mendel and a million monks could never have figured them out.

That's why possessing the complete DNA sequence of humans won't produce medical miracles any time soon. It's not just because of our variability. Genes make proteins and proteins interact in ways we don't understand. In a recent publication McKusick warned: "In general, the HGP [Human Genome Project] increases the gap between what we know how to diagnose and what we know how to treat. . . . There is also risk that the gap will be widened between what science really knows and what the public thinks is known."

But ever up-to-date, McKusick serves on the scientific advisory board of Celera, the private company that produced the genome sequence at the same time as the public effort. Like many other genomics companies, Celera plans to sell information about genes that may lead to new vaccines and drug therapies. Throughout the industry, human genes that may or may not be disease genes are being patented willy-nilly.

Does McKusick worry that the pharmaceutical industry's thirst for disease genes is distorting research priorities?

"Science is a self-correcting activity, where the truth will out," he says. "But competition within the biotech industry may also be a correcting factor. The profit motive isn't necessarily bad. It gets things done, as the sequencing projects have shown. The alliance between the academy and industry is essential."

He does allow that drug companies are neglecting the rare, single-gene aberrations—the very disorders he built his career on. "There are orphan diseases that might benefit from new enzyme therapies," he says. "But [the neglect] is not a new problem. Overall I'm happy with what I see. Medical genetics, or genetic medicine as we can call it now, has never been more exciting."

Discussion Questions

1. What is Marfan's syndrome? How is it inherited, and what are the symptoms? Why is it important that Marfan's syndrome be diagnosed early in a person's life?
2. What is Ellis–van Creveld syndrome? How is it inherited and what are the symptoms? Why is it more common among small communities of Amish people in Pennsylvania than in the general population?
3. Inbreeding (mating with close relatives) leads to children who are homozygous recessive for more gene pairs than they would typically have in an outbreeding population. Is it necessarily a bad thing to be homozygous recessive at many loci? Under what conditions does inbreeding lead to genetic problems?
4. Some alleles of genes increase a person's risk for developing certain diseases, such as breast cancer, diabetes, alcoholism, or bipolar disorder, under certain environmental conditions. However, not everyone who carries these alleles will develop the disease. Nor does a lack of these alleles mean that your risk of developing these diseases is zero. In general, do you think it would be useful to know exactly which alleles you carry that have been linked to disease? At what age should you learn this information? Who else should have access to such information—your employer, your insurance company, your spouse?
5. Will your answer to the above question change depending on whether there is any way you can affect your risk, such as through diet or exercise? What if there is nothing you can do to prevent or alleviate the symptoms of the disease or condition?
6. Should parents be able to choose in advance of conception whether their offspring will carry specific alleles? What sorts of negative characteristics would you choose to avoid in your offspring, if given the choice? What sorts of positive characteristics would you choose to endow your offspring, if given the choice?

7. If cloning can be perfected, what might be the advantages of being able to clone specific human beings? What might be the dangers or disadvantages?

8. McKusick implies that **medical genetics** and **genetic medicine** are converging now that the human genome has been sequenced. Why were these distinct fields before, and how has the sequencing of the genome helped bring them together?

 ## 7. 15 ANSWERS TO CREATIONIST NONSENSE

Many students struggle with reconciling their religious beliefs with what is known (and knowable) about the world through scientific reasoning, testing, and evidence. Anthropologists are scientists, and as such, try to understand the natural world without recourse to supernatural explanations. In "15 Answers to Creationist Nonsense," John Rennie addresses some of the most common "scientific" arguments raised against evolution.

When Charles Darwin introduced the theory of evolution through natural selection 143 years ago, the scientists of the day argued over it fiercely, but the massing evidence from paleontology, genetics, zoology, molecular biology and other fields gradually established evolution's truth beyond reasonable doubt. Today that battle has been won everywhere—except in the public imagination.

Embarrassingly, in the 21st century, in the most scientifically advanced nation the world has ever known, creationists can still persuade politicians, judges and ordinary citizens that evolution is a flawed, poorly supported fantasy. They lobby for creationist ideas such as "intelligent design" to be taught as alternatives to evolution in science classrooms. As this article goes to press, the Ohio Board of Education is debating whether to mandate such a change. Some antievolutionists, such as Philip E. Johnson, a law professor at the University of California at Berkeley and author of *Darwin on Trial,* admit that they intend for intelligent-design theory to serve as a "wedge" for reopening science classrooms to discussions of God.

Besieged teachers and others may increasingly find themselves on the spot to defend evolution and refute creationism. The arguments that creationists use are typically specious and based on misunderstandings of (or outright lies about) evolution, but the number and diversity of the objections can put even well-informed people at a disadvantage.

To help with answering them, the following list rebuts some of the most common "scientific" arguments raised against evolution. It also directs readers to further sources for information and explains why creation science has no place in the classroom.

1. Evolution is only a theory. It is not a fact or a scientific law.
Many people learned in elementary school that a theory falls in the middle of a hierarchy of certainty—above a mere hypothesis but below a law. Scientists do not use the terms that way, however. According to the National Academy of Sciences (NAS), a scientific theory is "a well-substantiated explanation of some aspect of the natural world that can incorporate facts, laws, inferences, and tested hypotheses." No amount of validation changes a theory into a law, which is a descriptive generalization about nature. So when scientists talk about the theory of evolution—or the

atomic theory or the theory of relativity, for that matter—they are not expressing reservations about its truth.

In addition to the **theory** of evolution, meaning the idea of descent with modification, one may also speak of the **fact** of evolution. The NAS defines a fact as "an observation that has been repeatedly confirmed and for all practical purposes is accepted as 'true.' " The fossil record and abundant other evidence testify that organisms have evolved through time. Although no one observed those transformations, the indirect evidence is clear, unambiguous and compelling. All sciences frequently rely on indirect evidence. Physicists cannot see subatomic particles directly, for instance, so they verify their existence by watching for telltale tracks that the particles leave in cloud chambers. The absence of direct observation does not make physicists' conclusions less certain.

2. Natural selection is based on circular reasoning: the fittest are those who survive, and those who survive are deemed fittest.

"Survival of the fittest" is a conversational way to describe natural selection, but a more technical description speaks of differential rates of survival and reproduction. That is, rather than labeling species as more or less fit, one can describe how many offspring they are likely to leave under given circumstances. Drop a fast-breeding pair of small-beaked finches and a slower-breeding pair of large-beaked finches onto an island full of food seeds. Within a few generations the fast breeders may control more of the food resources. Yet if large beaks more easily crush seeds, the advantage may tip to the slow breeders. In a pioneering study of finches on the Galápagos Islands, Peter R. Grant of Princeton University observed these kinds of population shifts in the wild [see his article "Natural Selection and Darwin's Finches," *Scientific American,* October 1991].

The key is that adaptive fitness can be defined without reference to survival: large beaks are better adapted for crushing seeds, irrespective of whether that trait has survival value under the circumstances.

3. Evolution is unscientific, because it is not testable or falsifiable. It makes claims about events that were not observed and can never be re-created.

This blanket dismissal of evolution ignores important distinctions that divide the field into at least two broad areas: microevolution and macroevolution. Microevolution looks at changes within species over time—changes that may be preludes to speciation, the origin of new species. Macroevolution studies how taxonomic groups above the level of species change. Its evidence draws frequently from the fossil record and DNA comparisons to reconstruct how various organisms may be related.

These days even most creationists acknowledge that microevolution has been upheld by tests in the laboratory (as in studies of cells, plants and fruit flies) and in the field (as in Grant's studies of evolving beak shapes among Galápagos finches). Natural selection and other mechanisms—such as chromosomal changes, symbiosis and hybridization—can drive profound changes in populations over time.

The historical nature of macroevolutionary study involves inference from fossils and DNA rather than direct observation. Yet in the historical sciences (which include astronomy, geology and archaeology, as well as evolutionary biology), hypotheses can still be tested by checking whether they accord with physical evidence and whether they lead to verifiable predictions about future discoveries. For instance, evolution implies that between the earliest-known ancestors of humans (roughly five million years old) and the appearance of anatomically modern humans (about 100,000 years ago), one should find a succession of hominid creatures with features progressively less apelike and more modern, which is indeed what the fossil record shows. But one should not—and does not—find modern human fossils embedded in strata from the Jurassic period (144 million years ago). Evolutionary biology routinely makes predictions far more refined and precise than this, and researchers test them constantly.

Evolution could be disproved in other ways, too. If we could document the spontaneous generation of just one complex life-form from inanimate matter, then at least a few creatures seen in the fossil record might have originated this way. If superintelligent aliens appeared and claimed credit for creating life on earth (or even particular species), the purely evolutionary explanation would be cast in doubt. But no one has yet produced such evidence.

It should be noted that the idea of falsifiability as the defining characteristic of science originated with philosopher Karl Popper in the 1930s. More recent elaborations on his thinking have expanded the narrowest interpretation of his principle precisely because it would eliminate too many branches of clearly scientific endeavor.

4. Increasingly, scientists doubt the truth of evolution.
No evidence suggests that evolution is losing adherents. Pick up any issue of a peer-reviewed biological journal, and you will find articles that support and extend evolutionary studies or that embrace evolution as a fundamental concept.

Conversely, serious scientific publications disputing evolution are all but non-existent. In the mid-1990s George W. Gilchrist of the University of Washington surveyed thousands of journals in the primary literature, seeking articles on intelligent design or creation science. Among those hundreds of thousands of scientific reports, he found none. In the past two years, surveys done independently by Barbara Forrest of Southeastern Louisiana University and Lawrence M. Krauss of Case Western Reserve University have been similarly fruitless.

Creationists retort that a closed-minded scientific community rejects their evidence. Yet according to the editors of *Nature, Science* and other leading journals, few antievolution manuscripts are even submitted. Some antievolution authors have published papers in serious journals. Those papers, however, rarely attack evolution directly or advance creationist arguments; at best, they identify certain evolutionary problems as unsolved and difficult (which no one disputes). In short, creationists are not giving the scientific world good reason to take them seriously.

5. The disagreements among even evolutionary biologists show how little solid science supports evolution.
Evolutionary biologists passionately debate diverse topics: how speciation happens, the rates of evolutionary change, the ancestral relationships of birds and dinosaurs, whether Neandertals were a species apart from modern humans, and much more. These disputes are like those found in all other branches of science. Acceptance of evolution as a factual occurrence and a guiding principle is nonetheless universal in biology.

Unfortunately, dishonest creationists have shown a willingness to take scientists' comments out of context to exaggerate and distort the disagreements. Anyone acquainted with the works of paleontologist Stephen Jay Gould of Harvard University knows that in addition to co-authoring the punctuated-equilibrium model, Gould was one of the most eloquent defenders and articulators of evolution. (Punctuated equilibrium explains patterns in the fossil record by suggesting that most evolutionary changes occur within geologically brief intervals—which may nonetheless amount to hundreds of generations.) Yet creationists delight in dissecting out phrases from Gould's voluminous prose to make him sound as though he had doubted evolution, and they present punctuated equilibrium as though it allows new species to materialize overnight or birds to be born from reptile eggs.

When confronted with a quotation from a scientific authority that seems to question evolution, insist on seeing the statement in context. Almost invariably, the attack on evolution will prove illusory.

6. If humans descended from monkeys, why are there still monkeys?
This surprisingly common argument reflects several levels of ignorance about evolution. The first mistake is that evolution does not teach that humans descended from monkeys; it states that both have a common ancestor.

The deeper error is that this objection is tantamount to asking, "If children descended from adults, why are there still adults?" New species evolve by splintering off from established ones, when populations of organisms become isolated from the main branch of their family and acquire sufficient differences to remain forever distinct. The parent species may survive indefinitely thereafter, or it may become extinct.

7. Evolution cannot explain how life first appeared on earth.
The origin of life remains very much a mystery, but biochemists have learned about how primitive nucleic acids, amino acids and other building blocks of life could have formed and organized themselves into self-replicating, self-sustaining units, laying the foundation for cellular biochemistry. Astrochemical analyses hint that quantities of these compounds might have originated in space and fallen to earth in comets, a scenario that may solve the problem of how those constituents arose under the conditions that prevailed when our planet was young.

Creationists sometimes try to invalidate all of evolution by pointing to science's current inability to explain the origin of life. But even if life on earth turned out to have a nonevolutionary origin (for instance, if aliens introduced the first cells billions of years ago), evolution since then would be robustly confirmed by countless microevolutionary and macroevolutionary studies.

8. Mathematically, it is inconceivable that anything as complex as a protein, let alone a living cell or a human, could spring up by chance.
Chance plays a part in evolution (for example, in the random mutations that can give rise to new traits), but evolution does not depend on chance to create organisms, proteins or other entities. Quite the opposite: natural selection, the principal known mechanism of evolution, harnesses nonrandom change by preserving "desirable" (adaptive) features and eliminating "undesirable" (nonadaptive) ones. As long as the forces of selection stay constant, natural selection can push evolution in one direction and produce sophisticated structures in surprisingly short times.

As an analogy, consider the 13-letter sequence "TOBEORNOTTOBE." Those hypothetical million monkeys, each pecking out one phrase a second, could take as long as 78,800 years to find it among the 2,613 sequences of that length. But in the 1980s Richard Hardison of Glendale College wrote a computer program that generated phrases randomly while preserving the positions of individual letters that happened to be correctly placed (in effect, selecting for phrases more like Hamlet's). On average, the program re-created the phrase in just 336 iterations, less than 90 seconds. Even more amazing, it could reconstruct Shakespeare's entire play in just four and a half days.

9. The Second Law of Thermodynamics says that systems must become more disordered over time. Living cells therefore could not have evolved from inanimate chemicals, and multicellular life could not have evolved from protozoa.

This argument derives from a misunderstanding of the Second Law. If it were valid, mineral crystals and snowflakes would also be impossible, because they, too, are complex structures that form spontaneously from disordered parts.

The Second Law actually states that the total entropy of a closed system (one that no energy or matter leaves or enters) cannot decrease. Entropy is a physical concept often casually described as disorder, but it differs significantly from the conversational use of the word.

More important, however, the Second Law permits parts of a system to decrease in entropy as long as other parts experience an offsetting increase. Thus, our planet as a whole can grow more complex because the sun pours heat and light onto it, and the greater entropy associated with the sun's nuclear fusion more than rebalances the scales. Simple organisms can fuel their rise toward complexity by consuming other forms of life and nonliving materials.

10. Mutations are essential to evolution theory, but mutations can only eliminate traits. They cannot produce new features.

On the contrary, biology has catalogued many traits produced by point mutations (changes at precise positions in an organism's DNA)—bacterial resistance to antibiotics, for example.

Mutations that arise in the homeobox (*Hox*) family of development-regulating genes in animals can also have complex effects. *Hox* genes direct where legs, wings, antennae and body segments should grow. In fruit flies, for instance, the mutation called *Antennapedia* causes legs to sprout where antennae should grow. These abnormal limbs are not functional, but their existence demonstrates that genetic mistakes can produce complex structures, which natural selection can then test for possible uses.

Moreover, molecular biology has discovered mechanisms for genetic change that go beyond point mutations, and these expand the ways in which new traits can appear. Functional modules within genes can be spliced together in novel ways. Whole genes can be accidentally duplicated in an organism's DNA, and the duplicates are free to mutate into genes for new, complex features. Comparisons of the DNA from a wide variety of organisms indicate that this is how the globin family of blood proteins evolved over millions of years.

11. Natural selection might explain microevolution, but it cannot explain the origin of new species and higher orders of life.

Evolutionary biologists have written extensively about how natural selection could produce new species. For instance, in the model called allopatry, developed by Ernst Mayr of Harvard University, if a population of organisms were isolated from the rest of its species by geographical boundaries, it might be subjected to different selective pressures. Changes would accumulate in the isolated population. If those changes became so significant that the splinter group could not or routinely would not breed with the original stock, then the splinter group would be **reproductively isolated** and on its way toward becoming a new species.

Natural selection is the best studied of the evolutionary mechanisms, but biologists are open to other possibilities as well. Biologists are constantly assessing the potential of unusual genetic mechanisms for causing speciation or for producing complex features in organisms. Lynn Margulis of the University of Massachusetts at Amherst and others have persuasively argued that some cellular organelles, such as the energy-generating mitochondria, evolved through the symbiotic merger of ancient organisms. Thus, science welcomes the possibility of evolution resulting from forces beyond natural selection. Yet those forces must be natural; they cannot be attributed to the actions of mysterious creative intelligences whose existence, in scientific terms, is unproved.

12. Nobody has ever seen a new species evolve.
Speciation is probably fairly rare and in many cases might take centuries. Furthermore, recognizing a new species during a formative stage can be difficult, because biologists sometimes disagree about how best to define a species. The most widely used definition, Mayr's Biological Species Concept, recognizes a species as a distinct community of reproductively isolated populations—sets of organisms that normally do not or cannot breed outside their community. In practice, this standard can be difficult to apply to organisms isolated by distance or terrain or to plants (and, of course, fossils do not breed). Biologists therefore usually use organisms' physical and behavioral traits as clues to their species membership.

Nevertheless, the scientific literature does contain reports of apparent speciation events in plants, insects and worms. In most of these experiments, researchers subjected organisms to various types of selection—for anatomical differences, mating behaviors, habitat preferences and other traits—and found that they had created populations of organisms that did not breed with outsiders. For example, William R. Rice of the University of New Mexico and George W. Salt of the University of California at Davis demonstrated that if they sorted a group of fruit flies by their preference for certain environments and bred those flies separately over 35 generations, the resulting flies would refuse to breed with those from a very different environment.

13. Evolutionists cannot point to any transitional fossils—creatures that are half reptile and half bird, for instance.
Actually, paleontologists know of many detailed examples of fossils intermediate in form between various taxonomic groups. One of the most famous fossils of all time is *Archaeopteryx,* which combines feathers and skeletal structures peculiar to birds with features of dinosaurs. A flock's worth of other feathered fossil species, some more avian and some less, has also been found. A sequence of fossils spans the evolution of modern horses from the tiny *Eohippus.* Whales had four-legged ancestors that walked on land, and creatures known as *Ambulocetus* and *Rodhocetus* helped to make that transition [see "The Mammals That Conquered the Seas," by Kate Wong, *Scientific American,* May]. Fossil seashells trace the evolution of various mollusks through millions of years. Perhaps 20 or more hominids (not all of them our ancestors) fill the gap between Lucy the australopithecine and modern humans.

Creationists, though, dismiss these fossil studies. They argue that *Archaeopteryx* is not a missing link between reptiles and birds—it is just an extinct bird with reptilian features. They want evolutionists to produce a weird, chimeric monster that cannot be classified as belonging to any known group. Even if a creationist does accept a fossil as transitional between two species, he or she may then insist on seeing other fossils intermediate between it and the first two. These frustrating requests can proceed ad infinitum and place an unreasonable burden on the always incomplete fossil record.

Nevertheless, evolutionists can cite further supportive evidence from molecular biology. All organisms share most of the same genes, but as evolution predicts, the structures of these genes and their products diverge among species, in keeping with their evolutionary relationships. Geneticists speak of the "molecular clock" that records the passage of time. These molecular data also show how various organisms are transitional within evolution.

14. Living things have fantastically intricate features—at the anatomical, cellular and molecular levels—that could not function if they were any less complex or sophisticated. The only prudent conclusion is that they are the products of intelligent design, not evolution.

This "argument from design" is the backbone of most recent attacks on evolution, but it is also one of the oldest. In 1802 theologian William Paley wrote that if one finds a pocket watch in a field, the most reasonable conclusion is that someone dropped it, not that natural forces created it there. By analogy, Paley argued, the complex structures of living things must be the handiwork of direct, divine invention. Darwin wrote *On the Origin of Species* as an answer to Paley: he explained how natural forces of selection, acting on inherited features, could gradually shape the evolution of ornate organic structures.

Generations of creationists have tried to counter Darwin by citing the example of the eye as a structure that could not have evolved. The eye's ability to provide vision depends on the perfect arrangement of its parts, these critics say. Natural selection could thus never favor the transitional forms needed during the eye's evolution—what good is half an eye? Anticipating this criticism, Darwin suggested that even "incomplete" eyes might confer benefits (such as helping creatures orient toward light) and thereby survive for further evolutionary refinement. Biology has vindicated Darwin: researchers have identified primitive eyes and light-sensing organs throughout the animal kingdom and have even tracked the evolutionary history of eyes through comparative genetics. (It now appears that in various families of organisms, eyes have evolved independently.)

Today's intelligent-design advocates are more sophisticated than their predecessors, but their arguments and goals are not fundamentally different. They criticize evolution by trying to demonstrate that it could not account for life as we know it and then insist that the only tenable alternative is that life was designed by an unidentified intelligence.

15. Recent discoveries prove that even at the microscopic level, life has a quality of complexity that could not have come about through evolution.

"Irreducible complexity" is the battle cry of Michael J. Behe of Lehigh University, author of *Darwin's Black Box: The Biochemical Challenge to Evolution.* As a household example of irreducible complexity, Behe chooses the mousetrap—a machine that could not function if any of its pieces were missing and whose pieces have no value except as parts of the whole. What is true of the mousetrap, he says, is even truer of the bacterial flagellum, a whiplike cellular organelle used for propulsion that operates like an outboard motor. The proteins that make up a flagellum are uncannily arranged into motor components, a universal joint and other structures like those that a human engineer might specify. The possibility that this intricate array could have arisen through evolutionary modification is virtually nil, Behe argues, and that bespeaks intelligent design. He makes similar points about the blood's clotting mechanism and other molecular systems.

Yet evolutionary biologists have answers to these objections. First, there exist flagellae with forms simpler than the one that Behe cites, so it is not necessary for all those components to be present for a flagellum to work. The sophisticated components of this flagellum all have precedents elsewhere in nature, as described by Kenneth R. Miller of Brown University and others. In fact, the entire flagellum assembly is extremely similar to an organelle that *Yersinia pestis,* the bubonic plague bacterium, uses to inject toxins into cells.

The key is that the flagellum's component structures, which Behe suggests have no value apart from their role in propulsion, can serve multiple functions that would have helped favor their evolution. The final evolution of the flagellum might then have involved only the novel recombination of sophisticated parts that initially evolved for other purposes. Similarly, the blood-clotting system seems to involve the modification and elaboration of proteins that were originally used in digestion, according to studies by Russell F. Doolittle of the University of California at San Diego. So some of the complexity that Behe calls proof of intelligent design is not irreducible at all.

Complexity of a different kind—"specified complexity"—is the cornerstone of the intelligent-design arguments of William A. Dembski of Baylor University in his books *The Design Inference* and *No Free Lunch.* Essentially his argument is that living things are complex in a way that undirected, random processes could never produce. The only logical conclusion, Dembski asserts, in an echo of Paley 200 years ago, is that some superhuman intelligence created and shaped life.

Dembski's argument contains several holes. It is wrong to insinuate that the field of explanations consists only of random processes or designing intelligences. Researchers into nonlinear systems and cellular automata at the Santa Fe Institute and elsewhere have demonstrated that simple, undirected processes can yield extraordinarily complex patterns. Some of the complexity seen in organisms may therefore emerge through natural phenomena that we as yet barely understand. But that is far different from saying that the complexity could not have arisen naturally.

"Creation science" is a contradiction in terms. A central tenet of modern science is methodological naturalism—it seeks to explain the universe purely in terms of observed or testable natural mechanisms. Thus, physics describes the atomic nucleus with specific concepts governing matter and energy, and it tests those descriptions experimentally. Physicists introduce new particles, such as quarks, to flesh out their theories only when data show that the previous descriptions cannot adequately explain observed phenomena. The new particles do not have arbitrary properties, moreover—their definitions are tightly constrained, because the new particles must fit within the existing framework of physics.

In contrast, intelligent-design theorists invoke shadowy entities that conveniently have whatever unconstrained abilities are needed to solve the mystery at hand. Rather than expanding scientific inquiry, such answers shut it down. (How does one disprove the existence of omnipotent intelligences?)

Intelligent design offers few answers. For instance, when and how did a designing intelligence intervene in life's history? By creating the first DNA? The first cell? The first human? Was every species designed, or just a few early ones? Proponents of intelligent-design theory frequently decline to be pinned down on these points. They do not even make real attempts to reconcile their disparate ideas about intelligent design. Instead they pursue argument by exclusion—that is, they belittle evolutionary explanations as far-fetched or incomplete and then imply that only design-based alternatives remain.

Logically, this is misleading: even if one naturalistic explanation is flawed, it does not mean that all are. Moreover, it does not make one intelligent-design theory more reasonable than another. Listeners are essentially left to fill in the blanks for themselves, and some will undoubtedly do so by substituting their religious beliefs for scientific ideas.

Time and again, science has shown that methodological naturalism can push back ignorance, finding increasingly detailed and informative answers to mysteries that once seemed impenetrable: the nature of light, the causes of disease, how the brain works. Evolution is doing the same with the riddle of how the living world took shape. Creationism, by any name, adds nothing of intellectual value to the effort.

Discussion Questions

1. Pick several of the 15 points to discuss in more detail. Have you heard people make these arguments? Have you made them yourself? Do you understand why they are not scientific?
2. Given that U.S. elementary and high school classrooms contain students of many different religious backgrounds—Jewish, Christian, Muslim, Ba'hai, Buddhist, Hindu, Shinto, Confucian, Navajo, Hopi, Miwok, Dogon, Zulu, and many others, in addition to agnostic and atheist students—is it possible to present a "balanced" view of Creationism in the classroom? Whose creationism?
3. Should comparative religious beliefs be taught in a science class? Should they be taught at all in public schools?
4. Is it necessary to view the scientific perspective on evolution as invalidating one's personal religious beliefs, or can they co-exist?
5. Many students come to their first anthropology class "knowing" things about evolution that are not true. Where do such ideas come from? What have you learned in your class so far that contradicts something you "knew" at the beginning of the semester?

Additional Resources

For Internet links related to this chapter, please visit our website at www.mhhe.com/dettwyler

GLEISER, MARCELO. *The Dancing Universe: From Creation Myths to the Big Bang.* New York: Plume Books, 1998.

GROCE, NORA ELLEN. *Everyone Here Spoke Sign Language: Hereditary Deafness on Martha's Vineyard.* Cambridge, MA: Harvard University Press, 1988.

President's Council on Bioethics. *Human Cloning and Human Dignity: An Ethical Inquiry.* Washington, DC: The President's Council on Bioethics, 2002.

RAPP, RAYNA. *Testing Women, Testing the Fetus: The Social Impact of Amniocentesis in America.* New York: Routledge, 2000.

SPROUL, BARBARA C. *Primal Myths: Creation Myths Around the World.* San Francisco, CA: Harper, 1992.

The Primates

Primatology, the study of the living nonhuman primates, has always been part of anthropology. Nonhuman primates are studied both for their own sakes and for the light that they can shed on human behavior and evolution. The 20th century saw numerous field studies of free-living nonhuman primates, and these studies revealed that the line between human and nonhuman primate is clearly one of degree, rather than kind. That is to say, humans rely most on learned behavior, but the nonhuman primates, especially our closest relatives the Great Apes, also rely on learned behavior to a much greater extent than people usually realize. Students watching films of nonhuman primates are often struck by how human-like they seem. The two articles in this chapter focus on the latest research from field studies of chimpanzees and orangutans.

 ## 8. APING CULTURE

*Many people will argue forcefully that humans are unique and distinct among creatures, different not merely in degree, but also in kind. They say that humans are fundamentally different from all other animals, including our close relatives, the chimpanzees. Meredith Small examines recent controversies in the study of chimpanzees, specifically the question of whether or not chimpanzees can be said to have culture. Much hinges on how one defines the concept of **culture**—is it merely "behavior passed down through observational learning rather than instinct" as Jane Goodall maintains, or is the term more properly used to mean only "the information that we share that tells us what's appropriate to do . . . not the act of baking a cake, but the recipe," as Lee Cronk contends? As we learn more and more about our closest relatives, the chimpanzees, we find fewer and fewer criteria that distinguish us from them.*

In the summer of 1960, a young Englishwoman stood on the shores of Lake Tanganyika looking into the hills of Gombe Stream Reserve with her mother. From the shore, Gombe seems impossible to negotiate: Steep, tree-covered ridges and their corresponding ravines rise from the beach as if a giant child had reached down with spread fingers and scraped the landscape upward. The pant-hoot calls of chimpanzees—husky puffs of noise that rise quickly into wild screams—echo across the ravines and taunt any visitor to follow the apes across the undulating terrain.

The young woman spent the first months trying to catch up with her subjects, scrambling up cliffs, grabbing onto roots, and then standing perfectly still so as not to scare them away. The only way the chimps would tolerate her presence, she eventually found, was if she lured them close with bananas. Thus began a decades-long effort to follow around groups of chimpanzees to figure out what they can tell us about ourselves.

Her name, of course, was Jane Goodall, and in the years that followed she would become an icon of both sober science and exotic adventure. The willowy figure dressed in green fatigues, the limp blonde hair drawn back in a ponytail, the quiet British voice narrating innumerable National Geographic specials—these images and sounds are inextricably bound to the public's understanding of chimp behavior. Before Goodall's work, chimpanzees were known mostly from studies on animals that had been captured and imported to indoor and outdoor laboratories. Although psychobiologists like Robert Yerkes knew that chimps were smart, no one was sure how they used those smarts in the wild.

"When I went to Gombe, nothing was known," Goodall said recently, "Chimps weren't allowed to have personalities—no names, no reasoning ability, no emotions. Until one recognized the individuals, you couldn't work out the social structure, nor could you make any sense of the communication. It was so confusing." Goodall's work changed all that. Her detailed daily records of individual chimpanzees—maintained these days by other primatologists and field assistants—resulted in the first chimp personality portraits, as well as startling discoveries of chimpanzee tool use, hunting practices, and even murder.

That was just the beginning. For the past four decades, an army of researchers from Europe, Japan, and the United States has observed chimpanzees at more than 40 sites. In 1966 Toshisada Nishida began a study in the Mahale Mountains, 90 miles south of Gombe, and went on to identify the basic social structure of chimpanzee communities. In the 1970s, researchers discovered that chimps living in Guinea and Ivory Coast, on the far western edge of their species's range, hunted and used tools differently from their eastern cousins. A decade later, Richard Wrangham, working in both Gombe and the Kibale National Park in Uganda, showed that chimps can act much the same even when they live in different habitats and have different diets. Takayoshi Kano and others, meanwhile, have cast a new light on chimpanzee behavior through studies of the bonobo, the chimpanzee's more peaceable, more egalitarian cousin.

Last summer, researchers from seven long-term field sites combined their results in a landmark report in the journal *Nature*. Led by primatologist Andrew Whiten of the University of St. Andrews in Scotland, they listed 39 chimpanzee behaviors that go beyond mere survival strategies. More important, those behaviors vary from group to group: In some areas, for instance, chimpanzees dip for ants with a long stick, swipe the ants into a ball, and then flick the ball into their mouths. At other sites they use a short stick and slurp the ants with their tongues. Some chimpanzees clip the edges of leaves as a display; others use the leaves as napkins. Perusing the total list is a bit like thumbing through a *Fodor's* travel guide. And that is exactly the point. Chimpanzees, Whiten and his colleagues concluded, have culture.

Critics wasted no time in raising objections. Culture means more than just a set of learned behaviors that vary from place to place, some argued; culture means history and tradition, art, philosophy, and religion—the last barrier, together with language, that separates humans from other species. Others voiced more subtle concerns: "Are we measuring what we really think we are measuring?" anthropologist John Mitani of the University of Michigan wonders. "Just because it's different at two different places—is it culture?"

The debate boils down to semantics as much as science, and it largely misses the point. The fact that different chimps learn different ways to act hardly makes them human—it may not even make them cultural. But it does raise a far more intriguing question, one that has long seemed unanswerable: What can those learned behaviors tell us about the origins and purpose of human culture?

The Bossou Nature Reserve in the Republic of Guinea pops up from the West African plain like a green thumb. It looks almost out of place—a leafy oasis in a sea of humanity, a spot of nature amid peasant villages and irrigated rice and manioc farms. But this forest was here long before the people began cutting down the trees, planting crops, and corralling the resident chimps toward their last stand. Today, a village sits at the base of the reserve, and villagers, looking up, can see the animals bounce among the trees. Their backyard is essentially a natural exhibit of chimpanzees.

And what curious chimps they are. As one walks up the hillside, out of the village and into the forest, the hubbub of talking, laughing, and shouting people fades away, and the air begins to ring with hollow knocks and smacks. It sounds as if workers in a factory are beating some product into shape, but a closer look shows that it's a group of chimpanzees sitting together cracking nuts. An old female grabs a heavy stone and makes sure it's flat, then wedges another stone underneath it to keep it from rocking. She places an oil palm nut on top, into a spot worn smooth from hours of smashing. Holding a lighter stone in her hand, she raises it high above her head and slams it down, crushing the nut to pieces. She then delicately picks out the nut meats and chews them contemplatively, clearly enjoying her fatty snack.

What makes this scene so interesting is not just that chimps are smart enough to figure out how to crack hard-shelled nuts, but that their method of doing so is specific to West Africa. In the Mahale Mountains in East Africa, chimpanzees walk right by those nuts, oblivious to their nutritious meats. Moreover, nut-cracking is clearly a learned behavior, since it takes years to master. When young chimps at Bossou try their hand at it, primatologist Tetsuro Matsuzawa has found, the nuts keep slipping off the flat stone, or the young chimps can't hit them, or they strike at a bad angle and the nut goes whizzing through the forest like an errant bullet. It takes years of watching how it's done, and lots of practice, before the youngsters get anywhere.

Nut-cracking has all the elements of a cultural behavior. It only occurs at some sites and is passed down by learning and imitation. But other presumed cultural differences are more subtle. For example, John Mitani has found that male chimpanzees' pant-hoots crescendo differently depending on where they live. At one site, the calls sound like a train slowly leaving the station—**chug-ah, chug-ah, chug-ah**—gradually accelerating toward a scream. Elsewhere the buildup is faster, higher-pitched, and more frantic. More intriguing still, males at each site seem to modulate their voices so that their calls sound alike. By doing so, they are presumably announcing their joint presence and confirming that they belong to the same group.

Mitani tentatively calls these different pant-hoots "dialects," but he acknowledges that what he hears may be a product of differences in body size, genes, or habitat. "It wouldn't be fair to compare the calls produced by West African chimps, who are larger and have deeper voices, with small East African chimps," he explains. Yet the calls don't seem to be tailored to their habitats either. In the Mahale Mountains, low-pitched calls would carry farthest, yet the chimps have relatively high voices; in Gombe's open woodland, high-pitched calls would travel best, but the chimps have low voices.

Even if the differences in calls are learned, some linguists might question Mitani's terms. When he says that chimpanzees have dialects, he means that different groups make different sounds even though their members can intermingle. But when people are said to speak a dialect, the term means more than just distinctive sounds. "Dialects are two versions of a language that are still mutually comprehensible," says Robbins Burling, a linguist at the University of Michigan. Or as Massachusetts Institute of Technology psychologist Steven Pinker puts it: "The standard definition is that a language is a dialect with an army and a navy." Pinker is quick to add that Mitani's use of the term is "innocuous." But even the most open-minded linguist or primatologist wouldn't say that chimpanzees speak a language.

One of the best examples of chimp culture can be seen in the Mahale Mountains of Tanzania and in Gombe, 90 miles to the north. Though the two areas lie on the same side of Lake Tanganyika, the chimpanzees have more elaborate grooming habits in Mahale. In Gombe, when a male chimp lumbers up to a friend and sprawls out on the ground, the friend will usually groom him by gently passing a hand through the fur on his back, chest, face, or leg. In Mahale, chimps prefer to face each other, lock hands, and raise their arms in a mutual salute. The same style is seen at several other sites across Africa, and in captive populations, but not in Gombe. Is the Mahale style simply the most efficient way to groom an armpit? Or is it the chimpanzee version of a secret handshake?

Anthropologist William McGrew has studied the Mahale chimps, and several other groups, for 20 years. He not only believes that their grooming is cultural, but also thinks there are grooming subcultures as well. Recently, when McGrew showed his students at Miami University in Ohio some old photographs of chimps grooming, he noticed something: One group at Mahale groomed the usual way while another group at the same site had a slightly different technique. "This is like the difference between the three-fingered salute by the Boy Scouts and the two-fingered salute by the Cub Scouts," McGrew says. "We are really dealing with nuances. But they're there."

McGrew hopes that such studies will help motivate people to protect chimpanzees in the wild. "There are chimpanzee cultures that are winking out as we speak," he says. "If we need any new impetus to keep us pushing, that's it: We are not just saving gene pools and we're not just saving individuals. We are saving something that approximates culture." But Jane Goodall, for one, is far less sanguine. "It's fine to work for the rights of chimps, but humans have rights that don't protect them," she says. "Look what is happening in Africa, look at the genocide. The Hutu won't deny that the Tutsi are cultural and have rational thoughts and emotions, and vice-versa, and they still kill each other."

Does it matter? Do chimpanzees have to be so much like humans to have culture? The answer depends on your definition of culture—and a dozen anthropologists will give you a dozen different definitions. If, as some say, culture is any learned behavior that is shared by a collective, chimpanzees easily make the grade. As Barbara Miller, a cultural anthropologist at the George Washington University, puts it: "If we take a broader approach to culture, as I do, and include foraging behavior and sex, much of what chimpanzees do would be considered culture." But other anthropologists are more discriminating. Culture, they argue, is what people say and think, not what they do; it deals with symbols and meaning rather than behavior. Practicing a religion is cultural, according to this definition; plowing a field is not.

If that's the case, chimpanzees will never join the culture club. "None of us," anthropologist William McGrew admits, "knows what significance chimpanzees attach to some of the weird and wonderful things they do." Still, Whiten and his colleagues have shown that chimps can imitate complex behaviors step by step (though they never teach one another deliberately). The longer primatologists study chimpanzees and the more their findings are compared, the longer the list of unique learned behaviors grows.

Taken together, those traits may open a window on early human behavior as well. For example, according to a recent survey of five long-term chimp studies, the most sociable chimps tend to be best at using tools (captive chimps, by the same token, are better with tools than wild chimps). That pattern may help explain how early hominids, despite their smaller brains, gradually developed complex cultures. After all, fossil evidence shows that early humans only began to use tools after their canines (which they may have used to fight one another) began to shrink.

To get a less theoretical sense of how chimp culture and human culture are related, you might try standing quietly in Kibale National Park and listening hard. Chances are, instead of the monotonous sound of nut-cracking, you'll hear something more complex: a hollow knocking, a double-time **thump-thumping** that echoes through the trees.

Chimpanzees, you'll find, can drum.

The trees at Kibale and other sites often have huge buttresses that rise several yards from the leafy litter to the canopy overhead. By slapping at the buttresses with their hands, chimps can create rhythmic patterns that can carry for more than a mile. Adam Clark Arcadi, an anthropologist at Cornell University, has spent four years collecting these sounds. To do so, he and his research assistants simply stand in the forest and point a directional microphone toward a drummer. Later, back in his lab, Arcadi runs the recording through a sophisticated computer program that creates images of the sound. From that image he can measure differences in rhythm and pitch among drummers.

Chimp drumming is a male thing, as far as we know. Males do it throughout the day, most often when on the move, with each bout lasting anywhere from a few seconds to almost half a minute. Like jazz drummers knocking out a riff, each chimp seems to have a signature beat. "There are differences in the speed at which they drum, and in slaps that come in pairs—**ba-dump-ba-dump-ba-dump**—versus single beats—**dump-dump-dump**," Arcadi explained one day, hitting his desk to demonstrate. Like people, chimps can be righties or lefties, and they probably favor their better hand when drumming. When Arcadi played some of his drumming tapes, spliced together into a continuous loop, it sounded like elementary jazz.

All chimpanzees presumably drum to communicate with one another (though no one knows what they're communicating). But Arcadi has found that males at Kibale often drum without calling, whereas males in Taï National Park usually pant-hoot as well. One could say, therefore, that chimpanzee drumming is multicultural. Maybe there's even a link between what chimps pound out in the forest and the sounds that their human counterparts make on a Saturday night.

To deepen our concept of their culture, primatologists will have to learn more about chimps' interpersonal relationships. Do chimps from various sites treat each other differently? Are the customs and manners of East African chimps as different from those of West African chimps as, say, Samoans' are from Icelanders'? Are males more repressive toward females at one site and more easygoing at another, echoing the variety of human male-female relationships across the globe? In the words of primatologist Frans B. M. de Waal, who observes chimpanzee social behavior at the Yerkes Primate Field Station in Atlanta: "Who fishes for ants and who doesn't, or who cracks nuts and who doesn't—that's the easy thing to see. But the social dynamics, that's much harder to put your finger on."

Who knows what's left to discover? "I now regard chimpanzees as a very big mystery," says anthropologist Vernon Reynolds, who works in Uganda's Budongo Forest. "The more we find out, the less we understand." McGrew agrees: "I have been struck by the richness of chimpanzee nature. There is always a new twist on an old theme that causes you to smile and revise yet another set of conclusions. There is such a wonderful wealth of stuff here."

Late in the fall, Jane Goodall took some time away from her most recent book tour—and plans for yet another African safari—to talk about the chimp culture studies. The new findings hardly come as a surprise, she said. "I wrote an article in 1973 saying that the big challenge now, the most important thing, is to learn about cultural variation." As for the definition of culture, she still uses the one she has always used: "It's simple. You just have to prove that the behavior is passed down through observational learning rather than instinct."

Nevertheless, the studies that Goodall set in motion so long ago are quickly carrying us beyond such simple answers. Perhaps chimpanzees are more guided by cultural rules in their day-to-day interactions than we realize. Or perhaps some of the activities that we consider patently cultural—in humans as well as chimps—are really shaped by the environment.

"I don't think everything humans do is cultural," says cultural anthropologist Lee Cronk of Rutgers University. In one Kenyan tribe, for instance, tradition dictates that boys are more desirable than girls, yet parents consistently treat girls better. The reason, Cronk says, is that girls in that area are more likely than boys to give their parents grandchildren. Culture may urge one behavior, but biology urges another—and the latter wins out.

"Culture isn't what we do," Cronk concludes, "it's the information that we share that tells us what's appropriate to do. It's not the act of baking a cake; it's the recipe." The trick is determining when we're improvising and when we're cooking by the book. What part of marriage, for instance, is biological and what part cultural? "Culture is complicated when it comes to humans," Cronk admits. "But with chimps it's relatively simple. You can get your mind around it. It allows you to see very clearly that they behave in many ways with no cultural input. When people see that, it's easier to convince them that, yeah, culture isn't the only thing that is influencing human behavior."

Discussion Questions

1. Why do the similarities between humans and chimpanzees seem threatening to so many people in the United States? Why is it important to some people to maintain the idea that humans are distinct and special in the natural world?
2. What does the term **culture** mean? Is Jane Goodall correct, or is Lee Cronk correct? Does culture include behavior or only what we think about behavior?
3. If culture is only what we think about behavior, then can we know if chimpanzees (or indeed any other nonhuman animal) have culture?
4. What sorts of behaviors differ between different groups of chimpanzees in different regions of Africa? If these behaviors are taught (not instinctive), then does this prove that chimpanzees have culture?
5. Do you think that if more people understood how similar chimpanzees are to humans they would work harder to protect chimpanzees from extinction?

9. DISTURBING BEHAVIORS OF THE ORANGUTAN

Studies of orangutans have shown two different patterns of adolescent growth and reproductive strategizing among males. Some males grow twice as big as females and develop elaborate secondary sexual characteristics that make them attractive to females and result in opportunities to mate with willing female partners. Other males exhibit arrested adolescence and remain similar in size and physical characteristics to females. These males can only mate through forced copulations—in other words, they rape female orangutans in order to reproduce, a strategy which can be quite successful. The authors warn against drawing parallels between orangutan rape and human rape.

The orangutan is one of humankind's closest relatives. One of the four great apes (the other three are gorillas, chimpanzees and bonobos), Pongo pygmaeus is exquisitely adapted for life in the forest canopies of the Southeast Asian islands of Borneo and Sumatra. With their long arms and hooklike hands, orangutans are adept at swinging from tree to tree in search of tropical fruits. They are among the most solitary of large primates and the only great apes found outside Africa. Orangutans are also notable for the striking size difference between males and females: the average weight of an adult male (about 90 kilograms, or 198 pounds) is more than twice that of a female.

An adult male orangutan is an impressive sight. The animal has a pair of wide cheek pads, called flanges, and a well-developed throat sac used for emitting loud cries known as long calls. The mature male also has long, brightly colored hair on its body and face. These are secondary sexual characteristics, the flamboyant signals that male orangutans flaunt to proclaim their fertility and fitness to the opposite sex. The features emerge during orangutan adolescence: males reach puberty at around seven to nine years of age, then spend a few years in a far-from-impressive "subadult" stage, during which they are about the same size as mature females. The males reach their adult size and develop secondary sexual traits by ages 12 to 14. Or at least that's what primate researchers used to think.

As stable social groups of orangutans were established in zoos, however, it became clear that an adolescent male could remain a subadult, in a state of arrested development, until his late teens. In the 1970s, studies of orangutans in the rain forests of Southeast Asia by Biruté M. F. Galdikas of Simon Fraser University in British Columbia and others produced the same finding: sometimes males were arrested adolescents for a decade or more, about half their potential reproductive lives. Variability of this magnitude is fascinating—it is like finding a species in which pregnancy could last anywhere from six months to five years.

Biologists are keenly interested in studying cases of arrested development because they often shed light on the processes of growth and maturation. In some instances, the cause of arrested development is a genetic disorder; for example, a mutation in the receptor for a growth factor in humans results in a form of dwarfism. Environmental factors can also slow or halt an organism's development. For instance, food shortages delay maturation in humans and many other animals. This response is logical from an evolutionary standpoint—if it is unclear whether you will survive another week, it makes no sense to waste calories by adding bone mass or developing secondary sexual characteristics. Gymnasts and ballet dancers who exercise to extremes and anorexics who starve themselves sometimes experience delayed onset of puberty.

Among male orangutans, though, the cause of arrested development seems to lie in the animals' *social* environment. The presence of dominant adult males appears to delay the maturation of adolescent males in the same vicinity. Until recently, researchers believed that they were observing a stress-induced pathology—that is, the adolescent orangutans stopped developing because the adult males bullied and frightened them. Over the past few years, however, we have conducted studies suggesting that arrested development among orangutans is not a pathology but an adaptive evolutionary strategy. The arrested adolescent males are capable of impregnating females, and by staying small and immature (in terms of secondary sexual features) they minimize the amount of food they need and lower the risk of serious conflict with adult males. But the strategy of these arrested adolescents has a disquieting aspect: they copulate forcibly with females. In other words, they rape.

Measuring Stress

The first investigations into this subject focused on groups of captive orangutans. Terry L. Maple of Zoo Atlanta and other zoo biologists found that adolescent males remained developmentally arrested as long as there was a mature male in their enclosure. If the researchers removed that dominant male, the adolescents soon began to develop into adults. This kind of social regulation had been observed previously in other species. Among mandrill monkeys, for instance, socially dominant males develop dramatic secondary sexual characteristics, such as large testes and high testosterone levels, whereas subordinate males do not. In tree shrews and many rodent species, puberty is delayed in the subordinate animals. In another example, elephant poaching in certain areas of Africa has recently produced orphaned males that grew up in a fairly unsocialized manner. When in "musth"—a male elephant's mating period—these animals become quite aggressive and dangerous. Some zoologists have reported an effective solution: introducing older, more dominant males into the region, which results in social suppression of musth in the rogue males.

In all these cases, researchers have generally agreed that the stress of being subordinate accounts for the developmental arrest. During a typical period of stress for a mammal—say, a sprint across the savanna to escape a predator—energy is mobilized to power the muscles. As part of this process, a variety of long-term building projects in the body are inhibited, including growth, tissue repair and reproductive functions. It is the logic of triage: the animal concentrates on survival during the emergency and resumes long-term tasks later, if there is a later. But when an animal undergoes chronic stress, such as that caused by social subordination, the triaging can have adverse consequences, such as decreased growth, lower levels of sex hormones, reduced fertility and delayed puberty. In humans, severe and prolonged psychological stress can cause growth to stop in children, a rare syndrome called psychogenic dwarfism.

At first glance, adolescent male orangutans also appear to be under chronic stress. Adult male orangutans are extremely aggressive to adolescents, particularly within the confines of a zoo. In the wild, orangutan males are dispersed and solitary, belligerently defending a large territory that encompasses several females' territories—sort of a scattered harem. But even there, adolescents are well aware of the threatening presence of a mature male. One signal is a musky odorant that adult males spread about their territories. In addition, mature male orangutans announce their presence by performing long calls; John C. Mitani of the University of Michigan has found that these resonant cries can travel for miles.

Researchers had made little effort, however, to test the hypothesis that the stress of being near a dominant male induces hormonal changes that arrest development in adolescents. In 1989 we began looking for a way to examine the hormones of arrested adolescent orangutans to determine whether these animals were indeed under chronic stress. Ideally one would want to measure the levels of relevant hormones in the orangutans' blood, but this was impossible to do, for ethical and practical reasons. So we took advantage of the fact that the average levels of various hormones in the animals' blood are reflected in a fairly parallel fashion in their urine. Getting urine from wild animals would be immensely difficult, so we studied captive populations. Thanks to the generous help of zookeepers, curators and veterinarians at 13 zoos, we obtained more than 1,000 urine samples from 28 male orangutans, along with information on their developmental status (juvenile, arrested adolescent, developing adolescent or adult), housing, diet, medical history and growth records. In collaboration with Nancy Czekala of the Center for Reproduction of Endangered Species at the San Diego Zoo, we measured the levels of nine hormones, comparing animals in different developmental stages.

First we focused on growth hormone, which is crucial for normal maturation. Among the juveniles, arrested adolescents and adults, growth hormone levels in the urine were low and extremely similar, within 15 percent of one another. In contrast, adolescent males that were maturing into adults had growth hormone levels approximately three times as high. This result basically served as an internal control, showing that the external assessments of an animal's development stage closely matched the hormonal profile relevant to growth. In other words, adolescent males going through a developmental spurt in terms of appearance—growing larger, increasing the size of their cheek flanges, and so on—were experiencing hormonal changes as well.

We then considered hormones that respond to stress. Probably the best known is adrenaline (also called epinephrine), which plays a central role in energy mobilization. Epinephrine, unfortunately, cannot be measured accurately in urine. We could, however, determine levels of another key class of stress hormones called the glucocorticoids, which can suppress growth, tissue repair and reproduction. In addition, we measured the levels of prolactin, a stress-indicative hormone that can inhibit reproduction.

This is where we got a surprise. Glucocorticoid levels did not differ among juveniles, arrested adolescents and adults. Prolactin levels did not differ either. But adolescents going through the developmental spurt had glucocorticoid and prolactin levels roughly double those of the other groups. It wasn't the developmentally arrested adolescents who seemed to be stressed—it was the **developing** adolescents.

We got another surprise when we examined reproductive hormones in these animals. As expected, adolescent males who were developing secondary sexual characteristics had hormonal profiles implying an active gonadal system. Developing males had higher levels of testosterone and luteinizing hormone (which stimulates the release of testosterone) than did the arrested adolescents. But the levels of these hormones in arrested adolescents were equivalent to those seen in adults. Moreover, arrested males had levels of follicle-stimulating hormone (FSH), which stimulates sperm maturation in males, equal to those of developing adolescents or adult males. And other investigators have found that arrested adolescents have mature functional sperm and that their testes are the same size as those of developing adolescents.

Evolutionary Strategies

These findings overturned some long-held assumptions about orangutans. Apparently, arrested adolescents are neither stressed nor reproductively suppressed. What is going on? It turns out that there is more than one way for a male orangutan to improve his chances of reproducing.

A cornerstone of modern evolutionary theory is that animal behavior has evolved not for the good of the species or the social group but to maximize the number of gene copies passed on by an individual and its close relatives. For a long time, the study of primates was dominated by simplistic models of how animals achieve this goal. According to these models, male behavior consists of virtually nothing but aggression and competition to gain access to females. If only one female is sexually receptive in a group with many males, this competition would result in the highest-ranking male mating with her; if two females are receptive, the males ranking first and second in the hierarchy would mate with them, and so on.

But this kind of behavior is rarely seen among social primates. Instead male primates can choose alternative strategies to maximize their reproductive success. Why should there be alternatives? Because the seemingly logical strategy—developing powerful muscles and dramatic secondary sexual characteristics to excel at male-male competition—has some serious drawbacks. In many species, maintaining those secondary characteristics requires elevated testosterone levels, which have a variety of adverse effects on health. The aggression that comes with such a strategy is not great for health either.

Furthermore, increased body mass means greater metabolic demands and more pressure for successful food acquisition. During famines, the bigger primates are less likely to survive. For an arboreal species such as the orangutan, the heavier body of the mature male also limits which trees and branches can be accessed for food. And the development of secondary sexual characteristics makes a male more conspicuous, both to predators and to other males that view those characteristics as a challenge.

The competition between adult males and developing adolescents probably explains the elevated levels of stress hormones in the latter. In the eyes of an adult male orangutan, a developing male is soon to be a challenger, so naturally he becomes a prime target for aggression. The same pattern is seen among horses and various other social ungulates: it is not until the young males start developing secondary sexual characteristics that the unrelated dominant males begin to harass them into leaving the group. Another example comes from work by one of us (Sapolsky) with wild baboons. Some socially subordinate male baboons have much higher glucocorticoid levels than do the dominant animals, primarily because these subordinates are actively challenging the high-ranking males.

In contrast, the key impression that a developmentally arrested male communicates to an adult male is a lack of threat or challenge, because the immature male looks like a kid. Arrested male orangutans are apparently inconspicuous enough to be spared a certain amount of social stress. What is more, the "low profile" of these animals may actually give them a competitive advantage when it comes to reproduction. In many primate species, the low-ranking males are actually doing a fair share of the mating. Genetic paternity testing of these primates has shown that the subordinate males are quite successful in passing on their genes. This finding extends to orangutans: studies of zoo populations have proved that arrested males mate and that these matings are fertile. More recently Sri Suci Utami of Utrecht University in the Netherlands has shown that arrested adolescents fathered approximately half of the orangutan babies at her Sumatran study site.

Why are these low-ranking males taking part in so many matings? In some primate species, such as the savanna baboon, the females can decide with whom they will mate, and they frequently choose males who exhibit strong male-female affiliation and parental behavior rather than male-male competition. Even when dominant male baboons stand guard to prevent low-ranking males from mating, the females often initiate surreptitious matings—sometimes referred to as "stolen copulations"—with the subordinates. For low-ranking male baboons, the strategy of pursuing affiliative "friendships" with females is a viable one because it avoids the metabolic costs, injuries and stress of male-male competition.

But arrested male orangutans do not engage in long-term affiliative relationships with females, although an arrested male may sometimes accompany a female for several days as she roams through the forest. Furthermore, the great majority of adult female orangutans are sexually receptive only to mature males. So how do the arrested males mate? Observations of orangutans both in the wild and in captive populations have indicated that the arrested males forcibly copulate with females. Rape is an apt term for these copulations: the adult females usually resist the arrested adolescents fiercely, biting the males whenever they can and emitting loud, guttural sounds (called rape grunts) that are heard only under these circumstances. Adult males sometimes rape, too, but not nearly as often as the arrested males. In a study conducted in Borneo during the early 1980s, Mitani and his field assistants observed 151 copulations by arrested males; 144 of the matings were forced.

Thus, two reproductive strategies appear to have evolved for adolescent male orangutans. If no fully mature males are nearby, the adolescent will most likely develop quickly in the hopes of attracting female attention. When adult males are present, however, a strategy of arrested development has its advantages. If the social environment changes—say, if the nearby adult males die off or migrate—the arrested males will rapidly develop secondary sexual features and change their behavior patterns. Researchers are now trying to determine exactly how the presence or absence of adult males triggers hormonal changes in the adolescents.

Unpleasant Findings

What are the lessons we can learn from the male orangutan? First, a situation that seems stressful from a human's perspective may not necessarily be so. Second, the existence of alternative reproductive strategies shows that the optimal approach can vary dramatically in different social and ecological settings. There is no single blueprint for understanding the evolution of behavior. Third, although the recognition of alternative strategies built around female choice has generally met with a receptive audience among scientists, the rape-oriented strategy of arrested male orangutans is not so pleasing. But the study of primates has demonstrated time and again that the behavior of these animals is far from Disney-esque. Just consider the strategic infanticide of langur monkeys or the organized aggression—sometimes called genocide—between groups of chimpanzee males.

One must be cautious, however, in trying to gain insights into human behavior by extrapolating from animal studies. There is a temptation to leap to a wrongheaded conclusion: because forcible copulation occurs in orangutans and something similar occurs in humans, rape has a natural basis and is therefore unstoppable. This argument ignores the fact that the orangutan is the only nonhuman primate to engage in forcible copulation as a routine means of siring offspring. Furthermore, close observations of orangutan rape show that it is very different from human rape: for example, researchers have never seen a male orangutan injure a female during copulation in an apparently intentional manner. Most important, the orangutan's physiology, life history and social structure are completely unlike those of any other primate. Orangutans have evolved a unique set of adaptations to survive in their environment, and hence it would be the height of absurdity to draw simpleminded parallels between their behaviors and those of humans.

Discussion Questions

1. What was the original hypothesis about why some orangutan males failed to develop physically into fully mature adult males?
2. Give examples of species in which the presence of a higher-ranking individual suppresses the sexual behavior of subordinate individuals.
3. Give examples of how environmental stresses such as lack of food or psychological stress can impair growth and development in humans.
4. How did Maggioncalda and Sapolsky study stress hormones in orangutans? What was their research methodology? Why didn't they study hormone levels from blood or urine samples of wild-living orangutans?

5. How did the hormone profiles differ among juveniles, arrested adolescents, developing adolescents, and adults in terms of growth hormone, glucocorticoids, and prolactin? What did this suggest was going on? In other words, who was the most stressed? Which males were capable of successful reproduction?

6. What are the disadvantages of developing into a fully mature adult male orangutan?

7. What are the similarities and differences between orangutan rape and human rape?

Additional Resources

For Internet links related to this chapter, please visit our website at www.mhhe.com/dettwyler

BEKOFF, MARC. *Minding Animals: Awareness, Emotions, and Heart.* New York: Oxford University Press, 2002.

DIXSON, ALAN F. *Primate Sexuality: Comparative Studies of the Prosimians, Monkeys, Apes, and Humans.* New York: Oxford University Press, 1999.

GOODALL, JANE. *Through a Window: My Thirty Years with the Chimpanzees of Gombe.* Boston: Houghton Mifflin, 1990. Reissued in 2000.

MATSUZAWA, TETSURO. *Primate Origins of Human Cognition and Behavior.* New York: Springer Verlag, 2001.

PARKER, SUE TYLOR, ROBERT W. MITCHELL, and H. LYN MILES, eds. *The Mentalities of Gorillas and Orangutans: Comparative Perspectives.* New York: Cambridge University Press, 1999.

WRANGHAM, RICHARD W., W. C. McGREW, and FRANS B. M. de WAAL, eds. *Chimpanzee Cultures.* Cambridge, MA: Harvard University Press in cooperation with the Chicago Academy of Sciences, 1994.

CHAPTER 6

Primate Evolution

10. IN THE REALM OF VIRTUAL REALITY, by Richard Conniff and Harry Marshall, *Smithsonian* 32, no. 6 (September 2001), pp. 70–79.

Nonhuman primate evolution is not the most thrilling topic in anthropology (although some people clearly love it!). Nor does the study of early fossil primates hold direct relevance for most students' lives today. As our selection for this topic, therefore, we did not pick an article about omomyid teeth or the evolution of middle-ear morphology in early lemuroids. Rather, we chose an article about the search for Yeti in Bhutan—both as a way to capture your attention and imagination, and as a springboard for discussing a number of related issues. Read the selection with an open mind, and think about what it would mean if Yeti (and/or Bigfoot/Sasquatch/the Abominable Snowman) should turn out to be a previously unknown nonhuman primate, surviving in the remote reaches of the Himalayas or the northwest United States and Canada.

*Western scientists often act as though a species has not been "discovered" until it is discovered and described by Western scientists. Thus, it has been reported that kangaroos were "discovered" by Captain Cook, though clearly Australian Aborigines knew of kangaroos thousands of years before Cook arrived. Likewise, numerous new primate species have been discovered in South America in the last few decades, and new species of a variety of mammals have been found in parts of Vietnam since the end of the Vietnam war. Additionally, it is quite possible that many "unknown" primates (known only to local peoples) have become extinct in the last 100 years, without ever becoming known to Western scientists, or being factored into our ideas about primate evolution. All of this suggests that the story of primate evolution is far from complete, and that stories of the **migoi** may represent an "undiscovered," cold-adapted, high-altitude primate, perhaps similar to a mountain gorilla, living in the mountains of Bhutan.*

In the courtyard of a monastery somewhere in central Bhutan, cockerels strut across the lattice of flagstones. A dozen temple dogs doze fitfully in the sun. A novice late for prayers scurries, sandals in hand, and vanishes into a doorway. Inside, it's cold and dark. The only light oozes down like buckwheat honey through a narrow atrium, dimly illuminating the weird figures painted on the heavy timbers, and the monstrous antlers of a supposedly extinct deer, the shou, lashed to a balcony railing.

From a black recess up ahead comes the low, sonorous sound of chanting, rising steadily in pitch and fervor. A horn made from a human femur goes **oh-woe-oh-oh-oh.** Cymbals stutter. A pair of short metallic horns put up a high-pitched, reedy sound. A drum beats. Our guide leads us into a narrow hall and then, after we remove our shoes, into the prayer room, where monks in maroon robes sit around the periphery and a smudge of incense drifts up from a censer. As our eyes adjust, strange animals shapes form vaguely out of the darkness: the dust-cloyed head of a tiger hanging on a wall, a huge, primitive-looking fish with long bony scales, a string of human hands. And off to one side of the altar, the thing we have come halfway round the world to see, a hanging figure with a white veil draped over its head.

Legend says a holy man brought Buddhism to the Himalayan kingdom of Bhutan 1,200 years ago, flying in on the back of a tigress. Today, you fly into Paro International Airport in a Druk Air 72-seat jet. It's reputed to be the most technically difficult landing in the world. "While flying in," the pilot announces on the initial descent, "you may find yourself coming closer to the terrain than is usual in a jet-liner. Much closer. This is normal. Don't be alarmed." Most pilots crash several times before learning how to thread their way down the corridor of valleys to the airstrip. Fortunately, they make their mistakes on a flight simulator before attempting an actual approach. Bhutan has always been a place where the virtual and the real happily coexist.

Having opened itself to the outside world only 40 years ago, the "Land of the Thunder Dragon" is also a place where tradition still shapes everyday life. In the terraced rice paddies of the Paro Valley, families thresh rice by hand, the sheaves swinging overhead, sending up plumes of dust, then down, **swot,** on a rock, over and over, until all the dry kernels of rice break loose and rain down in heaps. Chili peppers, another great national food, are spread out in bright red carpets on rooftops and hillsides to dry in the sun. Only about 700,000 people live in Bhutan, most of them in the fertile valleys. Uphill, beyond the last timbered farmhouse, the forest still covers 70 percent of a country the size of Switzerland (only more mountainous). Tigers, leopards and bears still wander there. So, too, according to legend, does the **migoi,** which is what the Bhutanese call the yeti.

Migoi literally means "wild man," and the idea that there might be an undiscovered primate, a hairy quasi-human biped, still living in Bhutan's uncharted mountains is, according to some members of our expedition, the stuff of great adventure. And to some of us it is utter bunk. We agree, at least, that seeking the migoi is a way to get beneath the surface of this intriguing culture, which is why a British-American television partnership has sent us here. The group includes an Oxford-trained evolutionary biologist, a primatologist who has spent years working with monkeys in West Africa, and a British technical wiz who will keep our gear in working order. We have come equipped with camera traps, plaster of paris for casting footprints, and laboratory jars for sending back hair, scat or tissue samples to be identified by DNA analysis. We've also got video cameras to record what the migoi means to the Bhutanese themselves. Our guide is Dasho Palden Dorji, a tall, chiseled 37-year-old who was educated at the University of California, Santa Barbara, and speaks English like an American. He's a true believer in the migoi, but patient with skeptics. Despite his easygoing manner, locals tend to trot when he issues an order. "Dasho" is a term of respect similar to "lord," and he is a first cousin to the king.

Other Bhutanese aren't so patient. When we note the failure of numerous previous attempts to find any hard evidence for the existence of the migoi, a forestry official wryly observes that Westerners only believe a species exists if a white man has given it a Latin name. In the 1950s a "new" primate was "discovered" in southern Bhutan and named with the help of a British naturalist, E. P. Gee. The golden langur, a gregarious monkey living in groups of 15 or 16 individuals, had been well known to the Bhutanese for centuries. But it is now immortalized in scientific literature as *Presbytis geei,* a name that still rankles some people in Bhutan. Local knowledge also got short shrift when yak herders reported seeing tigers in the mountains; science knew that tigers never go much above 6,000 feet. Then Bhutanese wildlife officials photographed a tiger crossing through a meadow at nearly 10,000 feet. So when locals who travel in the mountains say that a shy, solitary primate survives undetected there, isn't it a little arrogant to dismiss it as myth?

Maybe so, but our first few rounds of inquiry go to the skeptics. In a traditional farmhouse a few miles from the airport, a ritual purification ceremony is under way. The air is heavy with the smell of burning juniper and the sound of monks praying to drive unwanted spirits into intricate traps made of bamboo and ribbon. Dorji Tshering, the head of the household, sits cross-legged on the floor, fanning flies from his bowl of butter tea as he recalls his encounter with the migoi. The memory still gives him nightmares, though it happened 50 years ago. He and a friend had climbed the mountain behind the house in search of a suitable tree to saw into planks. Their journey took them through a glen called Migoi Shitexa and up to a shelter called Bandits' Cave. That night, as they collected firewood, they noticed strange footprints in the fresh snow. Tshering, now in his 80s, bow-legged, with a shock of white hair, taps his forearm at the elbow and then his knuckles, to show the length of the footprint. He knew what bear footprints looked like, he says, and this wasn't a bear. In the darkness, the two men heard the creaking and breaking of bamboo, followed by an eerie monotone call. Tshering imitates the sound. "This was definitely the migoi," he tells us. "We thought it was going to eat us up." "But what did you actually see?" we ask, and the answer is little more than a shape moving beyond the light of their fire, the size of a man, hairy, on two legs, its features indistinct in the darkness.

The stories told about the migoi are often like that, full of conviction but woefully short on detail. Or chock-full of plausible details, until a trapdoor suddenly drops open in the argument: a nomad digresses knowledgeably about the differences between migoi scat, which he says mainly contains bamboo, and bear scat, which is full of acorns. Then he adds that if you happen to go into the mountains when you are spiritually unclean, the migoi will bring typhoons and hailstorms down on your head. This odd mix of being so savvy about the natural world and yet so credulous is a little hard for outsiders like us to fathom. When we ask Tshering what "Migoi Shitexa" means, he says, "the place where the yeti scratches for lice." It is normal in Bhutan to be earthy and otherworldly at the same time.

The purification ceremony ends late in the day when the children carry the spirit traps out of the house and into the fields. The traps are laden with bread, fruit, money and strands of fabric to placate the evil spirits now bottled up within. "Ghostbusters for Buddhists," someone remarks. But in truth, the whole scene feels as if we've been set down in the middle of a Brueghel painting, in the Europe of 500 years ago: blue smoke in the air, a neat golden stack of rice straw in the farm-yard with a straw finial on top, a pervasive sense of religious faith, and a kind of ribald peasant contentment with the course of life. Standing outside, we can hear the monks raucously chanting their last few prayers. One of them turns his weath-ered face over his shoulder, grinning and shouting the words of the prayer out to us through a tiny arched window. A few minutes later, a mangy dog comes trotting back to the house from the field, a strand of ribbon trailing over its ears from its raid on the contents of a spirit trap.

The winding, one-lane mountain roads take us into central Bhutan, where the monastery called Gangtey Gompa is famous for two things: black-necked cranes forage in the broad wetlands below, and within the walls of the monastery itself is a mummified **mechume**, the putative remains of a small yeti.

The black-necked cranes are real enough, and by late October their **trum-trum** calls echo across the frosted marshes. In the brilliant white light of dawn, groups of them soar down, the sun glinting off their six-foot wingspans. In a country where the human life expectancy is about 50 years, the cranes live to be nearly half that and are revered as bodhisattva, or Buddhist deities. It's said that at the time of their de-parture each year, before their migration north to the Tibetan plateau, the cranes fly three times around the monastery, the clockwise ritual of any Buddhist pilgrim. There's a simpler explanation: ornithologists say the cranes are simply flying around trying to gain altitude. But for us, the symbolic and supernatural values are starting to become more intriguing. Coming from a world where we see the landscape in terms of lots and subdivisions, we're learning to envy the way people in Bhutan still tell stories about their own hills and valleys.

It's easy to get caught up in local values, especially within the darkened monastery itself, where the monks chant **Om ma ni pad me hung** ("Praise to the jewel in the lotus"), as they have chanted numberless times since the 12th century. Our guide, Dasho Palden, says no Westerner has ever entered the monastery's inner sanctum before, but the abbot has arranged this visit especially to show us the mechume. The atmosphere in the prayer room is somewhere between a reliquary and a rag-and-bone shop. By the flickering butter candles, we step gingerly around sacks hanging like punching bags from the rafters. Asked what's in them, Palden replies, "Diseases. If they get out, they will spread." The wide wooden floorboards have been polished by generations of barefoot pilgrims prostrating themselves be-fore the crowded altar. Dasho Palden prostrates himself, too, and then, according to custom, a monk hands him three dice to foresee the fate of the expedition we are about to undertake into the perilous high country. Palden rolls a 13. In the Eastern scheme of things, he assures us, this is a good, solid number.

Afterward, he leads us over to the far side of the altar, to examine the mechume. The story goes that roughly 200 years ago, in a village two days' hike from here, a series of killings occurred. A local holy man determined that this mechume was the culprit. He tracked it down and cut it in half with his sword, and the corpse has been hanging at Gangtey Gompa ever since. The head, no larger than a child's, slumps down, chin resting on the sack of skin that was once its chest. The withered hands and feet hang by threads and bits of dried flesh. The eyes are squeezed shut, and the mouth is stretched wide. Dasho Palden suggests that the mouth is making the sound of the mechume, **Woooooo.** But to us it looks as if the mouth has been frozen at the split second of this creature's death in an eternal wail of agony and despair. Either way, someone has stuffed an offering of **ngultrum**, the local currency, into its mouth.

That face continues to haunt us for days afterward, and one night around the campfire, the skeptics in our group develop an alternative theory about how it came to be at Gangtey Gompa: imagine a rural holy man beset by angry, terrified villagers demanding action. Was it practical to think he could have caught and killed a creature as elusive as the mechume, which the Bhutanese themselves sometimes describe as part god, part devil? Or did he simply find some poor scapegoat, a loner, a madman, someone who would not be missed—much as New Englanders once burned ordinary women as witches? In any case, we agree that what is hanging at Gangtey Gompa is unmistakably, unbearably, human.

"You'll have to excuse me," Kunzang Choden says, when she greets us at the front door of her family compound, "but I am expecting my uncle's reincarnation. He's an American boy, 14 now." He's due to arrive sometime before nightfall, and everyone's bustling around getting ready. Ugyen Choling Palace, where Choden's ancestors have lived since the 15th century, is at the end of the long, idyllic Tang Valley in central Bhutan. It's two hours by car from the nearest town, Bumthang, and a one-hour hike uphill from the nearest road. The palace once lorded over the valley, but almost all the rooms are empty now, with the wooden window panels drawn shut to keep out pigeons. Choden, who is 48, grew up before electricity, television and videotapes came to Bhutan, and the greatest pleasure of her childhood was listening to yak herders, back from the wild, telling their stories of the high country. She's now Bhutan's leading folklorist, and she's put together an anthology called *Bhutanese Tales of the Yeti.*

Choden accepts our impression that the migoi stories are much like European fairy tales. The migoi, like an ogre in a fairy tale, often comes to a gruesome end. "I also have my sympathies with the migoi," Choden admits. "I'm sure if the migoi could tell its story, these terrible things wouldn't happen." But humans tell the stories, and "even though we Bhutanese live in nature, we have to be able to be the masters somehow."

Is it possible that's why Bhutan still has its migoi stories? Because there's still wilderness, unmastered, just beyond the farmyard gate, much as there was dark forest in Europe back when the fairy-tale tradition there was strong? Choden replies that urbanized Western countries still have their credulous tales, only updated a little: "*Star Wars* and all that comes from the fact that they've lost the wilderness and they have to look beyond, whereas we still have our environment intact, and we know that there are spirits living under the trees, spirits residing on the mountaintops. So this is still a part of our reality."

As we talk, her pet Lhasa apso noses around. "Ignore him," she advises. "He is a most terrible attention-seeker." And then she continues, "The supernatural and the natural, we do not delineate. People in the villages still perform rituals to appease the spirits that they have harmed, knowingly or unknowingly. We have, I guess, a ritual world. We have so much that is not explained. And we do not want it explained.

What I fear most is that soon, with our children all going into Western schools and learning more about Western culture and beliefs, this will be lost."

Then, since our expedition is about to head off into the mountains, seeking explanations and evidence, she offers some parting advice: if we meet a female yeti, keep in mind that the yeti's long, sagging breasts make her top-heavy on a down slope. "So, yes, run downhill," Choden says. Then she grins and adds, "Go down the cliff, I think."

Next night, when our packhorses have been set free to graze, and our tents are staked down, the group gathers for dinner. We're in bear and tiger country now, our evolutionary biologist reminds us, and he gives each of us an "attack alarm." "It will produce a 107-decibel shriek, and that should scare off just about any animal." Then he pushes the trigger.

"The horses didn't twitch," someone says, when we have recovered enough to hear them contentedly tearing up the grass just beyond the light of our lanterns. We decide to put our faith instead in one of our guides, known simply as "303," for the battered old .303 Enfield rifle he keeps slung over one shoulder. The government has provided us with this armed protection because unpredictable Himalayan black bears often maul or kill unlucky yak herders.

We camp in an open meadow, but there's still forest all around. On the big old spruce trees, Spanish moss drifts in the breeze like an old man's wispy beard. Rhododendrons with leaves as big as fans grow in the understory, along with stunted little bamboo. Soft green moss carpets the floor and swells up in pom-pom clumps over broken branches. The forest itself feels as though animals—and spirits, too— have somehow taken root in the steep mountain soil. But our camera traps, with motion sensors and infrared gear for shooting by night as well as by day, turn up no big, dangerous animals. The movement of the vegetation sets them off. And once, some creature leaves its tantalizing shadow across a corner of the video frame.

Proving a species exists is relatively straightforward. The rule of habeas corpus applies: you must present a body or specimen, a holotype that other scientists can examine in a laboratory setting. Proving that a species doesn't exist, on the other hand, is near to impossible. This dawns on us, literally, at Rodong La, at 14,000 feet on the trek from Bumthang to Lhuentse.

According to Kunzang Choden, this lonely pass is one of the most frequent sites for yeti spottings. So one night two of our party, the skeptics, camp out alone at Rodong La, without 303 or any other protection, offering ourselves to the yeti as unbelievers. We spend the first part of the night holed up in a blind we've pitched in a shadowy stand of gnarled rhododendrons. It's cold and lonely. A cloud envelops us, and we have no moon or stars to give us the minimal light needed for the image intensifier on our video camera. Everything is damp and eerily silent, with no birds or insects. It feels as if the cloud has somehow sucked the sound out of the sky. On this remote spot, one of Choden's informants once saw a yeti face-to-face with a tiger.

We have no such luck. But when the lichen and moss have gone brittle with frost, the cloud lifts. The faint yellow light before dawn unveils the landscape around us, and then other hills and mountains, which gradually separate from one another as the sun rises. In the distance, brilliant orange light catches on the snowcapped peak of Gangkar Punsum. At 25,000 feet, it is the highest mountain in Bhutan, and no one has ever climbed it.

By now, we are out of the blind wandering in amazement. To the northeast, a wide lazy river of clouds flows through a valley, and at the end, the clouds spill down over a precipice like a waterfall, tumbling and steaming between two spruce promontories. Beyond that, other valleys, still forested and without people, delve toward infinity. It makes us realize that in this vast unexplored landscape anything is possible.

But not necessarily right now. In all our climbing up lonely mountain passes and down endless winding stairways built into the cliff face, we turn up nothing remotely like a yeti. The camera traps yield one squirrel, and a yak herder urinating by the side of the trail. Then one day we make the steep, sweaty descent into a valley, where the white noise of a river rises up to meet us, along with the cries of farm children. In the remote, roadless village of Khaine Lhakhang, we meet a man named Sonam Dhendup. He's 37 years old, with black hair just starting to go gray, a wispy goatee and short, rough, muscular legs, the product of a lifetime in the Himalayas.

Dhendup tells us he has worked for the past 12 years as a migoi-spotter for the government. He has yet to see a migoi himself. But he knows a place two days' hike away, where the migoi comes to eat bamboo each spring and where his droppings pile up in heaps. The season is wrong. But the mountains are tempting, and Dhendup tells us enough to convince us he knows the local wildlife.

Accompanied by 303, two of our party follow Dhendup back up until they are walking among the clouds at 12,000 feet. In the dense, sodden forest there, Dhendup kneels to indicate the fresh pugmarks of a large male tiger, a few minutes ahead. The worn bolt on the .303 Enfield slides home with a sharp click. A soft rain begins to fall. As Dhendup creeps barefoot through the forest, he points out more tiger prints, some wild boar grubbings, places where bears have clearly rubbed against trees. He's a connoisseur of Himalayan wildlife, able to distinguish black bear and brown bear by their paw marks alone. Why would he, as skeptics like to suggest, mistake either species for a yeti?

The hill fog closes in around them, and the bamboo forest becomes a dripping prison of crisscrossed stems and pungent leaf mold. They circle aimlessly for hours, until Dhendup veers off purposefully and they arrive at the hollow tree he has been seeking. As expected, the dung heaps he saw there last spring are long gone. But there's a cavity in the tree just large enough for a human, or some creature of similar size, to hunker down and find refuge. A careful inspection turns up hairs stuck in the rough sides of the cavity. Some of the strands are long and dark, others shorter and more bristly. Not bear, says Dhendup. The hairs are, at the very least, worth packing up and taking home for DNA analysis.

Months later, in a laboratory at Oxford University, geneticist Bryan Sykes is pleased with the samples we have brought back. The hairs have plump follicles, the part that contains the DNA. Prospects for identifying the source of these hairs seem good. Sykes starts with the plausible assumption that he is looking at bear DNA, or maybe wild pig. But the DNA seems to suggest otherwise. His laboratory simply cannot sequence it. "We normally wouldn't have any difficulty at all," says Sykes. "It had all the hallmarks of good material. It's not a human, it's not a bear, nor anything else that we've so far been able to identify. We've never encountered any DNA that we couldn't sequence before. But then, we weren't looking for the yeti." It is, he says, "a mystery, and I didn't think this would end in a mystery."

What a scientist cannot add is that sometimes a mystery is enough. The skeptics in our group had conceded as much that morning back in Rodong La. Watching the sunrise on the endless mountains, we agreed that if we had a choice—a land rich in wilderness, and rich in demons, too, or a land "civilized" and full of skeptics like us—we would gladly take Bhutan the way it is, yeti and all.

Discussion Questions

1. According to the Bhutanese, what is the **migoi**? Why do the Bhutanese believe the **migoi** exists? What evidence do they have of its existence?

2. For what two things is the monastery of Gantey Gompa famous? What is the **mechume** supposed to be, and how did it come to hang in the inner sanctum of the monastery?

3. How do the authors explain the **mechume**? How do they think it came to be in the monastery? Look up the photograph of the **mechume** in the original *Smithsonian* magazine article—does it look human to you?

4. What is the standard for proving that a new species exists? Why is it more difficult to prove that a species doesn't exist?

5. The research team recovers hair from inside a hollowed-out tree high in the dripping cloud forest mountains of Bhutan. What is the outcome of DNA analysis of the hair samples?

6. If the hair does not belong to any known species, does that mean it belongs to a giant primate, or ape-man?

7. We know that early *Homo erectus* populations in Southeast Asia interacted with *Gigantopithecus,* a genus of huge gorilla-like primates that became extinct in the region after the arrival of early hominids. Could memories of these encounters, passed down through the thousands of years since the extinction of *Gigantopithecus,* be the source of **migoi** stories?

8. Imagine that a live **migoi** has been captured in Bhutan and is available for study. What ethical issues are involved in doing research on a previously unknown species? Does it make any difference if the **migoi** turns out to be related to a bear, or if it is a surviving *Gigantopithecus* or even a *Homo erectus*?

9. Do you agree or disagree with this statement: "If populations of Yeti really do exist, they obviously don't want to interact with humans, and have taken great pains to hide from us. Therefore, we should leave them alone, instead of trying to find them and study them"?

Additional Resources

For Internet links related to this chapter, please visit our website at www.mhhe.com/dettwyler

CONNIFF, RICHARD, and HARRY MARSHALL. *Abominable Snowman: The Search for the Truth.* New York: The Learning Channel (documentary), 2001.

HEUVELMANS, BERNARD. *On the Track of Unknown Animals.* London: Kegan Paul Intl., 1995.

KAPPELER, PETER M., and MICHAEL ERIC PEREIRA, eds. *Primate Life Histories and Socioecology.* Chicago, IL: University of Chicago Press, 2003.

KIMBEL, WILLIAM H., and LAWRENCE B. MARTIN, eds. *Species, Species Concepts, and Primate Evolution.* New York: Plenum Pub. Corp., 1993.

SKUKER, KARL P. N. *The New Zoo: New and Rediscovered Animals of the Twentieth Century.* Poughkeepsie, NY: House of Stratus Inc., 2002.

CHAPTER 7

Early Hominids

11. "Not Out of Africa: Alan Thorne's Challenging Ideas about Human Evolution," by Joseph D'Agnese, *Discover* 23, no. 8 (August 2002), pp. 52–57.

12. "Eating Right: Lessons Learned from Our Prehistoric Ancestors," by Vaughn M. Bryant (2003).

Unraveling the prehistoric record of the earliest humans is a mystery that needs the keen investigation techniques worthy of Sherlock Holmes. Like a modern crime scene, the evidence of our earliest ancestors comes as tiny fragments of bone, or a few teeth, maybe a footprint, or even a few ancient tools. From these bits of information anthropologists must try to decide how old the fossils are, who were their ancestors and descendants, if they represent some new race or species of early hominid, or if the evidence belongs to some group that is already known. When fossil hunting began in earnest during the 1800s, anthropologists lacked many of the sophisticated techniques and tools we use today. Instead, they had to rely on bone structure, the stone tools they found, and on the hypotheses that abounded about where and how human evolution began. Charles Darwin was the first to propose that Africa was the birthplace of humankind, but few believed him. Instead, for nearly a century most researchers focused on Asia, which they believed contained the earliest evidence. As more remains were discovered and as new techniques emerged, the story of human evolution changed frequently. Finally, researchers believed they had solved the puzzle of human evolution because they found ways to examine human DNA. Scientists discovered that mitochondrial DNA (mtDNA) often survives the ravages of time, that the genetics are fairly easy to unravel because there are only 37 genes, and that mtDNA is inherited only through the maternal line. Quick testing and sampling of modern human populations showed that everyone has mtDNA that is related to modern Africans. This led to the "out of Africa" theory, the belief that all living humans could trace their ancestry back to a common ancient population that once lived in Africa. Along with this new idea came the belief that many of the fossil hominids, such as the Neanderthals, must have been "dead ends," and that they did not interbreed with the more modern peoples coming out of Africa.

The title of this article immediately tells the reader that it is going to dispute the widely held view that all modern humans are the product of a small group of people who left the continent of Africa somewhere between 120,000 and 250,000 years ago. It was the discovery of two partial skulls from some very old Australians that led to this challenge. Both the morphological features and the DNA evidence from these skulls present problems for the "out of Africa" believers. In an effort to dispute the "out of Africa" concept, the author weaves a convincing argument about his own beliefs concerning how early human populations emerged, when they left Africa, and what happened to them once they left. While doing so he also challenges the very core of the "out of Africa" hypothesis and suggests that things might not be as neat and tidy as the "out of Africa" group thinks.

She came to him in 1968, inside a small cheap suitcase—her burned and shattered bones embedded in six blocks of calcified sand. The field researchers who dug her up in a parched no-man's-land in southeastern Australia suspected that she was tens of thousands of years old. He was 28. Almost every day for the next six months, he painstakingly freed her remains from the sand with a dental drill, prizing out more than 600 bone chips, each no larger than a thumbnail. He washed them carefully with acetic acid, sealed them with a preservative, and pieced them together into a recognizable skeleton. Looking closely at skull fragments, bits of arm bone, and a hint of pelvis, he became convinced that two things were true. First, the bones were human, *Homo sapiens* for sure, and they had held together a young woman. As he assembled this "monster three-dimensional jigsaw puzzle," Alan Thorne, then a lecturer in the department of anatomy at the University of Sydney, began asking himself whose bones they might actually have been. He had no idea that many years later, the answer to that question would rock the world of anthropology.

Something else about this woman became clear early on—she had been important and powerful. The pattern of burn marks on her bones showed that after she died, her family burned the corpse, then smashed the bones. Later, they added more fuel and burned the bones a second time. This was an unusual ritual. Ancient Aboriginal women were typically buried without fuss. Thorne wondered if her descendants had tried to ensure that she did not return to haunt them; similar cremation rituals are still practiced by some Aboriginal groups today. As hours and days and months passed, he found himself thinking of her as a living, breathing person who'd spent her life encamped on the shores of Lake Mungo, in New South Wales. If this Mungo Lady turned out to be as ancient as field researchers thought, she would be the oldest human fossil ever found in Australia. To Thorne she was already the most mysterious.

In 1968 most anthropologists thought they had a grip on human evolution: Big-browed, thick-skulled humanoids had descended from walking apes. These hulking creatures were eventually replaced by the more advanced, fine-boned humans of our species—*Homo sapiens*. Throughout Australia, anthropologists had found only big-browed, thick-skulled fossils. That made Mungo Lady a puzzle. Lab analysis of her remains suggested she was 25,000 years old—old enough to be a grandmother to those specimens—but her skull bones were as delicate as an emu's eggshell. Thorne began to realize that she might be telling him a different story than the one he'd read in textbooks—that the delicate, fine-boned people had reached Australia before the big-brows.

That was an exotic thought, and now, many years later, it is fueling the debate within anthropology over a single huge question: Where did *Homo sapiens* come from? Most researchers accept a theory referred to as "out of Africa." It holds that numerous species of hominids—beginning with *Homo erectus*—began migrating out of Africa almost 2 million years ago and evolved into several species. Then a new species called *Homo sapiens* evolved in Africa and migrated between 100,000 and 120,000 years ago to Europe, Asia, and Australia, consigning all the earlier hominids it encountered to extinction.

Thorne preaches a revolutionary view called regional continuity. He believes that the species his opponents insist on calling *Homo erectus* was in fact *Homo sapiens,* and that they migrated out of Africa almost 2 million years ago and dispersed throughout Europe and Asia. As he sees it, there was no later migration and replacement: "Only one species of human has ever left Africa, and that is us."

Why does this matter? Because if Thorne and his camp are right, much of what we think we know about human evolution is wrong. In the world according to Thorne, the human family tree is not divided into discrete species such as *Homo erectus, Homo antecessor, Homo heidelbergensis,* and *Homo neanderthalensis.* They are all *Homo sapiens.* Yes, Thorne agrees, from the outside all these hominids look different from each other, but so do humans today—a Korean, a Nigerian, and a Dane hardly resemble each other. Our ancestors displayed great variety, but they were similar in the only way that mattered: They were the same species, which meant they could have sex with each other and produce fertile offspring.

Mungo Lady started Thorne down the road to regional continuity. Six years after he reassembled her, Thorne and three assistants unearthed another small-boned skeleton only 1,600 feet from where she had been found. At burial, this body had been laid on its right side, knees bent, arms tucked between its legs. Certain features—the skull, the shape of the pelvis, and the length of the long bones—told Thorne he was looking at Mungo Man, which thrilled him. As a general rule, female skeletons are more delicate than male ones, so doubts about the uniqueness of Mungo Lady's delicate bones would be quashed by having an equally delicate male counterpart to study.

Thorne's colleagues took their best guess at this specimen's age, as they had with Mungo Lady in 1968, based on radio-carbon dating and analysis of stratigraphy. They dated him to 30,000 years ago. As the oldest humans ever found down under, the finds were considered so important that the Australian government declared the sandy, bone-dry crater that was once Lake Mungo a national park in order to honor—and protect—the site. To the Aboriginal tribes, the pair became precious symbols of their early peopling of the continent.

But Thorne assigned a meaning to the bones that resonated beyond Australia. To his mind, the presence of two such unusual skeletons suggested that the peopling of the Pacific was a richer, more complex process than anyone had ever imagined. Anthropologists had long assumed that the first *Homo sapiens* to reach Australia were fishermen who left Indonesia and got blown off course, ending up on the new continent. Thorne began to wonder whether the first journey from Indonesia to Australia was not an accident but an adventure, undertaken with confidence by intelligent, mobile people. Mungo Lady and Mungo Man closely resembled skeletons of people living in China at the same time. Had these people migrated in boats to Australia? Had there been successive waves of immigration by different peoples over tens of thousands of years? To imagine such things, Thorne had to abandon familiar notions of early man as a blundering primitive.

He had already begun to do so. In the months he'd spent piecing together those braincases, he had begun to think of them as his elders, worthy of respect, capable of thought and imagination. That supposition was not an outrageous one for an Australian anthropologist to make. From childhood Thorne had grown up on a continent that was home to one of Earth's oldest continuous cultures. He'd learned a great deal about Aboriginal culture while working his way through college as a reporter at the *Sydney Morning Herald.* From where he stood, the ways of Mungo Man and Mungo Lady were not so different from those of modern Aborigines. He could easily picture two different tribes settling near Lake Mungo, one from nearby Java, another perhaps with roots in China. And once the two parties were encamped around the lake, it was not hard to imagine them crossbreeding.

Those who believe in regional continuity tend to have a view of sexuality that is more generous and more inclusive than that of the out-of-Africa proponents. In the latter view, *Homo sapiens* led a kind of search-and-replace mission as they spread around the planet; these researchers believe that members of the new species would not have been able to successfully reproduce with members of earlier species, no matter how hard they tried. Thorne thinks that's nonsense. "European scientists have dominated this field for 150 years," he says. "And they've got a big problem in Europe. Namely, they've got to account for those Neanderthals. My opponents would say that Cro-Magnons"—humans identical to us who lived during the Ice Age—"simply 'replaced' Neanderthals with no intermingling. That's the part I object to. 'No intermingling.' Now, I ask you, does that sound like the human beings you know?"

In the early 1970s, these ideas were pure speculation. Thorne had no proof of anything. The bones had told him what they could and then lapsed into silence. So he tucked them away and went on with his career. Three decades later, the bones spoke again.

In 1997 Thorne finally got the tool he needed to explore Mungo Lady and Mungo Man further. European scientists reported that they had successfully extracted fragments of mitochondrial DNA (mtDNA) from the remains of Neanderthal skeletons unearthed in Germany, Croatia, and Russia. This was stunning science; the Neanderthals had died out 35,000 years ago, and yet researchers had been able to harvest genetic matter from their bones as if they'd expired yesterday.

It was the beginning of a revolution in paleoanthropology. Geneticists were hooking up with bone men everywhere. They were focusing on mtDNA because the mitochondria, which lie outside the nucleus, are easier to study—in a human cell there are only 37 mitochondrial genes compared with 100,000 genes found in the nucleus—and because it is the only DNA anyone has been able to isolate and interpret in ancient fossils. For reasons not yet understood, mtDNA survives the ravages of time better than nuclear DNA. And it has another interesting attribute: It's inherited only through the maternal line. Scientists seized upon this characteristic to try to build genetic family trees. Almost two years ago, geneticists working in Sweden and Germany reported studying the mtDNA of 53 living people from around the world. Within this small sample, they found that Africans shared a characteristic sequence of mtDNA, and that everyone else carried at least some portion of that sequence in their cells. The research suggests that all living humans had their roots in Africa. But Thorne doesn't put much stock in this report. He thinks the conclusions are questionable because samples taken in Africa today could be from people whose ancestors were not African.

When the first Neanderthal studies were published in 1997, Thorne had already retired. He had traveled the world for 30 years, excavating sites and filming science documentaries for Australian television. His face and his ideas were as well known in Australia as Carl Sagan's once were in the United States. At the request of the Aboriginal council, Thorne still safeguarded the Mungo fossils. Because three more-sophisticated dating technologies were now available, he ordered new tests on 13 of the individuals in his care, and the results gave him a shock.

The ages came back first. Using the new technologies, his team found that the small-boned Mungo Lady and Mungo Man were actually 60,000 years old—twice as old as anyone had guessed. Thorne saw these dates as a crushing blow to the out-of-Africa theorists. No matter what his opponents said, there wasn't enough time on their 120,000-year clock for *Homo sapiens* to leave Africa, dash up to China, evolve from rugged Africans into small-framed Asians, invent boats, sail to Australia, march to the interior, get sick, and die. How much simpler everyone's life would be, he thought, if anthropologists could agree that some of the players in this drama had reached China 1.5 million years ago and continued to evolve there.

After the dating, Gregory Adcock, a doctoral student in genetics at Australian National University, decided to check all 13 fossils for mtDNA. But first he set up stringent procedures. It's easy to contaminate specimens: More than once, scientists have been embarrassed when the "ancient DNA" they extracted turned out to be their own. To avoid this catastrophe, Adcock alone handled the specimens. He alone traveled between two testing labs. He sampled his own DNA and Thorne's to use as a control. Before sampling the ancient specimens, he tested five modern human and animal bones to make sure he'd perfected handling techniques. Then he drilled into each fossil and took a sample from the bone's interior, where no one could ever have touched it. Of more than 60 samples he analyzed, he reported only three contaminations. Ten of the 13 yielded DNA.

The results were nothing less than remarkable: Among the 10 successful extractions was the world's oldest known human DNA—plucked from none other than Mungo Man. (No DNA was recovered from Mungo Lady, perhaps because she had been cremated.) Mungo Man also appeared to mock the findings of previous scientists: His mtDNA signature did not match anyone's, living or fossil, on Earth. There was no evidence that he was genetically related to ancient Africans.

The findings were published in January 2001 by Adcock, Thorne, and five other researchers. What followed was intense disagreement. "People just fell over when they read this new stuff," says Alan Mann, an anthropologist at Princeton University and a moderate in the human-origins debate. "The people at Mungo were totally modern looking and were expected to carry the DNA we have, but they didn't. I think that makes for an incredibly complicated story. It's a stunning development."

Thorne's critics were underwhelmed. "Alan is great at generating media interest. He's a former journalist, you know," says Chris Stringer, head of human origins at the Natural History Museum in London, a staunch advocate of the out-of-Africa model who is accustomed to his phone ringing off the hook every time Thorne fires another volley. "He has done some important work. I'm not saying his work is bad or wrong or whatever. Obviously, I have a different interpretation of it."

Stringer and his colleagues laid into Thorne. First, they said it was unlikely that 10 of the 13 skeletons had yielded mtDNA. This was an unprecedented success rate, so they believed that there had to be contamination. Even researchers at Oxford University, in one of the world's finest labs, had contaminated specimens. Then they said that mtDNA lines died out all the time; the Australians were making much ado about nothing. This part was true: Twenty-five to 30 percent of mankind's mtDNA has been lost over the past million years when women gave birth to boys or didn't reproduce at all.

Thorne concedes that mtDNA has evolved greatly over time, and all scientists working in this area have to be cautious. But as long as everyone is using mtDNA analysis as a basis for speculation, he asks why his work is regarded with such suspicion. Mungo Man and his alternative complement of genes were alive enough to make it to Australia and contribute to the peopling of a continent. Modern Aborigines didn't inherit Mungo Man's mtDNA, but they have certainly inherited the characteristics of his skull. "Eventually, all these people intermingled, and that's why the Aborigines have such diversity," he says.

Stringer, for his part, maintains that the out-of-Africa model could account for a settlement in southern Australia 60,000 years ago. Africans, he says, would have had to travel only one mile toward Australia each year for 10,000 years to make that possible. In other words, the *Homo sapiens* who left Africa 100,000 years ago would have reached Indonesia with plenty of time to sail to Australia.

In New York, Ian Tattersall, one of Thorne's closest friends, has long quibbled with his stance. "We've agreed to disagree," says Tattersall, curator of anthropology at the American Museum of Natural History. "I have a lot of respect for him; I just think he's barking up the wrong tree." Tattersall argues that Neanderthals were so obviously a separate species that *Homo sapiens* could not have bred with them.

Thorne says his lifelong study of animals has taught him otherwise. In captivity, for example, jaguars have mated with leopards and pumas and produced fertile female offspring—although all three animals supposedly belong to different species. Polar bears and brown bears, wolves and coyotes, dromedaries and Bactrian camels also cross-mate. Darwin himself dismissed **species** as a term that is "arbitrarily given, for the sake of convenience."

In recent months Thorne and his team have examined every human fossil from Australia and Asia they could get their hands on. They're retesting their Mungo Man work, hoping to confirm the findings and fill in some of the remaining gaps in the fossilized man's mtDNA profile. To satisfy their critics, they are allowing three rival labs to analyze Mungo Man extractions. Results will be available by the end of this year. When they are, they will most likely be debated. This science is still too inchoate for either side to declare victory.

Whatever the outcome, the bones from Lake Mungo have created change in Australia. The nation has committed to returning Lake Mungo and its environs to the Aborigines. Soon elders of the tribes living around Lake Mungo will decide when they will assume management of the land, artifacts, wildlife, and tourist trade. In 1991, standing near the metal stake that marks the spot where Mungo Lady was found, Thorne returned her bones to the elders of those tribes. At the time, elders debated whether to rebury her or preserve her. Thorne argued for the latter. "If you do away with her bones," he told them, "I'll always be right. You won't be able to refute my work. Someday there will be an aboriginal Alan Thorne, and he'll have a different way of looking at these bones. You have to give him that chance." The council voted for preservation. Today Mungo Lady inhabits a safe that can be opened only with a key, of which two copies exist. Aboriginal elders hold one; Thorne was presented with the other.

Despite Thorne's proselytizing, only a small fraction of the world's anthropologists accept his theories. But he couldn't care less. These days, he draws inspiration from the old Sherlock Holmes maxim: "Once you eliminate the impossible, whatever remains, no matter how improbable, must be the truth."

He points out that regional continuity is by far the simpler theory and can much more comfortably account for all the complicated twists and turns in the genetic evidence of human evolution now coming to light. "It argues that what is going on today is what has been going on for 2 million years, that the processes we see today are what have been going on in human populations for a very long time. You don't need a new species that has to extinguish all the other populations in the world. This is why out-of-Africa is the impossible, and regional continuity is not only not improbable but the answer and the truth."

Discussion Questions

1. In Australia where were the oldest bones of ancient humans found?
2. What is the "out-of-Africa" hypothesis?
3. Why are the ancient human bones found in Australia so puzzling? Why don't they fit the pattern people expected to find there?
4. Thorne, the anthropologist who found the Australian fossils, preaches a revolutionary view called regional continuity. What is that concept?
5. Besides the ancient bones from Australia, what other early pre-modern fossil humans have been examined for their mitochondrial DNA?
6. How old are the early human fossils from Australia and why is their age proving to be a problem for the "out-of-Africa" believers?
7. The "out-of-Africa" group believes there was no interbreeding between various groups of fossil humans. What evidence does Thorne provide to suggest it could have happened?
8. When the Australian Aborigines were given the bones of the ancient humans, what did they do with them?

 12. EATING RIGHT: LESSONS LEARNED FROM OUR PREHISTORIC ANCESTORS

The archaeological record and our recent studies of early aboriginal cultures present convincing evidence that until fairly recently most humans lived healthy lives and very few of them were fat. This is in sharp contrast to modern humans, especially those in the industrialized nations of the world, who are suffering from many diet-related problems and are becoming fatter every year. What happened to the human diet? Through an examination of the past and present the author explains what has happened to the modern human diet and why it is killing us. Humans evolved from tree-dwelling and fruit-eating primates in a region of the world where sodium was very scarce. Thus, the human digestive system developed to process and extract calories and minerals from the natural foods people gathered and ate. With the invention of agriculture this pattern changed. Varied diets low in sodium and sugars

were replaced with monotonous diets of ground cereals that lacked many of the needed minerals and vitamins found in natural foods. Later, abundant and inexpensive sources of salt, sugar, and fats flooded the human diet. Today, in many regions of the Western world food is so inexpensive that even once-impoverished groups often have ample to eat; however, the least expensive foods are now heavy in fats, sugar, and salt. As the author notes, we don't have to return to the caveman days to eat healthy diets, but we do need to adjust our current eating habits or humans will forever retain the title as being the fattest mammal on earth.

The United States is in the midst of a health crisis! Eighty percent of American women and 60 percent of the men say they are trying to lose weight or not gain more weight, and they are spending over 30 billion dollars a year in the process. Fewer and fewer of us are considered physically fit, at any age.

According to data collected by the CDC (Centers for Disease Control and Prevention) nearly 65% of all Americans are now overweight, a percentage that is rising each year. In that same group the number of people who are now considered obese (more than 20% over a person's ideal body weight) has nearly doubled since 1980 to an estimated 30% of the U.S. population. Even more alarming are the latest data showing that 25% of all children in the U.S. are now overweight and of those 13% are considered obese.

As Mark Sorensen of Northwestern University has noted, a European Neanderthal living in near-arctic conditions would have needed about 4,000 kilocalories (more commonly called calories) a day to sustain himself. This compares with the modern needs of a typical, urban American male of only 2,600 calories. The problem today is that many of us are still eating as if we were Neanderthals.

How did this happen? Jeffrey Koplan, director of the CDC, notes that during the past two decades the daily consumption of calories for women in America has increased by 7% and for men by 10%. This, he says, is the result of changes in our habits that now include a greater variety of fatty foods, foods with more calories, the expansion and availability of fast foods, the successful marketing of new high-calorie snack foods, and a tendency to use food and drink as the centerpiece while socializing. During these same two decades the percentage of adults who said they followed the CDC's recommendation to exercise at least 30 minutes three times a week dropped from 57% to 30%.

Greg Critser in his current book *Fat Land* says the turning point in American diets occurred around 1970 because of two important events. First, he says that during the early 1970s President Nixon and the Congress passed a series of farm support bills that created today's heavily subsidized agricultural industry. The consequence of that event was the production of abundant and inexpensive food, which has to be sold. The second event also occurred around the same time when the fast food industry realized that most customers were too embarrassed to purchase second helpings for fear others would think they were gluttons. On the other hand, the industry discovered that if customers were offered a choice between a regular size meal or a more expensive "super size" meal, many would gladly purchase the larger meals without any remorse. After that, super sizing, Big Gulps, and Whoppers became the standard size for adults and the pre-1970 "regular size" meals were now renamed "Happy Meals" and were considered children's meals.

Is there hope? Yes, but we need to look to earlier times for our answers. As an anthropologist, I have spent more than 35 years sifting through the remains of our prehistoric ancestors searching for information about how long they lived, how healthy they were, and what they ate. What I am finding indicates that most of them ate better diets and enjoyed better health than we do.

Humans evolved more than four million years ago, and for most of that time we have lived as nomadic hunters and gatherers. It has only been during the last 10,000 years that some groups abandoned foraging to pursue agriculture and animal herding. Throughout those early millions of years during the pre-agricultural era, life was physically demanding but healthy. Many died early, but their diet was not at fault. Accidents, infection, and a body worn out from a physically stressful lifestyle each took its toll.

The archaeological evidence—gleaned from skeletons, trash pits, the remains of meals found in preserved human feces (coprolites), and artifacts—tells us quite a bit about the lifestyles of our ancestors and questions the so-called dietary advances created by our lifestyle as farmers and herders.

Nutritionists and doctors tell us that our prehistoric ancestors ate "the perfect human diet and lived the perfect lifestyle," and that we need to return to many of those essential principles. Today the human body and digestive system are essentially the same as they were millions of years ago; yet for most of the people living in the world's most affluent nations, lifestyles and diets have changed radically.

The problem is our technology that has advanced far beyond the wildest dreams of our prehistoric ancestors; yet for all of our great advancements, we are still locked into a body style that is millions of years old. Our body and our digestive system were honed to perfection during that 99 percent of human existence when everyone was a nomadic hunter and gatherer. Then, 10,000 years ago in the Middle East our ancestors first domesticated plants and animals and settled down. Soon, this new lifestyle was found in other world areas such as West Africa, Southeast Asia, and to Central and South America. How these events affected and altered human cultures is phenomenal, yet human genetics and biology have changed very little.

Many claim that farming should be listed as the single greatest invention in all of human existence. Others, like physiologist and Pulitzer Prize winner Jared Diamond of UCLA, believe "the adoption of agriculture, supposedly our most decisive step towards a better life, was in many ways a catastrophe from which we have never recovered."

How can his statement be true? Aren't we taught that the growing of crops and raising of animals frees us from the perils of an uncertain food supply and provides us with ample leisure time to develop art, music, and science? For most of the affluent societies of the world, haven't the fruits of the agricultural revolution been a longer life span, electricity, central cooling and heating, automobiles, airplanes, television, computers, and a life of pampered comfort? For most of the world's wealthy people, doesn't their only strenuous physical exertion come from short periods of self-imposed exercise each week?

Should we trade our 21st century lifestyle for theirs just because we are told our pre-agricultural ancestors lived the "perfect lifestyle" and ate "the perfect diet?" I think not. But it is possible to change aspects of our current lifestyle and diets to mirror the lessons we are learning from the lives of our ancient ancestors. Shouldn't we try to improve our health and daily lives without sacrificing the technological achievements we now cherish?

Humans inherited a body that was originally designed for our tree-dwelling primate ancestors. Fortunately, some of those physical traits became advantages. Large brains, grasping hands, stereoscopic and color vision, and social lifestyles are just some of these. Humans also have the advantage of not being physically specialized, meaning that we can adapt to life in many different environments. It's true that some minor physiological changes have occurred in humans since we first developed. Some groups living at high altitudes have developed larger lung capacities while others living in hot desert regions have dark, protective skin color and tend to be tall and thin because it maximizes the body's ability to dissipate heat. Nevertheless, in cold climates we use warm clothes in place of body hair, to travel by sea we use boats in place of gills and flippers, and to travel long distances we use airplanes instead of wings.

Our bipedal form of walking (on two feet instead of four) made traveling long distances easier and less costly in terms of calories burned as energy. Our hairless bodies and ability to sweat allowed our ancestors to move around in safety during the heat of the day when most other large animals, and especially predators, had to rest in the shade or risk overheating and dying of sunstroke. Our ability to consume and digest both plant and animal foods is another advantage because it enables us to use many different resources and eat almost anything. More importantly, it helped our ancestors find enough food to feed the needs of our large brains.

The brain is a greedy organ that consumes a tremendous amount of energy. By weight, brain tissue uses about 16 times more energy per minute than does muscle tissue. Even when resting or sleeping, the human brain still consumes about 25% of the total energy being used by a human. During similar resting stages the smaller brains of most nonprimate mammals use only 3 to 5% of the total body's energy. These data have led anthropologists such as William Leonard of Northwestern University to suggest that human brains probably grew larger only after our earliest ancestors became skilled at finding sufficient amounts of high-calorie foods (protein and fats) to feed the voracious needs of their expanding brains. Even though an improved diet played a critical role, he notes that it was not the only factor that probably led to an increased brain size in humans.

The archaeological evidence left by our ancient ancestors attests to their skills as hunters and gives us important clues about their lifestyles, diets, and nutrition. In addition, when comparing the skeletons from ancient hunting and gathering societies to the skeletons of early farming cultures, we find chilling evidence of what happened to the lives and health of most of the world's early agricultural and, later, urban populations.

According to anthropologist George Armelagos of Emory University, high levels of bone porosity in the vault of the skull and around the eye orbits, called porotic hyperostosis, are considered good indicators of long-term anemia, commonly attributed to iron deficiency. Although porosity might be caused by other conditions, such as severe hookworm infections, the most frequent link is to long-term reliance on diets that are low in meat and high in carbohydrates—a common occurrence in early farming cultures where diets consisted mostly of cereal grains.

When Dr. Armelagos compared human skeletons from pre-agricultural foraging peoples who lived in the Illinois and Ohio River valleys with those of later farming cultures in the same region, the evidence of anemia in the farming group was overwhelming. He found a 400% increase in the occurrence of porotic hyperostosis among skeletons from the farming period, whose diets consisted mostly of maize.

Professor Jane Buikstra, of the University of New Mexico anthropology department, notes that humans who experience episodes of severe physical stress often carry a record of those events in the long bones of their arms and legs and in the enamel layers of their teeth. She identifies typical types of stress as periods of prolonged or serious famine, periods of severe infection, or stress caused by malnutrition.

One type of growth-related stress indicator is known as Harris lines, which can be seen during x-ray or cross-section examinations of human long bones. Although most common in the skeletons of farming cultures, Harris lines occasionally appear in the skeletons of some foragers. Many now believe that some types of Harris lines reflect relatively short periods of stress while other lines indicate prolonged periods of stress.

Dr. Buikstra has noted that studies of North American skeletons from foraging groups and from early farming cultures show noticeable differences. The long bones from the farming groups have thinner cortical thickness and are shorter, indicating a reduction in height. These, she believes, represent the physical effects of chronic malnutrition after the switch to farming.

Another reliable indicator of diet and nutritional-related stress is abnormal development in the enamel layer of teeth. One type of tooth abnormality is called **linear enamel hypoplasia** and seems to be caused by severe physical stress. This condition, which appears as depressed and pitted areas in the enamel layer of teeth, is more commonly seen in the teeth of early farming cultures than in those of foragers.

Wilson bands, another type of tooth enamel abnormality, are also linked to stress-induced growth disruptions and are much more prevalent in the skeletons from farming cultures than foraging ones. When the teeth from burials belonging to farming cultures are examined, they show large numbers of enamel abnormalities and large numbers of dental caries. By contrast, rarely is either of these conditions found in the teeth of earlier foraging groups.

Susceptibility to dental caries varies with individuals, but in all cases the potential for infection is greater on diets containing large amounts of refined carbohydrates, especially sugars. About 2% of the fossil teeth from ancient foraging cultures contain small or shallow areas of decay of the pit and fissure types, and these are found mostly on the occlusal (top) surface of teeth. However, after cultures turned to farming, the record of dental decay increased dramatically. Even so, it wasn't until the widespread use of factory-produced refined carbohydrates, including sugar, that human dental decay reached its current epidemic proportions. One study, conducted in 1900 of factory workers in England, revealed that 70% of their teeth contained caries. More importantly, most of the dental decay occurred in-between their teeth, which are locations associated almost exclusively with post-agricultural diets composed of finely ground cereals and sugars.

Examinations of preserved human coprolites provide another valuable source of information about our prehistoric ancestors. Coprolites are ideal records because they contain the nondigestible remains of human diets, such as fiber, insect parts, bones, hair, feathers, shells, seeds, pollen, and the leaves of foods that were actually eaten. In recent years, the scientific study of coprolites has provided valuable clues about the diets, health, and nutrition of ancient foraging peoples as well as those living in early agricultural communities.

Anthropologist Kristin Sobolik of the University of Maine has spent most of her career examining human coprolites found in prehistoric sites of the arid American southwest. She has found that for thousands of years ancient foragers ate diets composed mostly of nutritious plant foods that were high in fiber, such as sunflower seeds, ground mesquite pods, cactus seeds, acorns, walnuts, pecans, persimmons, grapes, dewberries, the soft basal leaf portion of desert plants such as sotol and agave, and cactus flowers, fruits, and pads. These ancient foragers balanced their mostly plant-food diets with about 15 to 30% meat protein and minimal amounts of fat obtained from tiny, lean animals such as mice, rabbits, birds, fish ranging from minnows to small catfish and gar, freshwater clams, small rock lizards, caterpillars, grasshoppers, bird eggs, and, when they were lucky, maybe a deer.

Karl Reinhard, an anthropologist at the University of Nebraska, is a leading authority on ancient human parasite infection. He notes that intestinal parasites can be debilitating and potentially fatal, especially when they infect a person who is already weakened by episodes of famine or prolonged malnutrition. His examination of human coprolites recovered from many regions of North and South America indicates that hunting and gathering populations were almost totally free of intestinal parasitic infections. However, once groups settled down and turned to farming, they became heavily infected. High population densities, poor sanitation, and the compactness of living spaces in small farming villages and pueblos skyrocketed the infection rates of nearly a dozen types of intestinal parasites, including pin worms, tapeworms, and thorny-headed worms.

The Human Body

Carbohydrates: Humans rely on three primary food sources to provide them with energy and needed building materials—carbohydrates, protein, and fats. The continual need to replenish these components is what gives us the desire to eat. In addition, our bodies also require certain other substances such as sodium, potassium, calcium, and a variety of other important minerals and vitamins.

Plants provide our primary source of carbohydrates and most of the calories we use as energy. Each gram of carbohydrate (about 1/28th of an ounce) provides four kilocalories of energy when it is completely digested. There are two main types of carbohydrates, simple and complex. The simple carbohydrates are sugars. They exist naturally as monosaccharides—different types of single-molecule sugars (glucose, dextrose, fructose, galactose), or as disaccharides—double-molecule sugars (sucrose, maltose, lactose). Our bodies digest both types and both are found naturally in fruits, flower nectar, and the sap of some plants. The complex carbohydrates come mostly from starch and cellulose.

Archaeological records note that carbohydrates have provided the majority of energy calories used by humans for more than four million years. Carbohydrates have been the mainstay of human diets since our earliest ancestors left the trees and began walking upright on the savannahs of Africa. However, significant changes have occurred in the types of carbohydrates humans now eat. Many of the carbohydrates we now eat have a high glycemic index (GI-index). The glycemic index, first introduced during the late 1970s, refers to how rapidly our bodies digest different types of carbohydrates. Foods with a high GI-index, such as some sugars and many foods made from refined flour, are digested quickly and cause a spike in the release of insulin needed to digest those foods. That type of cycle forces our body to either use or store the excess glucose it has produced. What isn't used is stored as fat. According to the authors of the recent book, *The Glucose Revolution,* foods with a high GI-index leave a person feeling hungry after only a few hours. Foods with a low GI-index are digested more slowly and provide a long and sustained source of energy, thus curbing a person's hunger pangs. Nutritionists say that our current diets, rich in high GI-index foods, are a main reason we are becoming the "fattest mammals on earth." One reason our ancestors didn't have weight problems was that they ate natural foods, most of which have a low GI-index.

Another problem we humans have is that our taste buds love sweet things. Perhaps this is because our primate ancestors learned that sweet fruits are rarely poisonous and are good sources of food. Tree fruits were a much sought-after food source by primates because, ounce for ounce, fruits offer more usable calories than do leaves, bark, or stems. In addition, the riper the fruit, the sweeter it becomes as its starch is converted to sugars.

The association of sweetness with good-tasting, ready-to-eat, high-calorie-value fruits served the early primates and our human ancestors well. It encouraged them to search for these tasty food sources and to avoid most sour and bitter-tasting fruits because those characteristics, then as now, often indicate that fruits are poisonous or not yet ripe. Our ancient ancestors never ate too much sugar. Except for small amounts of sugar found in fruits, in a few other natural foods, and an occasional lucky discovery of honey, our foraging ancestors, and even early farming peoples, had no access to sugar. No human forager, or early farmer, was ever in danger of overdosing on sugar. Perhaps this is why of the four essential taste sensations (sour, sweet, salty, bitter), humans usually avoid foods that are too sour, too salty, or too bitter, but rarely turn away from foods that are too sweet.

Two events increased our consumption of sugar. First, Columbus carried sugarcane to the New World and found that it grew well in the moist climate and fertile soils of the Caribbean. Second, the Spanish and Portuguese pioneered the importing of slaves as an inexpensive labor source for their plantations that soon produced tons of sugar at competitive market prices. For example, in England, the availability of inexpensive sugar from the New World reduced the per-pound cost from the equivalent price equal to the yearly salary of an average worker in 1600 to the same price as a dozen eggs by 1700. As the price of sugar dropped, consumption rose so that soon the United States and most European countries mirrored the English's rapid increase in the use of sugar.

By 1913 the annual consumption of sugar in the U.S. had reached 75 pounds per person. By 1976 U.S. sugar consumption had reached 125 pounds per person per year, which represents about 11% of the total daily calories eaten by each American. By 1998 sugar was supplying 16% of the total daily calories for each U.S. adult and 20% of children's daily calories. Anthropologist Sidney Mintz of Johns Hopkins University believes he knows why the U.S. and world sugar consumption continues to climb. He notes that only a small portion of each person's daily sugar consumption comes from spoonfuls or cubes of sugar those individuals add to foods or drink. Instead, most of the sugar we eat is hidden. Bakers add sugar to nonyeast-rising products because it makes cakes, cookies, and breads smoother, softer, and whiter. Sugars also improve the texture of baked goods. Manufacturers produce heavily sugared soft drinks because thicker syrup-like liquids are smoother and more appealing to the mouth and tongue than is flavored water. Sugar also slows staleness in bread, stabilizes the chemical contents of salt, cloaks the acidity of tomatoes in catsup, and, when added as a sauce to bland-tasting meats like fish and poultry, sugar makes them taste much better.

The complex carbohydrates have long chains of linked sugar molecules called polysaccharides. Humans can't digest some types, such as cellulose, so it becomes the fiber content of our diets. Other types of carbohydrates, such as starch, are digestible and can be converted to energy.

Paradoxically, until very recently, too much dietary fiber was a problem in most human diets. Our ancient ancestors pounded and ground plant foods, techniques that exposed starches but did not reduce the intake of high amounts of fiber. Dr. Boyd Eaton and his colleagues at the Emory University School of Medicine estimate that our foraging ancestors probably consumed about 150 grams of fiber each day as compared to the current USDA recommended daily allowance of 20 to 25 grams of fiber daily. Even so, the average American usually eats less than 10 grams of fiber each day.

My coprolite studies of pre-agricultural groups living in North and South America support Dr. Eaton's estimates of high fiber in ancient diets. In many instances, I find that nondigested fiber is the dominant component of ancient coprolites from pre-agricultural foragers. In some cases I find that fiber accounts for more than one-half of the total weight of each coprolite.

Our digestive system still needs lots of fiber. Fiber speeds the passage of food through our small intestines, adds needed bulk for our large intestine, stimulates peristalsis necessary for the excretion process, and minimizes the effects of ingested carcinogens, which might otherwise cause some of the DNA in our digestive tract to mutate into cancers. Low-fiber diets are also a factor in the occurrence of disorders such as spastic colon, diverticulosis, hiatal hernia, and hemorrhoids.

Animal Protein: All primates eat some type of animal protein, but humans eat the highest amounts. Protein is a high-calorie food that our ancient ancestors needed to feed the high-energy needs of our large brain. When eaten, 3.5 ounces of meat produces about 200 calories of energy, while the same amount of fruit yields less than 100 calories, and 3.5 ounces of leaves produces only 10 to 20 calories.

Anthropologist Richard Lee of the University of Toronto has spent a lifetime studying the diets of contemporary foraging societies. He estimates that most of today's foraging societies obtain about one-third of their daily calories from animal protein, with the other two-thirds coming from plant foods. That amount is considerably higher than the average diet of 5 to 7% animal protein eaten by our closest relatives, the chimpanzees. William Leonard and others note that larger-brained humans need more high-calorie foods than do the smaller-brained chimps. Lee also notes that among contemporary foragers a significant percentage of their meat often comes from small reptiles, birds, and mammals. My examination of ancient human coprolites confirms that reliance on meat protein mainly from small-animal hunting seems to be thousands of years old and may represent an essential pattern even from the beginning of humankind.

Humans need a constant supply of protein because, unlike fats and carbohydrates, our body cannot store protein as protein. Instead, humans store excess protein as fat. Meat from animals, fish, and fowl contains from 15 to 40% protein by weight and is considered a complete protein source. By contrast, most plant foods often contain meager amounts of about 2 to 10% protein and are considered incomplete proteins because plant sources often lack at least one or more essential amino acids needed by all humans.

The increased need for protein to feed our larger brains may explain why *Homo erectus,* the first of our species with a brain nearly as large as modern humans, left the grasslands of east Africa and soon ranged over much of Europe, Asia, and the rest of Africa. Anthropologist Susan Anton of Rutgers University and others estimate that by the time *Homo erectus* emerged somewhere between one to two million years ago, the human needs for food and especially protein meant that this new species needed 8 to 10 times more room to search for food than did their smaller-brained ancestors who were restricted to the continent of Africa.

How much protein do humans really need? Nutritionists say that about 10 to 20% of our diets should come from meat protein, a percentage that is within the minimal average eaten by most nonpoverty-level Americans. For many of our ancient foraging societies about one-third of their daily calories came from animal sources and most of that came from meat. Nevertheless, archaeological records also indicate that some of our ancient ancestors, especially the ones we call the big game hunters, probably relied on meat sources for as much as 50 to 60% of their total dietary calories.

Humans need protein because it provides the essential amino acids used by our bodies to build new tissues such as muscles, tendons, ligaments, and the walls of blood vessels. All of our growth from birth to death, as well as all repairs to our body, depends upon the amino acids we obtain from protein sources. Even our skin, hair, and nails cannot form properly without the correct amount and mixture of amino acids.

Fats: Until very recently human diets were low in fat. Fats are found in some plant foods, such as seeds and nuts, and in the meat of animals. In prehistoric times fat was a hard-to-find food source because most wild, land-dwelling animals have lean bodies with less than 4% fat. By contrast, 30% or more of the total butchered carcass weight of most American domestic cattle and pigs is fat.

Most fats are composed of long chains of triglyceride molecules. They get their name because each contains three fatty acids attached to one glycerol molecule. Cholesterol, sometimes mistakenly called a fat, is needed to produce numerous hormones and bile acids, but it is not really a fat. Instead, cholesterol is a complicated substance composed of molecule rings that reacts more like a wax than a true fat.

There are many types of fatty acids found in nature. Some fats are saturated and others are unsaturated; the unsaturated group is divided into mono or poly types, depending on whether they are linked with one, or more, double bonds of carbon. The chemistry of fatty acids is complex, so, for most of us, knowing how they work in the human body is more important. When digested, fats also offer the most energy calories (nine) per gram.

Some polyunsaturated fats are called structural fats because they are used to build and repair nearly all cell membranes. These fats are also important because they are used to build various types of hormones and utilize various vitamins that regulate our body functions. By contrast, most saturated fats occur as adipose tissue, which is where animals store excess amounts of fat for later use. In some animals, such as seals, whales, or bears, a thick layer of subcutaneous adipose fat is essential because it provides insulation against the cold or it becomes stored calories for use during hibernation. However, in most animals excess amounts of saturated fats are stored in other body locations, such as in the abdominal cavity or within muscle tissue where it can be converted into energy when needed.

The meat of wild animals provides much more protein than fat. Wild animals have small amounts of saturated fat that is often distributed uniformly throughout the body, yet most fat in wild animals is the unsaturated type. Animals raised in captivity, our pets, and steers raised in feed lots as food have one thing in common— they all have high amounts of saturated fat.

I often ask students in my classes to list their 10 favorite foods. With rare exception, all foods listed contain fats. Of the foods humans like most, the majority contains fats. It is unfortunate for humans that fats will satisfy our hunger pangs quicker than any other food source. Millions of years ago it was nature's way of encouraging our ancestors to find and eat this essential food item. This food craving served our foraging ancestors well, but it has become a liability for many of us today. What is worse is that nature designed our intestines to be very efficient at digesting fats, generally allowing no more than 5% to escape before being absorbed. This digestive advantage provided an essential advantage for our ancient ancestors, who rarely ate fat, but it is one of the factors that now contribute to making more than 65% of Americans overweight.

It is the amount of saturated fat and trans fat in our diet that should be cause for alarm. The U.S. Senate's Select Committee on Nutrition and Human Needs reports that the typical American diet consists of 42% fat and a majority of that is saturated fat. However, as nutritionist Walter Willett of Harvard University recently noted, the "amount" of fat we eat is less critical to our health than the "type" of fat we eat. He explains that eating monounsaturated fat (olive oil) is good for us, but eating high levels of saturated and trans fats adds not only pounds but can also ruin our health. He cites his research on trans fat by saying, "This kind of fat is found in many kinds of margarine and other foods, especially fast food." Trans fats, he points out, are created by hydrogenating vegetable oils and are the most commonly used types because they are inexpensive, add texture and taste to commercially prepared foods, and keep fried foods from going stale. By comparison, our ancient foraging ancestors ate meat containing mostly the healthy type of unsaturated fats, and their total daily calories from fat were rarely more than 20%.

Both the total amount of fat and the high percentage of saturated and trans fats make our modern diets so unhealthy. In addition to straining our heart and skeletal system, elevating our blood cholesterol levels, and increasing our chances of developing high blood pressure, being overweight is also the main cause for the recent rise in the number of people suffering from diabetes. Recent research has also linked being overweight with increased chances of developing a variety of cancers including prostate, breast, and colon cancer.

Dr. Boyd Eaton writes in his book, *The Paleolithic Prescription,* that he doubts our ancient ancestors ever had to worry about coronary heart disease, one of today's major killers, especially in the world's more developed countries. High levels of serum cholesterol, diet, age, sex, and genetics are all potential contributors to coronary atherosclerosis, yet, of these, we can potentially control only several, the food we eat and the levels of serum cholesterol.

Many people mistakenly believe that their serum cholesterol level is directly linked to the amount of cholesterol they eat. Ironically, a high cholesterol diet usually only slightly raises a person's serum cholesterol level. For example, the cattle-herding Masai tribe of east Africa drink large amounts of milk and have a daily intake of cholesterol that often exceeds 1,000 to 2,000 milligrams. However, most Masai warriors have low serum cholesterol levels of only 115 to 145 milligrams per deciliter, far less than the level of 200 that is recommended by most American doctors.

Like the Masai, our ancient ancestors probably had low serum cholesterol levels even though we suspect they may have consumed up to 1,000 milligrams of cholesterol daily, depending on their meat supply. Recent research confirms that genetics and a high-fat diet—especially one high in saturated and trans fats—have a much greater influence on raising serum cholesterol levels than does the amount of cholesterol a person eats.

Salt: Mammals normally consume more potassium than sodium (table salt is about 40% sodium). Dr. Henry Blackburn, a professor of physiology at the University of Minnesota's Medical School, points out that the human kidney is a marvelous organ for maintaining the delicate balance between sodium and potassium. However, because humans first developed in Africa where sodium has always been scarce, our kidneys were designed to **retain,** not **excrete** sodium.

One of the greatest changes in human diets from ancient times to the present has been the switch from ancient diets rich in potassium and low in sodium to modern diets high in salt. A typical prehistoric forager's diet of 3,000 calories, 60% coming from fresh plant foods (leaves, nuts, tubers, berries, fruits) and 40% from meat (large game, birds, fish, eggs, reptiles) would contain about 7,000 milligrams of potassium and 900 milligrams of sodium. By comparison, the U.S. National Academy of Sciences Food and Nutrition Board reports that the average American is now consuming 6,000 to 18,000 milligrams of salt per day. That, they say, is about 6 to 10 times too much sodium in the typical American diet that already lacks sufficient potassium.

Medical researchers believe that high sodium use, especially among people who have a genetic predisposition to retain much of the sodium they eat, is a primary cause of high blood pressure. Years ago some believed that the high levels of salt use in our diets resulted from a human craving for sodium. Today, most medical doctors believe that our salty diets are based strictly on an acquired taste, not on any type of physiological need.

Additional evidence links high blood pressure with high levels of salt use. Statistics reveal that the incidence of high blood pressure is greatest in countries with the highest per capita consumption of salt. Likewise, problems of high blood pressure do not seem to exist among many cultures with diets that are traditionally low in salt and high in potassium, such as the diets of the Yanomami of Venezuela, the Inuit of the Arctic, the San of the African Kalahari, and natives in areas of Polynesia that have not been affected by tourism. I believe the evidence is overwhelming. One reason our ancient ancestors were so healthy is that they were free from the health problems caused by high blood pressure because their potassium-rich diets contained little salt.

Exercise: Another important difference between our ancient ancestors and modern populations is exercise. Hunting and gathering are activities that require strength and stamina. Hunters often travel long distances in search of game. Once game was killed and butchered, the hunters carried the meat back to camp. Meanwhile, women spent their days digging for tubers, carrying young children, gathering other foods, finding water, and collecting firewood. Studies of modern foraging groups reveal those types of daily activities will ensure that individuals remain strong, retain great stamina, and will be slim even into their old age. Similar proof comes from the study of skeletons belonging to our ancient ancestors. Their weight-bearing leg bones and arm bones are thick and have pronounced rough areas where large muscles and tendons attached.

Once humans turned to farming, their skeletons reveal that they lived a less strenuous lifestyle. Skeletons dating from the early farming era about 10,000 years ago begin to lose these robust features, and skeletons from the period of early urbanization reveal that these robust features are almost entirely gone. The evidence suggests that even though early farmers may have worked long hours, their efforts no longer required the levels of physical stamina and endurance common in the lives of pre-agricultural cultures. As human strength was replaced by machines after the Industrial Revolution, many people, especially those of the affluent classes, enjoyed a life of leisure requiring little physical effort, stamina, or strength.

During the 1960s, muscular strength and endurance testing of high school and college-age Americans revealed they were considerably weaker than earlier generations at their same age. Much of this resulted from children having fewer opportunities in daily life to burn calories. In recent years some schools have reduced physical education activities, fewer children now walk to and from school, and even today's household chores are assisted by laborsaving machines. Studies conducted in 1997 revealed that children between the ages of 6 and 18 were spending an average of 38 hours per week playing video games or watching TV. The link between adults and exercise has also been declining. As a nation, Americans walk less and drive more and most now work in facilities that are increasingly automated.

The Future

These chilling comparisons can depress us or we can benefit from what we have learned. Until recently, medical professionals believed the degenerative process, seen in many of today's elderly, was a normal part of the aging process. However, the skeletal remains of our ancient ancestors and current medical evidence suggest that most of our degenerative processes are caused by a lifetime of neglect caused from years of eating the wrong foods and exercising little.

We don't have to give up the blessings of civilization, but we do need to live in harmony with our body's physiology. By selecting a diet that approximates the proportions of fats, fiber, protein, and complex carbohydrates eaten by our ancient ancestors, and by reducing our intake of sugar and sodium, we can benefit from eating a near perfect diet. Then, by adding regular exercise and avoiding tobacco and other harmful substances, we should be able to maintain good health with reasonable levels of strength and stamina as we age.

This doesn't mean we have to eat insects, mice, and coarse plant fibers, as our ancient ancestors once did, but it does mean we need to make intelligent decisions at the grocery store or when we eat out in restaurants. We can reject most fried foods and instead eat broiled chicken, turkey, and fish, which are high in protein and low in fats. Most lean red meats are high in both. Many fruits and fresh vegetables are rich in potassium and low in sodium, but their canned equivalents are often high in both sodium and sugars. Whole wheats and bran are rich in bulk and fiber while foods from refined flour are not.

If we are willing to make some dietary changes, if we try to exercise daily, and if we can balance the total number of calories we eat with the amount we burn, then we can enjoy the best aspects of the perfect foraging lifestyle as well as all the comforts of modern civilization.

Discussion Questions

1. According to the Centers for Disease Control and Prevention, why is there a crisis in American diets today?
2. In the book *Fat Land* the author says that the turning point in American diets was the early 1970s when two things happened. What are these?
3. Humans inherited a body that was designed for a tree-dwelling animal. How did this attribute help our ancestors survive? What are some of the advantages this gave all humans?
4. William Leonard believes that an important event had to occur before the human brain could expand in size. What was it?
5. The bones and teeth of our ancestors reveal that after the invention of agriculture the lives of our ancestors became much more stressful. What are the types of evidence our bones and teeth record?
6. What are coprolites and what do they tell us about ancient diets and health?
7. How and why did sugar suddenly become a major part of our diet? Why do so many modern foods add sugar?
8. Do humans have a natural craving for salt? What types of health problems do high-salt diets create?

Additional Resources

For Internet links related to this chapter, please visit our website at www.mhhe.com/dettwyler

AUDETTE, RAY, TROY GILCHRIST, and MICHAEL R. EADES. *Neanderthin: Eat Like a Caveman to Achieve a Lean, Strong, Healthy Body.* New York: St. Martins Press, 2000.

CORDAIN, LOREN. *The Paleo Diet: Lose Weight and Get Healthy by Eating the Food You Were Designed to Eat.* New York: John Wiley & Sons, 2001.

CRITSER, GREG. *Fat Land: How Americans Became the Fattest People in the World.* New York: Houghton Mifflin Co., 2003.

EATON, S. BOYD, M.D., MARJORIE SHOSTAK, and MELVIN J. KONNER, M.D. *The Paleolithic Prescription: A Program of Diet & Exercise and a Design for Living.* New York: Harper-Collins, 1989.

JOHANSON, DONALD, and JAMES SHREEVE. *Lucy's Child: The Discovery of a Human Ancestor.* New York: Avon, 1989.

LEONARD, WILLIAM. "Food for Thought: Dietary Change Was a Driving Force in Human Evolution." *Scientific American 287* (December 2002), pp. 106–115.

SCHWARTZ, JEFFREY H., and IAN TATTERSALL. *The Human Fossil Record, Volume 1, Terminology and Craniodental Morphology of Genus Homo (Europe).* New York: Wiley, 2001.

SCHWARTZ, JEFFREY H., and IAN TATTERSALL. *The Human Fossil Record, Volume 2, Craniodental Morphology of Genus Homo (Africa and Asia).* New York: Wiley, 2003.

TATTERSALL, IAN. *The Fossil Trail: How We Know What We Think We Know About Human Evolution.* New York: Oxford University Press, 1995.

THORNE, ALAN, and ROBERT RAYMOND. *Man on the Rim: The Peopling of the Pacific.* Sydney, Australia: Angus & Robertson, 1989.

WALKER, ALAN, and PATRICIA SHIPMAN. *The Wisdom of the Bones: In Search of Human Origins.* New York: Knopf, 1996.

WOLPOFF, MILFORD H. *Paleoanthropology.* 2nd edition. New York: McGraw-Hill, 1998.

WONG, KATE. "An Ancestor to Call Our Own: Controversial New Fossils Could Bring Scientists Closer Than Ever to the Origin of Humanity." *Scientific American,* January 2003.

CHAPTER 8

Modern Humans

13. "The Evolution of Human Birth," by Karen R. Rosenberg and Wenda R. Trevathan, *Scientific American* 285, no. 5 (November 2001), pp. 60–65.

14. "Care-Worn Fossils: Bones Reopen Controversy about Ancient Assistance," by Bruce Bower, *Science News* 162, no. 21 (2002), pp. 328–330.

The discovery of fossil hominid skeletal remains and archaeological materials often fires the imagination. We think about what life must have been like for our remote ancestors—how scary to be giving birth, how difficult to survive after a disabling injury. We ponder how they behaved, what they thought, and how they felt. There are limits to the degree and kind of interpretation that can be read from the bones and archaeological remains. We have to be careful not to let our modern cultural biases and personal experiences affect our views of the past. And yet the anatomy of the bones and studies of nonhuman primates can help us make sense of what we find, and can help us understand why our modern bodies work the way they do. They also illuminate how humans have used social and cultural accommodations to help compensate for the quirks of our bipedal gait.

 ## 13. THE EVOLUTION OF HUMAN BIRTH

In this selection, Karen Rosenberg and Wenda Trevathan explore how human childbirth differs physically from other primate birthing patterns. The combination of a pelvis designed for bipedal locomotion (usually walking on our hind limbs only) and offspring who have relatively large brains at birth means that human babies have to twist and turn in the pelvis as they are being born. Usually, they end up facing away from the mother, which makes it more difficult for her to help the baby emerge from the birth canal. This may help explain why "humans are the only primate species that regularly seeks assistance during labor and delivery." This is just one example of the many ways humans use cultural beliefs and behaviors to help compensate for their physical limitations.

Giving birth in the treetops is not the normal human way of doing things, but that is exactly what Sophia Pedro was forced to do during the height of the floods that ravaged southern Mozambique in March 2000. Pedro had survived for four days perched high above the raging floodwaters that killed more than 700 people in the region. The day after her delivery, television broadcasts and newspapers all over the world featured images of Pedro and her newborn child being plucked from the tree during a dramatic helicopter rescue.

Treetop delivery rooms are unusual for humans but not for other primate species. For millions of years, primates have secluded themselves in treetops or bushes to give birth. Human beings are the only primate species that regularly seeks assistance during labor and delivery. So when and why did our female ancestors abandon their unassisted and solitary habit? The answers lie in the difficult and risky nature of human birth.

Many women know from experience that pushing a baby through the birth canal is no easy task. It's the price we pay for our large brains and intelligence: humans have exceptionally big heads relative to the size of their bodies. Those who have delved deeper into the subject know that the opening in the human pelvis through which the baby must pass is limited in size by our upright posture. But only recently have anthropologists begun to realize that the complex twists and turns that human babies make as they travel through the birth canal have troubled humans and their ancestors for at least 100,000 years. Fossil clues also indicate that anatomy, not just our social nature, has led human mothers—in contrast to our closest primate relatives and almost all other mammals—to ask for help during childbirth. Indeed, this practice of seeking assistance may have been in place when the earliest members of our genus, *Homo,* emerged and may possibly date back to five million years ago, when our ancestors first began to walk upright on a regular basis.

Tight Squeeze

To test our theory that the practice of assisted birth may have been around for millennia, we considered first what scientists know about the way a primate baby fits through the mother's birth canal. Viewed from above, the infant's head is basically an oval, longest from the forehead to the back of the head and narrowest from ear to ear. Conveniently, the birth canal—the bony opening in the pelvis through which the baby must travel to get from the uterus to the outside world—is also an oval shape. The challenge of birth for many primates is that the size of the infant's head is close to the size of that opening.

For humans, this tight squeeze is complicated by the birth canal's not being a constant shape in cross section. The entrance of the birth canal, where the baby begins its journey, is widest from side to side relative to the mother's body. Midway through, however, this orientation shifts 90 degrees, and the long axis of the oval extends from the front of the mother's body to her back. This means that the human infant must negotiate a series of turns as it works its way through the birth canal so that the two parts of its body with the largest dimensions—the head and the shoulders—are always aligned with the largest dimension of the birth canal.

To understand the birth process from the mother's point of view, imagine you are about to give birth. The baby is most likely upside down, facing your side, when its head enters the birth canal. Midway through the canal, however, it must turn to face your back, and the back of its head is pressed against your pubic bones. At that time, its shoulders are oriented side to side. When the baby exits your body it is still facing backward, but it will turn its head slightly to the side. This rotation helps to turn the baby's shoulders so that they can also fit between your pubic bones and tailbone. To appreciate the close correspondence of the maternal and fetal dimensions, consider that the average pelvic opening in human females is 13 centimeters at its largest diameter and 10 centimeters at its smallest. The average infant head is 10 centimeters from front to back, and the shoulders are 12 centimeters across. This journey through a passageway of changing cross-sectional shape makes human birth difficult and risky for the vast majority of mothers and babies.

If we retreat far enough back along the family tree of human ancestors, we would eventually reach a point where birth was not so difficult. Although humans are more closely related to apes genetically, monkeys may present a better model for birth in prehuman primates. One line of reasoning to support this assertion is as follows: Of the primate fossils discovered from the time before the first known hominid, *Australopithecus,* one possible remote ancestor is *Proconsul,* a primate fossil dated to about 25 million years ago. This tailless creature probably looked like an ape, but its skeleton suggests that it moved more like a monkey. Its pelvis, too, was more monkeylike. The heads of modern monkey infants are typically about 98 percent the diameter of the mother's birth canal—a situation more comparable with that of humans than that of chimps, whose birth canals are relatively spacious.

Despite the monkey infant's tight squeeze, its entrance into the world is less challenging than that of a human baby. In contrast to the twisted birth canal of modern humans, monkeys' birth canals maintain the same cross-sectional shape from entrance to exit. The longest diameter of this oval shape is oriented front to back, and the broadest part of the oval is against the mother's back. A monkey infant enters the birth canal headfirst, with the broad back of its skull against the roomy back of the mother's pelvis and tailbone. That means the baby monkey emerges from the birth canal face forward—in other words, facing the same direction as the mother.

Firsthand observations of monkey deliveries have revealed a great advantage in babies' being born facing forward. Monkeys give birth squatting on their hind legs or crouching on all fours. As the infant is born, the mother reaches down to guide it out of the birth canal and toward her nipples. In many cases, she also wipes mucus from the baby's mouth and nose to aid its breathing. Infants are strong enough at birth to take part in their own deliveries. Once their hands are free, they can grab their mother's body and pull themselves out.

If human babies were also born face forward, their mothers would have a much easier time. Instead the evolutionary modifications of the human pelvis that enabled hominids to walk upright necessitate that most infants exit the birth canal with the back of their heads against the pubic bones, facing in the opposite direction as the mother (in a position obstetricians call "occiput anterior"). For this reason, it is difficult for the laboring human mother—whether squatting, sitting, or lying on her back—to reach down and guide the baby as it emerges. This configuration also greatly inhibits the mother's ability to clear a breathing passage for the infant, to remove the umbilical cord from around its neck or even to lift the baby up to her breast. If she tries to accelerate the delivery by grabbing the baby and guiding it from the birth canal, she risks bending its back awkwardly against the natural curve of its spine. Pulling on a newborn at this angle risks injury to its spinal cord, nerves and muscles.

For contemporary humans, the response to these challenges is to seek assistance during labor and delivery. Whether a technology-oriented professional, a lay midwife or a family member who is familiar with the birth process, the assistant can help the human mother do all the things the monkey mother does by herself. The assistant can also compensate for the limited motor abilities of the relatively helpless human infant. The advantages of even simple forms of assistance have reduced maternal and infant mortality throughout history.

Assisted Birth

Of course, our ancestors and even women today can and do give birth alone successfully. Many fictional accounts portray stalwart peasant women giving birth alone in the fields, perhaps most famously in the novel *The Good Earth* by Pearl S. Buck. Such images give the impression that delivering babies is easy. But anthropologists who have studied childbirth in cultures around the world report that these perceptions are highly romanticized and that human birth is seldom easy and rarely unattended. Today virtually all women in all societies seek assistance at delivery. Even among the !Kung of southern Africa's Kalahari Desert—who are well known for viewing solitary birth as a cultural ideal—women do not usually manage to give birth alone until they have delivered several babies at which mothers, sisters or other women are present. So, though rare exceptions do exist, assisted birth comes close to being a universal custom in human cultures.

The complicated configuration of the human birth canal is such that laboring women and their babies benefit—by lower rates of mortality, injury and anxiety—from the assistance of others. This evolutionary reality helps to explain why attended birth is a near universal feature of human cultures. Individual women throughout history have given birth alone in certain circumstances, of course. But much more common is the attendance of familiar friends and relatives, most of whom are women. (Men may be variously forbidden, tolerated, welcomed or even required at birth.) In Western societies, where women usually give birth in the presence of strangers, recent research on birth practices has also shown that a doula—a person who provides social and emotional support to a woman in labor—reduces the rate of complications. In many societies, a woman may not be recognized as an adult until she has had a baby. The preferred location of the delivery is often specified, as are the positions that the laboring women assume. The typical expectation in Western culture is that women should give birth lying flat on their backs on a bed, but in the rest of the world the most prevalent position for the delivery is upright—sitting, squatting or, in some cases, standing. Squatting is one of the most typical positions for women to give birth in non-Western cultures.

Knowing this (that assisted birth comes close to being a universal custom in human cultures)—and believing that this practice is driven by the difficulty and risk that accompany human birth—we began to think that midwifery is not unique to contemporary humans but instead has its roots deep in our ancestry. Our analysis of the birth process throughout human evolution has led us to suggest that the practice of midwifery might have appeared as early as five million years ago, when the advent of bipedalism first constricted the size and shape of the pelvis and birth canal.

A behavior pattern as complex as midwifery obviously does not fossilize, but pelvic bones do. The tight fit between the infant's head and the mother's birth canal in humans means that the mechanism of birth can be reconstructed if we know the relative sizes of each. Pelvic anatomy is now fairly well known from most time periods in the human fossil record, and we can estimate infant brain and skull size based on our extensive knowledge of adult skull sizes. (The delicate skulls of infants are not commonly found preserved until the point when humans began to bury their dead about 100,000 years ago.) Knowing the size and shape of the skulls and pelvises has also helped us and other researchers to understand whether infants were born facing forward or backward relative to their mothers—in turn revealing how challenging the birth might have been.

Walking on Two Legs

In modern humans, both bipedalism and enlarged brains constrain birth in important ways, but the first fundamental shift away from a nonhuman primate way of birth came about because of bipedalism alone. This unique way of walking appeared in early human ancestors of the genus *Australopithecus* about four million years ago [see "Evolution of Human Walking," by C. Owen Lovejoy; *Scientific American*, November 1988]. Despite their upright posture, australopithecines typically stood no more than four feet tall, and their brains were not much bigger than those of living chimpanzees. Recent evidence has called into question which of the several australopithecine species were part of the lineage that led to *Homo*. Understanding the way any of them gave birth is still important, however, because walking on two legs would have constricted the maximum size of the pelvis and birth canal in similar ways among related species.

The anatomy of the female pelvis from this time period is well known from two complete fossils. Anthropologists unearthed the first (known as Sts 14 and presumed to be 2.5 million years old) in Sterkfontein, a site in the Transvaal region of South Africa. The second is best known as Lucy, a fossil discovered in the Hadar region of Ethiopia and dated at just over three million years old. Based on these specimens and on estimates of newborns' head size, C. Owen Lovejoy of Kent State University and Robert G. Tague of Louisiana State University concluded in the mid-1980s that birth in early hominids was unlike that known for any living species of primate.

The shape of the australopithecine birth canal is a flattened oval with the greatest dimension from side to side at both the entrance and exit. This shape appears to require a birth pattern different from that of monkeys, apes or modern humans. The head would not have rotated within the birth canal, but we think that in order for the shoulders to fit through, the baby might have had to turn its head once it emerged. In other words, if the baby's head entered the birth canal facing the side of the mother's body, its shoulders would have been oriented in a line from the mother's belly to her back. This starting position would have meant that the shoulders probably also had to turn sideways to squeeze through the birth canal.

This simple rotation could have introduced a kind of difficulty in australopithecine deliveries that no other known primate species had ever experienced. Depending on which way the baby's shoulders turned, its head could have exited the birth canal facing either forward or backward relative to the mother. Because the australopithecine birth canal is a symmetrical opening of unchanging shape, the baby could have just as easily turned its shoulders toward the front or back of its body, giving it about a 50-50 chance of emerging in the easier, face-forward position. If the infant were born facing backward, the australopithecine mother—like modern human mothers—may well have benefited from some kind of assistance.

Growing Bigger Brains

If bipedalism alone did not introduce into the process of childbirth enough difficulty for mothers to benefit from assistance, then the expanding size of the hominid brain certainly did. The most significant expansion in adult and infant brain size evolved subsequent to the australopithecines, particularly in the genus *Homo*. Fossil remains of the pelvis of early *Homo* are quite rare, and the best-preserved specimen, the 1.5-million-year-old Nariokotome fossil from Kenya, is an adolescent often referred to as Turkana Boy. Researchers have estimated that the boy's adult relatives probably had brains about twice as large as those of australopithecines but still only two thirds the size of modern human brains.

By reconstructing the shape of the boy's pelvis from fragments, Christopher B. Ruff of Johns Hopkins University and Alan Walker of Pennsylvania State University have estimated what he would have looked like had he reached adulthood. Using predictable differences between male and female pelvises in more recent hominid species, they could also infer what a female of that species would have looked like and could estimate the shape of the birth canal. That shape turns out to be a flattened oval similar to that of the australopithecines. Based on these reconstructions, the researchers determined that Turkana Boy's kin probably had a birth mechanism like that seen in australopithecines.

In recent years, scientists have been testing an important hypothesis that follows from Ruff and Walker's assertion: the pelvic anatomy of early *Homo* may have limited the growth of the human brain until the evolutionary point at which the birth canal expanded enough to allow a larger infant head to pass. This assertion implies that bigger brains and roomier pelvises were linked from an evolutionary perspective. Individuals who displayed both characteristics were more successful at giving birth to offspring who survived to pass on the traits. These changes in pelvic anatomy, accompanied by assisted birth, may have allowed the dramatic increase in human brain size that took place from two million to 100,000 years ago.

Fossils that span the past 300,000 years of human evolution support the connection between the expansion of brain size and changes in pelvic anatomy. In the past 20 years, scientists have uncovered three pelvic fossils of archaic *Homo sapiens:* a male from Sima de los Huesos in Sierra Atapuerca, Spain (more than 200,000 years old); a female from Jinniushan, China (280,000 years old); and the male Kebara Neandertal—which is also an archaic *H. sapiens*—from Israel (about 60,000 years old). These specimens all have the twisted pelvic openings characteristic of modern humans, which suggests that their large-brained babies would most likely have had to rotate the head and shoulders within the birth canal and would thus have emerged facing away from the mother—a major challenge that human mothers face in delivering their babies safely.

The triple challenge of big-brained infants, a pelvis designed for walking upright, and a rotational delivery in which the baby emerges facing backward is not merely a contemporary circumstance. For this reason, we suggest that natural selection long ago favored the behavior of seeking assistance during birth because such help compensated for these difficulties. Mothers probably did not seek assistance solely because they predicted the risk that childbirth poses, however. Pain, fear and anxiety more likely drove their desire for companionship and security.

Psychiatrists have argued that natural selection might have favored such emotions—also common during illness and injury—because they led individuals who experienced them to seek the protection of companions, which would have given them a better chance of surviving [see "Evolution and the Origins of Disease," by Randolph M. Nesse and George C. Williams; *Scientific American,* November 1998]. The offspring of the survivors would then also have an enhanced tendency to experience such emotions during times of pain or disease. Taking into consideration the evolutionary advantage that fear and anxiety impart, it is no surprise that women commonly experience these emotions during labor and delivery.

Modern women giving birth have a dual evolutionary legacy: the need for physical as well as emotional support. When Sophia Pedro gave birth in a tree surrounded by raging floodwaters, she may have had both kinds of assistance. In an interview several months after her helicopter rescue, she told reporters that her mother-in-law, who was also in the tree, helped her during delivery. Desire for this kind of support, it appears, may well be as ancient as humanity itself.

Discussion Questions

1. What two anatomical features of humans account for the particularly tight squeeze that human babies experience during childbirth?
2. How does the shape of a typical nonhuman primate baby's skull differ from the shape of a human baby's skull? How does this affect the way the baby turns as it is being born?
3. Why are most human babies born face down?
4. Why is it difficult and/or risky for human mothers to help their babies emerge from the birth canal? Why are human babies not able to help in their own deliveries the way monkey babies do?
5. How common is unassisted childbirth in cultures around the world?
6. What evidence is there to suggest that midwifery (assistance during childbirth) has ancient roots in the hominid evolutionary lineage?
7. Rosenberg and Trevathan suggest that natural selection would have favored genes that led to the behaviors associated with seeking and giving assistance during childbirth. How does natural selection work on genes for behavior?
8. In most traditional (non-Western) cultures, women seek out the companionship of close friends and relatives during labor and delivery. How does this differ from the experience of a woman during a typical U.S. hospital birth?
9. Around the world, most women labor and give birth while standing, sitting, or squatting. The squatting position is the one that opens the pelvis to its widest dimensions, giving the baby's head the most room. Why, then, do most U.S. hospitals require women to lie on their backs with their feet up in stirrups during childbirth?
10. To what extent do U.S. cultural beliefs and practices (induction of labor, epidurals, lying on one's back, and strangers in the delivery room, among others) make it **more difficult** for women in the United States to labor safely?

14. CARE-WORN FOSSILS: BONES REOPEN CONTROVERSY ABOUT ANCIENT ASSISTANCE

Debate over the role of Neanderthals (Homo sapiens neanderthalensis) *in the ancestry of modern humans* (Homo sapiens sapiens) *divides many anthropologists into two camps. Proponents of the "Out of Africa" view think that modern humans (Cro-Magnons) arose in Africa relatively recently and spread out and replaced all previous hominids in the rest of the Old World, including the Neanderthals in Europe. Followers of this theoretical model usually describe Neanderthals as less intelligent, less culturally complex, and less adaptable than the Cro-Magnons. On the other hand, proponents of the "Regional Model" suggest that modern humans have evolved in situ in Africa, Asia, Europe, and Australia since the time of* Homo erectus *or very early* Homo sapiens, *with substantial migration and gene flow back and forth between populations. From this perspective, "Neanderthals are us," and they are usually described as intelligent, culturally complex, and both adaptable and successful. Some anthropologists see clear evidence of Neanderthal genetic contributions to modern human populations in the faces of living central and eastern Europeans and their descendants in the United States.*

Part of this debate has included a discussion of when evidence for compassion toward impaired members of the population first appears in the archaeological record. If an individual was born with spina bifida, or congenital dwarfism, or was injured in a hunting accident or rock fall, and yet survived for a number of years, some anthropologists have interpreted this as evidence of conspecific care—the beginnings not only of medical treatment, but of compassion and care for one's fellow beings, presumably a noble and advanced characteristic. The question is usually framed as one of whether Neanderthals were capable of such behavior, or if it did not evolve until fully modern Homo sapiens sapiens.

In 1991, one of us (KAD) published an article titled "Can Paleopathology Provide Evidence of 'Compassion'?" challenging the very notion that one can determine values and attitudes from the fossil remains or the archaeological record. The answer to the title question was clearly no, and for a number of years, people stopped writing about compassion in fossil hominids. In 2002, however, this viewpoint arose again, in an article by Serge Lebel and Erik Trinkaus about a partial Neanderthal jaw from France. This selection by Bruce Bower discusses the newly reopened debate.

Welcome to a messy tale of survival in the face of daunting physical challenges. Its protagonists include a nearly toothless adult of indeterminate sex, a man with a withered arm and one blind eye, a teenage dwarf, and a bunch of apes. No, it's not a screenplay for the next David Lynch movie—at least, not yet. It's a scientific inquiry into whether fossils of physically impaired individuals show that our ancient ancestors had a soft spot for the injured and infirm.

The latest chapter in this Stone Age saga began last year with a much-publicized report of a partial Neandertal jaw missing many of its teeth and marred by extensive bone damage *(SN: 9/15/01, p. 167)*. The newly discovered specimen, dated at between 169,000 and 191,000 years old, came from a man or woman who must have endured a mouthful of pain and was unable to chew food for at least 6 months, concluded coauthors Serge Lebel of the University of Quebec in Montreal and Erik Trinkaus of Washington University in St. Louis.

This person's survival hinged on having a support system, the researchers theorized. Neandertal comrades supplied fruit and other soft foods to him or her, and they probably pounded or cooked tougher fare—meat, in particular—so that it could be swallowed without chewing.

Not everyone who stares into the jaw, which was discovered in France, or examines other disfigured human fossils sees signs of prehistoric compassion, though. Lebel and Trinkaus ignored critical evidence that undermines their conclusion, contends David DeGusta, a doctoral student in anthropology at the University of California, Berkeley.

He has examined published reports of relatively recent wild monkeys and apes that exhibit as much or more tooth loss and bone disease as that reported for the French Neandertal find, he says. Skeletal scrutiny also indicates that these animals can survive a range of illnesses and injuries that cause permanent disabilities.

Such data haven't fueled any arguments that healthy monkeys and apes keep their disabled peers alive or to help make their lives easier. Neither can such evidence be used as a signature of social support among Stone Age folk, DeGusta concludes in the December *Journal of Archaeological Science*.

"The French jaw doesn't provide any evidence of increased Neandertal caregiving relative to nonhuman primates," he says. "This fossil individual could just as easily have provided or processed his or her food without help from others."

DeGusta, Trinkaus, and other scientists are re-examining data and specimens collected over the last century to try to clear up how Stone Age folk treated their weakened comrades.

Ancestral Aid

The French jaw, found at the Bau de l'Aubesier rock shelter and dubbed Aubesier 11, joins several other debilitated Stone Age individuals often regarded as recipients of social assistance. The French jaw represents the earliest evidence of caring for the disabled by our fossil ancestors, according to Lebel and Trinkaus. It also fits with broader attempts by some anthropologists to portray Neandertals as the cultural equals of modern people (*SN:* 12/15/01, p. 380).

"This is one more piece of the puzzle indicating that some type of social support occurred among Neandertals," Trinkaus says.

The most prominent case of Neandertal physical impairment is an adult male whose skeleton was found more than 30 years ago at Iraq's Shanidar Cave. Trinkaus' 1983 analysis indicated that the Shanidar man, who lived about 50,000 years ago, suffered many bone fractures and extensive arthritic damage to his joints. His withered right arm had been paralyzed, and damage to his left eye had probably left it blind.

Moreover, several Neandertals who inhabited Croatia's Krapina Cave around 130,000 years ago sustained skull fractures that would have knocked them unconscious and required life-saving aid from others for at least a few days, says Janet Monge of the University of Pennsylvania in Philadelphia. Monge and Princeton University anthropologist Alan Mann discovered the injuries when they recently took X rays of more than 800 Krapina fossils belonging to several dozen Neandertals.

Monge suspects that the Krapina Neandertals sustained skull fractures from pieces of the cave's roof falling on their heads. Other researchers think that the head injuries resulted from fights using clubs or other weapons.

Some Krapina cave dwellers also lived with considerable tooth loss. It's hard to know whether these individuals got special care from others, Monge holds. Some people today adapt to the pain of untreated dental disease and manage on their own, while others don't. Jawbones can't reveal telltale signs of either resilience or misery.

Neandertals weren't the only human ancestors that survived physical disabilities. Consider three separately discovered archaic *Homo sapiens* fossils dating to around 150,000 years ago. One individual grew to adulthood despite an inborn misalignment of head and neck, another tottered around on a misshapen hip, and a third had bony growths in the inner ear that would have interfered with balance and walking. The discoverers of these fossil individuals have assumed that they must have benefited from some type of social assistance.

An even more curious case involved the Romito boy, an 11,000-year-old human skeleton that was excavated in an Italian cave nearly 40 years ago. This 3-1/2-foot-tall individual, about 17 years old at the time of his death, experienced a severe growth deficiency and limited mobility, according to a 1987 study directed by anthropologist David W. Frayer of the University of Kansas in Lawrence. Comrades must have taken pains to feed the diminutive teen and bring him along on periodic moves through the area's rugged environment, Frayer's group concluded.

Nearly toothless, diseased jaws also appear in the skeletal remains of hunter-gatherers who lived in parts of North America several thousand years ago, according to research directed by anthropologist Clark S. Larsen of Ohio State University in Columbus. In his view, however, there's no evidence that these individuals—or the Aubesier Neandertal—received special care from their comrades.

Another anthropologist who studies Stone Age *Homo* species disagrees. Although it's hard to squeeze prehistoric behavior out of fossils, Lebel and Trinkaus "are on to something," remarks Karen Rosenberg of the University of Delaware in Newark.

Fossil evidence including the Aubesier jaw suggests that, beginning with Neandertals, social assistance of some kind enabled physically impaired individuals to survive longer than they could have in earlier species, such as *Homo erectus,* Rosenberg asserts.

Aping Human Injuries

"It's really reaching to interpret [the Aubesier] fossil's condition as a sign of social care among Neandertals," contends Berkeley anthropologist F. Clark Howell, DeGusta's academic advisor. He and DeGusta wondered whether apes, which anthropologists generally agree don't take care of injured companions, survive after similarly serious wounds.

Although DeGusta found that relatively few researchers have probed skeletal markers of disease and injury in nonhuman primates, he located several published instances of these creatures having lived with extensive tooth loss and bone-decaying oral ailments. These reports described recently deceased animals.

One of the most thorough investigations of primate skeletons occurred decades ago. In 1956, primatologist Adolph Schultz wrote that "the misnamed permanent dentition" frequently falls out or becomes unusable because of disease in apes and monkeys, as well as in people. Schultz noted that several freshly killed chimpanzees showed evidence of having survived for months and possibly years after the loss of the majority of their teeth.

DeGusta also located a 1936 investigation by another scientist that noted near-total tooth loss in a chimp and a monkey that had lived into old age in the wild.

Studies conducted more recently have found that nonhuman primates sometimes survive not only extensive tooth loss but also illnesses such as hepatitis, malaria, and poliomyelitis, DeGusta says.

They also endure a surprising number of injuries from guns. In 1993, anthropologist Bruce Latimer X-rayed chimp, gorilla, and orangutan skeletons held at the Cleveland Museum of Natural History. He determined that about 12 percent of injuries originally classified as naturally occurring fractures were instead healed gunshot wounds. These creatures had endured types of injuries that routinely put people in the hospital and sometimes prove fatal, Latimer says.

"Even a cursory examination of great ape skeletons demonstrates that these animals have a remarkable ability to survive trauma and infection," he holds.

The physical resilience of apes also casts a shadow over attempts to portray skeletal disease, such as that on the French Neandertal jaw, as a marker of social care. "I have no doubt that Neandertals had a sophisticated culture and social structure, but dental [disease] is not evidence of it," Latimer contends.

That hardly settles the issue. Lebel and Trinkaus defend their position in an upcoming *Journal of Human Evolution.*

Wild apes and monkeys have yet to provide any evidence of having lived for long periods with as much tooth loss as that observed on the French Neandertal jaw, the researchers assert. Most of the apes and monkeys in the studies that Lebel and Trinkaus have considered had lost fewer than 60 percent of their teeth. Those who survived the most extensive tooth loss lived in the tropics where they ate soft plants, a far more congenial diet than Neandertals' meat-laden menu, the researchers maintain.

Field observations of baboons and ring-tailed lemurs indicate that individuals that lose most or all of their teeth soon die or disappear from their groups, Trinkaus adds.

Handicapping Bones

The Aubesier jaw inspires a frustrated sense of déjà vu in Katherine A. Dettwyler. "Oh, brother," she says, "will people never learn?"

Dettwyler, an anthropologist who now works at the American Philosophical Association in Newark, Del., wrote a 1991 paper that challenged fossil-fueled scenarios of compassionate Stone Age caregivers. She says that the newer evidence doesn't change her position.

In her 1991 piece, she took special aim at scientists' interpretation of the Shanidar skeleton. This individual may not have been a good hunter, but he could have collected plants, processed and cooked food, and performed many other daily activities, Dettwyler argued. If loss of sight in one eye occurred after adulthood, the Shanidar Neandertal could have adjusted relatively easily to a narrower visual field, she added.

Dettwyler also challenged the conclusion that the Romito boy must have been helped along on his people's strenuous treks. Dettwyler notes that in some African hunter-gatherer groups, children as young as 5 years old walk with their mothers on long food-gathering trips. The Romito boy probably didn't march at the head of a traveling band, but he could have straggled along on his own. It's also possible that migrating group members left the Romito boy behind, and he then tracked them down at his own pace. There's no way to know from his bones, Dettwyler says.

Frayer has now reversed course and agrees with Dettwyler. Because apes and monkeys show so many skeletal signs of surviving major illnesses and injuries, it's dangerous to assume that the Romito boy or any other fossil ancestor displaying a physical disability benefited from special care, Frayer contends.

"A lot of researchers, including me, have been guilty of jumping to conclusions from fossil evidence about ancient caring behaviors," he says.

As the mother of a child with Down syndrome, Dettwyler has a personal stake in this debate. Researchers who study the Stone Age and draw lessons about ancient social care from fossils rely on a handful of inaccurate beliefs about disabilities in modern societies, she says.

First, scientists assume that nonproductive individuals are rare and hard to incorporate into most societies. Instead, human groups have much experience caring for needy individuals. These include babies, children, and women in the final stages of pregnancy and the weeks after giving birth.

Second, the notion that bones inevitably tell the story of a person's disabilities is belied by cases of blindness, deafness, mental retardation, and other impairments that don't always affect the skeleton.

Third, people with physical disabilities often live without others' assistance. In Mali, where Dettwyler has conducted fieldwork, many people develop disabilities from polio, leprosy, or untreated injuries. Yet these individuals can hold respected jobs, including caring for their relatives' children, spinning cotton, and serving as traditional healers.

On the other side of the coin, even modern people who survive physical impairments haven't necessarily been treated kindly. In Mali, Dettwyler observed some disabled individuals routinely beaten and jeered and children with crippling polio crawling to school. "The [fossil] record can't tell us whether disabled persons were treated with compassion, tolerance, or cruelty," Dettwyler says.

Skeleton Keys

At this point, the fossil record contains just enough to keep the scientific debate about prehistoric social support simmering at a slow boil.

If skeletal keys can conclusively unlock Stone Age behavior toward the disabled, they have yet to be found, remarks anthropologist Della C. Cook of Indiana University in Bloomington. Cook studies signs of disease in skeletal remains of people who lived between around 10,000 and 5,000 years ago.

The Aubesier jaw represents a classic example of skeletal ambiguity, she says. Lebel and Trinkaus make an "interesting and persuasive" case for Neandertal social support, according to Cook. However, she notes, DeGusta provides a "useful critique" that, of necessity, relies on a small number of ape and monkey studies.

"I'm not convinced by either argument," Cook says. "We need far more data than we're likely to have anytime soon to resolve this issue."

Discussion Questions

1. Why do Lebel and Trinkaus think that the mandible they discovered in France suggests that other Neanderthals were helping the individual survive?
2. What research methods does David DeGusta use to try to answer the question of whether survival with serious physical handicaps necessarily means conspecific care?

3. What have DeGusta's studies shown about survival in nonhuman primates?
4. With what other sorts of physical impairments did early humans survive? What sorts of extra help would they have benefited from?
5. What kinds of individuals in any typical population are not able to provide for all of their own needs? What percentage of the population do they constitute?
6. Is it necessarily the case that physically (or even mentally) impaired individuals are not capable of contributing anything to their society? What sorts of factors determine how much impaired people can contribute to their own survival and to society in general?
7. Is it possible that physically impaired individuals might receive help that allows them to survive and yet still be treated cruelly by some members of the group?
8. Is it always compassionate and morally right to facilitate the survival of a disabled individual? Are there circumstances under which it is more compassionate to let a severely disabled individual die?

Additional Resources

For Internet links related to this chapter, please visit our website at www.mhhe.com/dettwyler

AUEL, JEAN M. *The Clan of the Cave Bear.* New York: Crown, 1980.

DAVIS-FLOYD, ROBBIE. *Birth as an American Rite of Passage.* Berkeley, CA: University of California Press, 1993.

DEGUSTA, DAVID. "Comparative Skeletal Pathology and the Case for Conspecific Care in Middle Pleistocene Hominids." *Journal of Archaeological Science* 29, no. 12, 2002: 1435–1438.

DETTWYLER, KATHERINE A. "Can Paleopathology Provide Evidence for 'Compassion'?" *American Journal of Physical Anthropology* 84, no. 4, 1991: 375–384.

GOER, HENCI. *The Thinking Woman's Guide to a Better Birth.* New York: Perigee Press, 1999.

LEBEL, SERGE, and ERIK TRINKAUS. "Middle Pleistocene Human Remains from the Bau de l'Aubesier." *Journal of Human Evolution* 43, no. 5, 2002: 659–685.

ROSENBERG, KAREN R., and WENDA R. TREVATHAN. "Bipedalism and Human Birth: The Obstetrical Dilemma Revisited." *Evolutionary Anthropology* 4, no. 5, 1996: 161–168.

TATTERSALL, IAN. *The Last Neanderthal: The Rise, Success, and Mysterious Extinction of Our Closest Human Relatives.* Boulder, CO: Westview Press, 1999.

CHAPTER 9

Human Diversity and "Race"

15. "Race Counts," by David Berreby, *The Sciences,* (Sept./Oct., 2000), pp. 38–43.

16. "Interracial Generation: We Are Who We Are," by Daryl Strickland, *Seattle Times,* May 5, 1996.

The study of human variation is fascinating and informative. Most students are startled to learn that there are no biological races in humans—we all belong to the taxonomic category of Homo sapiens sapiens. *Variation within a single population is usually greater than the average amount of variation between populations. Some variation between populations is adaptive—members of populations living in hot climates tend to be taller and thinner than those living in cold climates. While being homozygous for sickle-cell anemia results in a devastating disease, the presence of the sickle-cell variant of hemoglobin B allows carriers in the population to have protection against malaria. Variation in skin color has been directly linked to variation in levels of ultraviolet radiation. Darker skin is a form of protection against damage caused by the sun's rays to circulating folic acid in the bloodstream. For every physical and physiological trait imaginable, humans vary. It's part of what makes being a physical anthropologist so interesting—to note and marvel at the vast array of human biological variation.*

Consider, for example, that all humans have the same basic body plan and facial features—bilateral symmetry, two arms, two legs, one head, two ears, two eyes, one nose, and one mouth (something we share with most fictional space aliens as well). Why then, does everyone look different? Why does the typical American privilege variation in some biological features, such as skin color and nose shape to define "racial" categories and ignore variation in other biological features, such as hair on the knuckles, left-handedness, height, possession of a "white forelock," or variations in a number of blood group systems? Ethnicity, of course, is cultural, and bears little relationship to the underlying biological variation in human populations. The two selections in this chapter focus on the inherent difficulties (and pointlessness) of assigning individuals to racial groups.

This essay by David Berreby is a review of a book by Clara E. Rodríguez, Changing Race: Latinos, the Census and the History of Ethnicity in the United States. *The central points of the essay revolve around the complexity of modern American ethnicity and the pitfalls of groupthink in various contexts. The problem of what categories to have on census questionnaires is particularly vexing, since almost all Americans have ancestors who came originally from a variety of different countries—we are all of mixed biological heritage. The case of Hispanics as a racial or ethnic category illustrates some of the complexities of the issue.*

They were waiting for the "walk" signal, two women in sundresses talking about their weekends, and one asked how it went on Saturday.

"Oh, well, you know," said the other. "She's Irish, so the food wasn't so good."

Her friend nodded, because she did know, and so did I. We were in Brooklyn, and if you're seeking gastronomical pleasures among the hyphenated Americans of that borough, you think of Chinese food and Italian food and foods Arab and Greek, but you don't think Irish. And, generally speaking, you're right. As a matter of pure logic, of course, that makes no sense, for Irish identity is not a brake on cooking skills. And even if it were, a tendency among the Irish to avoid the kitchen is no predictor that any particular Mrs. Ryan will be a lousy cook. Groups don't cook. Individuals cook, and individuals vary.

No matter. Any reader who knows how Americans classify different kinds of white people can grasp why the first half of the woman's sentence was relevant to the second. Yet it's a guilty grasp, because everybody knows that group traits are probabilities, not certainties (somewhere, no doubt, there's a Colleen who's the best cook on her multiethnic block). One can't even talk about the racial, ethnic, cultural, geographic or religious groups to which a person belongs without carving out exceptions for that person—as in "Yes, their name is Peterson, but they're a Puerto Rican family," or "Yes, he's from New York, but he's really polite," or "Yes, she's Irish, but she's a fabulous cook." That inescapable yes-buttering means it is impossible to know for sure that any given Irish woman is a bad cook or a good Catholic or anything else. And if one can't be certain that a given Irish person has any particular trait, one can't be certain that she even possesses all the traits that are typically used to define people as Irish. Human groups are inherently slippery.

In certain narrowly defined circumstances—on a passport, for instance—one's racial or ethnic identity can be specified by the artificial clarity of the law. Yet even such paperwork has its limits. As Clara E. Rodríguez notes in her rich trove of lore on how Americans classify Americans, the United Nations has a hard time comparing census data from various countries because each country pigeonholes people in surprisingly different, even incompatible, ways. One study of the censuses that were conducted in fifty-one New World nations during the past forty years showed that they had no shared definition of ethnicity. Sixteen countries did not even ask about it; moreover, in many countries people skipped the ethnicity questions altogether or complained that they could not answer them. Even within the United States, definitions vary. Hispanics are considered a race by the federal agencies that track civil-rights enforcement, but they are not a race to the Bureau of the Census. Thus even in the realm of written, official definitions, the answers to questions about race depend on what is being asked, who is asking it, and why.

The upshot is that when one tries to examine these overwhelmingly important entities to which every person belongs, they dissolve into exceptions, qualifications, coded speech and navel gazing. Each category is like a portrait that, held up too close, turns into flecks and dabs of paint. And those of us who persist in applying the categories anyway are like the family in the old joke that doesn't want to cure the cousin who thinks he's a chicken. We need the eggs.

Globalization makes the problem urgent: we are all being forced to rub elbows with people who seem somehow all wrong. The questions of what makes them seem that way, and of what marks our common humanity, are more relevant to more people than ever before. We want to talk coherently about race, ethnicity, class, nation, religion and "culture." But we don't know how because, when we try, we realize that we don't know what we're talking **about.**

To admit confusion about such social categories may be fine for the ordinary citizen, whose folk sociology is probably no more coherent than his folk physics or folk biology. But in academia the fuzziness in thinking about group concepts is an embarrassment if not a crisis. The basic question social scientists seek to answer is straightforward: How do people categorize other people, and how do they make predictions on the basis of those categories? Put that way, the question sounds readily amenable to the scientific method. And, in fact, most every useful tool of science, from the statistical analysis of populations to genetics to evolutionary theory, has been applied, soon after its inception, to the question of human groups.

That application of sophisticated scientific tools to the problem of human "groupthink" will no doubt continue. Last summer, for instance, two teams of social psychologists, neurobiologists and medical-imaging specialists brought the magnetic resonance imaging scanner into the fray. They focused on the amygdala, a region deep in each brain hemisphere that helps spotlight emotionally important information: things that are dangerous, unpredictable or sexually arousing. One team, based at Massachusetts General Hospital in Boston, reported that the amygdala shows more activation in white people viewing black faces, and vice versa, than it does when people look at faces of their own color. The other team, which was made up of investigators from New York University and Yale University, found that among volunteers who showed race-based differences in amygdala activation, the amount of that difference could predict how the volunteers scored on two unrelated psychological tests that measure unconscious racial attitudes.

No matter how many new technologies they apply, however, all social scientists face a second, confounding question about human groupthink. To understand how people categorize people and make predictions, the scientists themselves must categorize and make predictions. But how can scientists be sure that "scientific" categories are different from—more objective than—folk categories based on emotion, self-interest and bias, whether unwitting or otherwise? Until that conundrum is resolved, the dangers of wishful thinking and pseudoscience will always be close at hand.

All one can be sure of so far is that what seems to be good people-science in one epoch looks tainted a century later. American medical science, for instance, once included a diagnosis of "drapetomania"—a regrettable condition that afflicted slaves and whose defining symptom was a desire to run away. Yet an awareness of that history of egregious error has led some scholars to throw the baby out with the bathwater. In 1997, for instance, a trio of anthropologists, writing in the journal

Evolution and Human Behavior, declared tribes, clans, villages, societies and cultures to be the inventions of intellectuals, and unworthy of serious attention from evolutionary theorists. (The mass-market version of that idea is Margaret Thatcher's line: "There is no such thing as society. There are individual men and women, and there are families.")

Without a consensus on fundamentals, then, scholars who study groups are free to say whatever suits their purposes. Early in her book, Rodríguez observes that most scholarly writing on ethnicity is not particularly rigorous. In fact, she notes, a recent analysis of nearly 200 studies of ethnicity published by social scientists between 1974 and 1992 found that more than 80 percent of the studies did not adhere to a coherent theory of the subject. Slightly less than a quarter of them even acknowledged the central problem: people and the groups to which they belong are separate kinds of entities.

By definition, for instance, the group known as African-Americans is all African-American and nothing but. Any individual African-American, though, may be the holder of many other identities as well: man, father, veteran, lawyer, resident of the East Side and so on. Identity depends on who is asking, and for what purpose. And it is the process of asking the questions and getting the answers that is not understood: What is it about a trait that makes someone decide that all who possess it form a group? How do people determine that a stranger belongs to this group instead of that one? How much of that decision is even accessible to the conscious mind? How do people reconcile the exceptions with the rules? And how does the process of group making change with a person's—or a region's or a society's—circumstances?

Rodríguez writes that "many people have a core of identity, or a self, that is made up of multiple identities." She herself, Rodríguez explains, is "a light-skinned Latina with European features and hair texture . . . born and raised in New York City," and her first language was Spanish. In her South Bronx neighborhood her "natural tan" was attractive, whereas "downtown . . . it was 'otherizing.'" "In the United States today," she points out, "a person may be Puerto Rican or Mexican on a personal level, Latino on an instrumental level, and Hispanic to the government. Some people might classify this person as black, white or Asian." ("Hispanic" is a rather vague term, encompassing new immigrants from Spanish-speaking countries, as well as North Americans who speak no Spanish. The U.S. government uses the term to refer to people whose ancestors came from Central or South America. Many people, however, prefer the term "Latino," which, among other things, avoids labeling Portuguese-speaking Brazilians as "Hispanic.")

It is not, of course, merely interesting that no one quite grasps the relation between group and member. The consequences in law enforcement have become well known, thanks to the current campaign against "police profiling"—the practice of viewing members of one ethnic group with extra suspicion. The effects of group-think on the practice of medicine are also becoming better known. In a 1996 paper published in the *Annals of Internal Medicine,* for instance, Ritchie Witzig, a physician and epidemiologist, cited two relevant case histories: an eight-year-old boy who was scheduled for surgery because no one associated his stomach pains with their true cause, sickle-cell anemia (he wasn't black); and a twenty-four-year-old black man who was treated for sickle-cell anemia (which he didn't have), and then died of a bleeding peptic ulcer [see "Bred in the Bone?" by Alan H. Goodman, March/April 1997].

Rodríguez's sprawling yet intriguing book makes the case that there is a third arena in which a flawed understanding of groupthink affects contemporary Americans: the censuses conducted in the United States every ten years. Much more than a head count, each census since the first one in 1790 has been a taxonomy of the American people, with serious, practical effects on their lives: their taxes, their freedom of movement, even their right to stay in the country. As she puts it, the census categories "represent public consensus on how populations are viewed and counted." The census is an explicit social construction—debated, decided and recorded—and the classifications it makes are just as arbitrary as the ones imposed by law enforcement or medicine. But because it was so early in the country's history that the government came to believe in an absolute division of human beings into white and black, Rodríguez points out, the arbitrariness of classifications has been most apparent in the case of people who are neither.

Mexicans once constituted a race of their own, in the 1930 census. Armenians were "Asiatics" until a court decision in 1909 promoted them to "white." And the explicit construction of categories goes on: Before the 2000 census, Congress held hearings on a proposal to create a Middle Eastern/Arab group. The government decided against the proposal, because that rather remarkable category (it would lump Arabs, Turks, Iranians, Afghans and others into one unit) is still under construction.

But it is among Hispanics, Rodríguez argues, that the fluidity of ethnic identity in the United States is easiest to observe. For example, Hispanics were defined by language in the 1940 census, surname in the censuses of 1950 and 1960, and "origin" in the 1970 census.

To say race is a social construction is not to say it doesn't matter, any more than telling people that their chronic pain is psychosomatic makes it go away. Race and ethnicity are facts of people's lives. Most Hispanics feel discriminated against in American society, Rodríguez reports. Some of her informants recounted stingingly clear reminders of their status, having been treated as "white" until the sound of a name or an accent led someone to reclassify them. Race is a fact: it is just not the kind of fact—biological, inevitable, unchanging—that most Americans think it is. What kind of a fact it actually is is the unanswered question.

Rodríguez, a professor of sociology at Fordham University in New York City, brings several disparate methods to bear on the problem: surveys of Hispanics, in-depth case studies of individual Latinos, a historical analysis of the U.S. census, and an analysis of contemporary racial politics as reflected in government hearings on the 2000 census. Her argument can feel a bit scattered, but her accumulation of relevant evidence from so many different perspectives is, ultimately, a strength. That variety of approaches underscores an often-ignored fact that any successful theory of race and ethnicity must account for: On most any timescale you care to choose, be it the day, the week, the decade or the century, ethnic identity varies with the circumstances.

Americans are by now so used to defining themselves—in conversation, on official forms, in Web-based "user profiles"—that it may come as a shock to learn that until the 1980 census, respondents were not allowed to check their own racial or ethnic category from a list on the census form. Instead, race was reported—and, in all cases before 1970, decided—by the census taker who counted each household. The "race" question (though it was not explicitly labeled as such) on the 1980 U.S. census form asked: "Is this person_____?" followed by a list. The list included such categories as "Black or Negro," "White,"

"Hawaiian," "Korean," "Samoan" and so forth, and ended with the option "Other—specify." It did not include "Hispanic." Yet just three questions later the form asked, "Is this person of Spanish/Hispanic origin or descent?" The result was that some 40 percent of Hispanics—7.5 million people—checked "other" on their census forms, causing deep consternation among the tabulators.

In 1990 the Census Bureau changed its language, dropping the open-ended question used in 1980 in favor of one that explicitly mentioned the word "race." Yet in that census even more of the country's Hispanic population—43 percent, by then 9.7 million people—chose the "other race" box. The jump in the nonwhite numbers caught the imagination of the media. *TIME* magazine published a story titled, "The Browning of America," and American capitalism adjusted to the new kind of consumer it was told to expect. Companies changed their marketing plans, and an era of corporate-sponsored celebrations of "diversity" began.

All of that, Rodríguez shows, was overblown. A good part of the "browning of America" was the result of the shift, after the 1970 census, to self-reporting. Under the old system, census takers in 1970 classified 93.3 percent of Hispanics as white. In 1980, when people first categorized themselves, only 57.7 percent of Hispanics were white. Self-classification had revealed their reluctance to adopt the American racial taxonomy. They flocked to the "other" designation. And often they added explanatory notes, writing "Dominican" or "Honduran" or "Puerto Rican" in the box.

The trouble, Rodríguez argues, is that in the Latin tradition, culture, national origin and upbringing are also important factors in determining a person's race. North Americans tend to think instead primarily in terms of biology. That is not to say that Latin countries lack racial hierarchies—with whites at the top. Latinos who classify themselves as white fare better in the United States, and often they come from countries where white skin and traits are valued more highly than nonwhite ones. One of the case studies recounted in the book is that of a Mexican-American woman who recalled that the lightest-skinned of her sisters was always given the easy chores. At family gatherings even today, the darker sisters cook for hours, while *la favorita* brings the paper goods.

But the "pigmentocracies" of Latin America and the Caribbean are societies that recognize many gradations of racial category. Terms such as *moreno, indio, jabao* and *trigueño* signify people between the two ends of a black-white racial continuum. Rodríguez cites a study in Latin America that found eighty-two racial terms in use. Many Hispanics, she reports, react with puzzlement to America's few, immutable categories: black or white, for the most part, with a few Indians and Asian/Pacific islanders in the margins. As one of the people interviewed in Rodríguez's surveys said resignedly, "I do not consider myself white, but this is what the government says I am."

How did Americans get the way they are about black and white? Rodríguez's approach to the question through the history of the census is fascinating. Before the great waves of immigration in the early twentieth century, the story told by the census is not one of a melting pot but, rather, of a social group worried about keeping its advantage over people who were not part of the "governing race." The census results of 1870, 1880 and 1890 included maps showing the density of the "colored" populations of the states. A report on blacks in Maryland from the 1850 census stated that, given the growth rates of the black population in the first two decades after the first census was taken in 1790, "there was in 1810, reason for apprehension that, in another half century, the blacks would become the preponderating race."

One intriguing table in Rodríguez's book charts the categories for nonwhite people. "All other free persons" was the term of choice in 1790, 1800 and 1810; "free colored," between 1820 and 1840; "color," between 1850 and 1880; "color or race, whether white, black, mulatto, quadroon, octoroon, Chinese, Japanese, or Indian" was used in 1890; and "race," between 1900 and 1950. After 1950 those relative constancies gave way to irresolution. Census takers in 1960, running down a checklist, asked, "Is this person———?" In 1970 they asked for "color or race." The 1960 checklist reappeared in 1980, though, as I noted earlier, this time it was to be filled out by the respondents. The 1990 census simply asked for "race." As the questions change, so do the answers, both scientific and political.

So what kinds of questions is the census asking nowadays? Rodríguez relates how proposals to count Hispanics as a race in the 2000 census were dropped after detailed studies suggested that such a question would lower the numbers of both "Hispanics" and "whites." Instead, the race question was changed in a different way. This year's question is: "What is this person's race?"—but, for the first time, people are allowed to give more than one answer. The Office of Management and Budget estimates that fewer than 2 percent of the respondents will pick more than one racial category. Outside investigators think the number could be much higher. The consequences—for federal statistics, civil-rights programs and politics—could be far-reaching.

Changing Race presents the central problem of groupthink in all its complexities and contradictions, and relates it to a political concern that is just as important, in the long run, as policing and medicine. Rodríguez makes an excellent case that categories for people depend on context, and that context includes the category maker. Such a conclusion suggests that much of the accumulated so-called wisdom about group identity presents only half the picture: it provides categories, such as "African-American" or "gay person" or "soccer mom," without asking, Who made this category? What purpose of theirs does it serve? As Rodríguez shows, the decennial deliberations about the census are unusual in that they reveal both sides of the picture. In the records of those discussions one sees not only the categorized, but also the categorizers, doing in public what most of us usually do unconsciously, or at least in private.

In reaction to the terrible history of such categories as "the proletariat" and "the Aryan race," in whose name millions of innocent people have been killed, intellectual life is now, properly, oriented against the making of vast, all-explaining categories for people. The problem, though, is that such a taboo leaves people without any language for the generalizations they need to say anything about any aspect of human behavior. Rodríguez's book hints at a way around that impasse. Hers is an example of a study of groupthink that does not resort to simplifying assumptions. She does not claim that census categories are only of interest for what they say about the people who made them up. Neither does she say they are objectively real distinctions among people. After all, it is obvious that concepts about human groups, both folk and scientific, are useful in their context. For example, because the vast majority of the people who checked the "other" or "other race" boxes in the past two censuses were Hispanic, it is logical to look for a cause for that behavior that is rooted in that shared trait.

If, as Rodríguez makes clear, categories of people are not eternal, a science of human categories must explain how those categories come to be made and unmade—including how they are made and unmade within science. In place of the great master category, something else is needed: the self-aware, locally useful, answers-one-well-defined-question category. But the language hasn't been worked out.

What is clear, though, is this: The value of contemplating the abandoned pigeon-holes of the past is not in the cheap pleasure of tsk-tsk-ing the folly of long-dead people. Rather than shoring up contemporary smugness, Rodríguez's book teaches two useful lessons. First, what is important to understand is not the "objective" value of this or that category of person, but rather how the process of category formation works. Social science needs to understand how pigeonholes are made, not any particular pigeonhole.

Second, as citizens, we ought to be humble about our own certainties, which are as much a product of ill-understood processes as were those of 1850 or 1910. Our descendants will find our categories for people quaint and silly. But if our social science can decipher how we—and they—exercise the category-making system, then that science will have earned the kind of respect that is now accorded to physics and biology. The great social problem of the twenty-first century is waiting, in plain sight, to be solved.

Discussion Questions

1. Think about your first impressions of a new acquaintance. How important is his or her apparent "race" or ethnicity to you? Do you tend to assume certain personality traits on the basis of a person's physical appearance? What do you think your own appearance says to others?
2. Think of examples of human variation that are **not** usually considered "racial" characteristics, such as height, left-handedness, and the presence of hair on one's knuckles. Why don't we use this variation as the basis for "racial" categorization?
3. What are the dangers involved in assuming that all members of one "race" will have certain character traits in common? Give examples from law enforcement and from medicine.
4. Construct a chart showing how the census has classified people differently over the decades.
5. What happened to the structure of the census in 1980 that resulted in an apparent browning of America—meaning the sudden increase in the percent of the population that was Hispanic?
6. Imagine that there eventually comes a time when no one in the United States discriminates for or against anyone else because of their perceived racial or ethnic heritage. Would there then be any reason to gather such data on census forms?
7. What does Berreby mean when he refers to the pigmentocracies of Latin America and the Caribbean? Is there also a pigmentocracy among people in the United States who consider themselves African American?
8. In 1890 the U.S. census included such categories as mulatto, quadroon, and octoroon. These terms are seldom used anymore. What did they mean originally?
9. People who have even a single distant ancestor from Africa are usually described as African Americans, even if their facial features (and likewise an analysis of their genes) show a preponderance of European ancestry. Why is this the case?
10. Many U.S. college students (of primarily European ancestry) claim to have a "Cherokee grandmother." Why Cherokee? Why a grandmother? And why would people want to claim Native American ancestry, which almost always turns out to be fictitious?

16. INTERRACIAL GENERATION: WE ARE WHO WE ARE

This essay, written by a Seattle Times *staff reporter in 1996 when the racial and ethnic categories for the 2000 census were being debated, touches on some of the same issues as the previous selection. Strickland focuses particularly on children whose parents belong to two different ethnic categories. Are they the same race/ethnicity as their father or their mother? Or are they all of the above? People with multiple racial/ethnic heritages would like the option of choosing more than one category on the census. For the first time the census of 2000 allowed them to do just that. The state of Washington is one of the more diverse states in the United States, with especially diverse Asian immigrants from many different countries, as well as European Americans, African Americans, and so on.*

Fears of the masses all choosing more than one category turned out to be unfounded. Almost 275 million people (98 percent) chose just one racial category from among these choices: White, Black or African American, American Indian and Alaska Native, Asian, Native Hawaiian, Other Pacific Islander, and "Some other race." Another 6.3 million chose two categories and almost 500,000 chose three or more categories. "Hispanic" was not one of the racial options, but a separate question was asked about Hispanic ethnicity. Of people who indicated they were ethnically Hispanic, close to half said they were racially "White," while about 42 percent chose the "Some other race" category.

This selection voices the concerns of specific individuals who find the whole concept of racial categorization frustrating and pointless.

She is a scoop of Neapolitan ice cream, black, white and Native American swirled into one. A curious confection for those who view the world as single-dipped flavors, rather than triple-treats.

With shoulder-length hair, hazel green eyes and a tan complexion, Minty Nelson defies easy labeling. For as long as she can remember, others have stared at her, whispered about her, demanded of her: What color are you? Then one day, Uncle Sam wanted to know.

Describing her race on the latest U.S. Census form, Nelson marked three boxes instead of one. Within weeks, a Census counter appeared at her door, wondering which one was correct.

"All three," Nelson replied.

"Can't be all three," the middle-aged woman told her, "just one."

Back and forth they went, their patience ebbing. The woman rolled her eyes, sighing in gusts; Nelson spoke in monotones. Twenty minutes later, drained from the experience, Nelson stopped. She told the woman to pick a box, any box, herself.

"None of them was going to be accurate," said Nelson, a 27-year-old Seattle University employee and student, though the observer checkmarked something.

Odd thing was, Nelson couldn't remember what. Still can't.

Something Other than "Other"

From Mariah Carey singing it, to golfer Tiger Woods talking it, from campus and community support groups organizing over it, to a number of books, movies, magazines, conferences, and online sites educating about it, to more and more people coping with it, an **interracial generation** coalesces into prominence.

Wanting to be known as something other than "other," they are demanding that the government record multiracial heritages on U.S. Census forms more accurately. Further rousing support for that notion, an online magazine, *Interracial Voice,* has planned a July 20 rally in Washington, D.C.

If what's white is black, or red or yellow or brown, the issue could radically change the national dialogue on race, breaking down the notion of white racial purity, a chief underpinning of racism. It could change the way race, ethnicity and culture are viewed—even the way people see themselves.

But others believe a separate identity will divide the nation even more sharply along color lines. Laws and remedies, designed to ensure fairness, voting rights and equal opportunity, could be undermined. And the political and economic clout of minority groups could be diluted at a time when racial tensions have frayed over affirmative action, job cutbacks, welfare reform, the legal system, and race-based remedies in general.

"(Establishing a multiracial category) suggests we live in a color-blind society where people are considered as individuals, and on individual merit alone," said Gary Flowers of the Lawyers Committee for Civil Rights, a Washington, D.C.-based legal group, a leading advocate resisting the change. "But people are still discriminated against based on how they look."

A Richer Pot

Nearly everyone can trace racial mixture in their heritage as the nation's melting pot thickens, growing richer than ever before.

The rate of married **interracial** couples has jumped 275 percent since 1970, while the rate for same-race couples has grown only 16 percent. Almost two out of three Japanese-Americans marry outside their race. And since 1970, the white non-Hispanic population has declined 12 percent to 75 percent overall.

"Society is changing in a way that it hasn't changed in 100 years," said Rep. Thomas Sawyer (D-Ohio), who chaired hearings of the House Subcommittee on Census, Statistics and Postal Records into which racial categories should be listed on Census 2000. "We are arguably the most extraordinary mixture of humanity ever gathered under one flag. It means that we are producing succeeding generations that blur those lines even within nuclear families."

Washington state has followed a similar path. During the 1980s, the ethnic minority population grew three times faster than that of whites. And in a state that never barred matrimony between people of different races, 4 percent of the nation's mixed couples live here, according to the last census.

Significant change occurred in King, Pierce, and Snohomish counties as well. Consider that almost half of all African-American children in the tricounty area are born to **interracial** couples. That more than twice as many Native American children are born to white, not Native American, mothers. And that more Filipino infants are biracial than monoracial.

"Everybody knows somebody who's mixed: a friend, a relative, a co-worker, a neighbor, a grocer," said Maria P. P. Root, who teaches multiracialism at the University of Washington and who has written a book, *The Multiracial Experience:*

Racial Borders as the New Frontier. "It's becoming that common, and all the evidence points to more in the future."

During festivals and cultural events, books on multiracial identity sell briskly when Karen Maeda Allman points them out to curious parents often holding the hand of their biracial child. "A lot of times," said the outreach director at Red & Black Books, "they get excited because they don't know such a thing exists, especially if I'm in places like Richland, Puyallup or Mount Vernon."

The 37-year-old Allman, who is part Japanese and part Caucasian, has been described differently every decade on the Census, most recently as "other." As a child, she remembers her father arguing with a Census taker that young Allman should not be categorized as his race, white, which is what the enumerator wrote down anyway. Recently her father became a Census taker, to play a role in accurate recordings.

"It was a funny thing in our family," Allman said. "It was so obvious I was a part-Japanese kid." Given a choice, she would rather check a multiracial box instead of federal observers deciding her race. "I'd like the existence of people like me to be recognized."

Determining Categories

On the third floor of the Old Executive Building, next to the White House, stands the Office of Management and Budget, the agency that determines racial and ethnic standards in statistics and federal forms, like the Census.

Statistical Directive 15, established in 1977, recognizes four major races: White, Black, American Indian or Alaskan Native, Asian or Pacific Islander. Ethnicity also was divided into Hispanic Origin and Not of Hispanic Origin.

These categories, stamped on job applications, college entrance forms, mortgages and bank loans, also are used to enforce the Voting Rights Act, civil rights, and public health statistics.

Ever since Thomas Jefferson supervised the first Census in 1790, documented race has changed nearly decade to decade, reflecting temporal bias. Then, those with one drop of black blood were considered slaves, a rule that helped define racial superiority. Its legacy spread.

In the 1890 Census survey, for instance, there were categories for White, Black, Mulatto, Quadroon, Octaroon, Chinese, Japanese and Indian. By the 1930s, listings were changed to include Mexicans and Negroes, Hindus and Koreans. From 1920 to 1940, Asian Indians were considered Hindus; from 1950 to 1970 as white; and in the past two surveys, as Asian/Pacific Islander.

Since the 1960s, there has been a biracial baby boom, the result of liberal immigration laws and the U.S. Supreme Court's rejection of state bans on **interracial** marriage. By 1991, a Gallup Poll found for the first time that more Americans approved of marriage between whites and blacks (48 percent) than disapproved (42 percent), though blacks looked at it more favorably than whites.

The current conflict differs from the past in this way: Never have the categories remained fixed during a wave of population changes; but never have there been civil rights laws to protect the disadvantaged, which require rigid racial boundaries.

During public comment at the Census hearings two years ago, more than 750 letter writers asked for new categories, among them: Asian and Pacific Islanders wanting separate identities; native Hawaiians asking to be lumped with Native

Americans; Middle Easterners desiring distinction from whites; and even Germans clamoring for change.

"It's becoming clear that the categories are no longer adequate to meet the many ways people perceive themselves," said Sawyer, acknowledging that "enormous bias" in society requires safeguards against discrimination. "The most accurate thing we can say is that maybe we can diminish the distortions."

That leaves many biracials wanting to identify as they see themselves: as a blended individual. Take Scott Watanabe, who embraces his Japanese and African-American heritage. "It is other people who expect you to choose," he said.

Watanabe grew up with the family story of his African-American mother, just out of labor, waiting for the head nurse to lay her daughter in her arms. "Is there a Mrs. Watanabe?" the nurse announced in the room. When the mother answered, "That's me," the nurse asked the question again, and again, ignoring the mother's reply. Exasperated, the nurse found the father, who confirmed his wife and child.

"Even before I was born, race was a part of my life," said Watanabe, 26, who's moving to Japan this month to explore his heritage. He disdains generic racial categories that at best describe skin color—not the individual.

"The concept of race used today is garbage," he said. "It's good that people are trying to change the designations so that race is more accurate in reflecting reality." Ethnicity is a better gauge for accuracy since race is divisive, and lacks scientific merit. "Until we get to that point," he said, "I'll treat the idea of race with the respect it deserves—none."

Black—or White?

When Susan Graham's son was born 11 years ago, she wondered about things that perhaps more mothers find themselves worrying about: How would society perceive him? As black, like his father, or as white, like his mother?

As executive director of Georgia-based Project RACE (Reclassify All Children Equally), Graham has been advocating change ever since. Over the past five years, her voluntary group has testified before Congress and helped lobby seven states (Ohio, Illinois, Michigan, Indiana, North Carolina, Florida and Georgia) to include a "multiracial" box on state or school forms.

"(Choosing only one box) forces us to deny parents," said Graham, whose son has been listed as white on the Census, black at school and multiracial at home. She believes multiracials should have the option to honor their heritages. "The labels given to a group are important for self-identification and pride."

Maybe those labels would have helped Fredrick Cloyd, who grew up in Japan yearning for playmates but was shunned because of his African-American-Cherokee-Welsh-Japanese-Chinese-European ancestry. One day, four older boys said the 6-year-old Cloyd could join them on a hike. Out of sight, one of them asked: "Is your blood red like ours?" Suddenly, three of the boys grabbed his arms and legs, while the other beat him with a baseball bat, leaving him with a concussion and broken nose and finger.

The taunts and discrimination continued when he moved to America as a teenager, and even later as he coached U.S. Junior Olympic Volleyball. Critics described his training methods as "too Oriental," triggering a torrent of emotion stored up over a lifetime. At 27, he broke down. He quit the team and confined himself to his one-room apartment for six months.

"Almost all of my problems . . . 90 percent were due to race," said Cloyd, 42, who became a Buddhist monk for four years in hopes of finding spirituality. "All the apartments, or jobs I didn't get, the names I was called, were always racial. I had to find a way out."

Now, as owner of a self-development firm in Seattle, Cloyd prefers racial categories be abandoned, period. "I want to transcend the categories and the baggage that comes along with it. I'm not denying the racial categories; I just don't want to conform to what you think is black, or Japanese."

Others agree. "I'd love to get rid of the categories," said Ramona E. Douglass, president of the Association of MultiEthnic Americans, a California-based umbrella group of 17 affiliates nationwide. "But as long as we have them, I don't intend to be invisible."

Born to a Sicilian mother and a black and American Indian father, she marched in the South during the 1960s and sits on the 2000 Census Advisory Committee, which recommends what race and ethnicity should be included on the survey. She's offended by critics who say advocates are politically naive.

"I was on a radio show recently, and a woman called in saying, 'You need to realize you're black and to get on with life,' " Douglass said. "But if it were reverse, she'd call me a bigot. I'm defining myself and that's a right of any American. When we delineate on racial lines, no one wins; we all lose. My loyalty is to people of like minds, not colors."

Inclusion forms the heart of what G. Reginald Daniel, a sociologist at the University of California, Santa Barbara, calls "the new multiracial consciousness." Rather than a person passing for white, it is a desire to claim one's full heritage, seeing race in a spectrum of grays, promoting understanding, a peaceful role.

Aileen Wrothwell's project is an example. The Seattle University student will use a $21,500 scholarship from Rotary International to study Afro-German literature in Germany, searching for links between biracials in both cultures.

"I could be divided in half over ethnicity if I allowed myself to," said Wrothwell, a Seattle native who graduated from Lakeside School and believes a race category on the Census is not useful. She has Irish-British-German roots from her mother, and African-American and Native American heritage from her father.

"I've found a way to synthesize these different cultural heritages, and I believe it's possible for our larger society to come to some peaceful synthesis as well. Diversity can be a force for unity, and not separation."

Privilege through Skin Tones

Many civil-rights groups have banded together to oppose Census changes. While acknowledging the nation's evolving racial mixture, they believe society still treats people according to visual perceptions of race, and grants privilege by gradations of skin tones.

"We believe strongly that the OMB should not rush to institute the multiracial category when there is clear potential for increasing the racial segregation, discrimination and stigmatization of black Americans," read a statement signed by The Lawyers' Committee for Civil Rights Under Law, the National Association for the Advancement of Colored People, the Urban League and the Joint Center for Political and Economic Studies.

Seven years ago, civil-rights lawyers filed a class-action lawsuit against Shoney's Inc., a large restaurant chain accused of firing, belittling or not promoting blacks because of their skin color. White managers even described times when blacks were fired for being too visible.

Shoney's agreed to a series of commitments and eventually settled the suit for $134 million. But multiracial statistics would have confused the issue, said the Rev. Joseph E. Lowery, head of the Southern Christian Leadership Conference.

"I don't know how we could have dealt with them if we couldn't determine how many blacks they had hired. I don't know how we would have evaluated how fair its practices are in hiring and promotion," said Lowery, who helped found the organization with the Rev. Martin Luther King Jr. nearly 30 years ago. "We would be hard pressed to fight for racial justice if we were not able to identify people defined in certain categories."

While there is great mixture in the Asian, Native American and Hispanic communities, as well, not everyone is convinced change is called for. "We oppose the multiracial box. We're not sure what it does, how it's counted and what it means," said Eric Rodriguez, a policy analyst at the National Council of La Raza, an umbrella group representing more than 200 community-based groups and more than 2 million Hispanics.

For several years, those applying for state jobs have had the option of choosing their race, in broad terms, by checking as many boxes that applied to them, or selecting "multiracial." About one out of 25 applicants mark multiracial, said Roy Standifer, the state's workforce diversity manager, who was appointed to a five-member subcommittee that will study the practical effects if such a category were implemented on the Census.

There are varying estimates to the number of minorities across the country, especially African Americans, who would check a multiracial box. A *Newsweek* poll conducted a year ago showed that more blacks (49 percent) favored the category than whites (36 percent).

But the government, through polls and hearings, hasn't found anywhere near that kind of practical support yet. The latest survey, released last November, showed less than 2 percent chose multiracial.

Starting next month, another study will be launched in hopes of solving the issue by mid-1997. Among the deciding factors include whether the change justifies the cost of training observers, changing forms and maintaining continuity of records.

Relating to Everybody

A few years ago, Minty Nelson, working as a medical transcriber, waited for word of her next assignment. It was in South-Central Los Angeles, during the second day of the rioting, an area she had visited many times.

While watching the mayhem on television, her boss called, saying don't go. Puzzled, Nelson asked why. "We think they won't recognize you as a black woman in the car," her boss said, "and we don't want anything to happen to you." Nelson tried to brush off the remark, but it hurt too much. I'm not black enough. I don't belong! She just watched television, with tears in her eyes, until she fell asleep past midnight.

In her current job in Seattle University's Office of Minority Student Affairs, she feels she relates to everyone. "Not a whole lot of people can do that," said Nelson, who, having been adopted along with a Korean girl by white parents with a blond-haired boy of their own, feels steeped in tolerance.

For years she wished for an appearance that made her identity obvious, but she refuses to carry that baggage anymore. When she hugs her two daughters, commonly perceived as African Americans, she hopes they are proud of their heritage—not just a piece of it.

"I'd be so hurt if only part of me were acceptable to them," as if "only part of me were decent, and that's not true," Nelson said. "You are who you are, and you can't change it."

Discussion Questions

1. In 1996 what prompted the debate about the 2000 census categories?
2. Why were people excited about new categories for race and ethnicity?
3. What new choices were offered on the 2000 census? How was Hispanic-ness treated?
4. Study the paragraph that begins "Significant change occurred in King, Pierce and Snohomish counties as well." How does Strickland phrase his words to make his point? What model of inheritance of race/ethnicity is he clearly following here? Is he aware of it?
5. Until what decade did many U.S. states ban interracial marriages?
6. What does Scott Watanabe have to say about his experience as a child of a Japanese father and an African-American mother?
7. Why did Susan Graham start Project RACE? What are the goals of Project RACE?
8. How is Frederick Cloyd described? Why do you suppose he lists continents (Africa, Europe) and countries (Japan, China, Wales), but then specifies Cherokee ancestry, instead of saying Native American?
9. Why are many civil rights organizations opposed to the new categories?
10. Does anyone in class have ancestors who all came from a single country?

Additional Resources

For Internet links related to this chapter, please visit our website at www.mhhe.com/dettwyler

CAVALLI-SFORZA, LUIGI LUCA, and FRANCESCO CAVALLI-SFORZA. *The Great Human Diasporas: The History of Diversity and Evolution.* Cambridge, MA: Perseus Publishing, 1996.

COHEN, MARK NATHAN. *Culture of Intolerance: Chauvinism, Class, and Racism in the United States.* New Haven, CT: Yale University Press, 1999.

D'ALUISIO, FAITH, PETER MENZEL, and NAOMI WOLF. *Women in the Material World.* San Francisco, CA: Sierra Club Books, 1996.

EIBL-EIBESFELDT, IRENAUS, and FRANK K. SALTER, eds. *Ethnic Conflict and Indoctrination.* Oxford, England: Berghahn Books, 2001.

MENZEL, PETER, CHARLES C. MANN, and PAUL KENNEDY. *Material World: A Global Family Portrait.* San Francisco, CA: Sierra Club Books, 1995.

MOLNAR, STEPHEN. *Human Variation: Races, Types, and Ethnic Groups.* Upper Saddle River, NJ: Prentice Hall, 1997.

OLSON, STEVE. *Mapping Human History: Discovering the Past Through Our Genes.* New York: Houghton Mifflin Co., 2002.

RODRÍGUEZ, CLARA A. *Changing Race: Latinos, the Census and the History of Ethnicity in the United States.* New York: New York University Press, 2000.

ROOT, MARIA P. P., eds. *The Multiracial Experience: Racial Borders As the New Frontier.* Thousand Oaks, CA: Sage Publications, 1996.

The First Farmers

17. "First to Ride," by William Speed Weed, *Discover* 23, no. 3 (March 2002), pp. 54–61.

18. "Invisible Clues to New World Plant Domestication," by Vaughn M. Bryant, *Science* 299 (February 14, 2003).

19. "Who Were the First Americans?" by Sasha Nemecek, *Scientific American,* September 20, 2000 (from website www.sciam.com/article.cfm?article ID=000333F5-D417-1C73-9B81809EC588EF21).

Archaeologists do not agree on a number of points regarding the prehistory of humans and the changes humans have made in their environment. Before there were cities and state societies with their large agricultural complexes, people subsisted only by foraging and later by simple forms of farming and animal herding. One big question is, When, where, and how did early humans domesticate other animals? Were these animals domesticated for companionship, to help humans hunt, as captive hunting populations, or for transportation? What impact did domestication by humans have on the animal populations? What sort of impact, in turn, did the domestication of animals have on human culture and biology? Another big question is, When, where, and how did humans first domesticate plants? We know this happened independently on several continents, involving different plant species. Yet another big question is, When, where, and how did early humans cross from the Old World, the site of all early hominid evolution, to the New World? There is still little agreement on who, when, and how many humans first ventured into the New World of the Americas. There is even some dispute as to whether those first settlers arrived by sea in South America and then moved northward, or landed in boats along the coastal regions of Alaska and then moved southward. Another view claims these first Americans crossed over a land bridge between Siberia and Alaska and then walked southward all the way to the southern tip of South America. The three selections in this chapter provide a taste of ongoing research, discussions, and controversies in archaeology.

Dogs are believed to have been the first domesticated animals. How do we know this? Because we find signs of love and affection toward dogs as evidenced by dog burials that date as early as 12,000 to 13,000 years ago. Domestication also changed the shape of the dog's skull. Skeletal evidence proving domestication of other animals is more challenging. In horses, for example, modern domestic horse bones look identical to those of their wild ancestors thousands of years ago. If that is true, then how can archaeologists know when and where horses and other similar animals were first domesticated? The answers come not from changes in the bone structure, as they do in dogs, but from a study of thousands of animal bones in archaeological sites. The numbers and ratio of bones from one animal species, in terms of the total number of male versus female and young versus old, are often the best clues. This technique is now offering the best evidence of when and where horses were first domesticated—an event that some have called "a momentous turning point in human history."

Archaeologists have long known that horses were domesticated much later than some other well-known animals such as goats, sheep, pigs, and cattle. For many years, people believed that horses were first tamed and ridden in the Ukraine region near the Black Sea around 6,000 years ago. The evidence was a horse skull from an archaeological site that showed bit-wear on the teeth, a feature that one would expect to find only in a domestic horse. Recent radiocarbon dating of the bones, however, revealed that the skull is younger, perhaps only 2,400 years old. Meanwhile, other studies at sites farther east on the short-grass plains of Kazakhstan have unearthed the remains of 6,000-year-old Botai peoples who lived in pit houses and relied on horsemeat as their primary source of food,* The question that archaeologists are now trying to answer is whether those bones came from wild horses the Botai hunted or were from domestic horses that were corralled, killed, and then eaten as food.

Sandra Olsen stands knee-deep in summer grass on a sprawling plain in northern Kazakhstan, peering at horse herders creeping antlike over a golden hill miles away. Kazakhs have roamed this cold dry grassland on horseback for centuries and are renowned for their ability to shoot arrows with accuracy while bouncing atop galloping steeds. As Olsen watches mammoth clouds gathering on the horizon, she envisions a time thousands of years ago when these plains were inhabited by hardy hunter-gatherers who lived on horse meat but did not know how to ride the horses they hunted. She muses on how radically their world must have changed when one of them finally climbed aboard a horse, tamed it, and rode like the wind. "Prior to horseback riding, most people carried all their cargo on their shoulders, or they were restricted to using boats along rivers and coastlines," says Olsen, an archaeologist at the Carnegie Museum of Natural History in Pittsburgh. "Horses were swift of foot, could easily support one or two human passengers, carry heavy loads, and survive on very poor quality vegetation or fodder. They were our first form of rapid transit."

Ultimately, the taming of horses turned out to be a momentous turning point in human history. "Horses caused the first globalization," says Melinda Zeder, an archaeologist at the Smithsonian Institution in Washington, D.C. "They allowed cul-

*As evidenced by the bones of horses.

tures to grow from isolated pockets to interconnected spheres of influence." Archaeologists generally agree that this historical upheaval began in the only region on Earth where horses survived in significant numbers after the Ice Age: the vast Eurasian steppe that stretches from the Carpathian Mountains in Hungary to the Altaí Mountains in Mongolia thousands of miles away. Researchers also agree that domestication occurred before 3000 B.C., when horses suddenly started showing up in distant places like Turkey and Switzerland. But one of the most enduring archaeological mysteries has yet to be resolved. Who were the original horsemen, and what inspired them to straddle a 1,000-pound beast that could kick out their brains with one blow?

Every summer Olsen returns to this spot in the heart of the Eurasian steppe, hoping to prove that her version of history is correct. Beneath her black Reeboks and the knee-high grass lies a village that a primitive people known as the Botai lived in 6,000 years ago. Excavations at this site, dubbed Krasnyi Yar, and another site less than 100 miles to the west, have revealed that the Botai endured a harsh existence. They lived in pit houses dug into the ground and half-covered with some structure that has since rotted away. During winter, which lasts nearly nine months of the year, they dressed in the furs of various small mammals, huddled around fires, and ate horse meat. And they left behind some clues: Their pit houses are chock-full of bones, 90 percent of them from horses.

What's not immediately evident is whether those horses were wild or tame, or both. But after eight years of careful detective work, Olsen thinks she has deciphered the tale the bones have to tell. The Botai people not only hunted and herded horses for food, she says, they also used them as a means of transport. If she's right, then she has found the earliest-known horsemen and, quite possibly, the inventors of riding.

Olsen and her team have set up camp in a copse of windswept trees a few hundred yards from the ancient Krasnyi Yar site. There are two dozen sleep tents, a large circular-domed yurt that serves as the mess hall, and a rusty mobile home referred to by the Russian word *vagon*. The vagon is Olsen's lab, complete with microscopes, measuring tools, laptop computers, and a growling propane generator. It's the little house on the prairie where Olsen, a native Kansan, brings a long-lost world alive. "I don't care much for living horses," she says, conscious of the irony. "It's their bones I like."

Archaeologists who study the domestication of other animals have a much easier time analyzing skeletal artifacts. "With dogs, pigs, sheep, and cattle, you can see morphological changes in their bones" over time, says Olsen, sitting on a small wooden chair that looks like it was borrowed from a grade school. For example, when dogs were tamed and bred to be much more docile than their wild wolf cousins, their snouts and their brain cases changed shape. Likewise, domesticated cows are much smaller than the now-extinct aurochs from which they descended. Nothing like that happened with horses. "It would be great to pick up a bone and say, 'This was a wild horse, this was a tame horse,'" says Olsen as she plucks a phalanx (toe bone) from the plethora of skeleton parts scattered about the vagon. "But we can't. For all we know from its shape, it could be modern, it could be Ice Age, it could be Botai domesticated, it could be Botai wild."

Still, the bones do offer information. "For a long time, people thought they could get around the lack of morphological changes by looking for other marks that showed domestication, most notably bit-wear on the teeth," says Olsen. In the early 1960s Russian archaeologists excavated a 6,000-year-old site in Ukraine called Dereivka, where they found a stallion skull that had distinctive beveling on its teeth.

They thought that was unequivocal evidence of a riding bit. As a result, the Sredny Stog people who had inhabited the site in prehistoric times "went in all the textbooks," says Olsen, as the earliest known horseback riders. But some scientists, including Olsen, remained skeptical. "I mean, how are you going to get hard-metal scrape marks on a Copper Age tooth?" she asks, shaking her head. Then, three years ago, new radiocarbon-dating techniques revealed that the skull was actually 2,400 years old. "It was an Iron Age horse whose grave had been dug down into a more ancient settlement," says Olsen.

There will be no such obvious clues in Krasnyi Yar, but Olsen is quite content to slowly tease subtle evidence from her cache. After measuring the size of individual bones and carefully examining the teeth, she runs statistical tabulations for breakdowns of the horse population by sex and age at the time of death. Then she looks for mortality patterns that might help distinguish domesticated stock from victims of the hunt. Zeder of the Smithsonian pioneered this technique in a study of goat domestication at a site in Iran. She discovered that the people who lived there 9,000 years ago killed off most of the male goats by age 2, about the time they reached sexual maturity. The females were allowed to live past 4. If the people were killing wild goats, this mortality pattern wouldn't make any sense, says Zeder. "The hunter is after the bigger meat package. To maximize the hunt, he kills adult male goats, not 2-year-olds." The pattern makes sense for livestock and is still a standard practice of modern goat herders, who keep a few select males around for reproduction but kill off the rest before they start making trouble.

The mortality pattern Olsen has found among horses at the Botai sites is similar to the hunting pattern Zeder predicted for goats: The males are fully grown and slightly outnumber females. "But," Olsen says, "hunting horses is different from hunting goats, and domesticated horses are not just livestock." Wild horses live in two groups: families and bachelors. Families consist of a single stallion, a half-dozen females, and their young; bachelor pods consist of two or three young males. "The families stick together when they're attacked," Olsen says. "But the male twosomes have no loyalty. They'll just take off in opposite directions." The way to maximize a horse hunt is to attack the mostly female families. So if the Botai were just horse hunters, Olsen reasons, she'd be seeing many more female bones around their pit houses.

Olsen says one other difference between the mortality patterns of goats and horses may be more significant. Unlike goat herders, who can afford to cull young males because humans don't ride goats, ancient horsemen would likely keep young males alive and ride them, which suggests that a purely domestic mortality pattern for horses might be weighted heavily toward older males, Olsen says. But the Botai mortality pattern is more balanced. She offers a simple explanation: "They hunted wild horses from horseback."

In the process of measuring the Botai horse bones, Olsen says she found other, very large clues staring her in the face: "Full skeletons of horses, entire vertebral columns, and pelvises. The Botai didn't just leave behind horse parts. They've got whole horses." Olsen is tall and fit enough to lug water crates, dig trenches, and perform the various chores of running a dig in the middle of the wide-open steppe. But the muscle power required to heft giant horse bones on and off the measuring table made her think of the Botai in the same spot 6,000 years ago: How far would they have been willing to move whole horses? "I don't think they went out, miles overland on foot, killed a horse, and dragged the whole 1,000-pound thing back here," she says. They'd more likely butcher a wild horse in the field, divide up the meat for easy carrying, and leave heavy and nonnutritious parts behind. In that case, she argues, you wouldn't find the spine and hips in the Botai village pit houses. "Yet we find them," says Olsen, who suggests that the full skeletons are the remains of domesticated horses as well as wild horses hauled home whole by means of living horses. She calls this bit of reasoning "the schlep effect."

The schlep effect should also extend to other materials. Olsen is curious about quartzite stone scrapers she found at Krasnyi Yar, so she has sent out graduate students on geological surveys to find the quarry, which, even after 6,000 years, should still be visible. They haven't found it, and if it turns out to be a great distance away—more than 50 miles—she'll argue that the Botai must have had horses to go so far on a regular basis. But stone chips and flakes unearthed in recent excavations indicate that the Botai were carrying home chunks of rock larger than a human could carry long-distance.

A light rain falls as a monstrous thunderhead passes to the north, raising a rapid-fire din on the tin roof of the vagon and dousing the far-off horse herders. Meanwhile, Olsen, an avid outdoorswoman who is usually disappointed to be forced inside by nasty weather, uses the time to consider how the earliest riders may have developed the first horse tackle.

"They probably had a simple bridle made of hide or hemp," she says, drawing a little schematic of a rope looped around the front teeth of a horse's skull. They might also have had lassos, whips, tethers, and hobbles of the same material. Most of the tackle we now associate with horses, from saddles to stirrups, are sophistications that were invented well into the history of riding. Because of the Dereivka bit-wear fiasco, Olsen has had little interest in pursuing direct evidence for riding gear. Nonetheless, there is indirect evidence so plentiful among the Botai horse bones that she can't ignore it. Hundreds of jawbones have tiny rubbing marks on them. These marks aren't evidence of riding, Olsen says. That part of the jaw is covered in flesh when a horse is alive. But Olsen thinks the Botai may have used tools fashioned out of horse jawbones as a tool to make their riding ropes.

She grabs a boomerang-shaped horse jaw to explain. "This is a thong smoother," she says, pointing to the inside curve of the boomerang. "Using a scanning electron microscope, we've looked at this notch on dozens of these jawbones, and they've all been worn down by the rubbing of some sort of leather," she says. "If you put a strip of hide in the notch and pull it back and forth, any bendy piece will straighten out into strong usable leather," she explains. Without a thong smoother, the longest piece of straight leather one can make is the same length as a horsehide, about six feet. With a thong smoother, the hide can be cut in a spiral, then straightened to create a strip of leather a dozen yards long.

Olsen points out that the Botai had more thong smoothers than cooking pots. "It's a regular thong factory out here. I don't think they built their homes with them." Botai houses are 175-square-foot pits that would have been covered with thatch or adobe mud. "It's a deductive argument to say that they're making horse tackle. But they used them for something," she says.

Unable to avoid the rain any longer, Olsen dashes to the nearby yurt for lunch: a traditional bowl of buckwheat groats, called *gretchka,* which she and her colleagues Bruce Bradley and Alan Outram don't exactly love. "But it's pretty good for out here," says Outram, a proper young British lecturer in archaeology at Exeter University in England. Olsen tells Outram and Bradley about the artifacts she and other archaeologists unearthed at the other Botai site in the years before they joined her dig here at Krasnyi Yar. Among the hundreds of thong smoothers and stone scrapers, there are bird bones made into awls and beaver jaws used for woodworking. There are also lots of marmot foot bones, which suggest that the Botai wore marmot furs but didn't bother to debone the tiny feet. Most of the pit houses have dog burials near the west door: The dogs that guarded the house in life could ritually guard it after death.

Olsen turns excitedly to the topic of human burial, a subject archaeologists apparently deem suitable mealtime conversation. There aren't many human bones at the Botai sites, she says. Perhaps they didn't bury their dead, or perhaps they buried them some distance from the houses, and those graves haven't been found. But there is evidence from two ritual burials at the other Botai site, and the more she becomes convinced that the Botai rode horses, the more sense the burials make.

The evidence from one burial includes a decapitated human skull found in a pit, with traces of a yellow clay mask and two little holes bored through the crown. "I looked at the skull with a scanning electron microscope to see how they'd skinned him," Olsen says. "It was done with great respect, with slow, careful cuts. Then they put flesh-toned clay on him. Perhaps the holes were for tying on a wig of some sort so that the skull resembled him in life." The effigy was laid to rest in a pit with the tools of his trade: a thong smoother, a hunting arrow, and the jaws of a horse. In a second burial, two men, a woman, and a child were found in a large pit encircled with the skulls, vertebrae, and pelvises of 14 horses. "A family with their mounts," Olsen says. "It would be a truly remarkable ritual if these were 14 wild horses," especially because the schlep problem would have involved 14,000 pounds of horseflesh, says Bradley.

Outram's specialty is determining how ancient people used animal fats, and Olsen has asked him to investigate another line of evidence that could bolster her argument that the Botai rode horses. Modern-day Kazakhs make a lightly fermented mare's milk drink called koumiss. Olsen says it "tastes like stomach bile," but Kazakhs love it, and it has been a staple of the steppe horse herders' diet since before anyone can remember. Maybe, Olsen reasons, it goes all the way back to the Botai. So she has asked Outram to test Botai pottery shards for mare's milk.

Outram first journeyed into remote Kazakh villages to collect regional samples of mare's milk. The herders, most of whom had never seen a Westerner, obliged with proud smiles, milking their mares into wooden pails and pouring the thin white liquid into Outram's lab-sterile plastic bags. He also cut chunks of fat from carcasses at local meat stalls. Back in England, his laboratory task will be to distinguish lipid compounds found in horse fat (which could linger in the pots of people who only hunted horses) from lipid compounds found exclusively in the milk. If he can identify mare's-milk lipids in Botai pottery, then he has proof they were milking horses. "Unless you're going to tell me they're milking wild horses," says Olsen, laughing.

If Olsen's work convinces other archaeologists that the Botai rode horses—and others are beginning to accept the concept—she will have identified the earliest known riders. That still won't mean they were the first, she says: "Archaeologists tend not to ask the question 'Did it happen here first?' It's enough for us to say, 'This is the earliest evidence we've got.'"

Some archaeologists, like David Anthony of Hartwick College in upstate New York, find the Botai implausible first horse tamers. Anthony contends that "horses almost certainly were first domesticated for use as food animals, like cattle or pigs, by a culture, like the Sredny Stog, already practiced in the art of herding cattle." Olsen responds: "I think you get yourself into trouble if you start making presumptions about what is plausible and what is not. Human beings are weird and imaginative. They frequently do implausible things," such as get on the back of a creature that charges overland at 30 miles an hour.

Outside the yurt, the rain has passed. The bright sun on the summer grass is all the more beautiful for its contrast with the purple storm still lingering on the horizon. For horses this steppe is paradise, an endless sea of grass. For humans it is a harsh and unforgiving place. It's easy to see how, 6,000 years ago, the Botai people's reliance on horses could have been absolute. And it's not hard to imagine the immense benefits they would have gained by bringing the horse under their control, domesticating it. Horses in the corral are larder for the long winter. Horses that have been tamed for riding make the distance to the horizon, and the next wild horse, less daunting.

Most archaeologists dismiss as hindsight the notion that a people invented something because they knew the range of its benefits. Like the inventors of gunpowder, the cotton gin, or the Internet, the first horseback riders likely had no idea of the power of their discovery. Perhaps it was merely a daydreamer loafing in summer grass who envisioned mounting a horse. Perhaps it was a daredevil showing off to his friends, leaping from a tree onto the back of a colt and hanging on to the mane for his life. And, muses Olsen as the distant horse herders emerge from the storm, "perhaps it happened here."

Discussion Questions

1. Studies of domestic goat bones in early village sites suggest that the majority of bones come from male goats under the age of two years. Why do archaeologists believe these young male goat bones are the most common at those sites?
2. If the Botai people living in Kazakhstan 6,000 years ago ate mostly wild horses, what should be the dominant sex and age of horse bones found in their sites?
3. Digging into the remains of Botai pit houses, archaeologists find the spines and hipbones of horses. What does this pattern suggest to the archaeologists?
4. What do the archaeologists hope to discover by searching for the quarry source of the quartzite stone scrapers found in the Botai pit houses?
5. Why were the thong smoothers (made from horse jawbones) important to the Botai?
6. How were horse bones used by the Botai to mark human burials?
7. What do archaeologists hope to learn from conducting chemical tests of the pottery once used by the Botai peoples?
8. Is the primary archeologist working on Botai sites, Dr. Olsen, now convinced that the Botai are indeed the very first people ever to domesticate horses?
9. Discuss how changes in transportation technology can lead to changes in other aspects of culture, such as trade, marriage patterns, subsistence, health, and so on. Include the invention/discovery of simple rafts, more complex boats, sea-going boats, horse riding, bicycles, automobiles, and airplanes.
10. Discuss how your life would be different if you had to walk everywhere you went and could only carry things in your arms.

CHAPTER 10
The First Farmers

Most scientists agree that one of the most important events in all of human history was learning how to domesticate various types of plants and then improve food production even more through selective plant breeding. Archaeological and historical records attest that cultures in all regions of the world experimented with many different types of plants before they discovered the best ones for each type of environment and those that would produce the greatest amounts of food. One of these experimental regions was the New World, consisting of North, Central, and South America. By the time Columbus landed in the Bahamas in 1492, the peoples of the New World had already domesticated over 100 different plants. Some of these plants, such as maize (corn), beans, squash, white and sweet potatoes, peanuts, tomatoes, and chili peppers are now used throughout the world. In some regions, they provide the primary food staple for millions of people. Because of the tremendous cultural changes that accompanied plant domestication, archaeologists have wanted to find when and where the earliest New World domestication of plants began. This search, which started more than a century ago, was thought to have been resolved during the 1960s, when teams of archaeologists working in the highlands of south central Mexico found what seemed to be positive evidence for the earliest plant domestication. The next article in this chapter challenges that idea and discusses new evidence linking the earliest plant domestication with microscopic evidence found in the lowland tropical region of Ecuador.

Four decades ago, excavations in the Tehuacan Valley of Mexico convinced many archaeologists that they now had physical proof of how, when, and where plants were first domesticated in the New World. The proof came in the form of preserved seeds and fruits, maize (corn) kernels and cobs, fibers, and the rinds from cultivated gourds and squash found in cave soils and in preserved human feces originally dated as early as 7,500 to 9,000 years old. Little did these archaeologists realize that the puzzle of New World plant domestication was far from being resolved. Not only would the original plant materials be radiocarbon dated again during the 1980s and found to be much younger (4,700 years old), but later they would also learn that the most critical clues come not from the large and visual remains of plants, but from tiny microscopic particles that most archaeologists unknowingly discarded.

Fortunately, a few researchers were not convinced by the traditional story of New World plant cultigen origins. Dolores Piperno of the Smithsonian Institution and a few others devoted more than three decades to searching the archaeological soils of Central and South America for microscopic phytoliths (plant crystals), tiny starch grains from domesticated plants, and fossil pollen. As noted by Piperno and Stothert (2003) and by Piperno and Pearsall in a recent book (1998), these microscopic traces of plants reliably pinpoint the earliest use of domesticated plants.

Early speculation about the origins of New World plant domestication focused on the upland regions of Mexico and South America. These regions were favored because they were easy to reach, often contained caves or rock shelters filled with preserved plant remains, and already had yielded successes that ensured continued funding. Few archaeologists were willing to search for the origin of plant cultigens in lowland and jungle regions, where seeds, wood, gourd rinds, and corncobs did not preserve well. Many also wondered how tropical lowlands could have supported foragers making the switch to early sedentary farming. And most believed incorrectly that all lowland and jungle soils were infertile, similar to ones known from the non-flood plain regions of the Amazon basin. But Piperno and a few others remained convinced that the long search for cultigen origins in the New World had focused on the wrong areas and the wrong kind of clues.

It is true that, except for charcoal, the visual evidence of plant remains quickly disappears in most tropical soils. But some clues remain, if you know where to look. By the early 1990s, Piperno had shown that plant phytoliths were plentiful in the lowland soils of many regions of Central and South America. She noted that the size and shape of phytoliths were often unique to each family, genus, or species of plants. Piperno and Pearsall then led the way in developing phytolith keys to a wide variety of New World cultigens and tropical plants. Armed with this knowledge, scientists began to search for microscopic clues in the soils of early, well-dated archaeological sites throughout Central and South America.

New studies based on phytolith data soon began to contradict the long-held theory that plant domestication began in upland regions, where many envisioned cave-living foragers being the first to switch to raising cultigens. Archaeologists challenging the new discoveries pointed to potential errors in dating, saying that the phytolith evidence could not possibly be as old as the dates indicated. To quell the critics, phytolith researchers developed new ways of dating tiny bits of carbon trapped inside phytoliths as they were formed.

The new techniques, which use accelerator mass spectrometry (AMS) dating, require the careful collection and separation of many phytoliths. Precise phytolith identification is also critical. Piperno and Stothert collected and measured phytoliths from more than 150 mature fruits from wild and domesticated species of *Cucurbita* (squash and gourds) grown in 100 different tropical locations. They found that the phytoliths from domestic species were substantially larger than those from wild species. The authors then used phytolith size to confirm that domesticated squash and gourds were grown and used during the early Holocene (last 10,000 years) in coastal Ecuador, between 9,000 and 10,000 years ago.

Piperno has also been at the forefront of searching for archaeological evidence of cultigen starch grains. In tropical regions of Central and South America, root crops—including yams, sweet potatoes, and manioc—are the mainstay of many indigenous cultures. These high-calorie tuber crops grow well in the wet soils and areas created by recently cleared tropical forests. But it has been difficult to prove when and where these plants were first domesticated. Tuber-producing crops do not preserve or carbonize well; furthermore, most produce small amounts of pollen and many do not produce diagnostic types of phytoliths. However, they do produce copious numbers of water-insoluble granules called "reserve starch grains," which preserve well on the surfaces of food preparation implements and in many types of tropical soils. Starch grains from domesticated types of tubers recently have been identified on early Holocene grinding stones used by prehistoric groups in Colombia and central Panama.

In 1957, the British pollen analyst Geoffrey Dimbleby stated that soils with a pH above 6 are virtually useless for fossil pollen studies. Because the pH values of almost all tropical soils exceed 6, pollen analysts for decades rarely have searched the tropical soils of Central or South America. I was one of those pollen analysts who spent more than 30 years working at sites in Mexico and South America. I never found well-preserved pollen in any of those sites.

To the astonishment of many, John Jones of Texas A&M University and his colleagues recently recovered pollen from key archaeological sites in Central America. His pollen data confirm the use of early cultigens, including maize and manioc, from the San Andres site in the Mexican tropical lowlands near the Gulf of Mexico in the state of Tabasco. Radiocarbon dating shows that the archaeological deposits containing cultigen pollen are 5,800 to 6,200 years old.

Perhaps DNA studies of soils in archaeological sites may soon replace our current techniques. Until then, our best New World records for early plant domestication origins are coming from the invisible clues: phytoliths, starch grains, and fossil pollen.

Discussion Questions

1. What was the traditional wisdom about when and where the domestication of plants first occurred in the New World? What evidence was there for this view?
2. What are phytoliths? Why are they proving to be useful clues to early plant use?
3. For many years archaeologists searched for the earliest records of plant domestication only in the highland regions of Central and South America. Why?
4. How do researchers date phytoliths accurately?
5. Piperno claims that the earliest evidence of plant domestication in the New World occurred earlier than previously thought, and in the lowlands. How old is her evidence and where does it come from?
6. Working in the lowland regions of Central America, John Jones recently found the earliest pollen evidence of corn (maize) cultivation. Where did he find the pollen and how old is it?
7. The author says that perhaps an even newer technique may soon replace the ones currently used in the search for the earliest plant domestication in the New World. What is this new and potentially useful technique?

 ## 19. WHO WERE THE FIRST AMERICANS?

In the poem, "Paul Revere's Ride," by Henry Wadsworth Longfellow, one line reads, "One if by land, and two if by sea." In the poem the passage refers to a lantern hung from a church steeple that would signal Paul Revere whether British troops were leaving their garrison to march to battle, or if they instead embarked on ships that would carry them up the coastline in a surprise attack on American troops. Unfortunately, we do not have a lantern signal confirming how the Americas were settled. Instead, the peopling of the Americas has been, and continues to be, one of the most heated and debated topics in American archaeology. Until the 1920s there was little evidence to suggest that people had arrived much earlier than perhaps 3,000 or 4,000 years ago. However, as new sites were found showing clear associations between human hunters and long-extinct animals, the clock got pushed back. Some suggested that a group we now call the Clovis Culture were the first, and that they walked into North America from Siberia no earlier than perhaps 14,000 years ago. That view is now under attack based on archaeological evidence from South America and from sites in eastern North America such as Meadowcroft and Cactus Hills. These new bits of evidence suggest that the First Americans may have arrived 20,000 or 30,000 years ago, or perhaps even earlier. Recent DNA results, the diversities of language in the Americas, and a growing belief that the first people may have reached the Americas by sea, have each added fuel to this already heated debate.

The leaf-shaped spearpoint I'm holding is surprisingly dainty—for a deadly weapon. I let my mind wander, trying to imagine life some 14,700 years ago in the marshes of southern Chile, where this relic was found. The 30 or so people who lived there then, at the creekside campsite now known as Monte Verde, were some of the earliest inhabitants of South America—most likely descendants of people who reached North America by crossing the Bering land bridge from Asia at least 15,000 years ago, perhaps more. Did this roving crew realize they were such pioneers? Or are such musings reserved for people who don't have to worry about where to find their next meal?

My thoughts are interrupted by Tom Dillehay, professor of anthropology at the University of Kentucky and the man who in the 1970s uncovered Monte Verde, the oldest known site of human habitation in the Americas. In a basement classroom on the university's campus, Dillehay has spread out a gallery of artifacts from Monte Verde on the table before me. He directs my attention to a fragment of another spearpoint, which, were it still intact, would be virtually identical to the one I'm holding. "These were probably made by the same person," he says.

The misty images of primitive explorers evaporate, and I suddenly picture a single artisan spending hours, perhaps days, crafting these stone tools, each less than four inches long and half an inch wide. The workmanship is exquisite, even to my untrained eye: the series of tiny notches that form the sharp edges are flawlessly symmetrical. Whoever made these tools was clearly a perfectionist. The question of when people first reached the Americas has been an ongoing discussion in anthropology and archaeology circles for years. Yet how the first Americans actually lived—how my diligent toolmaker spent his (or her?) days—is only now receiving significant attention. The findings at Monte Verde shattered the previously accepted entry date into the Americas, which had been considered to be around 14,000 years ago. (Because of the significance of this shift in thinking, acceptance of the Monte Verde site was a slow process; the archaeological community did not endorse Dillehay's analysis until 1997, when a paper on the site was published in the journal *Science*. A handful of scholars still have reservations about the age of the site.)

Excavations under way in the eastern U.S. and throughout South America hint that humans' arrival date may have to be pushed back to as far as 20,000 or even 40,000 years ago. Such discoveries may very well do more than just alter our understanding of how long people have lived in the Americas. With every new artifact, researchers like Dillehay are slowly piecing together more about the day-to-day lives of the early Americans: how they hunted, what plants they ate, how they moved across vast stretches of land—in short, what life was really like for those men, women and children who originally settled in the New World.

The canonical view of how humans first reached the Americas can be traced back to 1589, when José de Acosta, a Jesuit missionary to South America, suggested that the original Americans had somehow migrated from Siberia many thousands of years ago. The theory persisted, and by the early part of the 20th century archaeologists had agreed on the identity of the very first Americans. The evidence seemed irrefutable. Archaeological sites dating to approximately 13,000 years ago had turned up all across the landscape; nothing older had yet been found. Moreover, the tools from these sites shared striking similarities, as though the people who created them had a common cultural background and had all moved onto the continent together. Researchers termed these people and their culture "Clovis" (after Clovis, N.M., where the first such artifact was found). Clovis spearpoints, for instance, can be found in Canada, across the U.S. and into Central America.

In certain parts of the U.S., particularly the desert Southwest, these Clovis points are nearly as common as cacti. Why would the Clovis people have needed so many weapons? Again, the answer seemed clear. They must have been voracious hunters, following their prey—big game animals like the woolly mammoth—across the Bering land bridge around 14,000 or 15,000 years ago, when the ice sheets extending from the North Pole had melted just enough to open a land passageway through Canada. The hunters pursued the animals relentlessly, taking around 1,000 years to spread through North and South America. The emphasis on hunting made sense—this was the Ice Age, after all, and meat from a mammoth or bison provided lots of much needed fat and protein for the entire family. And the fur hides could be fashioned into warm clothes.

Thomas Lynch, an expert on Clovis culture and director of the Brazos Valley Museum of Natural History in Bryan, Texas, points out another advantage: "The easiest way to get food is by hunting big game, in particular herding animals. And at first, the animals would not be afraid of humans." A quick sweep across the continent fits the pattern as well, Lynch argues, remarking that the hunters would have had to move fast "as the animals got spooked by humans."

The idea that the first Americans were Ice Age hunters has been accepted for decades, filling pages in both textbooks and scientific journals. But researchers have increasingly pointed to holes in the theory. David Meltzer, a professor of anthropology at Southern Methodist University who has studied Clovis culture extensively, suggests that this view of the first settlers is too simplistic, relying as it does on a stereotype that "people worked their way through the continent gnawing on mammoth bones." With closer scrutiny, he says, "this just doesn't hold up."

Meltzer contends that the small bands of 15 to 30 people, typical of nomadic tribes, were essentially always at risk of dying out, either from inbreeding or some sort of catastrophe. Hunting a mammoth was, of course, extremely dangerous, possibly even too perilous for these groups to have relied on it as their sole source of food. So they must have turned to other sources, particularly small game, nuts and berries, and maybe even fish and turtles. Indeed, a few archaeologists have discovered the remains of smaller animals, including deer, rabbits and snakes, at Clovis sites. Unfortunately, though, the technology associated with small-game hunting, fishing and gathering—the wooden tools, nets and baskets—generally don't survive as well as stone artifacts do.

One site in Pennsylvania, however, has yielded just these kinds of remains. James Adovasio, an archaeologist at Mercyhurst College, has spent almost 30 years excavating Meadowcroft Rockshelter southwest of Pittsburgh, where early settlers set up camp at least 12,900 years ago. He has found baskets that he believes would have been used to carry plants or even mussels from the nearby Ohio River. Adovasio has also uncovered parts of snares for catching small game, and bone awls for working textiles and hides.

For much of the past three decades, other archaeologists have disputed Adovasio's interpretation of these finds; even today some question the antiquity of the site, although a recent analysis of the site by an outside researcher may help resolve the issue. "We have found bone needles, and people would say, 'Oh, they used them to sew hides.' But you and I know they would snap!" Adovasio insists. Instead, he argues, these needles must have been for weaving lightweight fabrics made from plant material. "People make the mistake of thinking the Ice Age was cold all the time. They remember the 40,000 Januarys but forget the 40,000 Julys," he laughs.

And just who was sewing clothes for the warmer weather? Adovasio complains that the official mammoth-centric picture of early Americans completely neglects the role of women, children and grandparents. He points to the icon of the Ice Age hunter with his stone spears: "By focusing only on stones, we are ignoring 95 percent of what these people made and what they did." Look at more recent hunter-gatherer societies, he says. Women, children and older people of both sexes supply the vast majority of the food and carry out vital tasks such as making clothes, nets and baskets. Why would the earliest Americans have been any different?

Margaret Jodry, an archaeologist at the Smithsonian Institution, also cautions against overlooking the issue of how families traveled through the New World. Conventional wisdom has the Clovis people walking the entire way. But, Jodry asks, what about Clovis sites that have been found on both sides of a river? "Unless we're suggesting they would swim across" the river every day just to get home, she says incredulously, they must have relied on boats for transportation. "How are you going to swim the Missouri River with Grandma, your wife who's eight months pregnant, your kids and dogs?" Furthermore, she points out, humans had developed watercraft by at least 40,000 years ago, because by then they were in Australia.

Early American boats would have been constructed from animal skins or wood—again, fairly ephemeral substances. But Jodry thinks that archaeologists might be able to find distinct signatures of the boatbuilding process. Based on her observations of construction techniques used by modern indigenous groups of North America, she has proposed archaeological markers—a certain configuration of post holes encircled by stones, for instance—that might represent an ancient workshop for assembling boats.

Monte Verde in Chile—home to around 30 people some 12,500 years ago—is the oldest known site of human habitation in the Americas. Archaeologist Tom Dillehay and his colleagues have uncovered a variety of human artifacts from this ancient camp, which is not far from the Andes and the Pacific Ocean.

In response to these novel lines of reasoning, archaeologists are beginning to change how and where they dig. Jodry reports that some colleagues have told her they plan to revisit previously excavated sites, looking for evidence of boats. And finds at Meadowcroft and elsewhere have prompted archaeologists to hunt for more than just stones and bones. (At Monte Verde, Dillehay found knotted cords that he thinks were used to secure tents made of animal hides; remains of the tents turned up as well.)

But they'll have to change the types of sites they look for, according to Dillehay. "People concentrate on caves and open-air sites," he explains, where preservation of delicate artifacts is unlikely. "If you want to find another Monte Verde"—where a layer of peat from the nearby swamp covered the campsite and prevented oxygen from reaching the remains—"you've got to look where wet sites are preserved," he says.

This newfound emphasis on softer artifacts should help to substantiate the emerging picture of the first Americans as people with an intricate knowledge of their environment, who could not only spear a mammoth once in a while but who also knew how to catch fish, pick the right berries, weave plant fibers into clothes and baskets, and build boats for local travel.

And as researchers cast a wider net for artifacts, they may have to consider a range of explanations for what they find. Texas A&M University archaeologist and Clovis specialist Mike Waters notes that when the archaeological community accepted the 14,700-year-old date for Monte Verde just three years ago, the recognition "jump-started the whole debate about Clovis being first." As scholars digest the evidence from Monte Verde, they have been rethinking many long-held ideas on who populated the Americas and when and how they got here. For his part, Waters maintains three working hypotheses: that the Clovis people were in fact the first in the Americas, that there was a smattering of people in North America before Clovis but they left almost no trace or that there was a large pre-Clovis occupation we have yet to identify.

Transportation to the New World is a big topic for debate. If the early Americans did cruise around the continent in canoes and kayaks, might the first settlers have arrived by boat as well? For decades the archaeological community rejected this notion (Ice Age hunters could never have carried all their weapons and leftover mammoth meat in such tiny boats!), but in recent years the idea has gathered more support. One reason for the shift: the nagging problem of just how fast people can make the journey from Alaska to Tierra del Fuego.

Consider Dillehay's 14,700-year-old Monte Verde site. According to the previously accepted timeline, people could have made the journey from Asia on foot no earlier than 15,700 years ago (before this time, the ice sheets extending from the North Pole covered Alaska and Canada completely, making a land passage impossible). If this entry date is correct, the Monte Verde find would indicate that the first settlers had to make the 12,000-mile trip through two continents in only 1,000 years. In archaeological time, that's as fast as Marion Jones.

One way to achieve this pace, however, would be by traveling along the Pacific coastlines of North and South America in boats. Knut Fladmark, a professor of archaeology at Simon Fraser University in Burnaby, B.C., first suggested this possibility in the 1970s and remains an advocate of a coastal entry into the Americas. If people had a reason to keep moving, he says, they could have traversed both continents in 100 years. Fladmark estimates that traveling at a rate of 200 miles a month would have been quite reasonable; the settlers no doubt stopped during winter months and probably stayed in some spots for a generation or so if the local resources were particularly tempting.

Fladmark's theory, though enticing, won't be easy to prove. Rising sea levels from the melting Ice Age glaciers inundated thousands of square miles along the Pacific coasts of both continents. Any early sites near the ocean that were inhabited before 13,000 years ago would now be deep underwater.

Recently a few enterprising researchers have attempted to dredge up artifacts from below the Pacific. In 1997, for example, Daryl Fedje, an archaeologist with Parks Canada (which runs that country's national parks system), led a team that pulled up a small stone tool from 160 feet underwater just off the coast of British Columbia. The single tool, which Fedje estimates to be around 10,200 years old, does establish that people once lived on the now submerged land but reveals little about the culture there.

Excavating underwater sites might turn out to be the only way to prove when humans first arrived on this continent. And for many researchers this is still a very open question, with answers ranging from 15,000 years ago to as far back as 50,000 years ago. When Fladmark first proposed the idea of a coastal migration, the entry date of 14,000 or 15,000 years ago was orthodoxy. But many researchers have since speculated that humans must have been in the Americas for much, much longer.

Which brings me back to my skilled spearpoint designer from Monte Verde. Although his ancestors theoretically could have made it to the southern tip of Chile in just 100 years if they traveled in watercraft, practically speaking, the group wouldn't then have had much time to adapt to the new surroundings.

And for Dillehay, this distinction between theory and reality is crucial: The people living at Monte Verde 14,700 years ago, he says, "knew exactly where they were positioning themselves." They had been in the region long enough to set up camp on prime real estate, within an hour's walk of nearby wetlands, lush with edible plants. The ocean and the Andean foothills were both about a day's walk away. The group had carefully situated itself close to three different environments, all of which provided them with food and supplies.

Dillehay has found desiccated cakes, or "quids," of seaweed that the people sucked on, probably for the high iodine content in the plants (the quids are almost perfect molds of the top of a person's mouth—down to the impressions of molars). And based on the mastodon bones found at the site, Dillehay believes that the Monte Verdeans either killed or scavenged animals trapped in the nearby bogs. He also suspects they used rib bones from the animals as digging sticks to unearth tubers and rhizomes from the surrounding marshes.

Such elaborate knowledge of one's environment does not come quickly; it probably requires several generations at least. Precisely how long the folks at Monte Verde would have needed to gain such an understanding, though, is difficult to estimate. The arrival of modern humans into an unpopulated continent has happened only twice—in Australia and in the Americas—so we have little by way of reference. But Dillehay looks at the issue in a broader context. In places like the Indus Valley and China, it took tens of thousands of years for complex civilizations to arise. He remarks that unless Americans were "the most remarkable people in the world"—setting up the beginnings of civilization in only a couple thousand years—they must have been here for much longer. Dillehay suggests that an arrival time of around 20,000 years ago would have given the first Americans ample time to put down the roots of civilization.

Such an early entry date is bolstered by two other lines of evidence. Linguist Johanna Nichols of the University of California at Berkeley argues that the amazing diversity of languages among Native Americans could have arisen only after humans had been in the New World for at least 20,000 years—possibly even 30,000. Geneticists, including Theodore Schurr of the Southwest Foundation for Biomedical Research in San Antonio, Texas, and Douglas Wallace of Emory University, present a related argument based on genetic diversity. By comparing several DNA markers found in modern Native Americans and modern Siberians, Schurr and Wallace estimate that the ancestors of the former left Siberia for the New World at least 30,000 years ago.

These ancient dates—if they are correct—would have important implications. Experts on human origins believe that behaviorally modern humans left Africa for Europe and Asia around 50,000 or 60,000 years ago. So as archaeologists push back the arrival date of humans in the Americas, they move the peopling of the New World into the larger story of human evolution. As Robson Bonnichsen, director of the Center for the Study of the First Americans at Texas A&M University, has written, the occupation of the Americas should be "understood in respect to the process that led to the global expansion of modern humans."

Some evidence links the settling of the Americas to the migration of modern humans out of Africa. In perhaps one of the most startling finds of recent years, Walter Neves of the University of São Paulo determined that the oldest skeleton ever found in the Americas—a 13,500-year-old adult female from southeastern Brazil—resembles Africans and Australian aborigines more than modern Asians or Native Americans. Neves interprets this result (and similar ones from some 50 skulls dated to between 8,900 and 11,600 years old) to mean that non-Mongoloid migrants were among the first in the Americas.

Neves is quick to point out, though, that he does not think these people came directly from Africa or Australia but that they splintered off from the band moving slowly through Asia that eventually went south to Australia. According to the fossil record, Mongoloid groups arrived in South America around 9,000 years ago, where they appear to have replaced the previous population. "I don't have an answer for [what happened]," Neves says. "Maybe war, maybe killing, maybe they were absorbed" by all the intermixing that was surely going on, he suggests.

So it seems the New World has been a melting pot for millennia. Those famous Ice Age hunters no doubt did cross the Bering land bridge at some point and head onto the continent. But they probably were not the first ones to do so, and they most certainly were not the only ones. Thanks to recent archaeological finds, researchers are beginning to figure out what life was like for some of the other people here—the fisherfolk boating along the Pacific coast, the hunter-gatherers living in the temperate forests of North and South America.

In the meantime, investigators can't dig fast enough to keep pace with the rapid shifts in our knowledge of who the first Americans were. Archaeologists are scouring Alaska for remains of early inhabitants; geologists are trying to determine exactly when the glaciers melted enough for settlers to start moving into central Canada and the U.S. Others continue hunting for even earlier signs of Clovis in the U.S. The eastern U.S. is home to several important ongoing excavations: Cactus Hill in Virginia and the Topper Site in South Carolina. Preliminary finds at Cactus Hill suggest that a group possibly related to the Clovis people may have lived in the area around 18,000 years ago.

Al Goodyear, an archaeologist at the University of South Carolina, went back to a Clovis site at Topper, near the Savannah River, to see what was underneath (and thus older). The results surprised him: artifacts in the deeper layers at Topper are completely unlike Clovis technology. He has found no Clovis-type spearpoints, only tiny stone blades and scraping tools thought to be associated with the use of wood, bone and antlers.

Goodyear recounts how he "went into a mild state of shock" when he realized just how difficult it would be to explain who these people were. This summer he brought in two experts on determining the age of archaeological sites, Waters of Texas A&M and Tom Stafford of Stafford Research Laboratories in Boulder, Colorado, the leading carbon-14 dating facility in the country. The team is still unsure of how old the tools are—as Stafford says, they could be from just 100 years before Clovis—but the analysis continues. Goodyear hopes eventually to excavate in a nearby marshy area, where conditions should be more suited to the preservation of delicate items such as wooden tools or clothing fibers.

Other investigators working at sites in South America, including Dillehay, have described camps that could be as old as 30,000 years. Dillehay himself, however, is cautious about these dates, saying more spots must be found from this era before researchers can be certain these highly contested numbers are correct. But he has little doubt on another point: that the individuals who lived at Monte Verde and throughout the New World—whenever it was truly new—were part of "one of the most intricate, thrilling and inspiring episodes of the human adventure." In his book *The Settlement of the Americas* (Basic Books, 2000), he describes the expansion into new environments as the "high adventure that gave people a strong sense of mission"—analogous to having our space program continue for thousands of years.

But isn't this sort of self-awareness rather too modern? Wasn't the main adventure for these people trying to stay alive? Dillehay thinks perhaps they had more on their minds. "People pick the same good campsites over and over—rock-shelters, overlooks," he says, so it wouldn't have been strange to see the remains of previous inhabitants. "But there must have been some point when people realized that no one had been there before," he adds. "When they realized, 'We are the first.'"

Discussion Questions

1. Tom Dillehay may have found the earliest known site of human habitation in the Americas. Where is the site located, how old is it, and why is the site so important?
2. Who were the Clovis people and what types of food economy do most people associate with this group?
3. Archaeologist David Meltzer believes that some of the Clovis people were nomadic foragers, but why is that idea so difficult to prove?
4. At the Meadowcroft site they found bone needles that many believe were used to sew leather hides into clothing. James Adovasio believes otherwise. Why?
5. Why do some archaeologists believe that the Clovis cultures must have known about boats and could build them out of wood and hides?
6. What type of evidence supports the idea that perhaps the first humans to enter the Americas came by boat?
7. How are DNA studies and studies of Native American languages helping to resolve the question of when the first humans reached the Americas?
8. Why are the Cactus Hill site in Virginia and the Topper Site in South Carolina important sites when it comes to answering the question of when people first populated the Americas?
9. Do you think humans have a natural wanderlust—that is, that they always want to know what's over the next hill, where the river leads, what you can see from the top of the mountain, and where the ocean currents take you? How might this have influenced the settling of both the Old and New Worlds?

Additional Resources

For Internet links related to this chapter, please visit our website at www.mhhe.com/dettwyler

ADOVASIO, J. M., and JAKE PAGE. *The First Americans: In Pursuit of Archaeology's Greatest Mystery.* New York: Random House, 2002.

COHEN, MARK NATHAN, and GEORGE J. ARMELAGOS, eds. *Paleopathology at the Origins of Agriculture.* New York: Academic Press, 1984.

CLUTTON-BROCK, JULIET. *A Natural History of Domesticated Mammals,* 2nd edition. New York: Cambridge University Press, 1999.

COWAN, C. WESLEY, and PATTY JO WATSON. *The Origins of Agriculture: An International Perspective.* Washington, DC: Smithsonian Institution Press, 1992.

DILLEHAY, THOMAS D. *The Settlement of the Americas: A New Prehistory.* New York: Basic Books, 2000.

HARRIS, DAVID R., ed. *The Origins and Spread of Agriculture and Pastoralism in Eurasia.* Washington, DC: Smithsonian Institution Press, 1996.

HAYNES, GARY. *The Early Settlement of North America: The Clovis Era.* New York: Cambridge University Press, 2003.

HORNELL, JAMES. *Water Transport: Origins and Early Evolution.* Newton Abbot, Devon, UK: David & Charles Publishers Ltd., 1970.

OLSEN, SANDRA L., ed. *Horses Through Time.* Boulder, CO: Roberts Rinehart, Publishers for Carnegie Museum of Natural History, 1996.

PIPERNO, DOLORES R., and DEBORAH M. PEARSALL. *The Origins of Agriculture in the Lowland Neotropics.* New York: Academic Press, 1998.

PIPERNO, DOLORES R., and KAREN E. STOTHERT. "Phytolith Evidence for Early Holocene *Cucurbita* Domestication in Southwest Ecuador." *Science* 299 (February 14, 2003): 1054–1057.

PRICE, T. DOUGLAS, and ANNE BIRGITTE GEBAUER, eds. *Last Hunters–First Farmers: New Perspectives on the Prehistoric Transition to Agriculture.* Santa Fe, NM: School of American Research Press, 1995.

THOMAS, DAVID HURST. *Skull Wars: Kennewick Man, Archaeology, and the Battle for Native American Identity.* New York: Basic Books, 2001.

CHAPTER 11

The First Cities
and States

 20. 1491, by Charles C. Mann, *The Atlantic Monthly,* March 2002 (from website
www.theatlantic.com/issues/2002/03/mann.htm).

For three centuries history textbooks that have been written about the conquest and
European settling of the Americas have portrayed the view that the New World was
scarcely populated except by nomadic Indians and that, except for a few regions,
such as Mexico and Peru, there were no large urban centers of any consequence.
Early estimates of pre-1492 Indian populations in North America argue that per-
haps there were as many as 1.15 million of them. However, a few decades ago this
long-standing and conservative view was challenged by researchers who claimed
that there were instead over 18 million people in North America when Columbus ar-
rived, and that as many as 95 percent of all Indians in the New World died within
the first 130 years after Columbus arrived. Furthermore, they argued that for a num-
ber of reasons, including conscience and politics, it was more convenient to portray
the initial Europeanization of the Americas as being carried out by settlers who
found the region mostly empty, and except in a few cases, did not cause too much
hardship on the original Indian populations. Then, too, there is the controversy
about whether European or New World lifestyles and cities were the ideals of tech-
nology and living standards. A recent survey asked historians, anthropologists, and
archaeologists familiar with pre- and postcolonial life in the New World if they
would rather have been a European or an American Indian in 1491. Every one of
them selected to have been an American Indian.

Before it became the New World, the Western Hemisphere was vastly more populous and sophisticated than has been thought—an altogether more salubrious place
to live at the time than, say, Europe. New evidence of both the extent of the population and its agricultural advancement leads to a remarkable conjecture: the Amazon
rain forest may be largely a human artifact.

The plane took off in weather that was surprisingly cool for north-central Bolivia and flew east, toward the Brazilian border. In a few minutes the roads and houses disappeared, and the only evidence of human settlement was the cattle scattered over the savannah like jimmies on ice cream. Then they, too, disappeared. By that time the archaeologists had their cameras out and were clicking away in delight.

Below us was the Beni, a Bolivian province about the size of Illinois and Indiana put together, and nearly as flat. For almost half the year rain and snowmelt from the mountains to the south and west cover the land with an irregular, slowly moving skin of water that eventually ends up in the province's northern rivers, which are sub-subtributaries of the Amazon. The rest of the year the water dries up and the bright-green vastness turns into something that resembles a desert. This peculiar, remote, watery plain was what had drawn the researchers' attention, and not just because it was one of the few places on earth inhabited by people who might never have seen Westerners with cameras.

Clark Erickson and William Balée, the anthropologists, sat up front. Erickson is based at the University of Pennsylvania; he works in concert with a Bolivian archaeologist, whose seat in the plane I usurped that day. Balée is at Tulane University, in New Orleans. He is a cultural anthropologist, but as native peoples have vanished, the distinction between cultural anthropologists and archaeologists has blurred. The two men differ in build, temperament, and scholarly proclivity, but they pressed their faces to the windows with identical enthusiasm.

Dappled across the grasslands below was an archipelago of forest islands, many of them startlingly round and hundreds of acres across. Each island rose ten or thirty or sixty feet above the floodplain, allowing trees to grow that would otherwise never survive the water. The forests were linked by raised berms, as straight as a rifle shot and up to three miles long. It is Erickson's belief that this entire landscape—30,000 square miles of forest mounds surrounded by raised fields and linked by causeways— was constructed by a complex, populous society more than 2,000 years ago. Balée, newer to the Beni, leaned toward this view but was not yet ready to commit himself.

Erickson and Balée belong to a cohort of scholars that has radically challenged conventional notions of what the Western Hemisphere was like before Columbus. When I went to high school, in the 1970s, I was taught that Indians came to the Americas across the Bering Strait about 12,000 years ago, that they lived for the most part in small, isolated groups, and that they had so little impact on their environment that even after millennia of habitation it remained mostly wilderness. My son picked up the same ideas at his schools. One way to summarize the views of people like Erickson and Balée would be to say that in their opinion this picture of Indian life is wrong in almost every aspect. Indians were here far longer than previously thought, these researchers believe, and in much greater numbers. And they were so successful at imposing their will on the landscape that in 1492 Columbus set foot in a hemisphere thoroughly dominated by humankind.

Given the charged relations between white societies and native peoples, inquiry into Indian culture and history is inevitably contentious. But the recent scholarship is especially controversial. To begin with, some researchers—many but not all from an older generation—deride the new theories as fantasies arising from an almost willful misinterpretation of data and a perverse kind of political correctness. "I have seen no evidence that large numbers of people ever lived in the Beni," says Betty J. Meggers, of the Smithsonian Institution. "Claiming otherwise is just wishful thinking." Similar criticisms apply to many of the new scholarly claims about Indians, according to Dean R. Snow, an anthropologist at Pennsylvania State University. The problem is that "you can make the meager evidence from the ethnohistorical record tell you anything you want," he says. "It's really easy to kid yourself."

More important are the implications of the new theories for today's ecological battles. Much of the environmental movement is animated, consciously or not, by what William Denevan, a geographer at the University of Wisconsin, calls, polemically, "the pristine myth"—the belief that the Americas in 1491 were an almost unmarked, even Edenic land, "untrammeled by man," in the words of the Wilderness Act of 1964, one of the nation's first and most important environmental laws. As the University of Wisconsin historian William Cronon has written, restoring this long-ago, putatively natural state is, in the view of environmentalists, a task that society is morally bound to undertake. Yet if the new view is correct and the work of humankind was pervasive, where does that leave efforts to restore nature?

The Beni is a case in point. In addition to building up the Beni mounds for houses and gardens, Erickson says, the Indians trapped fish in the seasonally flooded grassland. Indeed, he says, they fashioned dense zigzagging networks of earthen fish weirs between the causeways. To keep the habitat clear of unwanted trees and undergrowth, they regularly set huge areas on fire. Over the centuries the burning created an intricate ecosystem of fire-adapted plant species dependent on native pyrophilia. The current inhabitants of the Beni still burn, although now it is to maintain the savannah for cattle. When we flew over the area, the dry season had just begun, but mile-long lines of flame were already on the march. In the charred areas behind the fires were the blackened spikes of trees—many of them, one assumes, of the varieties that activists fight to save in other parts of Amazonia.

After we landed, I asked Balée, Should we let people keep burning the Beni? Or should we let the trees invade and create a verdant tropical forest in the grasslands, even if one had not existed here for millennia?

Balée laughed. "You're trying to trap me, aren't you?" he said.

Like a Club Between the Eyes

According to family lore, my great-grandmother's great-grandmother's great-grandfather was the first white person hanged in America. His name was John Billington. He came on the Mayflower, which anchored off the coast of Massachusetts on November 9, 1620. Billington was not a Puritan; within six months of arrival he also became the first white person in America to be tried for complaining about the police. "He is a knave," William Bradford, the colony's governor, wrote of Billington, "and so will live and die." What one historian called Billington's "troublesome career" ended in 1630, when he was hanged for murder. My family has always said that he was framed—but we would say that, wouldn't we?

A few years ago it occurred to me that my ancestor and everyone else in the colony had voluntarily enlisted in a venture that brought them to New England without food or shelter six weeks before winter. Half the 102 people on the Mayflower made it through to spring, which to me was amazing. How, I wondered, did they survive?

In his history of Plymouth Colony, Bradford provided the answer: by robbing Indian houses and graves. The Mayflower first hove to at Cape Cod. An armed company staggered out. Eventually it found a recently deserted Indian settlement. The newcomers—hungry, cold, sick—dug up graves and ransacked houses, looking for underground stashes of corn. "And sure it was God's good providence that we found this corn," Bradford wrote, "for else we know not how we should have done." (He felt uneasy about the thievery, though.) When the colonists came to Plymouth, a month later, they set up shop in another deserted Indian village. All through the coastal forest the Indians had "died on heapes, as they lay in their houses," the English trader Thomas Morton noted. "And the bones and skulls upon the severall places of their habitations made such a spectacle" that to Morton the Massachusetts woods seemed to be "a new found Golgotha"—the hill of executions in Roman Jerusalem.

To the Pilgrims' astonishment, one of the corpses they exhumed on Cape Cod had blond hair. A French ship had been wrecked there several years earlier. The Patuxet Indians imprisoned a few survivors. One of them supposedly learned enough of the local language to inform his captors that God would destroy them for their misdeeds. The Patuxet scoffed at the threat. But the Europeans carried a disease, and they bequeathed it to their jailers. The epidemic (probably of viral hepatitis, according to a study by Arthur E. Spiess, an archaeologist at the Maine Historic Preservation Commission, and Bruce D. Spiess, the director of clinical research at the Medical College of Virginia) took years to exhaust itself and may have killed 90 percent of the people in coastal New England. It made a huge difference to American history. "The good hand of God favored our beginnings," Bradford mused, by "sweeping away great multitudes of the natives . . . that he might make room for us."

By the time my ancestor set sail on the Mayflower, Europeans had been visiting New England for more than a hundred years. English, French, Italian, Spanish, and Portuguese mariners regularly plied the coastline, trading what they could, occasionally kidnapping the inhabitants for slaves. New England, the Europeans saw, was thickly settled and well defended. In 1605 and 1606 Samuel de Champlain visited Cape Cod, hoping to establish a French base. He abandoned the idea. Too many people already lived there. A year later Sir Ferdinando Gorges—British despite his name—tried to establish an English community in southern Maine. It had more founders than Plymouth and seems to have been better organized. Confronted by numerous well-armed local Indians, the settlers abandoned the project within months. The Indians at Plymouth would surely have been an equal obstacle to my ancestor and his ramshackle expedition had disease not intervened.

Faced with such stories, historians have long wondered how many people lived in the Americas at the time of contact. "Debated since Columbus attempted a partial census on Hispaniola in 1496," William Denevan has written, this "remains one of the great inquiries of history." (In 1976 Denevan assembled and edited an entire book on the subject, *The Native Population of the Americas in 1492*.) The first scholarly estimate of the indigenous population was made in 1910 by James Mooney, a distinguished ethnographer at the Smithsonian Institution. Combing through old documents, he concluded that in 1491 North America had 1.15 million inhabitants. Mooney's glittering reputation ensured that most subsequent researchers accepted his figure uncritically.

That changed in 1966, when Henry F. Dobyns published "Estimating Aboriginal American Population: An Appraisal of Techniques With a New Hemispheric Estimate," in the journal *Current Anthropology*. Despite the carefully neutral title, his argument was thunderous, its impact long-lasting. In the view of James Wilson, the author of *The Earth Shall Weep* (1998), a history of indigenous Americans,

Dobyns's colleagues "are still struggling to get out of the crater that paper left in anthropology." Not only anthropologists were affected. Dobyns's estimate proved to be one of the opening rounds in today's culture wars.

Dobyns began his exploration of pre-Columbian Indian demography in the early 1950s, when he was a graduate student. At the invitation of a friend, he spent a few months in northern Mexico, which is full of Spanish-era missions. There he poked through the crumbling leather-bound ledgers in which Jesuits recorded local births and deaths. Right away he noticed how many more deaths there were. The Spaniards arrived, and then Indians died—in huge numbers, at incredible rates. It hit him, Dobyns told me recently, "like a club right between the eyes."

It took Dobyns eleven years to obtain his Ph.D. Along the way he joined a rural-development project in Peru, which until colonial times was the seat of the Incan empire. Remembering what he had seen at the northern fringe of the Spanish conquest, Dobyns decided to compare it with figures for the south. He burrowed into the papers of the Lima cathedral and read apologetic Spanish histories. The Indians in Peru, Dobyns concluded, had faced plagues from the day the conquistadors showed up—in fact, before then: smallpox arrived around 1525, seven years ahead of the Spanish. Brought to Mexico apparently by a single sick Spaniard, it swept south and eliminated more than half the population of the Incan empire. Smallpox claimed the Incan dictator Huayna Capac and much of his family, setting off a calamitous war of succession. So complete was the chaos that Francisco Pizarro was able to seize an empire the size of Spain and Italy combined with a force of 168 men.

Smallpox was only the first epidemic. Typhus (probably) in 1546, influenza and smallpox together in 1558, smallpox again in 1589, diphtheria in 1614, measles in 1618—all ravaged the remains of Incan culture. Dobyns was the first social scientist to piece together this awful picture, and he naturally rushed his findings into print. Hardly anyone paid attention. But Dobyns was already working on a second, related question: If all those people died, how many had been living there to begin with? Before Columbus, Dobyns calculated, the Western Hemisphere held ninety to 112 million people. Another way of saying this is that in 1491 more people lived in the Americas than in Europe.

His argument was simple but horrific. It is well known that Native Americans had no experience with many European diseases and were therefore immunologically unprepared—"virgin soil," in the metaphor of epidemiologists. What Dobyns realized was that such diseases could have swept from the coastlines initially visited by Europeans to inland areas controlled by Indians who had never seen a white person. The first whites to explore many parts of the Americas may therefore have encountered places that were already depopulated. Indeed, Dobyns argued, they must have done so.

Peru was one example, the Pacific Northwest another. In 1792 the British navigator George Vancouver led the first European expedition to survey Puget Sound. He found a vast charnel house: human remains "promiscuously scattered about the beach, in great numbers." Smallpox, Vancouver's crew discovered, had preceded them. Its few survivors, second lieutenant Peter Puget noted, were "most terribly pitted . . . indeed many have lost their Eyes." In *Pox Americana* (2001), Elizabeth Fenn, a historian at George Washington University, contends that the disaster on the northwest coast was but a small part of a continental pandemic that erupted near Boston in 1774 and cut down Indians from Mexico to Alaska.

Because smallpox was not endemic in the Americas, colonials, too, had not acquired any immunity. The virus, an equal-opportunity killer, swept through the Continental Army and stopped the drive into Quebec. The American Revolution would be lost, Washington and other rebel leaders feared, if the contagion did to the colonists what it had done to the Indians. "The small Pox! The small Pox!" John Adams wrote to his wife, Abigail. "What shall We do with it?" In retrospect, Fenn says, "One of George Washington's most brilliant moves was to inoculate the army against smallpox during the Valley Forge winter of '78." Without inoculation smallpox could easily have given the United States back to the British.

So many epidemics occurred in the Americas, Dobyns argued, that the old data used by Mooney and his successors represented population nadirs. From the few cases in which before-and-after totals are known with relative certainty, Dobyns estimated that in the first 130 years of contact about 95 percent of the people in the Americas died—the worst demographic calamity in recorded history.

Dobyns's ideas were quickly attacked as politically motivated, a push from the hate-America crowd to inflate the toll of imperialism. The attacks continue to this day. "No question about it, some people want those higher numbers," says Shepard Krech III, a Brown University anthropologist who is the author of *The Ecological Indian* (1999). These people, he says, were thrilled when Dobyns revisited the subject in a book, *Their Numbers Become Thinned* (1983)—and revised his own estimates upward. Perhaps Dobyns's most vehement critic is David Henige, a bibliographer of Africana at the University of Wisconsin, whose *Numbers From Nowhere* (1998) is a landmark in the literature of demographic fulmination. "Suspect in 1966, it is no less suspect nowadays," Henige wrote of Dobyns's work. "If anything, it is worse."

When Henige wrote *Numbers From Nowhere,* the fight about pre-Columbian populations had already consumed forests' worth of trees; his bibliography is ninety pages long. And the dispute shows no sign of abating. More and more people have jumped in. This is partly because the subject is inherently fascinating. But more likely the increased interest in the debate is due to the growing realization of the high political and ecological stakes.

Inventing by the Millions

On May 30, 1539, Hernando de Soto landed his private army near Tampa Bay, in Florida. Soto, as he was called, was a novel figure: half warrior, half venture capitalist. He had grown very rich very young by becoming a market leader in the nascent trade for Indian slaves. The profits had helped to fund Pizarro's seizure of the Incan empire, which had made Soto wealthier still. Looking quite literally for new worlds to conquer, he persuaded the Spanish Crown to let him loose in North America. He spent one fortune to make another. He came to Florida with 200 horses, 600 soldiers, and 300 pigs.

From today's perspective, it is difficult to imagine the ethical system that would justify Soto's actions. For four years his force, looking for gold, wandered through what is now Florida, Georgia, North and South Carolina, Tennessee, Alabama, Mississippi, Arkansas, and Texas, wrecking almost everything it touched. The inhabitants often fought back vigorously, but they had never before encountered an army with horses and guns. Soto died of fever with his expedition in ruins; along the way his men had managed to rape, torture, enslave, and kill countless Indians. But the worst thing the Spaniards did, some researchers say, was entirely without malice—bring the pigs.

According to Charles Hudson, an anthropologist at the University of Georgia who spent fifteen years reconstructing the path of the expedition, Soto crossed the Mississippi a few miles downstream from the present site of Memphis. It was a nervous passage: the Spaniards were watched by several thousand Indian warriors. Utterly without fear, Soto brushed past the Indian force into what is now eastern Arkansas, through thickly settled land—"very well peopled with large towns," one of his men later recalled, "two or three of which were to be seen from one town." Eventually the Spaniards approached a cluster of small cities, each protected by earthen walls, sizeable moats, and deadeye archers. In his usual fashion, Soto brazenly marched in, stole food, and marched out.

After Soto left, no Europeans visited this part of the Mississippi Valley for more than a century. Early in 1682 whites appeared again, this time Frenchmen in canoes. One of them was Réné-Robert Cavelier, Sieur de la Salle. The French passed through the area where Soto had found cities cheek by jowl. It was deserted—La Salle didn't see an Indian village for 200 miles. About fifty settlements existed in this strip of the Mississippi when Soto showed up, according to Anne Ramenofsky, an anthropologist at the University of New Mexico. By La Salle's time the number had shrunk to perhaps ten, some probably inhabited by recent immigrants. Soto "had a privileged glimpse" of an Indian world, Hudson says. "The window opened and slammed shut. When the French came in and the record opened up again, it was a transformed reality. A civilization crumbled. The question is, how did this happen?"

The question is even more complex than it may seem. Disaster of this magnitude suggests epidemic disease. In the view of Ramenofsky and Patricia Galloway, an anthropologist at the University of Texas, the source of the contagion was very likely not Soto's army but its ambulatory meat locker: his 300 pigs. Soto's force itself was too small to be an effective biological weapon. Sicknesses like measles and smallpox would have burned through his 600 soldiers long before they reached the Mississippi. But the same would not have held true for the pigs, which multiplied rapidly and were able to transmit their diseases to wildlife in the surrounding forest. When human beings and domesticated animals live close together, they trade microbes with abandon. Over time mutation spawns new diseases: avian influenza becomes human influenza, bovine rinderpest becomes measles. Unlike Europeans, Indians did not live in close quarters with animals—they domesticated only the dog, the llama, the alpaca, the guinea pig, and, here and there, the turkey and the Muscovy duck. In some ways this is not surprising: the New World had fewer animal candidates for taming than the Old. Moreover, few Indians carry the gene that permits adults to digest lactose, a form of sugar abundant in milk. Non-milk-drinkers, one imagines, would be less likely to work at domesticating milk-giving animals. But this is guesswork. The fact is that what scientists call zoonotic disease was little known in the Americas. Swine alone can disseminate anthrax, brucellosis, leptospirosis, taeniasis, trichinosis, and tuberculosis. Pigs breed exuberantly and can transmit diseases to deer and turkeys. Only a few of Soto's pigs would have had to wander off to infect the forest.

Indeed, the calamity wrought by Soto apparently extended across the whole Southeast. The Coosa city-states, in western Georgia, and the Caddoan-speaking civilization, centered on the Texas-Arkansas border, disintegrated soon after Soto appeared. The Caddo had had a taste for monumental architecture: public plazas, ceremonial platforms, mausoleums. After Soto's army left, notes Timothy K. Perttula, an archaeological consultant in Austin, Texas, the Caddo stopped building community centers and began digging community cemeteries. Between Soto's and La Salle's visits, Perttula believes, the Caddoan population fell from about 200,000 to about 8,500—a drop of nearly 96 percent. In the eighteenth century the tally shrank further, to 1,400. An equivalent loss today in the population of New York City would reduce it to 56,000—not enough to fill Yankee Stadium. "That's one reason whites think of Indians as nomadic hunters," says Russell Thornton, an anthropologist at the University of California at Los Angeles. "Everything else—all the heavily populated urbanized societies—was wiped out."

Could a few pigs truly wreak this much destruction? Such apocalyptic scenarios invite skepticism. As a rule, viruses, microbes, and parasites are rarely lethal on so wide a scale—a pest that wipes out its host species does not have a bright evolutionary future. In its worst outbreak, from 1347 to 1351, the European Black Death claimed only a third of its victims. (The rest survived, though they were often disfigured or crippled by its effects.) The Indians in Soto's path, if Dobyns, Ramenofsky, and Perttula are correct, endured losses that were incomprehensibly greater.

One reason is that Indians were fresh territory for many plagues, not just one. Smallpox, typhoid, bubonic plague, influenza, mumps, measles, whooping cough—all rained down on the Americas in the century after Columbus. (Cholera, malaria, and scarlet fever came later.) Having little experience with epidemic diseases, Indians had no knowledge of how to combat them. In contrast, Europeans were well versed in the brutal logic of quarantine. They boarded up houses in which plague appeared and fled to the countryside. In Indian New England, Neal Salisbury, a historian at Smith College, wrote in *Manitou and Providence* (1982), family and friends gathered with the shaman at the sufferer's bedside to wait out the illness—a practice that "could only have served to spread the disease more rapidly."

Indigenous biochemistry may also have played a role. The immune system constantly scans the body for molecules that it can recognize as foreign—molecules belonging to an invading virus, for instance. No one's immune system can identify all foreign presences. Roughly speaking, an individual's set of defensive tools is known as his MHC type. Because many bacteria and viruses mutate easily, they usually attack in the form of several slightly different strains. Pathogens win when MHC types miss some of the strains and the immune system is not stimulated to act. Most human groups contain many MHC types; a strain that slips by one person's defenses will be nailed by the defenses of the next. But, according to Francis L. Black, an epidemiologist at Yale University, Indians are characterized by unusually homogenous MHC types. One out of three South American Indians have similar MHC types; among Africans the corresponding figure is one in 200. The cause is a matter for Darwinian speculation, the effects less so.

In 1966 Dobyns's insistence on the role of disease was a shock to his colleagues. Today the impact of European pathogens on the New World is almost undisputed. Nonetheless, the fight over Indian numbers continues with undiminished fervor. Estimates of the population of North America in 1491 disagree by an order of magnitude—from 18 million, Dobyns's revised figure, to 1.8 million, calculated by Douglas H. Ubelaker, an anthropologist at the Smithsonian. To some "high counters," as David Henige calls them, the low counters' refusal to relinquish the vision of an empty continent is irrational or worse. "Non-Indian 'experts' always want to minimize the size of aboriginal populations," says Lenore Stiffarm, a Native American-education specialist at the University of Saskatchewan. The smaller the numbers of Indians, she believes, the easier it is to regard the continent as having been up for grabs. "It's perfectly acceptable to move into unoccupied land," Stiffarm says. "And land with only a few 'savages' is the next best thing."

"Most of the arguments for the very large numbers have been theoretical," Ubelaker says in defense of low counters. "When you try to marry the theoretical arguments to the data that are available on individual groups in different regions, it's hard to find support for those numbers." Archaeologists, he says, keep searching for the settlements in which those millions of people supposedly lived, with little success. "As more and more excavation is done, one would expect to see more evidence for dense populations than has thus far emerged." Dean Snow, the Pennsylvania State anthropologist, examined Colonial-era Mohawk Iroquois sites and found "no support for the notion that ubiquitous pandemics swept the region." In his view, asserting that the continent was filled with people who left no trace is like looking at an empty bank account and claiming that it must once have held millions of dollars.

The low counters are also troubled by the Dobynsian procedure for recovering original population numbers: applying an assumed death rate, usually 95 percent, to the observed population nadir. Ubelaker believes that the lowest point for Indians in North America was around 1900, when their numbers fell to about half a million. Assuming a 95 percent death rate, the pre-contact population would have been 10 million. Go up one percent, to a 96 percent death rate, and the figure jumps to 12.5 million—arithmetically creating more than two million people from a tiny increase in mortality rates. At 98 percent the number bounds to 25 million. Minute changes in baseline assumptions produce wildly different results.

"It's an absolutely unanswerable question on which tens of thousands of words have been spent to no purpose," Henige says. In 1976 he sat in on a seminar by William Denevan, the Wisconsin geographer. An "epiphanic moment" occurred when he read shortly afterward that scholars had "uncovered" the existence of eight million people in Hispaniola. Can you just invent millions of people? he wondered. "We can make of the historical record that there was depopulation and movement of people from internecine warfare and diseases," he says. "But as for how much, who knows? When we start putting numbers to something like that—applying large figures like ninety-five percent—we're saying things we shouldn't say. The number implies a level of knowledge that's impossible."

Nonetheless, one must try—or so Denevan believes. In his estimation the high counters (though not the highest counters) seem to be winning the argument, at least for now. No definitive data exist, he says, but the majority of the extant evidentiary scraps support their side. Even Henige is no low counter. When I asked him what he thought the population of the Americas was before Columbus, he insisted that any answer would be speculation and made me promise not to print what he was going to say next. Then he named a figure that forty years ago would have caused a commotion.

To Elizabeth Fenn, the smallpox historian, the squabble over numbers obscures a central fact. Whether one million or 10 million or 100 million died, she believes, the pall of sorrow that engulfed the hemisphere was immeasurable. Languages, prayers, hopes, habits, and dreams—entire ways of life hissed away like steam. The Spanish and the Portuguese lacked the germ theory of disease and could not explain what was happening (let alone stop it). Nor can we explain it; the ruin was too long ago and too all-encompassing. In the long run, Fenn says, the consequential finding is not that many people died but that many people once lived. The Americas were filled with a stunningly diverse assortment of peoples who had knocked about the continents for millennia. "You have to wonder," Fenn says. "What were all those people up to in all that time?"

Buffalo Farm

In 1810 Henry Brackenridge came to Cahokia, in what is now southwest Illinois, just across the Mississippi from St. Louis. Born close to the frontier, Brackenridge was a budding adventure writer; his *Views of Louisiana,* published three years later, was a kind of nineteenth-century *Into Thin Air,* with terrific adventure but without tragedy. Brackenridge had an eye for archaeology, and he had heard that Cahokia was worth a visit. When he got there, trudging along the desolate Cahokia River, he was "struck with a degree of astonishment." Rising from the muddy bottomland was a "stupendous pile of earth," vaster than the Great Pyramid at Giza. Around it were more than a hundred smaller mounds, covering an area of five square miles. At the time, the area was almost uninhabited. One can only imagine what passed through Brackenridge's mind as he walked alone to the ruins of the biggest Indian city north of the Rio Grande.

To Brackenridge, it seemed clear that Cahokia and the many other ruins in the Midwest had been constructed by Indians. It was not so clear to everyone else. Nineteenth-century writers attributed them to, among others, the Vikings, the Chinese, the "Hindoos," the ancient Greeks, the ancient Egyptians, lost tribes of Israelites, and even straying bands of Welsh. (This last claim was surprisingly widespread; when Lewis and Clark surveyed the Missouri, Jefferson told them to keep an eye out for errant bands of Welsh-speaking white Indians.) The historian George Bancroft, dean of his profession, was a dissenter: the earthworks, he wrote in 1840, were purely natural formations.

Bancroft changed his mind about Cahokia, but not about Indians. To the end of his days he regarded them as "feeble barbarians, destitute of commerce and of political connection." His characterization lasted, largely unchanged, for more than a century. Samuel Eliot Morison, the winner of two Pulitzer Prizes, closed his monumental *European Discovery of America* (1974) with the observation that Native Americans expected only "short and brutish lives, void of hope for any future." As late as 1987 *American History: A Survey,* a standard high school textbook by three well-known historians, described the Americas before Columbus as "empty of mankind and its works." The story of Europeans in the New World, the book explained, "is the story of the creation of a civilization where none existed."

Alfred Crosby, a historian at the University of Texas, came to other conclusions. Crosby's *The Columbian Exchange: Biological Consequences of 1492* caused almost as much of a stir when it was published, in 1972, as Henry Dobyns's calculation of Indian numbers six years earlier, though in different circles. Crosby was a standard names-and-battles historian who became frustrated by the random contingency of political events. "Some trivial thing happens and you have this guy winning the presidency instead of that guy," he says. He decided to go deeper. After he finished his manuscript, it sat on his shelf—he couldn't find a publisher willing to be associated with his new ideas. It took him three years to persuade a small editorial house to put it out. *The Columbian Exchange* has been in print ever since; a companion, *Ecological Imperialism: The Biological Expansion of Europe, 900–1900,* appeared in 1986.

Human history, in Crosby's interpretation, is marked by two world-altering centers of invention: the Middle East and central Mexico, where Indian groups independently created nearly all of the Neolithic innovations, writing included. The Neolithic Revolution began in the Middle East about 10,000 years ago. In the next few millennia humankind invented the wheel, the metal tool, and agriculture. The Sumerians eventually put these inventions together, added writing, and became the world's first civilization. Afterward Sumeria's heirs in Europe and Asia frantically copied one another's happiest discoveries; innovations ricocheted from one corner of Eurasia to another, stimulating technological progress. Native Americans, who had crossed to Alaska before Sumeria, missed out on the bounty. "They had to do everything on their own," Crosby says. Remarkably, they succeeded.

When Columbus appeared in the Caribbean, the descendants of the world's two Neolithic civilizations collided, with overwhelming consequences for both. American Neolithic development occurred later than that of the Middle East, possibly because the Indians needed more time to build up the requisite population density. Without beasts of burden they could not capitalize on the wheel (for individual workers on uneven terrain skids are nearly as effective as carts for hauling), and they never developed steel. But in agriculture they handily outstripped the children of Sumeria. Every tomato in Italy, every potato in Ireland, and every hot pepper in Thailand came from this hemisphere. Worldwide, more than half the crops grown today were initially developed in the Americas.

Maize, as corn is called in the rest of the world, was a triumph with global implications. Indians developed an extraordinary number of maize varieties for different growing conditions, which meant that the crop could and did spread throughout the planet. Central and Southern Europeans became particularly dependent on it; maize was the staple of Serbia, Romania, and Moldavia by the nineteenth century. Indian crops dramatically reduced hunger, Crosby says, which led to an Old World population boom.

Along with peanuts and manioc, maize came to Africa and transformed agriculture there, too. "The probability is that the population of Africa was greatly increased because of maize and other American Indian crops," Crosby says. "Those extra people helped make the slave trade possible." Maize conquered Africa at the time when introduced diseases were leveling Indian societies. The Spanish, the Portuguese, and the British were alarmed by the death rate among Indians, because they wanted to exploit them as workers. Faced with a labor shortage, the Europeans turned their eyes to Africa. The continent's quarrelsome societies helped slave traders to siphon off millions of people. The maize-fed population boom, Crosby believes, let the awful trade continue without pumping the well dry.

Back home in the Americas, Indian agriculture long sustained some of the world's largest cities. The Aztec capital of Tenochtitlán dazzled Hernán Cortés in 1519; it was bigger than Paris, Europe's greatest metropolis. The Spaniards gawped like hayseeds at the wide streets, ornately carved buildings, and markets bright with goods from hundreds of miles away. They had never before seen a city with botanical gardens, for the excellent reason that none existed in Europe. The same novelty attended the force of a thousand men that kept the crowded streets immaculate. (Streets that weren't ankle-deep in sewage! The conquistadors had never heard of such a thing.) Central America was not the only locus of prosperity. Thousands of miles north, John Smith, of Pocahontas fame, visited Massachusetts in 1614, before it was emptied by disease, and declared that the land was "so planted with Gardens and Corne fields, and so well inhabited with a goodly, strong and well proportioned people . . . [that] I would rather live here than any where."

Smith was promoting colonization, and so had reason to exaggerate. But he also knew the hunger, sickness, and oppression of European life. France—"by any standards a privileged country," according to its great historian, Fernand Braudel—experienced seven nationwide famines in the fifteenth century and thirteen in the sixteenth. Disease was hunger's constant companion. During epidemics in London the dead were heaped onto carts "like common dung" (the simile is Daniel Defoe's) and trundled through the streets. The infant death rate in London orphanages, according to one contemporary source, was 88 percent. Governments were harsh, the rule of law arbitrary. The gibbets poking up in the background of so many old paintings were, Braudel observed, "merely a realistic detail."

The Earth Shall Weep, James Wilson's history of Indian America, puts the comparison bluntly: "the western hemisphere was larger, richer, and more populous than Europe." Much of it was freer, too. Europeans, accustomed to the serfdom that thrived from Naples to the Baltic Sea, were puzzled and alarmed by the democratic spirit and respect for human rights in many Indian societies, especially those in North America. In theory, the sachems of New England Indian groups were absolute monarchs. In practice, the colonial leader Roger Williams wrote, "they will not conclude of ought . . . unto which the people are averse."

Pre-1492 America wasn't a disease-free paradise, Dobyns says, although in his "exuberance as a writer," he told me recently, he once made that claim. Indians had ailments of their own, notably parasites, tuberculosis, and anemia. The daily grind was wearing; life-spans in America were only as long as or a little longer than those in Europe, if the evidence of indigenous graveyards is to be believed. Nor was it a political utopia—the Inca, for instance, invented refinements to totalitarian rule that would have intrigued Stalin. Inveterate practitioners of what the historian Francis Jennings described as "state terrorism practiced horrifically on a huge scale," the Inca ruled so cruelly that one can speculate that their surviving subjects might actually have been better off under Spanish rule.

I asked seven anthropologists, archaeologists, and historians if they would rather have been a typical Indian or a typical European in 1491. None was delighted by the question, because it required judging the past by the standards of today—a fallacy disparaged as "presentism" by social scientists. But every one chose to be an Indian. Some early colonists gave the same answer. Horrifying the leaders of Jamestown and Plymouth, scores of English ran off to live with the Indians. My ancestor shared their desire, which is what led to the trumped-up murder charges against him—or that's what my grandfather told me, anyway.

As for the Indians, evidence suggests that they often viewed Europeans with disdain. The Hurons, a chagrined missionary reported, thought the French possessed "little intelligence in comparison to themselves." Europeans, Indians said, were physically weak, sexually untrustworthy, atrociously ugly, and just plain dirty. (Spaniards, who seldom if ever bathed, were amazed by the Aztec desire for personal cleanliness.) A Jesuit reported that the "Savages" were disgusted by handkerchiefs: "They say, we place what is unclean in a fine white piece of linen, and put it away in our pockets as something very precious, while they throw it upon the ground." The Micmac scoffed at the notion of French superiority. If Christian civilization was so wonderful, why were its inhabitants leaving?

Like people everywhere, Indians survived by cleverly exploiting their environment. Europeans tended to manage land by breaking it into fragments for farmers and herders. Indians often worked on such a grand scale that the scope of their ambition can be hard to grasp. They created small plots, as Europeans did (about 1.5 million acres of terraces still exist in the Peruvian Andes), but they also reshaped entire landscapes to suit their purposes. A principal tool was fire, used to keep down underbrush and create the open, grassy conditions favorable for game. Rather than domesticating animals for meat, Indians retooled whole ecosystems to grow bumper crops of elk, deer, and bison. The first white settlers in Ohio found forests as open as English parks—they could drive carriages through the woods. Along the Hudson River the annual fall burning lit up the banks for miles on end; so flashy was the show that the Dutch in New Amsterdam boated upriver to goggle at the blaze like children at fireworks. In North America, Indian torches had their biggest impact on the Midwestern prairie, much or most of which was created and maintained by fire. Millennia of exuberant burning shaped the plains into vast buffalo farms. When Indian societies disintegrated, forest invaded savannah in Wisconsin, Illinois, Kansas, Nebraska, and the Texas Hill Country. Is it possible that the Indians changed the Americas more than the invading Europeans did? "The answer is probably yes for most regions for the next 250 years or so" after Columbus, William Denevan wrote, "and for some regions right up to the present time."

When scholars first began increasing their estimates of the ecological impact of Indian civilization, they met with considerable resistance from anthropologists and archaeologists. Over time the consensus in the human sciences changed. Under Denevan's direction, Oxford University Press has just issued the third volume of a huge catalogue of the "cultivated landscapes" of the Americas. This sort of phrase still provokes vehement objection—but the main dissenters are now ecologists and environmentalists. The disagreement is encapsulated by Amazonia, which has become the emblem of vanishing wilderness—an admonitory image of untouched Nature. Yet recently a growing number of researchers have come to believe that Indian societies had an enormous environmental impact on the jungle. Indeed, some anthropologists have called the Amazon forest itself a cultural artifact—that is, an artificial object.

Green Prisons

Northern visitors' first reaction to the storied Amazon rain forest is often disappointment. Ecotourist brochures evoke the immensity of Amazonia but rarely dwell on its extreme flatness. In the river's first 2,900 miles the vertical drop is only 500 feet. The river oozes like a huge runnel of dirty metal through a landscape utterly devoid of the romantic crags, arroyos, and heights that signify wildness and natural spectacle to most North Americans. Even the animals are invisible, although sometimes one can hear the bellow of monkey choruses. To the untutored eye—mine, for instance—the forest seems to stretch out in a monstrous green tangle as flat and incomprehensible as a printed circuit board.

The area east of the lower-Amazon town of Santarém is an exception. A series of sandstone ridges several hundred feet high reach down from the north, halting almost at the water's edge. Their tops stand drunkenly above the jungle like old tombstones. Many of the caves in the buttes are splattered with ancient petroglyphs—renditions of hands, stars, frogs, and human figures, all reminiscent of Miró, in overlapping red and yellow and brown. In recent years one of these caves, La Caverna da Pedra Pintada (Painted Rock Cave), has drawn attention in archaeological circles.

Wide and shallow and well lit, Painted Rock Cave is less thronged with bats than some of the other caves. The arched entrance is twenty feet high and lined with rock paintings. Out front is a sunny natural patio suitable for picnicking, edged by a few big rocks. People lived in this cave more than 11,000 years ago. They had no agriculture yet, and instead ate fish and fruit and built fires. During a recent visit I ate a sandwich atop a particularly inviting rock and looked over the forest below. The first Amazonians, I thought, must have done more or less the same thing.

In college I took an introductory anthropology class in which I read *Amazonia: Man and Culture in a Counterfeit Paradise* (1971), perhaps the most influential book ever written about the Amazon, and one that deeply impressed me at the time. Written by Betty J. Meggers, the Smithsonian archaeologist, *Amazonia* says that the apparent lushness of the rain forest is a sham. The soils are poor and can't hold nutrients—the jungle flora exists only because it snatches up everything worthwhile before it leaches away in the rain. Agriculture, which depends on extracting the wealth of the soil, therefore faces inherent ecological limitations in the wet desert of Amazonia.

As a result, Meggers argued, Indian villages were forced to remain small—any report of "more than a few hundred" people in permanent settlements, she told me recently, "makes my alarm bells go off." Bigger, more complex societies would inevitably overtax the forest soils, laying waste to their own foundations. Beginning in 1948 Meggers and her late husband, Clifford Evans, excavated a chiefdom on Marajó, an island twice the size of New Jersey that sits like a gigantic stopper in the mouth of the Amazon. The Marajóara, they concluded, were failed offshoots of a sophisticated culture in the Andes. Transplanted to the lush trap of the Amazon, the culture choked and died.

Green activists saw the implication: development in tropical forests destroys both the forests and their developers. Meggers's account had enormous public impact—*Amazonia* is one of the wellsprings of the campaign to save rain forests.

Then Anna C. Roosevelt, the curator of archaeology at Chicago's Field Museum of Natural History, re-excavated Marajó. Her complete report, *Moundbuilders of the Amazon* (1991), was like the anti-matter version of *Amazonia*. Marajó, she argued, was "one of the outstanding indigenous cultural achievements of the New World," a powerhouse that lasted for more than a thousand years, had "possibly well over 100,000" inhabitants, and covered thousands of square miles. Rather than damaging the forest, Marajó's "earth construction" and "large, dense populations" had improved it: the most luxuriant and diverse growth was on the mounds formerly occupied by the Marajóara. "If you listened to Meggers's theory, these places should have been ruined," Roosevelt says.

Meggers scoffed at Roosevelt's "extravagant claims," "polemical tone," and "defamatory remarks." Roosevelt, Meggers argued, had committed the beginner's error of mistaking a site that had been occupied many times by small, unstable groups for a single, long-lasting society. "[Archaeological remains] build up on areas of half a kilometer or so," she told me, "because [shifting Indian groups] don't land exactly on the same spot. The decorated types of pottery don't change much over time, so you can pick up a bunch of chips and say, 'Oh, look, it was all one big site!' Unless you know what you're doing, of course." Centuries after the conquistadors, "the myth of El Dorado is being revived by archaeologists," Meggers wrote last fall in the journal *Latin American Antiquity,* referring to the persistent Spanish delusion that cities of gold existed in the jungle.

The dispute grew bitter and personal; inevitable in a contemporary academic context, it has featured vituperative references to colonialism, elitism, and employment by the CIA. Meanwhile, Roosevelt's team investigated Painted Rock Cave. On the floor of the cave what looked to me like nothing in particular turned out to be an ancient midden: a refuse heap. The archaeologists slowly scraped away sediment, traveling backward in time with every inch. When the traces of human occupation vanished, they kept digging. ("You always go a meter past sterile," Roosevelt says.) A few inches below they struck the charcoal-rich dirt that signifies human habitation—a culture, Roosevelt said later, that wasn't supposed to be there.

For many millennia the cave's inhabitants hunted and gathered for food. But by about 4,000 years ago they were growing crops—perhaps as many as 140 of them, according to Charles R. Clement, an anthropological botanist at the Brazilian National Institute for Amazonian Research. Unlike Europeans, who planted mainly annual crops, the Indians, he says, centered their agriculture on the Amazon's unbelievably diverse assortment of trees: fruits, nuts, and palms. "It's tremendously difficult to clear fields with stone tools," Clement says. "If you can plant trees, you get twenty years of productivity out of your work instead of two or three."

Planting their orchards, the first Amazonians transformed large swaths of the river basin into something more pleasing to human beings. In a widely cited article from 1989, William Balée, the Tulane anthropologist, cautiously estimated that about 12 percent of the nonflooded Amazon forest was of anthropogenic origin—directly or indirectly created by human beings. In some circles this is now seen as a conservative position. "I basically think it's all human-created," Clement told me in Brazil. He argues that Indians changed the assortment and density of species throughout the region. So does Clark Erickson, the University of Pennsylvania archaeologist, who told me in Bolivia that the lowland tropical forests of South America are among the finest works of art on the planet. "Some of my colleagues would say that's pretty radical," he said, smiling mischievously. According to Peter Stahl, an anthropologist at the State University of New York at Binghamton, "lots" of botanists believe that "what the eco-imagery would like to picture as a pristine, untouched Urwelt [primeval world] in fact has been managed by people for millennia." The phrase "built environment," Erickson says, "applies to most, if not all, Neotropical landscapes."

"Landscape" in this case is meant exactly—Amazonian Indians literally created the ground beneath their feet. According to William I. Woods, a soil geographer at Southern Illinois University, ecologists' claims about terrible Amazonian land were based on very little data. In the late 1990s Woods and others began careful measurements in the lower Amazon. They indeed found lots of inhospitable terrain. But they also discovered swaths of **terra preta**—rich, fertile "black earth" that anthropologists increasingly believe was created by human beings.

Terra preta, Woods guesses, covers at least 10 percent of Amazonia, an area the size of France. It has amazing properties, he says. Tropical rain doesn't leach nutrients from terra preta fields; instead the soil, so to speak, fights back. Not far from Painted Rock Cave is a 300-acre area with a two-foot layer of terra preta quarried by locals for potting soil. The bottom third of the layer is never removed, workers there explain, because over time it will re-create the original soil layer in its initial thickness. The reason, scientists suspect, is that terra preta is generated by a special suite of microorganisms that resists depletion. "Apparently," Woods and the Wisconsin geographer Joseph M. McCann argued in a presentation last summer, "at some threshold level . . . dark earth attains the capacity to perpetuate—even regenerate itself—thus behaving more like a living 'super'-organism than an inert material."

In as yet unpublished research the archaeologists Eduardo Neves, of the University of São Paulo; Michael Heckenberger, of the University of Florida; and their colleagues examined terra preta in the upper Xingu, a huge southern tributary of the Amazon. Not all Xingu cultures left behind this living earth, they discovered. But the ones that did generated it rapidly—suggesting to Woods that terra preta was created deliberately. In a process reminiscent of dropping microorganism-rich starter into plain dough to create sourdough bread, Amazonian peoples, he believes, inoculated bad soil with a transforming bacterial charge. Not every group of Indians there did this, but quite a few did, and over an extended period of time.

When Woods told me this, I was so amazed that I almost dropped the phone. I ceased to be articulate for a moment and said things like "wow" and "gosh." Woods chuckled at my reaction, probably because he understood what was passing through my mind. Faced with an ecological problem, I was thinking, the Indians fixed it. They were in the process of terraforming the Amazon when Columbus showed up and ruined everything.

Scientists should study the microorganisms in terra preta, Woods told me, to find out how they work. If that could be learned, maybe some version of Amazonian dark earth could be used to improve the vast expanses of bad soil that cripple agriculture in Africa—a final gift from the people who brought us tomatoes, corn, and the immense grasslands of the Great Plains.

"Betty Meggers would just die if she heard me saying this," Woods told me. "Deep down her fear is that these data will be misused." Indeed, Meggers's recent *Latin American Antiquity* article charged that archaeologists who say the Amazon can support agriculture are effectively telling "developers [that they] are entitled to operate without restraint." Resuscitating the myth of El Dorado, in her view, "makes us accomplices in the accelerating pace of environmental degradation." Doubtless there is something to this—although, as some of her critics responded in the same issue of the journal, it is difficult to imagine greedy plutocrats "perusing the pages of *Latin American Antiquity* before deciding to rev up the chain saws." But the new picture doesn't automatically legitimize paving the forest. Instead it suggests that for a long time big chunks of Amazonia were used nondestructively by clever people who knew tricks we have yet to learn.

I visited Painted Rock Cave during the river's annual flood, when it wells up over its banks and creeps inland for miles. Farmers in the floodplain build houses and barns on stilts and watch pink dolphins sport from their doorsteps. Ecotourists take shortcuts by driving motorboats through the drowned forest. Guys in dories chase after them, trying to sell sacks of incredibly good fruit.

All of this is described as "wilderness" in the tourist brochures. It's not, if researchers like Roosevelt are correct. Indeed, they believe that fewer people may be living there now than in 1491. Yet when my boat glided into the trees, the forest shut out the sky like the closing of an umbrella. Within a few hundred yards the human presence seemed to vanish. I felt alone and small, but in a way that was curiously like feeling exalted. If that place was not wilderness, how should I think of it? Since the fate of the forest is in our hands, what should be our goal for its future?

Novel Shores

Hernando de Soto's expedition stomped through the Southeast for four years and apparently never saw bison. More than a century later, when French explorers came down the Mississippi, they saw "a solitude unrelieved by the faintest trace of man," the nineteenth-century historian Francis Parkman wrote. Instead the French encountered bison, "grazing in herds on the great prairies which then bordered the river."

To Charles Kay, the reason for the buffalo's sudden emergence is obvious. Kay is a wildlife ecologist in the political science department at Utah State University. In ecological terms, he says, the Indians were the "keystone species" of American ecosystems. A keystone species, according to the Harvard biologist Edward O. Wilson, is a species "that affects the survival and abundance of many other species." Keystone species have a disproportionate impact on their ecosystems. Removing them, Wilson adds, "results in a relatively significant shift in the composition of the [ecological] community."

When disease swept Indians from the land, Kay says, what happened was exactly that. The ecological ancien régime collapsed, and strange new phenomena emerged. In a way this is unsurprising; for better or worse, humankind is a keystone species everywhere. Among these phenomena was a population explosion in the species that the Indians had kept down by hunting. After disease killed off the Indians, Kay believes, buffalo vastly extended their range. Their numbers more than sextupled. The same occurred with elk and mule deer. "If the elk were here in great numbers all this time, the archaeological sites should be chock-full of elk bones," Kay says. "But the archaeologists will tell you the elk weren't there." On the evidence of middens the number of elk jumped about 500 years ago.

Passenger pigeons may be another example. The epitome of natural American abundance, they flew in such great masses that the first colonists were stupefied by the sight. As a boy, the explorer Henry Brackenridge saw flocks "ten miles in width, by one hundred and twenty in length." For hours the birds darkened the sky from horizon to horizon. According to Thomas Neumann, a consulting archaeologist in Lilburn, Georgia, passenger pigeons "were incredibly dumb and always roosted in vast hordes, so they were very easy to harvest." Because they were readily caught and good to eat, Neumann says, archaeological digs should find many pigeon bones in the pre-Columbian strata of Indian middens. But they aren't there. The mobs of birds in the history books, he says, were "outbreak populations—always a symptom of an extraordinarily disrupted ecological system."

Throughout eastern North America the open landscape seen by the first Europeans quickly filled in with forest. According to William Cronon, of the University of Wisconsin, later colonists began complaining about how hard it was to get around. (Eventually, of course, they stripped New England almost bare of trees.)

When Europeans moved west, they were preceded by two waves: one of disease, the other of ecological disturbance. The former crested with fearsome rapidity; the latter sometimes took more than a century to quiet down. Far from destroying pristine wilderness, European settlers bloodily created it. By 1800 the hemisphere was chockablock with new wilderness. If "forest primeval" means a woodland unsullied by the human presence, William Denevan has written, there was much more of it in the late eighteenth century than in the early sixteenth.

Cronon's *Changes in the Land: Indians, Colonists, and the Ecology of New England* (1983) belongs on the same shelf as works by Crosby and Dobyns. But it was not until one of his articles was excerpted in *The New York Times* in 1995 that people outside the social sciences began to understand the implications of this view of Indian history. Environmentalists and ecologists vigorously attacked the anti-wilderness scenario, which they described as infected by postmodern philosophy. A small academic brouhaha ensued, complete with hundreds of footnotes. It precipitated *Reinventing Nature?* (1995), one of the few academic critiques of postmodernist philosophy written largely by biologists. *The Great New Wilderness Debate* (1998), another lengthy book on the subject, was edited by two philosophers who earnestly identified themselves as "Euro-American men [whose] cultural legacy is patriarchal Western civilization in its current postcolonial, globally hegemonic form."

It is easy to tweak academics for opaque, self-protective language like this. Nonetheless, their concerns were quite justified. Crediting Indians with the role of keystone species has implications for the way the current Euro-American members of that keystone species manage the forests, watersheds, and endangered species of America. Because a third of the United States is owned by the federal government, the issue inevitably has political ramifications. In Amazonia, fabled storehouse of biodiversity, the stakes are global.

Guided by the pristine myth, mainstream environmentalists want to preserve as much of the world's land as possible in a putatively intact state. But "intact," if the new research is correct, means "run by human beings for human purposes." Environmentalists dislike this, because it seems to mean that anything goes. In a sense they are correct. Native Americans managed the continent as they saw fit. Modern nations must do the same. If they want to return as much of the landscape as possible to its 1491 state, they will have to find it within themselves to create the world's largest garden.

Discussion Questions

1. When the settlers of the *Mayflower* arrived in New England, they found the area lightly populated. Had it always been that way?
2. How did the research by Henry Dobyns conflict with the existing views about the European conquest of North America?
3. What did General Washington do during the winter of 1778 at Valley Forge to ensure the survival of his army?
4. How can we explain the conflicting reports written by Hernando de Soto and Réné-Robert Cavelier Sieur de la Salle about the Indians living in the southern United States?
5. What were the main differences between the early farming cultures of the Middle East and those of the New World?

6. Why did the European colonists in the Americas believe they needed to import slaves from Africa rather than use Indians as slaves?
7. What is the controversy over **terra preta** and why is the outcome important?
8. Why have American Indians been called "keystone species"? Why are keystone species so important?
9. Which view of America before Columbus seems most probable? Or is the truth still out there somewhere?
10. Would you rather have been an American Indian, or a European, in 1491?

Additional Resources

For Internet links related to this chapter, please visit our website at www.mhhe.com/dettwyler

BARBER, ELIZABETH WAYLAND. *Mummies of Urumchi.* New York: W. W. Norton & Company, 2000.

COHEN, MARK NATHAN. *Health and the Rise of Civilization.* New Haven, CT: Yale University Press, 1991.

CRONON, WILLIAM. *Uncommon Ground: Rethinking the Human Place in Nature.* New York: W. W. Norton & Company, 1996.

FENN, ELIZABETH ANNE. *Pox Americana: The Great Smallpox Epidemic of 1775–82.* New York: Hill & Wang, 2001.

HENIGE, DAVID P. *Numbers From Nowhere: The American Indian Contact Population Debate.* Norman, OK: University of Oklahoma Press, 1998.

KRECH, SHEPARD, III. *The Ecological Indian: Myth and History.* New York: W. W. Norton & Company, 1999.

MAISELS, CHARLES KEITH. *Early Civilizations of the Old World: The Formative Histories of Egypt, the Levant, Mesopotamia, India and China.* New York: Routledge, 2001.

MCINTOSH, RODERICK JAMES. *The Peoples of the Middle Niger: The Island of Gold.* Oxford, UK: Blackwell Publishers, 1997.

PIKIRAYI, INNOCENT, and JOSEPH O. VOGEL. *The Zimbabwe Culture: Origins and Decline of Southern Zambezian States.* Walnut Creek, CA: Altamira Press, 2001.

ROOSEVELT, ANNA C. *Moundbuilders of the Amazon: Geophysical Archaeology on Marajo Island, Brazil.* New York: Academic Press, 1991.

THAKUR, UPENDRA. *Buddhist Cities in Early India: Buddha-Gaya: Rajagrha: Nalanda.* Columbia, MO: South Asia Books, 1995.

WILSON, JAMES. *The Earth Shall Weep: A History of Native America.* New York: Atlantic Monthly Press, 1998.

CHAPTER 12

Ethics and Methods in Cultural Anthropology

21. "Bad Breath, Gangrene, and God's Angels," by Katherine A. Dettwyler, from *Dancing Skeletons: Life and Death in West Africa*. Prospect Heights, IL: Waveland Press, 1994, pp. 91–99.

22. "Too Many Bananas, Not Enough Pineapples, and No Watermelon at All: Three Object Lessons in Living with Reciprocity," by David Counts, from *The Humbled Anthropologist: Tales from the Pacific,* edited by Philip R. DeVita. Belmont, CA: Wadsworth Publishing Company, 1990, pp. 18–24.

*When anthropologists go to the field to do research, they bring with them all their own cultural and personal baggage. Many things that we all take for granted as **normal** and **natural** turn out to be cultural—we just don't realize it until we go someplace where people take different things for granted. In these two selections, a number of fieldwork issues are raised, and the anthropologist-authors are exposed as real, living human beings, struggling to understand themselves, as well as members of another culture.*

21. BAD BREATH, GANGRENE, AND GOD'S ANGELS

This selection comes from my (Dettwyler) book Dancing Skeletons: Life and Death in West Africa, *based on research in Mali in 1989. It was my second trip to Mali and I was accompanied by my daughter Miranda, then nine years old, an undergraduate research assistant from Texas A&M (Heather Katz), and my field assistant/interpreter (Moussa Diarra). We had gone to a remote rural village to measure both children and adults. As often happened, I was faced with a number of issues that affected me personally, as well as professionally. As you read this selection, imagine how you might have felt and acted had you been the anthropologist.*

There is more than one kind of freedom. Freedom to and freedom from. In the days of anarchy, it was freedom to. Now you are being given freedom from. Don't underrate it.

—MARGARET ATWOOD (1986, *The Handmaid's Tale*)

I stood in the doorway, gasping for air, propping my arms against the door frame on either side to hold me up. I sucked in great breaths of cool, clean air and rested my gaze on the distant hills, trying to compose myself. Ominous black thunderclouds were massed on the horizon and moved rapidly toward the schoolhouse. They rolled down the hills like wads of dark cotton, like the fog blankets that regularly obliterate the hills around San Francisco Bay. Thunder growled; the smell of ozone permeated the air. Rain pounded the iron roof overhead, drowning out all thought, while great rivers of water streamed off the corners of the building. Gusts of wind whipped through the trees, blowing the rain into my face. I turned and plunged back inside, back into the fray.

The morning had begun pleasantly enough, with villagers waiting patiently under the huge mango tree in the center of the village. But before long, the approaching storm made it clear that we would have to move inside. The only building large enough to hold the crowd was the one-room schoolhouse, located on the outskirts of the village. Here adults learned to read and write the newly alphabetized written Bambara. General education for children was still a foreign concept.

Inside the schoolhouse, chaos reigned. It was 20 degrees hotter, ten times as noisy, and as dark as gloom. What little light there was from outside entered through the open doorway and two small windows. The entire population of the village crowded onto the rows of benches, or stood three deep around the periphery of the room. Babies cried until their mothers pulled them around front where they could nurse, children chattered, and adults seized the opportunity to converse with friends and neighbors. It was one big party, a day off from working in the fields, with a cooling rain thrown in for good measure. I had to shout the measurements out to Heather, to make myself heard over the cacophony of noise.

The stench in the room was incredible: hundreds of unwashed, sweaty bodies mingled with the ever-present undertones of wood smoke, tobacco, and spices. It was so dark inside the schoolroom that I had to shine a flashlight inside people's mouths, and peer closely, my face right in theirs, in order to count their teeth. Being this up close and personal made people understandably uncomfortable. They guffawed with embarrassment when I looked in their mouths, overwhelming me with the odor of rotting teeth. I had to keep retreating to the door of the schoolroom to compose myself and get some fresh air, to keep from throwing up. Halfway through the morning I gagged once again and turned to Heather in disgust. "I can't stand this anymore. I am absolutely giving up on looking for third molars in adults' mouths."

I was interested in third molar eruption as evidence that rural Malian adults had faces and jaws large enough to comfortably accommodate third molars (wisdom teeth). My hidden agenda was to argue that current understandings of human evolution were skewed, because they took modern Europeans, with relatively small faces, as the epitome of what "modern humans" looked like. Arguments over interpretations of the fossil record and the date of the first appearance of "modern humans" with "small faces" became irrelevant when the full range of modern humans was appreciated, including particularly West Africans with their large, projecting lower faces and fully operational sets of third molars.

I knew from studies in Magnambougou that most urban adults had beautiful, healthy teeth, including all four third molars, fully erupted and in perfect occlusion. The lack of refined sugar, and the use of traditional tooth-cleaning sticks in many parts of Mali resulted in few cavities. Every morning, adults walked around with the stub of a tooth-brushing stick protruding from one corner of their mouth. Only particular trees provided "tooth brushes"—sticks that were chewed to a frazzle at one end, then used to scrub and polish the teeth. Chemical analysis of these twigs showed that they had antibiotic and anticavity properties.

Apparently, the knowledge of this traditional mode of dental hygiene never made it to Merediela, and I found myself face-to-face with incredible dental wear, multiple cavities, exposed roots, and draining abscesses. I was familiar with all of these dental conditions from working with prehistoric Native American skeletal material, but I had never really pondered what they would be like in the flesh—what it meant for the living people who had to cope with teeth like that. Now I knew firsthand, and it was not a pretty sight, nor a pleasant smell. "It's no wonder kissing isn't big around here," I quipped, trying to find some humor in the situation. "From now on, I'm only looking in little kids' mouths. Next!"

A middle-aged man dressed in a threadbare pair of Levis shoved a crying child forward. I knelt down to encourage the little boy to step up onto the scales and saw that his leg was wrapped in dirty bandages. He hesitated before lifting his foot and whimpered as he put his weight onto it. "How old is this child?" I asked Heather. She consulted his birth certificate. "Four years old," she answered. By that time, he was crying loudly.

"What's the matter with his leg?" I asked his father.

"He hurt it in a bicycle accident," he said.

I rolled my eyes at Heather. "Let me guess. He was riding on the back fender, without wearing long pants, or shoes, and he got his leg tangled in the spokes." Moussa translated this aside into Bambara, and the man acknowledged that that was exactly what had happened.

Bicycle injuries of this kind were frequent, and they would often result in devastating wounds to children's legs and feet. In the country, children wear few or no clothes, and no shoes. They straddle the back of rickety bicycles, hanging on behind their father or older brother. A moment's inattention, and they get caught. Bicycle spokes can do nasty things to children's limbs.

The father set the little boy up on the table we were using as a desk, gently unwrapping the filthy dressings. The last few layers were crusted over and had to be teased away, exposing the wound. One glance and I had to turn my head away in horror and dismay. The room suddenly seemed hotter, the air thicker than ever.

The festering wound encompassed the boy's ankle and part of his foot, deep enough to see bone at the bottom. His entire lower leg and foot were swollen and putrid; it was obvious that gangrene had a firm hold.

"When did this happen?" I asked the father.

"About five days ago," he replied.

"How did you treat the wound?"

"We just covered it with this cloth."

"Why didn't you take him to a doctor?"

"We thought it would get better by itself," he said, turning to look pleadingly at the boy's mother.

"You have to take him to the hospital in Sikasso immediately," I explained.

"But we can't afford to," he balked.

"You can't afford not to," I cried in exasperation, turning to Moussa. "He doesn't understand," I said to Moussa. "Please explain to him that the boy is certain to die of gangrene poisoning if he doesn't get to a doctor right away. It may be too late already, but I don't think so. He may just lose his leg." Moussa's eyes widened with alarm. Even he hadn't realized how serious the boy's wounds were. As the father took in what Moussa was saying, his face crumpled.

While the boy's father ran to get his cache of carefully hoarded coins and bills, I dressed the wound with antibiotic cream and a clean gauze bandage. I gave him some chewable children's aspirin, as though it would help. I had to do something constructive. The little boy cringed when I touched him, but he no longer cried. Father and son were last seen leaving Merediela, the boy perched precariously on the back of a worn-out donkey hastily borrowed from a neighbor, while the father trotted alongside, shoulders drooping, urging the donkey to greater speed.

Lunch back at the animatrice's compound provided another opportunity for learning about infant feeding beliefs in rural Mali, through criticism of my own child feeding practices. This time it was a chicken that had given its life for our culinary benefit. As we ate, without even thinking, I reached into the center pile of chicken meat and pulled pieces of meat off the bone. Then I placed them over in Miranda's section of the communal food bowl and encouraged her to eat.

"Why are you giving her chicken?" Bakary asked.

"I want to make sure she gets enough to eat," I replied. "She didn't eat very much porridge for breakfast, because she doesn't like millet."

"But she's just a child. She doesn't need good food. You've been working hard all morning, and she's just been lying around. Besides, if she wanted to eat, she would," he argued.

"It's true that I've been working hard," I admitted, "but she's still growing. Growing children need much more food, proportionately, than adults. And if I didn't encourage her to eat, she might not eat until we get back to Bamako."

Bakary shook his head. "In Dogo," he explained, "people believe that good food is wasted on children. They don't appreciate its good taste or the way it makes you feel. Also, they haven't worked hard to produce the food. They have their whole lives to work for good food for themselves, when they get older. Old people deserve the best food, because they're going to die soon."

"Well, I applaud your respect and honor for the elderly, but health-wise, that's completely wrong. How do you expect children to grow up to be functioning adults if they only get millet or rice to eat?" Of course, many children don't grow up at all, on this diet. They die from malnutrition, or from diseases such as measles that wouldn't kill a well-nourished child. Studies of the long-term consequences of childhood malnutrition have shown that adults who have survived are functionally impaired when it comes to sustained work effort. They cannot work as long as adults who were not malnourished as children.

In Magnambougou, the prevailing idea in child nutrition was that children alone should decide when, what, and how much they wanted to eat, but they were usually offered whatever was available, including some of the meat and vegetables in the sauce. In rural southern Mali, "good food" (which included all the high protein/high calorie foods) was reserved for elders and other adults. Children subsisted almost entirely on the carbohydrate staples, flavored with a little sauce. My actions in giving Miranda my share of the chicken were viewed as bizarre and misguided—I was wasting good food on a mere child, and depriving myself.

Villagers' reactions to my behaviors were often very enlightening. This conversation was no exception, and I would have liked it to continue. However, it was interrupted by the arrival of a string of children with miscellaneous cuts and scrapes, coming for first aid. I quickly finished eating and went to attend to them. I did what I could with soap and water, antibiotic ointment and Band-Aids. One little boy sat straddling his mother's hip, his arms draped across her shoulders. She showed me an open sore on the back of one of his buttocks.

"What happened here?" I asked his mother.

"He had malaria, so I gave him an injection of Quinimax. Now the malaria is gone, but his leg is sore," she answered.

"But he can walk on it all right?" I asked, taking the boy's hand and leading him around to see if he could still use the leg.

"Oh yes, he can walk fine."

"Where did you get the needle for the shot?" I pressed, as I held the boy down and administered to the sore.

"From a neighbor," she answered.

In Mali, as in many medically underdeveloped places, injections are thought to be more effective than oral medicines. In many cases, the doctor merely prescribes the medicine to be purchased at the pharmacy; it is up to the patient to find a way to have the medicine injected. This often means tracking down a "neighborhood needle" and paying a small fee to borrow the needle. For a little extra, you can get someone to inject the medicine, or you can do it yourself. The needle may be rinsed in water between uses, but it certainly isn't sterilized. The multiple use of needles leads, not uncommonly, to minor infections at the injection site. As AIDS becomes more common in Mali, it will become even more dangerous. But as unsanitary as this method is, it may be better than having the injection done by the doctor at the clinic, as my friend from Magnambougou, Agnes, can attest.

During the rainy season of 1982, Agnes took her one-year-old daughter to the local maternal-child health clinic because she had a bad case of malaria. The doctor gave the infant an injection of Quinimax, a viscous oil-based chloroquine mixture, the strongest means of combating malaria. Oral chloroquine tablets probably would have done the job, but injections have that special cachet.

Unfortunately, the doctor, a Malian trained in France, had little understanding of anatomy. Instead of giving the shot into the fat and muscle tissue of the buttocks, or the front of the thigh, he administered it in the back of the thigh, directly into her sciatic nerve. This nerve, as thick as a finger, runs the length of the leg and provides communication between the brain and the leg muscles. Damage to the nerve had left the little girl crippled.

At one year of age, she had just learned how to walk, but she was immediately reduced to crawling again, dragging her useless leg behind her. Agnes fought back, though, taking her to Kati every month for acupuncture treatments and working with her for long hours every day, trying to strengthen her leg. It took more than a year, but eventually she was able to walk again. As horrible as her experience was, it had worse repercussions beyond her own family.

A few months after the Quinimax crippling episode, the little boy next door to Agnes came down with malaria. His mother faced a choice on her little boy's behalf: malaria or paralysis. He had already survived several bouts of malaria. From her perspective, a trip to the doctor carried a more certain risk of being crippled by an inept injection. She gambled, and kept him at home. She gambled, and lost. This time, he died of malaria. Maybe the real cause of death was the doctors' poor medical training, though. Being a good parent in a disadvantaged place is harder than most of us can know. This mother gambled bravely, she gambled intelligently, and she lost cruelly.

In N'tenkoni the next morning, we were given use of the men's sacred meeting hut for our measuring session. A round hut about twenty feet in diameter, it had a huge center pole made from the trunk of a tree that held up the thatched roof. Because it had two large doorways, it was light and airy and would provide protection in the event of another thunderstorm.

The roof poles were hung with a variety of objects—a bundle of cow bones above one door, a bundle of corncobs above the other. Numerous boys' circumcision toys were wedged into the rafters. Known as *sistrums,* these wooden toys are made from tree branches and strung with serrated discs made from calabashes. Newly circumcised boys wear special clothing and are allowed to parade through the village shaking the toys. The calabash discs make a loud clacking sound, alerting everyone to the impending arrival of the boys, and people come out to give them small presents in honor of their new status as circumcised boys. I had never seen so many in one place.

There was some initial confusion caused by the fact that people outside couldn't really see what we were doing, and everyone tried to crowd in at once. That was straightened out by the chief, however, and measuring proceeded apace, men, women, children, men, women, children. One family at a time filed into the hut through one door, had their measurements taken, and departed through the other door. It was cool and pleasant inside the hut, in contrast to the hot sun and glare outside. Miranda sat off to one side, reading a book, glancing up from time to time, but generally bored by the whole thing.

"Mommy, look!" she exclaimed in mid-morning. "Isn't that an *angel?*" she asked, using our family's code word for a child with Down syndrome. Down syndrome children are often (though not always!) sweet, happy, and affectionate kids, and many families of children with Down syndrome consider them to be special gifts from God, and refer to them as angels. I turned and followed the direction of Miranda's gaze. A little girl had just entered the hut, part of a large family with many children. She had a small round head, and all the facial characteristics of a child with Down syndrome—"Oriental"-shaped eyes with epicanthic folds, a small flat nose, and small ears. There was no mistaking the diagnosis. Her name was Abi, and she was about four years old, the same age as my son Peter.

I knelt in front of the little girl. "Hi there, sweetie," I said in English. "Can I have a hug?" I held out my arms, and she willingly stepped forward and gave me a big hug.

I looked up at her mother. "Do you know that there's something 'different' about this child?" I asked, choosing my words carefully.

"Well, she doesn't talk," said her mother, hesitantly, looking at her husband for confirmation. "That's right," he said. "She's never said a word."

"But she's been healthy?" I asked.

"Yes," the father replied. "She's like the other kids, except she doesn't talk. She's always happy. She never cries. We know she can hear, because she does what we tell her to. Why are you so interested in her?"

"Because I know what's the matter with her. I have a son like this." Excitedly, I pulled a picture of Peter out of my bag and showed it to them. They couldn't see the resemblance, though. The difference in skin color swamped the similarities in facial features. But then, Malians think all white people look alike. And it's not true that all kids with Down syndrome look the same. They're "different in the same way," but they look most like their parents and siblings.

"Have you ever met any other children like this?" I inquired, bursting with curiosity about how rural Malian culture dealt with a condition as infrequent as Down syndrome. Children with Down syndrome are rare to begin with, occurring about once in every 700 births. In a community where 30 or 40 children are born each year at the most, a child with Down syndrome might be born only once in twenty years. And many of them would not survive long enough for anyone to be able to tell that they were different. Physical defects along the midline of the body (heart, trachea, intestines) are common among kids with Down syndrome; without immediate surgery and neonatal intensive care, many would not survive. Such surgery is routine in American children's hospitals, but nonexistent in rural Mali. For the child without any major physical defects, there are still the perils of rural Malian life to survive: malaria, measles, diarrhea, diphtheria, and polio. Some, like Peter, have poor immune systems, making them even more susceptible to childhood diseases. The odds against finding a child with Down syndrome, surviving and healthy in a rural Malian village, are overwhelming.

Not surprisingly, the parents knew of no other children like Abi. They asked if I knew of any medicine that could cure her. "No," I explained, "this condition can't be cured. But she will learn to talk, just give her time. Talk to her a lot. Try to get her to repeat things you say. And give her lots of love and attention. It may take her longer to learn some things, but keep trying. In my country, some people say these children are special gifts from God." There was no way I could explain cells and chromosomes and nondisjunction to them, even with Moussa's help. And how, I thought to myself, would that have helped them anyway? They just accepted her as she was.

We chatted for a few more minutes, and I measured the whole family, including Abi, who was, of course, short for her age. I gave her one last hug and a balloon and sent her out the door after her siblings. I turned to Moussa and Heather and said, "Guys, I need a break. I'll be right back."

I walked out of the hut, past the long line of villagers waiting patiently for their turn to be measured. They turned to stare as I passed. I went behind the animatrice's compound and sat down on a fallen log. I took several deep breaths, trying to get my emotions under control. Finally I gave in, hugged my knees close to my chest, and sobbed. I cried for Abi—what a courageous heart she must have; just think what she might have achieved given all the modern infant stimulation programs available in the West. I cried for Peter—another courageous heart; just think of what he might achieve given the chance to live in a culture that simply accepted him, rather than stereotyping and pigeonholing him, constraining him because people didn't think he was capable of more. I cried for myself—not very courageous at all; my heart felt as though it would burst with longing for Peter, my own sweet angel.

There was clearly some truth to the old adage that ignorance is bliss. Maybe pregnant women in Mali had to worry about evil spirits lurking in the latrine at night, but they didn't spend their pregnancies worrying about chromosomal abnormalities, the moral implications of amniocentesis, or the heart-wrenching exercise of trying to evaluate handicaps, deciding which ones made life not worth living. Women in the United States might have the freedom to choose not to give birth to children with handicaps, but women in Mali had freedom from worrying about it. Children in the United States had the freedom to attend special programs to help them overcome their handicaps, but children in Mali had freedom from the biggest handicap of all—other people's prejudice.

I had cried myself dry. I splashed my face with cool water from the bucket inside the kitchen and returned to the task at hand.

Discussion Questions

1. Why was the measuring session in Merediela held in the schoolhouse? What difficulties did this create for the researcher?
2. What kinds of dental problems did the people in Dogo experience? Why did they have such rotten teeth, when so many peoples in Third World countries have strong, straight teeth?
3. How did the little boy hurt his leg? What did the researcher suggest his parents should do? Should she have done more to help him? In more general terms, what are the obligations of an ethnographer to use his or her superior resources (knowledge, money, transportation) to help people in the study community? How does one draw the line, both in practical terms of getting one's research accomplished and in ethical terms of helping in some circumstances but not in others?
4. Why did Bakary object to the author's giving her daughter choice pieces of chicken to eat? Can you think of parallels in American society? For example, if you go to an expensive restaurant, do you order steak and lobster for your toddler? Why not?
5. What are the nutritional consequences for a child in the United States who orders off the "kids" menu? What are the nutritional consequences for a child in Mali who doesn't have access to enough protein?
6. How is it possible that injections of quinine for malaria can leave children crippled?
7. What was unusual about Abi in N'tenkoni? Why do children with Down syndrome usually not survive in Third World societies?
8. Compare the relative advantages and disadvantages of life in Mali and in the United States for children with Down syndrome. What advantages do children with Down syndrome have in the United States? What advantages do they have in Mali?
9. Why was the author looking at adult third molar eruption patterns in the adult Malians? What was her hidden agenda in collecting these data?

22. TOO MANY BANANAS, NOT ENOUGH PINEAPPLES, AND NO WATERMELON AT ALL: THREE OBJECT LESSONS IN LIVING WITH RECIPROCITY

There is a true story about a group of American businessmen who went to Japan to complete the final negotiations on a large industrial contract. After working out most of the details, the Japanese host and his colleagues invited the American business team to dinner at a very expensive restaurant. After dinner, in an effort to demonstrate their appreciation, the leader of the American team offered a toast to seal the deal and then handed a credit card to the head waiter and said, "Hey, guys, the meal's on us!" The next day the American group returned to the Japanese company but was told politely that the deal was off and that they should return to America. The shocked Americans left in bewilderment. Weeks later the American team discovered that their Japanese host was terribly embarrassed that his guests had "paid the bill" and therefore he had "lost face" in front of everyone at dinner. As a result, he felt too embarrassed to continue his business deal with the American team. A similar type of cultural misunderstanding is the focus of the next article.

No Watermelon At All

The woman came all the way through the village, walking between the two rows of houses facing each other between the beach and the bush, to the very last house standing on a little spit of land at the mouth of the Kaini River. She was carrying a watermelon on her head, and the house she came to was the government "rest house," maintained by the villagers for the occasional use of visiting officials. Though my wife and I were graduate students, not officials, and had asked for permission to stay in the village for the coming year, we were living in the rest house while the debate went on about where a house would be built for us. When the woman offered to sell us the watermelon for two shillings, we happily agreed, and the kids were delighted at the prospect of watermelon after yet another meal of rice and bully beef. The money changed hands and the seller left to return to her village, a couple of miles along the coast to the east.

It seemed only seconds later that the woman was back, reluctantly accompanying Kolia, the man who had already made it clear to us that he was the leader of the village. Kolia had no English, and at that time, three or four days into our first stay in Kandoka Village on the island of New Britain in Papua New Guinea, we had very little Tok Pisin. Language difficulties notwithstanding, Kolia managed to make his message clear: The woman had been outrageously wrong to sell us the watermelon for two shillings and we were to return it to her and reclaim our money immediately. When we tried to explain that we thought the price to be fair and were happy with the bargain, Kolia explained again and finally made it clear that we had missed the point. The problem wasn't that we had paid too much; it was that we had paid at all. Here he was, a leader, responsible for us while we were living in his village, and we had shamed him. How would it look if he let guests in his village **buy** food? If we wanted watermelons, or bananas, or anything else, all that was necessary was to let him know. He told us that it would be all right for us to give little gifts to people who brought food to us (and they surely would), but **no one** was to sell food to us. If anyone were to try—like this woman from Lauvore—then we should refuse. There would be plenty of watermelons without us buying them.

The woman left with her watermelon, disgruntled, and we were left with our two shillings. But we had learned the first lesson of many about living in Kandoka. We didn't pay money for food again that whole year, and we did get lots of food brought to us . . . but we never got another watermelon. That one was the last of the season.

LESSON 1: In a society where food is shared or gifted as part of social life, you may not buy it with money.

Too Many Bananas,
Not Enough
Pineapples, and No
Watermelon at All:
Three Object
Lessons in Living
with Reciprocity

In the couple of months that followed the watermelon incident, we managed to become at least marginally competent in Tok Pisin, to negotiate the construction of a house on what we hoped was neutral ground, and to settle into the routine of our fieldwork. As our village leader had predicted, plenty of food was brought to us. Indeed, seldom did a day pass without something coming in—some sweet potatoes, a few taro, a papaya, the occasional pineapple, or some bananas—lots of bananas.

We had learned our lesson about the money, though, so we never even offered to buy the things that were brought, but instead made gifts, usually of tobacco to the adults or chewing gum to the children. Nor were we so gauche as to haggle with a giver over how much of a return gift was appropriate, though the two of us sometimes conferred as to whether what had been brought was a "two-stick" or a "three-stick" stalk, bundle, or whatever. A "stick" of tobacco was a single large leaf, soaked in rum and then twisted into a ropelike form. This, wrapped in half a sheet of newsprint (torn for use as cigarette paper), sold in the local trade stores for a shilling. Nearly all of the adults in the village smoked a great deal, and they seldom had much cash, so our stocks of twist tobacco and stacks of the Sydney *Morning Herald* (all, unfortunately, the same day's issue) were seen as a real boon to those who preferred "stick" to the locally grown product.

We had established a pattern with respect to the gifts of food. When a donor appeared at our veranda we would offer our thanks and talk with them for a few minutes (usually about our children, who seemed to hold a real fascination for the villagers and for whom most of the gifts were intended) and then we would inquire whether they could use some tobacco. It was almost never refused, though occasionally a small bottle of kerosene, a box of matches, some laundry soap, a cup of rice, or a tin of meat would be requested instead of (or even in addition to) the tobacco. Everyone, even Kolia, seemed to think this arrangement had worked out well.

Now, what must be kept in mind is that while we were following their rules—or seemed to be—we were **really still buying food.** In fact we kept a running account of what came in and what we "paid" for it. Tobacco as currency got a little complicated, but since the exchange rate was one stick to one shilling, it was not too much trouble as long as everyone was happy, and meanwhile we could account for the expenditure of "informant fees" and "household expenses." Another thing to keep in mind is that not only did we continue to think in terms of our buying the food that was brought, we thought of them as **selling it.** While it was true they never quoted us a price, they also never asked us if we needed or wanted whatever they had brought. It seemed clear to us that when an adult needed a stick of tobacco, or a child wanted some chewing gum (we had enormous quantities of small packets of Wrigley's for just such eventualities) they would find something surplus to their own needs and bring it along to our "store" and get what they wanted.

By late November 1966, just before the rainy season set in, the bananas were coming into flush, and whereas earlier we had received banana gifts by the "hand" (six or eight bananas in a cluster cut from the stalk), donors now began to bring bananas, "for the children," by the **stalk!** The Kaliai among whom we were living are not exactly specialists in banana cultivation—they only recognize about thirty varieties, while some of their neighbors have more than twice that many—but the kinds they produce differ considerably from each other in size, shape, and taste, so we were not dismayed when we had more than one stalk hanging on our veranda. The stalks ripen a bit at a time, and having some variety was nice. Still, by the time our accumulation had reached **four** complete stalks, the delights of variety had begun to pale a bit. The fruits were ripening progressively and it was clear that even if we and the kids ate nothing but bananas for the next week, some would still fall from the stalk onto the floor in a state of gross overripeness. This was the situation as, late one afternoon, a woman came bringing yet another stalk of bananas up the steps of the house.

Several factors determined our reaction to her approach: one was that there was literally no way we could possibly use the bananas. We hadn't quite reached the point of being crowded off our veranda by the stalks of fruit, but it was close. Another factor was that we were tired of playing the gift game. We had acquiesced in playing it—no one was permitted to sell us anything, and in turn we only gave things away, refusing under any circumstances to sell tobacco (or anything else) for money. But there had to be a limit. From our perspective what was at issue was that the woman wanted something and she had come to trade for it. Further, what she had brought to trade was something we neither wanted nor could use, and it should have been obvious to her. So we decided to bite the bullet.

The woman, Rogi, climbed the stairs to the veranda, took the stalk from where it was balanced on top of her head, and laid it on the floor with the words, "Here are some bananas for the children." Dorothy and I sat near her on the floor and thanked her for her thought but explained, "You know, we really have too many bananas— we can't use these; maybe you ought to give them to someone else. . . ." The woman looked mystified, then brightened and explained that she didn't want anything for them, she wasn't short of tobacco or anything. They were just a gift for the kids. Then she just sat there, and we sat there, and the bananas sat there, and we tried again. "Look," I said, pointing up to them and counting, "we've got four stalks already hanging here on the veranda—there are too many for us to eat now. Some are rotting already. Even if we eat only bananas, we can't keep up with what's here!"

Rogi's only response was to insist that these were a gift, and that she didn't want anything for them, so we tried yet another tack: "Don't **your** children like bananas?" When she admitted that they did, and that she had none at her house, we suggested that she should take them there. Finally, still puzzled, but convinced we weren't going to keep the bananas, she replaced them on her head, went down the stairs, and made her way back through the village toward her house.

As before, it seemed only moments before Kolia was making his way up the stairs, but this time he hadn't brought the woman in tow. "What was wrong with those bananas? Were they no good?" he demanded. We explained that there was nothing wrong with the bananas at all, but that we simply couldn't use them and it seemed foolish to take them when we had so many and Rogi's own children had none. We obviously didn't make ourselves clear, because Kolia then took up the same refrain that Rogi had—he insisted that we shouldn't be worried about taking the bananas, because they were a gift for the children and Rogi hadn't wanted anything for them. There was no reason, he added, to send her away with them—she would be ashamed. I'm afraid we must have seemed as if we were hard of hearing or thought he was, for our only response was to repeat our reasons. We went through it again—there they hung, one, two, three, **four** stalks of bananas, rapidly ripening and already far beyond our capacity to eat—we just weren't ready to accept any more and let them rot (and, we added to ourselves, pay for them with tobacco, to boot).

Kolia finally realized that we were neither hard of hearing nor intentionally offensive, but merely ignorant. He stared at us for a few minutes, thinking, and then asked: "Don't you frequently have visitors during the day and evening?" We nodded. Then he asked, "Don't you usually offer them cigarettes and coffee or milo?" Again, we nodded. "Did it ever occur to you to suppose," he said, "that your visitors might be hungry?" It was at this point in the conversation, as we recall, that we began to see the depth of the pit we had dug for ourselves. We nodded, hesitantly. His last words to us before he went down the stairs and stalked away were just what we were by that time afraid they might be. "When your guests are hungry, *feed them bananas!*"

LESSON 2: **Never refuse a gift, and never fail to return a gift. If you cannot use it, you can always give it away to someone else—there is no such thing as too much—there are never too many bananas.**

Not Enough Pineapples

During the fifteen years between that first visit in 1966 and our residence there in 1981 we had returned to live in Kandoka village twice during the 1970s, and though there were a great many changes in the village, and indeed for all of Papua New Guinea during that time, we continued to live according to the lessons of reciprocity learned during those first months in the field. We bought no food for money and refused no gifts, but shared our surplus. As our family grew, we continued to be accompanied by our younger children. Our place in the village came to be something like that of educated Kaliai who worked far away in New Guinea. Our friends expected us to come "home" when we had leave, but knew that our work kept us away for long periods of time. They also credited us with knowing much more about the rules of their way of life than was our due. And we sometimes shared the delusion that we understood life in the village, but even fifteen years was not long enough to relieve the need for lessons in learning to live within the rules of gift exchange.

In the last paragraph I used the word **friends** to describe the villagers intentionally, but of course they were not all our friends. Over the years some really had become friends, others were acquaintances, others remained consultants or informants to whom we turned when we needed information. Still others, unfortunately, we did not like at all. We tried never to make an issue of these distinctions, of course, and to be evenhanded and generous to all, as they were to us. Although we almost never actually refused requests that were made of us, over the long term our reciprocity in the village was balanced. More was given to those who helped us the most; while we gave assistance or donations of small items even to those who were not close or helpful.

One elderly woman in particular was a trial for us. Sara was the eldest of a group of siblings and her younger brother and sister were both generous, informative, and delightful persons. Her younger sister, Makila, was a particularly close friend and consultant, and in deference to that friendship we felt awkward in dealing with the elder sister.

Sara was neither a friend nor an informant, but she had been, since she returned to live in the village at the time of our second trip in 1971, a constant (if minor) drain on our resources. She never asked for much at a time. A bar of soap, a box of matches, a bottle of kerosene, a cup of rice, some onions, a stick or two of tobacco, or some other small item was usually all that was at issue, but whenever she came around it was always to ask for something—or to let us know that when we left, we should give her some of the furnishings from the house. Too, unlike almost everyone else in the village, when she came, she was always empty-handed. We ate no taro from her gardens, and the kids chewed none of her sugarcane. In short, she was, as far as we could tell, a really grasping, selfish old woman—and we were not the only victims of her greed.

Having long before learned the lesson of the bananas, one day we had a stalk that was ripening so fast we couldn't keep up with it, so I pulled a few for our own use (we only had one stalk at the time) and walked down through the village to Ben's house, where his five children were playing. I sat down on his steps to talk, telling him that I intended to give the fruit to his kids. They never got them. Sara saw us from across the open plaza of the village and came rushing over, shouting, "My bananas!" Then she grabbed the stalk and went off gorging herself with them. Ben and I just looked at each other.

Finally it got to the point where it seemed to us that we had to do something. Ten years of being used was long enough. So there came the afternoon when Sara showed up to get some tobacco—again. But this time, when we gave her the two sticks she had demanded, we confronted her.

First, we noted the many times she had come to get things. We didn't mind sharing things, we explained. After all, we had plenty of tobacco and soap and rice and such, and most of it was there so that we could help our friends as they helped us, with folktales, information, or even gifts of food. The problem was that she kept coming to get things, but never came to talk, or to tell stories, or to bring some little something that the kids might like. Sara didn't argue—she agreed. "Look," we suggested, "it doesn't have to be much, and we don't mind giving you things—but you can help us. The kids like pineapples, and we don't have any—the next time you need something, bring something—like maybe a pineapple." Obviously somewhat embarrassed, she took her tobacco and left, saying that she would bring something soon. We were really pleased with ourselves. It had been a very difficult thing to do, but it was done, and we were convinced that either she would start bringing things or not come. It was as if a burden had lifted from our shoulders.

It worked. Only a couple of days passed before Sara was back, bringing her bottle to get it filled with kerosene. But this time, she came carrying the biggest, most beautiful pineapple we had seen the entire time we had been there. We had a friendly talk, filled her kerosene container, and hung the pineapple up on the veranda to ripen just a little further. A few days later we cut and ate it, and whether the satisfaction it gave came from the fruit or from its source would be hard to say, but it was delicious. That, we assumed, was the end of that irritant.

We were wrong, of course. The next afternoon, Mary, one of our best friends for years (and no relation to Sara), dropped by for a visit. As we talked, her eyes scanned the veranda. Finally she asked whether we hadn't had a pineapple there yesterday. We said we had, but that we had already eaten it. She commented that it had been a really nice-looking one, and we told her that it had been the best we had eaten in months. Then, after a pause, she asked, "Who brought it to you?" We smiled as we said, "Sara!" because Mary would appreciate our coup—she had commented many times in the past on the fact that Sara only **got** from us and never gave. She was silent for a moment, and then she said, "Well, I'm glad you enjoyed it—my father was waiting until it was fully ripe to harvest it for you, but when it went missing I thought maybe it was the one you had here. I'm glad to see you got it. I thought maybe a thief had eaten it in the bush."

LESSON 3: Where reciprocity is the rule and gifts are the idiom, you cannot demand a gift, just as you cannot refuse a request.

It says a great deal about the kindness and patience of the Kaliai people that they have been willing to be our hosts for all these years despite our blunders and lack of good manners. They have taught us a lot, and these three lessons are certainly not the least important things we learned.

Discussion Questions

1. What happened when the visiting anthropologists tried to buy a watermelon?
2. Among whom and where were the anthropologists doing their fieldwork?
3. What was the policy they had to follow about getting the food they needed?
4. What items did the anthropologists most often give the villagers as presents?
5. Why did bananas become a real food problem for the anthropologists?
6. Who was Sara and why did the anthropologists hate to see her come to visit?
7. How did the anthropologists get a pineapple?
8. What were the villagers' views about giving gifts? Did the anthropologists believe that gift-giving was free, or did they think it carried some other obligation?

Additional Resources

For Internet links related to this chapter, please visit our website at www.mhhe.com/dettwyler

CASSELL, JOAN, and SUE ELLEN JACOBS. *Handbook on Ethical Issues in Anthropology.* Washington, DC: American Anthropological Association, Special Publication No. 23, 1987.

DETTWYLER, KATHERINE A. *Dancing Skeletons: Life and Death in West Africa.* Prospect Heights, IL: Waveland Press, 1994.

DEVITA, PHILIP R., ed. *The Humbled Anthropologist: Tales from the Pacific.* Belmont, CA: Wadsworth Publishing Company, 1990.

GEERTZ, CLIFFORD. *Available Light: Anthropological Reflections on Philosophical Topics.* Princeton, NJ: Princeton University Press, 2001.

GRAY, ANN. *Research Practice for Cultural Studies: Ethnographic Methods and Lived Cultures.* New York: Sage Publications, 2002.

GRINDAL, BRUCE T., and FRANK SALAMONE, eds. *Bridges to Humanity: Narratives on Anthropology and Friendship.* Prospect Heights, IL: Waveland Press, 1995.

CHAPTER 13

Culture

23. "Thinking Inside the Box," by Caroline Kettlewell, from *The Washington Post*, July 15, 2002.

24. "A Woman's Curse? From Taboo to Time Bomb: Rethinking Menstruation," by Meredith Small, *The Sciences*, January/February 1999, pp. 24–29.

Culture is a profound and powerful force in the life of every human. What we eat, what we wear, the music we listen to, our beliefs about the universe, our beliefs about human nature, our beliefs about our bodies, our physical and mental health—all are influenced by the cultural beliefs and practices that we absorb growing up in our native cultures, as well as by ideas and influences from other cultures that affect us throughout our lives. Some cultural beliefs are general and all-pervasive; for example, the value most Americans place on the independence of individuals and political freedom, or the Bambara belief that spirits animate old baobab trees and live at the bottom of the Niger River. Other cultural beliefs are specific and, some would say, trivial, such as whether French fries are properly eaten with ketchup or vinegar or mayonnaise, or whether it is proper for women to wear pants. Some cultural beliefs and practices survive across many generations and even after the original populations have migrated to other places. Other cultural beliefs and practices are ephemeral—they last only a short time, and are quickly discarded when something more appealing comes along. Some cultural beliefs have little impact on our health, while others affect it in significant ways.

The selections for this chapter could have been about any cultural topic. We chose these pieces as interesting examples of how culture works, how it changes, and how it affects us.

 ## 23. THINKING INSIDE THE BOX

*Contact between different cultures has always involved the sharing of ideas, attitudes, and technology. Anthropologists speak of the **diffusion** of culture from one area to another. People take their food, their clothes, their music, their religions, and much more with them when they travel; and they learn about other ways of viewing*

the world, other ways of doing things from those who visit them, or those they meet on their travels. Diffusion of ideas is facilitated by various advances in our means of communication, from writing and printing presses and snail mail, to the telephone, telegraph, fax machine, and, more recently, email and the Internet. As transportation has improved; as migration has increased between communities, regions, and countries; as more and more people learn English for business purposes, or to use the Internet, the influence of other cultures continues to grow. An idea that previously might have taken centuries (literally) to diffuse from China to France can now be transmitted within minutes not only to France, but to every place on the planet via the Internet.

*In 1998 an article on an obscure British pastime known as **letterboxing** was published in* Smithsonian *magazine. Letterboxing can trace its roots back to 1854 and has been popular only among a small group of eccentrics in the British countryside who spread the idea and the rules by word of mouth, for the most part. In the* Smithsonian *article, letterboxing was presented as a quaint and unusual British pastime involving tramping over the moors searching for hidden boxes with unique, hand-carved rubber stamps inside them. Following the publication of the article, two Americans began a U.S. version of letterboxing on a modest scale. From humble beginnings, the sport has morphed into a variety of different forms, including the high-tech version known as **geocaching** which uses GPS systems, websites, and email alerts, the urban-literary version known as **bookcrossing,** and the minimalist* **Where's George?** *version. Within just a few years, letterboxing, geocaching, bookcrossing, and other variants have exploded in popularity in the United States, and have spread to other countries as well. The first reading for this chapter is a story published in 2002 in* The Washington Post *newspaper, and chronicles the beginning of letterboxing in the United States.*

We were on a forest trail, following clues written by a stranger we knew only by a code name, and things weren't going very well. We couldn't seem to locate a key landmark identified by the cryptic phrase, "Stop at the 'bat tree/J + B heart.' " Was it a tree that looked like a bat? An ash, from which baseball bats are made? Not, I would have to admit, that I'd know an ash from an oak from a maple. We presumed "J + B heart" was a romantic gesture unkindly carved into a tree, but we didn't see anything like that either.

We retraced our steps, turned around in circles a few times, stared furrow-browed at the clue as though it might yield further hints, and finally felt our way almost by instinct to a nondescript forked tree. I took a quick look; in a hollow between the forks, well disguised against casual discovery, the box was there.

"We found it!" I called out, enjoying a happy, triumphant thrill.

Two people came around the bend toward us on the pathway, but they passed by, too engrossed in conversation to notice us only 30 feet away. I pulled the box out. It was grimy and weathered, but the contents appeared safe. We crouched down. I unpacked my supplies.

It took us only a few minutes to accomplish what we came for. We restored the box carefully to its hiding place and slipped back onto the pathway.

This is letterboxing, a hybrid of art, orienteering and cerebral treasure hunt, a whimsical quest that can reward you with the discovery of beautiful places you never knew before. It's a British import that has caught on quickly in the past four years in the United States. Letterboxing, unembellished, is this: Armed with an unruled notebook, an ink pad, and a rubber stamp (preferably one you've carved yourself—but we'll get to that in a minute), off you go hunting for a letterbox.

A letterbox is a small, waterproof container holding another rubber stamp and paper pad. It has been hidden somewhere—generally, but not always, in a park or other public outdoor location—by a fellow letterboxer, whose clues you will attempt to follow to find the box. Should you succeed in your quest, you mark your victory by inking your stamp onto the letterbox notepad and the letterbox stamp onto your own notepad. Then you replace and carefully conceal the box just where you found it. That's it.

Letterboxing's roots are in England, where it is generally confined to the environs of Dartmoor National Park in Devon and traces its history to a 19th-century gentleman who left his card in a bottle in a remote part thereof. On this side of the pond, you can hunt letterboxes in every state as well as in Canada, Central America, Mexico, Bermuda, the Virgin Islands and the District of Columbia—so far—and almost all of those boxes have been placed since 1998. To try it for yourself, all you need is Internet access, an afternoon, a spirit of adventure and a handful of supplies you can easily acquire for under $30.

In the course of two agreeable days recently, my husband, son and I carved two stamps, hunted for six boxes, collected five stamps, discovered four parks we'd never before visited and picked up three deer ticks. We trod warily through verdant poison ivy and downwind of at least one discomfited skunk, and tallied sightings of all manner of wildlife, all within a half-hour's drive (okay, maybe not during rush hour) of Capitol Hill.

To start our quest, we went online to Letterboxing North America (LbNA) at www.letterboxing.org. LbNA is a true virtual community; it was born as a Web site, it has helped forge enduring friendships among people who never have met in person, and its history exists almost entirely in e-mail format, "in three hard drives scattered around my house," LbNA co-founder Erik Davis says.

In April 1998, *Smithsonian* magazine ran a story about a quirky British pastime called letterboxing and the passionate devotees who would happily tramp endless miles through Dartmoor in execrable weather in pursuit of hidden stamps.

Davis, a self-described "urban refugee" who escaped to Vermont in the 1970s, says of the article, "It just hit me. It's so great—it involves families out hiking with their kids, the mystery of the hunt and the search and the clues, and it involves an art form in terms of the stamp you make and how it relates to where you hide the box. I thought 'There's got to be a way to do this.' So I got on the Internet."

He found his way to a couple of Dartmoor letterboxing Web sites and e-mailed to ask if they knew of anybody letterboxing in the states. They didn't. But a week later, Davis got an e-mail from a Minnesotan named Dan Servatius, another *Smithsonian* reader intrigued by the letterboxing story. "I just talked to these people from Dartmoor and they gave me your name," Servatius said.

Within little more than a week, Servatius and Davis had hatched Letterboxing North America with "a very modest sort of page" on the Web, a place where clues and information could be shared to help inspire letterboxing in the United States. Davis hid the first LbNA box that same month, at Prayer Rock, near Bristol, Vt. (where you can still find it).

According to Davis, "Our founding principle was that any child could go on any public access computer and find their way in and find the clues to take their family on an adventure." Although the LbNA site has greatly expanded, and there is a "talk list" with 500 subscribers and new clues added almost daily, it's still all maintained by a small volunteer group, is determinedly nonprofit and has a friendly, come-one-and-all spirit.

The first stop you'll want to make at Letterboxing.org is the FAQ's (Frequently Asked Questions) page. Here you can find everything you need to know to begin letterboxing yourself, from obtaining supplies to interpreting clues to following good letterboxing etiquette. When you're ready to try your first hunt, return to the home page and click on the image of the book to go to the list of letterboxing clues, organized by location.

As the FAQ's page warns, "Clues come in all shapes and styles, from the simple to the cryptic to the poetic to the bizarre." The variety is endlessly imaginative, with new variations cropping up regularly. In addition to "traditional" letterboxes, there are coveted Hitchhikers (a stamp and pad without an official home, placed in an existing box to be picked up and moved along to another box by the next letterboxer to find them) and Mystery Boxes (the mystery is where to begin looking for them; sometimes the clue gives you the state, but sometimes all you know is that the box is somewhere on planet Earth). One of the most recent innovations is "virtual letterboxing," a hunt that takes place entirely online.

For our first letterboxing attempt, we decided to go looking for several boxes hidden in the Accotink Bay Wildlife Refuge by an avid Virginia-based letterboxer known as the "Jolly G-Man." (Adopting a pseudonymous "nom de stamp"—as Erik Davis, aka the "Vermont Viking," calls it—is an English letterboxing tradition, a lighthearted cloak-and-dagger touch taken up by many U.S. enthusiasts.) The G-Man has hidden nearly 60 boxes around the country, and his clues run the gamut from simple and straightforward to downright dastardly. We opted for the former.

The Accotink Bay Wildlife Refuge is on the grounds of the Fort Belvoir Army base in Virginia. A very nice MP with a very serious M-16 directed us to the refuge's parking lot, where we paused for an instructive visit to the spare but clean composting restrooms; picked up a map to the 1,856-acre refuge at the small kiosk at the edge of the parking lot; and then plunged into the woods.

The trail threaded first through low-lying woods that in wetter times would probably be boggy; we were immediately besieged by a cloud of iridescent green flies incessantly buzzing around our heads like a pack of joyriding hoodlums. Because letterboxing usually takes place in the great outdoors, a realm notorious for harboring all manner of unpredictable elements, animal, vegetable and otherwise, you will find that things that slither, bite, and itch figure regularly in letterboxing discussions. If you are not fond of nature unfettered, letterboxing is possibly not for you. For others, a measure of suffering is half the fun; after all, do we not go into the wilderness to be tested and emerge stronger? Do we not go in order to regale our sofa-bound friends with tales of epic travails that are generally almost true? I think so.

Perhaps a half-hour's walk took us within range of the first box. The traffic noise from nearby Route 1 faded as we moved deeper into the refuge, and presently we emerged in a meadow leading to a hilltop where the last step called for a compass reading (a common feature in many letterboxing clues). We read. We proceeded. A grove of scruffy, largely indistinguishable trees presented itself to us. We stepped up smartly to the tree to which our compass pointed us, and there, amazingly, behind that very tree, was our very first letterbox.

It is when you find that first box that you discover how ridiculously fun this delightfully pointless adventure of letterboxing really is.

"It is a wonderful feeling of accomplishment," says Amanda "Amanda from Seattle" Arkebauer, a flight attendant and prolific letterboxer. She has "stamped into" 250 boxes and placed about 30 in the United States, Canada and Central America. After her first find, on a Seattle mountaintop, she says, she was hooked.

Virginian Robin Russ, of Norfolk, says that when her family tried its first letterboxing hunt, "It took us an hour or two, but when we found the little box, we screamed. It was so much fun. The joy of discovery is intoxicating."

Giddy with surprise and satisfaction at our own first success, we set about putting the inaugural stamp in our logbook. I also marked the G-Man's log with my personal stamp, which I'd carved only the day before.

We collected all three of the Jolly G-Man's "McCarty Farm" stamps that afternoon, on an extended circuit hike through a hardwood forest and by the water's edge of Accotink Bay. Along the way we sighted herons and egrets, a large box turtle, several camouflaged toads hopping along the forest floor and one wild turkey scurrying off into the underbrush at our approach. Nearly back where we had started, we made a short detour for a fourth G-Man box, this one placed along a wheelchair-accessible paved pathway.

"Hey look," I said, thumbing through the logbook. " 'Amanda from Seattle' was here!" Each of the Jolly G-Man's boxes was well concealed by some combination of rocks, deadwood and fallen leaves, but easily retrieved once we'd found the correct spot. Letterboxers point out that you should never dig holes or in any way damage the surrounding landscape to hide or hunt for boxes, and Letterboxing.org advocates Leave No Trace principles (see them at www.lnt.org) for respectful stewardship of outdoor resources. A number of letterboxers I spoke with also thought it was a good idea to obtain permission and even work together with land owners and managers to develop letterboxing activities appropriately within their parks and properties.

"This doesn't want to be a nuisance," Davis stresses.

As letterboxing has grown, debate has arisen about whether the act of planting a human artifact in a wild place actually contradicts the essence of the Leave No Trace philosophy; the prevailing letterboxing sentiment seems to be that a small container, invisible to anyone not expressly searching for it, is acceptable. And the truth is that a letterbox isn't necessarily easy to find even when you think you know where you're supposed to be looking; with the third G-Man box, we spent several minutes peering behind various oaks to locate the particular one indicated in the clues.

Gale Zucker, a professional photographer and letterboxer from Connecticut, recalls, "Once we had no compass and had a set of clues that included looking for a boulder that resembled 'Wimpy's favorite food.' Talk about frustrating—almost every boulder looks a little like a hamburger if you squint at it the right way."

The Jolly G-Man says that unpredictability is all part of the game. "You can read directions wrong or the letterbox can have moved or disappeared. Things can change in the environment too." And of course, he notes with a jolly laugh, "Some people's abilities to give you directions are . . . better than others."

On our second hunt, a week later, we discovered the unpredictability factor for ourselves. We were searching for two boxes placed in Huntley Meadows Park in Alexandria by a letterboxer known as "Two Gray Squirrels." The park is a delightful, tranquil spot, a pocket of woods and wetlands in the middle of suburbia. Here we saw a black rat snake, dark as jet, long and languid, sunning on a weathered gray branch, as well as ducks, geese and other birds, turtles, one very small woodland toad and fat, emerald green frogs plopping happily through the silty muck of the marsh.

What we didn't find was the second box. Because I'd forgotten the compass, I cannot say for certain that we were looking in exactly the right clump of trees, and we weren't altogether certain we had even followed the clues correctly that far. But our failure was a momentary vexation; it was hard to complain about a pleasant walk in the outdoors just because we didn't get a stamp at the end.

Ultimately, that's what letterboxing is all about—the fun of the hunt, the pleasure of the outdoors, experiencing, as the Jolly G-Man says, "other people's favorite places."

"Letterboxing has provided for some of the best moments we've had as a family in the past months," Zucker says. "It has caused us to head out together and explore wonderful trails and breathtakingly beautiful spots that we'd never have heard of—much less found or made the time to look for—were we not in search of a little plastic box with a stamper."

"People are participating from all over the country," Davis says. "Where it has gone has totally amazed me."

Stamps of Approval

It would be difficult to underestimate my artistic talents, as several art teachers over the years have pointedly observed. And when it comes to projects, I'm strictly from the measure-once-and-cut-twice school, short on patience and inclined to start itching to skip to the end somewhere around Step 2. So to be honest, the stamp-carving part wasn't what first drew me to letterboxing. But it's the art part that makes letterboxing more than just a walk in the woods, and as you begin collecting stamps in your logbook, you see why.

When you make the stamp yourself, it can be utterly unique, carved to reflect your personality or the setting or the theme of a particular letterbox. "I really encourage people to take the time to carve their own stamps," says Erik Davis, and many other letterboxers feel the same way.

In the interest of full journalistic inquiry, then, I tried my hand at carving. The Letterboxing North America FAQ's page at www.letterboxing.org includes ample information on stamping materials and a link to the very helpful "How to make a rubber stamp" by Mitch "Der Mad Stamper" Klink, an Oregon graphic designer and letterboxer. (His directions can be found via hyperlink from the letterboxing FAQ's page, or directly at members.aol.com/Letterboxr/carving.html). You can find stamping materials at art supply stores; at the Jolly G-Man's recommendation, I went to Pearl Discount Art & Craft at 5695 Telegraph Road in Alexandria (at Lenore Avenue, just off I-95/495; 703/960-3900), which has a range of carving media, ink pads in a broad spectrum of colors, and acid-free pads and notebooks for your logbook.

If you want to get fancy about carving, there are all kinds of tools and techniques and Internet groups and whatnot, but I kept it simple. (A links page and stamping information provided by the Carving Consortium can be found at www.negia.net/~unity/newbie.htm). I followed Der Mad Stamper's directions and used a small, rectangular, white vinyl Factis eraser; an X-Acto knife; and a design guaranteed not to raise my standing among those former art teachers. I sketched the outline on a piece of paper, blacked it in heavily with a No. 2 pencil, then pressed the darkened side against the eraser and rubbed vigorously with a blunt object, thus transferring the image in reverse onto the eraser. Cut away the parts where the design isn't and voila! You've got your stamp.

Whittling away at that eraser turned out to be much more entertaining than I had expected—and not nearly as difficult. But apparently I'd gotten a little carried away with my slicing and dicing, as by week two, letterbox five, my stamp had disintegrated into a small pile of white vinyl chunks.

No matter; I'd already carved my second.

Discussion Questions

1. What does traditional British letterboxing involve?
2. Why do you think people in England participate in letterboxing?
3. How did letterboxing come to the United States? What modes of communication were involved?
4. Visit the Letterboxing North America website (www.letterboxing.org). How does American letterboxing, as started by Davis and Servatius, differ from the original? What cultural spin did these two Americans put on an obscure British pastime?
5. Why does Caroline Kettlewell say that her family enjoys letterboxing?
6. Visit the Geocaching website at www.geocaching.com/. How does geocaching differ from letterboxing?
7. Visit the Bookcrossing website at www.bookcrossing.com. How does bookcrossing differ from geocaching and letterboxing?
8. Visit the "Where's George?" website at www.wheresgeorge.com. How does this variant differ from the others? Does it, perhaps, not belong in the same category of behavior?
9. In what ways does geocaching reflect American culture, in contrast to its British ancestor, letterboxing? Who participates in bookcrossing—different people than those participating in geocaching?
10. Discuss other examples of how the Internet and email have increased the speed of cultural diffusion. Is the world becoming more culturally homogeneous? Why or why not?

 24. A WOMAN'S CURSE? FROM TABOO TO TIME BOMB: RETHINKING MENSTRUATION

Menstruation, like lactation, is a biological phenomenon, part of normal development for all human females. At the same time, like lactation, it is heavily culturized. Different cultures celebrate or denigrate menstruation and hold diverse beliefs about what it means, what effects it has on society and the individual, and how you should talk about it and feel about it. Additionally, our experiences of menstruation are affected by our cultural beliefs and practices concerning pregnancy and lactation. Our cultural beliefs sometimes contradict our biology, leading to biological problems with a cultural origin. In this selection, physical anthropologist Meredith Small examines Beverly Strassmann's recent research on menstruation among the Dogon of Mali, showing how a typical American woman's experience of menstruation differs from that of a woman living in a traditional subsistence agricultural society, and how it differs from what our bodies have been selected to expect and experience over millions of years of natural selection.

187

A Woman's Curse?
From Taboo to Time
Bomb: Rethinking
Menstruation

The passage from girlhood to womanhood is marked by a flow of blood from the uterus. Without elaborate ceremony, often without discussion, girls know that when they begin to menstruate, their world is changed forever. For the next thirty years or so, they will spend much energy having babies, or trying not to, reminded at each menstruation that either way, the biology of reproduction has a major impact on their lives.

Anthropologists have underscored the universal importance of menstruation by documenting how the event is interwoven into the ideology as well as the daily activities of cultures around the world. The customs attached to menstruation take peculiarly negative forms: the so-called menstrual taboos. Those taboos may prohibit a woman from having sex with her husband or from cooking for him. They may bar her from visiting sacred places or taking part in sacred activities. They may forbid her to touch certain items used by men, such as hunting gear or weapons, or to eat certain foods or to wash at certain times. They may also require that a woman paint her face red or wear a red hip cord, or that she segregate herself in a special hut while she is menstruating. In short, the taboos set menstruating women apart from the rest of their society, marking them as impure and polluting.

Anthropologists have studied menstrual taboos for decades, focusing on the negative symbolism of the rituals as a cultural phenomenon. Perhaps, suggested one investigator, taking a Freudian perspective, such taboos reflect the anxiety that men feel about castration, an anxiety that would be prompted by women's genital bleeding. Others have suggested that the taboos serve to prevent menstrual odor from interfering with hunting, or that they protect men from microorganisms that might otherwise be transferred during sexual intercourse with a menstruating woman. Until recently, few investigators had considered the possibility that the taboos—and the very fact of menstruation—might instead exist because they conferred an evolutionary advantage.

In the mid-1980s the anthropologist Beverly I. Strassmann of the University of Michigan in Ann Arbor began to study the ways men and women have evolved to accomplish (and regulate) reproduction. Unlike traditional anthropologists, who focus on how culture affects human behavior, Strassmann was convinced that the important role played by biology was being neglected. Menstruation, she suspected, would be a key for observing and understanding the interplay of biology and culture in human reproductive behavior.

To address the issue, Strassmann decided to seek a culture in which making babies was an ongoing part of adult life. For that she had to get away from industrialized countries, with their bias toward contraception and low birthrates. In a "natural-fertility population," she reasoned, she could more clearly see the connection between the physiology of women and the strategies men and women use to exploit that physiology for their own reproductive ends.

Strassmann ended up in a remote corner of West Africa, living in close quarters with the Dogon, a traditional society whose indigenous religion of ancestor worship requires that menstruating women spend their nights at a small hut. For more than two years Strassmann kept track of the women staying at the hut, and she confirmed the menstruations by testing urine samples for the appropriate hormonal changes. In so doing, she amassed the first long-term data describing how a traditional society appropriates a physiological event—menstruation—and refracts that event through a prism of behaviors and beliefs.

What she found explicitly challenges the conclusions of earlier investigators about the cultural function of menstrual taboos. For the Dogon men, she discovered, enforcing visits to the menstrual hut serves to channel parental resources into the upbringing of their own children. But more, Strassmann, who also had training as a reproductive physiologist, proposed a new theory of why menstruation itself evolved as it did—and again, the answer is essentially a story of conserving resources. Finally, her observations pose provocative questions about women's health in industrialized societies, raising serious doubts about the tactics favored by Western medicine for developing contraceptive technology.

Menstruation is the visible stage of the ovarian cycle, orchestrated primarily by hormones secreted by the ovaries: progesterone and a family of hormones called estrogens. At the beginning of each cycle (by convention, the first day of a woman's period) the levels of the estrogens begin to rise. After about five days, as their concentrations increase, they cause the blood- and nutrient-rich inner lining of the uterus, called the endometrium, to thicken and acquire a densely branching network of blood vessels. At about the middle of the cycle, ovulation takes place, and an egg makes its way from one of the two ovaries down one of the paired fallopian tubes to the uterus. The follicle from which the egg was released in the ovary now begins to secrete progesterone as well as estrogens, and the progesterone causes the endometrium to swell and become even richer with blood vessels—in short, fully ready for a pregnancy, should conception take place and the fertilized egg become implanted.

If conception does take place, the levels of estrogens and progesterone continue to rise throughout the pregnancy. That keeps the endometrium thick enough to support the quickening life inside the uterus. When the baby is born and the new mother begins nursing, the estrogens and progesterone fall to their initial levels, and lactation hormones keep them suppressed. The uterus thus lies quiescent until frequent lactation ends, which triggers the return to ovulation.

If conception does not take place after ovulation, all the ovarian hormones also drop to their initial levels, and menstruation—the shedding of part of the uterine lining—begins. The lining is divided into three layers: a basal layer that is constantly maintained, and two superficial layers, which shed and regrow with each menstrual cycle. All mammals undergo cyclical changes in the state of the endometrium. In most mammals the sloughed-off layers are resorbed into the body if fertilization does not take place. But in some higher primates, including humans, some of the shed endometrium is not resorbed. The shed lining, along with some blood, flows from the body through the vaginal opening, a process that in humans typically lasts from three to five days.

Of course, physiological facts alone do not explain why so many human groups have infused a bodily function with symbolic meaning. And so in 1986 Strassmann found herself driving through the Sahel region of West Africa at the peak of the hot season, heading for a sandstone cliff called the Bandiagara Escarpment, in Mali. There, permanent Dogon villages of mud or stone houses dotted the rocky plateau. The menstrual huts were obvious: round, low-roofed buildings set apart from the rectangular dwellings of the rest of the village.

The Dogon are a society of millet and onion farmers who endorse polygyny, and they maintain their traditional culture despite the occasional visits of outsiders. In a few Dogon villages, in fact, tourists are fairly common, and ethnographers had frequently studied the Dogon language, religion and social structure before Strassmann's arrival. But her visit was the first time someone from the outside wanted to delve into an intimate issue in such detail.

189

A Woman's Curse?
From Taboo to Time
Bomb: Rethinking
Menstruation

It took Strassmann a series of hikes among villages, and long talks with male elders under the thatched-roof shelters where they typically gather, to find the appropriate sites for her research. She gained permission for her study in fourteen villages, eventually choosing two. That exceptional welcome, she thinks, emphasized the universality of her interests. "I'm working on all the things that really matter to [the Dogon]—fertility, economics—so they never questioned my motives or wondered why I would be interested in these things," she says. "It seemed obvious to them." She set up shop for the next two and a half years in a stone house in the village, with no running water or electricity. Eating the daily fare of the Dogon, millet porridge, she and a research assistant began to integrate themselves into village life, learning the language, getting to know people and tracking visits to the menstrual huts.

Following the movements of menstruating women was surprisingly easy. The menstrual huts are situated outside the walled compounds of the village, but in full view of the men's thatched-roof shelters. As the men relax under their shelters, they can readily see who leaves the huts in the morning and returns to them in the evening. And as nonmenstruating women pass the huts on their way to and from the fields or to other compounds, they too can see who is spending the night there. Strassmann found that when she left her house in the evening to take data, any of the villagers could accurately predict who she would find in the menstrual huts.

The huts themselves are cramped, dark buildings—hardly places where a woman might go to escape the drudgery of work or to avoid an argument with her husband or a co-wife. The huts sometimes become so crowded that some occupants are forced outside—making the women even more conspicuous. Although babies and toddlers can go with their mothers to the huts, the women consigned there are not allowed to spend time with the rest of their families. They must cook with special pots, not their usual household possessions. Yet they are still expected to do their usual jobs, such as working in the fields. Why, Strassmann wondered, would anyone put up with such conditions?

The answer, for the Dogon, is that a menstruating woman is a threat to the sanctity of religious altars, where men pray and make sacrifices for the protection of their fields, their families and their village. If menstruating women come near the altars, which are situated both indoors and outdoors, the Dogon believe that their aura of pollution will ruin the altars and bring calamities upon the village. The belief is so ingrained that the women themselves have internalized it, feeling its burden of responsibility and potential guilt. Thus violations of the taboo are rare, because a menstruating woman who breaks the rules knows that she is personally responsible if calamities occur.

Nevertheless, Strassmann still thought a more functional explanation for menstrual taboos might also exist, one closely related to reproduction. As she was well aware, even before her studies among the Dogon, people around the world have a fairly sophisticated view of how reproduction works. In general, people everywhere know full well that menstruation signals the absence of a pregnancy and the possibility of another one. More precisely, Strassmann could frame her hypothesis by reasoning as follows: Across cultures, men and women recognize that a lack of menstrual cycling in a woman implies she is either pregnant, lactating or menopausal. Moreover, at least among natural-fertility cultures that do not practice birth control, continual cycles during peak reproductive years imply to people in those cultures that a woman is sterile. Thus, even though people might not be able to pinpoint ovulation, they can easily identify whether a woman will soon be ready to conceive on the basis of whether she is menstruating. And that leads straight to Strassmann's insightful hypothesis about the role of menstrual taboos: information about menstruation can be a means of tracking paternity.

"There are two important pieces of information for assessing paternity," Strassmann notes: timing of intercourse and timing of menstruation. "By forcing women to signal menstruation, men are trying to gain equal access to one part of that critical information." Such information, she explains, is crucial to Dogon men, because they invest so many resources in their own offspring. Descent is marked through the male line; land and the food that comes from the land are passed down from fathers to sons. Information about paternity is thus crucial to a man's entire lineage. And because each man has as many as four wives, he cannot possibly track them all. So forcing women to signal their menstrual periods, or lack thereof, helps men avoid cuckoldry.

To test her hypothesis, Strassmann tracked residence in the menstrual huts for 736 consecutive days, collecting data on 477 complete cycles. She noted who was at each hut and how long each woman stayed. She also collected urine from ninety-three women over a ten-week period, to check the correlation between residence in the menstrual hut and the fact of menstruation.

The combination of ethnographic records and urinalyses showed that the Dogon women mostly play by the rules. In 86 percent of the hormonally detected menstruations, women went to the hut. Moreover, none of the tested women went to the hut when they were not menstruating. In the remaining 14 percent of the tested menstruations, women stayed home from the hut, in violation of the taboo, but some were near menopause and so not at high risk for pregnancy. More important, none of the women who violated the taboo did it twice in a row. Even they were largely willing to comply.

Thus, Strassmann concluded, the huts do indeed convey a fairly reliable signal, to men and to everyone else, about the status of a woman's fertility. When she leaves the hut, she is considered ready to conceive. When she stops going to the hut, she is evidently pregnant or menopausal. And women of prime reproductive age who visit the hut on a regular basis are clearly infertile.

It also became clear to Strassmann that the Dogon do indeed use that information to make paternity decisions. In several cases a man was forced to marry a pregnant woman, simply because everyone knew that the man had been the woman's first sexual partner after her last visit to the menstrual hut. Strassmann followed one case in which a child was being brought up by a man because he was the mother's first sexual partner after a hut visit, even though the woman soon married a different man. (The woman already knew she was pregnant by the first man at the time of her marriage, and she did not visit the menstrual hut before she married. Thus the truth was obvious to everyone, and the real father took the child.)

In general, women are cooperative players in the game because without a man, a woman has no way to support herself or her children. But women follow the taboo reluctantly. They complain about going to the hut. And if their husbands convert from the traditional religion of the Dogon to a religion that does not impose menstrual taboos, such as Islam or Christianity, the women quickly cease visiting the hut. Not that such a religious conversion quells a man's interest in his wife's fidelity: far from it. But the rules change. Perhaps the sanctions of the new religion against

191

A Woman's Curse?
From Taboo to Time
Bomb: Rethinking
Menstruation

infidelity help keep women faithful, so the men can relax their guard. Or perhaps the men are willing to trade the reproductive advantages of the menstrual taboo for the economic benefits gained by converting to the new religion. Whatever the case, Strassmann found an almost perfect correlation between a husband's religion and his wives' attendance at the hut. In sum, the taboo is established by men, backed by supernatural forces, and internalized and accepted by women until the men release them from the belief.

But beyond the cultural machinations of men and women that Strassmann expected to find, her data show something even more fundamental—and surprising—about female biology. On average, she calculates, a woman in a natural-fertility population such as the Dogon has only about 110 menstrual periods in her lifetime. The rest of the time she will be prepubescent, pregnant, lactating or menopausal. Women in industrialized cultures, by contrast, have more than three times as many cycles: 350 to 400, on average, in a lifetime. They reach menarche (their first menstruation) earlier—at age twelve and a half, compared with the onset age of sixteen in natural-fertility cultures. They have fewer babies, and they lactate hardly at all. All those factors lead women in the industrialized world to a lifetime of nearly continuous menstrual cycling.

The big contrast in cycling profiles during the reproductive years can be traced specifically to lactation. Women in more traditional societies spend most of their reproductive years in lactation amenorrhea, the state in which the hormonal changes required for nursing suppress ovulation and inhibit menstruation. And it is not just that the Dogon bear more children (eight to nine on average); they also nurse each child on demand rather than in scheduled bouts, all through the night as well as the day, and intensely enough that ovulation simply stops for about twenty months per child. Women in industrialized societies typically do not breastfeed as intensely (or at all), and rarely breastfeed each child for as long as the Dogon women do. (The average for American women is four months.)

The Dogon experience with menstruation may be far more typical of the human condition over most of evolutionary history than is the standard menstrual experience in industrialized nations. If so, Strassmann's findings alter some of the most closely held beliefs about female biology. Contrary to what the Western medical establishment might think, it is not particularly "normal" to menstruate each month. The female body, according to Strassmann, is biologically designed to spend much more time in lactation amenorrhea than in menstrual cycling. That in itself suggests that oral contraceptives, which alter hormone levels to suppress ovulation and produce a bleeding, could be forcing a continual state of cycling for which the body is ill-prepared. Women might be better protected against reproductive cancers if their contraceptives mimicked lactation amenorrhea and depressed the female reproductive hormones, rather than forcing the continual ebb and flow of menstrual cycles.

Strassmann's data also call into question a recently popularized idea about menstruation: that regular menstrual cycles might be immunologically beneficial for women. In 1993 the controversial writer Margie Profet, whose ideas about evolutionary and reproductive biology have received vast media attention, proposed in *The Quarterly Review of Biology* that menstruation could have such an adaptive value. She noted that viruses and bacteria regularly enter the female body on the backs of sperm, and she hypothesized that the best way to get them out is to flush them out. Here, then, was a positive, adaptive role for something unpleasant, an evolutionary reason for suffering cramps each month. Menstruation, according to Profet, had evolved to rid the body of pathogens. The "anti-pathogen" theory was an exciting hypothesis, and it helped win Profet a MacArthur Foundation award. But Strassmann's work soon showed that Profet's ideas could not be supported because of one simple fact: under less-industrialized conditions, women menstruate relatively rarely.

Instead, Strassmann notes, if there is an adaptive value to menstruation, it is ultimately a strategy to conserve the body's resources. She estimates that maintaining the endometrial lining during the second half of the ovarian cycle takes substantial metabolic energy. Once the endometrium is built up and ready to receive a fertilized egg, the tissue requires a sevenfold metabolic increase to remain rich in blood and ready to support a pregnancy. Hence, if no pregnancy is forthcoming, it makes a lot of sense for the body to let part of the endometrium slough off and then regenerate itself, instead of maintaining that rather costly but unneeded tissue. Such energy conservation is common among vertebrates: male rhesus monkeys have shrunken testes during their nonbreeding season, Burmese pythons shrink their guts when they are not digesting, and hibernating animals put their metabolisms on hold.

Strassmann also suggests that periodically ridding oneself of the endometrium could make a difference to a woman's long-term survival. Because female reproductive hormones affect the brain and other tissues, the metabolism of the entire body is involved during cycling. Strassmann estimates that by keeping hormonal activity low through half the cycle, a woman can save about six days' worth of energy for every four nonconceptive cycles. Such caloric conservation might have proved useful to early hominids who lived by hunting and gathering, and even today it might be helpful for women living in less affluent circumstances than the ones common in the industrialized West.

But perhaps the most provocative implications of Strassmann's work have to do with women's health. In 1994 a group of physicians and anthropologists published a paper, also in *The Quarterly Review of Biology,* suggesting that the reproductive histories and lifestyles of women in industrialized cultures are at odds with women's naturally evolved biology, and that the differences lead to greater risks of reproductive cancers. For example, the investigators estimated that women in affluent cultures may have a hundredfold greater risk of breast cancer than do women who subsist by hunting and gathering. The increased risk is probably caused not only by low levels of exercise and a high-fat diet, but also by a relatively high number of menstrual cycles over a lifetime. Repeated exposure to the hormones of the ovarian cycle—because of early menarche, late menopause, lack of pregnancy and little or no breastfeeding—is implicated in other reproductive cancers as well.

Those of us in industrialized cultures have been running an experiment on ourselves. The body evolved over millions of years to move across the landscape looking for food, to live in small kin-based groups, to make babies at intervals of four years or so and to invest heavily in each child by nursing intensely for years. How many women now follow those traditional patterns? We move little, we rely on others to get our food, and we rarely reproduce or lactate. Those culturally initiated shifts in lifestyle may pose biological risks.

Our task is not to overcome that biology, but to work with it. Now that we have a better idea of how the female body was designed, it may be time to rework our lifestyles and change some of our expectations. It may be time to borrow from our distant past or from our contemporaries in distant cultures, and treat our bodies more as nature intended.

Discussion Questions

1. How is menstruation "marked" in societies around the world? Discuss some of the early anthropological explanations for its negative symbolism.
2. How did Beverly Strassmann gather data to test whether menstrual taboos among the Dogon of Mali might be adaptive?
3. What is the nature of menstrual taboos among the Dogon? What is the purpose of the taboos, according to the Dogon?
4. What is the purpose of the taboos according to Beverly Strassmann? In other words, what significant information about reproductive status do women's visits to the menstrual huts convey to members of the village?
5. What is the relationship between a man's religion and his wife's visits to the menstrual hut?
6. Compare the number of menstrual periods experienced by a Dogon woman versus a woman in the United States. Why do American women have so many menstrual periods?
7. What is the relationship between breastfeeding (lactation) and menstruation?
8. What was Margie Profet's 1993 theory about the adaptive value of menstrual cycling for women? What does Strassmann have to say about Profet's theory?
9. In what way is menstruation an energy-saving adaptation?
10. What is the link between numerous menstrual cycles over a lifetime and a woman's risk of reproductive cancers?
11. How might women in the United States change their lifestyles to reduce their risk of reproductive cancers?

Additional Resources

For Internet links related to this chapter, please visit our website at www.mhhe.com/dettwyler

BENEDICT, RUTH. *Patterns of Culture.* New York: Mariner Books (reprint), 1989.

BUCKLEY, THOMAS, and ALMA GOTTLIEB, eds. *Blood Magic: The Anthropology of Menstruation.* Berkeley, CA: University of California Press, 1988.

CRONK, LEE. *That Complex Whole: Culture and the Evolution of Human Behavior.* Boulder, CO: Westview Press, 1999.

DE WAAL, FRANS B. M., ed. *Tree of Origin: What Primate Behavior Can Tell Us about Human Social Evolution.* Cambridge, MA: Harvard University Press, 2002.

DONOHUE-CAREY, PATRICIA. "Solitary or Shared Sleep: What's Safe?" *Mothering,* September–October: 39–47.

DUNBAR, R. I. M., CHRIS KNIGHT, and CAMILLA POWER, eds. *The Evolution of Culture: An Interdisciplinary View.* New Brunswick, NJ: Rutgers University Press, 1999.

FERNEA, ELIZABETH WARNOCK. *Guests of the Sheik: An Ethnography of an Iraqi Village.* New York: Anchor, 1969. Originally published in 1965.

GRANSTROM, CHRIS. "They Live and Breathe Letterboxing," *Smithsonian* 29, no. 1, (April 1998), pp. 82–91.

GROCE, NORA ELLEN. *Everyone Here Spoke Sign Language: Hereditary Deafness on Martha's Vineyard.* Cambridge, MA: Harvard University Press, 1988.

HERMAN, ANDREW, and THOMAS SWISS, eds. *The World Wide Web and Contemporary Cultural Theory: Magic, Metaphor, Power.* New York: Routledge, 2000.

MEAD, MARGARET. *Sex and Temperament in Three Primitive Societies.* New York: Quill, 1988. Originally published in 1935.

MILLER, DANIEL, and DON SLATER. *The Internet: An Ethnographic Approach.* New York: New York University Press, 2002.

QUINN, DANIEL. *Ishmael.* New York: Bantam Books, 1995.

ZHA, JIANYING, and TRANYING ZHA. *China Pop: How Soap Operas, Tabloids and Bestsellers are Transforming a Culture.* New York: New Press, 1996.

CHAPTER 14

Ethnicity

25. "País de mis Sueños: Reflections on Ethnic Labels, Dichotomies, and Ritual Interactions," by Gisela Ernst, from *Distant Mirrors: American as a Foreign Culture,* Philip R. DeVita and James D. Armstrong, eds. Belmont, CA: Wadsworth Publishing Company 2001, pp. 102–109.

26. "People of the Reindeer," by John F. Ross, *Smithsonian* 31, no. 9 (December 2000), pp. 54–64.

Ethnicity and bigotry have often been linked. Because some groups of people have a different skin color, dress differently, speak differently, or practice different religious beliefs, they are sometimes the targets of bigotry. Between 1890 and 1920 more than 18 million immigrants came to America. They represented many different ethnic groups. Some had non-English names that were difficult to pronounce and spell. Others could not speak English. Both groups were often assigned new American-sounding names, which immigration agents hoped would speed the loss of those peoples' ethnicity and cause their assimilation as Americans. This concept even became the central focus of a popular play in 1908, called The Melting Pot. *The play, written by a Jewish immigrant named Israel Zangwill, was an instant success and carried the powerful message that all immigrants should transform themselves into citizens by stripping away all vestiges of their original ethnicity. The play professed that those actions would produce a "new alloy" called Americans that would be forged in the "crucible of democracy." Most new immigrants arriving during the 19th and 20th centuries learned that their success often depended on blending in and following the norms of American society instead of remaining ethnically separate. Today, however, attitudes have changed. During the last half-century many immigrants coming to America have remained proud of their individual ethnicity and want to express homage to their roots. This has now created a new set of cultural problems because of existing ingrained ethnic divisions within America.*

25. PAÍS DE MIS SUEÑOS: REFLECTIONS ON ETHNIC LABELS, DICHOTOMIES, AND RITUAL INTERACTIONS

Americans tend to view their culture ethnocentrically; they tend to believe that their culture and their democratic way of life should be the standards for all other cultures. Americans are shocked to learn that members of other nations often do not think American culture is the best, nor do those people especially want to mold their culture in ways to imitate it. This type of realization is the focus of the article written by Gisela Ernst. She came to the United States, the country of her dreams, only to discover that American culture is different in many ways from the culture she grew up knowing in Peru. Her examination of American culture, from an outsider's viewpoint, is both eye opening and enlightening. She found, for example, that ethnic labeling has become a system-maintaining device used in America for social and political reasons. Most important, this article should cause each of us to rethink our ethnocentric view that our culture is superior to any other.

Like Saint Paul, I have seen the light. It happened while I was finishing my master's degree, when I was introduced to sociolinguistics; what I learned about language, language use, and culture literally changed the direction of my career. I had found an area of study that allowed me to grapple with the interplay of linguistic, social, and cultural factors in human communication. During my doctoral program at the University of Florida, I had the opportunity to think more deeply about why people use language the way they use it and why language can be clear and precise. At the same time, language often can be characterized by vagueness, ambiguity, and imprecision.

Perhaps nowhere is the interplay of language and culture more "fuzzy" (to use Lakoff's term) than in the labels we use to define ourselves and others. In this chapter I will share some of my experiences, and my subsequent reflections upon those experiences, with the use of labels and terms used to refer to a person's ethnic, cultural, and racial background. Within this context I will share my feelings about, and explore the connotations of, the made-in-the-U.S.A. label "Hispanic." Then I will explore the use of dichotomies and negative constructions in English. These structures will be better understood by contrasting them to Spanish. This comparison will illustrate that the existence in English of extreme dichotomies can often influence how native English speakers voice and manage their relations with others. Finally, I would like to illustrate how some of us "foreigners" can often be taken in by the friendliness of people in the United States.

Ethnic Labels: "I Came as a Peruvian and Immediately Became a Hispanic"

I was a fortunate child who grew up in Lima, Peru. I was brought up in an upper-middle-class environment, attended private schools, lived in a handsome neighborhood, and was surrounded by a protected haven of mostly well-educated friends and acquaintances. Like many others in Peru, I was a *mestiza,* the daughter of an Austrian father and a Peruvian mother, the product of an encounter of two continents, of two races. Like many others, I had European names and Peruvian looks, spoke more than one language, and was proud to be a Peruvian who also had knowledge about and appreciation for her father's homeland.

In spite of my good fortune, I also encountered my share of problems, sorrow, and broken dreams. This is why, like many others who leave their familiar lands in search of better lives, I too left mine in search of *el país de mis sueños* (the land of my dreams). I had little money but lots of hope, confidence, and a clear sense of national identity as a Peruvian woman. Therefore I set off happily, in June of 1985, unaware of the need for "clear" labels to identify my ethnicity, race, and culture. Soon after my arrival in Florida, I did what many other foreign students have to do if they want to get into graduate school in the United States: fill out multiple forms. Throughout this process I discovered two things: first, the momentousness of the written word in this society, and second, the importance of race and ethnicity as forms of social classification in the United States. It quickly dawned on me that my avowed national identity was of little relevance to the society at large. I realized that I was seldom considered a Peruvian but was most often either "Hispanic," "legal alien," "Latino," "Spanish-speaking," "South American," "Spanish," or, what is worse, "Other"! Within the context of official forms, institutionalized inquiries, and government requirements, I was faced with having to find the appropriate label to describe my nationality, culture, and background. The following question about ethnic origin will help illustrate my feeling of dubiousness, doubtfulness, and diffidence as I attempted to answer what, for some, might be just another question on a form.

Ethnic Origin (mark one)

__White (not Hispanic origin)

__Asian or Pacific Islander

__Black (not Hispanic origin)

__American Indian or Alaskan Native

__Hispanic

__Other

Not only did I find the emphasis on racial categorizations in the United States perplexing, but I felt that the selection offered was limited and problematic. I felt that I had to summarize my nationality, ethnicity, upbringing, language, culture—in sum, my whole existence—in one fixed and unappealing label. I was not only appalled but also confused. For example, given the categories mentioned above, I could have marked the first option since I appeared "white" in both of my passports (Peruvian and Austrian). Yet, at the same time, that option would be incorrect since I am also what could be called "Hispanic."

I thought about marking "American Indian" or "Alaskan Native" since, in fact, I was born in (South) America and there is some Indian blood in my mother's ancestry (even though she might not want to admit to it). But these labels did not reflect all my other influences: my mother's descent from Spain, my father's Austrian and German blood, and the fact that I do not speak the languages nor share the cultures of Peruvian Indians. Because I had to use my European passport, on which I appeared as "white" (it included my visa and my "alien" number), I felt that no available categories encompassed my national and cultural identity.

My confusion grew as the smorgasbord of categories changed—from form to form and from institution to institution, and I often found myself spending considerable time trying to select the most appropriate label. After several months and many more forms, I opted to leave the question unmarked (when possible) or to mark "Other" (if there was such an option). On some occasions, depending on my mood, when the question asked for "race," I would write "Cocker Spaniel," "German Shepherd," or "unknown" on the blank line next to "Other." Because there often was an indication that this information was optional, I did not feel any remorse for perhaps skewing some demographic data. On the contrary, this simple act provided me with an opportunity to show my dissent toward questions that limited my individuality to a generic label.

Do the classifications recognized by the U.S. Census Bureau offer us a useful way of understanding our national and cultural experiences? Do terms such as *black, Asian American,* and *Hispanic* have any real substance to them, or are they the creation of media czars and political impresarios? Let's examine the official definition of Hispanic (according to the 1990 U.S. census):

> A person is of Spanish/Hispanic origin if the person's origin (ancestry) is Mexican, Mexican-American, Chicano, Puerto Rican, Dominican, Ecuadorian, Guatemalan, Honduran, Nicaraguan, Peruvian, Salvadoran; from other Spanish-speaking countries of the Caribbean or Central or South America; or from Spain.

The ethnic label "Hispanic" began to be used heavily by state agencies in the early 1970s to refer to all people in this country whose ancestry is predominantly from one or more Spanish-speaking countries. As a result, millions of people of a variety of national and cultural backgrounds are put into a single arbitrary category. No allowances are made for our varied racial, linguistic, and national experiences, nor for whether we are recent immigrants, long-time residents, or belong to an associated territory. Furthermore, using "Hispanic" to refer to those who are of Spanish-speaking origin can be problematic in that it excludes a considerable sector of the population in Latin America for whom Spanish is not a first language. Many "Hispanic" immigrants come from regions that are not necessarily predominantly Spanish. This is the case of those who speak Nahuatl and Tiwa in Indian villages in Mexico; Kanjobal and Jacaltec in the southern part of Guatemala; Quechua and Aymara in the highlands of Peru and Bolivia; Guarani, Chulupi, and Mascoi in the Chaco region of Paraguay; Tukano and Tuyukaf in the swamps of Venezuela and Colombia; and others from predominantly non-Spanish-speaking regions. Thus, given that their native language may not be Spanish, it is inaccurate to call these people of "Spanish-speaking origin."

Furthermore, as Berkeley social scientist Carlos Muñoz writes, the term *Hispanic* is derived from *Hispania,* which was the name the Romans gave to the Iberian peninsula, most of which became Spain, and "implicitly emphasizes the white European culture of Spain at the expense of the nonwhite cultures that have profoundly shaped the experience of all Latin Americans" through its refusal to acknowledge "the nonwhite indigenous cultures of the Americas, Africa, and Asia, which historically have produced multicultural and multiracial peoples in Latin America and the United States" (1989: 11). It is a term that ignores the complexities within and throughout these various groups.

Dichotomies and Negative Constructions: "I Didn't Realize I Was a Minority Until I Came to the United States"

As mentioned earlier, I always felt special and different among my fellow Peruvians. However, it was only when I came to this country that a label for being different was assigned to me: I became a minority! I must say that being labeled as such has not always been that bad; on occasion I have received some special treatment just because I fit the category of minority. However, the term *minority* has heavy connotations, especially when we realize that it signifies differences from those who make up the majority in this country. In other words, my status was assigned to me because I am not part of the majority, so therefore I should be part of the minority. The term *minority,* like other terms used to identify people's racial, ethnic, and cultural backgrounds, is defined in opposition to another term.

The same can be said about the term *Hispanic.* In contemporary discourse the term *Hispanic* has come to be used as a nonwhite racial designation. It is not unusual to read or hear people use the terms *whites, blacks,* and *Hispanics* as if they were mutually exclusive when, in fact, the 1990 census states that 52 percent of Hispanics identify themselves as white, 3 percent as black, and 43 percent as "other race."

The English language is constructed as a system of differences organized as extreme dichotomies—white/black, majority/minority, good/bad, dark/fair, and so on. The existence of this polarization influences how English speakers manage their relations with others. Consider the case of qualifiers or adjectives. The heavy emphasis on opposites often compels speakers of English to use one of two opposite adjectives when formulating questions. As a result, people in the United States commonly use evaluative terms in questions and descriptions, and find it easier to be critical rather than positive or neutral. For example, let's compare pairs of adjectives in English and in Spanish:

English		Spanish	
old	young	viejo	joven
long	short	largo	corto
far	near	cerca	lejos

At first, it may seem as if both the English and Spanish pairs contain words that are opposite in meaning but equal in their power to describe a point on a continuum. However, this is not the case. Consider how the English adjectives are used in asking questions: "How old is he?" "How long is that ruler?" and "How far do we have to go?" Questions are not phrased using the secondary term, as in "How young is he?" (unless in reference to a baby or small child), "How short is that ruler?" and "How near do we have to go?" In all of these questions one of the terms is designated as the defining term—for age, *old;* for size, *long;* and for distance, *far.*

To the Spanish speaker, these same dichotomies do not have the same dependent hierarchy; rather, these pairs enjoy symmetry. This weaker polarization of Spanish pairs is evident in the way questions are phrased. In Spanish, "How old is he?" becomes *"¿Qué edad tiene él?"* which can be literally translated as "What is his age?" The question "How long is that ruler?" becomes *"¿Cuánto mide esa regla?"*—that is, "What's the measurement of that ruler?"—and so on. In Spanish, the emphasis is placed on the middle ground of the continuum rather than on one of its ends.

Thus, one important aspect of opposing adjectives in English is that the primary term appears as the defining term or the norm of cultural meaning, while the secondary term is much more specific or derives its meaning from its relation to the first one. Examples of the "good-bad" dichotomy help to illustrate this point. If you ask a friend to help you with a new software program, you will probably say, "How good are you with MacMisha 5.1?" rather than "How bad are you with MacMisha 5.1?"

That is, the use of the term *good* reflects a more general qualifier, while the use of the term *bad* already suggests that something is not good; thus this latter term is more specific (in a negative sense).

This same polarity can be applied to some of the qualifiers used in discussing issues of race and ethnicity. For example, in the case of pairs of labels, as in white/black, majority/minority, resident/nonresident, white/colored, and American/other, the defining term of the norm is given by the primary term; the secondary term represents what is different, alien, or abnormal.

The negative precision of English qualifiers yields a linguistic base for qualifying as negative whatever appears to be different. Thus, the labels and distinctions made among different ethnic and racial groups perpetuate a hierarchical system where some groups are the norm while the others, by default, do not fit the norm.

Ritual Interactions: "People Are Incredibly Friendly!"

My brother, who recently visited me from Peru, shared with me his thoughts about American friendliness after spending two days wandering around a large northwestern city. He was taken aback by the Pacific Northwest because he found people to be "incredibly friendly." He went on to say that during his three-week stay in this part of the country, a number of people on the street, on the road, and in the parks had smiled or said "hello" to him. He found it "kind of strange because you just don't see that in Lima, New York, Vienna, or Paris." I was a bit taken aback myself when I heard the story, thinking to myself, "Is the difference tangible?" After pondering a moment, I answered my own question, "Absolutely!" There's a unique, friendly spirit you find throughout the Pacific Northwest. I think we sometimes lose sight of that fact. When you live something every day, there's a chance you'll start taking it for granted. My brother's comments were somewhat of a wake-up call for me and reminded me of my first months in the United States.

Although at that time I was in northern Florida, I can recall having similar feelings about this unusual kind of friendliness. I clearly remember feeling incredibly special when someone would welcome me to the town, ask me how I was feeling, and wish me a pleasant day. Furthermore, I still remember how shocked I was when an auto mechanic spent almost two hours trying to install a tiny plastic hook in the door of my 1966 VW bug and charged me only $1.50 for the part. And, in perhaps the most startling demonstration of American "friendliness," I vividly recall how, just two months after my arrival in this country, a smiling police officer said, "Welcome to America," after she gave me two (undeserved, I must add) traffic tickets.

Instances like these remind me of an incident recounted by British-born journalist Henry Fairlie in an article entitled "Why I Love America":

> One spring day, shortly after my arrival, I was walking down the long, broad street of a suburb, with its sweeping front lawns (all that space), its tall trees (all that sky), and its clumps of azaleas (all that color). The only other person on the street was a small boy on a tricycle. As I passed him, he said "Hi"—just like that. No four-year-old boy had ever addressed me without an introduction before. Yet here was this one, with his cheerful "Hi!" Recovering from the culture shock, I tried to look down stonily at his flaxen head, but instead, involuntarily, I found myself saying in return: "Well—hi!" He pedaled off, apparently satisfied. He had begun my Americanization. (1983: 12)

For Fairlie the word "Hi!" had an important meaning:

> (I come from a country where one can tell someone's class by how they say "Hallo!" or "Hello!" or "Hullo," or whether they say it at all.) But [in America] anyone can say "Hi!" Anyone does.

Like my brother and Henry Fairlie, I was also very impressed with the friendliness of people in this part of the globe, in particular the friendliness and concern of store clerks and waiters, who would often introduce themselves by their first names and treat me in a casual, friendly manner, even asking how I was feeling today. I was really taken by this caring manner. I remember thinking, How can you not feel special in this great nation if everyone is always trying to see if you are okay? In Lima, where everyone is in a hurry (and sometimes trying to take advantage of others), store clerks and waiters barely say "thank you," if they speak to you at all. And of course, as a customer, you would not spend time chatting or exchanging greetings with those who are in such unsuccessful positions.

One day, however, I was struck by a somewhat sad discovery: What I thought was true concern and friendliness was just a ritual interaction. On that day, I had just learned that Max, my roommate's Golden Retriever, was at a veterinary hospital; he had been run over by a car. On my way home, I stopped by the grocery store to get some milk. As on other days, a friendly clerk checked my groceries, and when she asked me, "How are you?" I responded, "A bit sad." To my surprise, the friendly clerk said, "Great! Have a nice day." After a few seconds of puzzlement, I grabbed my paper sack and left the store. Later, my roommate, a native Floridian, explained that this type of greeting was routine and that stores often require their employees to display "extreme friendliness" with customers. It was only after this explanation that I realized that the caring tone used by clerks and others working with the public was routine chat, part of a ritual exchange.

Ritual exchanges such as "How are you?" "I'm fine, thank you," "Nice meeting you," "Hope you have a nice day," and other similar phrases are, like any ritual exchange, more about form than substance. In other words, questions and answers are (or should be) the same, regardless of the participants in the interactions and their feelings. In the above incident, even though I responded candidly with an unscripted answer to the customary "How are you" question, I got a conventional short and scripted answer.

The brevity and formulaic aspects of these ritual exchanges, I believe, have little to do with whether people are friendly or not. Rather, this behavior might be related to an informal, egalitarian approach to others characteristic of American culture. It might also have to do with the brevity, informality, and practicality that characterize the American style of communication (which, by the way, reminds me of the typical monosyllabic answers that I receive from my students when I ask even complex questions: "Sure," "OK," or "Nope").

Ritual interactions, like many other aspects of language and communication, vary from culture to culture and from country to country. This becomes evident when contrasting the little and often impersonal ritual exchanges of Americans with the long and personal ritual interactions of Peruvians. In Peru, ritual exchanges like those mentioned above are not as common as in the United States. When they do occur, however, one generally asks about family members' health. On these occasions, one needs to be accurate in one's questioning and attentive in one's listening, not only in terms of asking about the appropriate family members (for instance, not asking a widow about her husband's health), but also in relation to the substance of the answer (for example, showing some empathy when someone mentions an illness in the family).

Some Final Thoughts

The study of communication and miscommunication across cultures is a relatively new area of research and one that holds much promise in terms of what it can teach us about language and intercultural communication. In this piece I have shared my experiences and reflections about the powerful role played by some terms and ethnic labels in the construction of people's social identity. In addition, I have also discussed some aspects of face-to-face interaction that vary from culture to culture and, as in the case of ritual interactions, provide fertile ground for miscommunication. My intent has been not only to illustrate how individual misunderstandings emerge but also to signal how these interactional processes reproduce and reinforce larger patterns within a society.

All in all, my years in the United States have for the most part unfolded like a dream. Sure, I encountered some problems, misunderstandings, and barriers, and often I had to adjust my expectations and appeal to my flexibility in order to keep going. But then, that is life. I am still learning about how to survive in this, my new home, and in the process I am trying to figure out why we use language the way we use it and why language can make things fuzzier and/or less fuzzy.

Discussion Questions

1. Why did the author want to leave the country of her birth and want to go to America?
2. When she arrived in Florida in 1985, what shocked her about the social classification system she found on all the forms she had to fill out?
3. What does the author mean when she says, "I find the emphasis on racial categorizations in the United States perplexing . . . limited and problematic"?
4. What are the author's views about the term **other** in reference to race?
5. What problem did the author find with the use of the term **Hispanic**?
6. The author says that qualifiers in the English language often convey a negative opinion about anything that differs from the norm. Explain why she feels this way.
7. When the author first arrived in America, she found everyone to be incredibly friendly. How did she learn that this friendliness was only ritual, not sincere?
8. The author later says that the typical "brief and formalistic responses" one often gets during conversations in America don't seem to reflect whether a person is friendly or not. Instead, what does the author believe they reflect?

 26. PEOPLE OF THE REINDEER

During the past few decades many ethnic groups throughout the world have begun to express pride in their ethnicity and their desire to hold on to their cultural uniqueness. Because many ethnic groups represent minorities within larger cultures, their desire to remain ethnically different is sometimes the basis for racial and ethnic bigotry. An example of this problem is seen in the following article written about the reindeer

herders who still live in northwestern Siberia. As their numbers dwindle, some are try-ing to retain their ethnic identity. However, these groups are now under attack by the country's majority who see these ethnic groups as obstacles standing in the way of progress. The question remains: Should minority ethnic groups be permitted to retain their identity, or should they be forced to blend into the culture of a nation's majority?

Although we're traveling over land, the view from the shuddering orange and blue Mi-8 Russian helicopter is of water. Water defines the pine and bog forests, or taiga, of northwestern Siberia, just south of the Arctic tundra. The rivers corkscrew madly upon themselves, forming oxbow lakes that, in turn, are often pierced by other rivers. Ponds spread across the taiga like craters from bombing runs. Patches of cedar, pine and larch resemble islands pinched between great swathes of ice-crusted lakes. It's May.

Not a single mountain, town or road interrupts the flat, wet expanse. A trackless wilderness spreads below me, so vast that it defies comprehension. If all of Siberia were detached from Asia and formed into its own country, it would be far larger than China, yet it would contain only 2.5 percent of China's population. It is a place that can swallow people, as Joseph Stalin knew all too well when he sent many millions to the gulags here.

After a couple of hours, the helicopter drops us near a lake onto a boggy patch of peat and moss. We are still miles from where we're supposed to be, but the pilots can't locate the camp, and the helicopter has run low on fuel. They touch down for 45 seconds and drop us off, ungraciously it seems to me, without a wave. The only piece of high-tech equipment that I've brought, a global positioning system receiver, reveals that we're 1,100 miles northeast of Moscow and 200 miles south of the Arctic Circle. This section of northwestern Siberia, known as the Khanty-Mansiisk District of the Tiumen Oblast, is split by one of the world's longest rivers, the Ob', as it searches for the sea.

Our crew heads into the forest: photographer Scott Warren and I, translator Nuriya Rakhimkulova, 27-year-old Misha Moldanov, his wife, Lena, their 5-year-old daughter, Vika, and a two-week-old white puppy of indeterminate lineage. Our job now is to find Misha's father and mother, who are located somewhere nearby in their temporary spring camp. We all wear rubber boots and haul loaded packs. I've come here to spend some time with a forest-dwelling Khanty family, seminomadic reindeer herders who are members of one of some 33 groups of indigenous peoples spread across Russia's Far North.

Months earlier, Scott Warren had shown me some photographs he had taken of the Khanty (pronounced HANT-ee). The smiling faces of these people, Scott explained, belied a dire situation—oil and natural gas interests, running wild after the collapse of the Soviet Union, are aggressively mining Siberia's vast underground petroleum wealth. This once pristine and remote corner of the world has become one of the world's most extensive petroleum developments. The Russian fever for black gold has hit the Khanty people hard, displacing them from their hunting grounds, polluting their rivers and interrupting the reindeer herder economy. Their traditional way of life as hunters, fishermen and sometimes reindeer herders, practiced for centuries, is drawing to a close in less than a generation. I felt like Karl Bodmer or George Catlin, the painters of the 19th century who traveled west to capture the faces of the American Plains Indians before they vanished. Like Scott, I wanted not only to witness traditional Khanty culture before time ran out but also to learn about the impact of oil drilling and exploration on their lives. Scott mentioned that his friend Misha, a Khanty teacher, would be willing to act as a guide and take us out to visit his parents, who herd reindeer. Scott and I picked up Misha in the remote Siberian village of Kazym and took the helicopter to the camp. Now, with the bog threatening to suck off my boots with each step, I wonder at the wisdom of my decision. But the orange translucence of the bark on the pines lifts my spirits, and the cool sweetness of the air begins to ease my doubts. I learn to step precisely in Misha's footsteps, so as to avoid patches of bog where I could end up sinking to my waist.

We have been slogging along in this fashion for more than an hour and a half when, off in the distance, I see several Siberian reindeer clumped around a dark object in the moss. They are larger than white-tailed deer and are covered with mottled gray, brown and white fur. Unlike other species of deer, females as well as males grow antlers. As we draw closer, several reindeer bound off in an amusing high-stepped gait, as though they dislike touching the peat. One deer remains, her head cocked in concern. She hurriedly nudges a small, dark creature, which stands up on four spindly legs near its purple placenta. The newborn calf trembles with effort, then promptly falls on its face. By tomorrow it will be able to outrun any of us easily—and have a chance at fleeing from the large brown bears, wolves and golden eagles that haunt the taiga.

Even though skittish, these reindeer are semidomesticated and the property of Misha's parents. Humans have formed a long relationship with reindeer. Paleolithic dig sites reveal that Neanderthals depended on them for food 40,000 years ago; by 15,000 years ago, reindeer featured in cave paintings. Scientists theorize that humans domesticated reindeer between 5,000 and 7,000 years ago, an event that may even predate the domestication of the horse. In the north, where cattle and swine cannot survive temperatures that can plunge to –58 degrees Fahrenheit, reindeer (known as caribou in North America) became the central food source of many peoples of the north, such as the Saami of Scandinavia and Russia, formerly referred to as Laplanders, and the tundra Nentsi of Russia. Two forms of reindeer husbandry evolved, one in the tundra and the other in the forest. The open tundra enabled people to move large herds of reindeer sometimes hundreds of miles between winter and summer pastures. Herders who lived in the forests of the taiga, however, could not easily supervise large herds, so they managed with a smaller number of animals and supplemented their diet with fish and other game. Khanty and other herders in the Siberian taiga are seminomadic, moving among established seasonal camps that may be separated by several miles. Such migration is necessary to ensure that vegetation grows back after reindeer have depleted an area.

During my spring visit, the reindeer browse freely in the wilderness and females deliver their fawns. Come summer, the Khanty will lure the deer back into corrals by burning great piles of wet peat. The thick and acrid smoke created by these fires gives the deer—and the Khanty as well—relief from the clouds of relentless mosquitoes.

After struggling across the flooded taiga for several hours, we finally locate the camp, a simple compound centered around a tall tepee-like structure, known as a *chum* (pronounced CHOOM). Misha runs ahead, like a little boy, to meet his parents, and a trio of dogs erupts with a chorus of barks. We are all greeted as long-lost relatives: I'm hugged and kissed by Misha's mother, Dusya, who barely comes up to my stomach, and by his father, white-haired Alexei, whose wild eyebrows animate his otherwise impassive features.

We stoop and enter the chum. Pine boughs and white reindeer furs with gray highlights cover the ground. No spot inside is more than ten feet away from the squat metal stove in the center. The tent's skeleton, 26 pine poles, is covered by felt and animal hide. A piece of the bright afternoon sky peeks into the hole created where the poles meet 15 feet above our heads. Alexei brings out a bottle of vodka and pours shots into cups for the guests. Shooing a dog outside, he starts chanting in a low voice, then picks up a mug and throws its contents into the open stove. The inside of the chum explodes with bright orange light. In that moment, the severed wings of an eagle and duck that hang on the wall appear as birds in mid-flight.

"A prayer to the invisible people," Alexei says solemnly, addressing the fire. He chants for the next five minutes, running down a list of various spirit masters representing animals, forests and rivers. Later, he confides that there are as many spirits as trees in the forest. We drink to the parents of the sun and moon, and to the all-powerful bear. Alexei Moldanov is among the most prosperous of the Khanty reindeer herders living in the vicinity of the village of Kazym. In his seven-plus decades, he has endured Stalin's repressive policies of the 1930s and Soviet attempts after World War II to collectivize reindeer breeders. He and other herders were forced to work together in large state farms. Members of his family participated in a local rebellion that was brutally snuffed out by Stalin's minions. He has watched helplessly as Khanty spiritual leaders, or shamans, who act as intermediaries between the earthly and spiritual worlds, were persecuted, and even executed, as threats to the state. Upon the collapse of the Soviet Union, Alexei came full circle and started keeping his own herds, only to see his people challenged in new ways by petroleum exploration.

Not long after the drinking commences, Alexei shows me his bear. In the homes of most Khanty herders, a bearskin and head occupy a place of honor. Alexei's bear sits outside on a sled. It's the partial remains of an immense Siberian brown bear: a head and paws with skull, bones and flesh removed. Even when dried and flattened to the size of a large pizza platter, the bear still exudes raw power.

The Khanty explain that the bear is the son of Torum, master of the upper, or sacred, region of the cosmos. One day long ago, Alexei relates, the bear looked down from his vantage high above Earth and became intoxicated with the rich tapestry of green, brown and yellow colors. He asked his father for permission to visit, but Torum forbade it. After much discussion, however, Torum agreed, on the condition that the bear not disturb Khanty reindeer herds, storage sheds and burial places. The bear promised, and a cradle lowered him to Earth.

Attacked by voracious mosquitoes, and constantly wet and hungry, the bear cried, "Where is that beautiful carpet I saw from above?" In his hunger he forgot his father's admonitions and killed reindeer, attacked storage sheds and, finally, in the anger of his impotence, desecrated a Khanty cemetery. Mother Earth decreed that the bear must be punished, and so a Khanty hunter killed it. One of the bear's multiple spirits flew into the sky to be with Torum, while the rest remained on Earth, scattering to populate sacred places. As Alexei tells me this Khanty legend, I reflect that even the gods acknowledge that life in the Siberian taiga is anything but easy.

Khanty hunters don't actively hunt bears, although they are permitted to kill a bear if they encounter one. Unlike Westerners, who are taught to wear bells on their shoelaces and talk loudly on trails in bear country, the Khanty walk quietly and talk softly in the forests, out of reverence for the bear. Traditionally, a bear killing launches a multi-day ceremony in which the story of the bear serves as a narrative device in songs and dances to express the Khanty worldview, geography and ancestry. The Khanty people have more than 100 different words and terms for bear, including my favorite, which translates as "host of the forest."

Work resumes the next morning: women cook bread in a large outside oven and carry water from the lake a hundred yards away. Alexei trims a bloody growth that covers a deer's right eye while Misha immobilizes the terrified creature in a headlock. A yearling named Butterfly wanders by for a look, along with White Nose, Baby and My Bull. As any good shepherd, Alexei knows not only the names of all of the deer in his 200-head herd but their personalities, ages and genealogy as well.

Like gentle apparitions, several reindeer always seem to hover in the vicinity of camp, and I get used to their benign presence and their frequent snorting and coughing. Occasionally one will poke its long head through the flap of the chum. It's springtime, so soft velvet covers their short antlers. One afternoon as I am brushing my teeth outside, I look up and am startled to find a reindeer with a bright white coat staring at me intently from only a few feet away. Its black eyelashes seem to float on its milk-white face. White-coated reindeer are not common in the forest and are a sign of a wealthy Khanty herder.

During the day, few moments are wasted. Misha and I head off to go fishing. He drags a tiny Khanty aluminum canoe across the bog to a lake where a larger boat that I'll use is waiting. The boat is barely big enough to hold my frame; only three inches of clearance separates me from the chill water.

We wet our hair with cold water from the lake, and Misha teaches me a Khanty prayer, which translates, I later find out, as "so that the boat floats on the water like on grease," a supplication to the spirit of the water. We pass from the lake into a maze of small waterways, marsh grass rising up on either side of us. Eventually we come to a length of river flanked with two tall poles, one near each bank. Between them hangs a net, filled with pike and perch. We start at opposite poles, working our way toward the center of the river, pulling the net up against our boats until we are soaked and shivering, and we untangle the fish from the net.

As the fish splash us, Misha tells me that his wife, Lena, is pregnant. He has an eager grin, a wiry frame and adventurous dreams of paddling across the Bering Strait in a small boat. Although he makes his living as a teacher in the village of Kazym, he feels drawn to forest life, he confides, and would like to take over his parents' herd. Yet his wife and daughter want not only the creature comforts of the village but its opportunities as well. To them, life in the forest represents hardship. In Kazym, where I first meet Misha, he had seemed edgy. Out here he comes alive.

I've gone on several walks with him after dinner when the extended dusk of the high latitudes, known as white nights, turns the taiga into a soft sea of pastels well past midnight. But the hikes turn into many-hour ordeals, and soon I tire of them. He seems to be walking to escape from something, and I can't keep up. The new pregnancy translates to more responsibility and the need to keep his job in the village. He'd rather be working with the reindeer, but that would mean separation from his daughter and wife. Of the approximately 20,000 Khanty, only about 60 percent speak their native language, and a much smaller percent live in the forest, and both numbers are declining. Of Alexei and Dusya's five children, only Misha is interested in living in the forest.

When our boats touch in the middle of the river, Misha dumps most of his catch into my canoe. The lower half of my body is obscured by still-twitching fish; I ride even lower in the water than before. Although the Khanty depend on fish in their diet, most of this catch will go to the reindeer, who have a fondness for dried fish. Misha tells me that the fish his parents give the reindeer often enable the animals to survive the winter.

Back at camp, Alexei has tethered a reindeer to the trunk of a pine in the deep moss near the edge of the lake and sits nearby sharpening his knife. A cool, brisk wind blows off the lake while Dusya brings out the ceremonial bear head, wrapped in a red scarf, and places it in the branch of a tree with a good view of this impromptu stage. Misha makes a fire, struggling to keep it from blowing into a nearby bush. Lena brings out a square table with stubby six-inch legs, a kettle and a bucket. Dusya throws fungal growths taken from birch trees into the fire, where they smolder and give off a woodsy smell.

Misha and I each wind a rope around the reindeer's neck and step back and apart, holding the animal so it can't move. The victim, Alexei explains, is a 13-year-old deer that belongs to one of his sons. Without missing a beat, Alexei picks up an ax and, with a powerful blow, knocks the dull end against the top of the bull's skull. It sinks to the moss and dies. We all turn clockwise seven times, bowing and yelling "ooohh!" Then Dusya and Alexei chant the names of gods: "Goddess of the earth, accept this spirit from us; Spirit of the forest, accept this spirit from us. . ." Alexei flings the rope that held the bull into the branches of a nearby tree. If a knot forms when he pulls it down later, the spirits will have been satisfied with our efforts.

The butchering begins, a surprisingly quick process that is largely bloodless after Alexei ties off several arteries. They take extra care with the fur at the hooves, which will be used to fashion winter boots. Every part of the animal will be used, from the bone (for knife handles) to the sinews (for sewing). Although Alexei and Dusya are subsistence herders, they will occasionally sell live reindeer and reindeer meat to buy necessities they can't manufacture themselves. Then Alexei's knife exposes the large nasal cavity. Inside, a fist-size mass of yellow, pulpy maggots writhes and seethes, the larvae of flies that have crawled in through the nose. I suddenly understand why the reindeer snort so much: they must be trying to expel these maggots from deep within their sinuses.

Raw reindeer meat is rich, chewy and gamy, and it sticks uncomfortably in my throat. I welcome a proffered cup of tea as an excuse to move away from the bloody table. When everyone is finished, Misha digs a hole in the moss and places the meat next to the frozen earth. The sinews running along the backbone are hung up in a tree to dry for eventual use in sewing and lacing. The skin will be scraped, cured with a mixture of fish guts, and used for bedding on a sled. We carry the bucket of blood back to the chum. The following day we make blood bread, bright-pink pancakes fried over the fire. It's then that we taste the blood, thin and rich like liquid meat.

For the past few days, Alexei has walked with a grimace, his arm pressed to his lower back. I learn that another herder had struck him savagely in the back with a log during a dispute over a reindeer years ago. Old age and a life of labor have aggravated the injury. Each day, he lines up a veritable arsenal of medicines: an elixir of Siberian ginseng and ground-up deer antler; black gunpowder that he rubs in his eyes; rancid bear fat smoothed onto his chest; chewing tobacco cut with ashes from the fire. I offer to give him a massage and a couple of tablets of ibuprofen.

His back is scarred terribly, his skin thin and bloodless. But the massage seems to provide him a few hours of ease, and later I give him a couple more. The third time something peculiar occurs. I feel as though I've sucked his aches right through my fingertips into my own body. I'm a man of modern medicine, with not much patience for New Age explanations, but my body feels heavy.

When I mention this to Misha, he says in a matter-of-fact tone that his father has spirits in him that have moved to me. He pulls some birch fungus from the fire, places it in a bowl and directs me to stand with one foot raised. Misha passes the smoking bowl under my foot. Then I lift the other foot, and he repeats the motion seven times. As Misha predicts, the spirits flow out of me into the ground where they belong: the heaviness leaves me within a half hour. Had an incident of this sort happened at home, I would have shrugged it off as nothing more than the power of suggestion at work. Yet out in the taiga and immersed in the Khanty world, where every action resonates with spiritual significance, such things take on a different cast.

Later that day, Alexei notices that a rope has moved from where he placed it. "Must be the invisible people," he says. And that launches a discussion of missing puppies, lost axes and strange events that have occurred over the course of his life. He and many Khanty attribute such mysterious events to a group of spirit people who are like them, only invisible. Sometimes these spirits become visible, and occasionally they can lure a person over to their world. Khanty children are told never to have dinner with strangers in the woods, because they may be invisible people who have materialized. Just sitting down to one meal, the Khanty say, can erase one's memory of being human.

Some anthropologists might say that the Khanty have invented the spirits and invisible people out of necessity, to explain the inexplicable in an environment both harsh and capricious. Certainly, many of their beliefs and legends do contain information vital for survival, such as not eating with strangers. After spending time here, however, I'm not so sure that strict pragmatism is the sole explanation for their rich spiritual life. Out in this Siberian wilderness it's not possible to tell where the practical ends and the mystical begins.

I'm also forced to reexamine my assumption that the people of the remotest corners of Siberia have been closed off from the rest of the world by their geography. In fact, the Khanty have had a great deal of contact with outsiders over the millennia. From archaeological, linguistic and folkloric evidence, Georgetown University anthropologist Marjorie Mandelstam Balzer surmises that some of the Khanty's nomadic ancestors came north from the steppe in the ninth century, perhaps fleeing Christianization. Linguistically, they speak an Ob-Ugrian language of the Finno-Ugric branch of the Uralic family. They share the Ugrian language with their indigenous neighbors, the Mansi, and the Hungarians. It appears that the Khanty learned reindeer herding in the 15th century from the Nentsi people who live to their north. Over time, Turks, Persians, Cossacks and Russians have forced them to adapt; often the Khanty have incorporated major elements of the dominant culture while at the same time maintaining the integrity of their own. A Christlike god as well as a Turkic god inhabit their pantheon, yet the Khanty remain neither Christian nor Islamic. "The Judeo-Christian outlook," Hungarian anthropologist Eva Schmidt tells me, "doesn't make sense to the Khanty, who are nomadic and fighting for their lives every day in a harsh environment." Their oral history remains remarkably fluid, and information gleaned one day from a radio broadcast may be incorporated into a legend the next day.

Recent events, however, may prove more overwhelming than anything these resilient people have endured to date. The collapse of the Soviet Union opened up Siberia to wholesale drilling by private oil companies. Alexei tells of the time when Russian geologists came to this area during perestroika in the late 1980s. They drilled for oil near a river, and it soon became polluted and many fish died. The oil workers shot reindeer from helicopters for the fun of it. And someone's cabin burned down. These interlopers were loud and disrespectful in the forests and angered the invisible people, Alexei says. During one of our conversations, Alexei declares that dying trees and dead ponds in one area resulted from acid rain created by refineries to the south.

Even more worrisome are the oil derricks that have displaced a Khanty family and destroyed a sacred grove 150 miles to the west. Alexei has good reason to be alarmed. Russian scientist Dmitri Syrovatski estimates that the reindeer population has decreased 28 percent between 1991 and 1997 in the Khanty-Mansiisk region and even more in other parts of Siberia. Natural gas exploration removes large tracts of grazing pasture, forcing reindeer to forage on increasingly smaller parcels of land. This results in overgrazing and the destruction of habitat. Two Russian scientists estimate that gas and oil fields and main pipelines have destroyed 965 square miles of plant cover in northwestern Siberia. It's especially difficult for the fragile taiga ecosystem to rebound after such depredation. For the past several years, Andrew Wiget of New Mexico State University, and independent Russian scholar Olga Balalaeva, have led an effort to establish a large reserve for the Khanty, but it's unclear whether their work will be too late.

Later, after I take the helicopter back to Kazym, Alexei's daughter-in-law, Tatiana Moldanova, tells me about her and her husband's group, Save the Ugric People. They are working to establish cooperatives wherein Khanty herders can sell reindeer meat, and pool resources. They've consulted with the oil companies on how to minimize the effects of drilling, roads and pipelines, and have recommended establishing corridors for the reindeer and the Khanty to travel seasonally. But she is not optimistic. "In the next ten years," she says, "reindeer herding by the Khanty will be vastly reduced or will disappear altogether. Most of the traditional ways of the Khanty will vanish."

I play devil's advocate and tell her about the group of Khanty and Nentsi children that I canvassed in Kazym, the location of a regional boarding school for indigenous children, some on leave from their herding families in the forests. Did they want to herd reindeer when they grew up, I asked? The students looked uncomfortable when I posed the question, but they almost uniformly said no. The pull of the village and its creature comforts prove too strong a draw over the tough life of herding. Times change, I tell Tatiana: What's the matter with the Khanty changing, too, and adapting Khanty customs to life in the village?

She answers my pushy question sagely, with a metaphor. Do I know of the maroshka berry, she asks? I do. It's a yellow fruit that grows in the bog. On our long treks, I look eagerly for this and other berries: I find them rejuvenating, tart and refreshing, cutting the dryness from my mouth during long slogs. "This particular berry," she says, "will never grow in a greenhouse, like a rose. It needs stinky swamp air and wet, boggy conditions. Otherwise it will die, even with the purest of water and the best fertilizer. In this world, you need not only the beautiful rose but the maroshka too."

On the last day I spend in camp, the mosquitoes come, rising from the earth like an early morning fog. And I know that this is only the beginning. According to Alexei, the mosquitoes become so dense that they kill reindeer calves, making them so weak that they succumb to disease. "But," he says with a smile, "the mosquitoes also keep away the outsiders." Whether or not the mosquitoes will help protect the Khanty from the newest threats only time will tell. In the meantime I marvel at the ingenious partnership that Alexei, his family and the Khanty people have forged with this beautiful but harsh land.

Discussion Questions

1. Who are the Khanty?
2. Why is the Russian government so interested in the region of northwestern Siberia where the reindeer herders live?
3. When do anthropologists believe that reindeer were first domesticated?
4. What are reindeer called in North America?
5. What is the **taiga** and why does it limit the size of domestic reindeer herds?
6. What is a **chum**?
7. Who are the invisible people, why do the reindeer people worry about them, and what are some of the things the invisible people get blamed for?
8. According to the reindeer people, the mosquito is a bane as well as a blessing. Why?

Additional Resources

For Internet links related to this chapter, please visit our website at www.mhhe.com/dettwyler

COHEN, MARK NATHAN. *Culture of Intolerance: Chauvinism, Class, and Racism in the United States.* New Haven, CT: Yale University Press, 1998.

FAIRLIE, HENRY. "Why I Love America." *The New Republic,* July 4, 1983, p. 12.

GOULD, STEVEN J. *The Mismeasure of Man.* 2nd ed. New York: W. W. Norton & Company, 1996.

KIDD, COLIN. *British Identities before Nationalism: Ethnicity and Nationhood in the Atlantic World, 1600–1800.* Cambridge, England: Cambridge University Press, 1999.

MIN, PYONG GAP, ed. *The Second Generation: Ethnic Identity Among Asian Americans.* Walnut Creek, CA: Altamira Press, 2002.

MUÑOZ, CARLOS, JR. *Youth, Identity, Power: The Chicano Movement.* London: Verso Books, 1989.

MUÑOZ, CARLOS, JR. *The Chicano Movement: Youth, Identity, Power.* 2nd ed. London: Verso Books, 2003.

OBELER, S. *Ethnic Labels, Latino Lives: Identity and the Politics of (Re)presentation in the United States.* Minneapolis, MN: University of Minnesota Press, 1995.

PEDRAZA, SILVIA, and RUBEN RUMBAUT. *Origins and Destinies: Immigration, Race, and Ethnicity in America.* New York: Wadsworth Publishing Company, 1995.

CHAPTER 15

Language and Communication

27. "Face the Music," by Susan Milius, *Natural History* 110, no. 10 (December/January 2001–2002), pp. 48–56.

28. "Last Words," by Payal Sampat, *World Watch,* May/June 2001, pp. 34–40.

Humans are by far the most flexible and adept of all the species when it comes to communicating complex ideas, including abstract and hypothetical (nonconcrete) notions. We communicate with symbolic spoken and written language, with sign language, with body language, and with music as well as noises such as a sigh or a click of the tongue. As with all other aspects of human existence, an individual or group's means of communication is the result of a complex interplay between our evolved biological and physiological capabilities and the cultural milieu in which we were raised. There continues to be much scholarly debate about the origins and development of spoken human language, of gestural communication, and of singing and musical instruments. Likewise, while some communicative functions of language and music are obvious, others are more complex and subtle. The two articles in this chapter focus our attention on music and on the many spoken languages in the world that are in danger of becoming extinct.

27. FACE THE MUSIC

Every known culture has music of some kind, both instrumental and vocal (using the human voice as the instrument). Within this cultural universal, however, one finds a huge variety of types of music, instruments, context, and meaning. In Susan Milius's "Face the Music," she explores a number of different theories, proposed by scientists with different perspectives, about how music first arose as a part of the human cultural repertoire. Is music adaptive in an evolutionary sense, or is it merely the "mind at play"? What adaptive functions might music serve?

"In our village there was a man who had a daughter, and a guy wanted to marry her," reminisces Dadie Aime Loh, from southwestern Ivory Coast. The suitor was of another religion, however. "The father said the guy must change his religion. He did. They made a song about it in the village, and everybody was singing it. They were making fun of him: 'Just to have a wife, you gave up your religion.' People back home make songs about everything."

For the Dida people, Loh asserts, music is not the same thing it is for most contemporary Westerners, and not just because the drums and bells, calls and responses, sound a different beat. Loh, who demonstrates and teaches Dida music at the University of California, Santa Barbara, conjures up a world in which gifted singers may be celebrated but the talents of a few don't silence the voices of everyone else. "If you can speak, if you can think, you can make a song," he says.

The truth is that just about everybody everywhere is musical. The most off-key croakers among us respond to music, feeling the chill in a dirge, quickening to the frolic in a reel, or waiting nervously for a twenty-foot spider to jump out of the darkness when a movie soundtrack turns jittery. Human beings appear to be musical beings—but why? Does music have a biological function? Has musicality mattered in the evolution of our species?

The first challenge faced by any theory about the origins of our musical capacity, emphasizes David Huron, head of the Cognitive and Systematic Musicology Laboratory at Ohio State University, is to explain why music is not just widespread but truly universal. Every culture that anthropologists have observed has its own music. (Music may be forbidden in some cultures at some points in their history, but repression of music is not the same as the absence of the desire to make it.) Styles of singing and types of instruments vary enormously—to the delight of fans of "world music"—but some form of music is present, often as part of important cultural traditions, from the arctic tundra to the tropical rainforests, whether for pursuing seals or for communicating with the spirits of birds.

Pervasiveness alone, of course, does not mean that a trait matters a lot in evolution. Music could be just a happy accident, notes psychologist Steven Pinker, of the Massachusetts Institute of Technology. Think about food. The vagaries of prehistoric nutrition may have favored hominids with a taste for fruit or for calorie-packed fats. Nowadays we can titillate those tastes whenever we want, but it's hard to argue that survival advantages drove humanity to evolve an enthusiasm for strawberry cheesecake. In theory, Pinker maintains, music, too, could tickle pleasure out of cognitive circuitry that evolved for more practical purposes, such as sorting out individual sounds from a noisy environment. In his 1997 book *How the Mind Works,* he writes, "I suspect that music is auditory cheesecake."

So far, that has been a hard statement to prove or disprove. But it is a view that Ian Cross, university lecturer in music at the University of Cambridge, disputes. Cross argues that dismissing music as a useless frill smacks of ethnocentricity. He concedes that the view is perhaps a fair description of "what music has become over the last hundred years within technologized and capitalistic Western society," in which a booming industry for recording and selling sounds has turned music into "a commodity to be consumed, dispensable on demand." But elsewhere in the world, people turn to music for reasons other than entertainment—from keeping workers on task to powering spiritual events.

David Huron agrees, pointing to the Mekranoti Indians in the Amazon rainforest of Brazil as an example. Mekranoti women settle down on palm leaves and sing during months-long naming ceremonies. The men typically gather to sing in the predawn hours; their singing helps keep them roused and ready for any attack. Slugabeds get roundly taunted.

Huron describes himself as open minded on the question of an evolutionary value for music. "I think we should investigate matters further before we dismiss the notion," he says. But where to look? If music is indeed a universal human trait, then clues about its functions and origin may reside in our brains. One optimist searching for brain tissue devoted to musical matters is neuropsychologist Isabelle Peretz, of the University of Montreal. Peretz has studied people who suffered brain injuries that shut down their musicality but left other mental faculties intact. For instance, she has tested three people who, after recovering from ruptured aneurysms, were able to speak normally and even to recognize sounds in the environment (barking dogs, cars rumbling by) but could not recognize the tunes of songs they once knew, such as Christmas carols or "Happy Birthday." One of these people said she still enjoyed music, however, and Peretz found that even though the woman couldn't recognize a tune, she was able to rate the happiness or sadness of a composition as readily as an uninjured listener could. (A different misfortune struck Russian composer Vissarion Shebalin: a severe stroke deprived him of almost all his language ability, yet he went on to compose his Fifth Symphony.)

Recently Peretz has begun to work with ten people who have no visible sign of brain injury but who describe themselves as profoundly tone deaf. Indeed, her tests have confirmed that these individuals cannot discriminate among pitches well enough to distinguish one tune from another. Such a limitation should not influence their conversation, Peretz points out, since speech, while often inflected and modulated, does not require the fine distinctions that music does. Peretz suspects, based on memoirs, that Latin American revolutionary leader Che Guevara shared their condition. Despite remarkable abilities in other areas, he remained unable to distinguish one musical piece from another—an awkward problem when it came to standing up for the national anthem.

Another intriguing line of inquiry focuses on babies' considerable responsiveness to music. Much of this research takes advantage of their tendency to react to something novel—by turning their head or body toward it—but to get bored with and stop responding to the familiar. Sandra Trehub, of the University of Toronto, for example, has found that infants can distinguish very small changes in musical patterns. Interestingly, six-month-olds react much as adults do to changes in pitch and pitch relations.

Jenny Saffran, of the University of Wisconsin–Madison, has explored babies' sense of pitch. She and her colleagues tested both adults and eight-month-olds with a series of bell tones. The infants proved far sharper than the adults at noticing sequences with the same relative pitches but different absolute pitches. Saffran proposes that people may be born with perfect pitch but lose the ability as they mature.

If such research does confirm built-in musicality, we're back to asking why. Charles Darwin addressed this question in his 1871 *Descent of Man:* "As neither the enjoyment nor the capacity of producing musical notes are faculties of the least use to man in reference to his daily habits of life, they must be ranked amongst the most mysterious with which he is endowed." Darwin suggested one answer: that music evolved as part of courtship. Initially he proposed to explain birdsong as a display, enabling a discerning female to select a mate from among a number of males. "They charm the female by vocal or instrumental music of the most varied kinds," he wrote. This process, which Darwin called sexual selection, enabled traits for the sexiest display to spread through the population. Darwin then extended his idea to the origins of human music: "[I]t appears probable that the progenitors of man, either the males or females or both sexes, before acquiring the power of expressing their mutual love in articulate language, endeavoured to charm each other with musical notes and rhythm."

In recent years, evolutionary psychologist Geoffrey Miller, of the University of New Mexico, has taken a fresh look at Darwin's notion that music arose through sexual selection. If Darwin was right, music might have evolved as a display, bursting forth naturally. And, claims Miller, so it does:

> "Music differs clearly from other human abilities such as proving mathematical theorems, writing legal contracts, or piloting helicopters, which depend on a tiny minority of individuals being able to acquire counterintuitive skills through years of difficult training." Ultimately, Miller says, he's trying to explain why "music is so primordially sexy. A wonderful musician is just more compelling than the world's best tax accountant or a man who's assembled the world's largest ball of string."

While understanding the visceral messages of music and developing enough skill to warble a recognizable "Happy Birthday" may be easy for most people, reaching the heights of musical prowess takes time and effort and, Miller suggests, special genetic gifts. As a result, music might serve as an opportunity for sexual competition.

Ellen Dissanayake, an independent scholar in Seattle who writes on the origins of artistic elaboration (see "Birth of the Arts," December 2000/January 2001), agrees but says, "Geoffrey's argument doesn't explain enough." She finds a much stronger case for music's origins in its power to foster cooperation. The cradle of music, she argues, literally was the cradle, and in human evolution, music came from the bonding duets between mothers and infants. Modern humans evolved to bear especially helpless young, compared with those of other primates, so anything that strengthened the bond between mother and infant would have had strong, immediate survival benefits and would have spread widely.

Dissanayake sees evidence for this hypothesis in the tendency of caregivers around the world to engage infants in cooing, crowing, and peekabooing interactions that display many of the components of music. In many cultures, adults playing with babies tend to pump up the high inflections and drop the lows, so that the sounds they make take on a melodic quality. Think, for example, of simple statements such as "Look at YOU-oooo" and of many nursery games, such as the one that ends with "THIS little piggy went WEE-WEE-WEE all the way home." In addition, phrases are repeated, and adult and baby fall into rhythms.

Experiments have shown how important this timing can be. In one experiment, mothers and babies were in separate rooms but able to see and hear each other via closed-circuit television. All proceeded smoothly—mother and baby happily gazing and chirping back and forth—until the researchers manipulated the tapes so that the baby was watching a replay of an earlier reaction from its mother. When the rhythms of the mother's actions and reactions were out of sync with the baby's reactions, the baby showed signs of distress by fussing and frowning. As soon as the researchers restored real-time communication, the baby resumed gurgling and kicking its feet contentedly. The motions in such duets matter as much as the sounds, Dissanayake says.

Perhaps the most sweeping view of music's benefits for emerging humanity comes from Cross. He proposes that music evolved as what he calls a "play-space" for the mind. Cross offers due respect to our predecessor species, some of which had superb skills in certain domains, such as understanding inanimate materials well enough to shape them into tools. But modern humans seem to possess a trait found in no other species—immense mental flexibility. As Cross puts it, modern humans can transfer insights from one domain to another, often to a domain that is metaphoric or symbolic. As a result, a tool is no longer just a tool. Take a knife, for example. It can slice through a slab of meat, but it can also suggest purely mental operations, such as cutting through an argument to the main point.

If music played any kind of conceptual role for our ancestors, it must have deep roots in the evolution of our species. Archaeological evidence now suggests such roots. The earliest unambiguously musical object that Cross recognizes is a bone pipe found in southern Germany. (He discounts another flutelike find, from Slovenia, as being not clearly musical. Besides, he points out, it is from a Neanderthal site.) The German pipe, which was found along with other signs of modern humans, dates back to about 36,000 years ago—toward the end, Cross has written, "of the sudden efflorescence of visual art and symbolic artifacts that marks the undoubted emergence of modern human capacities."

Cross has also begun a quest for other kinds of early musical instruments. He was intrigued by stalagmite structures in some of the caves in France, Spain, and Portugal that were frequented by people some 30,000 years ago. These stalagmites—some of which show signs of ancient decorations, such as red ocher dots, as well as chipped spots and other traces of wear—ring with resonant tones when struck. Cross proposes that ancient peoples may have "played" stalagmites like chimes. He and two archaeologist colleagues suggest that flint tools of this era might likewise have served early rock musicians. Inspired by the pleasant ringing sound that many tools make when struck, the researchers experimentally tapped a lot of rocks to get an idea of the kinds of wear marks that music-making would leave. Now Cross and his colleagues will be looking for those marks on ancient tools.

Regardless of the outcome of the rock project, the old German flute has already convinced Cross that "musicality is human and ancient"—so ancient, he says, that it could easily have played a role in that quantum leap in mental flexibility. The reason music might be an excellent promoter of mental flexibility, says Cross, is that it isn't inherently **about** anything, the way language is. Play around with language . . . *ooglu, oggli, ugly* . . . and you might be in big trouble if your word play gets overheard by someone big and cranky. Stick to instruments or meaningless sounds such as *la la la,* however, and you're safe.

Looked at slightly differently, Cross observes, music can be about many things. A musician might muse about how a melody that rises and falls is like a wave breaking on a beach or a bird soaring and then diving for a fish. That's a shift from one domain to another. The melody has led the musician through a bit of cognitive acrobatics. And therein lies the value of the musical playspace: it provides opportunities to experiment with conceptual leaps while incurring little risk that anyone will spear you for doing so.

That's a difficult hypothesis to test, Cross admits. "Music leaves few traces except in the minds of those who engage in it." Of course, the agility of human thought and the ability to take one kind of idea and recast it for another domain might be just the sorts of traces he's hoping to find. "Without music," he says, "it could be that we would never have become human."

But maybe looking at how music benefits individuals is narrowing the focus too much, says Steven Brown, of the University of Texas Health Science Center at San Antonio. Like Dissanayake, Brown holds music's salient feature to be its fostering of strong bonds, although he focuses not on the mother-infant duo but on groups of people.

Singing together, dancing, even listening to the same music can help weld individuals into a team, a village, a nation. Before anybody gets too sentimental about the blessings of music, however, Brown points out that music can also transform crowds into a dangerous mob. But whatever kind of solidarity music promotes, he argues, members of such groups are more likely to survive and reproduce than are members of ragtag assemblages prone to infighting.

That train of thought assumes that evolution operates at the level of the group as well as that of the gene or the individual. The idea of group selection has been much criticized as woolly thinking in the past. Brown is not deterred, finding the evidence convincing that evolution plays favorites at many levels: "Multilevel selection is a fact of biology," he says.

One of group selection's longtime proponents, David Sloan Wilson, of Binghamton University in New York, says that he sees modern formulations of the idea increasingly invoked in studies of sex ratios and of disease virulence. "Now **denying** the role of group selection is beginning to appear like woolly thinking," he says.

Wilson heartily endorses Brown's assertion that group-level benefits might have driven the evolution of musicality. "I think it's entirely plausible," he says. Music strikes Wilson as a particularly promising place to look for group selection, because (unlike Geoffrey Miller) he finds the evidence for individual-level selection weak. "Music is employed in many ways that seem to benefit the whole group more than the relative fitness of the individual musician within the group," he says.

Brown agrees, drawing support for his hypothesis from what he calls the "groupishness" of music, especially outside Western societies. "In the rest of the world, there's not this 'I love you so much I can't live without you' stuff," he says. Instead of emphasizing individual travail, especially in romance, much of the planet's music addresses group concerns. The Aka pygmies of central Africa, for example, sing some two dozen kinds of music, each for a different occasion. Brown lists categories of songs—for hunting, for gathering, for the death of an elephant—and points out the predominance of topics that affect the welfare of the group.

Even in Western societies, Brown finds, music often functions as social glue. In 1941 Dmitri Shostakovich composed a work, now called the Leningrad Symphony, to rally support for the city's 872-day resistance to the German siege. A live radio broadcast of the piece in 1942 was considered so important that soldiers with musical training were temporarily excused from front-line duty so they could play in the concert. A recognition of music's bonding power led Nazi occupiers in Poland and Czechoslovakia to issue a very different order—the disbanding of the national symphonies.

Solidifying membership within a group fulfills only one of music's roles, however, Brown maintains. Music also conveys information, with goose bumps added. It creates the visceral rush solemnifying the news that a child has reached adulthood, that a man and a woman are now one couple, that a community prays for healing. Loh offers examples from his village. "We sing when someone dies. The singing is about the life of the person, what he did bad, what was good. Also when we have a baby, there is special music, praying for him, telling him to be polite."

Catharsis is another group use of music. Brown argues that it channels grief or rage or other nearly overwhelming emotions for shared public release. Just ask people who watched the collapse of the World Trade Center towers how it felt to sing the national anthem in the following days. Most—even those who are neither religious nor nationalistic and who may be against the use of military force—are likely to say that singing with others who were going through the same experience brought some sort of relief.

Such groupish powers arise from the very structure of music, Brown maintains. "Conversation is about one person speaking and then the other," he says. "Music is about blending pitches, entraining to rhythms." If divided we fall, united we sing.

Discussion Questions

1. Compare the different theories of the origins of music proposed by Steven Pinker, Ian Cross, and David Huron. What sort of evidence could you search for to test each of these theories?
2. Describe the types of musical impairment found in people who have suffered brain injuries. What does this tell us about the relationship between music and language?
3. List as many examples as you can of music that has widespread, specific meaning in traditional American (U.S.) culture. For example, start with the tunes to "Happy Birthday," the national anthem, your college's fight song, the theme song from "Gilligan's Island," the musical sounds that denote that one is entering the "Twilight Zone," the sounds that mean "Nanny nanny boo boo," and "Mary Had a Little Lamb." Are there students in the class who are not familiar with some of these songs and their meanings? Is it because they grew up in a different country, or did not have access to television? How many more examples can you think of?
4. Why does Ellen Dissanayake think that music might have started as a way to strengthen the bonds between mother and child? What evidence supports her view?
5. What is sexual selection? On which sex (male or female) does it work? How could musical talents have evolved through sexual selection?
6. Why does Ian Cross think that music is so important for the modern human brain?
7. What evidence supports the view that music originated about 30,000 years ago, at the same time as the Upper Paleolithic flowering of visual art?
8. Why does Cross dismiss the early flute from Slovenia? Is this simply anti-Neanderthal bias?
9. Are you convinced by the notion that early humans might have played stalagmites in caves and stone tools to create early forms of music?
10. How does Steven Brown explain the adaptiveness of music? How is his group selection view different from that of other scientists? What are some of the group functions of music?
11. Discuss the ability of music to evoke certain emotions, from joy and happiness to sadness, fear, rage, and group spirit. Discuss examples of each type.
12. Can music sometimes divide as well as unite? Can it function as a marker of group or generational boundaries? How do different genres of music in the United States (classical, country, folk, pop, rap, rock, ska, World Music, and many others) correlate with other subcultural or demographic differences?

28. LAST WORDS

Most people born and raised in the United States speak only one language fluently—English. And English is well on its way to being the lingua franca *of international business, science, and popular culture, including email and the Internet. Second-language learning in the U.S. public school system usually doesn't start until junior high or high school, even though we know that infancy and toddlerhood are the best times to learn multiple languages. At the same time, in the rest of the world, approximately two-thirds of the children continue to grow up in multilingual (not just bilingual) environments. And while many languages are becoming extinct, in some areas people are also working to preserve and protect endangered languages and even to revive languages that have been recently lost. As you read this article, think about your own experiences with language learning, as well as those of your ancestors and your children and grandchildren. How will these experiences differ?*

Marathi. Gujarati. Hindi. English. Kutchi. In Bombay, where I grew up, I used these languages every day. To get by on the streets, to get directions, to interact with people—I had to be able to speak Marathi. To go to a corner store to buy rice or tomatoes for dinner, I had to speak a little Gujarati, the language of many local shopkeepers. Kids in my school came from so many different linguistic backgrounds that we conversed either in English, the language of instruction, or Hindi, India's most widely-spoken tongue. And my grandparents spoke Kutchi, the language of our ancestors, who came from the deserts of western India.

Despite their best efforts, I did anything I could to avoid responding to my grandparents in Kutchi. After all, they could converse fluently in a number of Bombay's working languages. And I sensed from a very early age that Kutchi wasn't useful in any obvious way. It couldn't help me make friends, follow what was on TV, or get me better grades. So by default, I abandoned the language of my ancestors, and chose instead to operate in the linguistic mainstream.

Marathi, Gujarati, Hindi, and English are each spoken by at least 40 million Indians. Kutchi, on the other hand, has perhaps 800,000 speakers—and that number is declining as more and more Kutchi-speaking young people switch to Gujarati or English. This decline makes the language increasingly vulnerable to other pressures. Last January, western India suffered a catastrophic earthquake, which had its epicenter in Kutch. Kutchi lost an estimated 30,000 speakers.

India is a densely polyglot country. Estimates of the number of languages spoken there vary widely, depending on where one draws the line between language and dialect. But a conservative reckoning would put the number of native Indian tongues at roughly 400; of these, about 350 are rapidly losing speakers. The same is true for thousands of other languages all over the world. And most of these fading tongues don't come anywhere near Kutchi in terms of the number of speakers: of the world's 6,800 extant languages, nearly half are now spoken by fewer than 2,500 people. At the current rate of decline, experts estimate that by the end of this century, at least half of the world's languages will have disappeared—a linguistic extinction rate that works out to one language death, on average, every two weeks. And that's the low-end estimate; some experts predict that the losses could run as high as 90 percent. Michael Krauss, a linguist at the Alaskan Native Language Center and an authority on global language loss, estimates that just 600 of the world's languages are "safe" from extinction, meaning they are still being learned by children.

It's believed that the human faculty for language arose at some point between 20,000 and 100,000 years ago. Many languages have come and gone since then, of course, but it's unlikely that the global fund of languages has ever before gone into so extensive and chronic a decline. This process seems to have originated in the 15th century, as the age of European expansion dawned. At least 15,000 languages were spoken at the beginning of that century. Since then, some 4,000 to 9,000 tongues have disappeared as a result of wars, genocide, legal bans, and assimilation. Many anthropologists see the decline as analogous to biodiversity loss: in both cases, we are rapidly losing resources that took millennia to develop.

Today, the world's speech is increasingly homogenized. The 15 most common languages are now on the lips of half the world's people; the top 100 languages are used by 90 percent of humanity. European languages have profited disproportionately from this trend. Europe has a relatively low linguistic diversity—just 4 percent of the world's tongues originated there—yet half of the 10 most common languages are European. Of course, as a first language, the world's most common tongue is not European but Asian: Mandarin Chinese is now spoken by nearly 900 million people. But English is rapidly gaining ground as the primary international medium of science, commerce, and popular culture. Most of the world's books, newspapers, and e-mail are written in English, which is now spoken by more people as a second language (350 million) than as a native tongue (322 million). According to one estimate, English is used in some form by 1.6 billion people every day.

Most languages, in contrast, have a very limited distribution. Much of the world's linguistic diversity is concentrated in just a few regions—all of which are extremely rich in biodiversity as well. The Pacific region in particular has produced an amazing diversity of the spoken word. The island of New Guinea, which the nation of Papua New Guinea shares with the Indonesian state of Irian Jaya, has spawned some 1,100 tongues. New Guinea is home to just 0.1 percent of the world's people—yet those people speak perhaps one sixth of the world's languages. Another 172 languages are spoken in the Philippines, and an astounding 110 can be heard on the tiny archipelago of Vanuatu, which is inhabited by fewer than 200,000 people. Over all, more than half of all languages occur in just eight countries: Papua New Guinea and Indonesia have 832 and 731 respectively; Nigeria has 515; India has about 400; Mexico, Cameroon, and Australia have just under 300 each; and Brazil has 234. (These figures come from the *Ethnologue,* a database published by the Summer Institute of Linguistics in Austin, Texas; some totals may include languages that have recently gone extinct.)

Some of these linguistic "hot spots" appear to be on the verge of a kind of cultural implosion. Take Australia, for example. About 90 percent of the country's 250 aboriginal languages are near extinction; only seven have more than 1,000 speakers and only two or three are likely to survive the next 50 years or so. It's apparent from the *Ethnologue* that Australia is hemorrhaging languages. Most of Queensland's 50 or so native tongues are listed as having fewer than 20 speakers, or as already extinct. The future appears equally bleak for the many languages of Western and South Australia; people whose parents spoke Mangala or Tyaraity, for instance, prefer aboriginal English or Kriol, an English-based hybrid tongue. But this type of linguistic hemorrhaging is hardly confined to the hot spot regions. Serious decline can be found virtually everywhere, as a brief survey of the world's continents will show.

In North America, the linguistic richness that still characterizes Mexico was once the norm over much of the continent. In 1492, the year Columbus first crossed the Atlantic, some 300 languages could be heard in the region that is now the United States. Today, only five of them have more than 10,000 speakers. Of the 260 native tongues still spoken in the United States and Canada, 80 percent are no longer being learned by children. Idaho's Coeur D'Alene has just five speakers. Marie Smith is the last remaining speaker of Eyak, which is native to the coast of Prince William Sound, Alaska. And when Roscinda Nolasquez of Pala, California, died in 1994, Cupeño went extinct. California is considered one of the world's linguistic treasure troves; it has produced perhaps 100 languages, including Esselen from Carmel and Obispeño from Santa Barbara—both now extinct. Only 50 Californian languages remain, and just two or three have as many as 200 speakers.

In South America, hundreds of languages were wiped out following the Spanish conquest, but the continent's remaining 640 tongues are still remarkably diverse. One way to gauge this diversity is to think in terms of stocks, groups of related languages. (Stocks are a more finely tuned and comprehensive set of categories than conventional language families, such as Indo-European or Sino-Tibetan.) Johanna Nichols, the linguist at the University of California, Berkeley who developed this concept, has found that South American native languages derive from 93 stocks, compared with the six stocks native to Europe, or the 20 in Africa. (Nichols has identified 250 different stocks for the world as a whole.) About 80 percent of South America's native languages are spoken by under 10,000 people and 27 percent are approaching extinction. In Brazil, one of the "hot spot" countries, 42 languages are already extinct, and most of the remaining ones are rapidly being replaced by Portuguese. The country has lost a number of "isolates"—languages that have no contemporary relative. In the Amazon region, few native languages have more than 500 speakers any longer and many are down to less than a hundred. Karahawyana, for instance, has 40 remaining speakers; Katawixi has 10; and Arikapu has just six.

In Africa, the birthplace of 30 percent of the world's tongues, 54 languages are believed dead; another 116 are near extinction. Among the languages that have already been lost are Aasáx, which was spoken by a group of hunter-gatherers in northern Tanzania until 1976. This culture has now been assimilated into the Masai and other Bantu groups. In Ethiopia, Gafat, a language native to a region near the Blue Nile, has been replaced by the national language Amharic, which is spoken by 17 million people.

In Asia, more than half the native languages have fewer than 10,000 speakers, despite the fact that the continent is home to 3 billion people. The list of endangered Asian languages includes Brokskat, which is limited to 3,000 speakers in the Ladakh region of northern India; Burmeso, an isolate spoken by 250 people in Irian Jaya; and Onge, the tongue of a traditional fishing community of 96 people on the Andaman Islands. In the Philippines, Arta is down to its last three families.

Nor is Europe immune to the decline, despite the dominance of its major languages. Manx, once spoken on the Isle of Man, went extinct in 1974 with the death of its last speaker, Ned Maddrell. And when the Turkish farmer Tefvik Esenc died in 1992, so did Ubykh, a language from the Caucasus region that had the highest number of consonants ever recorded.

It is true that the past couple of centuries have seen the emergence of a number of new languages. But by and large, these developments have done little to mitigate the general linguistic loss. A few of the new languages are wholly artificial. Esperanto, for example, was introduced in 1887; its inventors hoped it would become a universal tongue, even though they derived it entirely from Indo-European languages. There are also some 114 sign languages used around the world; many of them have acquired the innovative, expressive power of spoken natural languages, but they are used almost exclusively by the deaf. Among the new natural languages are 81 creoles, 17 pidgins, and numerous trade languages. All of these are the product of two or more languages, one of them usually a European colonial tongue. Pidgins and trade languages have highly simplified grammars and limited vocabularies; they are always second languages. Creoles are sometimes complex enough to serve as mother tongues.

About 80 percent of the world's languages are spoken only in their country of origin and virtually all endangered languages are endemic to a single area (that is, they are spoken nowhere else). As with living things, endemism increases vulnerability. In Thailand, for instance, dams built on the Kwai River in the late 1970s flooded the villages of the Ugong-speaking people, forcing them to migrate to Thai-speaking areas. Today, perhaps 100 speakers of this isolate remain. And had Kutchi had fewer speakers, the recent earthquake could easily have extinguished it.

Endemic languages are vulnerable to much more than just landscape disturbance. A language can disappear for many reasons, but as the biologist, historian, and linguistic scholar Jared Diamond notes, "the most direct way . . . is to kill almost all its speakers." This is how all the native languages of Tasmania, for example, were eliminated, as British colonists extended their control over the island during the period 1803–1835. Ubykh's extinction was the delayed result of another act of genocide: most of its 50,000 speakers were killed or forced to flee following Russian conquest of the northern Caucasus in the 1860s.

Elsewhere, governments have banned minority languages in favor of linguistic conformity. Many countries require children to be educated in the dominant language—policies that have the unfortunate (and sometimes intended) effect of discouraging acquisition of the native tongue. Until recently, for instance, the United States required that all classroom instruction on Native American reservations be in English. It was illegal to teach in Hawaiian in the islands' public schools until 1986—even though Hawaiian had been taught in 150 schools until the late 1880s, prior to U.S. annexation. In the former Soviet Union, Russian was enforced as the language of education and government during the entire Soviet era. This effort was extremely successful: in Russia today, 90 percent of the population speaks Russian, while roughly 70 of the country's nearly 100 other native languages are near extinction. Many of these are Siberian tongues. Gilyak, for example, is a Siberian isolate with just 400 speakers. Udihe has only 100 speakers—all of them adults who were resettled into Russian-speaking regions. Yugh is now spoken by just two or three people.

Promoting a single language is often seen as a way to foster national identity, especially in ethnically diverse countries that were not unified until colonial rule. East African governments have favored Swahili, for instance, which has overpowered such local tongues as Alagwa in Kenya and Zalamo in Tanzania. But as the linguists Daniel Nettle and Suzanne Romaine note in their book, *Vanishing Voices,* a common language hardly guarantees political unity. The troubles in

Northern Ireland, for instance, are not alleviated by the fact that both sides speak English. Similarly, Somalia's high degree of linguistic uniformity does not appear to have constrained that country's chronic civil war.

Language loss is obviously a form of cultural impoverishment, but the damage extends far beyond the communities immediately affected. There are several reasons why widespread linguistic decline is a matter of concern for all humanity. In the first place, there is the loss to linguistics itself—and to the other sciences that draw upon it, such as psychology and anthropology. Already, linguists are lamenting the fading opportunity to analyze the extraordinary variety of grammar and speech that they are finding in the world's languages. As with species extinction, we do not even know what we are losing. Uncertainties over how to analyze India's tongues, for instance, have led to huge disparities in estimating the number of languages native to that country: the count ranges from 400 to 1,600. India may be an extreme case in this regard, but it's hard to say how extreme because most other centers of linguistic diversity have received even less attention. In Papua New Guinea, for example, only about a dozen of the 830 or so languages have been studied in any detail. And despite their proximity to each other, many of these languages are isolates. Diamond writes of his travels through the island: "Every 10 or 20 miles I pass between tribes with languages as different as English is from Chinese."

A second general consequence of the declines involves our ability to understand our past. Languages hold important clues to the history of our species. For example, by analyzing words for various crops and farm implements, the Berkeley linguist Johanna Nichols has traced the modern people of the Caucasus back to the ancient farmers of the Fertile Crescent. Similarly, the distribution of Austronesian languages is being used to map the prehistoric migration out of Taiwan and onto the islands of the open Pacific.

Finally, by relinquishing our linguistic diversity, we are also diminishing our understanding of biological diversity. Native inhabitants of regions with high biodiversity have developed elaborate vocabularies to describe the natural world around them—collective "field guides" that reflect the ecological knowledge of, in some cases, hundreds of generations. Native Hawaiians, for example, named fish species for their breeding seasons, medicinal uses, and methods of capture. When the marine biologist R. E. Johannes interviewed a Palauan fisherman born in 1894, he found that the Pacific islander had names for over 300 different species of fish, and knew the lunar spawning cycles of several times as many species as had then been described in the scientific literature. Many of these treasure houses of local knowledge are being replaced by more simplified forms of speech. For instance, New Guinean pidgin English, which is popular with young people, has just two names to describe birds—*pisin bilong de* (bird seen by day) and *pisin bilong nait* (bird seen by night)—whereas native Papua New Guinean languages have an extensive vocabulary for the island's many bird species.

A few languages are slowly making a comeback, with the help of community groups, governments, and linguists. In 1999, four students in Hawaii graduated from high school educated exclusively in Hawaiian—the first to do so in the century since U.S. annexation. Their achievement was made possible largely by Punana Leo, a nonprofit organization dedicated to reviving the language, which now has 1,000 speakers. Cornish, the language of Cornwall (southwestern England), has been revived since its last "natural" speaker died in 1777; it now has 2,000 speakers.

Nationalism has been a powerful force for such revivals, as in the case of Gaelic or Hebrew. During the last century, Hebrew has grown from a purely written language to Israel's national tongue, with 5 million speakers. In Mexico, the Zapatistas are urging a revival of Mayan languages as part of their campaign for local autonomy. Efforts are also under way to revive Welsh, Navajo in the United States, New Zealand's Maori, and several native Botswanan languages.

Most languages, of course, aren't going to get that kind of attention. (Fewer than 4 percent of the world's languages have any official status in their country of origin.) Many experts believe that the best way to conserve linguistic wealth is to foster multilingualism. Certainly, different peoples need to understand each other, which is why some languages have always served as *linguae francae.* But among minority language speakers, multilingualism has always been the norm—my grandparents in Bombay are a good example. And despite the wide linguistic variations found in Papua New Guinea, it's believed that most of the country's people speak five or more languages.

Even today, it's estimated that two thirds of all children are still growing up in multilingual environments. Removing the fetters that have been placed on minority languages in the last two or three centuries might help revive the linguistic heritage of many countries. Norway's Saami Language Act of 1992, for example, is an effort to preserve the culture of the people most commonly known as "Laplanders" (a term they themselves view as pejorative). Or again, why shouldn't Breton, Caló, and Corsican become officially recognized languages in France, the country where their speakers traditionally reside? The revival of these tongues would hardly threaten the status of French as the national language, but it could be a substantial help in preserving the country's cultural vibrancy.

Millennia of human experience are wrapped up in the planet's many languages, and this linguistic diversity may be as essential to our cultural health as biological diversity is to our physical health. No language is an exact map of any other; each is, in a sense, its own world. By allowing so many of these worlds to slip away, we may be forfeiting a lot more than just words.

Discussion Questions

1. According to the author, why did he balk at learning and using Kutchi, the language of his grandparents?
2. At what rate are languages becoming extinct? What does it mean to say that a language is safe from extinction?
3. How do Mandarin Chinese and English compare: Which one has the greater number of native speakers, and which one is spoken by the greatest number of people as either a native tongue or as a second language?
4. Some regions of the world—designated linguistic hot spots—exhibit remarkable linguistic diversity, including Papua New Guinea, the Philippines, Vanuatu, Indonesia, Nigeria, India, Mexico, (aboriginal) California, Cameroon, Australia, and Brazil. What factors might contribute to a particular region's developing many different languages? What factors might contribute to a region's having relatively few languages?
5. A variety of factors contribute to the extinction of languages, including coercive forces such as killing most or all of the native speakers, forbidding the use of the language, and providing formal schooling only in the language of the colonizers. Discuss examples of each of these methods. Are any of these currently in use in the United States?

6. Sometimes people willingly give up the language of their ancestors, especially if they have migrated to a new place. Discuss examples of situations in which people might willingly make this choice. Is this currently happening in the United States?

7. How can natural disasters such as earthquakes and human modifications of the environment, such as the building of a dam, contribute to the extinction of languages?

8. Is there any relationship between having a common language and political unity?

9. Why does it matter if many of the world's languages become extinct? What is lost when entire languages disappear?

10. How have different groups tried to protect languages from extinction? Are there any examples of successful movements to recover dying or dead languages?

Additional Resources

For Internet links related to this chapter, please visit our website at www.mhhe.com/dettwyler

CAMPBELL, PATRICIA SHEEHAN. *Songs in Their Heads: Music and its Meaning in Children's Lives.* New York: Oxford University Press, 1998.

CROTTY, JAMES MARSHALL. *How to Talk American: A Guide to Our Native Tongues.* New York: Mariner Books, 1997.

DEACON, TERRENCE W. *Symbolic Species: The Co-Evolution of Language and the Brain.* New York: W. W. Norton & Company, 1998.

DICKSON, PAUL. *The Hidden Language of Baseball.* New York: Walker & Company, 2003.

GROCE, NORA ELLEN. *Everyone Here Spoke Sign Language.* Harvard, MA: Harvard University Press, 1988.

HALL, EDWARD T. *The Silent Language.* New York: Anchor Books, 1973.

LORIZY, DONALD. *How the Brain Evolved Language.* New York: Oxford University Press, 2002.

MITHEN, STEVEN. *The Prehistory of the Mind: The Cognitive Origins of Art, Religion and Science.* London: Thames & Hudson, 1999.

NETTLE, DANIEL, and SUZANNE ROMAINE. *Vanishing Voices: The Extinction of the World's Languages.* New York: Oxford University Press, 2000.

PADDEN, CAROL, and TOM HUMPHRIES. *Deaf in America: Voices from a Culture.* Cambridge, MA: Harvard University Press, 1990.

PAUL, DORIS A. *The Navajo Code Talkers (25th Anniversary Edition).* Pittsburgh, PA: Dorrance Publishing Co., Inc., 1998.

PINKER, STEVEN. *How the Mind Works.* New York: W. W. Norton & Company, 1999.

SETON, ERNEST THOMPSON. *Sign Talk of the Cheyenne Indians and Other Cultures.* Mineola, NY: Dover Publications, 2000.

TITON, JEFF TODD, LINDA K. FUJIE, DAVID LOCKE, DAVID P. McALLESTER, DAVID B. RECK, JOHN M. SCHECHTER, MARK SLOBIN, and R. ANDERSON SUTTON, eds. *Worlds of Music: An Introduction to the Music of the World's Peoples.* New York: Schirmer Books, 2001.

WIERZBICKA, ANNA. *Understanding Cultures Through Their Key Words: English, Russian, Polish, German, and Japanese.* New York: Oxford University Press, 2002.

CHAPTER 16

Making a Living

29. "Sea Hunters of Lamalera," by Fred Bruemmer, *Natural History* 110, no. 8 (October 2001), pp. 54–59.

30. "A Fair Share of the Pie," by Bruce Bower, *Science News* 161, no. 7 (February 16, 2002), pp. 104–106.

Many people in Western society believe that the rest of the world dreams of becoming like the urbanites living in the big cities of highly industrialized countries. Anthropologists, however, have discovered that for many cultures this is neither their dream nor their goal. Likewise, most people in Western society have lost touch with the basics of making a living as our early ancestors once did. Some of these people try to recapture the past by fishing and hunting on the pretense that they are providing food for their families. Others spend afternoons collecting wild berries and mature nuts in their quest to forage from nature such as all humans once did. Some even camp out in their tents or recreational vehicles in an effort to live in the outdoors like all humans once did. Psychologists point to these actions as proof that urban dwellers have a longing to return to a time when making a living depended on a person's skill and wits against the perils of nature. What about those millions of people who now make a living by depending on the ups and downs of stock markets, global trade, or a market economy? For most of them the quest for money and profits has become their single focus. In the recent movie Wall Street *the CEO of a large corporation brags that profits should be the only goal and that "greed is good." Is this what earning a living has become for most humans? The two articles in this chapter offer a fresh perspective on some modern cultures in which profits are not always the goal of economic exchanges and where the challenges and perils of hunting using ancient techniques are still the mainstay of a culture's economy.*

A dying breed of skilled sea hunters lives in an isolated village on an island in the Pacific Ocean. They are the survivors of what was once a more prevalent way of life. They are the sea hunters who leave their village each day in search of whales, great white and whale sharks, and a variety of smaller fish, including manta rays. They do this in narrow wooden boats that are handmade using only stone tools. They treat their boats with great respect and often mourn the loss of a boat for months. They hunt not for pleasure but to feed their hungry families. They use what excess meat they have to barter for fruits and vegetables, which they do not grow. Hunting is the center of their economy and it is their life. During the 1970s the United Nations sent a Norwegian whaling ship to the island to help the ancient sea hunters. After three years the UN withdrew their assistance because it had nearly wrecked the culture's society and economy. The UN admitted that the ancient ways were indeed the best suited for the culture.

Their boats are sacred and, they believe, immortal. Their prey is gigantic and dangerous. They are the sea hunters of Lamalera, an isolated village on the tiny Indonesian island of Lembata, 1,200 miles due east of Jakarta.

To the 150 or so hunters and the rest of the village's 2,000 people, each of the fifteen boats that operate out of Lamalera (formerly known as Lomblen) is a living being that links them to their ancestors and their ancestral home. That home, as legend has it, was to the north, on an island destroyed centuries ago by a tidal wave. After a long journey, two boatloads of survivors landed on the harsh, volcanic coast of Lembata, where they built a village above a crescent beach facing the turbulent but rich Sawu Sea. One of the two boats that brought their ancestors to Lamalera was, say the villagers, the *Kebako Pukã.*

In Lamalera I often traveled in a boat also called the *Kebako Pukã,* which, according to its crew, was identical in every detail to the original (the model for subsequent boats). When a boat dies—in a storm, of old age, smashed by a furious whale—the villagers mourn for two months while a replacement is built. It takes eighteen trees to build one. Root ends are used to make the stern, so that their life force will flow toward the head of the boat. Planks are carefully adzed—never bent—to the correct curve. The planks are caulked with palm-fiber oakum. Hand-carved wooden pegs—never nails, screws, or anything else metal—are driven in with stone hammers. Carved crosspieces are lashed to the frame with rattan. Finally a sacred symbol is painted on the prow; a common one is eyes that search unceasingly for prey. On the prow of the *Kebako Pukã* a snake coils around a mountain, symbolizing the tidal wave that destroyed the Lamalerans' ancestral home.

The boats are made by *ata molã,* highly skilled craftsmen from the village's nineteen boatbuilding clans. Robert Barnes, professor of social anthropology at the University of Oxford and an expert on Lamalera's history and customs, has noted that the term *ata molã* is also used to refer to a priest.

The finished boat is heavy and sturdy. Thirty feet long, six feet wide in the beam, tapered at both bow and stern, it has a false keel of softwood that can easily be replaced if damaged in rough landings, a frequent occurrence. Its huge rectangular sail is woven from the leaves of gebang palm and suspended from a twenty-five-foot-high bipod bamboo mast. Two outriggers give the vessel great stability. Beyond the bow juts a narrow, five-foot-long, bamboo-and-plank platform. This is the precarious place from which the boat's single harpooner will launch his *kāfés*, harpoons at the tip of ten-foot poles.

In Lamalera, animistic beliefs in the sanctity and spirituality of hunted animals exist in syncretic harmony with devout Catholicism. (Jesuit missionaries began visiting the village in the 1800s, and a permanent Catholic mission was established there in 1913.) Custom and conduct are governed by an ancient oral code. With little agriculture—villagers grow some corn and manioc—and no other industry, it is hardly surprising that the hunt is the center of life. Each May, after the priest has blessed the fleet and prayers have been offered to Kotekema, the spirit of the sperm whale, the hunting season begins. It will last until October.

Lamalerans hunt several species of whales, the most feared, most respected, most sought after of which is the sperm whale. The annual catches peaked at fifty-six in 1969. But then, say the villagers, they sold one of the sacred sperm whale skulls lining the beach to tourists from a passing ship. This offended the whale's spirit, and for years afterward, no more than ten sperm whales a year were harvested. Catches have increased since 1990, however.

Today the sea hunters take mostly young male sperm whales, twenty to forty feet long, which eat the abundant Sawu Sea squid. Crews are leery of the full-grown sperm whale bull (up to sixty feet in length), a rarer sight. In 1994 two Lamaleran boats sank after being struck by a whale that had towed them for miles, almost to the island of Timor. A third boat picked up the crews and drifted for days until it was rescued by a passing ship.

Rejecting spinner dolphins (too fast) and baleen whales (taboo), Lamalerans hunt several species of sharks, including the great white but most often the large and lethargic whale shark (known to them as the stupid fish). They also go after sunfish, marlin, and dorado, as well as manta rays (the largest of all the rays, these can weigh up to one and a half tons). The hunt is hard work. The crews are out all day beneath the burning sun—and often return with nothing to show for their day at sea. They rarely eat or drink on board, so I learned to fill myself with liquids, camel-like, before going out with them.

Weather permitting, the fleet sails at dawn every day except Sunday. On a slipway of hardwood logs, the heavy boat is slid from its palm-leaf-thatched shelter at the back of the beach down to the lethal-looking, pounding surf where the crew calmly waits for the highest wave. With one mighty shove from them, the boat rides out. The men quickly slide aboard, otter-smooth. They pole out beyond the breakers, settle on the thwarts, then row with all their strength to an ancient rhythmic chant, *"Hilabé, hilabé, héla, héla/hilabé, héla, héla. . . ."* Farther out, the chant changes into a song that translates as "We are the men from Lamalera/We are the hunters of the whale."

Suddenly, a few miles from shore, they stop while the harpooner sharpens his *kāfés*. The men remove their hats and pray, first a paternoster in Lamaholot (the language of Lamalera, Lamaholot is one of many languages of eastern Indonesia), then a final plea: "Lord bless our hunt and let us return alive." With this ritual, the hunt becomes holy. The mast is raised, the great golden sail is unfurled, and the boat sails farther out into the Sawu Sea—often up to eight miles. There the crew tacks and jibes, ever alert for the telltale spout of a distant whale, the curled tip of a manta ray's wing, the sheen of a shark near the surface.

Out there, with nothing to distract from the lazy roll of oily swells, the boat's dull creaking, the faint flapping of the sail, the burning sun, I learned what Samuel Taylor Coleridge meant by "As idle as a painted ship/Upon a painted ocean." Then, at a sudden cry, the crew swings into action, rowing and paddling to the rapid cadence of time-honored chants. On his perch the harpooner is at ease, even when the boat pitches, slews, and yaws in stormy weather. Finally he tenses and, in a great leap, flings himself on the prey and drives in the harpoon. Yes, the harpooner always jumps onto the back of the whale, shark, or ray—such leaping greatly increases his accuracy and killing power. Although pulled along by the frantic animal, he swiftly grabs an outrigger and slides smoothly back on board.

I watched once as a wounded manta ray dived rapidly, the wrist-thick palm-fiber rope attached to the harpoon pole flying overboard in spinning coils, lethal to anyone who might get caught in them. At last the rope went slack, and as the men strained to haul up the struggling fish that must literally have weighed a ton, they sang a loud song that they believe is heard by a ray's spirit. "We do not hunt for fun," they sang. "We desperately need your meat to live, to feed our hungry children." Part incantation, part plea, such a song must appease the ray's spirit before the fish can be killed. When the ray was near the surface, several men jumped overboard. Looking for a quick kill—a ray's thrashing wings can span twenty-five feet and break both men and boat—they dived beneath the massive fish and stabbed it with long-bladed, bamboo-handled knives. The fish was cut into chunks at sea; the rest of the butchering would be done on dry land. When a whale or shark is caught, it's lashed alongside the boat and hauled slowly to shore.

In Lamalera, life is lived on the seashore. Children play in the surf; old men sit in the shade, smoking thin cigarettes rolled with strips of lontar palm leaf, talking about long-ago hunts, weaving new sails, or braiding new ropes. But the instant a boat rides in on a soaring swell, all the males, from tots to aged men, rush to help haul the boat up onto the beach. Then the kill is cut up and divided among members of the boat clan, as well as the sailmakers and boatbuilders. Shares are determined by custom, with the biggest portion going to the harpooner. His share is called *leí nakē,* "the wages of his feet," in tribute to his balance on the narrow platform; he in turn is obliged to present his share to the oldest male in his direct paternal line.

The meat and fat are sun-dried on racks, and every part of the animal is used. It is considered sinful—and an offense to the dead animal's spirit—to waste anything. About half the bounty is kept in the village. The rest is traded: Lamalera, an almost moneyless society, depends primarily on barter.

Every Saturday at dawn, the women and girls walk five miles to a market at Wulan Doni, where they trade with women from many mountain villages. Carrying heavy basins of meat and fat on their heads, they proceed straight-backed along a path used by untold generations. At the market, women from the mountain villages spread agricultural produce under the trees. The women of Lamalera sit apart. Once they and the others have paid a tiny tribute to a few families that keep the market area clean, a whistle shrills and the bartering begins. There is little or no haggling, because every item has a traditional value: a piece of dried whale meat two fingers wide and a hand-length long, for example, is worth twelve bananas. In the afternoon, the Lamalerans set off for home with basins of maize, rice, yams, bananas, cassava, and other fruits and vegetables.

In 1973, in an effort to modernize the sea hunt, the UN's Food and Agriculture Organization (FAO) sent a whaling ship, along with a Norwegian master whaler, to Lamalera. The experiment lasted three years, and it nearly wrecked the barter-based economy and harmony of the village. The FAO's final report concluded that the hunters "have evolved a method of whaling which suits their natural resources, cultural tenets and style." Many Lamalerans have left in search of a different life, of course. Several are Catholic priests, some ordained in Rome and Berlin; other emigrants include a professor of linguistics, a general in the Indonesian army, the captain of a luxury liner, civil servants, and businessmen working throughout Indonesia. But in Lamalera the boats still sail at dawn, the golden sails unfurl, and sunburned men invoke the blessings of God and the ancient spirits so that their hunt may be successful and they may make it home alive.

Discussion Questions

1. What is the name of the island where these people live and where is it located?
2. What do the people think links them with their ancestors and with their ancestral homeland?
3. Describe one of their hunting boats. About how many trees does it take to make a boat and how long does it take to make one?
4. How do they kill the sea animals they hunt? Who kills them?
5. Have any missionaries visited the group or established a mission?
6. About how many large sperm whales do the sea hunters kill each year?
7. How is the meat they get from hunting divided among the villagers?
8. Describe how they trade meat for other goods. Where do they go to make the trades?

30. A FAIR SHARE OF THE PIE

In the second article in this chapter, Bruce Bower examines different methods of economic commerce and exchange systems among some non-Western cultures. He points out that there are often hidden reasons for making economic exchanges. Using various types of psychological tests, the author notes that some cultures promote concepts that lead to stinginess, while other cultures strive for equality and fairness as their primary goals in making economic exchanges.

Hadza hunter-gatherers in Tanzania chow down on gazelle meat, fruit, honey, and other mealtime staples without spending a dime. The Au and Gnau foragers of Papua New Guinea generously give food and other gifts to their neighbors without bothering to take out bank loans. Kazakh herders in western Mongolia monitor the weather and their animals' health but ignore the ups and downs of international stock markets.

These groups have little need for the colored paper and bits of metal known lovingly as money in industrialized nations. Nonetheless, small societies lying outside the Western world's corporate bustle are hotbeds of economic activity. In fact, more than a dozen such groups, including those just mentioned, have yielded insights into social forces that may shape economic behavior from Tennessee to Timbuktu.

There's a simple explanation for this unlikely development: Experimental economics has gone native. Until now, this academic exercise in controlled financial exchanges has rarely strayed from the laboratory. Researchers typically recruit college students to play games in which two or more strangers divvy up a sum of money using a set of ground rules.

In a break from this tradition, 11 anthropologists and an economist spent the past couple of years probing how people in diverse cultures play economic games. Initial results come from 15 small-scale societies located in 12 countries that span the globe. Participating groups consist of three hunting-and-foraging societies, six communities that rely primarily on slash-and-burn agriculture, four nomadic-herding groups, and two farm villages.

This extension of experimental economics far beyond the realm of indentured undergraduates has proven enlightening, says project director Joseph Henrich, an anthropologist at the Institute for Advanced Study in Berlin. Henrich and several other project scientists described themes emerging from their data in a session at last November's annual meeting of the American Anthropological Association, held in Washington, D.C.

Traditional economic theory assumes that basic human self-interest lies at the heart of commerce. As a result, regardless of his or her cultural background, a volunteer who receives a wad of money in an economics experiment should offer as little as possible to a partner, even if both players will be left penniless if that partner rejects the offer. In theory, a self-interested partner should accept even a stingy offer since it's better than nothing.

However, a chief discovery of the project, Henrich says, is that nowhere do individuals behave out of pure self-interest, whether they live in college dorms or thatched huts. In one group after another, a person given a chunk of money or other valuable stuff tends to offer a substantial, although highly variable, share to an anonymous partner. Moreover, the partner often rejects any offer perceived as too low and contentedly departs empty-handed.

Cross-cultural results indicate that economic games tap into collective notions of what makes for a fair transaction. These flexible rules of thumb for sharing resources run circles around any brute instinct for self-interest.

In economic games, members of societies that feature lots of bargaining and bartering gravitate toward dividing available goods equally. Communities in which families are isolated come closest to exhibiting the traditional economic model.

As bastions of market economies and cooperative business ventures, industrialized nations promote a stronger ethic of fairness than do many of the traditional societies studied so far, Henrich notes.

These findings raise profound issues that have been little explored, says economist Colin Camerer of the California Institute of Technology in Pasadena, a participant in the cross-cultural project.

"The opportunity to trade in economic markets may create social expectations about sharing and trust that exist over and above individual decisions and motivations," Camerer remarks. "Such findings can show us how to look at economic-game data with a fresh eye."

Take It or Leave It

The idea of going global with experimental economics grew out of Henrich's initial findings among a community in Peru. Each forest-dwelling Machiguenga family lives in near-isolation and subsists on slash-and-burn farming, hunting, foraging, and fishing.

Henrich administered to pairs of unrelated Machiguenga volunteers a version of the so-called ultimatum game. Each duo had at its disposal a relatively large sum of money, equal to about 2 day's worth of labor by a Machiguenga adult. The first player, the proposer, was free to offer any part of the total to the other player, the responder. If the responder accepted the offer, each player received those amounts; if the responder turned it down, neither player got anything.

Machiguenga proposers displayed a greater streak of self-interest than any college student had in previous laboratory studies (*SN:* 3/28/98, p. 205). The Peruvian forest dwellers usually offered 15 percent to 25 percent of the pot. Responders agreed to nearly all offers, including those below 15 percent. In contrast, undergraduate proposers in the United States and elsewhere usually tender 30 percent to 40 percent of the total, and most of their responders reject anything below 20 percent.

Rules for fair behavior with nonfamily members have little chance to flourish among the Machiguenga, according to Henrich. A nomadic existence in which goods are exchanged only within families results in a relatively self-interested approach to the ultimatum game played by unrelated people. Even the Machiguenga, though, don't display purely selfish behavior in this situation.

Research elsewhere underscores the impact of everyday opportunities for exchanging goods and participating in cooperative activities, such as hunting and food growing, on how people play economic games.

Consider the Hadza. These hunter-gatherers treat meat and other food as public property if it's brought back to camp and others see it. The Hadza enforce extensive sharing through gossip and outright punishment of cheaters. Occasionally hunters beat the system by eating part of their kills in the field and sneaking some of the rest into their families' shelters at night.

In ultimatum games conducted by Harvard University's Frank Marlowe, Hadza players displayed their tension between resenting forced sharing and wanting to punish those who defied it. When dealing with an anonymous partner, Hadza proposers made offers almost as low as those of the Machiguenga. In turn, Hadza responders usually turned up their noses at offers.

Individual traits, such as age, sex, and number of children, did not affect how the Hadza played the ultimatum game, Marlowe says. However, members of a particularly large camp made much higher offers as proposers than did members of several smaller camps. The Harvard researcher suspects that the large camp had developed the harshest sanctions against those who tried to flout food sharing.

"The Hadza have donor fatigue," Marlowe says. "When they have a chance to escape from forced sharing, they do."

Yet donor fatigue doesn't create all-out selfishness. In dictator games, where proposers simply give what they want to another player who has to accept the offer, Hadza players forked over around 10 percent of the pot rather than keeping it all.

Paraguay's Aché foragers provide an interesting contrast to the Hadza. Aché hunters often leave their killed prey outside of camp to be discovered by others, so as to avoid looking boastful. Game then gets distributed equally among all households.

In ultimatum games conducted by Kim Hill of the University of New Mexico in Albuquerque, Aché proposers usually offered either 40 percent or 50 percent of a sizable sum. Many others offered as much as 70 percent. There were no rejected offers.

When carving up the experimental pie, Aché proposers perceived themselves as parceling out meat that they or a male member of their family had hunted, Hill proposes.

Whatever the case, the contrasting ways in which the Aché and the Hadza play the ultimatum game "seem to reflect their differing patterns of everyday life, not any underlying logic of hunter–gatherer social organization," Henrich contends.

Whale of a Deal

The whale-hunting Lamalera of Indonesia made the most generous offers of all in the ultimatum game, according to Michael Alvard of Texas A&M University in College Station. A majority of Lamalera proposers, who exchanged packs of cigarettes, offered half or more of their booty. Offers lower than 50 percent were frequently rejected.

Because the cigarette account in Lamalera experiments represented 10 days' wages, making an offer was like dividing up a whale, Alvard says. Lamalera players refused to use money in order to avoid the appearance of gambling, an act frowned upon in their community.

Again, volunteers played the game with their daily interactions in mind. When a Lamalera whaling team returns with a whale or other big catch, a specially designated crewmember separates it into preassigned parts for the harpooner, other hunt participants, the sail maker, and nonhunting community members. In other words, Lamalera hunters are accustomed to getting a modest portion of the booty they secure.

Ultimatum exchanges take a radically different turn when players are accustomed to giving and getting gifts that come with strings attached. Unlike any other groups, the Au and Gnau speakers of Papua New Guinea's northern coast avidly rejected both stingy and generous offers, says David Tracer of the University of Colorado at Denver. Like the Hadza, these foraging villages relentlessly enforce food sharing. Selfish offenders face physical attacks that can result in severe injury or death.

Moreover, Au and Gnau frequently give gifts of food and other items to neighbors in order to cement local alliances and to create social debts that they can later collect on when, say, food runs low or fighters are needed to wage warfare.

Au and Gnau responders feared incurring such debts if they accepted large offers from proposers, Tracer holds. "They either didn't believe that an anonymous windfall was real or feared the consequences of taking it," he says.

Unusual findings also occurred in Mongolia, where Francisco Gil-White of the University of Pennsylvania in Philadelphia studied two neighboring groups of nomadic herders, Mongols and Kazakhs. Proposers in both populations offered relatively high amounts—on average, 40 percent—although responders demonstrated a willingness to accept even extremely low offers. This pattern makes sense in light of the herders' great concern for nurturing a good personal reputation with others and smoothing over interpersonal conflicts, Gil-White says.

In violation of numerous Western social psychology experiments documenting ingroup favoritism, Mongols made higher offers to Kazakhs than to players from their own ethnic group. Kazakh proposers also upped their offers when they knew they were dealing with a Mongol. Concern for avoiding conflict between closely interacting groups may have sparked this surprising generosity across populations, Gil-White suggests.

Market-Based Trust

A few researchers in the project have extended their work beyond the ultimatum and dictator games. For instance, Jean Ensminger of the California Institute of Technology administers the "trust game" to pairs of anonymous players. Each player receives $40 or an equivalent sum. Player 1 gives any part of his or her pot to Player 2. The experimenter then triples Player 2's total. Player 2 can then give any portion of that much larger sum back to Player 1. In this game, the more money Player 2 returns to Player 1, the more trust exists between them.

So far, the most trusting players have been from a rural Missouri town, Ensminger says. Among these folk, on average, Player 2 gave back enough to Player 1 to create roughly equal final shares.

Returns to Player 1 were somewhat less among the Orma, a group of African livestock herders studied by Ensminger. In other experiments, college students have displayed relatively low trust, with Player 2 usually keeping the entire bonus.

"There seems to be more trust and greater concern about fairness and going for 50-50 splits in places where people are somehow involved in a market economy," Ensminger contends.

Her argument that a society's structure molds its members' selfish and altruistic behavior clashes with evolutionary as well as economic theory. Many evolutionary biologists hold that natural selection has favored individuals who are genetically inclined to act out of self-interest in order to propagate their own genes.

Henrich theorizes that throughout humanity's evolution, groups that devised the most successful social guidelines for pursuing fair interactions left competing groups in the dust. This process advanced genetic traits in the surviving groups that proved conducive to hashing out equitable deals.

"This new cross-cultural research is cutting-edge stuff," comments anthropologist Stuart Plattner of the National Science Foundation in Arlington, Virginia. "It will advance economic theory." NSF has funded a second phase of the project. A larger contingent of researchers will study additional societies and probe economic behavior using food and other nonmonetary items.

It's encouraging, Henrich notes, that all people studied so far treat the economic games as if they're genuine encounters. Once they grasp the point, nomads, foragers, and farmers draw on their own group-specific assumptions about fairness and sharing.

Henrich and his colleagues have yet to formulate an airtight case for group differences in concepts of fair exchange, remarks economist Kevin McCabe of George Mason University in Fairfax, Virginia. The cross-cultural findings may instead reflect disparities in researchers' ability to articulate the point of economic games to players and to administer the games consistently, he contends.

McCabe suspects that much cooperative behavior represents a form of delayed gratification, in which individuals forgo immediate self-interest to work with others for a greater personal payoff in the future. "Still, the cross-cultural work is provocative and interesting," he says. "It's definitely worth pursuing."

Discussion Questions

1. Aside from cultures that have market economies, what other types of communities tend to exhibit similar concepts of fairness?
2. Among the Machiguenga families of Peru, what did the experimenters discover when they asked them to play the ultimatum game?
3. How did the Machiguenga players of the ultimatum game differ from traditional undergraduate players in the United States?
4. How did the Hadza players differ from the Machiguenga players when each group played the ultimatum game?

5. What type of reactions did the Aché players from Paraguay exhibit during the ultimatum game?
6. Of all the cultural groups, which exhibited the most generous offers during the ultimatum game?
7. Why did players from the Au and Gnau cultures of New Guinea refuse to accept any offers during the ultimatum game?
8. The author remarks that throughout human evolution it appears that fair trading guidelines have been the most successful. Why?
9. How would you have played the ultimatum game?

Additional Resources

For Internet links related to this chapter, please visit our website at www.mhhe.com/dettwyler

BARKER, JAMES H., and ROBIN BARKER. *Always Getting Ready, Upterrlainarluta: Yup'lk Eskimo Subsistence in Southwest Alaska.* Seattle, WA: University of Washington Press, 1993.

CHAGNON, NAPOLEON. *The Yanomamö.* 5th ed. New York: Holt, Rinehart & Winston, 1997.

CRONK, LEE. "Strings Attached," *The Sciences,* May–June, 1989, pp. 2–4.

ENGLISH-LUECK, J. A. *Cultures@SiliconValley.* Stanford, CA: Stanford University Press, 2002.

HARRIS, DAVID R., ed. *The Origins and Spread of Agriculture and Pastoralism in Eurasia.* Washington, DC: Smithsonian Institution Press, 1996.

HOLTZMAN, JON D. *Nuer Journeys, Nuer Lives: Sudanese Refugees in Minnesota.* Boston, MA: Allyn & Bacon, 1998.

KELLY, ROBERT L. *The Foraging Spectrum: Diversity in Hunter-Gatherer Lifeways.* Washington, DC: Smithsonian Institution Press, 1995.

PANTER-BRICK, CATHERINE, ROBERT H. LAYTON, and PETER ROWLEY-CONWY, eds. *Hunter-Gatherers: An Interdisciplinary Perspective.* New York: Cambridge University Press, 1997.

ROCHE, JUDITH, and MEG MCHUTCHISON. *First Fish, First People: Salmon Tales of the North Pacific Rim.* Seattle, WA: University of Washington Press, 1998.

TURNBULL, COLIN. *The Forest People: A Study of the Pygmies of the Congo.* New York: Simon & Schuster, 1961.

WILK, R. R. *Economies and Cultures: An Introduction to Economic Anthropology.* Boulder, CO: Westview, 1996.

YOUNG, WILLIAM. *The Rashaayda Bedouin: Arab Pastoralists of Eastern Sudan.* New York: Wadsworth Publishing Company, 1994.

CHAPTER 17

Political Systems

31. "The Social Psychology of Modern Slavery," by Kevin Bales, *Scientific American*, April 2002 (from website www.sciam.com/article.cfm?articleID=0005F839-CC6-B4A8809EC588EEDF).

32. "A Tribal Chair's Perspective on Inherent Sovereignty," by Billy Evans Horse and Luke Eric Lassiter, *St. Thomas Law Review* 10 (Fall 1997), pp. 79–86.

Political systems can be thought of as the systems by which some people control how other people behave, usually by limiting their choices and options. This can include official government structures, formal legal systems, and local rules and regulations. Behavior can be controlled through positive sanctions (rewards for doing what those in power want) or negative sanctions (punishments for not doing what those in power want, or for doing what is forbidden to do). Rewards and punishments can involve physical force or freedom or economic repercussions. There are also numerous unofficial and informal systems of political control.

*When thinking about political systems, a useful distinction is that between "freedom to" and "freedom from." For example, most people in the United States grow up thinking that "freedom to" is more important than "freedom from," while people in some other cultures view "freedom from" as more important than "freedom to." This can lead to misunderstandings, both of one's own cultural beliefs and practices (and the costs they may entail) and of the cultural beliefs and practices of others (and the advantages they may entail). For example, most women in the United States have the **freedom to** be seen in public without having to cover their hair, heads, hands, or legs. Women in Muslim countries that require women to be veiled in public have **freedom from** being sexually harassed or judged by, and valued for, their body size and shape and physical beauty. Most women in the United States have a lot of **freedom to** choose who they will marry, while most women in Africa and Asia have **freedom from** having to worry about whether or not they will ever marry, whether or not they will pick the right man, and whether or not their marriage will last. They can enjoy their pre-adult years, secure in the knowledge that*

*they will be married and have a spouse and children, that their marriage will last,
and that their parents will choose an appropriate spouse for them.*

*Understanding this important distinction, and looking for the advantages and
disadvantages of any particular system, will help you to appreciate both your own
and others' cultural beliefs and practices.*

 ## 31. THE SOCIAL PSYCHOLOGY OF MODERN SLAVERY

*As Kevin Bales's article clearly shows, slavery—in different forms—is alive and well
in the world today. Most people think of slavery as the owning of one person by another, backed up by force or threat of force. However, there are many different forms
of slavery, including outright ownership of another person whose life and labor one
can command, sexual slavery, economic slavery, and hereditary debt-bondage. People sometimes choose to remain indentured to their owners, who provide some "freedom froms" in exchange for labor, the goods or money that result from that labor,
and the relinquishing of certain "freedom tos." As you read Bales's selection, think
about the political, economic, social, and psychological forces that lead to the perpetuation of modern slavery.*

For Meera, the revolution began with a single rupee. When a social worker came
across Meera's unmapped village in the hills of Uttar Pradesh in India three years
ago, he found that the entire population was in hereditary debt bondage. It could
have been in the time of their grandfathers or great-grandfathers—few in the village
could remember—but at some point in their past, the families had pledged themselves to unpaid labor in return for loans of money. The debt passed down through
the generations. Children as young as five years old worked in quarry pits, making
sand by crushing stones with hammers. Dust, flying rock chips and heavy loads had
left many villagers with silicosis and injured eyes or backs.

Calling together some of the women, the social worker proposed a radical plan.
If groups of 10 women agreed to set aside a single rupee a week from the tiny sums
the moneylenders gave them to buy rice, he would provide seed money and keep the
funds safe. Meera and nine others formed the first group. The rupees slowly
mounted up. After three months, the group had enough to pay off the loan against
which Meera was bonded. She began earning money for her work, which greatly increased the amount she could contribute to the group. In another two months, another woman was freed; the following month, a third came out of bondage.

At that point, the other members, seeing that freedom was possible, simply re-
nounced their debts and declared themselves free. The moneylenders quickly moved
against them, threatening them and driving them from the quarries. But the women
were able to find jobs in other quarries. New groups followed their example. The social worker has taken me to the village twice, and on my second visit, all its inhabitants were free and all their children in school.

Less than 100 kilometers away, the land turns flat and fertile. Debt bondage is
common there, too. When I met Baldev in 1997, he was plowing. His master called
him "my halvaha," meaning "my bonded plowman." Two years later I met Baldev

again and learned that because of a windfall from a relative, he had freed himself from debt. But he had not freed himself from bondage. He told me:

> After my wife received this money, we paid off our debt and were free to do whatever we wanted. But I was worried all the time—what if one of the children got sick? What if our crop failed? What if the government wanted some money? Since we no longer belonged to the landlord, we didn't get food every day as before. Finally, I went to the landlord and asked him to take me back. I didn't have to borrow any money, but he agreed to let me be his halvaha again. Now I don't worry so much; I know what to do.

Lacking any preparation for freedom, Baldev reenrolled in slavery. Without financial or emotional support, his accidental emancipation didn't last. Although he may not bequeath any debt to his children, his family is visibly worse off than unbonded villagers in the same region.

To many people, it comes as a surprise that debt bondage and other forms of slavery persist into the 21st century. Every country, after all, has made it illegal to own and exercise total control over another human being. And yet there are people like Baldev who remain enslaved—by my estimate, which is based on a compilation of reports from governments and nongovernmental organizations, perhaps 27 million of them around the world. If slaveholders no longer own slaves in a legal sense, how can they still exercise so much control that freed slaves sometimes deliver themselves back into bondage? This is just one of the puzzles that make slavery the greatest challenge faced by the social sciences today. Despite being among the oldest and most persistent forms of human relationships, found in most societies at one time or another, slavery is little understood. Although historians have built up a sizable literature on antebellum American slavery, other types have barely been studied. It is as if our understanding of all arachnids were based on clues left by a single species of extinct spider. In our present state of ignorance, we have little hope of truly eradicating slavery, of making sure that Meera, rather than Baldev, becomes the model.

The New Slavery

Researchers do know that slavery is both evolving and increasing in raw numbers. Like spiders, it permeates our world, typically hidden in the dark spaces of the economy. Over the past few years, journalists and activists have documented numerous examples. Human trafficking—the involuntary smuggling of people between countries, often by organized crime—has become a huge concern, especially in Europe and Southeast Asia. Many people, lured by economic opportunities, pay smugglers to slip them across borders but then find themselves sold to sweatshops, brothels or domestic service to pay for their passage; others are kidnapped and smuggled against their will. In certain areas, notably Brazil and West Africa, laborers have been enticed into signing contracts and then taken to remote plantations and prevented from leaving. In parts of South Asia and North Africa, slavery is a millennia-old tradition that has never truly ended.

The plight of these people has drawn the attention of governments and organizations as diverse as the Vatican, the United Nations, the International Organization for Migration, and Amnesty International. Two years ago the U.S. government established a central coordinating office to deal with human trafficking. Academic researchers are beginning to conduct intensive studies. The anecdotal and journalistic approach is slowly transforming into the more rigorous inquiry of social science. For example, Urs Peter Ruf of the University of Bielefeld in Germany has documented the evolution of master-slave relations in modern Mauritania. Louise Brown of the University of Birmingham in England has studied women forced into prostitution in Asia. David Kyle of the University of California at Davis and Rey Koslowski of Rutgers University have explored human smuggling. I have posited a theory of global slavery and tested it through case studies in five countries.

A common question is why these practices should be called slavery rather than just another form of superexploitation. The answer is simple. Throughout history, slavery has meant a loss of free will and choice backed up by violence, sometimes exercised by the slaveholder, sometimes by elements of the state. That is exactly what other researchers and I have observed. Granted, workers at the bottom of the economic ladder have few options to begin with, but at some point on the continuum of exploitation, even those options are lost. These workers are unable to walk away.

Human suffering comes in various guises, yet slavery has a distinctive horror that is evident to those of us who have seen it in the flesh. Even when it does not involve beating or other physical torture, it brings about a psychological degradation that often renders victims unable to function in the outside world. "I've worked in prisons and with cases of domestic violence," says Sydney Lytton, an American psychiatrist who has counseled freed slaves. "This is worse."

Although each of the manifestations of slavery has unique local characteristics, one of the aims of social scientists is to understand their universal features, so that therapies developed in one place can be applied elsewhere. Foremost among these commonalities is the basic economic equation. In 1850 an agricultural slave cost $1,500 in Alabama (around $30,000 in today's dollars). The equivalent laborer can be had for around $100 today. That payment might be made as part of a "loan" or as a "fee" to a trafficker. A young woman in Southeast Asia or eastern Europe might be sold several times, through a series of brokers and pimps, before she ends up in a brothel.

One should not read too much into these specific dollar amounts, because what the slaveholder purchases is somewhat different in each case. The basic point is that forced labor represents a much smaller percentage of business expenses than it used to. It took 20 years of labor for an antebellum American slave to repay his or her purchase price and maintenance costs; today it takes two years for a bonded laborer in South Asia to do the same. This fall in price has altered not only the profitability of slavery but also the relationship between slave and master. The expensive slave of the past was a protected investment; today's slave is a cheap and disposable input to low-level production. The slaveholder has little incentive to provide health care or to take care of slaves who are past their prime.

Several trends could account for this shift. The world's population has tripled since World War II, producing a glut of potential slaves. Meanwhile the economic transformation of the developing world has, whatever its benefits, included the loss of community and social safety nets, matched by the erection of vast shantytowns. But the vulnerability of large numbers of people does not make them slaves; for that, you need violence. The key factor in the persistence of slavery is the weak rule of law in many regions. Widespread corruption of government and police allows violence to be used with impunity even when slavery is nominally illegal.

A second commonality among different forms of slavery is the psychological manipulation they all involve. The widely held conception of a slave is someone in chains who would escape if given half a chance or who simply does not know better. But Meera's and Baldev's stories, among numerous others, suggest that this view is naive. In my experience, slaves often know that their enslavement is illegal. Force, violence and psychological coercion have convinced them to accept it. When slaves begin to accept their role and identify with their master, constant physical bondage becomes unnecessary. They come to perceive their situation not as a deliberate action taken to harm them in particular but as part of the normal, if regrettable, scheme of things.

One young woman I met in northeastern Thailand, Siri, has a typical story. A woman approached her parents, offered to find their 14-year-old daughter a job, and advanced them 50,000 baht (at the time, about $2,000) against her future income. The broker transferred Siri to a low-end brothel for twice that sum. When she tried to escape, her debt was doubled again. She was told to repay it, as well as a monthly rent of 30,000 baht, from her earnings of 100 baht per customer.

Siri had little idea what it meant to be a prostitute. Her initiation took the form of assault and rape. Shattered, the teenager had to find a way to carry on with life. In the world in which she lived, there were only those with total power and those with no power. Reward and punishment came from a single source, the pimp. Young women in Siri's position often find building a relationship with the pimp to be a good survival strategy. Although pimps are thugs, they do not rely solely on violence. They are adept at fostering insecurity and dependence.

Cultural norms have prepared these young women for control and compliance. A girl will be told how her parents will suffer if she does not cooperate and work hard, how the debt is on her shoulders and must be repaid. Thai sex roles are clearly defined, and women are expected to be retiring, nonassertive and obedient—as the women are repeatedly reminded. The pimps also cite religion. The young women are encouraged to believe that they must have committed terrible sins in a past life to deserve their enslavement and abuse. They are urged to accept this karmic debt, to come to terms with it and to reconcile themselves to their fate.

To live in slavery, the young women often redefine their bondage as a duty or a job or a form of penance. To accept their role and the pimp's, they must try to diminish their view of themselves as victims who have been wronged. They must begin to see their enslavement from the point of view of the slaveholder. At the time of my visit, the women in Siri's brothel were at various stages in this process of submission. Some were even allowed to visit their families during holidays, for they always came back.

A similar psychology operates in a different form of slavery, one that involves domestic servants that African and Asian diplomats and business executives have brought with them to Europe and North America. As an employee of the Committee against Modern Slavery, Cristina Talens worked for several years to free and rehabilitate domestic slaves who had been brought to Paris. She told me that liberating the body was much easier than freeing the mind:

> In spite of the violence, and the living and working conditions, people in slavery
> have their own mental integrity and their own mechanisms for surviving. Some may

actually like different aspects of their life, perhaps the security or their understanding of the order of things. When you disrupt this order, suddenly everything is confused. Some of the women who were freed have attempted suicide. It is easy to assume that this happened because of the abuse they had lived through. But for some of these women, slavery had been the major psychological building block in their lives. When that was destroyed, the meaning of their life was like a bit of paper crushed up and thrown away. They were told: "No, this is not the way it is supposed to be. Start all over again." It was as though their life had no meaning.

Plausible Deniability

The psychology of the slave is mirrored by that of the slaveholder. Slavery is not a simple matter of one person holding another by force; it is an insidious mutual dependence that is remarkably difficult for slaveholder as well as slave to break out of. Branding the slaveholder as pure evil may in some way comfort us, but maintaining that definition becomes difficult when one meets actual slave masters.

Almost all the slaveholders I have met and interviewed in Pakistan, India, Brazil and Mauritania were family men who thought of themselves simply as businessmen. Pillars of the local community, they were well rewarded financially, well integrated socially, and well connected legally and politically. Their slaveholding was not seen as a social handicap except, possibly, by "outsiders" who, they felt, misunderstood the local customs of business and labor.

How is it that such nice men do such bad things? A government official in Baldev's district who held bonded workers was frank about his slaveholding:

> Of course I have bonded laborers: I'm a landlord. I keep them and their families, and they work for me. When they aren't in the fields, I have them doing the household work washing clothes, cooking, cleaning, making repairs, everything. After all, they are from the Kohl caste; that's what they do, work for Vaisyas like me. I give them food and a little land to work. They've also borrowed money, so I have to make sure that they stay on my land till it is paid back. They will work on my farm till it is all paid back. I don't care how old they get; you can't just give money away!
>
> After all, there is nothing wrong in keeping bonded labor. They benefit from the system, and so do I. Even if agriculture is completely mechanized, I'll still keep my bonded laborers. You see, the way we do it, I am like a father to these workers. It is a father-son relationship; I protect them and guide them. Of course, sometimes I have to discipline them as well, just as a father would.

Other slaveholders also have told me that their slaves are like their children, that they need close control and care. They make the argument of tradition: because the practice has been going on for so long, it must be the natural order of things. For others, it is a simple question of priorities: they say that enslaving people is unfortunate but that their own family's welfare depends on it. Often slaveholders have interposed many layers of management between themselves and the slaves. They purposely deny themselves the knowledge of what they are doing and thus the responsibility for it.

Forty Acres and a Mule

All this points to the need for a highly developed system of rehabilitation for freed slaves and slaveholders alike. Physical freedom is not enough. When slaves were emancipated in the U.S. in 1865, the government enacted no such rehabilitation. General William Tecumseh Sherman's promise to give each former slave "forty acres and a mule" never materialized. The result was four million people dumped into a shattered economy without resources and with few legal protections. It can be argued that America is still suffering from this liberation without rehabilitation.

Human-rights worker Vivek Pandit of the Vidhayak Sansad organization in India has been liberating bonded laborers for more than 20 years. He is adamant that real liberation takes place in the mind, that physical freedom isn't enough—as was the case with Baldev. Conversely, mental freedom can bring about physical freedom—as it did for Meera.

Pandit's organization has devised a program of education that prepares former bonded laborers for a life of freedom. They are taught basic science to promote their curiosity and attention to detail; role-playing to stimulate problem solving; and games to develop strategic thinking and teamwork. This training comes after a challenging public dialogue in which the laborer recounts and renounces his or her bondage. The renunciation is recorded and read out in the village. "When the ex-slave has fixed his thumbprint to this public document," Pandit says, "they can't go back."

The experience of these programs suggests that a combination of economic support, counseling and education can lead to stable, sustainable freedom. This kind of work is still in its early stages, though. No systematic evaluations of these programs have been carried out. No social scientist has explored a master-slave relationship in depth.

Slave economics are another puzzle. How can would-be liberators crack the dark economy and trace the slave-made products to our homes? Why are such large numbers of people being trafficked across continents, how many of these people really are enslaved, and why are these flows apparently increasing? What is the impact of this workforce on national economies? What are the links among the traffic in people, drugs and guns?

Studying bondage can be socially and politically controversial. Researchers in the field face numerous ethical dilemmas, and clarity and objectivity are all the more difficult to achieve when individuals and governments seek to conceal what they are doing. If there is good news, it is the growing recognition of the problem. The plight of enslaved child workers has drawn significantly increased funding, and new partnerships between antislavery organizations and industries that use slave-made commodities provide an innovative model for abolition. But if our figures are correct, only a small fraction of slaves are reached and freed every year. Our ignorance of their hidden world is vast.

Discussion Questions

1. Many Americans have ancestors (recent or distant) who came to the United States as slaves or indentured servants. Others have ancestors who came to the United States fleeing slavery or indentured servitude or seeking greater economic or educational opportunities than were available to them in their homelands. Other than students of Native American heritage, are there any students in class whose ancestors came to the United States (or who came themselves as adults) for any other reasons?

2. Discuss examples of different forms of slavery, including sexual slavery, economic slavery, and hereditary debt-bondage. How do these forms of slavery differ?

3. Which of these forms of slavery can be found in the United States?
4. What economic, social, and psychological forces lead to the perpetuation of modern slavery?
5. Why might a person prefer indentured servitude to freedom? Are there advantages to being taken care of (**freedom froms**), even if you have to give up some **freedom tos**?
6. Are there any parallels between a woman in the United States being a wealthy man's "trophy wife" and garden-variety indentured servitude?
7. Why would a poor person from another country willingly take on years of debt and the possibility of death in order to be smuggled into the United States?

32. A TRIBAL CHAIR'S PERSPECTIVE ON INHERENT SOVEREIGNTY

People don't always agree about who has legitimate authority in certain contested arenas. For example, the Kurds in the Middle East do not recognize the national governments of either Iraq or Turkey. Likewise, the Christian and animist peoples of the southern Sudan do not recognize the Muslim government in Khartoum as having legitimate leadership over them. Many of the tribal groups of Afghanistan never have recognized the national government in Kabul, whether it was Russian- or British-backed, led by the Taliban, or led by the current president, Hamid Karzai. When governments claim legitimacy and rights through religious fiat—as in the wording from the U.S. Declaration of Independence: "We hold these truths to be self-evident, that all men are created equal, that they are endowed by their Creator with certain inalienable Rights, that among these are Life, Liberty, and the pursuit of Happiness"—they are bound to come into conflict with other groups claiming inherent sovereignty from their own God or gods. In this selection, Billy Evans Horse and Luke Eric Lassiter describe some of the conflicts between the traditional and modern Kiowa political worldview and the U.S. government's view of Native American sovereignty, as well as conflicts within the Kiowa over how best to preserve their cultural heritage and political autonomy.

Many years ago, my grandfather, William "Cornbread" Tanedooah, who was one of the last Kiowa doctors—or as we say in English, "medicine men"—passed to me one of his bundles, a bundle possessing buffalo medicine. And with it, my grandfather told me the following story:

> When the Kiowas were still free on the Plains following the buffalo, there was once a young orphan boy who had no family. He befriended another orphan of sorts: a widowed woman who had been deserted by her relatives. She asked the boy to live with her. She would take care of him if he would take care of her. As was the practice, they took each other as relatives: the boy called the woman "grandmother" and she called him "grandson."
>
> The widow and her grandson were very poor. They had holes in their tipi and in their clothing. With no family to provide for them, they struggled day after day to find food. What made matters worse, the Kiowas had fallen on bad times. It was the dead of winter and no one had seen any buffalo. The camp chiefs announced that everyone would have to "tighten up" and eat as little as possible until they found buffalo again.
>
> The widow and her grandson had only one wooden bowl and one buffalo horn spoon. That's all they had. One day, the orphaned boy was playing and came running into the tipi and accidentally stepped on their spoon and broke it in half. His

grandmother became very angry. "Don't you know we've just got one spoon," she yelled. "We have no buffalo to make another!"

The little boy had never been scolded before and he was very hurt. He sank to the ground and cried and cried. While he lay there in the tipi crying, under the bottom part of the tipi, the wind blew in a smell. It startled the boy, for the smell was that of a buffalo. He sat up, but saw nothing. He lay back down, and again, he smelled buffalo. While he lay there, he thought to himself, "I know I smell a buffalo. I wonder if there are any out there?"

The boy jumped up and ran outside into the snow. But he saw nothing. He ran back into the tipi, wiping the tears from his eyes. "Grandma," he said, "I smell buffalo."

"Ya! Don't say that! Don't talk like that! We're poor. If anybody hears you, they'll kill us because you don't know what you're talking about."

"Come on grandma," he said. "I want to show you." He kneeled down on the ground again and pointed to a little opening in the tipi. They both neared the hole to smell.

"Yes," the boy's grandmother said. "I smell it. And it smells like buffalo alright!"

"I'm going out to see them."

"No! Don't go out grandson. The snow is too deep and it's too cold. You don't know how far you'll have to go."

The boy was persistent. "I'm going to see for myself," he said.

He ran out of the tipi and into the snow, following the scent. When he came over the second big hill, he saw hundreds of buffalo migrating in the valley below. As he stood there watching, something spoke to him. The voice told him what he needed to do to have the buffalo.

"Take this medicine," the spirit said, "and go around the buffalo and it will trap the buffalo where they stand."

The boy did just that. And the voice spoke again: "Good, now the buffalo can't run away."

The boy then ran back to his grandmother's tipi. "I found the buffalo! They're fat and there is plenty to eat for everyone!"

"Don't say that grandson! They'll kill us if they go out there and the buffalo are gone."

But the boy remained persistent. "We have to tell them grandma! There is plenty of buffalo!"

"All right. But remember, they'll kill us if you're not telling the truth."

So the two ran around and told everyone in the camp. The chiefs came out of their tipis, and the boy told them what he had seen. But the chiefs didn't believe him. "You're just an orphan!" they said to the boy. And they said to the old woman, "Take this boy back to your tipi and calm him down."

The boy was persistent. "I'm going to sing a song given to me by the spirit," he said. So the boy sang the song:

I smell buffalo in my nostrils.
This is the song I sing if I want something.
That's what the spirit told me.

The boy sang the song through four times. When he finished, one of the chiefs said, "This boy could be telling us the truth. Maybe we should see for ourselves."

So the Kiowas went to the second hill and in the valley below were buffalo as far as the eye could see. And as they moved, they traveled in a circle as if barricaded by an invisible wall. So the chiefs turned to the boy and asked, "How do you propose we might kill these buffalo? Are we to chase them?"

"No, no," said the boy. "Whoever wants to kill a buffalo, listen to me. Kill all you want to eat. This will save our people. When you're finished, I'll let them out."

So the people went in among the buffalo and killed all that they needed. When they were finished, they went back to the top of the hill. They all watched as the boy did the reverse of what the spirit first told him to do. He encircled the buffalo with the medicine, and as he did, the remaining buffalo dispersed.

It was said for years to come that this little orphaned boy saved the tribe. As he grew up, he became known as the "buffalo medicine man." People came to him when they needed help. Whatever they needed, he used his medicine and gave it to them.

The medicine this boy used is the bundle that was passed down through the generations to my grandfather, the bundle that my grandfather passed on to me. I sing its songs, tell its stories, and carry on its calling to help those in need, just as my grandfather and his grandfather before him did.

My rights to this bundle and its accompanying responsibilities always point back to Daw-Kee, literally meaning, in English, "Throwing Power"—or more simply put—God. This bundle is only a minute part of all that Daw-Kee has given to the Kiowa people. Our language, dances and songs, oral traditions—in a word, "culture"—all come from Him. Daw-Kee first granted the Kiowas their very existence by "throwing" these powers to them. Indeed, these powers are intrinsic to our ability to have survived as long as we have.

My grandparents used to say that long ago, before they had a culture, the Kiowas lived in darkness. They lived in chaos. But one day they saw a light, and in this light, they saw what looked like a human being. They saw a hand and it beckoned them towards the light. They entered into a world through a hole in the ground. On the other side, they entered upon the earth, and it was here that they began to speak a language, sing songs, and tell stories. My grandparents also used to say that the Kiowas were originally from "the north country." They moved onto the northern Plains several hundred years ago. Following the seasonal migration of the buffalo, the Kiowa people, along with the Kiowa Apache—who had followed the Kiowas from "the north country"—eventually moved south and with the Comanches nearly ruled the southern Plains. All of this changed, however, with the Medicine Lodge Treaty of 1867. The Kiowas, along with the Comanches and Kiowa-Apaches, agreed to settle on a reservation in southwestern Indian territory, which is today Oklahoma. Reservation life was hard and the promises made by the United States at Medicine Lodge never fully materialized. Even those which they promised for their so-called "assimilation" of Kiowas—schools, for example—were only partially carried out. By the close of the nineteenth century, the buffalo had all but completely disappeared, and the Kiowas faced an era of poverty and desperation. That's not to say, however, that they fully accepted the reservation. My great-great grandfather, Satethieday—in English, White Bear—resisted its establishment until the day he died in 1878. (The government said he committed suicide while in prison, which, to this day, Kiowas have never accepted. My grandfathers said he was murdered while in prison.) In the first decade of the twentieth century, the U.S. government abolished the reservation, allotted the land, and opened up over two-thirds of the reservation to American settlement.

The United States took away our freedom and our land, but the Kiowas never lost that which was given to them by Daw-Kee—our culture. What we have is what makes us Kiowas, specifically and uniquely. Without it, we, as a people, are nothing. As Kiowa Tribal Chairman, I see these traditions given and authorized by Daw-

Kee as being at the heart of what it means to be Kiowa. But it is also the foundation of our inherent sovereignty. What do I mean by this? The political and economic sovereignty of the Kiowa Tribe of Oklahoma has been defined within certain limits by the United States government and the State of Oklahoma under the Indian Reorganization Act of 1934 (IRA) and the Oklahoma Indian Welfare Act of 1936, respectively. Furthermore, tribal sovereignty is generally defined in a number of ways by a number of people and it takes shape very differently from tribal community to tribal community. This is the **tribal** sovereignty that my tribal business committee and I negotiate with the federal and state government everyday. But our **inherent** sovereignty is not defined by the United States or the State of Oklahoma. Inherent sovereignty means having those rights like language and buffalo medicine, rights that form the very foundation of who we are as Kiowa people. Kiowas like myself hold these rights to be as self-evident and unalienable as those rights upon which the United States was originally founded. These are **our** rights to life, liberty, and the pursuit of happiness. Just as the founding fathers of the United States saw their rights to be endowed by their Creator, I too see my peoples' rights to exist and govern as being endowed by my Creator.

I believe that such rights are endowed to all people. All that is needed is respect for one another's inherent sovereignty. Such a philosophy, of course, is at direct odds with the normal behavior of most human beings. It's certainly not to be found in the history of the dealings of the United States with the Kiowas. Still yet, it is the philosophy that I use to direct my decisions as Kiowa Tribal Chairman. In practical terms, maintaining inherent sovereignty is quite a struggle, not only within the limits of tribal sovereignty as defined by the federal and state governments, but even among my own people. While it may not be very difficult to understand why the federal government has yet to recognize our inherent sovereignty, many Kiowa people do not fully understand the impact of what the loss of our language and other traditions may mean to our very existence as a people.

One example stands out in my mind. When the Kiowas were free on the Plains, each summer, the bands gathered to hold their annual K'aw-tow. In English, K'aw-tow literally means "gathering," but it is more commonly known as the so-called "Sun Dance." The Kiowas' last Sun Dance was in 1890 when the United States government halted it with military force. The Kiowas never held a Sun Dance again. Several years ago, a few Kiowa people began meeting and talking about reviving the Sun Dance, but it never fully materialized. When one family announced that they would have a Sun Dance on their trust property in the summer of 1997, however, some Kiowas exhibited enthusiasm and some did not. Most Kiowas seemed to be indifferent; I was neither for it nor against it. God handles such things in His own way. Nevertheless, those that opposed the dance did so with great force, initiating a media blitz against the gathering. A handful of elderly men, calling themselves "the Kiowa Elders," opposed the dance so vehemently that they eventually brought suit against the family in federal court, arguing that the family had no rights to Sun Dance. The men based their argument on what they called an "agreement" with the United States government, made in 1890. In June 1997, the Code of Federal Court of Indian Offenses ruled in favor of the "Kiowa elders," citing tribal tradition (i.e., respect for elders) as the basis of the decision.

On one level, this event may be easily interpreted as a victory of tribal sovereignty over individual rights to worship as defined by the Constitution of the United

States. On another level, what my people were also debating—I believe unknowingly—was inherent sovereignty. The right to worship God—whether as a Christian or as a Sun Dance participant—is endowed by Daw-Kee and cannot be negotiated. Any government, whether the Kiowa Tribe of Oklahoma or the United States government, cannot tell you that you can or cannot worship. Yet as we well know, we as human beings believe we can indeed debate whether people have such rights. We do so regularly. And this case is a prime example.

I grew up in the Native American Church. My grandfathers taught me how to speak to Daw-Kee in our language, the language that He gave to us specifically. Daw-Kee expects to hear us talk to Him in this way. It is our special connection. Like my language, the bundles, and my stories, the Native American Church belongs to me and my people and is authorized by God, not any government. Again, it is part of our inherent sovereignty. Yet my rights to worship in the tipi and partake of peyote are regularly debated in United States courts. As I see it, the United States government granting or not granting me the right to worship in the tipi is as absurd as the so-called "Kiowa elders" insisting that other Kiowas do not have rights to Sun Dance. It's like Kiowas granting the Pope the right to serve wine.

Ultimately, to compromise our inherent sovereignty is to compromise our very survival as a people. To question the rights of religious freedom is to question God. Yet, on a more fundamental level, we are losing our language, our dances, our songs, our bundles, our stories. In my children's lifetime, the Kiowa language will surely become extinct. Very few Kiowas still speak the language. I wonder what this means for the future of my people and our inherent sovereignty? Indeed, at the core of who we are as a people is our language. When Daw-Kee pulled the Kiowas out of darkness, He said, "I give you a language and I want you to speak this language. When you stop speaking this language, there will be no more Kiowas." I believe the same holds true for all of our other traditions. With this in mind, how can we, then, argue for tribal sovereignty if we have lost the consecrated foundation upon which we stand? Such questions have come to define for me an even greater urgency for cultural preservation. Instead of arguing about the Sun Dance, Kiowas should be working to insure that our inherent sovereignty will have significance and meaning beyond the tribal sovereignty defined by outsiders.

Such a realization is nothing new. My grandfathers also spoke of this. When I was just a boy, one of my grandfathers told this story at a Native American Church meeting:

> Here is what is coming ahead. Toward where the sun rises, I saw a commotion. Before the sun came up, I could see what looked like a wagon rolling towards me. Its body was a green box, and it rested on four silver wheels. Nobody was pulling or pushing it. But the wheels were still rolling. As it got in clear view, I could see all the people of the world. And among them were Kiowas. All of them were riding on this wagon, fighting with one another over the very wagon itself. As the wagon came closer, I realized its body was a dollar bill and its wheels silver dollars.
>
> There will come a time when you will kill your own mother to be on this wagon. Brothers will kill their sisters. Sisters will kill their brothers. You will kill anyone just to be on this wagon.

This is a prophecy that I have thought much about as I have grown older. And I see it coming true, not just for Kiowas, but for all the people of the world. The force of the money wagon may be more consequential than anything the Kiowas have ever faced before. The reservation era pales when compared to it. For me, however, this new reality means that there must be new action. I believe that I must help my people understand that we must carry on what we have left. But a sad reality continues to raise its ugly head: What if my own people choose to jump on the money wagon? And what can be done to safeguard our inherent sovereignty if no one wants to be Kiowa anymore? These are extremely difficult questions for me. For I do indeed believe my grandfathers and the charge that Daw-Kee has thrown to me and my people. Surely, to throw away our culture is to throw away our inherent sovereignty. Close behind, I believe, is the loss of our tribal sovereignty.

Discussion Questions

1. What is the significance of the "bundle possessing buffalo medicine" that Billy Evans Horse inherited from his grandfather? What is the purpose of the story that goes along with the bundle? How is the owner of the medicine bundle supposed to use it?

2. Who is Daw-Kee? Is the name 'Daw-Kee' simply the Kiowa word for the same entity referred to by English-speaking Christians as 'God', by French-speaking Christians as 'Dieu', by Muslims as 'Allah', and by the ancient Greeks as 'Zeus'? Or does each cultural conception of a Supreme Being refer to something completely different? How can you know?

3. The Kiowas say that they emerged from a hole in the ground, from darkness into light, and also that they came from "the north country." Many Native American creation stories include the darkness-to-light motif, as well as the north-to-south migration motif. Some anthropologists think these stories reflect memories of a migration across the Bering Land Bridge from northeastern Asia/Siberia into the New World via Alaska (where winters are long and dark), and thence south to the sunlight of the temperate and tropical regions of the New World. Do you think it is possible for memories of actual events this long ago (12,000 to 30,000 plus years) to persist as part of creation stories? If not, how else could one account (from a scientific perspective) for these motifs and stories?

4. How did the Kiowas end up on a reservation in Oklahoma?

5. What does Billy Evans Horse mean by inherent sovereignty as opposed to the Kiowas' political and economic tribal sovereignty as defined by the U.S. government and the state of Oklahoma?

6. Even within the Kiowa tribal organization, people differ in their interpretation of what their inherent sovereignty means. Discuss the example of the Sun Dance controversy and how it illuminates issues of different types of sovereignty.

7. Do you think the U.S. government has the authority to tell the Kiowas how they may or may not practice their religion? Why or why not?

8. Billy Evans Horse is worried that too many Kiowas will cease to speak their native language, cease to worship as Daw-Kee told them to, and will "jump on the money wagon." What does he mean by the money wagon? Is the assimilation of Native American cultures into modern capitalist mainstream U.S. culture inevitable? Is it something to be lamented or something to be celebrated? From whose perspective?

9. Imagine that intelligent beings from another planet have conquered Earth, and, in the United States, have forbidden the speaking of English, destroyed all books written in English, destroyed the telephone and computer network systems, and outlawed all human religious beliefs. The aliens expect all Earthlings to learn to speak the aliens' language and to worship the aliens' deities. How willing do you think people in the

United States would be to go along with such plans? Would you be a collaborator or a member of the resistance movement? What forms might resistance take? If it was not possible to resist, what emotional consequences might follow for Americans and other Earthlings?

Additional Resources

For Internet links related to this chapter, please visit our website at www.mhhe.com/dettwyler

BARTH, FREDRIK. *Political Leadership Among Swat Pathans.* 5th ed. London: Athlone Press, 1965.

COLLIER, GEORGE A., and ELIZABETH LOWERY QUARATIELLO. *Basta! Land and the Zapatista Rebellion in Chiapas.* Rev. ed. Oakland, CA: Food First Books, 1999.

EVANS-PRITCHARD, E. E. *The Nuer: A Description of the Modes of Livelihood and Political Institutions of a Nilotic People.* New York: Clarendon Press, 1968.

MOORE, SALLY FALK. *Law As Process: An Anthropological Approach.* London: LIT Verlag, 2001.

NADER, LAURA. *Law in Culture and Society.* Berkeley, CA: University of California Press, 1997.

ROTHENBERG, DANIEL. *With These Hands: The Hidden World of Migrant Farmworkers To-day.* Berkeley, CA: University of California Press, 2000.

WARREN, KAY B. and JEAN E. JACKSON, eds. *Indigenous Movements, Self-Representation, and the State in Latin America.* Austin, TX: University of Texas Press, 2003.

WRIGHT, ROBIN B. *The Last Great Revolution: Turmoil and Transformation in Iran.* New York: Vintage Books, 2001.

CHAPTER 18

Families, Kinship, and Descent

 33. "SOUP NIGHT": COMMUNITY CREATION THROUGH
FOODWAYS, by Lin T. Humphrey, from Theodore C. Humphrey and Lin
T. Humphrey, eds., *We Gather Together: Food and Festival in American Life*. Logan, UT:
Utah State University Press, 1988, pp. 53–68.

*Most introductory anthropology textbooks have long, complicated chapters de-
scribing how different societies organize themselves using various systems of kinship. It is important for U.S. college students to understand how critical these
kinship systems are because they form the basis for much of the social organization
of other societies around the world. Most people, in most cultures, interact on a daily
basis not with hordes of strangers and/or casual acquaintances or people in con-
tractual relationships, but with well-known, multiply related individuals. Each individual (known in anthropological terminology as EGO, and typically viewed as a
male) serves as the central point of his or her own kinship network, based on ties of
biology (consanguineal relatives) and culture (through marriage, affinal relatives).
Each individual can trace his or her genetic relationships up through ascending
generations (parents, grandparents, great-grandparents, aunts and uncles, etc.),
across their own generation (siblings, cousins, second cousins, etc.), and down
through descending generations (children, grandchildren, great-grandchildren,
nieces and nephews, etc.). Similarly, they can trace their affinal relationships
through their own spouse (wife/husband, mother- and father-in-law, brother- and
sister-in-law, etc.) and through the spouses of all their consanguineal (genetic, or
"of the same blood") relatives.*

Different kinship systems choose to emphasize some aspects of relatedness and ignore others. There are four main aspects to choose to stress, downplay, or ignore altogether: type of relationship (consanguineal or affinal), sex of the relative, sex of the link(s) between EGO and the relative, and genealogical distance from EGO to the relative (number of links). In many modern U.S. communities, especially for people whose ancestors immigrated many generations ago, biological kinship is important only for the immediate family. It is important primarily in childhood and becomes increasingly less important as more generations accumulate in the new country, as divorces interrupt more and more nuclear biological families, and as families become smaller and smaller (fewer children) and more mobile in the modern economy.

However, just because we don't necessarily have large, intimate communities of consanguineal and affinal relatives to interact with on a daily basis doesn't mean we don't have a vital need for the community of support and friendship provided in more traditional societies by such groups of relatives. In nonkinship-based societies, people often create their own communities, based on geographic proximity, similarities of age or stage of life, or common interests or problems. These nonkinship-based communities can even be virtual—existing only in cyberspace, through the magic of the Internet. Kinship-based societies may also have nonkinship-based organizations, but in Western cultures, especially in the United States, and most especially among European-Americans, nonkinship-based communities become much more important than kinship-based communities.

In her selection, "Soup Night," Lin T. Humphrey describes in great detail how she and her husband Ted created a community of friends through the weekly sharing of food at their house. Although an informal get-together, Soup Night was bound by many rules and expectations of the participants, and it served a number of functions. Humphrey's focus is on the importance of sharing food to create community— a theme found in many different cultures and in many religious rituals. The Humphreys went to extraordinary lengths to create and maintain a circle of friends to serve as surrogate kin, and Soup Night persisted, week in and week out, for over 20 years. In 1987, one of us (Dettwyler) participated in an NEH summer seminar for college professors—focusing on food—in Charlottesville, Virginia. Other participants that summer included the Humphreys, and they hosted a special Soup Night for the participants in the seminar. As you read the selection, think about the many and various ways that modern Americans create community to fulfill the basic human needs for support and friendship that kinship networks serve in many other cultures. Think also about the role of food and music in creating and reinforcing community.

Soup Night, a contemporary small group festive gathering, began in my kitchen in Claremont, California in 1974. It grew out of my perceived need to spend time with friends in a less formal, less time-consuming format than the formal, sit-down, reciprocal dinner party. Although this had been the main avenue for social exchange among most of our friends, many of the women, including myself, had returned to jobs and interrupted careers, and we did not want to spend our weekends preparing fancy dinners and keeping track of reciprocity. After a successful New Year's Day Hoppin' John celebration in which we managed to feed close to a hundred people from one large pot of black-eyed peas and rice, I initiated Soup Night, or Soup, as it is frequently called. As "chief kitchen person" I invited the people, arranged the table, made the soup, and actively participated in the consuming of the food and the conversation that accompanied it. Out of this has grown a sense of community and group identity based on the sharing and consuming of food once a week. The balance and tension between individual and shared power, the limits of hospitality and reciprocity, the flexibility and portability of the event, and the need for *communitas* and commensality in a modern, urbanized society maintain this food-centered event and create a viable, recognizable community of participants for whom Soup expresses values and social identity.

The people who compose the community are not the same ones who started it; only a few of the original "soupers" are still active in the group. There are, however, several constants. The main foodstuff is soup; participants bring bread or wine or both; we provide bowls, wine glasses, spoons, knives, butter, napkins, bottle openers and corkscrews (although in truth, many of the bowls, glasses, spoons, and openers are gifts from various members of the group). My husband always serves the first bowl of soup to guests (except for the year he spent in Oklahoma when I took over the task). And there is a toast that is always made before everyone settles down to eating and talking. Since this event takes place in my home, since the participants are, for the most part, good, and in some cases, intimate friends, and since I initiated and maintain it, the idea of objectivity in my analysis of it is absurd. Yet these very problems, conflicts, and biases provide a basis for an intense esoteric view of this community.

The Soup Group has few of the traditional ties that bind groups together such as kinship, economic dependency, work or neighborhood affiliations. Generally speaking, the members are liberal in both religion and politics, concerned about the environment, and about individual health and fitness. More than half of those who usually frequent Soup were born and educated outside the state of California. Many, but not all, are teachers at all levels from kindergarten to university. Others are artists, designers, lawyers, chiropractors, office managers, occasional students, and sheriffs. Many do not live in Claremont but come from 20 or 30 miles away. There are regulars who have been coming every Thursday night for thirteen years; others come by once a month or so. "Going to Soup" becomes a password which designates those who belong to the community. The group maintains itself even during the summer through a series of salad potlucks that rotate from house to house depending on individual schedule and whim. This flexible community is balanced on a subtle hierarchy maintained by the tension between hospitality and power and a mutually understood but largely unspoken value system and code of behavior, both of which can be and have been broken. Within the experience and within the food consumed can be seen the structure, function, values and world view of the community known as "The Soup Group."

Having established that there is indeed a group of people who not only view themselves as a community bonded together by sharing food, but name themselves after the food that they share, let us look at the food involved in a typical Soup Night. In "Deciphering a Meal," Mary Douglas defines a meal as "a mixture of solid food accompanied by liquids." A quick glance through any number of cookbooks confirms that soup, indeed, consists of blending "soup liquids with your favorite meats, beans, vegetables, and fruits." Douglas (1972) goes on to say that "Meals properly require the use of at least one mouth-entering utensil per head." We eat our soup with large soup or table spoons, one per person. Soup is physical food; the eating of soup together constitutes a physical meal; and the process satisfies the physical need for sustenance. According to Charles Camp's typography in his dissertation, "America Eats: Toward a Social Definition of American Foodways," Soup fits into his Type Three category: "The foods prepared for these events are not the sort prepared for the everyday world, and the foods themselves serve as the reason for special gatherings." He goes on to say that structurally such a semi-public food event in which a single individual is responsible for the event but in which this person also participates can be delineated as "A = A + B +." Even Mary Douglas gives credence to the one-dish meal if it preserves the minimum structure of a meal—"vegetable soup with noodles and grated cheese" (1972). Peter Farb and George Armelagos (1980) also assert that soup is a meal which fits the pattern A + 2b (central ingredient together with two [and usually many more] unstressed ingredients). But Soup is primarily a meal because the participants define it as such. Furthermore, the food is so important that it names the event, Soup Night, and the people who attend refer to themselves as "The Soup Group" or as "Soupers."

Soup, however, is a very common, economical, ordinary food which, in most cultures, can be dressed up or down. Why is the soup served on Soup Night to the Soup Group special? Charles Camp argues that food is used along with other signs and symbols to execute implicit and explicit social strategies; thus the same food served at different occasions will have different intentions and different meaning and values (Camp 1978, 6). On a more practical level, soup serves well as the main foodstuff for an indeterminant number of people. It can be, and usually is, inexpensive; the ingredients seldom cost more than ten or twelve dollars. A twenty-quart pot will hold enough to feed as many as 35 or 40 people, and when the crowd is smaller (the average attendance is about 20), there is plenty for seconds or even thirds or to give to departing guests to take home afterward. Soup is also relatively easy to prepare, especially on a grand scale, for there is space and time to make and correct errors in seasoning, etc. On the other hand, this need for space and time may be seen as impractical in a rushed, fast-paced, urban society. For the Soup Group and for the cook, the very fact that making and consuming soup requires one to stop rushing around is both an implicit and explicit value. Thursday afternoons are sacred times for me, time set aside for making soup. I refuse committee appointments or meetings that conflict with that time. The afternoon is devoted to chopping, slicing, simmering, and thinking about soup. To paraphrase Claude Levi-Strauss, "Soup is good to think."

When one thinks about the physical aspect of soup, it becomes a metaphor for the event of Soup Night itself. Roger Abrahams suggests that "the currencies of exchange of primary importance in culture are . . . food, sex, talk," which include values, meaning, an etiquette, a decorum system, symbolic objects, and actions that "carry the most profound, if everyday, cultural messages." Soup is a mixture of many and various ingredients: vegetables, meats, liquids, cereals, and seasonings blend together to make something other than what each ingredient is by itself. It is a food of harmony and cooperation, almost always warm and aromatic. Furthermore, the increase in quantity, the large "mother" pot full of food for all-comers is the symbolic center of the event. Mary Douglas writes in the Introduction to *Food in the Social Order* that food can be given more meaning or the meaning can be changed not just by altering the quality of the food served but by changes in the quantity of food available; thus the greater the quantity of food, the greater the investment in cost, time, thought, and space (1984, p. 15).

The community created by and around Soup Night is also flexible in size. The number of people who attend varies from as few as ten to as many as forty or more. Part of the fun, the freedom, and the tension is in not knowing who will be there. As far as can be determined, there are no exclusionary barriers to Soup. People come because they are friends with others who come; certainly one would not come if one hated everyone there. Ted and I have never told anyone not to come, and Ted in particular tends to invite everyone he meets. People who come and do not enjoy themselves usually do not return. Somehow in this process freedom and hospitality are compromised. Hospitality is not the sole responsibility of the host or hostess, but an action wherein many of the participants seize power. The door is always unlocked and the porch light is on; returning participants let themselves in. If someone knocks or rings the doorbell, whoever is handy lets him or her in. Over the years, this has occasionally led to strangers being escorted in when actually they were looking for another address. Usually people greet each other with hugs, especially if someone has not been around for a while. People are invited formally once by either Ted or myself or by other guests; after that they are free to decide whether or not it is their "cup of soup." Friends usually feel free to bring along another friend, although sometimes they will call in the afternoon to let me know that someone new will be there. This may be a ritual of politeness or a way of noting the presence of someone unfamiliar to us and to the event itself.

Guests begin to arrive about 6:30 or shortly thereafter. Early birds often bring a bottle of "good" wine to share before everyone else comes. Most participants have a glass of wine before dinner and check on the kind of soup simmering on the stove. Wine glasses, open bottles of wine, and openers are handy on the main table. Bread is taken to the kitchen to be warmed. At seven, give or take a few minutes, when the house seems sufficiently crowded, Ted shouts, in his loudest voice, "Soup's On!," and most people pick up bowls stacked on the kitchen table and line up. (Although this may suggest soup lines during the Depression, most of the participants are too young to remember this except in books and films.) Participants crowd around the main table, which will seat a tight thirteen (no significance to the number, although we sometimes joke about it), sit on the floor and the furniture in the living room around a round coffee table, stand in the kitchen; or if it is warm enough, sit outside on the patio. Bread and butter (depending on what people bring) are available at both tables, and everyone is free to move around at will. Part of the feeling of free access is in the way the soup is served. After Ted serves himself and sits down, anyone who comes late or who wants more simply helps him/herself. Often a good-hearted "souper" will offer to get a bowl for another person, but in general each person is responsible for his or her own soup. Spoons, knives, glasses, and paper napkins are already on the main tables. In this curious, complex coming together of food and food-eaters, it is sometimes difficult to determine who is in charge. The lines of responsibility and power between host and guest are quite blurred. Strangers brought by other people may go half the evening before meeting both my husband and me. Certainly the open door, the nonspecified seating arrangement (with the exception of the seats reserved by custom—no place cards—for host and hostess), the access to food, utensils and beverages, and the free movement from room to room and table to table encourage, if not create, this division of power. A very important factor is the actual responsibility of the guests to provide important parts of the meal: i.e. the bread and the wine. Bread and wine, incidentally are not mandatory or inclusive; guests often bring dessert, cheese, crackers, or occasionally come empty-handed, promising to make up for it next time. The understanding and the acceptance of this shared power and responsibility is in part what holds this group together. Otherwise the limits of hospitality and reciprocity would be too overburdened for the event to continue.

Contributing to an event gives participants some power in shaping the event. In *Consuming Passions: The Anthropology of Eating,* Farb and Armelagos state, "The important metaphorical associations a society has are usually with the staples. In the Near East and Europe [and in America], the staple is bread," our so-called "staff of life." The power and responsibility for bread rest almost entirely on the shoulders of the other participants. We eat whatever bread is brought to the house. When little or no bread turns up, some of the guests may make a quick "bread-run" to the store, but more often, we simply share what is there. Invariably, the next week we will have far more bread than can be consumed in one evening. I save most of what is left over, especially if the loaves have not been opened, in the freezer and bring it out the next week. Occasionally someone will bring actual "homemade" bread, but most often it comes from local bakeries or grocery stores. There is a definite hierarchy of values given to the loaves of bread; dark bread, those made from whole grains, large round, brown loaves, fancy cheese or braided bread inevitably are eaten first, with some grabbing and finally sharing of the last small portions. Most bread arrives at the table, warm from the microwave, but uncut. We simply pass it around and tear off hunks or ask someone to pass a certain kind. Loud verbal praise is given to those who brought especially good bread, and a common question resounding around the room is, "Who brought the big loaf of pumpernickel?" The preference for dark, whole-grained bread is probably the result of the emphasis on healthy foods that influences nearly everyone who comes to Soup; this appreciation for healthy food (i.e., no fat, no sugar, whole grains, fresh vegetables) is one of the values held by the group as a whole. Camp affirms the idea that there is more to bread than good food when he says there are "symbolic and religious elements in the breaking of bread among friends or fellow worshippers which has little to do with the recipe from which the dough was made or the kind of oven in which it was made" (Camp 1978).

An equally important substance for which guests are also responsible is wine or other beverages. As with the bread, it is often "feast or famine"—everyone brings wine or no one does. I also will set on the table any wine left over from the week before; unfortunately, what is left is what no one wanted to drink in the first place. Here again judgements are made about the quality of what people bring. Most wine-bringers bring an inexpensive bottle of California wine that they themselves like. Most people prefer white, but in warm weather they have trouble getting it chilled before coming to Soup because it is something they usually pick up on the way. Good reds are actually rarer and much appreciated. Some guests bring a large bottle every other week or so, depending on specials at the local stores. Participants set the bottles on the long dining room table where openers are handy. Sex role transitions and accommodations appear here. Some women hand bottles to men to open; others pride themselves on their mastery of the wine cork. Once on the table, the wine, like the bread, belongs to everyone, and some people rush around to insure getting a glass of the "good stuff" which they or someone else brought. As a whole, we are not wine connoisseurs, but the tastes run generally to dry chablis, French Colombards, and hearty, dry reds, while quite a few of the women profess a fondness for white zinfandel or other so-called "blush wines." But not everyone drinks wine. A few bring beer which they stash in the refrigerator in the kitchen; some drink mineral water, apple cider, or diet soda. The point here is that the wine is important to the meal and it is almost completely in the hands of the participants, other than the host and hostess. Unopened bottles find their way into our wine rack from which they may emerge the next week. We tend to drink the opened bottles during the week, or use them for cooking. (Wine is almost always one of the ingredients in the soup.)

Bringing together bread and wine in a Western country inevitably raises the question of religious symbol and ritual. Indeed, what ritual we do maintain does involve the wine, but the degree to which it is overtly religious seems insignificant. Douglas notes that ritual performs several functions: it focuses attention by framing; it enlivens memory and links the present with the relevant past; it aids perception of an event; and it controls and modifies our experience of the outer world. The main ritual at Soup is quite simple, a toast given at the beginning of the meal in a call-and-response mode by my husband and me. In order for this ritual to be effective, it is necessary that we be seated at opposite ends of the main table—these are the only two seats "set aside" during the event. When nearly everyone is seated and has managed to get a glass of something to drink, a spoon, a knife, and a piece of bread, but before too much soup has actually been eaten, Ted raises his glass and says, "To friends who are present," and I respond, "And those who are not." Glasses clink, we usually raise our glasses to "those at the lower table," and we drink. This is not the first drink of the evening, as most guests have consumed a glass of wine or two before dinner, but it is important. At that moment there is a unity of focus that does not occur at any other time during the evening. The toast began at the same time that Soup began. It came from our realization and recognition that friends come and go in many ways. About the time Soup started, a good friend of mine, a former dance teacher who was important to many of the women in the group, died. "Those who are not" includes those who will never be at Soup or anywhere else again, but it also signifies those who simply are not present for various reasons, those who used to come but come no more, those who have moved away, perhaps those yet to come. It is all inclusive within the limits of friendship. Thus, Soup is a celebration of friendship, of community which transcends the here and now. Farb and Armelagos suggest that ritual provides comfort, security, and the reassurance that there will be no surprises (1980, 217). For those who come to Soup it is a moment of contact, recognition, and appreciation. I am not suggesting that all those who share the toast understand its meaning. We don't talk about it; we just do it. After the toast is the time for announcements, subsequent toasts, invitations, and applause. Toasts are made by anyone present to anyone else who has won an award, celebrated a birthday, written a paper, published book, bought a house. Participants also use this time to invite people to other social or civic events. If any cards or letters have come to "the Soup Group," they are read and passed around. Thus we move quickly from the spiritual to the secular.

One way of looking at this event suggests the more primitive idea of "potlach." We—the "chief" or "big man," my husband, aided and abetted by "the chief kitchen person," me—create, control, and maintain a network of friends in a loose pattern of allegiance. But allegiance to whom or to what? We are not plotting a political coup in the city of Claremont. It may be an unspoken allegiance to a way or life or a set of values that Soup represents. Certainly there is a great deal of ego-satisfaction when twenty people praise my soup and express what a good time they are having in our house. I enjoy the prestige of being known as "the Soup Lady" and the reputation of being a good cook, but suburban Claremont, located 35 miles from Los Angeles, is not a rural community where wives are ranked on the basis of their culinary skill or clean houses. Nearly all the men and women who come to Soup are college educated, professional people whose values do not center on domestic traditions. Soup may be seen as looking back at older values or a former lifestyle, lost in many modern urban communities. Because Soup Night takes place in a modern, post-industrial suburban location, the group experience is not like that in pre- or nonindustrial tribal life. A tribal or "family" feeling is created among individuals who are not blood-related by down-playing status. The emphasis is on contact and a feeling of community. Since Soup Night is not regulated by seasons or weather cycles, it is not a "natural" celebration. Instead it conforms to the so-called academic calendar, ceasing during school holidays and summer vacations. Occasionally it is cancelled so that my husband and I can go to various academic conferences.

Of course, there are some Thursdays when I would prefer not to have to spend the afternoon making soup or when there is something else going on that I would like to do instead, but there is a balance between pleasure and duty that Soup seems to satisfy. The enjoyment of sharing my house and soup with friends is balanced by spending Thursday afternoon not just making soup, which is creative fun, but in straightening the rest of the house, arranging furniture, and setting the table. Sometimes, once the soup is made and the table set, I have considered simply crawling into bed with a book and glass of wine, letting the event happen without me. Both Ted and I experience some Soup Nights in which we feel alienated and left out; we look at each other and nonverbally say, "Who are these people and why are they here?" Of course, these feelings are not common or we would stop having Soup. Furthermore, there are some people who come or have come to Soup that we do not like. And some of them do not like each other. But on Thursday night, we are not the sole owners of the house. It belongs to the Soup Group, which is large enough and complex enough to include ex-husbands and wives who are not speaking or, occasionally, several individuals that other guests may not enjoy particularly. However, the participants manage to maneuver and mingle so that there are very rarely unpleasant confrontations or outbursts. Part of the control is the reverse of what I just said—even though we have turned our house over to a community, because it is still a "private" home, no one can ask anyone else not to come or to leave. Neither Ted nor I have ever exercised that power; one of the basic tenets of the evening is that it is open to anyone who likes it.

Nevertheless, I know there is subtle weeding-out that takes place under what seems to be a self-selecting process. Soup does not suit everyone, yet many participants have stated that it can and does meet varied needs. If one is tired and depressed, it is all right to come by, have a bowl of soup, and go home; if one wishes to celebrate a birthday or anniversary, Soup provides a built-in party; if one is sad and needs comforting, there are people who will freely dispense hugs and advice. When Soup Night first began, most of the participants did not have extended family groups to which they belonged. Soup was often expanded, moved, and modified to cover Thanksgiving, Christmas, and Easter dinners. As the group has changed, several of the members have brought their mothers, brothers, and sisters to Soup, and the need for Soup to provide holiday meals has diminished. On the other hand, several people have told me that sometimes Soup is "just too much." Indeed the mood and noise level at Soup Night is jovial. Implicit in the freedom and flow are rules, codes, and structures that are understood and enforced by the "in-group" who assume the responsibility for making Soup work and the community continue. It is not a one-person show.

The shape, consistency, ritual, and the needs of all the participants create and maintain the etiquette and protocol of Soup Night. Since these rules are not written down or delivered orally, since there is no code for proper conduct or prescription for a successful Soup, the rules must be implicit in the behavior of the participants. As an insider, I have internalized, and perhaps created, the proper behavior, so it is difficult to sort out the appropriate and inappropriate ways to behave. Often we are aware of these only when they are violated. Anthropologists who have studied less industrialized societies are able to discern meaning in the structure of a meal by looking at the seating arrangements, the time span, and the interaction of the participants. For example, Tony Whitehead, in looking at how food behavior reveals culturally perceived needs, states: "The timing, seating arrangements, and dispensing protocol of a meal reflect ideas regarding role allocations, gender orientation, social order, status, and control." Richard Mirsky, in his study of food habits, goes even further and claims that "Food sharing events have been interpreted as occasions when the members of a social unit join together to express symbolically and to maintain social cohesion as opportunities for the establishment of social prestige through demonstrations of superior wealth and property, as elements in systems of property distribution which tend to minimize individual differences in wealth, and as expression of friendship or covert hostility." This does not apply to the small group festive gathering in a modern suburban setting. There is agreement among most food scholars that food events which involve sharing food within a small group are important in maintaining social cohesion. Jack Goody, quoting Robertson Smith, says that "the act of eating and drinking together is the solemn and stated expression of the fact that all those who share the meal are brethren and that all the duties of friendship and brotherhood are implicitly acknowledged in their common act." Understanding these "duties" determines the behavior code at Soup.

The unwritten rules of Soup Night are not handed down arbitrarily from on high. The protocol actually begins with the cook who is subject to the expectations of the community of soup eaters. The decision concerning the kind of soup to prepare is complicated by group considerations: who hates parsnips? who is allergic to oysters? are the vegetarians likely to be there? how hot can I make the curry? This may be complicated further by the knowledge that it is someone's birthday and thus special consideration should be given to the honored person. Of course, the ultimate decision may be based on what is easy, whether time is a factor, or what is cheap this week at the store. Thus power and responsibility must be compromised before the soup is made. There is also an important liminal period preceding Soup. The afternoon is a solitary time, devoted to cooking and watching soap operas on television. At various times well-intentioned friends have dropped by to lend a helping hand. Although they are treated politely and usually given a cup of coffee or iced tea, it is no doubt obvious that they are neither helpful nor welcome. To prepare for twenty or thirty guests, solitude is best. The half hour right before Soup is, for the cook, one of the high points of the event. With Soup made, table set, door unlocked, and drink in hand, I can sit down (often the first time all afternoon) and read until the first guest arrives. In Claremont, at least with this group, hardly anyone is ever on time, let alone early. Six-thirty means anytime between 6:30 and 7:00. As the days lengthen in springtime, guests arrive later. If someone comes early, he/she often sits alone in the living room, drinking wine while I run around showering or grating cheese. Sometimes a close friend may come by early in order to have a quiet, private conversation before the others arrive. But there is no punishment for being early; we laugh. This is a community of friends, of family. The rules are family rules. Dress codes are nonexistent. If someone arrives dressed up from work or on the way to a fancier function, the other guests notice, especially if a man arrives wearing a tie, but for the most part the emphasis is on comfort; after all, many people end up sitting on the floor. As already noted, the door is unlocked. Newcomers may knock and be let in, but most people simply walk in and greet those already there. There is, however, one written rule on the outside of the front door, a request that no one smoke in the house. Smokers smoke outside on the patio or on the front steps, but there are fewer than three people who come to Soup that smoke anywhere. Since we have three cats and a Scottish terrier who run around the house, friends with allergies or who do not like animals have to work out the frequency of their participation. It is possible to simply avoid the cats and dog. Children are another issue. Most of the Soupers have grown or at least teenage children. Even back when my own and others' children were younger, Soup has been an "adult" event. My own son and daughter never have and still do not like homemade soup. As preteens, I think they were embarrassed to see their parents and their friends' parents laughing and joking and drinking wine. There are exceptions, times when friends of my children would be there, but they usually spent all evening in the bedroom or went out for walks or to run around the neighborhood. Now when a few of the children come home from college, they come to Soup and are accepted as part of the group. The group has never banned children, but no accommodation has been made for them. At present, a younger couple, who have been coming to Soup for several years, even before they were married, have a one-year-old daughter whom they have brought all during the first year of her life. Most people, their own baby-producing years well behind them, enjoy holding her for a little while, but generally the parents come and leave early. They are aware that Soup Night is geared for adults.

There is no limit to the number of bowls of soup anyone may have, but we very rarely run out of soup. If someone comes by about nine o'clock, he/she may have to scrape the bottom of the pan and add a little water, but more often there are several quarts left over and some participants take it home in coffee cans or plastic butter dishes. There is no mother-figure insisting that you clean your bowl. Some people drink a lot of wine or beer; some drink only a little or none at all. Only one person in the history of this event ever got so drunk that it was obvious. He stood up, threw up and went home; the remaining Soupers pitched in and cleaned up the mess. Table manners at Soup are casual, informal to a fault. Farb and Armelagos state that "under special conditions . . . Western people consciously imitate an earlier stage in culture at a picnic, fish fry or campfire—. . . [they] still tear food apart with their fingers and their teeth, in a nostalgic renactment of eating behavior long vanished. Today's neighborhood barbecue recreates a world of sharing and hospitality that becomes rarer every year" (1980, 208).

The making and serving of coffee has developed into a small ritual over the years. One of the regular Soupers started making the coffee at the end of the meal several years ago. In the past year, because of personal and business commitments, he was not present at most Soup Nights. It took months before we finally realized that the "coffee-maker" was not there and that someone else had better take over that job. At first Ted or I did it, reasserting ourselves as providers. Recently, a friend who is now married to the ex-wife of the former coffee-maker has assumed the job, primarily because he likes coffee after a meal. When the former coffee-maker comes to Soup, the job is returned to him. About 9 o'clock, hospitality begins to wear a little thin. Most participants depart between 8:30 and 9:00 because Friday is a working day. Two hours of good food and good company are sufficient for supper. Occasionally a few linger on. The conversation, facilitated by the wine, creates intimacy and intensity that they are reluctant to break. Sometimes several guests will leave together and go somewhere else to dance or just talk some more. Lingering is especially tempting when one is sitting in the hot tub. But at 9:00, Ted and I are tired. We flip the lights off and on, turn off the jets in the tub, push people off our bed, and send them home. If only Ted is tired, he may simply crawl in bed, leaving me to sit and talk as long as I like. By 10, we are usually reading in bed, exchanging information and opinions gleaned at Soup. The behavior code of Soup, then, fits Camp's rubric: "The social organization . . . is ordered by the selectivity of participation . . . who may or may not be involved, and relationships—the determination and assumption of formal and informal roles with regard to the event. The social rules governing the determination of participation in turn give shape to the meal and establish the significance of the occasion" (Camp 1978, 5). Those who choose to come to Soup both set, accept, and enforce a necessary, but flexible and unwritten, etiquette and protocol of Soup Night.

Soup, wine, and bread make a simple supper. By themselves, eaten alone, they fulfill the requirements of a meal, but little else. Soup Night imbues these foodstuffs with meaning and power, and they in turn explain and reinforce the values and identity of the Soup Group. If bread and wine create communion, what does this communion mean? In one collection of essays on foodways and eating habits, the editors assert that "once we have associated food with social experience, and have attributed meaning and significance to preparing or serving a dish, then food becomes symbolic. Experiencing food with others often results in a transference to food of assessments and valuations of those experiences" (Jones, Giuliano, and Krell 1983, 41–42). The bread and the wine are bonding devices; sharing the food is an acknowlegement that one is willing to share oneself. Because the bread and wine are provided by the participants themselves, each becomes an active part of the event, inviting others to share what he/she has brought to the meal. Instead of merely taking soup from the host, they are reciprocating at the same time they are receiving. Thus, the communion is a communion of good and equal fellowship. The aspect of communion is emphasized early in the event with the ritual of the toast. The act of eating together is both powerful and symbolic. Eating a common food, in this case soup, creates a communion of common values. In addition, this eating event extends the boundaries of the core community. Newcomers are invited to become members through the simple act of taking part. In taking part, they may become part of a network. This past fall, a new couple came to Soup. The husband was a new faculty member at the college where my husband teaches, the wife, an unemployed children's librarian. They apparently enjoyed Soup and were soon present at spin-off occasions such as birthday celebrations at local restaurants with some, but not all, of the Soup Groupers. In addition, she became part of a women's Saturday morning breakfast group and also participated in Sunday morning bike rides with four or six of us. A couple of months ago, they decided to separate. The Soup community is supportive of both; both still come to Soup. Certainly one of the motivating forces behind why Soup works is the human need to belong. Fieldhouse asserts, "Food readily becomes an expression of the search for belongingness." His earlier contention that "Recurrent exchange and sharing [of food] is a feature of societies where community solidarity is maximal" (Fieldhouse 1986, 75) says something about the intentionality of Soup. Soup was conceived as a meal for the coming together of friends once a week in order to maintain contact and intimacy at a time when work and other obligations did not allow such contact to happen naturally. Mary Douglas states, "Meals are for family, close friends, honored guests. The ground operator of the system is the line between intimacy and distance. . . . The meal expresses close friendship" (Douglas 1972, 256). The assertion that Soup is a meal, not a party, is an extremely important distinction. In spite of divorces, dislike, aggravation, and frustration with the world and with each other, the people who come to Soup Night believe on some level that they are friends, good friends. They call on each other when cars break down or when they need help moving heavy furniture; they share good news and bad. In a town of 32,000 people, surrounded by 8 million others, the Soup Group bind themselves together through the act of eating. "Eating is symbolically associated with the most deeply felt human experiences, and thus expresses things that are sometimes difficult to articulate in everyday language" (Farb and Armelagos 1980, 111).

Soup Night is a time, a place, a meal, and a community. The tension between individual power and the concept of hospitality establishes the invisible but viable limits for behavior during this small group festive gathering. Hospitality is generally thought of as a part of a reciprocal exchange. Giving away food unilaterally would make an unbalanced and, hence, unpleasant relationship. The constant guest becomes a beggar (Douglas 1984, 10). But my guests must bring and pour their own wine, provide and serve their own bread, ask for butter or knives to be passed around the table, and freely share with others. I am relieved of nearly all the duties of being a hospitable hostess. When people need things that are not visible on the table, I tell them to look in the kitchen in various places. We become, at least for part of the evening, a family, with each member responsible for his/her own happiness. This engenders a feeling of freedom and cooperation not generally possible at a more formal dinner party. According to Paul Fieldhouse, "The act of eating together indicates some degree of compatibility or acceptance; food is offered as a gesture of friendship. . . . Offering to share food is to offer to share a bit of oneself; to refuse food when offered is easily seen as a rejection of friendship" (p. 82). The tension between hospitality and power is also evident here. When participants refuse to have soup, pleading nonhunger or having eaten elsewhere, there is consternation, not just from my husband and me, but from other guests. Often participants may come by early, before they have to be somewhere else, and eat a solitary bowl of soup while everyone else is sipping wine—a way of taking part in the gathering as much as possible. Or someone may come by late, after everyone else has eaten and sit and have a bowl of soup while everyone else winds down. Neither of these activities is considered rude or unorthodox. Group hospitality keeps the evening going and accepts the responsibility for social ease and enjoyment. Participants let others in, greet them at the door, help clear the table, load the dishwasher, and mingle with whomever they wish. These are the acts of family and friends.

Unlike traditional communities, the participants at Soup Night cannot rely on kinship networks to hold the group together, nor are they tied to each other by neighborhood or work affiliations. Other soup nights have been started in other parts of the country—New Paltz, New York, Little Rock, Arkansas. There is even a similar group in Claremont whose members are part of the local Unitarian Society. The survival of these and other communal activities depends on the needs of the participants. The Claremont Soup Group continues. Here's "To Friends who are present, and those who are not."

Discussion Questions

1. How many students in the class know more than 20 biological relatives intimately? How many students in the class can name all of their first cousins (parents' siblings' children)? How many have met all of their first cousins? How important are consanguineal and affinal relatives in each student's daily life?

2. Write down (anonymously) a list of all the different sets of people you interact with on a weekly or monthly basis. In addition to consanguineal and affinal relatives, this might include, for example, one's religious community, one's co-workers, one's friends from the dormitory or apartment complex, campus clubs or organizations, other students with the same major, civic organizations, volunteer organizations, and online virtual communities. Exchange lists throughout the class and then tally up the different sets of people. Where and how do college students create community?

3. Why does food play such an important role in the creation of community? Discuss examples from different cultures, religions, families, and other groups of how food is used to promote community solidarity.

4. Imagine that a natural disaster has left you homeless and penniless. To whom could you turn for help in such a time of crisis? Your consanguineal relatives? Your affinal relatives? Your friends? Your religious community? Local or federal government agencies?

5. What happens to the elderly in most traditional cultures? Are they cared for by strangers in private or government-subsidized nursing homes, or are they cared for at home? What advantages and disadvantages are there to the different systems?

6. In China, the national government has instituted and tried to enforce a "One Child" policy (married couples are only allowed to have one child). This creates social problems for couples whose one child is a daughter, because traditionally it was the son or sons who took care of the elderly parents. Without a son, elderly parents will have no one to care for them, and there are few government programs to fill in the gap. This is one of the main reasons that so many baby girls are abandoned at birth in China (some of whom are adopted by American families). What are the possible solutions to this dilemma? Which are more likely to be successful?

7. In what contexts has biological/genetic kinship become more important in the United States in the past few decades? In what contexts has it become less important?

8. Can you develop a definition of **family** that would work cross-culturally?

For Internet links related to this chapter, please visit our website at www.mhhe.com/dettwyler

BROOKS, JAMES F. *Captives and Cousins: Slavery, Kinship, and Community in the Southwest Borderlands*. Chapel Hill, NC: University of North Carolina Press, 2002.

CAMP, CHARLES. *America Eats: Toward a Social Definition of Foodways*. Ph.D. dissertation, Folklore and Folklife, University of Pennsylvania, 1978.

CARSTEN, JANET, ed. *Cultures of Relatedness: New Approaches to the Study of Kinship*. New York: Cambridge University Press, 2000.

CRONK, LEE. "Parental Favoritism Toward Daughters," *American Scientist* 81:272–279, 1993.

DOUGLAS, MARY, ED. *Food in the Social Order: Studies of Food and Festivities in Three American Communities*. New York: Russell Sage Foundation, 1984.

FARB, PETER, and GEORGE ARMELAGOS. *Consuming Passions: The Anthropology of Eating*. New York: Houghton Mifflin Co., 1980.

FIELDHOUSE, PAUL. *Food & Nutrition: Customs & Culture*. London: Helm, 1986.

FRANKLIN, SARAH, and SUSAN MCKINNON, eds. *Relative Values: Reconfiguring Kinship Studies*. Durham, NC: Duke University Press, 2002.

JONES, MICHAEL OWEN, BRUCE S. GIULIANO, and ROBERTA KRELL. "Prologue," "The Sensory Domain," "The Social Dimension," "Resources and Methods," and "Epilogue." In *Foodways and Eating Habits: Directions for Research,* pp. vii–xii, 1–3, 41–44, 91–93, and 134–137, respectively. Los Angeles, CA: California Folklore Society 40, no. 1, of *Western Folklore;* 1981, reprinted 1983.

JOYCE, ROSEMARY A., and SUSAN D. GILLESPIE, eds. *Beyond Kinship: Social and Material Reproduction in House Societies*. Philadelphia, PA: University of Pennsylvania Press, 2000.

KATZ, SOLOMON H., and DAVID F. ARMSTRONG. "Cousin Marriage and the X-Chromosome: Evolution of Longevity and Language." In *Biological Anthropology and Aging: Perspectives on Human Variation over the Life Span*. Edited by Douglas E. Crews and Ralph M Garruto. New York: Oxford University Press, 1997, pp. 101–123.

KEISER, LINCOLN. *Friend by Day, Enemy by Night: Organized Vengeance in a Kohistani Community*. New York: International Thomson Publishing, 1997.

LEWIS, IOAN M. *Blood and Bone: The Call of Kinship in Somali Society*. Lawrenceville, NJ: Red Sea Press, 1994.

SALTER, FRANK K., ed. *Risky Transactions: Trust, Kinship and Ethnicity*. Oxford & New York: Berghahn Books, 2002.

STACK, CAROL B. *All Our Kin*. Boulder, CO: Westview Press, 1997.

STONE, LINDA, ed. *New Directions in Anthropological Kinship*. Lanham, MD: Rowman & Littlefield Publishing, 2000.

WESTON, KATH. *Families We Choose: Lesbians, Gays, Kinship*. New York: Columbia University Press, 1997.

CHAPTER 19

Marriage

 34. LAND OF THE WALKING MARRIAGE, by Lu Yuan and Sam Mitchell,
Natural History 109, no. 9 (November 2000), pp. 58–65.

*Marriage is one of the most interesting topics to study cross-culturally because of
the sheer amount of variety to be found. Almost all human societies have some form
of officially sanctioned relationships between adults (though not always limited to
one man and one woman), but marriage is **not** a cultural universal. Yet, clearly, some
system of marriage has been found useful by most human societies. Marriage as an
institution can be used to solve a number of problems, including: putting some restrictions on sexual behavior; providing an economic unit for the production and
consumption of food and other goods; providing a stable environment for the raising of children and the passing on of cultural values from generation to generation;
and providing at least one other person who is supposed to keep you company, help
meet your needs, take care of you when you are sick, and so on. For most men, marriage is the only way they can acquire legitimate descendants. For most women,
marriage is the only way they can acquire legitimate status as respectable adults in
their society.*

*Marriages can be between one man and one woman, between one man and
more than one woman (most common), or between one woman and more than one
man (rarest). In addition, there are female-female marriages that have nothing to do
with homosexuality, but have everything to do with children and inheritance. Marriages can be arranged by others and be expected to last a lifetime, or they can be
self-arranged, in which case they often don't last very long at all! The article we*

*have selected for this chapter takes a look at one of the few cultures where tradi-
tional marriages as we usually think of them do not exist—the Mosuo/Nari of China.
As you read this selection, think of the advantages and disadvantages of the Mo-
suo/Nari system, compared to the advantages and disadvantages of the system(s)
with which you are more familiar.*

> There are so many skillful people,
>> but none can compare with my mother.
> There are so many knowledgeable people,
>> but none can equal my mother.
> There are so many people skilled at song and dance,
>> but none can compete with my mother.

We first heard this folk song around a blazing fire in southwestern China in the
spring of 1995. It was sung enthusiastically by women of Luoshui village—members of the Nari, an ethnic group more commonly known to outsiders as the Mosuo.
During the past few years, we have returned several times to visit these people, who
celebrate women in more than song. Although the majority of China's ethnic groups
follow a strong patrilineal tradition, the Mosuo emphasize matrilineal ties, with ma-
trilineally related kin assisting one another to farm, fish, and raise children. Women
also head most households and control most family property.

Marriage as other cultures know it is uncommon among the Mosuo; they prefer
a visiting relationship between lovers—an arrangement they sometimes refer to in
their language as *sisi* (walking back and forth). At about the age of twelve, a Mosuo
girl is given a coming-of-age ceremony, and after puberty, she is free to receive male
visitors. A lover may remain overnight in her room but will return in the morning to
his own mother's home and his primary responsibilities. Children born from such a
relationship live with their mother, and the male relatives responsible for helping to
look after them are her brothers. Many children know who their fathers are, of
course, but even if the relationship between father and child is quite close, it involves
no social or economic obligation. And lovers can end their relationship at any time;
a woman may signal her change of heart by simply no longer opening the door.
When speaking Chinese, the Mosuo will call the *sisi* arrangement *zou hun* (walking
marriage) or *azhu hunyin* (friend marriage, *azhu* being the Mosuo word for friend);
nevertheless, the relationship is not a formal union.

Chuan-kang Shih, an anthropologist at the University of Illinois at
Urbana–Champaign and an authority on the Mosuo, points out that many aspects of
their family system have parallels elsewhere in the world. For example, although in
most societies a husband and wife live together (usually near his relatives or hers),
in others they continue to live in separate households, and one spouse must make
overnight nuptial visits. Matrilineal kinship systems, in which a man looks after the
interests of his sisters' children, are also well known. And although men commonly
wield the power, even in matrilineal societies, women may play important political
and economic roles. But the absence of a formal marital union may quite possibly
be unique to the Mosuo. In this respect, only the precolonial practices of the matrilineal Nayar of southern India come close. As Shih explains, among some Nayar
groups, a woman would take lovers (with due regard for social class), who would
establish and maintain their relationships to her through a pattern of gift giving. De-

spite being expected to acknowledge paternity, the lovers incurred no obligations to their offspring. Still, the Nayar had a vestigial form of marriage: shortly before puberty, a girl would be wed to a young man; although this marriage lasted only three days and was often purely ceremonial in nature, the union marked the girl's transition to adult life and legitimized the birth of her children.

In Luoshui we stayed with thirty-year-old A Long, who runs a small guesthouse. His family consisted of his mother, grandmother, younger brother and sister, and his sister's two-year-old son. Each evening A Long departed with his small overnight bag; each morning he returned to help his mother and sister. After several days of eating with the family and becoming friendly with them, we asked A Long what he thought about the *sisi* system. " 'Friend marriage' is very good," he replied. "First, we are all our mother's children, making money for her; therefore there is no conflict between the brothers and sisters. Second, the relationship is based on love, and no money or dowry is involved in it. If a couple feels contented, they stay together. If they feel unhappy, they can go their separate ways. As a result, there is little fighting." A Long told us that he used to have several lovers but started to have a stable relationship with one when she had her first child.

"Are you taking care of your children?" we asked.

"I sometimes buy candy for them. My responsibility is to help raise my sister's children. In the future, they will take care of me when I get old."

A Long's twenty-six-year-old sister, Qima, told us that the Mosuo system "is good because my friend and I help our own families during the daytime and only come together at night, and therefore there are few quarrels between us. When we are about fifty years old, we will not have 'friend marriage' anymore."

Ge Ze A Che is the leader of Luoshui, which has a population of more than 200 people, the majority of them Mosuo, with a few Han (China's majority ethnic group) and Pumi as well. He spoke proudly of this small settlement: "I have been the leader of the village for five years. There has been little theft, rape, or even argument here. 'Friend marriage' is better than the husband-wife system, because in large extended families everyone helps each other, so we are not afraid of anything. It is too hard to do so much work in the field and at home just as a couple, the way the Han do."

The Mosuo live in villages around Lugu Lake, which straddles the border between Yunnan and Sichuan provinces, and in the nearby town of Yongning. They are believed to be descendants of the ancient Qiang, an early people of the Tibetan plateau from whom many neighboring minority groups, including the Tibetans themselves, claim descent. As a result of Han expansion during the Qin dynasty (221–206 B.C.), some Qiang from an area near the Huang (Yellow) River migrated south and west into Yunnan. The two earliest mentions of the Mosuo appear during the Han dynasty (A.D. 206–222) and the Tang dynasty (618–907), in records concerning what is now southwestern China.

The Mosuo do not surface again in historical accounts until after Mongol soldiers under Kublai Khan subjugated the area in 1253. During the Yuan dynasty (1279–1368), a period of minority rule by the Mongols, the province of Yunnan was incorporated into the Chinese empire, and many Mongol soldiers settled in the Mosuo region. In fact, during the 1950s, when the government set out to classify the country's minority nationalities, several Mosuo villages surrounding Lugu Lake identified themselves as Mongol, and some continue to do so today. When we walked around the lake, as the Mosuo do each year in the seventh lunar month—a ritual believed to ensure good fortune during the coming year—we passed through villages that identified themselves variously as Mosuo, Mongol, Naxi, Pumi, and Han. The "Mongol" people we encountered dressed the same as the Mosuo and spoke the same language. Their dances and songs, too, were the same, and they sometimes even referred to themselves as Mosuo.

Tibetan Buddhism first entered the region in the late thirteenth century and has greatly influenced the lives and customs of the Mosuo. Before the area came under the control of the Communist government, at least one male from almost every family joined the monastic community. The local practice of Buddhism even incorporated aspects of the *sisi* system, although the women did the "commuting." On the eighth day of the fifth lunar month, monks traveling to Tibet for religious study would camp in front of Kaiji village. That night, each monk would be joined by his accustomed lover—a ceremonial practice believed to enable the monks to reach Lhasa safely and to succeed in completing their studies. And the local Mosuo monks, each of whom lived with his own mother's family, could also receive lovers. Such arrangements seem to defy the injunctions of many schools of Tibetan Buddhism, but by allowing the monks to live and work at home, outside the strict confines of monastic life, they helped the Mosuo maintain a stable population and ensure an adequate labor force to sustain local agriculture.

The area around Lugu Lake did not come under the full control of China's central government until 1956, seven years after the founding of the People's Republic. In 1958 and 1959, during the Great Leap Forward, the nearby monasteries, notably the one at Yongning, were badly damaged. Now, however, with a combination of government funds and donations from local people, they are slowly being rebuilt. One element of recent religious revival is the Bon tradition, which is accepted by the Dalai Lama as a school of Tibetan Buddhism but believed by many scholars to be derived from an earlier, animist tradition. During our walk around Lugu Lake, we witnessed a Bon cremation ceremony and visited the Bon temple on the eastern shore of the lake. The Mosuo also retain a shamanic and animist tradition of their own, known as Daba.

In the twentieth century, the West became acquainted with the Mosuo through the work of French ethnographers Edouard Chavannes and Jacques Bacot and through the contributions of Joseph Rock, a Vienna-born American who first journeyed to Yunnan in 1922 while on a botanical expedition. A flamboyant character, Rock traveled through remote Tibetan borderlands accompanied by trains of servants and bodyguards and equipped with such dubious necessities as a collapsible bathtub and a silver English tea set. He made the Naxi town of Lijiang his home for more than twenty years, until the victory of the Chinese Communist Party in 1949 spelled an end to foreign-funded research and missionary activity in the area.

Besides conducting botanical surveys and collecting plant and animal specimens, Rock took many photographs and became the West's foremost expert on the region's peoples and their shamanic practices. He identified the Mosuo as a subgroup of the Naxi, who, although their kinship system is patrilineal, speak a language closely related to that of the Mosuo. The Mosuo strongly contest this classification, but it has been retained by the present government, which has been reluctant to assign the Mosuo the status of a distinct minority. The Communists claim that the Mosuo do not fit the criteria for nationality status as defined for the Soviet Union by Joseph Stalin. According to Stalin, as he phrased it in a 1929 letter, "A nation is a historically constituted, stable community of people, formed on the basis of the common possession of four principal characteristics, namely: a common language, a common territory, a common economic life, and a common psychological make-up manifested in common specific features of national culture."

In keeping with Marxist interpretations of historical development, Chinese ethnologists have also regarded Mosuo society as a "living fossil," characterized by ancient marriage and family structures. This view draws on theories of social evolution formerly embraced by Western anthropologists, notably the American ethnologist Lewis Henry Morgan (1818–81). Morgan proposed that societies pass through successive natural stages of "savagery" and "barbarism" before attaining "civilization." He also proposed a sequence of marriage forms, from a hypothetical "group marriage" of brothers and sisters to monogamy. Chinese scholars have argued that a minority such as the Mosuo, with its unusual kinship system, fits into this scheme and thus validates Marxist views. Of course, the application of Morgan's theories to minority cultures in China has also enabled the Han majority to see itself as more advanced in the chain of human societal evolution. This kind of thinking, long discredited in the West, is only now beginning to be reexamined in China.

With the coming of the Cultural Revolution (1966–76), the Mosuo were pressured to change their way of life. According to Lama Luo Sang Yi Shi (a Mosuo who holds a county-government title but is primarily a spiritual leader), "during the Cultural Revolution, the governor of Yunnan came to Yongning. He went into Mosuo homes and cursed us, saying that we were like animals, born in a mess without fathers. At that time, all of the Mosuo were forced to marry and to adopt the Han practice of monogamy; otherwise, they would be punished by being deprived of food." During this period Mosuo couples lived with the woman's family, and divorce was not permitted. But even though they held marriage certificates and lived with their wives, the men kept returning to their maternal homes each morning to work.

Luo Sang Yi Shi criticized this attempt to change the Mosuo and explained that "at the end of the Cultural Revolution, the Mosuo soon returned to their former system of 'friend marriage.' A small family is not good for work. Also, mothers and their daughters-in-law cannot get along well."

Today the Mosuo maintain their matrilineal system and pursue *sisi* relationships. Yet how long will this remain the case? The government of Yunnan recently opened Lugu Lake to tourism, and vans full of visitors, both Chinese and foreign, are beginning to arrive. To some degree, this added exposure threatens to envelop the Mosuo in a society that is becoming increasingly homogeneous. Yet the tourists are drawn not only by the beauty of the lake but by the exotic qualities of the Mosuo people. Ironically, their unique qualities may well enable the Mosuo to endure and prosper.

We asked Ge Ze A Che, the Luoshui village leader, if tourism would change the lives of the Mosuo. "It has already changed their lives to some extent," he observed. "Our young people now like to wear Han clothes, speak Chinese, and sing Chinese songs. In the future they will lose our people's traditions and customs."

And what would happen to "friend marriage"? we wondered.

"It will also change—but very, very slowly!"

Discussion Questions

1. Where do the Mosuo/Nari live?
2. What consequences do matrilineal kinship and *sisi* relationships have for the Mosuo?
3. Who takes care of children in Mosuo culture? Where do men sleep and where do they work?
4. What are the advantages for Mosuo women of having few restrictions on their sexual behavior and having their brothers help raise their children? Are there any disadvantages?
5. What are the advantages for Mosuo men of having lovers instead of wives, and of raising their sister's children instead of their own biological children? Are there any disadvantages?
6. From the perspective of the village leader, what are the advantages of their system compared to the more typical monogamous marriage system of the Han?
7. How do the Mosuo combine Tibetan Buddhism, Bon, and Daba religious practices?
8. Describe Lewis Henry Morgan's theory about the stages of social evolution. Why do most anthropologists consider this theory no longer valid?
9. According to the Mosuo, how will the opening of the lake region to tourism change the *sisi* marriage system and other aspects of Mosuo culture?
10. Would you want to live in a society with a *sisi* system? Why or why not?

Additional Resources

For Internet links related to this chapter, please visit our website at www.mhhe.com/dettwyler

BOCK, MONIKA, and APARNA RAO, eds. *Culture, Creation, and Procreation: Concepts of Kinship in South Asian Practice.* New York: Berghahn Books, 2001.

COONTZ, STEPHANIE, MAYA PARSON, and GABRIELLE RALEY, eds. *American Families: A Multicultural Reader.* New York: Routledge, 1998.

EVANS-PRITCHARD, E. E. *Kinship and Marriage Among the Nuer.* New York: Oxford University Press, 1985.

GOLDSTEIN, MELVYN C. "When Brothers Share a Wife," *Natural History,* March 1987, pp. 39–48.

HOODFAR, HOMA. *Between Marriage and the Market: Intimate Politics and Survival in Cairo.* Berkeley, CA: University of California Press, 1997.

HUA, CAI, and ASTI HUSTVEDT (translator). *A Society without Fathers or Husbands: The Na of China.* New York: Zone Books, 2001.

KENDALL, LAUREL. *Getting Married in Korea: Of Gender, Morality, and Modernity.* Berkeley, CA: University of California Press, 1996.

MACCORMACK, CAROL P. *Ethnography of Fertility and Birth.* Prospect Heights, IL: Waveland Press, 1994.

SIMPSON, BOB. *Changing Families: An Ethnographic Approach to Divorce and Separation.* New York: Berg Pub. Ltd, 1998.

SMALL, MEREDITH F. *Our Babies, Ourselves: How Biology and Culture Shape the Way We Parent.* New York: Dell Pub. Co., 1999.

STOCKARD, JANICE E. *Marriage in Culture: Practice and Meaning Across Diverse Societies.* New York: Wadsworth Publishing, 2001.

TOWNSEND, NICHOLAS W. *The Package Deal: Marriage, Work, and Fatherhood in Men's Lives.* Philadelphia, PA: Temple University Press, 2002.

Gender

Typically, most people born and raised in the United States think that humans come in two clear-cut sexes, female (XX) and male (XY), with distinct genitalia that reflect their underlying chromosomes. They also think these two sexes generally correspond with two genders, feminine (for females) and masculine (for males), although they may allow for some overlap for girls who act more like boys (tomboys). However, as the two articles in this chapter demonstrate, both sex and gender are much more complicated than two simple categories of male and female. At both biological and cultural levels, human sexuality and gender identity encompass a huge amount of variation. Many cultural systems easily accommodate individuals who don't fit the two standard sex and gender categories (female/male, feminine/masculine), while other cultural systems are more restrictive. One's gender identity does not have to match with one's sexual preferences. As you read these articles, think of how you and your overlapping circles of culture (family, friends, city, state, country, religious affiliation, etc.) handle these issues. Think of what the ideal cultural system might be that would accommodate everyone and ensure that all humans are respected.

 ## 35. THE FIVE SEXES, REVISITED

In 1993 Anne Fausto-Sterling wrote an article for The Sciences, *titled "The Five Sexes." In 2000 she revisited the issue with a subsequent essay on the same subject. In this, her latter essay, she explains the many variations that exist between*

female/XX/female genitalia/feminine gender identity, on the one hand, and male/XY/male genitalia/masculine gender identity, on the other. Some children are born with ambiguous external genitalia, or with external genitalia that, while not ambiguous, do not match their chromosomal sex. These variations can be due to genetic factors or to environmental (usually hormonal) influences during prenatal development. She describes the different combinations as being "points in a multi-dimensional space" rather than a continuum between male and female. Gender is culturally constructed and adds yet more layers of complexity to an individual's sexual identity. Fausto-Sterling points out how much has changed in the United States, culturally, between 1993 and 2000 due to the efforts of activists, including the adoption of the International Bill of Gender Rights (1995) and the founding of NATFI (North American Task Force on Intersexuality, 1999).

As Cheryl Chase stepped to the front of the packed meeting room in the Sheraton Boston Hotel, nervous coughs made the tension audible. Chase, an activist for intersexual rights, had been invited to address the May 2000 meeting of the Lawson Wilkins Pediatric Endocrine Society (LWPES), the largest organization in the United States for specialists in children's hormones. Her talk would be the grand finale to a four-hour symposium on the treatment of genital ambiguity in newborns, infants born with a mixture of both male and female anatomy, or genitals that appear to differ from their chromosomal sex. The topic was hardly a novel one to the assembled physicians.

Yet Chase's appearance before the group was remarkable. Three and a half years earlier, the American Academy of Pediatrics had refused her request for a chance to present the patients' viewpoint on the treatment of genital ambiguity, dismissing Chase and her supporters as "zealots." About two dozen intersex people had responded by throwing up a picket line. The Intersex Society of North America (ISNA) even issued a press release: "Hermaphrodites Target Kiddie Docs."

It had done my 1960s street-activist heart good. In the short run, I said to Chase at the time, the picketing would make people angry. But eventually, I assured her, the doors then closed would open. Now, as Chase began to address the physicians at their own convention, that prediction was coming true. Her talk, titled "Sexual Ambiguity: The Patient-Centered Approach," was a measured critique of the near-universal practice of performing immediate, "corrective" surgery on thousands of infants born each year with ambiguous genitalia. Chase herself lives with the consequences of such surgery. Yet her audience, the very endocrinologists and surgeons Chase was accusing of reacting with "surgery and shame," received her with respect. Even more remarkably, many of the speakers who preceded her at the session had already spoken of the need to scrap current practices in favor of treatments more centered on psychological counseling.

What led to such a dramatic reversal of fortune? Certainly, Chase's talk at the LWPES symposium was a vindication of her persistence in seeking attention for her cause. But her invitation to speak was also a watershed in the evolving discussion about how to treat children with ambiguous genitalia. And that discussion, in turn, is the tip of a biocultural iceberg—the gender iceberg—that continues to rock both medicine and our culture at large.

Chase made her first national appearance in 1993, in these very pages, announcing the formation of ISNA in a letter responding to an essay I had written for

The Sciences, titled "The Five Sexes" [March/April 1993]. In that article I argued that the two-sex system embedded in our society is not adequate to encompass the full spectrum of human sexuality. In its place, I suggested a five-sex system. In addition to males and females, I included "herms" (named after true hermaphrodites, people born with both a testis and an ovary); "merms" (male pseudohermaphrodites, who are born with testes and some aspect of female genitalia); and "ferms" (female pseudohermaphrodites, who have ovaries combined with some aspect of male genitalia).

I had intended to be provocative, but I had also written with tongue firmly in cheek. So I was surprised by the extent of the controversy the article unleashed. Right-wing Christians were outraged, and connected my idea of five sexes with the United Nations–sponsored Fourth World Conference on Women, held in Beijing in September 1995. At the same time, the article delighted others who felt constrained by the current sex and gender system.

Clearly, I had struck a nerve. The fact that so many people could get riled up by my proposal to revamp our sex and gender system suggested that change—as well as resistance to it—might be in the offing. Indeed, a lot has changed since 1993, and I like to think that my article was an important stimulus. As if from nowhere, intersexuals are materializing before our very eyes. Like Chase, many have become political organizers, who lobby physicians and politicians to change current treatment practices. But more generally, though perhaps no less provocatively, the boundaries separating masculine and feminine seem harder than ever to define.

Some find the changes under way deeply disturbing. Others find them liberating.

Who is an intersexual—and how many intersexuals are there? The concept of intersexuality is rooted in the very ideas of male and female. In the idealized, Platonic, biological world, human beings are divided into two kinds: a perfectly dimorphic species. Males have an X and a Y chromosome, testes, a penis and all of the appropriate internal plumbing for delivering urine and semen to the outside world. They also have well-known secondary sexual characteristics, including a muscular build and facial hair. Women have two X chromosomes, ovaries, all of the internal plumbing to transport urine and ova to the outside world, a system to support pregnancy and fetal development, as well as a variety of recognizable secondary sexual characteristics.

That idealized story papers over many obvious caveats: some women have facial hair, some men have none; some women speak with deep voices, some men veritably squeak. Less well known is the fact that, on close inspection, absolute dimorphism disintegrates even at the level of basic biology. Chromosomes, hormones, the internal sex structures, the gonads and the external genitalia all vary more than most people realize. Those born outside of the Platonic dimorphic mold are called intersexuals.

In "The Five Sexes" I reported an estimate by a psychologist expert in the treatment of intersexuals, suggesting that some 4 percent of all live births are intersexual. Then, together with a group of Brown University undergraduates, I set out to conduct the first systematic assessment of the available data on intersexual birthrates. We scoured the medical literature for estimates of the frequency of various categories of intersexuality, from additional chromosomes to mixed gonads, hormones and genitalia. For some conditions we could find only anecdotal evidence; for most, however, numbers exist. On the basis of that evidence, we calculated that for every 1,000 children born, seventeen are intersexual in some form.

That number—1.7 percent—is a ballpark estimate, not a precise count, though we believe it is more accurate than the 4 percent I reported.

Our figure represents all chromosomal, anatomical and hormonal exceptions to the dimorphic ideal; the number of intersexuals who might, potentially, be subject to surgery as infants is smaller—probably between one in 1,000 and one in 2,000 live births. Furthermore, because some populations possess the relevant genes at high frequency, the intersexual birthrate is not uniform throughout the world.

Consider, for instance, the gene for congenital adrenal hyperplasia (CAH). When the CAH gene is inherited from both parents, it leads to a baby with masculinized external genitalia who possesses two X chromosomes and the internal reproductive organs of a potentially fertile woman. The frequency of the gene varies widely around the world: in New Zealand it occurs in only forty-three children per million; among the Yupik Eskimo of southwestern Alaska, its frequency is 3,500 per million.

Intersexuality has always been to some extent a matter of definition. And in the past century physicians have been the ones who defined children as intersexual— and provided the remedies. When only the chromosomes are unusual, but the external genitalia and gonads clearly indicate either a male or a female, physicians do not advocate intervention. Indeed, it is not clear what kind of intervention could be advocated in such cases. But the story is quite different when infants are born with mixed genitalia, or with external genitals that seem at odds with the baby's gonads.

Most clinics now specializing in the treatment of intersex babies rely on case-management principles developed in the 1950s by the psychologist John Money and the psychiatrists Joan G. Hampson and John L. Hampson, all of Johns Hopkins University in Baltimore, Maryland. Money believed that gender identity is completely malleable for about eighteen months after birth. Thus, he argued, when a treatment team is presented with an infant who has ambiguous genitalia, the team could make a gender assignment solely on the basis of what made the best surgical sense. The physicians could then simply encourage the parents to raise the child according to the surgically assigned gender. Following that course, most physicians maintained, would eliminate psychological distress for both the patient and the parents. Indeed, treatment teams were never to use such words as "intersex" or "hermaphrodite"; instead, they were to tell parents that nature intended the baby to be the boy or the girl that the physicians had determined it was. Through surgery, the physicians were merely completing nature's intention.

Although Money and the Hampsons published detailed case studies of intersex children who they said had adjusted well to their gender assignments, Money thought one case in particular proved his theory. It was a dramatic example, inasmuch as it did not involve intersexuality at all: one of a pair of identical twin boys lost his penis as a result of a circumcision accident. Money recommended that "John" (as he came to be known in a later case study) be surgically turned into "Joan" and raised as a girl. In time, Joan grew to love wearing dresses and having her hair done. Money proudly proclaimed the sex reassignment a success.

But as recently chronicled by John Colapinto, in his book *As Nature Made Him*, Joan—now known to be an adult male named David Reimer—eventually rejected his female assignment. Even without a functioning penis and testes (which had been removed as part of the reassignment) John/Joan sought masculinizing medication, and married a woman with children (whom he adopted).

Since the full conclusion to the John/Joan story came to light, other individuals who were reassigned as males or females shortly after birth but who later rejected their early assignments have come forward. So, too, have cases in which the reassignment has worked—at least into the subject's mid-twenties. But even then the aftermath of the surgery can be problematic. Genital surgery often leaves scars that reduce sexual sensitivity. Chase herself had a complete clitoridectomy, a procedure that is less frequently performed on intersexuals today. But the newer surgeries, which reduce the size of the clitoral shaft, still greatly reduce sensitivity.

The revelation of cases of failed reassignments and the emergence of intersex activism have led an increasing number of pediatric endocrinologists, urologists and psychologists to reexamine the wisdom of early genital surgery. For example, in a talk that preceded Chase's at the LWPES meeting, the medical ethicist Laurence B. McCullough of the Center for Medical Ethics and Health Policy at Baylor College of Medicine in Houston, Texas, introduced an ethical framework for the treatment of children with ambiguous genitalia. Because sex phenotype (the manifestation of genetically and embryologically determined sexual characteristics) and gender presentation (the sex role projected by the individual in society) are highly variable, McCullough argues, the various forms of intersexuality should be defined as normal. All of them fall within the statistically expected variability of sex and gender. Furthermore, though certain disease states may accompany some forms of intersexuality, and may require medical intervention, intersexual conditions are not themselves diseases.

McCullough also contends that in the process of assigning gender, physicians should minimize what he calls irreversible assignments: taking steps such as the surgical removal or modification of gonads or genitalia that the patient may one day want to have reversed. Finally, McCullough urges physicians to abandon their practice of treating the birth of a child with genital ambiguity as a medical or social emergency. Instead, they should take the time to perform a thorough medical workup and should disclose everything to the parents, including the uncertainties about the final outcome. The treatment mantra, in other words, should be therapy, not surgery.

I believe a new treatment protocol for intersex infants, similar to the one outlined by McCullough, is close at hand. Treatment should combine some basic medical and ethical principles with a practical but less drastic approach to the birth of a mixed-sex child. As a first step, surgery on infants should be performed only to save the child's life or to substantially improve the child's physical well-being. Physicians may assign a sex—male or female—to an intersex infant on the basis of the probability that the child's particular condition will lead to the formation of a particular gender identity. At the same time, though, practitioners ought to be humble enough to recognize that as the child grows, he or she may reject the assignment—and they should be wise enough to listen to what the child has to say. Most important, parents should have access to the full range of information and options available to them.

Sex assignments made shortly after birth are only the beginning of a long journey. Consider, for instance, the life of Max Beck: Born intersexual, Max was surgically assigned as a female and consistently raised as such. Had her medical team followed her into her early twenties, they would have deemed her assignment a success because she was married to a man. (It should be noted that success in gender assignment has traditionally been defined as living in that gender as a heterosexual.)

Within a few years, however, Beck had come out as a butch lesbian; now in her mid-thirties, Beck has become a man and married his lesbian partner, who (through the miracles of modern reproductive technology) recently gave birth to a girl.

Transsexuals, people who have an emotional gender at odds with their physical sex, once described themselves in terms of dimorphic absolutes—males trapped in female bodies, or vice versa. As such, they sought psychological relief through surgery. Although many still do, some so-called transgendered people today are content to inhabit a more ambiguous zone. A male-to-female transsexual, for instance, may come out as a lesbian. Jane, born a physiological male, is now in her late thirties and living with her wife, whom she married when her name was still John. Jane takes hormones to feminize herself, but they have not yet interfered with her ability to engage in intercourse as a man. In her mind Jane has a lesbian relationship with her wife, though she views their intimate moments as a cross between lesbian and heterosexual sex.

It might seem natural to regard intersexuals and transgendered people as living midway between the poles of male and female. But male and female, masculine and feminine, cannot be parsed as some kind of continuum. Rather, sex and gender are best conceptualized as points in a multidimensional space. For some time, experts on gender development have distinguished between sex at the genetic level and at the cellular level (sex-specific gene expression, X and Y chromosomes); at the hormonal level (in the fetus, during childhood and after puberty); and at the anatomical level (genitals and secondary sexual characteristics). Gender identity presumably emerges from all of those corporeal aspects via some poorly understood interaction with environment and experience. What has become increasingly clear is that one can find levels of masculinity and femininity in almost every possible permutation. A chromosomal, hormonal and genital male (or female) may emerge with a female (or male) gender identity. Or a chromosomal female with male fetal hormones and masculinized genitalia—but with female pubertal hormones—may develop a female gender identity.

The medical and scientific communities have yet to adopt a language that is capable of describing such diversity. In her book *Hermaphrodites and the Medical Invention of Sex,* the historian and medical ethicist Alice Domurat Dreger of Michigan State University in East Lansing documents the emergence of current medical systems for classifying gender ambiguity. The current usage remains rooted in the Victorian approach to sex. The logical structure of the commonly used terms "true hermaphrodite," "male pseudohermaphrodite" and "female pseudohermaphrodite" indicates that only the so-called true hermaphrodite is a genuine mix of male and female. The others, no matter how confusing their body parts, are really hidden males or females. Because true hermaphrodites are rare—possibly only one in 100,000—such a classification system supports the idea that human beings are an absolutely dimorphic species.

At the dawn of the twenty-first century, when the variability of gender seems so visible, such a position is hard to maintain. And here, too, the old medical consensus has begun to crumble. Last fall the pediatric urologist Ian A. Aaronson of the Medical University of South Carolina in Charleston organized the North American Task Force on Intersexuality (NATFI) to review the clinical responses to genital ambiguity in infants. Key medical associations, such as the American Academy of Pediatrics, have endorsed NATFI. Specialists in surgery, endocrinology, psychology, ethics, psychiatry, genetics and public health, as well as intersex patient-advocate groups, have joined its ranks.

One of the goals of NATFI is to establish a new sex nomenclature. One proposal under consideration replaces the current system with emotionally neutral terminology that emphasizes developmental processes rather than preconceived gender categories. For example, Type I intersexes develop out of anomalous virilizing influences; Type II result from some interruption of virilization; and in Type III intersexes the gonads themselves may not have developed in the expected fashion.

What is clear is that since 1993, modern society has moved beyond five sexes to a recognition that gender variation is normal and, for some people, an arena for playful exploration. Discussing my "five sexes" proposal in her book *Lessons from the Intersexed,* the psychologist Suzanne J. Kessler of the State University of New York at Purchase drives this point home with great effect:

> The limitation with Fausto-Sterling's proposal is that . . . [it] still gives genitals . . . primary signifying status and ignores the fact that in the everyday world gender attributions are made without access to genital inspection. . . . What has primacy in everyday life is the gender that is performed, regardless of the flesh's configuration under the clothes.

I now agree with Kessler's assessment. It would be better for intersexuals and their supporters to turn everyone's focus away from genitals. Instead, as she suggests, one should acknowledge that people come in an even wider assortment of sexual identities and characteristics than mere genitals can distinguish. Some women may have "large clitorises or fused labia," whereas some men may have "small penises or misshapen scrota," as Kessler puts it, "phenotypes with no particular clinical or identity meaning."

As clearheaded as Kessler's program is—and despite the progress made in the 1990s—our society is still far from that ideal. The intersexual or transgendered person who projects a social gender—what Kessler calls "cultural genitals"—that conflicts with his or her physical genitals still may die for the transgression. Hence legal protection for people whose cultural and physical genitals do not match is needed during the current transition to a more gender-diverse world. One easy step would be to eliminate the category of "gender" from official documents, such as driver's licenses and passports. Surely attributes both more visible (such as height, build and eye color) and less visible (fingerprints and genetic profiles) would be more expedient.

A more far-ranging agenda is presented in the International Bill of Gender Rights, adopted in 1995 at the fourth annual International Conference on Transgender Law and Employment Policy in Houston, Texas. It lists ten "gender rights," including the right to define one's own gender, the right to change one's physical gender if one so chooses and the right to marry whomever one wishes. The legal bases for such rights are being hammered out in the courts as I write and, most recently, through the establishment, in the state of Vermont, of legal same-sex domestic partnerships.

No one could have foreseen such changes in 1993. And the idea that I played some role, however small, in reducing the pressure—from the medical community as well as from society at large—to flatten the diversity of human sexes into two diametrically opposed camps gives me pleasure.

Sometimes people suggest to me, with not a little horror, that I am arguing for a pastel world in which androgyny reigns and men and women are boringly the same. In my vision, however, strong colors coexist with pastels. There are and will continue to be highly masculine people out there; it's just that some of them are women. And some of the most feminine people I know happen to be men.

Discussion Questions

1. In her first article, "The Five Sexes," what were Fausto-Sterling's five sexes? How did her original article contribute to the founding of the Intersex Society of North America?
2. What percentage of children are considered intersexual at birth?
3. What role did psychologist John Money play in the treatment of intersexual infants throughout the second half of the 20th century? What were his views on gender identity and sex reassignment?
4. How did the case of John/Joan prove that Money's ideas were faulty?
5. What contributions has medical ethicist Laurence McCullough made to changing the way intersexed infants are treated?
6. Do you think parents should have the right to assign a sex and gender identity to their infants? Should parents of "normal" children (not intersexual, not having ambiguous genitalia) push them to fit into the two standard gender categories?
7. What are the consequences of living in a culture that has no place for intersexuals or people whose genitals don't match their gender?
8. What are the consequences of not fitting very well the gender categories available in one's culture?
9. Using www.google.com or any other Internet search engine, look up the International Bill of Gender Rights. What are the 10 rights? Pick several to discuss in more detail. Which are most likely to become reality in the near future?

 ## 36. MULTIPLE GENDERS AMONG NORTH AMERICAN INDIANS

This article comes from Serena Nanda's book, Gender Diversity: Cross-Cultural Variations. *In her book, Nanda gives many examples of the way cultures in different regions of the world define (or have defined in the past) gender categories and sexual identities. In this chapter, she focuses on North American Indian cultures, both past and present. She points out that hermaphrodites (intersexuals) and transvestites are different; that gender-variants can be defined by dress and occupation instead of, or in addition to, sexual preferences. She also makes it clear that many Native American cultures had more than two gender categories—it wasn't just a matter of letting some men act like women, or vice versa. There were additional gender categories that were considered as legitimate as the standard masculine/male and feminine/female categories. In some Native American cultures, male gender variants gained both power (political and/or religious) and respect by virtue of their difference. Female gender variants were rarer, but still existed, and were more accepted in most traditional Native American cultures than they would be today by mainstream U.S. culture. As you read this article, think about how the proliferation of gender categories allows for more flexibility in defining oneself in the world.*

The early encounters between Europeans and Indian societies in the New World, in the fifteenth through the seventeenth centuries, brought together cultures with very different sex/gender systems. The Spanish explorers, coming from a society where sodomy was a heinous crime, were filled with contempt and outrage when they recorded the presence of men in American Indian societies who performed the work of women, dressed like women, and had sexual relations with men (Lang 1996; Roscoe in 1995).

Europeans labeled these men "berdache," a term originally derived from an Arabic word meaning male prostitute. As such, this term is inappropriate and insulting, and I use it here only to indicate the history of European (mis)understanding of American Indian sex/gender diversity. The term berdache focused attention on the sexuality associated with mixed gender roles, which the Europeans identified, incorrectly, with the "unnatural" and sinful practice of sodomy in their own societies. In their ethnocentrism, the early European explorers and colonists were unable to see beyond their own sex/gender systems and thus did not understand the multiple sex/gender systems they encountered in the Americas. They also largely overlooked the specialized and spiritual functions of many of these alternative sex/gender roles and the positive value attached to them in many American Indian societies.

By the late-nineteenth and early-twentieth centuries, some anthropologists included accounts of North American Indian sex/gender diversity in their ethnographies. They attempted to explain the berdache from various functional perspectives, that is, in terms of the contributions these sex/gender roles made to social structure or culture. These accounts, though less contemptuous than earlier ones, nevertheless largely retained the emphasis on berdache sexuality. The berdache was defined as a form of "institutionalized homosexuality," which served as a social niche for individuals whose personality and sexual orientation did not match the definition of masculinity in their societies, or as a "way out" of the masculine or warrior role for "cowardly" or "failed" men (see Callender and Kochems 1983).

Anthropological accounts increasingly paid more attention, however, to the association of the berdache with shamanism and spiritual powers and also noted that mixed gender roles were often central and highly valued in American Indian cultures, rather than marginal and deviant. These accounts were, nevertheless, also ethnocentric in misidentifying indigenous gender diversity with European concepts of homosexuality, transvestism, or hermaphroditism, which continued to distort their indigenous meanings.

In American Indian societies, the European homosexual/heterosexual dichotomy was not culturally relevant and the European labeling of the berdache as homosexuals resulted from their own cultural emphasis on sexuality as a central, even defining, aspect of gender and on sodomy as an abnormal practice and/or a sin. While berdache in many American Indian societies did engage in sexual relations and even married persons of the same sex, this was not central to their alternative gender role. Another overemphasis resulting from European ethnocentrism was the identification of berdache as **transvestites.** Although berdache often cross-dressed, transvestism was not consistent within or across societies. European descriptions of berdache as **hermaphrodites** were also inaccurate.

Considering the variation in alternative sex/gender roles in native North America, a working definition may be useful: the berdache in the anthropological literature refers to people who partly or completely take on aspects of the culturally defined role of the other sex and who are classified neither as women nor men, but as genders of their own (see Callender and Kochems 1983:443). It is important to note here that berdache thus refers to variant gender roles, rather than a complete crossing over to an opposite gender role.

In the past twenty-five years there have been important shifts in perspectives on sex/gender diversity among American Indians and anthropologists, both Indian and non-Indian (Jacobs, Thomas, and Lang 1997: Introduction). Most current research rejects institutionalized homosexuality as an adequate explanation of American Indian gender diversity, emphasizing the importance of occupation rather than sexuality as its central feature. Contemporary ethnography views multiple sex/gender roles as a normative part of American Indian sex/gender systems, rather than as a marginal or deviant part (Albers 1989:134; Jacobs et al. 1997; Lang 1998). A new emphasis on the variety of alternative sex/gender roles in North America undercuts the earlier treatment of the berdache as a unitary phenomenon across North (and South) America (Callender and Kochems 1983; Jacobs et al. 1997; Lang 1998; Roscoe 1998). Current research also emphasizes the integrated and often highly valued position of gender variant persons and the association of sex/gender diversity with spiritual power (Roscoe 1996; Williams 1992).

A change in terminology has also taken place. Berdache generally has been rejected, but there is no unanimous agreement on what should replace it. One widely accepted suggestion is the term **two-spirit** (Jacobs et al. 1997; Lang 1998), a term coined in 1990 by urban American Indian gays and lesbians. Two-spirit has the advantage of conveying the spiritual nature of gender variance as viewed by gay, lesbian, and transgendered American Indians and also the spirituality associated with traditional American Indian gender variance, but the cultural continuity suggested by two-spirit is in fact a subject of debate. Another problem is that two-spirit emphasizes the Euro-American gender construction of only two genders. Thus, I use the more culturally neutral term, variant genders (or gender variants) and specific indigenous terms wherever possible.

Distribution and Characteristics of Variant Sex/Gender Roles

Multiple sex/gender systems were found in many, though not all, American Indian societies. Male gender variant roles (variant gender roles assumed by biological males) are documented for 110 to 150 societies. These roles occurred most frequently in the region extending from California to the Mississippi Valley and upper-Great Lakes, the Plains and the Prairies, the Southwest, and to a lesser extent among the Northwest Coast tribes. With few exceptions, gender variance is not historically documented for eastern North America, though it may have existed prior to European invasion and disappeared before it could be recorded historically (Callender and Kochems 1983; Fulton and Anderson 1992).

There were many variations in North American Indian gender diversity. American Indian cultures included three or four genders: men, women, male variants, and female variants (biological females who by engaging in male activities were reclassified as to gender). Gender variant roles differed in the criteria by which they were defined; the degree of their integration into the society; the norms governing their behavior; the way the role was acknowledged publicly or sanctioned; how others were expected to behave toward gender variant persons; the degree to which a gender changer was expected to adopt the role of the opposite sex or was limited in doing so; the power, sacred or secular, that was attributed to them; and the path to recruitment.

In spite of this variety, however, there were also some common or widespread features: transvestism, cross-gender occupation, same sex (but different gender) sexuality, some culturally normative and acknowledged process for recruitment to the role, special language and ritual roles, and associations with spiritual power.

Transvestism

The degree to which male and female gender variants were permitted to wear the clothing of the other sex varied. Transvestism was often associated with gender variance but was not equally important in all societies. Male gender variants frequently adopted women's dress and hairstyles partially or completely, and female gender variants partially adopted the clothing of men; sometimes, however, transvestism was prohibited. The choice of clothing was sometimes an individual matter and gender variants might mix their clothing and their accoutrements. For example, a female gender variant might wear a woman's dress but carry (male) weapons. Dress was also sometimes situationally determined: a male gender variant would have to wear men's clothing while engaging in warfare but might wear women's clothes at other times. Similarly, female gender variants might wear women's clothing when gathering (women's work), but male clothing when hunting (men's work) (Callender and Kochems 1983:447). Among the Navajo, a male gender variant, *nádleeh,* would adopt almost all aspects of a woman's dress, work, language and behavior; the Mohave male gender variant, called *alyha,* was at the extreme end of the cross-gender continuum in imitating female physiology as well as transvestism (the transvestite ceremony is discussed later in this chapter). Repression of visible forms of gender diversity, and ultimately the almost total decline of transvestism, were a direct result of American [meaning European-American] prohibitions against it.

Occupation

Contemporary analysis emphasizes occupational aspects of American Indian gender variance as a central feature. Most frequently a boy's interest in the implements and activities of women and a girl's interest in the tools of male occupations signaled an individual's wish to undertake a gender variant role (Callender and Kochems 1983:447; Whitehead 1981). In hunting societies, for example, female gender variance was signaled by a girl rejecting the domestic activities associated with women and participating in playing and hunting with boys. In the arctic and subarctic, particularly, this was sometimes encouraged by a girl's parents if there were not enough boys to provide the family with food (Lang 1998). Male gender variants were frequently considered especially skilled and industrious in women's crafts and domestic work (though not in agriculture, where this was a man's task) (Roscoe 1991; 1996). Female gender crossers sometimes won reputations as superior hunters and warriors.

Male gender variants' households were often more prosperous than others, sometimes because they were hired by whites. In their own societies the excellence of male gender variants' craftwork was sometimes ascribed to a supernatural sanction for their gender transformation (Callender and Kochems 1983:448). Female gender variants opted out of motherhood, so were not encumbered by caring for children, which may explain their success as hunters or warriors. In some societies, gender variants could engage in both men's and women's work, and this, too, accounted for their increased wealth. Another source of income was payment for the special social activities of gender variants due to their intermediate gender status, such as acting as go-betweens in marriage. Through their diverse occupations, then, gender variants were often central rather than marginal in their societies.

Early anthropological explanations of male gender variant roles as a niche for a "failed" or cowardly man who wished to avoid warfare or other aspects of the masculine role are no longer widely accepted. To begin with, masculinity was not associated with warrior status in all American Indian cultures. In some societies, male gender variants were warriors and in many others, males who rejected the warrior role did not become gender variants. Sometimes male gender variants did not go to war because of cultural prohibitions against their using symbols of maleness, for example, the prohibition against their using the bow among the Illinois. Where male gender variants did not fight, they sometimes had other important roles in warfare, like treating the wounded, carrying supplies for the war party, or directing postbattle ceremonials (Callender and Kochems 1983:449). In a few societies male gender variants became outstanding warriors, such as Finds Them and Kills Them, a Crow Indian who performed daring feats of bravery while fighting with the United States Army against the Crow's traditional enemies, the Lakota Sioux (Roscoe 1998:23).

Gender Variance and Sexuality

Generally, sexuality was not central in defining gender status among American Indians. But in any case, the assumption by European observers that gender variants were homosexuals meant they did not take much trouble to investigate or record information on this topic. In some American Indian societies same-sex sexual desire/practice did figure significantly in the definition of gender variant roles; in others it did not (Callender and Kochems 1983:449). Some early reports noted specifically that male gender variants lived with and/or had sexual relations with women as well as men; in other societies they were reported as having sexual relations only with men, and in still other societies, of having no sexual relationships at all (Lang 1998:189–95).

The bisexual orientation of some gender variant persons may have been a culturally accepted expression of their gender variance. It may have resulted from an individual's life experiences, such as the age at which he or she entered the gender variant role, and/or it may have been one aspect of the general freedom of sexual expression in many American Indian societies. While male and female gender variants most frequently had sexual relations with, or married, persons of the same biological sex as themselves, these relationships were not considered homosexual in the contemporary Western understanding of that term. In a multiple gender system the partners would be of the same sex but different genders, and homogender, rather than homosexual, practices bore the brunt of negative cultural sanctions. The sexual partners of gender variants were never considered gender variants themselves.

The Navajo are a good example (Thomas 1997). The Navajo have four genders; in addition to man and woman there are two gender variants: masculine female-bodied nádleeh and feminine male-bodied nádleeh. A sexual relationship between a female nádleeh and a woman or a sexual relationship between a male-bodied nádleeh and a man were not stigmatized because these persons were of different genders, although of the same biological sex. However, a sexual relationship between two women, two men, two female-bodied nádleeh or two male-bodied nádleeh was considered homosexual, and even incestual, and was strongly disapproved of.

The relation of sexuality to variant sex/gender roles across North America suggests that sexual relations between gender variants and persons of the same biological sex were a result rather than a cause of gender variance. Sexual relationships between a man and a male gender variant were accepted in most American Indian societies, though not in all, and appear to have been negatively sanctioned only when it interfered with child-producing heterosexual marriages. Gender variants' sexual relationships varied from casual and wide-ranging (Europeans used the term promiscuous), to stable, and sometimes even involved life-long marriages. In some societies, however, male gender variants were not permitted to engage in long-term relationships with men, either in or out of wedlock. In many cases, gender variants were reported as living alone.

There are some practical reasons why a man might desire sexual relations with a (male) gender variant: in some societies taboos on sexual relations with menstruating or pregnant women restricted opportunities for sexual intercourse; in other societies, sexual relations with a gender variant person were exempt from punishment for extramarital affairs; in still other societies, for example, among the Navajo, some gender variants were considered especially lucky and a man might hope to vicariously partake of this quality by having sexual relations with them (Lang 1998:349).

Biological Sex and Gender Transformations

European observers often confused gender variants with hermaphrodites. Some American Indian societies explicitly distinguished hermaphrodites from gender variants and treated them differently; others assigned gender variant persons and hermaphrodites to the same alternative gender status. With the exception of the Navajo, in most American Indian societies biological sex (or the intersexedness of the hermaphrodite) was not the criterion for a gender variant role, nor were the individuals who occupied gender variant roles anatomically abnormal. The Navajo distinguished between the intersexed and the alternatively gendered, but treated them similarly, though not exactly the same (Thomas 1997; Hill 1935).

And even as the traditional Navajo sex/gender system had biological sex as its starting point, it was only a starting point, and Navajo nádleeh were distinguished by sex-linked behaviors, such as body language, clothing, ceremonial roles, speech style, and work. Feminine, male-bodied nádleeh might engage in women's activities such as cooking, weaving, household tasks, and making pottery. Masculine, female-bodied nádleeh, unlike other female-bodied persons, avoided childbirth; today they are associated with male occupational roles such as construction or firefighting (although ordinary women also sometimes engage in these occupations). Traditionally, female-bodied nádleeh had specific roles in Navajo ceremonials (Thomas 1997).

Thus, even where hermaphrodites occupied a special gender variant role, American Indian gender variance was defined more by cultural than biological criteria. In one recorded case of an interview with and physical examination of a gender variant male, the previously mentioned Finds Them and Kills Them, his genitals were found to be completely normal (Roscoe 1998).

If American Indian gender variants were not generally hermaphrodites, or conceptualized as such, neither were they conceptualized as transsexuals. Gender transformations among gender variants were recognized as only a partial transformation, and the gender variant was not thought of as having become a person of the opposite sex/gender. Rather, gender variant roles were autonomous gender roles that combined the characteristics of men and women and had some unique features of their own. This was sometimes symbolically recognized: among the Zuni a male gender variant was buried in women's dress but men's trousers on the men's side of the graveyard (Parsons quoted in Callender and Kochems 1983:454; Roscoe 1991:124, 145). Male gender variants were neither men—by virtue of their chosen occupations, dress, demeanor, and possibly sexuality—nor women, because of their anatomy and their inability to bear children. Only among the Mohave do we find the extreme imitation of women's physiological processes related to reproduction and the claims to have female sexual organs—both of which were ridiculed within Mohave society. But even here, where informants reported that female gender variants did not menstruate, this did not make them culturally men. Rather it was the mixed quality of gender variant status that was culturally elaborated in native North America, and this was the source of supernatural powers sometimes attributed to them.

Sacred Power

The association between the spiritual power and gender variance occurred in most, if not all, Native American societies. Even where, as previously noted, recruitment to the role was occasioned by a child's interest in occupational activities of the opposite sex, supernatural sanction, frequently appearing in visions or dreams, was also involved. Where this occurred, as it did mainly in the Prairie and Plains societies, the visions involved female supernatural figures, often the moon. Among the Omaha, for example, the moon appeared in a dream holding a burden strap—a symbol of female work—in one hand, and a bow—a symbol of male work—in the other. When the male dreamer reached for the bow, the moon forced him to take the burden strap (Whitehead 1981). Among the Mohave, a child's choice of male or female implements heralding gender variant status was sometimes prefigured by a dream that was believed to come to an embryo in the womb (Devereux 1937).

Sometimes, by virtue of the power associated with their gender ambiguity, gender variants were ritual adepts and curers, or had special ritual functions (Callender and Kochems 1983:453, Lang 1998). Gender variants did not always have important sacred roles in native North America, however. Where feminine qualities were associated with these roles, male gender variants might become spiritual leaders or healers, but where these roles were associated with male qualities they were not entered into by male gender variants. Among the Plains Indians, with their emphasis on the vision as a source of supernatural power, male gender variants were regarded as holy persons, but in California Indian societies, this was not the case and in some American Indian societies gender variants were specifically excluded from religious roles (Lang 1998:167). Sometimes it was the individual personality of the gender variant rather than his/her gender variance itself, that resulted in occupying sacred roles (see Commentary following Callender and Kochems 1983). Nevertheless, the importance of sacred power was so widely associated with sex/gender diversity in native North America that it is generally agreed to be an important explanation of the frequency of gender diversity in this region of the world.

In spite of cultural differences, some significant similarities among American Indian societies are particularly consistent with multigender systems and the positive value placed on sex/gender diversity (Lang 1996). One of these similarities is a cosmology (system of religious beliefs and way of seeing the world) in which transformation and ambiguity are recurring themes. Thus a person who contains both masculine and feminine qualities or one who is transformed from the sex/gender assigned at birth into a different gender in later life manifests some of the many kinds of transformations and ambiguities that are possible, not only for humans, but for animals and objects in the natural environment. Indeed, in many American Indian cultures, sex/gender ambiguity, lack of sexual differentiation, and sex/gender transformations play an important part in the story of creation (Lang 1996:187). American Indian cosmology may not be "the cause" of sex/gender diversity but it certainly (as in India) provides a hospitable context for it.

The Alyha: A Male Gender Variant Role among the Mohave

One of the most complete classic anthropological descriptions of a gender variant role is from the Mohave, a society that lives in the southwest desert area of the Nevada/California border. The following description, based on interviews by anthropologist George Devereux (1937) with some old informants who remembered the transvestite ceremony and had heard stories about gender variant individuals from their elders, indicates some of the ways in which gender variance functioned in native North America.

The Mohave had two gender variant roles: a male role called alyha and a female role called *hwame*. In this society, pregnant women had dreams forecasting the anatomic sex of their children. Mothers of a future alyha dreamt of male characteristics, such as arrow feathers, indicating the birth of a boy, but their dreams also included hints of their child's future gender variant status. A boy indicated he might become an alyha by "acting strangely" around the age of 10 or 11, before he had participated in the boys' puberty ceremonies. At this age, young people began to engage seriously in the activities that would characterize their adult lives as men and women; boys, for example, learned to hunt, ride horses, make bows and arrows, and they developed sexual feelings for girls. The future alyha avoided these masculine activities. Instead he played with dolls, imitated the domestic work of women, tried to participate in the women's gambling games, and demanded to wear the female bark skirt rather than the male breechclout.

The alyha's parents and relatives were ambivalent about this behavior. At first his parents would try to dissuade him, but if the behavior persisted his relatives would resign themselves and begin preparations for the transvestite ceremony. The ceremony was meant to take the boy by surprise; it was considered both a test of his inclination and an initiation. Word was sent out to various settlements so that people could watch the ceremony and get accustomed to the boy in female clothing. At the ceremony, the boy was led into a circle of onlookers by two women, and the crowd began singing the transvestite songs. If the boy began to dance as women did, he was confirmed as an alyha. He was then taken to the river to bathe and given a girl's skirt to wear. This initiation ceremony confirmed his changed gender status, which was considered permanent.

After this ceremony the alyha assumed a female name (though he did not take the lineage name that all females assumed) and would resent being called by his former, male name. In the frequent and bawdy sexual joking characteristic of Mohave culture, an alyha resented male nomenclature being applied to his genitals. He insisted that his penis be called a clitoris, his testes, labia majora, and anus a vagina. Alyha were also particularly sensitive to sexual joking, and if they were teased in the same way as women they responded with assaults on those who teased them. Because they were very strong, people usually avoided angering them.

Alyha were considered highly industrious and much better housewives than were young girls. It is partly for this reason that they had no difficulty finding spouses, and alyha generally had husbands. Alyha were not courted like ordinary girls, however (where the prospective husband would sleep chastely beside the girl for several nights and then lead her out of her parents' house), but rather courted like widows, divorcees, or "wanton" women. Intercourse with an alyha was surrounded by special etiquette. Like Mohave heterosexual couples, the alyha and her husband practiced both anal and oral intercourse, with the alyha taking the female role. Alyha were reported to be embarrassed by an erection and would not allow their sexual partners to touch or even comment on their erect penis.

When an alyha found a husband, she would begin to imitate menstruation by scratching herself between the legs with a stick until blood appeared. The alyha then submitted to puberty observations as a girl would, and her husband also observed the requirements of the husband of a girl who menstruated for the first time. Alyha also imitated pregnancy, particularly if their husbands threatened them with divorce on the grounds of barrenness. At this time they would cease faking menstruation and follow the pregnancy taboos, with even more attention than ordinary women, except that they publicly proclaimed their pregnancy, which ordinary Mohave women never did. In imitating pregnancy, an alyha would stuff rags in her skirts, and near the time of the birth, drank a decoction to cause constipation. After a day or two of stomach pains, she would go into the bushes and sit over a hole, defecating in the position of childbirth. The feces would be treated as a stillbirth and buried, and the alyha would weep and wail as a woman does for a stillborn child. The alyha and her husband would then clip their hair as in mourning.

Alyha were said to be generally peaceful persons, except when teased, and were also considered to be cowards. They did not have to participate in the frequent and harsh military raids of Mohave men. Alyha did participate in the welcoming home feast for the warriors, where, like old women, they might make a bark penis and go through the crowd poking the men who had stayed home, saying, "You are not a man, but an alyha."

In general, alyha were not teased or ridiculed for being alyha (though their husbands were teased for marrying them), because it was believed that they could not help it and that a child's inclinations in this direction could not be resisted. It was believed that a future alyha's desire for a gender change was such that he could not resist dancing the women's dance at the initiation ceremony. Once his desires were demonstrated in this manner, people would not thwart him. It was partly the belief that becoming an alyha was a result of a "temperamental compulsion" or predestined (as forecast in his mother's pregnancy dream) that inhibited ordinary Mohave from ridiculing alyha. In addition, alyha were considered powerful healers, especially effective in curing sexually transmitted diseases (also called alyha) like syphilis.

The alyha demonstrates some of the ways in which gender variant roles were constructed as autonomous genders in North America. In many ways the alyha crossed genders, but the role had a distinct, alternative status to that of both man and woman (as did the hwame). Although the alyha imitated many aspects of a woman's role—dress, sexual behavior, menstruation, pregnancy, childbirth, and domestic occupations—they were also recognized as being different from women. Alyha did not take women's lineage names; they were not courted like ordinary women; they publicly proclaimed their pregnancies; and they were considered more industrious than other women in women's domestic tasks.

In spite of the alyha's sexual relations with men, the alyha was not considered primarily a homosexual (in Western terms). In fact, among ordinary Mohave, if a person dreamed of having homosexual relationships, that person would be expected to die soon, but this was not true of the alyha. Most significantly, the alyha were believed to have special supernatural powers, which they used in curing illness.

Female Gender Variants

Female gender variants probably occurred more frequently among American Indians than in other cultures, although this has been largely overlooked in the historic and ethnographic record (but see Blackwood 1984; Jacobs et al. 1997; Lang 1998; Medicine 1983).

Although the generally egalitarian social structures of many American Indian societies provided a hospitable context for female gender variance, it occurred in perhaps only one-quarter to one-half of the societies with male variant roles (Callender and Kochems 1983:446; see also Lang 1998:262–65). This may be explained partly by the fact that in many American Indian societies women could—and did—adopt aspects of the male gender role, such as warfare or hunting, and sometimes dressed in male clothing, without being reclassified into a different gender (Blackwood 1984; Lang 1998:261ff; Medicine 1983).

As with males, the primary criteria of changed gender status for females was an affinity for the occupations of the other gender. While this inclination for male occupations was often displayed in childhood, female gender variants entered these roles later in life than did males (Lang 1998:303). Among some Inuit, "men pretenders" would refuse to learn women's tasks and were taught male occupations when they were children, by their fathers. They played with boys and participated in the hunt. Among the Kaska, a family who had only daughters might select one to "be like a man"; by engaging in the male activity of hunting, she would help provide the family with food. Among the Mohave, too, hwame refused to learn women's work, played with boys, and were considered excellent providers, as well as particularly efficient healers (Blackwood 1984:30; Lang 1998:286). Among the Cheyenne, the *hetaneman* (defined as a hermaphrodite having more of the female element) were great female warriors who accompanied the male warrior societies into battle. In all other groups, however, even outstanding women warriors were not recast into a different gender role (Roscoe 1998:75). Female gender variants also sometimes entered specialized occupations, becoming traders, guides for whites, or healers. The female preference for male occupations might be motivated by a female's desire to be independent, or might be initiated or encouraged by a child's parents, and in some societies was sanctioned through supernatural omens or in dreams.

In addition to occupation, female gender variants might assume other characteristics of men. Cocopa *warrhameh* wore a masculine hairstyle and had their noses pierced, like boys (Lang 1998:283). Among the Maidu, the female *suku* also had her nose pierced on the occasion of her initiation into the men's secret society. Mohave hwame were tattooed like men instead of women. Transvestism was commonly though not universally practiced: it occurred, for example, among the Kaska, Paiute, Ute, and Mohave.

Like male gender variants, female gender variants exhibited a wide range of sexual relationships. Some had relationships with other females, who were generally regarded as ordinary women. Only rarely, as among a southern Apache group, was the female gender variant (like her male counterpart) defined in terms of her sexual desire for women. Mohave hwame engaged in sexual and marriage relationships with women, although they courted them in a special way, different from heterosexual courtships. If a hwame married a pregnant woman, she could claim paternity of the child, although the child belonged to the descent group of its biological father (Devereux 1937:514). Like an alyha's husband, a hwame's wife was often teased, and hwame marriages were generally unstable. Masahai Amatkwisai, the most well known hwame, married women three times and was also known to have sexual relationships with many men. Masahai's wives were all aggressively teased by male Mohave who viewed "real" sexual relations only in terms of penetration by a penis. At dances Masahai sat with the men, described her wife's genitals, and flirted with girls, all typical male behavior. Masahai's masculine behavior was ridiculed, and the men gravely insulted her (though never to her face), by referring to her by an obscene nickname meaning the female genitals. The harassment of Masahai's wives apparently led to the eventual breakup of her marriages.

Sexual relationships between women in American Indian societies were rarely historically documented, but in any case, were generally downplayed in female gender variant roles, even when this involved marriage. One female gender variant, for example, Woman Chief, a famous Crow warrior and hunter, took four wives, but this appeared to be primarily an economic strategy: processing animal hides among the Crow was women's work, so that Woman Chief's polygyny (multiple spouses) complemented her hunting skills.

While most often American Indian women who crossed genders occupationally, such as Woman Chief, were not reclassified into a gender variant role, several isolated cases of female gender transformations have been documented historically. One of these is Ququnak Patke, a "manlike woman" from the Kutenai (Schaeffer 1965). Ququnak Patke had married a white fur trader and, when she returned to her tribe, claimed that her husband had transformed her into a man. She wore men's clothes, lived as a man, married a woman and claimed supernatural sanction for her role change and her supernatural powers. Although whites often mistook her for a man in her various roles as warrior, explorer's guide, and trader, such transformations were not considered a possibility among the Kutenai, and many thought Ququnak Patke was mad. She died attempting to mediate a quarrel between two hostile Indian groups.

It is difficult to know how far we can generalize about the relation of sexuality to female gender variance in precontact American Indian cultures from the lives of the few documented female gender variants. These descriptions (and those for males, as well) are mainly based on ethnographic accounts that relied on twentieth-century informants whose memories were already shaped by white hostility toward gender diversity and same-sex sexuality. Nevertheless, it seems clear that although American Indian female gender variants clearly had sexual relationships with women, sexual object choice was not their defining characteristic. In some cases, female gender variants were described "as women who never marry," which does not say anything definitive about their sexuality; it may well be that the sexuality of female gender variants was more variable than that of men.

Occasionally, as with Masahai and Ququnak Patke, and also for some male gender variants, contact with whites opened up opportunities for gender divergent individuals (see Roscoe 1988; 1991). On the whole, however, as a result of Euro-American repression and the growing assimilation of Euro-American sex/gender ideologies, both female and male gender variant roles among American Indians largely disappeared by the 1930s, as the reservation system was well under way. And yet, its echoes may remain. The current academic interest in American Indian multigender roles, and particularly the testimony of contemporary two-spirits, remind us that alternatives are possible and that understanding American Indian sex/gender diversity in the past and present makes a significant contribution to understandings of sex/gender diversity in the larger society.

Discussion Questions

1. What is a **berdache**? Where does the word come from, and where did ideas about them originate? How does it relate to the newer term **"two-spirit"**?
2. What is the difference between a hermaphrodite and a transvestite?
3. How are sexual preferences (the biological sex of the person with whom you want to have sexual relations) related to intersexuality, transvestitism, and gender identity? Is there any necessary relationship between any of these aspects of sex/gender identity?
4. Discuss examples of how occupation played a greater role than sexuality in defining gender among North American Indians.
5. How did gender variants attain special sacred power? How was this manifested (i.e., what did this mean that they could do that ordinary people could not do)?

6. What does Nanda mean when she says that transformation and ambiguity are recurring themes in Native American cosmology?
7. What behavioral traits characterized the males known as **alyha** among the Mohave?
8. What led a person to become an alyha, and how were they treated? Did they have special powers? Why did they pretend to be pregnant?
9. Why were female gender variants less common than male gender variants? What sorts of roles did they fill?
10. How have sex/gender variant roles changed among Native Americans from precontact times to the 1930s? How are they expressed today?

Additional Resources

For Internet links related to this chapter, please visit our website at www.mhhe.com/dettwyler

BRETTELL, CAROLINE B., and CAROLYN F. SARGENT, eds. *Gender in Cross-Cultural Perspective.* 3rd ed. Englewood Cliffs, NJ: Prentice Hall, 2000.

COLAPINTO, JOHN. *As Nature Made Him: The Boy Who Was Raised as a Girl.* New York: Perennial, 2001.

DREGER, ALICE DOMURAT. *Hermaphrodites and the Medical Invention of Sex.* Cambridge, MA: Harvard University Press, 2000.

FAUSTO-STERLING, ANNE. *Sexing the Body: Gender Politics and the Construction of Sexuality.* New York: Basic Books, 2000.

HERDT, GILBERT H. *Guardians of the Flutes: Idioms of Masculinity.* New York: Columbia University Press, 1987.

HERDT, GILBERT H., ed. *Third Sex, Third Gender: Beyond Sexual Dimorphism in Culture and History.* New York: Zone Books, 1996.

KESSLER, SUZANNE J. *Lessons from the Intersexed.* Rutgers, NJ: Rutgers University Press, 1998.

LEWIS, OSCAR. "Manly-Hearted Women among the North Piegan." *American Anthropologist* 43(1941), pp. 173–187.

MASCIA-LEES, FRANCES E., and NANCY JOHNSON BLACK. *Gender and Anthropology.* Prospect Heights, IL: Waveland Press, 2002.

NANDA, SERENA. *Neither Man Nor Woman: The Hijras of India.* New York: Wadsworth Publishing, 1990.

NANDA, SERENA. *Gender Diversity: Crosscultural Variations.* Prospect Heights, IL: Waveland Press, 1990.

ORTNER, SHERRY B. *Making Gender: The Politics and Erotics of Culture.* Boston, MA: Beacon Press, 1997.

CHAPTER 21

Religion

37. "The Religious Success Story," by Jared Diamond, *The New York Review of Books,* November 7, 2002 (from website: www.nybooks.com/articles/15798).

38. "'From Here On, I Will Be Praying to You': Indian Churches, Kiowa Hymns, and Native American Christianity in Southwestern Oklahoma," by Luke Eric Lassiter, *Ethnomusicology* 45, no. 2 (Spring/Summer 2001), pp. 338–352.

There are more than 75 distinct religious groups that are known to function in the United States, and more than two-thirds of its population claims membership in some church, synagogue, mosque, or other organized religious group. America is not unique in this aspect because anthropologists have found that every culture practices some form or forms of religion. If so, when did humans first discover religion and why did it become a cultural universal? Textbooks define religion as "the beliefs and behavior concerned with supernatural beings, powers, and forces." The "father of anthropology," Edward Tylor, claimed that religion was invented to help people control fear. Sigmund Freud claimed religion was invented to provide a way for humans to seek and obtain forgiveness. More recently, David Wilson claims that religion developed by group selection and that today's formal and organized religions owe their origins to the early days of civilizations when dictators and kings discovered religion was a convenient way to control the masses and keep themselves in power.

 ## 37. THE RELIGIOUS SUCCESS STORY

The following article examines the culture of religion. It is a review, by Jared Diamond, of a recently published best-seller Darwin's Cathedral: Evolution, Religion, and the Nature of Society, *written by David Sloan Wilson. The book, which takes a look at religious origins and explores why religion has become a cultural universal, is considered by some to be controversial. For example, members of some of the*

fundamentalist religious groups may not agree with the book's contention that religions arose strictly as a function of group selection and that they were expanded into the types and denominations we have today strictly as convenient ways for governments to control the masses. As you read the article, see how the views that are expressed compare with your own views of religion.

"In the beginning, all people lived around a great ironwood tree in the jungle, speaking the same language. One man whose testes were enormously swollen from infection with a parasitic worm spent his time sitting on a branch of the tree, so that he could rest his heavy testes on the ground. Out of curiosity, animals of the jungle came up and sniffed at his testes. Hunters then found the animals easy to kill, and everyone had plenty of food and was happy.

"Then, one day, a bad man killed a beautiful woman's husband, in order to get the woman for himself. Relatives of the dead husband attacked the murderer, who was defended in turn by his own relatives, until the murderer and his relatives climbed into the ironwood tree to save themselves. The attackers tugged on lianas hanging from one side of the tree, in order to pull the tree's crown down towards the ground and get at their enemies.

"Finally, the lianas snapped in half, causing the tree to spring back with tremendous force. The murderer and his relatives were hurled out of the tree in many different directions. They landed so far away, in so many different places, that they never found each other again. With time, their languages became more and more divergent. That is why people today speak so many different languages and cannot understand each other, and why it is hard work for hunters to catch animals for food."

That story was related to me by Sikari people, a tribe of six hundred New Guineans. The story exemplifies a widespread class of myths called origin myths, familiar to us through accounts of the Garden of Eden and the Tower of Babel in the Bible's Book of Genesis. Despite those parallels with Judeo-Christian religions, traditional Sikari society lacked churches, priests, and sacred books. Why is the Sikari belief system so reminiscent of Judeo-Christian religions in its origin myth, yet so different in other respects?

All known human societies have had "religion," or something like it. But what really defines "religion"? Scholars have been debating this and related questions for centuries. For a belief system to constitute a religion, must it include belief in a god or gods, and does it necessarily include anything else? When, in human evolutionary history, did religion appear? Human ancestors diverged from the ancestors of chimpanzees around six million years ago. Whatever religion is, we can agree that chimps don't have it, but was there already religion among our Cro-Magnon ancestors of 40,000 years ago? Were there different historical stages in the development of religions, with creeds like Christianity and Buddhism representing a more recent stage than tribal belief systems like that of the Sikaris? These longstanding questions have become acute to all of us reeling from recent terrorist attacks, and struggling to comprehend the fanaticism that drove them. We tend to associate religion with humanity's noble side, not with its evil side: Why does religion sometimes preach murder and suicide?

If we are to answer these questions, David Sloan Wilson tells us in *Darwin's Cathedral,* we must recognize that religions are human institutions and belief systems evolving by the process which biologists term "group selection." Religions potentially offer practical, social, and motivational benefits to their adherents. But religions differ among themselves in the degree to which they motivate their adherents to have children, to rear those children to become productive members of society, and to convert or kill believers in competing religions. Those religions that are more successful in these respects will tend to spread, and gain and retain adherents, at the expense of other religions. Two quotations from Wilson's book will serve to summarize his thesis:

> Something as elaborate—as time-, energy-, and thought-consuming—as religion would not exist if it didn't have secular utility. Religions exist primarily for people to achieve together what they cannot achieve alone. The mechanisms that enable religious groups to function as adaptive units include the very beliefs and practices that make religion appear enigmatic to so many people who stand outside of them.
>
> Demographic change in a population depends upon births, deaths, immigration [i.e., conversion in the case of religion], and emigration [i.e., abandoning one's religion]. The balance of these inputs and outputs must be positive for any religion to persist, but their relative importance can vary widely. As one extreme example, the Shakers were successful for a brief period of time based purely on immigration, and without any births. Based on immigration alone, Judaism is at a large disadvantage compared to proselytizing Christian and Islamic religions, which accounts in part for its minority status. Despite its disadvantage with respect to immigration, however, Judaism has persisted on the strength of the other factors that contribute to demographic growth (high birth rate, low death rate, and low emigration).

Wilson introduces his argument with two chapters examining religion from the twin perspectives of group evolutionary biology and the social sciences. The next four chapters test his hypothesis against some actual religions: early Calvinism, Bali's water temple system, Judaism, the early Christian Church, the Houston Korean Church, and the Christian doctrine of forgiveness. These discussions are full of new perspectives on institutions seemingly so well known that one might think there was nothing new to say about them.

For example, why, among the innumerable tiny Jewish sects competing with each other and with non-Jewish groups within the Roman Empire in the first century AD, did Christianity emerge as the dominant religion three centuries later? Early Christianity's distinctive features contributing to this result included its active proselytizing (unlike mainstream Judaism), its practices promoting having more babies and enabling more of them to survive (unlike contemporary Roman society), its opportunities for women (in contrast to contemporary Judaism and Roman paganism and to later Christianity), its social institutions resulting in lower death rates of Christians than of Romans from plagues, and the Christian doctrine of forgiveness. That doctrine, which is often misunderstood as the simplistic notion of indiscriminately turning the other cheek, actually proves to be part of a complex, context-dependent system of responses ranging from forgiveness to retaliation. Under certain circumstances, experimental tests carried out by playing simulated games show that forgiving someone who has done you one wrong may really be the response most likely to gain you advantages in the future.

Obviously, the main subject of *Darwin's Cathedral*—religion—is widely contentious. In addition, many of the subjects on which Wilson draws to interpret religion—subjects such as group selection, adaptation, hypothesis testing, and how to "do" science—are contentious among scientists. Discussions of these subjects tend to be partisan, oversimplified, and riddled with misstatements. A great virtue of Wilson's book is the scrupulous fairness with which he treats controversial matters. He is careful to define concepts, to assess both their range of applicability and their limitations, and to avoid posturing, misrepresentations, exaggerated claims, and cheap rhetorical devices. Thus, Wilson's book is more than just an attempt to understand religion. Even to readers with no interest in either religion or science, his book can serve as a model of how to discuss controversial subjects honestly.

It seems to me that what we think of as "religion" encompasses four different, originally unrelated, elements: explanation, standardized organization, moral rules of good behavior toward in-groups, and (all too often) rules of bad behavior toward out-groups. Those elements served different functions; they appeared or began to disappear at different times in human history; and they came together only within the last eight thousand years. Most efforts to define religion begin with one element: belief in a god or gods. But that definition immediately plunges us into difficulties, as Wilson notes:

> Religion is sometimes defined as a belief in supernatural agents. However, other people regard this definition as shallow and incomplete. The Buddha refused to be associated with any gods. He merely claimed to be awake and to have found a path to enlightenment.

Some Jews and Unitarian Universalists as well, and many Japanese people, are agnostics or atheists but still consider themselves to belong to a religion. Conversely, many tribal societies believe in agents that we Westerners think of as spirits rather than as gods. What do these agents have in common?

An essential feature shared by the Judeo-Christian God, ancient Greek gods, and tribal spirits could be formulated as follows: "a postulated supernatural agent for whose existence our senses can't give us evidence, but which is invoked to explain things of which our senses do give us evidence." Quite a few Americans today believe God to be a "first cause" that created the universe and its laws and explains their existence, but that let the universe run thereafter without divine interference. Creationists invoke God to explain a lot more, including the existence of every plant and animal species, but most creationists wouldn't invoke God to explain every sunrise, tide, and wind. Yet the ancient Greeks did invoke gods or supernatural agents to explain sunrises, tides, and winds. The New Guinean societies in which I have lived go further and have supernatural explanations for the songs of each bird species (as the voices of former people transformed into birds).

Clearly, in modern Western society, religion's explanatory role has gradually become usurped by science. Where Sikaris and Old Testament believers invoke origin myths (like the ironwood tree and the Tower of Babel) to explain linguistic diversity, modern linguists instead invoke historical processes of language change. Explanations of sunrises, tides, and winds are now left to meteorologists and astronomers. For modern scientists, the last bastion of religious explanation is God-as-First-Cause: science still has nothing to say about why the universe exists at all. From my freshman year at Harvard in 1955, I recall the great theologian Paul Tillich defying his class of hyper-rational undergraduates to come up with a scientific answer to his simple question: "Why is there something, when there could have been nothing?"

Besides a belief in God, a second defining feature of religions that we take for granted is standardized organization. Most modern religions have full-time priests (alias rabbis, ministers, or whatever else they may be called) who receive either a salary or else life's necessities. Modern religions also have churches (alias temples, synagogues, mosques, etc.). Within any given sect, all those churches use standardized sacred books (Bibles, Torahs, Korans, etc.), rituals, art, music, architecture, and clothing. None of those features applies to New Guinea tribal beliefs.

Historically, those organizational features of religion arose to solve a new problem emerging as ancient human societies became richer and more populous. In recent times all Europeans have lived under political systems termed states, which European scholars initially assumed to be the natural form of political organization. But after 1492 AD, as Europeans spread over the world, they encountered peoples living under simpler and less populous political systems variously termed chiefdoms, tribes, and bands. From buried artifacts preserved at archaeological sites (such as recognizable trappings of chiefs and kings), archaeologists infer that the first chiefdoms emerged from tribal societies in the Fertile Crescent of western Asia around 5500 BC, and that the first states with kings emerged from chiefdoms around 3500 BC.

Band and tribal societies are too small and unproductive to generate food surpluses that could feed full-time priests, chiefs, tax collectors, potters, or specialists of any sort. Instead, every adult in the band or tribe has to acquire his or her own food by hunting, gathering, or farming himself or herself. Only larger and more productive societies generate surpluses that can be used to feed chiefs and other leaders or crafts specialists, none of whom grows or hunts for food.

How did such a diversion of food come about? A dilemma results from the confluence of three facts: populous societies are likely to defeat small societies; but populous societies require full-time leaders and bureaucrats; and full-time leaders and bureaucrats must be fed. In Wilson's words,

> . . . purely from the group-level functional standpoint, societies must become differentiated [into leaders and followers] as they increase in size. Thirty people can sit around a campfire and arrive at a consensual decision; thirty million people cannot.

But how does the chief get the peasants to tolerate what is basically the theft of their food by classes of social parasites? This problem is familiar to the citizens of any democracy, who ask themselves the same question at each election: What have the incumbents done since the last election to justify the fat salaries that they pay themselves out of the public coffers?

The solution devised by every known chiefdom and early state society—from ancient Egypt to Polynesian Hawaii to the Inca Empire—was to proclaim an organized religion with the following tenets: the chief or king is related to the gods; he or she can intercede with the gods on behalf of the peasants (e.g., to send rain or ensure a good harvest). In return for those services, the peasants should feed the chief and his priests and tax collectors. Standardized rituals, carried out at standardized temples, serve to teach these religious tenets to the peasants so that they will obey the chief and his lackeys. As early theocratic states evolved into the empires of ancient Babylon and Rome and commandeered more and more food and labor, the architectural trappings of state religions became ever more elaborate.

Of course, within recent centuries in the Judeo-Christian world, this trend has been reversed, and religion is much less than before the handmaiden of the state; politicians rely instead on other means to persuade or coerce all of us peasants. But the fusion of religion and state persists in some Muslim countries, Israel, and (until recently) Japan and Italy. Even the U.S. government invokes God on its currency and places official chaplains in Congress and in the armed forces.

Yet a third function of religion that we take for granted is to justify or reinforce moral precepts. All major world religions teach what is right, what is wrong, and how one should behave. Hence it will surprise most Jews, Christians, and Muslims to learn that this link between religion and morality is entirely absent in the New Guinean societies of which I have experience. It is not that New Guinean societies are amoral: most of them have stricter codes of social obligations than do European and American societies. Yet in all my years in traditional New Guinean societies, I have never heard any invocation of a god or spirit to justify how people should behave toward others. Instead, social obligations depend on relationship. Because a band or tribe contains only a few dozen or a few hundred individuals respectively, everyone in the band or tribe knows everyone else and their relationships. One owes different obligations to different blood relatives, to relatives by marriage, to members of one's own clan, and to fellow villagers belonging to a different clan.

Those relationships determine, for instance, whether you may refer to people by their names, marry them, or demand that they share their food and house with you. If you get into a fight with another tribe member, everyone else in the tribe is related to or knows both of you and pulls you apart. The problem of behaving peacefully toward unfamiliar individuals never arises, because the only unfamiliar individuals are members of enemy tribes. Should you happen to meet an unfamiliar person in the forest, of course you try to kill him or else to run away; our modern custom of just saying hello and starting a friendly chat would be suicidal.

Thus a new problem arose around 7,500 years ago, when some tribal societies evolved into chiefdoms comprising thousands of individuals—a far greater number than any single person can know by name and relationship. Emerging chiefdoms and states faced big problems of potential instability, because the old tribal rules of behavior no longer sufficed. If you encountered an unfamiliar member of your chiefdom and fought with him according to tribal rules of behavior, a brawl would result as your relatives jumped in on your side and his relatives jumped in on his side. A death in such a brawl would spark efforts by the victim's relatives to kill one of the murderer's relatives in revenge. What's to save the society from collapsing in an incessant orgy of brawls and revenge murders?

The solution to this dilemma of large societies is the one used in our own society, and documented in all chiefdoms and early states for which we have information. Rules of peaceful behavior apply between all members of the society and are enforced by the political leaders (chiefs or kings) and their agents, who justify the rules by a new function of religion. The gods or supernatural agents are presumed to be the authors of the rules. People are taught from childhood onward to obey the rules, and to expect severe punishment for breaking them (because now an attack on another person is also an offense against the gods). Prime examples familiar to Jews and Christians are the Ten Commandments.

It nevertheless troubles skeptics that each religion's account of its moral code's supernatural origins seems implausible to outsiders. For example, non-Mormons doubt Joseph Smith's claim that the angel Moroni appeared to him on September 21, 1823, to reveal golden plates buried on a hilltop near Manchester Village in western New York State and awaiting translation. Non-Mormons also doubt the sworn statements of eight witnesses (Christian Whitmer, Hiram Page, and six others) who claimed to have seen and handled the plates. But what, really, is the difference between the statements of Joseph Smith and his witnesses, and the biblical accounts of divine revelations to Moses and Jesus, except for millennia of elapsed time and our differing skepticisms derived from our differing upbringings? As Wilson points out, the success of a religion's moral code depends on whether the code motivates the religion's adherents to constitute a smoothly functioning society, not on whether the religion's claims happen to be fictitious: "Even massively fictitious beliefs can be adaptive, as long as they motivate behaviors that are adaptive in the real world"; "... factual knowledge is not always sufficient by itself to motivate adaptive behavior. At times a symbolic belief system that departs from factual reality fares better."

In recent secularized societies, such rules of moral behavior within society have moved beyond their religious origins. The reasons why atheists, as well as many believers, now don't kill their enemies derive from values instilled by society, and from fear of the potent hand of the law rather than fear of the wrath of God. But from the rise of chiefdoms until the recent rise of secular states, religion justified codes of behavior and thereby enabled people to live harmoniously in large societies where one encounters strangers frequently.

Another new problem faced by emerging chiefdoms and states, but not by the bands and tribes of previous history, involves wars. Because tribes use relationship by blood or marriage, not religion, to justify moral rules, tribesmen face no moral dilemmas in killing members of other tribes with whom they have no relationship. But once a state invokes religion to require peaceful behavior toward fellow citizens with whom one has no relationship, how can a state convince its citizens not to apply those same precepts during wartime? States permit, indeed they command, their citizens to steal from and kill citizens of other states against which war has been declared. After a state has spent eighteen years teaching a boy "Thou shalt not kill," how can the state turn around and say "Thou must kill, under the following circumstances," without getting its soldiers hopelessly confused and prone to kill the wrong people (e.g., fellow citizens)?

Again, in recent as in ancient history, religion comes to the rescue with the last of its four elements. The Ten Commandments apply only to one's behavior toward fellow citizens within the chiefdom or state. Most religions claim that they have a monopoly on the truth and that all other religions are wrong. Commonly in the past, and all too often today as well, citizens are taught that they are permitted or obliged to kill and steal from believers in those wrong religions. That's the dark side of all those noble patriotic appeals: for God and country, *por Dios y España,* etc. It in no way diminishes the guilt of the current crop of murderous religious fanatics to acknowledge that they are heirs to a long, widespread, vile tradition.

This basic hypocrisy of religions seems at first to defy explanation. Mr. Wilson's response is that a religion's success (or its "fitness," to use the language of evolutionary biology) can be defined only by comparison with the successes of other religions. Whether one likes it or not, religions can, and often have, increased their success (the number of their adherents) by killing or forcibly converting adherents of other religions:

> Whenever I strike up a conversation about religion, I am likely to receive a litany of evils perpetrated in God's name. In most cases, these are horrors committed by religious groups against other groups. How can I call religion adaptive in the face of such evidence? The answer is "easily," as long as we understand fitness in relative terms. It is important to stress that a behavior can be explained from an evolutionary perspective without being morally condoned.

The Bible, especially the Old Testament, is full of exhortations to be cruel to heathens. *Deuteronomy* 20:10–18, for example, explains the obligation of the Israelites to practice genocide: when your army approaches a distant city, you should enslave all its inhabitants if it surrenders, and kill all its men and enslave its women and children and steal their cattle and everything else if it doesn't surrender. But if it's a city of the Canaanites or Hittites or any of those other abominable believers in false gods, then the true God commands you to kill everything that breathes in the city. The Book of Joshua describes approvingly how Joshua became a hero by carrying out those instructions, slaughtering all the inhabitants of over four hundred cities. The book of rabbinical commentaries known as the Talmud analyzes the potential ambiguities arising from conflicts between those two principles of "Thou shalt not kill [believers in thine own God]" and "Thou must kill [believers in another god]." For instance, according to some Talmudic commentators, an Israelite is guilty of murder if he intentionally kills a fellow Israelite; is innocent if he intentionally kills a non-Israelite; and is also innocent if he kills an Israelite while throwing a stone into a group consisting of nine Israelites plus one heathen (because he might have been aiming at the one heathen).

In fairness, this outlook is more characteristic of the Old Testament than of the New Testament, whose moral principles have moved far in the direction of defining one's dealings with anyone—at least in theory. In practice, of course, some of history's most extensive genocides were committed by European colonialists against non-Europeans, relying for moral justification on the New Testament. The New Testament itself provides some explicit support for this policy: Revelations 9:4–5, for instance, says that it's okay to torture heathens for five months, though not to kill them.

Interestingly, among New Guineans, religion is never invoked to justify killing members of an out-group. Many of my New Guinean friends have described to me their participation in genocidal attacks on neighboring tribes. In all those accounts, I have never heard the slightest hint of any religious motive, of dying for God or the true religion, or of sacrificing oneself for any idealistic reason whatsoever. The religion-supported ideologies that accompanied the rise of states instilled into their citizens the obligation to obey the ruler ordained by God, to obey moral precepts like the Ten Commandments only with respect to fellow citizens, and to be prepared to sacrifice their lives while fighting against other states (i.e., heathens). That's what makes societies of religious fanatics so dangerous: a tiny minority of their adherents (e.g., nineteen of them) die for the cause, and the whole society of fanatics thereby succeeds at killing far more of its perceived enemies (e.g., 3,025 of them) [reference is to 9/11/01].

Wilson explains that fanatical religious sects, such as expansionist Islam and Christianity, spread as a result of group selection operating at the level of human societies: those early state societies whose religions were especially effective at motivating their citizens to sacrifice themselves succeeded in defeating societies with less motivating religions. Fictitious beliefs—such as the belief that a heaven populated by beautiful virgins awaits those who die for the cause—can contribute powerfully to effective motivation.

Rules of bad behavior toward out-groups reached their high point in the last 1,500 years, as fanatical Christians and Muslims inflicted death, slavery, or forced conversion on the heathen. Within the twentieth century, European states have turned instead to secular grounds to justify killing millions of citizens of other European states, but religious fanaticism is still strong in some other societies.

Where does this leave us in relation to religion's future in modern societies that are increasingly permeated by a scientific outlook? According to Wilson,

> There is no evidence that scientific understanding replaces religious belief in modern cultures. America has become more religious over the course of its history, not less, despite the influence of science and engineering . . . A very high proportion of scientists themselves profess a belief in God and participate in organized religions . . . Clearly, we must think of religious thought as something that coexists with scientific thought, not as an inferior version of it.

Wilson's thought-provoking book will stimulate each reader to examine his or her personal view of religion's future, and I can't resist doing so either. Personally, I accept purely secular reasons to pay taxes and to refrain from murder and theft, so that societies can promote the happiness of their citizens. I deny a religious need to kill members of out-groups, and I accept a secular need to do so under extreme circumstances, where the alternative would be worse. I remain uneasy about relying on religion to justify morality: today, as in the past, it's too small a step from there to justifying the killing of adherents of other religions. I accept the possibility of scientific explanations for almost every mystery of the natural world—but not for the greatest mystery of all. I still have no scientific answer, and expect there never to be one, to that challenge which Paul Tillich posed to me and my skeptical classmates: "Why is there something, when there could have been nothing?" Religion will thrive as long as there are human beings alive to reflect on the mystery of the First Cause.

Discussion Questions

1. For many Americans, the Old Testament's story of the Tower of Babel explains why there are diverse languages today. However, the Sikari peoples of New Guinea believe this happened another way. How does their story differ?
2. What is "group selection" and why do some think it led to the creation of religion?
3. The author says that there are two major proselytizing religions today. What are these?
4. Why does the author believe that early Christianity became so successful as a new religion?
5. The author says he believes that religion encompasses four different essential elements. What are they?
6. Modern science has explained many things that were once thought to be controlled by the gods. What do today's scientists say is the "last bastion of religious explanation"?
7. Why was religious belief so essential to early chiefdoms and state societies?
8. Religions often have as a tenet of their belief, "Thou shall not kill." Nevertheless, those same religions also justify and encourage the mass killing of others under certain circumstances. How do these religions explain this paradox?

38. "FROM HERE ON, I WILL BE PRAYING TO YOU": INDIAN CHURCHES, KIOWA HYMNS, AND NATIVE AMERICAN CHRISTIANITY IN SOUTHWESTERN OKLAHOMA

The Kiowa of Oklahoma, a Native American tribe, say that they are unable to express their complete love of God when they sing Christian hymns in English. Instead, they say that their true and deep love of God can only be expressed adequately through songs that they create and sing in their native language. If this is true, then our current textbooks that write about the beliefs of Native Americans and about how they have accepted Christian religion are missing some important facts. Eric Lassiter says that past researchers have missed some of the most important aspects of native spirituality because they did not examine the importance of hymns created and sung in native languages. The Kiowa, for example, explain that they have created hymns for all occasions and have ones that express solutions to all types of emotional and spiritual needs. They also point out that the songs and the words must be created and spoken in their native language and that there are no adequate ways to translate the songs into English or any other language. What worries some of today's Kiowa hymn singers is that many of the younger Kiowa are not interested in singing hymns or maintaining these important parts of their culture. Worst of all, the current hymn singers wonder how future generations will be able to understand the deep meaning of their hymns unless they make an effort to learn them now.

On a hot Sunday morning in mid-June 1998, Ralph Kotay and I drove to the J. J. Methvin Memorial United Methodist Church of Anadarko, Oklahoma—a small Indian church named after the missionary John Jasper Methvin who worked among the Kiowas from 1887 to 1908. We arrived in the church's parking lot with time to spare. Often Ralph and I took this interval to talk about Kiowa hymns or to discuss the previous night's powwows, but this morning's heat drove us out of the car and into the air conditioned church. Several other cars sat empty as well, attesting that the heat had perhaps driven more into the morning's Sunday School than usual.

Ralph and I walked through the back doors of the small church and made our way up the narrow hallway to the kitchen. There seated around a small table several of the elder members were in an intense discussion about the morning's Bible reading from Job. They bid a brief hello to Ralph and me and continued their debate about witnessing to the unsaved. The smell of freshly brewed coffee immediately diverted my attention, however. And Ralph's as well. We both headed for the coffee pot, filled our cups, and then made our way into the sanctuary. We greeted and shook hands with friends, and with coffee cups in hand, settled into our normal spot near the back and close to the kitchen door: Here, we could have easy access to the coffee pot.

The small sanctuary was cool and inviting; sipping our hot coffee on this already sultry morning seemed a little less contradictory in here. Echoing the low-pitched hum of the air conditioner, the ceiling fans whirled at full speed. But the carpeted floor seemed to deaden the sound. More immediately audible were those entering the church. A dozen or so people slowly made their way into the sanctuary from both the kitchen and the church's main entryway. They shook hands and talked as they began taking their seats in the cushioned pews, two rows of which flanked the edges of the aisle leading to the front of the church. There, on a platform raised just a few feet above the floor, a sheet covered an altar with preparations for this month's Holy Communion. Above, firmly attached to the exact center of the wall, a large wooden cross spanning a few feet wide and several more high faced back to the incoming congregation. To its right and left, the American and United Methodist flags stood, respectively. A few feet on either side of the flags two modestly crafted and cushioned chairs sat empty. Two pulpits, one on each side of the stage, framed this arrangement. And on its outermost edges, a piano and organ rested, now silent.

The window's shades were open, the sunlight danced across the soft white walls, which were simply adorned with a few wall hangings and pictures. A velvet image of Christ holding a lamb and leading a herd of sheep caught my eye this morning. I turned my attention back to the service's program which Ralph and I each now had in hand, reading. On its cover, below the words "bathed with tears," a color drawing depicted a water-filled bowl—its ringed ripples suggesting that it had been filled by droplets of tears. It rested atop a table, a towel at its base. A quick glance to the day's Bible readings written verbatim on the back of the program confirmed that the illustration referenced the day's Gospel reading, *Luke* 7:36–50—the story of Jesus forgiving the sins of a woman who bathed his feet with her tears and dried them with her hair. Inside, I glanced over announcements, the monthly calendar, prayer requests, and the Order of Worship. With the exception of the Holy Communion, the service was to proceed like most J. J. Methvin Sunday morning services. Following a musical "Prelude," a spoken "Welcome & Prayer," and "Sunday School Report," the service would begin with a "Call to Worship," recited from the program in unison. On this Sunday, the service would then turn to a "Hymn of Praise" from the gospel tradition, a "Hymn" from the Methodist hymnal, and three Bible readings entitled "First Lesson," "Second Lesson," and "Gospel Reading." Next, the congregation would sing "Native hymns," which at J. J. Methvin almost always meant Kiowa hymns (although at times other tribal hymns are sung as well). Following this singing, the church service would turn to the announcement of members' "Birthdays"—which was often followed by the Kiowa Birthday hymn—and "Joys and Concerns," which church member offered aloud to the rest of the congregation. Finally, after the "Pastoral Prayer," "Tithes & Offerings," and the musical "Doxology," the "Sermon" on this day would preface the "Holy Communion." The final invocation, or "Benediction" would end the program.

By this time, J. J. Methvin's pastor, Robert Pinezaddleby, had risen, walked to the front of the sanctuary, and had begun to greet all those in attendance. "I want to welcome you today," said Pinezaddleby after a while. "I believe we're ready for this morning's worship. As we prepare, we pray that the Holy Spirit will work with us, that the Holy Spirit will help us and **guide** us as we leave and as we go today." Several people continued visiting and talking as the service was slowly taking shape. Reverend Pinezaddleby turned toward the still dormant piano, silently acknowledging that the pianist had not yet arrived. The conventional musical prelude would not happen this Sunday. "We would like to have an opening hymn," Pinezaddleby said as a silence fell across the congregation. He looked over to where Ralph sat and motioned for him to start the song. Ralph took a deep breath, and on his exhale, the Kiowa words from the first stanza of the hymn resonated throughout the room (here translated in English): "If you are following the Christian way of life, be happy."

Several in the congregation joined in unison as Ralph progressed through the hymn's second, third, and fourth stanzas:

> If you are following Jesus' way, be happy.
> When you mention His name, He will give you salvation.
> If you are following Jesus' way, there is joy.

After singing the song through once, Ralph started it again. As we sang the song through three more times, I thought about why Ralph may have decided to sing this particular song: he always seemed to carefully choose the appropriate hymn for the occasion. With this in mind, I immediately thought back to what he had said the first time I heard him speak about this hymn in his weekly Kiowa hymn class: "The first time that the Indians began to get together, to worship in our modern day churches that were brought way back in the 1800s—the Baptist churches, the Methodist churches—they sing this. It's an old, favorite song" (Kotay 1994a).

"These Songs Will Somehow Work with You": A Meeting of Ralph Kotay's Kiowa Hymn Class

One evening in early January, 1994, a small group gathered for Ralph Kotay's weekly hymn class in Anadarko, Oklahoma. Soon after those assembled sat down, Ralph spoke briefly about why he started his class on Kiowa Christian hymns. In the early 1990s, he had felt compelled to preserve a song tradition practiced by many of the Indian churches since before the turn of the twentieth century. Born in 1927, Ralph had grown up speaking the Kiowa language and singing traditional Kiowa hymns; now, fewer and fewer people were learning either the Kiowa language or the songs. "These songs need to go on," Ralph said as he started his class.

Ralph talked for a few moments about class logistics, then turned attention back to hymns. "This first song I'll sing, it belongs to my uncle. He has a mind where that he's always thinking about the Almighty. I think that really helps him. . . ." Many of those gathered—young and old alike—turned their recorders on and Ralph sang the hymn. A few others joined in the singing. When Ralph finished, he translated the hymn's words into English, then reflected on their broader meanings. "The words in that," he began, "it says: 'It is good that I have recognized You as my God. From here on I will be praying to You'. Then it repeats that same wording, over and over." Ralph paused.

"You know," he continued, "if you're really a true believer, you're sincere about Christianity; these songs will somehow work with you. The words are **so** precious. The words get you to start thinking about your own life. That's the way **all** these songs are, no matter what tribe you're from. . . .

"[These Indian tribes] all have their different songs they like to sing. Say, for example, I sing around the drum, too. . . ." Ralph talked about his many years of pow-wow singing. "I've been around this singing **so** long," he said after a short while, "but **this** is the best type of singing that I do. I always praise, I always thank God for it, because I mention His name in every song; every time I'm in church. I mention His name. Sometimes I sing a song, it's for myself: how I've come through all the hardships, things like that—when my family gets sick. I pray to Him every day. And it makes you feel **good** to sing these songs. There are songs of thanksgiving, there are songs of sorrow, for people that are down and with sicknesses. We've got songs of **all** kinds."

Ralph returned to the song he had sung just a few minutes before. "So this song says you have recognized Him as our God; **my** God: 'From here on I will pray to You'. That's what it has in that" (Kotay 1994b).

"We've Got Songs of **All** Kinds": Singing Hymns in Southwestern Oklahoma

Throughout southwestern Oklahoma, Indian churches are a significant part of Native American community life. The variety of churches found here reflect the variety that one would find in most American communities. But while Indian churches share basic doctrine with their denominational counterparts in other American communities, their obvious differences in membership, individual church histories, and the use of tribal language in speech and song have brought about a unique Christian practice that situates these Indian churches specifically within an American Indian experience.

In southwestern Oklahoma where Ralph Kotay lives and teaches his hymn class, Indian churches serve a diverse Native population, including Kiowa, Kiowa-Apache, Chiricahua Apache, Caddo, Wichita, Comanche, and Delaware peoples. While several of these churches are comprised of "intertribal" memberships (also including non-Indians), many churches are comprised of tribal-specific memberships, and may serve primarily Kiowa or Comanche or Caddo congregations. In these congregations—and to a certain extent in those with intertribal congregations—the singing of traditional Indian hymns is an important component of each and every service.

Indian hymns are only one kind of song sung at these Indian churches, however. They share their place in any given service with English hymns (sung from hymnals) and, in some churches, gospel song. While hymnal songs and those that spring from a gospel tradition are most often sung in English, Indian hymns are almost always rendered in a specific tribal language. Indian hymns not only differ from English hymns and gospel in language and content; they also differ in their performance as well. English hymns are frequently assisted by hymnals, accompanied by a piano or organ, and often sung while standing; gospel is sometimes prompted by sheet music, may include guitars and microphones, and is usually performed at the front of the church; but Indian hymns generally have no accompaniment (except in some Pentecostal churches where a small drum is sometimes used), are most often sung while seated, and recalled completely from memory.

When Indian hymns are called for in a service, either from the written program or spontaneously, an individual "starts" the song. That individual is usually a man, but women sometimes start songs, too. After the first several words of the song's first stanza are sung through aloud and congregants have ascertained what song the individual is singing—for many songs have similar "starts"—those who know the song join in unison.

When the congregation completes the song once, the song's "starter" either repeats all or part of the hymn anew (depending on the hymn's form), and the song is sung through in unison again. The hymn is usually sung through two to four times with the song's starter ending the song, simply, by not starting it again. After a hymn is completed, the same (or another) individual might lead another song if one is called for, or if the Spirit is moving the service.

A singer working within most Indian hymn traditions has an enormous range of possibilities from which to choose a song. As Ralph Kotay says above, speaking of Kiowa hymns: "We've got songs of **all** kinds." But a singer doesn't necessarily just randomly choose any song. Singers like Ralph, being led by the Spirit of the service, often carefully select the appropriate hymn for the appropriate occasion. "The words that are put in there [in these hymns]," says Ralph, "they're for every occasion . . . There's a song for everything" (Kotay 1998). From baptismal hymns to funeral, prayer, and even birthday hymns, this wide range of songs thus engages a wide range of purposes, helping to clarify and deepen the sentiments associated with any given moment within any given church service.

Generally, Indian hymns in southwestern Oklahoma's Indian community—in sound, structure, performance, and use—are not entirely unlike many other Indian hymn traditions. But with regards to meaning, Indian hymns are located within very particular tribal traditions. Hymns belong to larger tribal song repertoires as much as they belong to Christian song repertoires. "Every tribe that we have," says Ralph, ". . . they have their own songs" (Kotay 1994d). In this way, hymns simultaneously communicate a combination of Christian and tribal-specific experience—pointing us to a deep level of experiential encounter that reaches beyond discrete musicological categories such as musical sound, structure, performance, and use.

"The Words Are **So** Precious": On Language and Story

But just what do Indian hymns communicate about this experiential encounter? The unique and complex intersection between Christianity, specific tribal histories, and individuals is clarified by the "language of hymns," which includes both what the language in song explicitly relates and communicates and the language surrounding song—that is, the voiced stories and sentiments that hymns invoke. Taken together, the language in and surrounding song provides an important window into the deeper meanings of Indian hymns in southwestern Oklahoma. Consider, for example, the following Kiowa hymn (here translated in English line by line):

> It is good that God made my spirit feel good. I am glad.
> It is Him: He is the One that made my spirit feel good. I am glad.
> It is good that God made my spirit feel good.
> One day, I felt so bad and so lonely.
> It is good that God made my spirit feel good.
>
> It is Him: He is the One that made my spirit feel good. I am glad.
> It is good that God made my spirit feel good.
> One day, I felt so bad and so lonely.
> It is good that God made my spirit feel good.

The words in this song obviously communicate a positive experience in which God turned sadness into joy. But this song, as sung in the communicative context of knowledgeable listeners, also references more than this. Ralph says of the hymn:

I heard this [song] a **long** time ago. My uncle, he's a good singer. He's made some songs. . . . This one particular song, he was telling me: "You know nephew, when I was young, I went to church—and I also went to the Native American Church. We **all** pray about the same thing, about something in our lives. This one time, this particular time, my wife had gone away. God had taken her away. I was really depressed. I was sitting there in the room by myself and thinking about things in my life. Later on, this song came to me. It came to me through the gladness of my heart. I'm glad I sung [it] because it seemed to lift all that depression off of me." (Kotay 1993)

While the language in this hymn generally communicates a relationship between God and an individual, the language surrounding this song extends the relationship further and situates it between Ralph and his uncle, and between Ralph's uncle and God. But that which this song references is not limited to Ralph's story. This (and every) song summons many layers of spoken interpretations, narratives, and individual sentiments. All of this is to say, therefore, that a song's meaning is not just encapsulated by the words in the song; the words are the symbolic foundation on which broader narrative meanings are built.

Given this, Ralph and others explain that there is much more to the significance and meaning of hymns in their community, especially in regards to the significance of language itself. In southwestern Oklahoma, fewer and fewer people use Native languages in everyday conversation, but Native language continues to command a central place in public events. While most every single person who gathers at any given powwow, peyote meeting, or church service speaks English, Native language emerges not just in song, but also in prayer and oral presentations. Obviously, language has a communicative role at these events; many elders, for example, say that some things just can't be spoken (or sung) in English as they can "in Indian." But Native language fulfills much more than its obvious communicative role, especially because most everyone gathered at any given event may not fully understand the Native language being publically vocalized. The use of Native language also communicates a connection to that which came before, that which is traditional, and, for many, that which is godly. Many elders say they pray in their Native language because it is the language that God gave to them specifically and uniquely. "Father, we consider that **You** have given everything that we see, and have done everything for us that is good," prays one individual in English at a powwow before praying in his Native language, "You have given us our language, dear Father, and this great gift of music."

The language in hymns, then, provides not only referents for individual stories; for many people—especially but not limited to elders—the sung performance of tribal language in hymns also enacts a larger, shared community experience with God and Christianity, and experiential relationship echoed in many songs. Expressions **in** songs, like "God made my spirit feel good" are regularly heard in Kiowa hymns, but they are not as ambiguous as they sound. For many Kiowa singers and listeners, this seemingly vague sentiment actually emerges from a very particular manifestation of God's presence in the lives of a very specific people. "If you **understand** the **real** meaning, the **deep** meaning—that's what makes these songs so beautiful . . . ," says Ralph. "When this Christianity came into our area, they [i.e., Kiowas] were so dedicated to this Christianity that these songs [came to them]. They don't compose these songs. They come to them through the Spirit. That's the reason why they're so beautiful. **All** these songs" (Kotay 1994c). For those like

Ralph, the "deep meanings" of hymns is that which simultaneously encompasses and transcends the multiplicity of individual interpretations, stories, and specific histories of individual songs: a long-established relationship with God as expressed and felt in song, a felt encounter that Ralph and others express in English as "Spirit."

"And It Makes You Feel **Good** to Sing These Songs": On Spirit

When talking about hymns in southwestern Oklahoma's Indian community, "Spirit" implies a godly encounter with song particularly framed by a Christian experience. This Christian experience, however, is a relatively recent addition to a broader narrative of encounter with the godly; in community-wide conversations, talk about Spirit denotes a godly encounter with all song—not just hymns—and it precedes the institution of Christianity in the community (see Lassiter 1998:200ff.). "Anytime we sing a song on His Behalf," says Ralph, reflecting on the relationship between all Kiowa song and God, "we mention God, *Daw-Kee*. That's always the way it's been, even before the missionaries came. . . . The Kiowa religious songs that we have, those songs that were sung, even before the missionaries came, all the songs pertain to God—the words are in there" (Kotay 1994d).

While the Kiowa word *Daw-Kee* now denotes the English "God," it is important to note that the root for both Daw-Kee and the Kiowa word for song, *daw-geab* is "power"; *daw* was and is that which materializes in song as Spirit (cf. Lassiter 1998: 187–90). Those like Ralph say that Kiowa song affirms a relationship that was established long ago in time immemorial, when the first Kiowa song was sung. Today, all Kiowa song—from peyote to powwow—maintains this relationship with the godly. Kiowa singers, whether singing hymns or peyote songs, thus further this relationship through singing; but God also reciprocates by continually giving songs to Kiowa people. As Ralph states above: "They don't compose these songs. They come to them through the Spirit" (Kotay 1994c). Understood in this light, song itself is an unfolding testimony of a long-established relationship between Daw-Kee and Kiowa people, individually expressed to those like Ralph's uncle, but made relevant to a larger community of believers through the act of singing.

Kiowa hymns obviously express a unique Christian component of this unfolding and ongoing relationship: "Everything that we sing in our Kiowa hymns now," says Ralph, "modern-day songs, it's always mentioned about Daw-Kee. When the missionaries came, that's where we learned about Jesus, the Son of God. He's the one that God created—Him, just like we are now, when He walked the earth. He was called the Son of God, Jesus" (Kotay 1994d). While the language in song engages a long-established relationship between Kiowa people and the godly, the language surrounding hymns—whether stories told in English or testimonies delivered in Kiowa—help to clarify the emergence of a unique Christian practice in the community since before the turn of the twentieth century.

"These Songs Need to Go On": On Maintaining and Preserving a Godly Relationship

Language, story, and song are thus at the heart of maintaining a specific connection to the godly that is generations old but that continues to materialize in the here and now. At church services, this godly connection emerges in prayer, testimony, and song—deepening the ever-emerging story about God, Indian people, and Christianity. "I feel like our forefathers, our grandmothers and them, they prayed a lot," says an individual at one of Ralph's hymn classes:

> And they were with the Lord a lot. We don't do that today. And I don't feel like we've composed songs like that. But **they** really were believers in the Holy Spirit. I feel like that's **why** they were given these songs. For us. (Blackbear 1994; as excerpted from Lassiter 1998:139)

While language, story, and song sharpen a connection to the past, to tribal memory, and to God, these expressions also provide the foundation for building the future of this relationship. For many like Ralph, some of the most meaningful components of this godly connection are threatened. "We don't have that many song leaders any more . . . ," says Ralph to his Kiowa hymn class. "Our young men, they don't seem to care [about being song leaders in the churches]. Even our language, a lot of us don't understand. . . . In our time, we're just too busy. We're all young and we don't care to learn these words [of the hymns]. That's where we're at [today]" (Kotay 1994c).

Ralph's sentiments do not just represent an elder generation bemoaning the passing of "old times." On the contrary, those like Ralph acknowledge that maintaining Kiowa language, story, and song not only means the continuance of a particular way of understanding and articulating experience; it also means maintaining a specific and precious relationship with God. Ralph's hymn class, then, is not just about preserving song or language or story; but also about that which these expressions sustain: a unique American Indian Christian practice in southwestern Oklahoma.

"That's the Way **All** These Songs Are, No Matter What Tribe You're From": On Native American Christian Identity

Understanding the deeper significance of Indian hymns—in this case, Kiowa hymns—opens a window onto the multifaceted intersection between the institution of Christianity and American Indian experience. But this window looks out on an experiential and phenomenological landscape; one which offers a much different perspective than that often explored by scholars who write about Christianity in Native communities.

Some of the most profound changes experienced in Native North America over the last several centuries have been religious; indeed, Christianity has had an enormous impact on Indian communities (see, e.g., Beaver 1988; Bowden 1981; Prucha 1984). Our scholarly descriptions and understandings of these changes, however, have been largely (but certainly not entirely) dictated by academically-positioned models, models like "assimilation" that emphasize broad sweeping changes and ignore the deeper experiential complexities that have emerged from this multidimensional encounter (cf. Schultz 1999:5–8). For example, many of our academic stories "attack missionaries as ill-informed and malicious," writes Clyde Ellis about missionary work among the Kiowas around the turn of the twentieth century. But the encounter between missionaries and Kiowas was much more complicated than this. "For their part," Ellis argues, "the Kiowas recognized that accepting Christianity need not come at the cost of their larger cultural identity, but did much to shape the contours of twentieth-century Kiowa life" (Ellis 1998:xvi).

When one listens to Ralph Kotay talk about Indian hymns and what it means to be a Christian, then, models like assimilation do more to obscure encounter and experience than elaborate it. When we begin to consider more deeply the intersection of Christianity and American Indian identity through the lens of experience, a more elaborate understanding of Native American Christian identity in general and Kiowa Christian identity in particular begins to unfold. This of course requires that we as students of Native American studies conceptualize and describe identity in more complex ways; as James Clifford writes:

> Stories of cultural contact and change have been structured by a pervasive dichotomy: absorption by the other **or** resistance to the other. . . . Yet what if identity is conceived not as a boundary to be maintained but as a nexus of relations and transactions actively engaging a subject? The story or stories of interaction must then be more complex, less linear and teleological. (Clifford 1988:344)

Expounding upon the language **in** and **surrounding** Indian hymns, I believe, invokes stories of interaction that are necessarily more complex and less linear and teleological than that often portrayed in the literature. Indeed, anthropologists, ethnomusicologists, and folklorists have written little about Indian hymns compared to what they have written about so-called "traditional songs." It often seems that Christian song repertoires are regarded as "less traditional," "less Indian," and therefore "less Other." The result? As Thomas McElwain argues, writing about Iroquois Christian hymns, "researchers have been blind to a rich source of information on native spirituality in the native Christian traditions" (McElwain 1990:83).

How can we correct this blind spot? How might we enhance our understanding of Indian hymns, experience, and Native American Christian identity—not just in the Kiowa community or the Southern Plains, but in all Native communities? On a broad level, we should continue the already initiated work of examining the epistemological assumptions that we carry about culture, change, and identity. But more to the point, the struggle of ethnographic understanding—that of being fully committed to elaborating the "native point of view"—continues to offer the most viable model for positively complicating and enriching the wider conversation about Native American experience and identity. Conceptualized in this way, ethnography necessarily broadens the framework of our discussions about culture to include our ethnographic consultants—people like Ralph Kotay, who in their talk about God, encounter, and experience force us to reconsider how we in the academy have traditionally understood Native American Christian identity. When, for example, a Kiowa elder suggests that "we lost our Christianity because we turned towards the White Man's ways" (Bointy 1998), we are immediately forced to reexamine the limitations of academically-constructed models like assimilation and consider instead the nexus of relations and transactions that engender deep meaning.

"**Deep** meaning," says Ralph, "that's what makes these songs so beautiful" (Kotay 1994c).

Discussion Questions

1. Who was the missionary John Jasper Methvin?
2. Who is Ralph Kotay and what does he do to try to ensure that the Kiowa don't forget their religious hymns?
3. According to Kotay the hymns that the Kiowa sing will "work for you" provided what happens?
4. Christian hymnal songs and gospel songs are sung differently and have different types of accompaniments in the Native American churches than do Native American hymns. What are those differences?
5. When an Indian hymn is called for in a service, who begins it and then what happens?
6. How do new Kiowa hymns generally originate?
7. Why do the Kiowa insist that their hymns must be sung in their native language?
8. How do the Kiowa view their acceptance of Christianity?

Additional Resources

For Internet links related to this chapter, please visit our website at www.mhhe.com/dettwyler

FITZGERALD, FRANCES. *Vietnam: Spirits of the Earth.* New York, NY: Bulfinch Press, 2001.

LASSITER, LUKE ERIC. *The Power of Kiowa Song: A Collaborative Ethnography.* Tucson, AZ: University of Arizona Press, 1998.

LASSITER, LUKE ERIC, CLYDE ELLIS, and RALPH KOTAY. *The Jesus Road: Kiowas, Christianity, and Indian Hymns.* Lincoln, NE: University of Nebraska Press, 2002.

MALINOWSKI, BRONISLAW. *Magic, Science and Religion, and Other Essays.* Garden City, NY: Doubleday/Anchor Books, 1954.

NASH, JUNE. "Judas Transformed." *Natural History,* March 1994, pp. 46–53.

NORBECK, EDWARD. *Religion in Human Life: Anthropological Views.* New York: Holt, Rinehart and Winston, 1974.

STARK, RODNEY. *The Rise of Christianity.* San Francisco, CA: HarperCollins, 1997.

STOLLER, PAUL, and CHERYL OLKES. *In Sorcery's Shadow: A Memoir of Apprenticeship Among the Songhay of Niger.* Chicago, IL: University of Chicago Press, 1989.

WILSON, DAVID SLOAN. *Darwin's Cathedral: Evolution, Religion, and the Nature of Society.* Chicago, IL: University of Chicago Press, 2002.

CHAPTER 22

The Arts

39. MYSTERIOUS ISLAND, by Paul Trachtman, *Smithsonian* 32, no.12 (March 2002), pp. 90–100.

In every culture, the arts are intrinsically multisensorial, appealing to us through all of our senses—sight, sound, smell, taste, touch, and movement. Whether we look at a painting or a dance performance or a play, listen to drums or an orchestra or a singer or a story-teller, perform or participate or observe from the sidelines, the arts engage us physically, cognitively, and emotionally. Art embodies our history, our culture, our religious and political and economic traditions. It is difficult to replicate that experience with words only on a printed page. The selection we chose for this chapter was one of the few we could find that (we hoped) could stand alone without pictures or sound to accompany it. In part, this is because the subject matter, Rapa Nui (Easter Island) art, is generally well known and readily available for viewing via the Internet. In addition, the famous Rapa Nui art involves mostly prehistoric and early historic giant stone statues. This is stationary art, rather than the fluid, living art of music or dance or storytelling; yet the legacy of Rapa Nui art continues today in many forms; it has not disappeared completely.

As you read this selection, think about the role of art in culture. Think about how art reflects and shapes cultural identity and how the revival of Rapa Nui artistic expression helps modern descendants of the original inhabitants of the island express their cultural legacy.

"There exists in the midst of the great ocean, in a region where nobody goes, a mysterious and isolated island," wrote the 19th-century French seafarer and artist Pierre Loti. "The island is planted with monstrous great statues, the work of I don't know what race, today degenerate or vanished; its great remains an enigma." Named

Easter Island by the Dutch explorer Jacob Roggeveen, who first spied it on Easter Day 1722, this tiny spit of volcanic rock in the vast South Seas is, even today, the most remote inhabited place on earth. Its nearly 1,000 statues, some almost 30 feet tall and weighing as much as 80 tons, are still an enigma, but the statue builders are far from vanished. In fact, their descendants are making art and renewing their cultural traditions in an island renaissance.

To early travelers, the spectacle of immense stone figures, at once serenely godlike and savagely human, was almost beyond imagining. The island's population was too small, too primitive and too isolated to be credited with such feats of artistry, engineering and labor. "We could hardly conceive how these islanders, wholly unacquainted with any mechanical power, could raise such stupendous figures," the legendary British mariner Captain Cook wrote in 1774. He freely speculated on how the statues might have been raised, a little at a time, using piles of stones and scaffolding; and there has been no end of speculation, and no lack of scientific investigation, in the centuries that followed. By Cook's time, the islanders had toppled many of their statues and were neglecting those left standing. But the art of Easter Island still looms on the horizon of the human imagination.

Just 14 miles long and 7 miles wide, the island is more than 2,000 miles off the coast of South America and 1,100 miles from its nearest Polynesian neighbor, Pitcairn Island, where mutineers from the *HMS Bounty* hid in the 19th century. Too far south for a tropical climate, lacking coral reefs and perfect beaches, and whipped by perennial winds and seasonal downpours, Easter Island nonetheless possesses a rugged beauty—a mixture of geology and art, of volcanic cones and lava flows, steep cliffs and rocky coves. Its megalithic statues are even more imposing than the landscape, but there is a rich tradition of island arts in forms less solid than stone— in wood and bark cloth, strings and feathers, songs and dances, and in a lost form of pictorial writing called *rongorongo,* which has eluded every attempt to decipher it.

This remarkable diversity is now on display in an exhibition at the Metropolitan Museum of Art in New York City. "Splendid Isolation: Art of Easter Island," which opened in December and runs through August 4, 2002, is the first showing of Easter Island art ever held in North America. More than a third of the 50 or so objects on display have never been exhibited before. Among the treasures are three spectacular feather headdresses that have been kept in storage at the Smithsonian Institution ever since the *USS Mohican* brought them back from the island around 1887, along with the huge stone head of a statue, also in the show, that hasn't been exhibited in 50 years. Two slabs of stone incised with "birdman" petroglyphs— human figures with bird heads, icons of a religious cult that replaced veneration of the stone giants—are also in the exhibition.

In a society of hereditary chiefs, priests, clans, and guilds of specialized craftsmen, many objects served as tokens of status and power. Wooden clubs, for example, could be ornately carved as ceremonial symbols of authority, or wielded in battle. Also on view are wood carvings of ancient spirits, or *akuaku,* in the form of lizard men, and fragile human images, made of a paperlike bark cloth, which may have been ancestor effigies. In his introduction to the show's catalog, exhibition curator Eric Kjellgren notes that the Polynesians who first landed on Easter Island early in the first millennium "lived in virtual isolation for the next thousand years." Their art, though distinctly Polynesian, he says, reflects their "splendid isolation."

History, as much as art, made this island unique. But attempts to unravel that history have produced many interpretations and arguments. The missionary's anecdotes, the archaeologist's shovel, the cultural anthropologist's oral histories, and the physical anthropologist's boxes of bones, have all revealed something of the island's story. But by no means all. When did the first people arrive? Where did they come from? Why did they carve such enormous statues? How did they move them and raise them up onto platforms? Why, after centuries, did they topple these idols? Such questions have been answered again and again, but the answers keep changing.

The islanders' origins were the subject of decades of debate after the great Norwegian adventurer Thor Heyerdahl and five companions made a daring voyage from Peru to Polynesia in 1947, drifting with wind and ocean currents aboard the wooden raft *Kon-Tiki* and finally crashing on a reef east of Tahiti. Seeing similarities between the stone art and architecture of Easter Island and that of the ancient Indian ruins in Bolivia and Peru, Heyerdahl was trying to prove that the original Easter Islanders could have sailed from South America. But there were so many holes in Heyerdahl's theory that it would have sunk quickly but for his own charisma and ability to patch leaky arguments with new speculations. Yet, to his great credit, Heyerdahl brought to the island a group of archaeologists and other researchers who, in turn, launched the modern era of scientific investigation.

Over the past few decades, archaeologists have assembled evidence that the first settlers came from another Polynesian island, but they can't agree on which one. Estimates of when people first reached the island are as varied, ranging from the first to the sixth century A.D. And how they ever found the place, whether by design or accident, is yet another bone of contention.

Some argue that the navigators of the first millennium could never have plotted a course over such immense distances without modern precision instruments. Others contend that the early Polynesians were among the world's most skilled seafarers—masters of the night sky and the ocean's currents. One archaeoastronomer suggests that a new supernova in the ancient skies may have pointed the way. But did the voyagers know the island was even there? For that, science has no answer. The islanders, however, do.

Benedicto Tuki is a tall 65-year-old master wood-carver and keeper of ancient knowledge. His piercing eyes are set in a deeply creased, mahogany face. He introduces himself as a descendant of the island's first king, Hotu Matu'a, who, he says, brought the original settlers from an island named Hiva in the Marquesas. He claims his grandmother was the island's last queen. He'll tell me about Hotu Matu'a, he says, but only from the center of the island, at a platform called Ahu Akivi with its seven giant statues. There he can tell the story in the right way.

In Tuki's native tongue, the island—like the people and the language—is called Rapa Nui. Platforms are called *ahu* and the statues that sit on them, *moai* (mo-eye). As our jeep negotiates a rutted dirt road, the seven moai loom into view. Their faces are paternal, all knowing and human—forbiddingly human. These seven, Tuki says, are not watching over the land like those with their backs to the sea. These stare out beyond the island, across the ocean to the west, remembering where they came from. When Hotu Matu'a came to the island, he brought seven different races with him, which became the seven tribes of Rapa Nui. These moai represent the original ancestor from the Marquesas, and the kings of other Polynesian islands. Tuki himself stares into the distance as he chants their names. "This is not written down," he says.

"My grandmother told me before she died." His is the 68th generation, he adds, since Hotu Matu'a.

Anthropologists have collected many variations of this legend. As Tuki tells it, because of fighting at home, the young chief Hotu Matu'a gathered his followers for a voyage to a new land. His tattooist and priest, Hau Maka, had flown across the ocean in a dream and saw Rapa Nui and its location, which he described in detail. Hotu Matu'a and his brother-in-law set sail in long double canoes, loaded with people, food, water, plant cuttings and animals. After a voyage of two months, they sailed into Anakena Bay, which was just as the tattooist had described it.

In the minds of the native people, science and legend seem to weave themselves together. The names of early anthropologists—among them England's Katherine Routledge (1914–15) and Switzerland's Alfred Métraux (1934–35)—who collected legends, recorded customs and restored some of the ahu by raising the fallen statues, are as familiar as the names of ancient kings. Instrumental in the rebirth of the island, they have become cultural heroes. One of the archaeologists Thor Heyerdahl brought to the island in the 1950s, William Mulloy, became a kind of father figure to a small band of students who continued his work.

Sometimes, says Cristián Arévalo Pakarati, an island artist in a New York Yankees cap who has worked with several archaeologists, the old stories hold as much truth as anything the scientists unearth. He tells me this as we climb up the cone of the volcano called Rano Raraku to the quarry where the great moai were once carved. The steep path winds through an astonishing landscape of moai, standing tilted and without order, many buried up to their necks, some fallen facedown on the slope, about 70 in all, apparently abandoned here before they could be moved across the island to the ahu for which they were carved. Pakarati is dwarfed by a stone head as he stops to lean against it. "It's hard to imagine," he says, "how the carvers must have felt when they were told to stop working. They'd been carving these statues here for centuries, until one day the boss shows up and tells them to quit, to go home, because there's no more food, there's a war, and nobody believes in the statue system anymore!" Pakarati identifies so strongly with his forebears because, working with UCLA archaeologist Jo Anne Van Tilburg, he's spent many years making detailed drawings and measurements of all the island's moai. Now, as we climb into the quarry itself, he shows me where the carving was done.

The colossal figures are everywhere, in every stage of completion, laid out on their backs with a sort of stone keel attaching them to the bedrock. Carved from a soft stone called lapilli tuff, a compressed volcanic ash, several figures lie side by side in a niche. "These people had absolute control over the stone," Pakarati says. "They could move statues from here to Tahai, which is 15 kilometers away, without breaking the nose, the lips, the fingers or anything." Then he points to a few broken heads and bodies on the slope below and laughs. "Obviously, accidents were allowed."

When a statue was almost complete, the carvers drilled holes through the keel to break it off from the bedrock, then slid it down the slope into a big hole, where they could stand it up to finish the back. Eye sockets were carved once a statue was on its ahu, and white coral and obsidian eyes were inserted during ceremonies, to awaken the moai's power. In some cases, the statues were adorned with huge cylindrical hats or topknots of red scoria, another volcanic stone. But first a statue had to be moved over one of the roads that led to the island's nearly 300 ahu. How that was done is still a matter of debate. Rapa Nui legends say the moai "walked" with the help of a chief or priest who had mana, or supernatural power. On the island in 1986, a crew put together by Thor Heyerdahl and Czech engineer Pavel Pavel walked an upright moai by rocking it from side to side, like a refrigerator. Archaeologists have proposed other methods for moving the statues, using various combinations of log rollers, sledges and ropes. Cristián Pakarati points out that the word "mana" can also mean technology or intelligence, so the old legends and modern science may not be so far apart. "Maybe those old people are right to say the statues were moved with mana," he muses.

Trying to sort out the facts of the island's past has led researchers into one riddle after another—from the meaning of the monuments to the reasons for the outbreak of warfare and the cultural collapse after a thousand years of peace. Apart from oral tradition, there is no historical record before the first European ships arrived. But evidence from many disciplines, such as the excavation of bones and weapons, the study of fossilized vegetation, and the analysis of stylistic changes in the statues and petroglyphs allows a rough historical sketch to emerge: The people who settled on the island found it covered with trees, a valuable resource for making canoes and eventually useful in transporting the moai. They brought with them plants and animals to provide food, although the only animals that survived were chickens and tiny Polynesian rats. Artistic traditions, evolving in isolation, produced a rich imagery of ornaments for the chiefs, priests and their aristocratic lineages. And many islanders from the lower-caste tribes achieved status as master carvers, divers, canoe builders or members of other artisan's guilds. Georgia Lee, an archaeologist who spent six years documenting the island's petroglyphs, finds them as remarkable as the moai. "There's nothing like it in Polynesia," she says of this rock art. "The size, scope, beauty of designs, and workmanship, is extraordinary."

At some point in the island's history, when both the art and the population were increasing, the island's resources were overtaxed. Too many trees had been cut down. "Without trees you've got no canoes," says Pakarati. "Without canoes you've got no fish, so I think people were already starving when they were carving these statues. The early moai were thinner, but these last statues have great curved bellies. What you reflect in your idols is an ideal, so when everybody's hungry, you make them fat, and big." When the islanders ran out of resources, they threw their idols down and started killing each other over what was left.

Some archaeologists point to a layer of subsoil with many obsidian spear points as a sign of sudden warfare. Islanders say there was probably cannibalism, as well as carnage, and seem to think no less of their ancestors because of it. Smithsonian forensic anthropologist Douglas Owsley, who has studied the bones of some 600 individuals from the island, has found numerous signs of trauma, such as blows to the face and head. But only occasionally, he says, did these injuries result in death. In any case, a population that grew to as many as 20,000 was reduced to only a few thousand at most when the captains of the first European ships counted them in the early 18th century. Over the next 150 years, with visits by European and American sailors, French traders and missionaries, Peruvian slave raiders, Chilean imperialists and Scottish ranchers (who introduced sheep and herded the natives off the land, fencing them into one small village), the Rapa Nui people were all but destroyed. By 1877 there were only 110 natives left on the island.

When Katherine Routledge arrived in 1914, she found that "the inhabitants of to-day are less real than the men who have gone; the shadows of the departed builders still possess the land." Such poetry popularized the mystery of the island, while the Rapa Nui remained confined to a single area, according to Routledge, "to secure the safety of the livestock." Although the population rebounded steadily through the 20th century, native islanders still don't own their land. The Chilean government claimed possession of Easter Island in 1888 and, in 1935, designated it as a national park, to preserve some 6,000 archaeological sites. Today, there are about 2,000 native people, and about as many Chileans, crowded into the island's only village, Hanga Roa, and its outskirts. Under growing pressure, the Chilean government is giving back a small number of homesteads to native families, alarming some archaeologists and stirring intense debate. But though they remain largely dispossessed, the Rapa Nui people have reemerged from the shadows of the past, recovering and reinventing their ancient art and culture.

Carving a small wooden moai in his yard, Andreas "Panda" Pakarati is part of that cultural renewal. "I'm the first professional tattooist on the island in 100 years," he says, soft eyes flashing under a rakish black beret. Panda's interest was stirred by pictures he saw in a book as a teenager, and tattoo artists from Hawaii and other Polynesian islands taught him their techniques. He has taken most of his designs from Rapa Nui rock art and from Georgia Lee's 1992 book on the petroglyphs. "Now," says Panda, "the tattoo is reborn."

Other artists of Panda's generation are also breathing new life into old art. In his small studio that doubles as living space, the walls lined with large canvases of Polynesian warriors and tattooed faces, Cristián Silva paints Rapa Nui themes with his own touch of swirling surrealism. "I paint because I appreciate my culture," he says. "The moai are cool, and I feel connected to ancestral things. On this island you can't escape that! But I don't copy them. I try to find a different point of view."

The dancers and musicians of the Kari Kari company, shouting native chants and swaying like palms in the wind, are among the most striking symbols of a cultural renewal. "We're trying to keep the culture alive," says Jimmy Araki, one of the musicians. "We're trying to recuperate all our ancient stuff and put it back together, and give it a new uprising." Dancer Carolina Edwards, 22, arrives for a rehearsal astride a bright red all-terrain vehicle, ducks behind some pickup trucks on a hill overlooking one of the giant statues, and emerges moments later in the ancient dress of Rapa Nui women, a bikini made of tapa, or bark cloth. "When I was little they used to call me *tokerau* which means wind, because I used to run a lot, and jump out of trees," she says, laughing. "Most of the islanders play guitar and know how to dance. We're born with the music." The dancers rehearse or perform four nights a week, and most have other jobs as well. Edwards teaches dance and works in her father's tourism business. "Everybody creates the dances," she says. "We all talk about the story, the song, the meaning, what kind of movement to use. People are very happy with what they have here. That's why, when tourists come from different countries, we're saying, like, 'Ha! See my island. This is **my** island!' "

Smithsonian anthropologist Adrienne Kaeppler suggests in an essay for the Metropolitan Museum exhibition catalog that the performing arts will become Easter Island's featured form of cultural expression in the 21st century. But some scholars, and some islanders, say the new forms have less to do with ancient culture than with today's tourist dollars. "What you have now is reinventing," says Rapa Nui archaeologist Sergio Rapu, a former governor of the island. "But the people in the culture don't like to say we're reinventing. So you have to say, 'OK, that's Rapa Nui culture.' It's a necessity. The people are feeling a lack of what they lost."

Even the oldest and most traditional of artisans, like Benedicto Tuki, agree that tourists provide the essential support for their culture. But he insists that the culture is intact—that its songs and skills carry the ancient knowledge into the present. Grant McCall, an anthropologist from the University of New South Wales in Australia, concurs. When I ask McCall, who has recorded the genealogies of island families on visits since 1968, how a culture could be transmitted through only 110 people, he tugs at his scruffy blond mustache. "Well, it only takes two people," he says, "somebody who is speaking and somebody who is listening."

Since many families' claims to land are based on their claim to knowledge of ancestral boundaries, the argument is hardly academic. Chilean archaeologist Claudio Cristino, who spent 25 years documenting and restoring the island's treasures, frames the debate dramatically. "There are native people on the island, and all over the world, who are using the past to recover their identities, land and power," he says. Contemplating the present from his office at the University of Chile in Santiago, he is not sanguine. "As a scientist, with all my deficiencies, I've spent half my life there. It's my island! And now people are already clearing land and plowing it for agriculture, destroying archaeological sites. Behind the statues you have people with their dreams, their needs to develop the island. Are we as scientists responsible for that? The question is, who owns the past?"

Who, indeed? The Rapa Nui mayor of Hanga Roa, Petero Edmunds, opposes the Chilean government's plans for giving away land. He wants the entire park returned to Rapa Nui control, to be kept intact. "But they won't listen," he says. "They've got their fingers in their ears." And who should look after it? "The people of Rapa Nui who have looked after it for a thousand years," he answers. He becomes pensive. "The moai are not silent," he says. "They speak. They're an example our ancestors created in stone, of something that is within us, which we call spirit. The world must know this spirit is alive."

Discussion Questions

1. Where is Rapa Nui (Easter Island) located? When was it first "discovered" by Europeans? When was it first settled by humans and where did they come from?
2. What was the occasion for the publication of this article in March 2002?
3. In what different forms did traditional (prehistoric) Easter Island art appear? Hint: It isn't just the giant stone statues.
4. What is *rongorongo*? Do you think it will ever be deciphered?
5. What material are the *moai* made from? How were they carved and transported to the *ahu* platforms?
6. What factors are thought to have led to the collapse of the island's thriving society and the abandonment of the tradition of carving *moai*? What happened to the remaining islanders after the arrival of Europeans and their descendants?
7. Who has political control of the island today?
8. How are the modern islanders revitalizing, reinventing, and changing their ancestors' artistic legacy?
9. Why does anthropologist Grant McCall say that it only takes two people to keep a culture going?

10. What are the current controversies over land ownership, use, and development on the island? Who do you think should make decisions about the island's future?

11. Can the multiple meanings of art that originate in one cultural context and time period ever be fully understood by people from another culture and another time? Why would people in the United States want to go look at art and cultural objects from the prehistoric peoples of Rapa Nui?

Additional Resources

For Internet links related to this chapter, please visit our website at www.mhhe.com/dettwyler

ALMEIDA, BIRA. *Capoeira, a Brazilian Art Form: History, Philosophy, and Practice.* 2nd ed. Berkeley, CA: North Atlantic Books, 1986.

ARNOLDI, MARY JO. *Playing With Time: Art and Performance in Central Mali.* Bloomington, IN: Indiana University Press, 1995.

BARZ, GREGORY F., and TIMOTHY J. COOLEY, eds. *Shadows in the Field: New Perspectives for Fieldwork in Ethnomusicology.* New York: Oxford University Press, 1996.

BOYD, CAROLYN. *The Rock Art of Ancient Texas.* College Station, TX: Texas A&M University Press, 2003.

CAMPHAUSEN, RUFUS C. *Return of the Tribal: A Celebration of Body Adornment: Piercing, Tattooing, Scarification, Body Painting.* Rochester, VT: Inner Traditions Int'l. Ltd., 1997.

DRAKE, ALAN, and GEORGIA LEE. *Easter Island: The Ceremonial Center of Orongo.* New York: Cloud Mountain Publishers, 1992.

FELD, STEVEN. *Sound and Sentiment: Birds, Weeping, Poetics, and Song in Kaluli Expression.* 2nd ed. Philadelphia, PA: University of Pennsylvania Press, 1989.

GRONING, KARL. *Decorated Skin: A World Survey of Body Art.* London: Thames & Hudson, 2002.

KELLY, MICHAEL. *Iconoclasm in Aesthetics.* New York: Cambridge University Press, 2003.

KJELLGREN, ERIC, JO ANNE VAN TILBURG, and ADRIENNE KAEPPLER. *Splendid Isolation: Art of Easter Island.* New Haven, CT: Yale University Press, 2001.

LEE, GEORGIA. *Rock Art of Easter Island: Symbols of Power, Prayers to the Gods.* Los Angeles, CA: University of California, Los Angeles, Institute of Archaeology, 1992.

MCCALL, GRANT. *Rapanui: Tradition and Survival on Easter Island.* Honolulu, HI: University of Hawai'i Press, 1981.

MCCARTY, CARA, JOHN EMIGH, JOHN W. NUNLEY, and LESLEY K. FERRIS. *Masks: Faces of Culture.* New York: Harry N. Abrams, Inc., 1999.

MERRIAM, ALAN P. *Anthropology of Music.* Chicago, IL: Northwestern University Press, 1964.

ROVINE, VICTORIA L. *Bogolan: Shaping Culture through Cloth in Contemporary Mali.* Washington, DC: Smithsonian Institution Press, 2001.

VOGEL, SUSAN MULLIN. *Baule—African Art, Western Eyes.* New Haven, CT: Yale University Press, 1997.

WIBER, MELANIE G. *Erect Men/Undulating Women: The Visual Imagery of Gender, "Race" and Progress in Reconstructive Illustrations of Human Evolution.* Waterloo, Ontario, Canada: Wilfrid Laurier University Press, 1998.

CHAPTER 23

The Modern World System

40. TRADING PLACES, by Paul Stoller, *Natural History* 111, no. 6 (July/August 2002), pp. 48–55.

Today's economic and political worlds reflect the ever-accelerating pace of migration—both of people and of ideas—between and among the world's different regions, countries, and cultures. Ideas and goods are imported from all regions of the world for sale in the United States, and vice versa. Hop in a cab in any big U.S. city and you are likely to encounter a cab driver who was born in another country—Eritrea, Afghanistan, Iran, Greece, Lithuania, Peru—and trained for a very different occupation in his homeland (often that of a doctor or a lawyer or a businessman). Other new immigrants continue their traditional occupations, but in new cultural and economic settings. Visit the Shabazz Market in New York City, and you might find Issifi Mayaki, whose cultural roots in Islam and West African commercial trading practices help him survive and flourish as a market trader in the United States.

Paul Stoller, the author of this selection, is a cultural anthropologist who has spent many years studying the Songhay in Niger (cf. In Sorcery's Shadow by Paul Stoller and Cheryl Olkes, 1989). Recently, he has studied the West African immigrants who work as market traders in New York City and "the bush" (more rural regions of the United States), and who form one part of the United States' vast informal economic sector. As you read this piece, think about how cultural beliefs, especially religious beliefs and kinship systems, help the West African immigrants succeed in their new homes.

Born in Niger, Issifi Mayaki learned his father's trade: selling indigenous African cloth, including antique textiles. With his impeccable French, he developed a clientele among French expatriates in the city of Abidjan, Côte d'Ivoire, and after picking up English he successfully cultivated members of Abidjan's English-speaking diplomatic community as well as African American visitors. Then in 1992, at the age of thirty, Mayaki began eyeing the lucrative market in the United States. Deciding to take a gamble, he packed up and airfreighted much of his stock to New York City, bought a round-trip ticket (as required for a six-month business visitor's visa), and set out to make his fortune.

At first, things went well. Upon arriving, Mayaki found lodging with fellow traders at a rundown, ostensibly single-room-occupancy hotel on West 77th Street in Manhattan and started making contacts. But several weeks later, after he sent out a large shipment of Ghanaian *kente* cloth, the recipient refused to pay. Mayaki's telephone calls and faxes went unanswered. Much of the inventory of valuable fabrics that had taken him years to collect in Africa was thus lost in a matter of weeks. In fact, he was stranded: to meet expenses, he had already sold the return portion of his air ticket.

Mayaki turned to his compatriots for assistance, and they pooled money to provide him with a loan. Adapting quickly to new circumstances, he decided to stock up on rap, rhythm and blues, and jazz cassettes to market to African Americans in Harlem. He set up a table on West 125th Street near the famed Apollo Theater and eventually took up residence with another trader living nearby. After city authorities cleared out the 125th Street market area, Mayaki relocated to the Malcolm Shabazz Harlem Market on West 116th Street, where he rented a stall for seven dollars a day and began to sell textiles along with cassettes and a few CDs. In time, he again became a cloth merchant.

"Was it difficult to negotiate the crossroads of New York City?" I once asked him.

"Life in New York is filled with uncertainties," he answered. "If I fall sick, will I be able to get help? Will Immigration detain and deport me? Will I make enough money to send to my family in Niger and Côte d'Ivoire? Will I make enough to pay my bills? So far, God has blessed me. The only certainty is that I have always been a trader and will always be a trader."

Two integrated aspects of his cultural heritage have enabled Mayaki to walk the myriad economic and social paths of New York City: the practices of West African trade and the teachings of Islam. Throughout the history of West Africa, specialized traders have, through kinship or patron-client relations, established large corporate networks. The most notable of these professional traders belong to two ethnic groups, the Hausa (Mayaki's group) and the Malinke, sometimes referred to as the Dyula. Other major players are Songhay from Niger and Mali, Wolof from Senegal, and Soninke from Gambia. Like their ancestors, West African traders in New York City have well-established procedures and organizations for obtaining informal credit and raising capital, and they adhere to Islamic precepts concerning commercial transactions.

From the earliest years of the *ummah* (the Muslim community of believers), which was established by the prophet Muhammad in the early seventh century A.D., traders were urged to interact in cooperative ways that would increase commerce. Various passages in the Qur'an speak of manifesting goodwill, providing correct weight, and not giving false oaths in transactions. More emphatically, Muhammad opposed monopolistic practices that could undermine cooperative relations. So when Mayaki (who regularly studies the Qur'an and the Hadith, or record of the Prophet's sayings) speaks of hard work, honest commercial relations, and trust, these beliefs derive directly from Islam.

Boubé Mounkaila is a Songhay, not a Hausa, but like Mayaki, he came to New York City from Niger by way of Abidjan. At the Malcolm Shabazz Harlem Market, he sells wristwatches as well as leather sacks and handbags made in Niger. Mounkaila's watches adopt the styles and trademarks of DKNY, Gucci, Rolex, and Swiss Army brands, but he makes no secret of the fact that his are counterfeits.

"I must be honest in my dealings," he told me. "I let everyone know that what I sell are copies, not originals."

"They probably know anyway, from the price," I said. "I mean, it's hard to get a real Rolex for twenty-five dollars."

"It doesn't matter," replied Mounkaila. "I must tell them anyway. That is our way. I am a merchant, and I try to establish trust with my clients. That way, they will, *Inshallah*—God willing—come back." He connected his trading practices to Islam. "I try to be a good Muslim. I say my prayers five times a day, avoid alcohol and pork, and give to the unfortunate. I try to be honest in trade. That is our way, and it makes me a better trader."

While the founding of Islam triggered the expansion of trade from Arabia to North and West Africa, the extension of kinship ties—both fictive and real—provided a customary means of enlarging trade networks. The practices that made long-distance trade possible in West Africa hold today in New York City. Mayaki's network consists, first of all, of his paternal kin. He is obliged to send money to the family head (his father) and to look after his mother and brothers. But Mayaki also feels a social and economic loyalty to his "brother" traders. His most important transactions and dealings are with fellow Hausa from Niger whom he knows from Abidjan. To lesser degrees, his sense of trust and comfort extends to other Hausa traders and then to other West African traders. He can expect to give and receive a small amount of credit from any of these people, no matter their actual proximity to his informal personal trade network, which also includes Korean, Chinese, and Afghani suppliers. "Islam makes us traders strong, resilient, and disciplined," Mayaki says. "It encourages our creativity in new lands. It creates a climate of trust."

There are even several economic networks of Hausa and Songhay traders that sponsor "trade children" in New York City. In West Africa, established elder traders, or "fathers," pay airfare, procure visas, and provide investment capital for enterprising young men. In return, they receive a percentage of the profits that their "children" earn. One of these elder traders is El Hadj Soumana Tondi, who travels from West Africa to New York City every six weeks to, as he puts it, check up on his children at the Shabazz Market.

Tens of thousands of West Africans, most of them men, have poured into the United States during the past fifteen years, usually settling in New York City or elsewhere on the East Coast. They are part of the wave of "new immigrants," consisting of people from developing countries affected by the economic and social dislocations brought on by globalization. Those who are literate and have work permits may drive yellow cabs or use their profits from vending to open a restaurant, boutique, or import-export business. But the majority enter a legal limbo, overstaying their visas. They become a vital part of the ever-growing informal sector, or underground economy, which evades the reach of government regulation and therefore goes untaxed.

Lower-income neighborhoods in New York City are major arenas of such economic activity. Like Ralph Ellison's "invisible man," many new immigrants walk in the shadows, their life stories and cultural backgrounds virtually unknown to the mainstream citizenry. Typical underground workers include the Trinidadian day-care employee for whom no Social Security forms are completed; the Guinean "gypsy cab" driver, possibly unlicensed or underinsured, who cruises parts of the city neglected by the yellow taxis; the Peruvian carpenter who crafts furniture in a space not zoned for manufacturing; the Thai woman who sews teddy bears in a poorly lit suburban garage; and, of course, the unlicensed Senegalese street vendor who shares informal market space in downtown Brooklyn or Lower Manhattan with African Americans, Jamaicans, Vietnamese, Ecuadorians, and a host of others.

Although he has become a pragmatic player in the global economy, Issifi Mayaki maintains a judicious distance from a society whose values he finds both fascinating and disturbing. As it is, during his time in New York City, he has been torn by conflicting allegiances—to his wife and children; to Monique, the girlfriend he has acquired, and her child; to his mother, father, and brothers; and to his own desires. One warm January day, I went to the Shabazz Market to see Mayaki, and we got into a discussion about his family, whom he had not seen in five years. "I miss Africa so much that I've become a nasty person, giving everybody a hard time," he lamented. "I really want to go back and see my family."

Mayaki's wife, children, and mother live near Maradi, Niger, in West Africa's hot, dusty, windswept Sahel. His father and three of his brothers are merchants who live in Abidjan. At the time of our conversation, a fourth brother, who had trained as a schoolteacher in Niger, was living in Melbourne, Australia, where he worked in a boutique specializing in African art.

Talk of his family compelled Mayaki to think of his mother. "For me," he said, "there is no more important person than my mother. You know how it is between sons and mothers. I really miss my mother. But when I tell this to Monique, she thinks that I really miss my wife. I care very much for Monique, and I respect my wife, but my mother is more important. We are of the same blood."

Mayaki reiterated that Americans couldn't understand why family is so important to Africans. "**You** understand," he said to me, "because you lived there for seven years. But Monique?" He shook his head. "Maybe next year I'll go back," he went on. "One of my brothers will come here. After I train him, I'll go back to Abidjan and he'll stay here."

For some reason, the unusual warmth that day hadn't drawn many customers to the market. Passing merchants offered their greetings to us. A young African American woman asked if Mayaki had Dutch Wax cloth. He searched through the bolts and found some. The woman didn't like the color scheme and sauntered away. Mayaki turned back to me, and we continued our conversation.

"There are two important things in my life: family and things that stir my heart. I sell my products to any person, Christian or Muslim, pastors or drug dealers, for if I am honest, money has no smell. If God grants me money in exchange for hard work, I must first make sure that my family is okay, that they're well fed, well clothed, well housed, and in good health. Then, if there is something left, I buy things that stir my heart." Mayaki pointed to his black leather jacket and said he had bought it at the Gap. He touched his corduroy trousers. "The Gap. I bought three pair." He unzipped his jacket to reveal a rust-colored linen shirt. "The Gap also," he said, smiling.

Mayaki was able to make these purchases because of a successful winter holiday season—a season that in much of the United States now includes Kwanzaa, a recently established African American community and cultural celebration spanning December 26 through January 1. Mayaki had rented space at the Jacob K. Javits Convention Center, the site of New York City's annual Kwanzaa Fest, and had sold a great deal of cloth to African Americans who wished to honor African values and to buy African products.

In the current climate, marked by suspicion and vilification of all things Muslim, Mayaki and his brother traders present a positive and dynamic portrait of how Islam bolsters the growth of trade and social relations. During their time in New York City, West Africans have established new partnerships, mastering the culture of capitalism while reinforcing traditions of long-distance African trading. They have staked out individual space in a market culture while engaging in the cooperative economics dictated by Islam and by long-standing West African commercial practices. They have adapted to the unfamiliar stresses of big-city life in the United States while reaffirming their African identities. Traders like Mayaki have much to teach us about how urban society works in contemporary America.

From April through October, some West Africans pack vans with African leather goods, textiles, and jewelry, along with Chinese- or Korean-made baseball caps and T-shirts that display logos of U.S. sports teams. Thus equipped, they tour through what they call "the bush"—Indianapolis, Kansas City, Detroit—following the circuit of African American trade shows and Third World cultural fairs. With his newly purchased van, Issifi Mayaki has recently become one of these mobile merchants. Although he travels the side roads of America, he is by no means isolated, for his beeper and cell phone enable him to stay connected to business associates, friends, and family in the United States and Africa. And if, by chance, his successful travels in the American bush transport him to the Gap, he might well follow his heart to browse and perhaps buy.

Discussion Questions

1. Describe the different stages of Issifi Mayaki's route from his homeland in Niger to New York City. What happened to his first attempt to be a cloth merchant?
2. What are "the practices of West African trade" that helped Mayaki cope with the complexities of life as a merchant in New York?
3. What are "the teachings of Islam" that helped Mayaki cope with the complexities of life as a merchant in New York?
4. The word "customer" is derived from the idea of a person developing a **custom** of buying from one particular merchant because of a personal relationship with that merchant. In the United States, how many people develop personal relationships with the people from whom they purchase goods or services? Do you know the person who works at the gas station where you buy gas? Do you even have a customary gas station that you always go to? What about other goods such as groceries, textbooks, and clothing, or services such as hair cuts, dry cleaning, or car washes? Assuming that you want to, why is it often difficult to establish such long-term personal relationships with merchants in the modern U.S. economy?
5. What role do kinship ties, both fictive and real, play in enlarging trade networks among West African traders, whether in West Africa or in the United States? With whom does Mayaki have his closest ties?

6. What are **trade children**? How is being a trade child different from being an apprentice in a skilled trade? How is it different from the modern U.S. system of training doctors? How is it different from parents subsidizing their child's college education?

7. Give examples of the informal sector, or underground economy, that many new immigrants belong to. Why is it referred to as being underground?

8. Discuss Mayaki's feelings towards his wife in Africa, his girlfriend in New York, and his mother in Africa. Why does he feel the most loyalty to his mother? Why does he say Stoller can understand his feelings toward his mother, while his girlfriend misinterprets them?

9. Mayaki uses his income to take care of his obligations to his family. If he has money left over, he buys things that "stir his heart," such as clothes from The Gap. Does his choice of clothes from The Gap (as something that "stirs his heart") surprise you?

10. Europeans and Americans often refer to rural, sparsely settled regions of West Africa as "the bush." Where is "the bush" for Mayaki in the United States and why does he travel there?

11. Do you see any parallels between the resurgence of Rapa Nui art and the importing of African art objects for sale to African Americans? How are people using such objects to express their cultural roots?

Additional Resources

For Internet links related to this chapter, please visit our website at www.mhhe.com/dettwyler

DIALLO, KADIATOU, and CRAIG WOLFF. *My Heart Will Cross This Ocean: My Story, My Son.* New York: One World/Ballantine, 2003.

PACKER, GEORGE. "How Susie Bayer's T-Shirt Ended up on Yusuf Mama's Back," *The New York Times,* March 31, 2002.

ROBBINS, RICHARD H. *Global Problems and the Culture of Capitalism.* Boston, MA: Allyn and Bacon, 2001.

STOLLER, PAUL, and CHERYL OLKES. *In Sorcery's Shadow: A Memoir of Apprenticeship Among the Songhay of Niger.* Chicago, IL: University of Chicago Press, 1989.

WARD, TERENCE. *Searching for Hassan: A Journey to the Heart of Iran.* New York: Anchor Books, 2003.

CHAPTER 24

Colonialism and Development

 41. **THE HIMBA AND THE DAM,** by Carol Ezzell, *Scientific American* June 2001 (from website: www.sciam.com/print_version.cfm?articleID=0005596A-DE68-1C6F-84A9809EC588EF21).

Colonialism began with greed—greed for land, greed for power, greed for natural resources, and greed for the control of labor. For several centuries, a small number of European countries used their more sophisticated military power, transportation technology, and political scheming to wrest control of vast regions of the world away from its original inhabitants. Under the European colonial system, the colonies provided raw materials, agricultural products, manufactured goods, and cheap labor for the colonial rulers. The colonial rulers and their compatriots at home in Europe prospered, while many native peoples were killed outright, killed indirectly through disease, or forced into slavery or low-wage jobs against their will. Although most former European colonies fought for and achieved political independence from their European rulers in the latter half of the 20th century (1951–2000), the legacy of colonialism continues to be felt around the world. Political independence has not necessarily meant political or economic stability.

One of the lingering after-effects of colonialism is the existence today of modern nation-states composed of peoples who do not share a single system of cultural beliefs. In some cases, numerous populations—with different ethnic heritages, modes of subsistence, languages, kinship, economic, and political systems, and religious beliefs—were lumped together and expected to coexist peacefully as citizens of the artificially created nation-states. In other cases, people from one cohesive culture were split into two or more different nation-states, because country boundaries were based on watersheds, or rivers, or lines of latitude and longitude. In many instances, descendants of the original colonial rulers continue to live on and control land taken by their ancestors—generations in the past—from the original inhabitants, whose own descendants still live in the region, often in the areas considered too poor or worthless for colonial attention. In a few instances, one particular minority ethnic group cooperated with the colonial rulers and amassed great wealth and power over members of other, larger, ethnic groups. All of these factors have led to continued struggles for peaceful relations amongst peoples in every region of the world.

Another lingering after-effect of colonialism has been, and continues to be, the process of **development,** *whereby the developed countries (former colonial powers and other Western industrial countries such as the United States), try to provide economic and technological aid to developing countries, in order, ostensibly, to improve the local standard of living. While many development schemes have been well intentioned, they have often been poorly planned, not least because the people in charge of the planning didn't understand the fundamental and far-reaching cultural differences between themselves and the people they were trying to help. In other instances, what sounded like an excellent idea at the time turned out to have disastrous economic, political, health, or environmental consequences that no one predicted.*

One of the most difficult cultural gaps to bridge has been that of Westerners trying to understand the value that many traditional peoples put on **place,** *on the landscape and physical geography of their traditional homelands, and their attachment to their traditional lifestyles even in the 21st century. The selection below is about the Himba of northwest Namibia in Africa and how they will be displaced by the building of a hydroelectric dam. It is a story that has been told over and over in different regions of the world—a story that continues to be told, in Africa, in Asia, and in South America—of indigenous peoples' lands and lifeways being sacrificed for "progress" they don't necessarily desire.*

> In our world a dam is a small thing that gives cattle water. What you are talking about is something else and will finish the Himba.
>
> —Chief Katjira Muniombar

Not until we stand on a ridge overlooking the Kunene River—which forms part of the border between the southern African nations of Angola and Namibia—does tribal leader Jakatunga Tjiuma comprehend the immensity of the proposed dam. "Look there," I tell him with the help of an interpreter, pointing to a distant notch in the river gorge that a feasibility study says would be the most likely site of the wall of concrete. "That's where the dam would be."

Turning, I point to hills in the east. "And the water would back up behind the dam to make a lake that would stretch to there." I can see the shock and incredulity in his eyes as he begins to understand how high the water would rise up the faraway hillsides, flooding more than 140 square miles of Himba settlements, grazing land and grave sites. He clutches a blanket around his shoulders and crouches on a rock, speechless.

Tjiuma is a counselor to one of the headmen for the Himba tribe, an essentially self-sufficient band of 16,000 people who eke out an existence from the barren, rocky terrain of northwest Namibia, living off the milk and meat of their cattle and goats, along with the occasional pumpkin or melon. The Himba are sometimes called the Red People because they traditionally cover their bodies, hair and the animal skins they wear with a mixture of butterfat and a powder ground from the iron ore ocher. They say they use the ocher-butter mixture because they like the way it looks, although it undoubtedly also protects their skin against the arid climate.

For decades, the Himba have lived in relative isolation. No other tribes wanted their hardscrabble land, and the Germans who colonized the area in the late 19th century rarely interacted with them. More recently, the Himba's main contact with outsiders has been with soldiers during the fight for Namibia's independence from South Africa (which was won in 1990), with marauding combatants spilling over from Angola's ongoing civil war, and with the occasional caravan of hippie Americans or Europeans. But if the Namibian government has its way, by 2008 more than 1,000 foreign workers will have settled in a temporary village just downstream from Epupa Falls, the site the government favors for the dam.

With them will come a cash economy, alcohol, prostitution and AIDS—as well as improved roads, better access to medical care, schools and perhaps even electricity.

The situation surrounding the proposed dam on the Kunene River can be viewed as a microcosm of dam projects around the world that are affecting indigenous peoples. A survey by the World Commission on Dams, which issued its controversial final report last November, found that 68 of the 123 dams worldwide they studied would displace people, many of them in tribes that had little prior contact with the technological world. The largest dam project, the massive Three Gorges Dam on the Yangtze River, will require the resettlement of up to two million Chinese. Nearly all the dams will change local peoples' livelihoods and cultures—for good or ill, or some combination of the two.

How should global society weigh the right of such peoples to be left alone against, in some cases, the very real necessity for developing countries to take advantage of their resources? Should such countries have the autonomy to decide what is in the best interests of all their citizens, even if some of them don't want to change? Perhaps most important, how can traditional peoples decide such issues for themselves when they have only a shaky idea of how more developed societies live and what they might be getting themselves into?

Into the Desert

Kaokoland, the corner of Namibia where the Himba live, is truly the back of beyond. We arrive at Epupa Falls, the modest waterfall on the Kunene River that would be inundated by the dam's reservoir, two days after leaving the last tarred road. Our 4x4 truck is packed with everything from jerricans of gasoline (the closest gas pump is a day's drive away) to cases of bottled water, spare tires, emergency medical supplies, camping gear, and small gifts of tobacco, sugar and blankets. Tied to the top of our vehicle is a brand-new bicycle—the payment requested by our Himba translator, Staygon Reiter, in exchange for his services, although how he will use it in this inhospitable landscape I don't know. He has asked specifically that the bicycle come equipped with a carrier basket large enough to hold a goat.

Much of our journey is bumpy, jerky and slow as we attempt to follow the rough track while swerving to avoid washouts and potentially tire-puncturing rocks. More than once we get stuck in sand while trying to cross a dry riverbed, our tires spinning and squealing until we jump out to deflate them a bit or to stuff branches behind them for traction. At one point we stop to look at a particularly large scorpion in our path; I comment that I've seen smaller lobsters.

The settlement at Epupa Falls, where we camp, is a kind of crossroads, a no-man's-land where Namibian Himba mix with their Himba relatives from across the river in Angola and with other tribes such as the Herero—to whom the Himba are closely related—as well as with the Zemba, Thwa and Ngambwe. There is a modest thatched church built by missionaries; a tiny but deluxe safari camp; a corrugated-metal store that sells mostly bags of cheap tobacco, maize meal, and tepid Coke, Sprite and Fanta; and a community-run campsite where visitors like us can pitch a tent under the palmlike omerungu trees for 50 Namibian dollars (about US$6) per night. Scarcely any people live at the settlement permanently: the Himba come for a few weeks or months at a time and build temporary huts while they attend funerals, divide inheritances, sell cattle, conduct other business, and visit with friends and relatives.

Our first stop is to meet Chief Hikuminwe Kapika at his compound near Epupa Falls, which is part of the territory he controls. It is immediately clear that Kapika—who is one of roughly a dozen Himba chiefs—is sick of talking about the proposed dam with outsiders but eager for us to appreciate the importance of his rank. From his shock of grayish hair and weathered face, I guess him to be in his 70s, although Himba don't have a calendar system, so they usually don't know the year in which they were born. He keeps us standing beside his white metal camp chair (the only one in his compound) swatting flies from our faces as I try to catch his attention long enough to answer my questions. Several times during our interview he spits through a gap in his front teeth created in his teens when, in keeping with Himba tradition, his lower two central incisors were knocked out and the top two filed to create a V-shaped opening. He makes a point of demonstrating what a busy man he is by continuing to sew a black fabric loincloth and interrupting our translator to correct a group of rowdy children.

Eventually Kapika tells us that he vehemently opposes the proposed dam. He is afraid that the people who will come to build it will steal the Himba's cattle—not an irrational fear, because the Himba were nearly wiped out at the end of the 19th century as a result of cattle raids by the Nama tribe, which lives to the south. And cattle theft continues today. He is also worried that the newcomers will take valuable grazing land, which the Himba are careful not to overuse. Family groups move their households several times a year so that extensively grazed regions can grow back. The area around Kapika's compound illustrates the need for such conservation: the cattle and goats have eaten everything green they can reach, leaving the bushes and trees top-heavy with scraggly growth overhanging trunks like lollipop sticks.

Himba leaders also object to the dam because it would flood hundreds of graves, which play a central role in the tribe's religious beliefs and social structure. In times of crisis, family patriarchs consult their forebears through special ceremonies at grave sites, and graves are often used to settle disputes over access to land. Acreage is owned communally, but each permanent settlement is guarded by an "owner of the land," usually the oldest man of the family who has lived at that place for the longest time. When deciding who should be able to graze their cattle in a particular area, Himba compare the number of ancestors they have buried there. They ask, "Whose ancestral graves are older, ours or theirs?"

Kapika says the Himba will resist and fight "with stones and spears" if the Namibian government tries to build a hydroelectric dam at Epupa Falls. "I'm a big man," he tells us. "I'm a man who can stand on his own."

Dammed If They Do

How do you describe a megadam to someone who has never seen electricity? Or a building more than one story high? The dam planned for Epupa Falls would rise 535 feet—only 15 feet shorter than the massive Grand Coulee Dam in Washington State. It would generate 360 megawatts of electricity per day and cost more than US$500 million to build.

A dam was first proposed near Epupa Falls in 1969, when Namibia was South West Africa, a territory of South Africa. The idea went nowhere, but it was revived in 1991, a year after Namibia's independence, when Namibia and Angola commissioned a feasibility study to evaluate such a scheme. The study considered two sites for the dam: Epupa Falls and a spot in the Baynes Mountains farther downstream. It concluded that Epupa Falls made more economic sense, but Angola has favored the Baynes site in part because building a dam there would mean that the country would also get funds to renovate a dam on an Angolan tributary that was damaged during the civil war. That cost is one reason the Baynes site would be more expensive.

When the study's consultants first came to discuss the intended dam with the Himba, the tribal leaders initially had no objections, thinking it was going to be a small earthen dam like the ones they built to help water their cattle. The degree of miscommunication took a while to become apparent. Margaret Jacobsohn of Integrated Rural Development and Nature Conservation, a Namibian journalist turned anthropologist who worked on the social impact part of the feasibility study, recalls a telling incident a few months into the process. She went to visit a Himba family compound near Epupa Falls and began asking their views about the proposed dam. Oddly, they didn't seem to know anything about it, even though the Namibian government had told her that they had been informed. As she finished her questionnaire, a family member asked her to help them with a mysterious piece of paper they had received some time before. When the man brought an ocher-smeared envelope out of his hut, she recognized it as a letter about the dam in English that they had never even opened. After she translated it for them, an old man of the family shook his head and said, "You're talking about the great death of the Himba."

Lifeways of the Himba

The Himba are one of the last tribes of traditional people who are generally self-supporting and fully or partially isolated from global society. Anthropologists find them particularly interesting because they observe a system of bilateral descent. Every tribe member belongs to two clans, one through the father (a patriclan) and another through the mother (a matriclan). Tribes that practice bilateral descent are rare: besides the Himba, the custom occurs among only a few peoples in West Africa, India, Australia, Melanesia and Polynesia.

Each Himba patriclan is led by the oldest man in the family. Sons live with their fathers; following marriage, daughters leave to join their husband's family's household and become a member of that patriclan. But the inheritance of material wealth—in the Himba's case, primarily cattle—is determined by the matriclan. Accordingly, a son does not inherit his father's cattle but his maternal uncle's instead.

Bilateral descent is particularly advantageous for tribes that live in precarious environments, such as the drought-prone region of the Himba, because during a crisis it allows an individual to rely on two sets of relatives spread over different areas. The system could also play a role in alleviating inbreeding among Himba livestock. Various patriclans have taboos prohibiting their members from owning cattle or goats of a certain color or coat pattern. When cattle are born that violate a patriclan's taboos, they must be swapped with nonoffending cattle from another patriclan.

The religion of the Himba is also organized according to bilateral descent and is practiced through an individual's patriclan. Himba believe in a god-creator, but that entity is very remote from human affairs and can be petitioned only by invoking dead paternal ancestors to act as intercessors. The tribe's religious observances center on holy fires that were initially kindled at the graves of ancestors and are maintained by the leader of each respective patriclan in his family compound.

The holy fire is small, often just a smoldering log surrounded by several rocks. It is always located between the opening of the headman's hut and the corral where the cattle are penned at night. That area of the compound is considered sacred: strangers cannot cross between the holy fire and the corral or between the holy fire and the headman's hut without first asking permission. Traditionally, the headman keeps the fire going during the day as he sits by it to commune with his ancestors about any problems facing the family. At night, the headman's wife takes an ember of the fire into the main hut; in the morning, the ember is taken outside to the hearth again.

The Himba are also intriguing to anthropologists as subjects of rapid social change. One way in which this change is manifesting itself is in patterns of dress. Many more Himba men than Himba women have adopted Western clothing and hairstyles. At Epupa Falls, where Himba occasionally have contact with outsiders, a Himba man can be seen one day bare-chested and wearing a Himba apron-skirt and jewelry, and the next day dressed in pants and a shirt. Few young men there wear the "bachelor ponytail" that is traditional for unmarried men, and even fewer married men follow the custom of not cutting their hair and of covering their heads with a cloth. And it is extremely rare to find a Himba man at Epupa Falls who wears ocher: indeed, many wash daily in the Kunene River using soap.

Himba women, however, are much more conservative in their dress. Even at Epupa Falls, most of the women go bare-breasted and wear traditional apron-skirts made of calfskins or goatskins; they smear themselves liberally from head to toe every morning with the ocher-butter mixture and almost never use water to wash. Young girls wear their hair in two thick braids that drape over their foreheads and faces, whereas women have a cascade of long, thin braids, each of which they coat with a mud mixture that dries to a hard shell.

According to anthropologists, Himba women are not merely clinging passively to their traditional dress: they are actively rejecting change because it is the only way they can maintain their prestige and value. Himba men occasionally earn money doing menial jobs or selling livestock, but Himba women have not had such opportunities. By preserving their ocher-covered bodies, braids and calfskin skirts, Himba women are engaged in what modern anthropological theory calls "change through continuity" or "active conservatism." "Remaining apparently traditional can be a strategic—and rational—response to modern events," Margaret Jacobsohn says.

The recent report by the World Commission on Dams declares that tribal peoples such as the Himba, whether they are actively conservative or not, often get caught between a dam and a hard place. Such projects have "inadequately addressed the special needs and vulnerabilities of indigenous and tribal peoples," the report concludes, adding that the effects of a dam on local peoples are "often not acknowledged or considered in the planning process." It calls for improving existing water and energy facilities rather than constructing new megadams and stipulates that sponsoring countries and international lenders base their decisions to build new dams on agreements with affected communities.

But in February the World Bank said it would use the commission's guidelines only as "reference points" rather than as binding procedures for financing large dam projects. A group of 150 nongovernmental organizations from 39 countries—including Namibia—countered in March with a letter to World Bank president James Wolfensohn to reconsider that stance and to place a moratorium on funding new dams until the bank implements the commission's guidelines. The organizations are requesting that the bank conduct independent reviews of planned and ongoing projects and set up procedures for providing reparations to people harmed by earlier dams. In the letter, they insinuate that the World Bank helped create the World Commission on Dams in 1998 with the World Conservation Union—IUCN only "to deflect opposition or to buy time." Unless the bank amends its position, they write, they "may be less inclined to engage in future . . . dialogues with the World Bank." According to the commission, the bank has provided an estimated $75 billion for 538 large dams in 92 countries.

So what is the case for a dam at Epupa Falls? Jesaya Nyamu, Namibia's minister of mines and energy, emphasizes that his country currently imports 60 percent of its power from South Africa and needs to pull the plug as a matter of national sovereignty. "No one seems to see our need for independent power," he laments.

Ensconced in the deep upholstery of a sofa in his cabinet minister's office in Windhoek, Namibia's capital, he labels the foreign environmental groups that oppose the dam as meddlers with a double standard: one for their own industrial countries and another for countries they consider untouched and exotic. "The whole of Europe and America is dammed," Nyamu says. "These people live in their own countries on hydropower."

Indeed, according to a trade group of dam builders, the International Commission on Large Dams, the U.S. has the second-largest number of large dams (higher than 90 meters) in the world, after China. And the American experience with dams and indigenous peoples is less than laudatory: the Grand Coulee Dam inundated the lands of Native Americans from the Colville and Spokane tribes and ruined their salmon fishery. The tribes sued for reparations in 1951, but the government took 43 years to settle the lawsuit. In 1994 the tribes accepted a $54-million lump sum and $15 million per year as long as the dam produces electricity.

But Katuutire Kaura, president of Namibia's main opposition party, the Democratic Turnhalle Alliance/United Democratic Front Coalition, contends that another dam on the Kunene River is "absolutely not necessary." An existing dam that was built in the 1970s upstream at Ruacana is running at less than 20 percent capacity, he points out. And the recently discovered Kudu gas field off Namibia's southern coast is estimated to contain 20 trillion cubic feet of natural gas—more than enough for Namibia's needs. "The Kudu gas field can last us 25 to 30 years," Kaura asserts. Shell Oil and the Namibian government are currently working to tap those gas fields.

Kaura adds that the Himba will reap few of the dam's benefits while paying high costs. They are not qualified to work on the dam, so it will not bring them jobs. They are also unlikely to get electricity from the project. Electricity did not come to the residents of Opuwo, the town closest to the Ruacana Dam, until 1994, more than 20 years after it was built. In the meantime, a dam at Epupa Falls would destroy the Himba's livelihood. It "will dislocate the Himba to the margins of society where they cannot survive," predicts Phil Ya Nangoloh, executive director of Namibia's National Society for Human Rights.

In a way, the dam will take the river away from the Himba and confer its benefits to people outside Kaokoland. According to the World Commission on Dams report, "Dams take a set of resources . . . generating food and livelihood for local people and transform them into another set of resources . . . providing benefits to people living elsewhere. There is a sense, therefore, in which large dams export rivers and lands."

Toward a Struggle?

One morning when Tjiuma comes to our camp to share a cup of coffee, I ask him what he really thinks will happen if the government goes ahead with its plans for the proposed dam. I know he is no stranger to combat, having been drafted as a tracker to fight on South Africa's side during the war for independence. As we gaze over the Kunene River in the still of the early morning, he admits that the Himba have a plan for resistance. More than 50 of the Himba headmen were in the military during the war, he says, and they still have their old .303 rifles in their compounds.

A week later, when I visit the minister of mines and energy in Windhoek, I tentatively ask him what the Namibian government would do if the Himba resist with violence. His response is chilling: "We know them; they cannot do anything. If they try anything, we will neutralize them, of course. But I don't think it will come to that."

Discussion Questions

1. Where do the Himba live? How much contact, and of what kind, do the Himba have with global society?
2. Briefly describe their traditional lifeways.
3. Why does the Namibian government want to build a dam that will flood Himba lands?
4. What will be the advantages of the dam for the Himba and for the country of Namibia? What will be the disadvantages for each?
5. Why does Chief Kapika oppose the dam? Are his fears justified?
6. What difference will it make if rising waters behind the dam flood the Himba's ancestral gravesites?
7. How did the Namibian government tell the Himba about their plans for the dam? Why was this not a very effective means of communication?
8. Describe the kinship and descent system of the Himba. Why are the Himba said to be of particular interest to anthropologists?
9. What is the significance of the holy fire?
10. What differences are there between the degree of cultural change, or assimilation to Western ways of dress, between Himba men and women? Why have the women refused to change?
11. Why does the Namibian national government say that the dam is necessary? What other sources of electrical power might they use?

12. Do you think the Himba can be successful at resisting the government's plan to build a dam?

13. Like the Himba, the Gwich'In of North America want to continue to follow their traditional lifeways, which are based on reindeer herds. Drilling for oil in this region, as proposed repeatedly by Republicans in the U.S. government over the past decade, will lead to environmental destruction, the loss of breeding grounds for the reindeer, and the end of traditional Gwich'In lifeways. Some people think that is a small price to pay for a potential domestic supply of energy. Think about how to place a value on the persistence of the traditional lifeways of a small group of people, versus the value of creating electricity for a nation-state to use in development. Whose rights should prevail? Who gets to decide? Are compromises or alternative solutions feasible?

14. After you read the final selection in this reader, "Patio Man and the Sprawl People," revisit this issue and think about what the people in the United States will most likely do with the oil from Gwich'In reserves. If there are "Patio People" in Namibia, are their needs for electricity worth the demise of the Himba?

Additional Resources

For Internet links related to this chapter, please visit our website at www.mhhe.com/dettwyler

BODLEY, JOHN H. *Anthropology and Contemporary Human Problems.* 3rd ed. New York: McGraw-Hill, 1994.

BODLEY, JOHN H. *Victims of Progress.* 4th ed. New York: McGraw-Hill, 1998.

CHETHAM, DEIRDRE. *Before the Deluge: The Vanishing World of the Yangtze's Three Gorges.* New York: Palgrave Macmillan, 2002.

CRANDALL, DAVID P. *The Place of Stunted Ironwood Trees: A Year in the Lives of the Cattle-Herding Himba of Namibia.* New York: Continuum Pub. Group, 2000.

CROSBY, ALFRED W. *Ecological Imperialism: The Biological Expansion of Europe, 900–1900.* New York: Cambridge University Press, 1993.

CURTIN, PHILIP D. *The World and the West: The European Challenge and the Overseas Response in the Age of Empire.* New York: Cambridge University Press, 2002.

FLYVBJERG, BENT, NILS BRUZELIUS, and WERNER ROTHENGATTER. *Megaprojects and Risk: An Anatomy of Ambition.* New York: Cambridge University Press, 2003.

HESSLER, PETER. "Letter from China: Underwater," *The New Yorker,* July 7, 2003.

LUCKE, LEWIS W. *Waiting for Rain: Life and Development in Mali, West Africa.* Hanover, MA: Christopher Publishing House, 1998.

LUK, SHIU-HUNG, and JOSEPH WHITNEY, eds. *Megaproject: A Case Study of China's Three Gorges Project.* Armonk, NY: M. E. Sharpe, 1993.

MADSEN, KEN, and NORMA KASSI. *Under the Arctic Sun: Gwich'In, Caribou, and the Arctic National Wildlife Refuge.* Englewood, CO: Westcliffe Publishers, 2002.

QING, DAI. *The River Dragon Has Come!: The Three Gorges Dam and the Fate of China's Yangtze River and Its People.* Armonk, NY: M. E. Sharpe, 1998.

CHAPTER 25

Cultural Exchange and Survival

42. "Birth," by Anne Fadiman, *The Spirit Catches You and You Fall Down: A Hmong Child, Her American Doctors, and the Collision of Two Cultures.* New York: Farrar, Straus & Giroux (1997).

43. "Patio Man and the Sprawl People," by David Brooks, *The Weekly Standard,* August 12/August 19, 2002 issue (from website: www.weeklystandard.com/ Content/Public/Articles/000/000/001/531wlvng.asp).

For the final chapter of our reader, we have chosen two very different selections that illustrate themes of cultural exchange and survival in the United States. The United States is, in many ways, a unique place in which to live and grow up. We are mostly a nation of immigrants. People have come from all over the world, starting with Native Americans migrating from Asia across the Bering Land Bridge on foot or in boats along the north Pacific coast many thousands of years ago. My (KAD) father's ancestors came from Scotland in the mid-1700s, my mother's from England via Canada in the mid-1800s; my husband's grandparents immigrated to the United States from Switzerland through Ellis Island in 1923. Since 1492 there has been a steady stream of immigrants from Europe (first, western and northern Europe; later, central, southern, and eastern Europe) and West Africa (mostly via the slave trade), followed by people from every region of the world. People still immigrate to the United States in large numbers. People come here for economic and educational opportunities, seeking better health and better lives. Some people come as refugees, fleeing difficult political situations in their homelands.

Once people arrive, bringing with them different traditions and ways of doing things, they begin to change and adapt. Some of this change is voluntary and some, coerced. Some aspects of culture change relatively quickly, while others persist for generations (especially language and foodways). Some aspects of a particular culture, or people from some particular regions, may fit easily into the multicultural, multiethnic hodgepodge of beliefs and behaviors that comprise modern American culture. As we saw in Stoller's article in Chapter 23, people may be able to move right into a community of their compatriots who migrated earlier. They can move into a neighborhood where people speak the language, eat the foods, practice the religion, and generally follow the cultural patterns of the home country. As time passes, immigrants may change drastically, or hardly at all, or they may keep moving, always seeking to improve their lot in life and to provide a good life for their children. Sometimes this process is easy, and sometimes it is immensely difficult.

As you read the following book excerpt and magazine article, think about how cultural beliefs and traditions come into conflict in the United States, a nation of immigrants, and how the descendants of immigrants continue to change and adapt through the generations.

42. BIRTH

Our first selection, "Birth," is the first chapter of Anne Fadiman's 1997 book The Spirit Catches You and You Fall Down: A Hmong Child, Her American Doctors, and the Collision of Two Cultures. *The book tells the story of the Lees, a family of Hmong refugees in central California, whose daughter Lia develops a particularly complicated and intractable seizure disorder, which her family attributes to "soul loss." The book divides its time between descriptions of Hmong culture and history, especially the role Hmong played as U.S. allies during the Vietnam War, and an in-depth examination of the fallout for one family from the "collision of two cultures." The two cultures were those of the Lees and her U.S. medical providers. Both groups of people wanted to help Lia recover from her seizures, but the cultural gaps were unbridgeable—not just in terms of language, education, and economic status, but in terms of fundamental differences in beliefs about the nature of the world, the nature of illness, the nature of healing, what constitutes a valuable life, and what makes a good parent or a good doctor.*

This excerpt from the book constitutes only the beginning of Lia Lee's story, starting with her birth in 1982. When the book ends, she is in a vegetative state due to a series of massive seizures in 1986 (the simple, Western medical explanation). As of 2003, Lia is still alive, still in a vegetative state, and still living at home in California, lovingly cared for by her family. Anne Fadiman writes today: "The period the book is mainly about is the early to mid-1980s—in other words, the years right after the first Hmong refugees arrived in the United States . . . The beliefs of Hmong-Americans are far less homogeneous in 2003 than they were then. Older, traditional Hmong are likely to hew to most of the beliefs and practices described in the book; younger Hmong, born and educated in the United States, are more likely today to follow a mixture of traditional and Americanized beliefs and practices." We hope that you will be inspired to read the rest of the book on your own.

If Lia Lee had been born in the highlands of northwest Laos, where her parents and twelve of her brothers and sisters were born, her mother would have squatted on the floor of the house that her father had built from ax-hewn planks thatched with bamboo and grass. The floor was dirt, but it was clean. Her mother, Foua, sprinkled it regularly with water to keep the dust down and swept it every morning and evening with a broom she had made of grass and bark. She used a bamboo dustpan, which she had also made herself, to collect the feces of the children who were too young to defecate outside, and emptied its contents in the forest. Even if Foua had been a less fastidious housekeeper, her newborn babies wouldn't have gotten dirty, since she never let them actually touch the floor. She remains proud to this day that she delivered each of them into her own hands, reaching between her legs to ease out the head and then letting the rest of the body slip out onto her bent forearms. No birth attendant was present, though if her throat became dry during labor, her husband, Nao Kao, was permitted to bring her a cup of hot water, as long as he averted his eyes from her body. Because Foua believed that moaning or screaming would thwart the birth, she labored in silence, with the exception of an occasional prayer to her ancestors. She was so quiet that although most of her babies were born at night, her older children slept undisturbed on a communal bamboo pallet a few feet away, and woke only when they heard the cry of their new brother or sister. After each birth, Nao Kao cut the umbilical cord with heated scissors and tied it with string. Then Foua washed the baby with water she had carried from the stream, usually in the early phases of labor, in a wooden and bamboo pack-barrel strapped to her back.

Foua conceived, carried, and bore all her children with ease, but had there been any problems, she would have had recourse to a variety of remedies that were commonly used by the Hmong, the hilltribe to which her family belonged. If a Hmong couple failed to produce children, they could call in a *txiv neeb,* a shaman who was believed to have the ability to enter a trance, summon a posse of helpful familiars, ride a winged horse over the twelve mountains between the earth and the sky, cross an ocean inhabited by dragons, and (starting with bribes of food and money and, if necessary, working up to a necromantic sword) negotiate for his patients' health with the spirits who lived in the realm of the unseen. A *txiv neeb* might be able to cure infertility by asking the couple to sacrifice a dog, a cat, a chicken, or a sheep. After the animal's throat was cut, the *txiv neeb* would string a rope bridge from the doorpost to the marriage bed, over which the soul of the couple's future baby, which had been detained by a malevolent spirit called a *dab,* could now freely travel to earth. One could also take certain precautions to avoid becoming infertile in the first place. For example, no Hmong woman of childbearing age would ever think of setting foot inside a cave,,because a particularly unpleasant kind of *dab* sometimes lived there who liked to eat flesh and drink blood and could make his victim sterile by having sexual intercourse with her.

Once a Hmong woman became pregnant, she could ensure the health of her child by paying close attention to her food cravings. If she craved ginger and failed to eat it, her child would be born with an extra finger or toe. If she craved chicken flesh and did not eat it, her child would have a blemish near its ear. If she craved eggs and did not eat them, her child would have a lumpy head. When a Hmong woman felt the first pangs of labor, she would hurry home from the rice or opium fields, where she had continued to work throughout her pregnancy. It was important to reach her own house, or at least the house of one of her husband's cousins, because if she gave birth anywhere else a *dab* might injure her. A long or arduous labor could be eased by drinking the water in which a key had been boiled, in order to unlock the birth canal; by having her family array bowls of sacred water around the room and chant prayers over them; or, if the difficulty stemmed from having treated an elder member of the family with insufficient respect, by washing the offended relative's fingertips and apologizing like crazy until the relative finally said, "I forgive you."

Soon after the birth, while the mother and baby were still lying together next to the fire pit, the father dug a hole at least two feet deep in the dirt floor and buried the placenta. If it was a girl, her placenta was buried under her parents' bed; if it was a boy, his placenta was buried in a place of greater honor, near the base of the house's central wooden pillar, in which a male spirit, a domestic guardian who held up the roof of the house and watched over its residents, made his home. The placenta was always buried with the smooth side, the side that had faced the fetus inside the womb, turned upward, since if it was upside down, the baby might vomit after nursing. If the baby's face erupted in spots, that meant the placenta was being attacked by ants underground, and boiling water was poured into the burial hole as an insecticide. In the Hmong language, the word for placenta means "jacket." It is considered one's first and finest garment. When a Hmong dies, his or her soul must travel back from place to place, retracing the path of its life geography, until it reaches the burial place of its placental jacket, and puts it on. Only after the soul is properly dressed in the clothing in which it was born can it continue its dangerous journey, past murderous *dabs* and giant poisonous caterpillars, around man-eating rocks and impassable oceans, to the place beyond the sky where it is reunited with its ancestors and from which it will someday be sent to be reborn as the soul of a new baby. If the soul cannot find its jacket, it is condemned to an eternity of wandering, naked and alone.

Because the Lees are among the 150,000 Hmong who have fled Laos since their country fell to communist forces in 1975, they do not know if their house is still standing, or if the five male and seven female placentas that Nao Kao buried under the dirt floor are still there. They believe that half of the placentas have already been put to their final use, since four of their sons and two of their daughters died of various causes before the Lees came to the United States. The Lees believe that someday the souls of most of the rest of their family will have a long way to travel, since they will have to retrace their steps from Merced, California, where the family has spent fifteen of its seventeen years in this country; to Portland, Oregon, where they lived before Merced; to Honolulu, Hawaii, where their airplane from Thailand first landed; to two Thai refugee camps; and finally back to their home village in Laos.

The Lees' thirteenth child, Mai, was born in a refugee camp in Thailand. Her placenta was buried under their hut. Their fourteenth child, Lia, was born in the Merced Community Medical Center, a modern public hospital that serves an agricultural county in California's Central Valley, where many Hmong refugees have resettled. Lia's placenta was incinerated. Some Hmong women have asked the doctors at MCMC, as the hospital is commonly called, if they could take their babies' placentas home. Several of the doctors have acquiesced, packing the placentas in plastic bags or take-out containers from the hospital cafeteria; most have refused, in some cases because they have assumed that the women planned to eat the placentas, and have found that idea disgusting, and in some cases because they have feared the possible spread of hepatitis B, which is carried by at least fifteen percent of the Hmong refugees in the United States. Foua never thought to ask, since she speaks no English, and when she delivered Lia, no one present spoke Hmong. In any case, the Lees' apartment had a wooden floor covered with wall-to-wall carpeting, so burying the placenta would have been a difficult proposition.

When Lia was born, at 7:09 p.m. on July 19, 1982, Foua was lying on her back on a steel table, her body covered with sterile drapes, her genital area painted with a brown Betadine solution, with a high-wattage lamp trained on her perineum. There were no family members in the room. Gary Thueson, a family practice resident who did the delivery, noted in the chart that in order to speed the labor, he had artificially ruptured Foua's amniotic sac by poking it with a foot-long plastic "amni-hook"; that no anesthesia was used; that no episiotomy, an incision to enlarge the vaginal opening, was necessary; and that after the birth, Foua received a standard intravenous dose of Pitocin to constrict her uterus. Dr. Thueson also noted that Lia was a "healthy infant" whose weight, 8 pounds 7 ounces, and condition were "appropriate for gestational age" (an estimate he based on observation alone, since Foua had received no prenatal care, was not certain how long she had been pregnant, and could not have told Dr. Thueson even if she had known). Foua thinks that Lia was her largest baby, although she isn't sure, since none of her thirteen elder children were weighed at birth. Lia's Apgar scores, an assessment of a newborn infant's heart rate, respiration, muscle tone, color, and reflexes, were good: one minute after her birth she scored 7 on a scale of 10, and four minutes later she scored 9. When she was six minutes old, her color was described as "pink" and her activity as "crying." Lia was shown briefly to her mother. Then she was placed in a steel and Plexiglas warmer, where a nurse fastened a plastic identification band around her wrist and recorded her footprints by inking the soles of her feet with a stamp pad and pressing them against a Newborn Identification form. After that, Lia was removed to the central nursery, where she received an injection of Vitamin K in one of her thighs to prevent hemorrhagic disease; was treated with two drops of silver nitrate solution in each eye, to prevent an infection from gonococcal bacteria; and was bathed with Safeguard soap.

Foua's own date of birth was recorded on Lia's Delivery Room Record as October 6, 1944. In fact, she has no idea when she was born, and on various other occasions during the next several years she would inform MCMC personnel, through English-speaking relatives such as the nephew's wife who had helped her check into the hospital for Lia's delivery, that her date of birth was October 6, 1942, or, more frequently, October 6, 1926. Not a single admitting clerk ever appears to have questioned the latter date, though it would imply that Foua gave birth to Lia at the age of 55. Foua is quite sure, however, that October is correct, since she was told by her parents that she was born during the season in which the opium fields are weeded for the second time and the harvested rice stalks are stacked. She invented the precise day of the month, like the year, in order to satisfy the many Americans who have evinced an abhorrence of unfilled blanks on the innumerable forms the Lees have encountered since their admission to the United States in 1980. Most Hmong refugees are familiar with this American trait and have accommodated it in the same way. Nao Kao Lee has a first cousin who told the immigration officials that all nine of his children were born on July 15, in nine consecutive years, and this information was duly recorded on their resident alien documents.

When Lia Lee was released from MCMC, at the age of three days, her mother was asked to sign a piece of paper that read:

I CERTIFY that during the discharge procedure I received my baby, examined it and determined that it was mine. I checked the Ident-A-Band® parts sealed on the baby and on me and found that they were identically numbered 5043 and contained correct identifying information.

Since Foua cannot read and has never learned to recognize Arabic numerals, it is unlikely that she followed these instructions. However, she had been asked for her signature so often in the United States that she had mastered the capital forms of the seven different letters contained in her name, Foua Yang. (The Yangs and the Lees are among the largest of the Hmong clans; the other major ones are the Chas, the Chengs, the Hangs, the Hers, the Kues, the Los, the Mouas, the Thaos, the Vues, the Xiongs, and the Vangs. In Laos, the clan name came first, but most Hmong refugees in the United States use it as a surname. Children belong to their father's clan; women traditionally retain their clan name after marriage. Marrying a member of one's own clan is strictly taboo.) Foua's signature is no less legible than the signatures of most of MCMC's resident physicians-in-training, which, particularly if they are written toward the end of a twenty-four-hour shift, tend to resemble EEGs. However, it has the unique distinction of looking different each time it appears on a hospital document. On this occasion, FOUAYANG was written as a single word. One A is canted to the left and one to the right, the Y looks like an X, and the legs of the N undulate gracefully, like a child's drawing of a wave.

It is a credit to Foua's general equanimity, as well as her characteristic desire not to think ill of anyone, that although she found Lia's birth a peculiar experience, she has few criticisms of the way the hospital handled it. Her doubts about MCMC in particular, and American medicine in general, would not begin to gather force until Lia had visited the hospital many times. On this occasion, she thought the doctor was gentle and kind, she was impressed that so many people were there to help her, and although she felt that the nurses who bathed Lia with Safeguard did not get her quite as clean as she had gotten her newborns with Laotian stream water, her only major complaint concerned the hospital food. She was surprised to be offered ice water after the birth, since many Hmong believe that cold foods during the postpartum period make the blood congeal in the womb instead of cleansing it by flowing freely, and that a woman who does not observe the taboo against them will develop itchy skin or diarrhea in her old age. Foua did accept several cups of what she remembers as hot black water. This was probably either tea or beef broth; Foua is sure it wasn't coffee, which she had seen before and would have recognized. The black water was the only MCMC-provided food that passed her lips during her stay in the maternity ward. Each day, Nao Kao cooked and brought her the diet that is strictly prescribed for Hmong women during the thirty days following childbirth: steamed rice, and chicken boiled in water with five special postpartum herbs (which the Lees had grown for this purpose on the edge of the parking lot behind their apartment building). This diet was familiar to the doctors on the Labor and Delivery floor at MCMC, whose assessments of it were fairly accurate gauges of their general opinion of the Hmong. One obstetrician, Raquel Arias, recalled, "The Hmong men carried these nice little silver cans to the hospital that always had some kind of chicken soup in them and always smelled great." Another obstetrician, Robert Small, said, "They always brought some horrible stinking concoction that smelled like the chicken had been dead for a week." Foua never shared her meals with anyone, because there is a postpartum taboo against spilling grains of rice accidentally into the chicken pot. If that occurs, the newborn is likely to break out across the nose and cheeks with little white pimples whose name in the Hmong language is the same as the word for "rice."

Some Hmong parents in Merced have given their children American names. In addition to many standard ones, these have included Kennedy, Nixon, Pajama, Guitar, Main (after Merced's Main Street), and, until a nurse counseled otherwise, Baby Boy, which one mother, seeing it written on her son's hospital papers, assumed was the name the doctor had already chosen for him. The Lees chose to give their daughter a Hmong name, Lia. Her name was officially conferred in a ceremony called a *hu plig,* or soul-calling, which in Laos always took place on the third day after birth. Until this ceremony was performed, a baby was not considered to be fully a member of the human race, and if it died during its first three days it was not accorded the customary funerary rites. (This may have been a cultural adaptation to the fifty-percent infant mortality rate, a way of steeling Hmong mothers against the frequent loss of their babies during or shortly after childbirth by encouraging them to postpone their attachment.) In the United States, the naming is usually celebrated at a later time, since on its third day a baby may still be hospitalized, especially if the birth was complicated. It took the Lee family about a month to save enough money from their welfare checks, and from gifts from their relatives' welfare checks, to finance a soul-calling party for Lia.

Although the Hmong believe that illness can be caused by a variety of sources—including eating the wrong food, drinking contaminated water, being affected by a change in the weather, failing to ejaculate completely during sexual intercourse, neglecting to make offerings to one's ancestors, being punished for one's ancestors' transgressions, being cursed, being hit by a whirlwind, having a stone implanted in one's body by an evil spirit master, having one's blood sucked by a *dab,* bumping into a *dab* who lives in a tree or a stream, digging a well in a *dab's* living place, catching sight of a dwarf female *dab* who eats earthworms, having a *dab* sit on one's chest while one is sleeping, doing one's laundry in a lake inhabited by a dragon, pointing one's finger at the full moon, touching a newborn mouse, killing a large snake, urinating on a rock that looks like a tiger, urinating on or kicking a benevolent house spirit, or having bird droppings fall on one's head—by far the most common cause of illness is soul loss. Although the Hmong do not agree on just how many souls people have (estimates range from one to thirty-two; the Lees believe there is just one), there is a general consensus that whatever the number, it is the life-soul, whose presence is necessary for health and happiness, that tends to get lost. A life-soul can become separated from its body through anger, grief, fear, curiosity, or wanderlust. The life-souls of newborn babies are especially prone to disappearance, since they are so small, so vulnerable, and so precariously poised between the realm of the unseen, from which they have just traveled, and the realm of the living. Babies' souls may wander away, drawn by bright colors, sweet sounds, or fragrant smells; they may leave if a baby is sad, lonely, or insufficiently loved by its parents; they may be frightened away by a sudden loud noise; or they may be stolen by a *dab.* Some Hmong are careful never to say aloud that a baby is pretty, lest a *dab* be listening. Hmong babies are often dressed in intricately embroidered hats (Foua made several for Lia) which, when seen from a heavenly perspective, might fool a predatory *dab* into thinking the child was a flower. They spend much of their time swaddled against their mothers' backs in cloth carriers called *nyias* (Foua made Lia several of these too) that have been embroidered with soul-retaining motifs, such as the pigpen, which symbolizes enclosure. They may wear silver necklaces fastened with soul-shackling locks. When babies or small children go on an outing, their parents may call loudly to their souls before the family returns home, to make sure that none remain behind. Hmong families in Merced can sometimes be heard doing this when they leave local parks after a picnic. None of these ploys can work, however, unless the soul-calling ritual has already been properly observed.

Lia's *hu plig* took place in the living room of her family's apartment. There were so many guests, all of them Hmong and most of them members of the Lee and Yang clans, that it was nearly impossible to turn around. Foua and Nao Kao were proud that so many people had come to celebrate their good fortune in being favored with such a healthy and beautiful daughter. That morning Nao Kao had sacrificed a pig in order to invite the soul of one of Lia's ancestors, which was probably hungry and would appreciate an offering of food, to be reborn in her body. After the guests arrived, an elder of the Yang clan stood at the apartment's open front door, facing East 12th Street, with two live chickens in a bag on the floor next to him, and chanted a greeting to Lia's soul. The two chickens were then killed, plucked, eviscerated, partially boiled, retrieved from the cooking pot, and examined to see if their skulls were translucent and their tongues curled upward, both signs that Lia's new soul was pleased to take up residence in her body and that her name was a good one. (If the signs had been inauspicious, the soul-caller would have recommended that another name be chosen.) After the reading of the auguries, the chickens were put back in the cooking pot. The guests would later eat them and the pig for dinner. Before the meal, the soul-caller brushed Lia's hands with a bundle of short white strings and said, "I am sweeping away the ways of sickness." Then Lia's parents and all of the elders present in the room each tied a string around one of Lia's wrists in order to bind her soul securely to her body. Foua and Nao Kao promised to love her; the elders blessed her and prayed that she would have a long life and that she would never become sick.

Discussion Questions

1. Where are the Lees from? Where were they living in the 1980s?
2. Compare Foua's experiences giving birth to her first 12 children in her house in Laos with Lia's birth at the Merced Community Medical Center. How do they differ in terms of who was present, what role the mother played in the birth, the position she assumed for the deliveries, and what happened to her and the baby during labor and delivery and after the birth?
3. What is a *txiv neeb?* What is a *dab?*
4. What do the Hmong believe about the placenta? What do they do with it after the baby is born? What role does it play after a person dies?
5. Imagine that traditional Hmong beliefs about the role of the placenta after death are correct. What does that mean for the souls of all the babies of every ethnicity born in U.S. hospitals, whose placentas are disposed of (incinerated) as medical waste?
6. Why does Fadiman say that "an abhorrence of unfilled blanks" on forms is an American trait? What experiences have you had with providing information about yourself to others for various purposes? Is this American trait—of the government gathering information about its citizens—weakening or becoming stronger in the United States today?
7. What did Foua think of her hospital birth?

8. What did the doctors think of the traditional postpartum chicken soup that Hmong husbands brought their wives after the delivery? How would anthropologists characterize Hmong beliefs about eating various foods during pregnancy and after delivery— are they examples of sympathetic or contagious magic?

9. What is a *hu plig* ceremony? What is its purpose?

10. According to traditional Hmong beliefs, how can a person lose his or her soul? Why are babies particularly susceptible? What are the possible consequences of soul loss for a person's health and happiness?

11. How do the Hmong guard against soul loss in babies?

12. List different ways that parents in the United States try to guard their children against illness and harm. Are there differences among various ethnic groups? Does it depend on how long the family has been in the United States? Why might parents in the United States feel that they have more control over their children's health than traditional Hmong parents had in Laos? Do they really have more control, or is it only an illusion?

43. PATIO MAN AND THE SPRAWL PEOPLE

The next story in this chapter is a wonderful allegory of upper-middle- and upper-class American culture and ideals. In the story, the writer tells us about "Patio Man," a person who has picked up his roots and moved his family to a new suburb called "Sprinkler City." The author points out that at the core of American culture there has always been a frontier spirit. Early in our history, during the 1600s and 1700s, American colonists settled east of the Appalachians, forming many small towns. Soon many of the small towns grew into large cities. With the cities came overcrowding, crime, dirt and grime, and waves of new immigrants. Rather than stay behind and try to fix or change the problems in the growing cities, those who could afford to do so left and headed west to build new towns.

Again and again during the history of the United States this process repeated itself as people built new towns that soon became overcrowded cities with all of the problems inherent to urbanism. One of the last great waves of movement occurred during the 1950s, with the beginning of the American interstate highway system and the economic boom of post–World War II industrialization. Many upper-middle class families left the cities during the 1950s and moved to newly created suburbs with their uniform-looking, ticky-tacky houses lined in neat rows along new, clean streets. Everyone had small, postage-size yards and a house with a garage. Houses were located close enough so that the kids could walk to brand-new schools. Life in the suburbs soon became the American Dream for all those who could afford to move to these new utopias. Left behind in the cities were the growing problems of urbanism and the millions of poor families who could not afford to leave.

As the years passed and those once-new suburbs began to age, the glitter wore off, the houses no longer portrayed the latest fashions, some lawns were always unkempt, and the schools were no longer shiny-new. As the richer families began to leave, they were replaced by waves of new and poorer immigrants. Many of the children, whose parents had first moved from the cities to the new suburbs, now did the "American thing." Rather than stay behind and try to improve the suburbs in which they lived, those who could afford to leave did so. People, such as Patio Man, packed up and headed further out to the new suburbs where they could buy bigger, multi-gabled houses with two or three garages large enough to hold several new SUVs with storage space to spare, mousepad-size yards, and best of all, wide, wooden decks built to support giant barbecue grills for weekend parties. For the new arrivals, this was the new American nirvana. This was Sprinkler City.

The author, David Brooks, is a senior editor at The Weekly Standard, *a contributing editor at* Newsweek *and* The Atlantic Monthly, *and the "Machine Age" columnist for* The New York Times Magazine. *He is also a regular commentator on National Public Radio, CNN's "Late Edition" and "The NewsHour with Jim Lehrer."*

I don't know if you've ever noticed the expression of a man who is about to buy a first-class barbecue grill. He walks into a Home Depot or Lowe's or one of the other mega hardware complexes and his eyes are glistening with a faraway visionary zeal, like one of those old prophets gazing into the promised land. His lips are parted and twitching slightly. Inside the megastore, the grills are just past the racks of affordable-house plan books, in the yard-machinery section. They are arrayed magnificently next to the vehicles that used to be known as rider mowers but are now known as lawn tractors, because to call them rider mowers doesn't really convey the steroid-enhanced M-1 tank power of the things.

The man approaches the barbecue grills and his face bears a trance-like expression, suggesting that he has cast aside all the pains and imperfections of this world and is approaching the gateway to a higher dimension. In front of him are a number of massive steel-coated reactors with names like Broilmaster P3, The Thermidor, and the Weber Genesis, because in America it seems perfectly normal to name a backyard barbecue grill after a book of the Bible.

The items in this cooking arsenal flaunt enough metal to suggest they have been hardened to survive a direct nuclear assault, and Patio Man goes from machine to machine comparing their features—the cast iron/porcelain coated cooking surfaces, the 328,000-BTU heat-generating capacities, the 1,600-degree-tolerance linings, the multiple warming racks, the lava rock containment dishes, the built-in electrical meat thermometers, and so on. Certain profound questions flow through his mind. Is a 542-square-inch grilling surface really enough, considering that he might someday get the urge to roast an uncut buffalo steak? Though the matte steel overcoat resists scratching, doesn't he want a polished steel surface on his grill so he can glance down and admire his reflection as he is performing the suburban manliness rituals, such as brushing tangy sauce on meat slabs with his right hand while clutching a beer can in an NFL foam insulator ring in his left?

Pretty soon a large salesman in an orange vest who looks like a human SUV comes up to him and says, "Howyadoin'," which is, "May I help you?" in Home Depot talk. Patio Man, who has so much lust in his heart it is all he can do to keep from climbing up on one of these machines and whooping rodeo-style with joy, manages to respond appropriately. He grunts inarticulately and nods toward the machines. Careful not to make eye contact at any point, the two manly suburban men have a brief exchange of pseudo-scientific grill argot that neither of them understands, and pretty soon Patio Man has come to the reasoned conclusion that it really does make sense to pay a little extra for a grill with V-shaped metal baffles, ceramic rods, and a side-mounted smoker box. Plus the grill he selects has four insulated drink holders. All major choices of consumer durables these days ultimately come down to which model has the most impressive cup holders.

Patio Man pays for the grill with his credit card, and is told that some minion will forklift his machine over to the loading dock around back. It is yet another triumph in a lifetime of conquest shopping, and as Patio Man heads toward the parking lot he is glad once again that he's driving that Yukon XL so that he can approach the loading dock guys as a co-equal in the manly fraternity of Those Who Haul Things.

He steps out into the parking lot and is momentarily blinded by sun bouncing off the hardtop. The parking lot is so massive that he can barely see the Wal-Mart, the Bed Bath & Beyond, or the area-code-sized Old Navy glistening through the heat there on the other side. This mall is in fact big enough to qualify for membership in the United Nations, and is so vast that shoppers have to drive from store to store, cutting diagonally through the infinity of empty parking spaces in between.

As Patio Man walks past the empty handicapped and expectant-mother parking spots toward his own vehicle, wonderful grill fantasies dance in his imagination: There he is atop the uppermost tier of his multi-level backyard patio/outdoor recreation area posed like an admiral on the deck of his destroyer. In his mind's eye he can see himself coolly flipping the garlic and pepper T-bones on the front acreage of his new grill while carefully testing the citrus-tarragon trout filets that sizzle fragrantly in the rear. On the lawn below he can see his kids, Haley and Cody, frolicking on the weedless community lawn that is mowed twice weekly by the people who run Monument Crowne Preserve, his townhome community.

Haley, 12, is a Travel Team Girl, who spends her weekends playing midfield against similarly pony-tailed, strongly calved soccer marvels. Cody, 10, is a Buzz Cut Boy, whose naturally blond hair has been cut to a lawn-like stubble and dyed an almost phosphorescent white. Cody's wardrobe is entirely derivative of fashions he has seen watching the X-Games.

In his vision, Patio Man can see the kids enjoying their child-safe lawn darts with a gaggle of their cul de sac friends, a happy gathering of Haleys and Codys and Corys and Britneys. It's a brightly colored scene: Abercrombie & Fitch pink spaghetti-strap tops on the girls and ankle length canvas shorts and laceless Nikes on the boys. Patio Man notes somewhat uncomfortably that in America today the average square yardage of boys' fashion grows and grows while the square inches in the girls' outfits shrink and shrink, so that while the boys look like tent-wearing skateboarders, the girls look like preppy prostitutes.

Nonetheless, Patio Man envisions his own adult softball team buddies lounging on his immaculate deck furniture watching him with a certain moist envy in their eyes as he mans the grill. They are fit, sockless men in dock siders, chinos, and Tommy Bahama muted Hawaiian shirts. Their wives, trim Jennifer Aniston women, wear capris and sleeveless tops that look great owing to their many hours of sweat and exercise at Spa Lady. These men and women may not be Greatest Generation heroes, or earthshaking inventors like Thomas Edison, but if Thomas Edison had had a Human Resources Department, and that Human Resources Department had organized annual enrichment and motivational conferences for mid-level management, then these people would have been the marketing executives for the back office outsourcing companies to the meeting-planning firms that hooked up the HR executives with the conference facilities.

They are wonderful people. And Patio Man can envision his own wife, Cindy, a Realtor Mom, circulating amongst them serving drinks, telling parent-teacher conference stories and generally spreading conviviality while he, Patio Man, masterfully runs the grill—again, to the silent admiration of all. The sun is shining. The people are friendly. The men are no more than 25 pounds overweight, which is the socially acceptable male paunch level in upwardly mobile America, and the children are well adjusted. It is a vision of the sort of domestic bliss that Patio Man has been shooting for all his life.

And it's plausible now because two years ago Patio Man made the big move. He pulled up stakes and he moved his family to a Sprinkler City.

Sprinkler Cities are the fast-growing suburbs mostly in the South and West that are the homes of the new style American Dream, the epicenters of Patio Man fantasies. Douglas County, Colorado, which is the fastest-growing county in America and is located between Denver and Colorado Springs, is a Sprinkler City. So is Henderson, Nevada, just outside of Las Vegas. So is Loudoun County, Virginia, near Dulles Airport. So are Scottsdale and Gilbert, Arizona, and Union County, North Carolina.

The growth in these places is astronomical, as Patio Men and their families—and Patio retirees, yuppie geezers who still like to grill, swim, and water ski—flock to them from all over. Douglas County grew 13.6 percent from April 2000 to July 2001, while Loudoun County grew 12.6 percent in that 16-month period. Henderson, Nevada, has tripled in size over the past 10 years and now has over 175,000 people. Over the past 50 years, Irving, Texas, grew by 7,211 percent, from about 2,600 people to 200,000 people.

The biggest of these boom suburbs are huge. With almost 400,000 people, Mesa, Arizona, has a larger population than Minneapolis, Cincinnati, or St. Louis. And this sort of growth is expected to continue. Goodyear, Arizona, on the western edge of the Phoenix area, now has about 20,000 people, but is projected to have 320,000 in 50 years' time. By then, Greater Phoenix could have a population of over 6 million and cover over 10,000 square miles.

Sprinkler Cities are also generally the most Republican areas of the country. In some of the Sprinkler City congressional districts, Republicans have a 2 or 3 or 4 to 1 registration advantage over Democrats. As cultural centers, they represent the *beau ideal* of Republican selfhood, and are becoming the new base—the brains, heart, guts, and soul of the emerging Republican party. Their values are not the same as those found in either old-line suburbs like Greenwich, Connecticut, where a certain sort of Republican used to dominate, or traditional conservative bastions, such as the old South. This isn't even the more modest conservatism found in the midwestern farm belt. In fact, the rising prominence of these places heralds a new style of suburb vs. suburb politics, with the explosively growing Republican outer suburbs vying with the slower-growing and increasingly Democratic inner suburbs for control of the center of American political gravity.

If you stand on a hilltop overlooking a Sprinkler City, you see, stretched across the landscape, little brown puffs here and there where bulldozers are kicking up dirt while building new townhomes, office parks, shopping malls, AmeriSuites guest hotels, and golf courses. Everything in a Sprinkler City is new. The highways are so clean and freshly paved you can eat off them. The elementary schools have spic and span playgrounds, unscuffed walls, and immaculate mini-observatories for just-forming science classes.

The lawns in these places are perfect. It doesn't matter how arid the local land-scape used to be, the developers come in and lay miles of irrigation tubing, and the sprinklers pop up each evening, making life and civilization possible.

The roads are huge. The main ones, where the office parks are, have been given names like Innovation Boulevard and Entrepreneur Avenue, and they've been built for the population levels that will exist a decade from now, so that today you can cruise down these flawless six lane thoroughfares in traffic-less nirvana, and if you get a cell phone call you can just stop in the right lane and take the call because there's no one behind you. The smaller roads in the residential neighborhoods have pretentious names—in Loudoun County I drove down Trajan's Column Terrace—but they too are just as smooth and immaculate as a blacktop bowling alley. There's no use relying on a map to get around these places, because there's no way map pub-lishers can keep up with the construction.

The town fathers try halfheartedly to control sprawl, and as you look over the landscape you can see the results of their ambivalent zoning regulations. The homes aren't spread out with quarter-acre yards, as in the older, close-in suburbs. Instead they are clustered into pseudo-urban pods. As you scan the horizon you'll see a densely packed pod of townhouses, then a stretch of a half mile of investor grass (fields that will someday contain 35,000-square-foot Fresh-Mex restaurants but for now are being kept fallow by investors until the prices rise), and then another pod of slightly more expensive detached homes just as densely packed.

The developments in the southeastern Sprinkler Cities tend to have Mini-McMansion Gable-gable houses. That is to say, these are 3,200-square-foot middle-class homes built to look like 7,000-square-foot starter palaces for the nouveau riche. And on the front at the top, each one has a big gable, and then right in front of it, for visual relief, a little gable jutting forward so that it looks like a baby gable leaning against a mommy gable.

These homes have all the same features as the authentic McMansions of the mid-'90s (as history flows on, McMansions come to seem authentic), but signifi-cantly smaller. There are the same vaulted atriums behind the front doors that never get used, and the same open kitchen/two-story great rooms with soaring palladian windows. But in the middle-class knockoffs, the rooms are so small, especially up-stairs, that a bedroom or a master-bath suite would fit inside one of the walk-in clos-ets of a real McMansion.

In the Southwest the homes tend to be tile and stucco jobs, with tiny mousepad lawns out front, blue backyard spas in the back, and so much white furniture inside that you have to wear sunglasses indoors. As you fly over the Sprinkler Cities you begin to see the rough pattern—a little pseudo-urbanist plop of development, a blank field, a plop, a field, a plop. You also notice that the developers build the roads and sewage lines first and then fill in the houses later, so from the sky you can see cul de sacs stretching off into the distance with no houses around them.

Then, cutting through the landscape are broad commercial thoroughfares with two-tier, big-box malls on either side. In the front tier is a line of highly themed chain restaurants that all fuse into the same Macaroni Grill Olive Outback Cantina Charlie Chiang's Dave & Buster's Cheesecake Factory melange of peppy servers, superfluous ceiling fans, free bread with olive oil, and taco salad entrees. In the 21st-century migration of peoples, the food courts come first and the huddled masses follow.

Then in the back row are all the huge, exposed-air-duct architectural behemoths, which are the big-box stores.

Shopping experiences are now segregated by mood. If you are in the mood for some titillating browsing, you can head over to a Lifestyle Center, which is one of those instant urban streetscapes that developers put up in suburbia as entertainment/ retail/community complexes, complete with pedestrian zones, outdoor cafes, roller rinks, multiplexes, and high-attitude retail concepts such as CP Shades, a chain store that masquerades as a locally owned boutique.

If you are buying necessities, really shopping, there are Power Malls. These are the big-box expanses with Wal-Marts, Kmarts, Targets, price clubs, and all the various Depots (Home, Office, Furniture, etc.). In Sprinkler Cities there are archipelagoes of them—one massive parking lot after another surrounded by huge boxes that often have racing stripes around the middle to break the monotony of the windowless exterior walls.

If one superstore is in one mall, then its competitor is probably in the next one in the archipelago. There's a Petsmart just down from a Petco, a Borders nearby a Barnes & Noble, a Linens 'n Things within sight of a Bed Bath & Beyond, a Best Buy cheek by jowl with a Circuit City. In Henderson, there's a Wal-Mart superstore that spreads over 220,000 square feet, with all those happy greeters in blue vests to make you feel small-town.

There are also smaller stores jammed in between the mega-outlets like little feeder fish swimming around the big boys. On one strip, there might be the ostentatiously unpretentious Total Wine & More, selling a galaxy of casual Merlots. Nearby there might be a Michaels discount women's clothing, a bobo bazaar such as World Market that sells raffia fiber from Madagascar, Rajasthani patchwork coverlets from India, and vermouth-flavored martini onions from Israel, and finally a string of storefront mortgage bankers and realtors serving all the new arrivals. In Sprinkler Cities, there are more realtors than people.

People move to Sprinkler Cities for the same reasons people came to America or headed out West. They want to leave behind the dirt and toxins of their former existence—the crowding and inconvenience, the precedents, and the oldness of what suddenly seems to them a settled and unpromising world. They want to move to some place that seems fresh and new and filled with possibility.

Sprinkler City immigrants are not leaving cities to head out to suburbia. They are leaving older suburbs—which have come to seem as crowded, expensive, and stratified as cities—and heading for newer suburbs, for the suburbia of suburbia.

One of the problems we have in thinking about the suburbs is that when it comes to suburbia the American imagination is motionless. Many people still have in their heads the stereotype of suburban life that the critics of suburbia established in the 1950s. They see suburbia as a sterile, dull, Ozzie and Harriet retreat from the creative dynamism of city life, and the people who live in the suburbs as either hopelessly shallow or quietly and neurotically desperate. (There is no group in America more conformist than the people who rail against suburbanites for being conformist—they always make the same critiques, decade after decade.)

The truth, of course, is that suburbia is not a retreat from gritty American life, it is American life. Already, suburbanites make up about half of the country's population (while city people make up 28 percent and rural folk make up the rest), and America gets more suburban every year.

According to the census data, the suburbs of America's 100 largest metro areas grew twice as fast as their central cities in the 1990s, and that was a decade in which many cities actually reversed their long population slides. Atlanta, for example, gained 23,000 people in the '90s, but its suburbs grew by 1.1 million people.

Moreover, newer suburbs no longer really feed off cities. In 1979, 74 percent of American office space was located in cities, according to the Brookings Institution's Robert Puentes. But now, after two decades in which the biggest job growth has been in suburban office parks, the suburbs' share of total office space has risen to 42 percent. In other words, we are fast approaching a time when the majority of all office space will be in the suburbs, and most Americans not only will not live in cities, they won't even commute to cities or have any regular contact with city life.

Encompassing such a broad swath of national existence, suburbs obviously cannot possibly be the white-bread places of myth and literature. In reality, as the most recent census shows, suburbs contain more non-family houses—young singles and elderly couples—than family households, married couples with children. Nor are they overwhelmingly white. The majority of Asian Americans, half of Hispanics, and 40 percent of American blacks live in suburbia.

And so now there are crucial fault lines not just between city and suburb but between one kind of suburb and another. Say you grew up in some southern California suburb in the 1970s. You graduated from the University of Oregon and now you are a systems analyst with a spouse and two young kids. You're making $65,000 a year, far more than you ever thought you would, but back in Orange County you find you can't afford to live anywhere near your Newport Beach company headquarters. So your commute is 55 minutes each way. Then there's your house itself. You paid $356,000 for a 1962 four-bedroom split level with a drab kitchen, low ceilings, and walls that are chipped and peeling. Your mortgage—that $1,800 a month—is like a tapeworm that devours the family budget.

And then you visit a Sprinkler City in Arizona or Nevada or Colorado—far from the coast and deep into exurbia—and what do you see? Bounteous roads! Free traffic lanes! If you lived here you'd be in commuter bliss—15 minutes from home on Trajan's Column Terrace to the office park on Innovation Boulevard! If you lived here you'd have an extra hour and a half each day for yourself.

And those real estate prices! In, say, Henderson, Nevada, you wouldn't have to spend over $400,000 for a home and carry that murderous mortgage. You could get a home that's brand new, twice the size of your old one, with an attached garage (no flimsy carport), and three times as beautiful for $299,000. The average price of a single-family home in Loudoun County, one of the pricier of the Sprinkler Cities, was $166,824 in 2001, which was an 11 percent increase over the year before. Imagine that! A mortgage under 200 grand! A great anvil would be lifted from your shoulders. More free money for you to spend on yourself. More free time to enjoy. More Freedom!

Plus, if you moved to a Sprinkler City there would be liberation of a subtler kind. The old suburbs have become socially urbanized. They've become stratified. Two sorts of people have begun to move in and ruin the middle-class equality of the development you grew up in: the rich and the poor.

There are, first, the poor immigrants, from Mexico, Vietnam, and the Philippines. They come in, a dozen to a house, and they introduce an element of unpredictability to what was a comforting milieu. They shout. They're less tidy. Their teenage boys seem to get involved with gangs and cars. Suddenly you feel you will lose control of your children. You begin to feel a new level of anxiety in the neighborhood. It is exactly the level of anxiety—sometimes intermingled with racism—your parents felt when they moved from their old neighborhood to the suburbs in the first place.

And then there are the rich. Suddenly many of the old ramblers are being knocked down by lawyers who proceed to erect 4,000-square-foot arts and crafts bungalows with two-car garages for their Volvos. Suddenly cars in the neighborhoods have window and bumper stickers that never used to be there in the past: "Yale," "The Friends School," "Million Mom March." The local stores are changing too. Gone are the hardware stores and barber shops. Now there are Afghan restaurants, Marin County bistros, and environmentally sensitive and extremely expensive bakeries.

And these new people, while successful and upstanding, are also . . . snobs. They're doctors and lawyers and journalists and media consultants. They went to fancy colleges and they consider themselves superior to you if you sell home-security systems or if you are a mechanical engineer, and in subtle yet patronizing ways they let you know it.

I recently interviewed a woman in Loudoun County who said she had grown up and lived most of her life in Bethesda, Maryland, which is an upscale suburb close to Washington. When I asked why she left Bethesda, she hissed "I hate it there now" with a fervor that took me by surprise. And as we spoke, it became clear that it was precisely the "improvements" she hated: the new movie theater that shows only foreign films, the explosion of French, Turkish, and new wave restaurants, the streets choked with German cars and Lexus SUVs, the doctors and lawyers and journalists with their educated-class one-upmanship.

These new people may live in the old suburbs but they hate suburbanites. They hate sprawl, big-box stores, automobile culture. The words they use about suburbanites are: synthetic, bland, sterile, self-absorbed, disengaged. They look down on people who like suburbs. They don't like their lawn statuary, their Hallmark greeting cards, their Ethan Allen furniture, their megachurches, the seasonal banners the old residents hang out in front of their houses, their untroubled attitude toward McDonald's and Dairy Queen, their Thomas Kinkade fantasy paintings. And all the original suburbanites who were peacefully enjoying their suburb until the anti-suburban suburbanites moved in notice the condescension, and they do what Americans have always done when faced with disapproval, anxiety, and potential conflict. They move away. The pincer movements get them: the rich and the poor, the commutes and the mortgages, the prices and the alienation. And pretty soon it's Henderson, Nevada, here we come.

George Santayana once observed that Americans don't solve problems, they just leave them behind. They take advantage of all that space and move. If there's an idea they don't like, they don't bother refuting it, they just go somewhere else, and if they can't go somewhere else, they just leave it in the past, where it dies from inattention.

And so Patio Man is not inclined to stay and defend himself against the condescending French-film goers and their Volvos. He's not going to mount a political campaign to fix the educational, economic, and social woes that beset him in his old neighborhood. He won't waste his time fighting a culture war. It's not worth the trouble. He just bolts. He heads for the exurbs and the desert. He goes to the new place where the future is still open and promising. He goes to fresh ground where his dreams might more plausibly come true.

The power of this urge to leave and create new places is really awesome to behold. Migration is not an easy thing, yet every year 43 million Americans get up and move. And it sets off a chain reaction. The migrants who move into one area push out another set of people, who then migrate to another and push out another set of people, and so on and so on in one vast cycle of creative destruction. Ten years ago these Sprinkler Cities didn't really exist. Fifteen years ago the institutions that dot them hadn't been invented. There weren't book superstores or sporting goods superstores or Petsmart or Petco, and Target was just something you shot arrows at. And yet suddenly metropolises with all these new stores and institutions have materialized out of emptiness. It's as if some Zeus-like figure had appeared out of the ether and slammed down a million-square-foot mall on the desert floor, then a second later he'd slammed down a 5,000-person townhome community, then a second later an ice rink and a rec center and soccer fields and schools and community colleges. How many times in human history have 200,000-person cities just materialized almost instantaneously out of nowhere?

The people who used to live in these empty places don't like it; they've had to move further out in search of valleys still pristine. But the sprawl people just love it. They talk to you like born-again evangelists, as if their life had undergone some magical transformation when they made the big move. They talk as if they'd thrown off some set of horrendous weights, banished some class of unpleasant experiences, and magically floated up into the realm of good climate, fine people, job opportunities, and transcendent convenience. In 2001, Loudoun County did a survey of its residents. Ninety-eight percent felt safe in their neighborhoods. Ninety-three percent rated their county's quality of life excellent or good. Only a third of the county's residents, by the way, have lived there for more than 10 years.

These people are so happy because they have achieved something that human beings are actually quite good at achieving. Through all the complex diversity of society, they have managed to find people who want pretty much the same things they want.

This is not to say they want white Ozzie and Harriet nirvana. The past 40 years happened. It never occurs to them to go back before rock, rap, women working, and massive immigration. They don't mind any of these things, so long as they complement the core Sprinkler City missions of orderly living, high achievement, and the bright seeking of a better future.

Recently three teams from the Seneca Ridge Middle School in Loudoun County competed in the National Social Studies Olympiad. The fifth grade team finished fifth out of 242 teams, while the eighth grade team finished twenty-third out of 210. Here are some of the names of the students competing for Loudoun: Amy Kuo, Arshad Ali, Samanth Chao, Katie Hempenius, Ronnel Espino, Obinna Onwuka, Earnst

Ilang-Ilang, Ashley Shiraishi, and Alberto Pareja-Lecaros. At the local high school, 99 percent of seniors graduate and 87 percent go on to higher education.

When you get right down to it, Sprinkler Cities are united around five main goals: The Goal of the Together Life. When you've got your life together, you have mastered the complexities of the modern world so thoroughly that you can glide through your days without unpleasant distractions or tawdry failures. Instead, your hours are filled with self-affirming reminders of the control you have achieved over the elements. Your lawn is immaculate. Your DVD library is organized, and so is your walk-in closet. Your car is clean and vacuumed, your frequently dialed numbers are programmed into your cell phone, your telephone plan is suited to your needs, and your various gizmos interface without conflict. Your wife is effortlessly slender, your kids are unnaturally bright, your job is rewarding, your promotions are inevitable, and you look great in casual slacks.

You can thus spend your days in perfect equanimity, the Sprinkler City ideal. You radiate confidence, like a professional golfer striding up the 18th fairway after a particularly masterful round. Compared with you, Dick Cheney looks like a disorganized hothead. George W. Bush looks like a self-lacerating neurotic. Professionally, socially, parentally, you have your life together. You may not be the most intellectual or philosophical person on the planet, but you are honest and straightforward. You may not be flamboyant, but you are friendly, good-hearted, and considerate. You have achieved the level of calm mastery of life that is the personality equivalent of the clean and fresh suburban landscape.

The Goal of Technological Heroism. They may not be stereotypical rebels, and nobody would call them avant-garde, but in one respect many Sprinkler City dwellers have the souls of revolutionaries. When Patio Man gets out of his Yukon, lowers his employee-badge necklace around his neck, and walks into his generic office building, he becomes a technological radical. He spends his long workdays striving to create some technological innovation, management solution, or organizing system breakthroughs that will alter the world. Maybe the company he works for has one of those indecipherable three-initial names, like DRG Technologies or SER Solutions, or maybe it's got one of those jammed together compound names that were all the rage in the 1990s until WorldCom and MicroStrategy went belly up.

Either way, Patio Man is working on, or longs to be working on, a project that is new and revolutionary. And all around him there are men and women who are actually achieving that goal, who are making that leap into the future. The biotech revolution is being conducted in bland suburban office parks by seemingly unremarkable polo-shirt-and-chino people at firms like Celera and Human Genome Sciences. Silicon Valley is just one long string of suburban office parks jutting out from San Jose. AOL is headquartered in Loudoun County. You walk down a path in a Sprinkler City corporate center and it leads you to a company frantically chasing some market-niche innovation in robotics, agricultural engineering, microtechnology, or hardware and software applications.

There are retail-concept revolutionaries, delivery-system radicals, market-research innovators, data-collection pioneers, computer-game Rembrandts, and weapons-systems analysts. They look like bland members of some interchangeable research team, but many of them are deeply engrossed in what they consider a visionary project, which if completed will help hurtle us all further into the Knowledge Revolution, the Information Millennium, the Age of MicroTechnology, the Biotech Century, or whatever transplendent future it is you want to imagine. They have broken the monopoly that cities used to have, and they have made themselves the new centers of creativity.

The Goal of Relaxed Camaraderie. The critics of suburbia believe that single-family homeowners with their trimmed yards and matching pansies are trying to keep up with the Joneses. But like most of what the critics assert, that's completely wrong. Sprinkler City people are competitive in the marketplace and on the sports field, but they detest social competition. That's part of why these people left inner-ring suburbs in the first place.

They are not emulating the rich; they are happy to blend in with each other. One of the comforts of these places is that almost nobody is far above you socially and almost nobody is far below. You're all just swimming in a pond of understated success.

So manners are almost aggressively relaxed. Everybody strives overtime to not put on airs or create friction. In style, demeanor, and mood, people reveal the language and values they have in common. They are good team members and demonstrate from the first meeting that they are team-able. You could go your entire life, from home to church to work to school, wearing nothing but Lands' End—comfortable, conservative, non-threatening activewear for people with a special fondness for navy blue. The dominant conversational tone is upbeat and friendly, like banter between Katie Couric and Matt Lauer on the "Today" show. The prevailing style of humor is ironic but not biting and owes a lot to ESPN's "SportsCenter."

The Goal of the Active Leisure Lifestyle. Your self-esteem is based on your success at work, but since half the time it's hard to explain to people what the hell it is you do, your public identity is defined by your leisure activities. You are the soccer family, engrossed by the politics and melodrama of your local league, or you are the T-ball coach and spend your barbecue conversations comparing notes on new $200 titanium bat designs (there's a new bat called The Power Elite—even C. Wright Mills has been domesticated for the Little League set). You are Scuba Woman and you converse about various cruises you have taken. You are Mountain Bike Man and you make vague references to your high altitude injuries and spills. Or you are a golfer, in which case nobody even thinks of engaging you in conversation on any topic other than golf.

Religion is too hot a subject and politics is irrelevant, so if you are not discussing transportation issues—how to get from here to there, whether the new highway exit is good or bad—you are probably talking about sports. You're talking about your kids' ice hockey leagues, NBA salary levels, or the competition in your over-70 softball league—the one in which everybody wears a knee brace and it takes about six minutes for a good hitter to beat out a double. Sports sets the emotional climate of your life. Sports provides the language of easy camaraderie, self-deprecating humor, and (mostly) controlled competition.

The Goal of the Traditional, but Competitive, Childhood. Most everything in Sprinkler Cities is new, but much of the newness is in the service of tradition. The families that move here are trying to give their children as clean and upright and traditional a childhood as they can imagine. They're trying to move away from parents who smoke and slap their kids, away from families where people watch daytime TV shows about transvestite betrayals and "My Daughter is a Slut" confessions, away from broken homes and, most of all, away from the company of children who are not being raised to achieve and succeed.

They are trying to move instead to a realm of clean neighborhoods, safe streets, competitive cheerleading, spirit squads, soccer tots academies, accelerated-reader programs, and adult-chaperoned drug-free/alcohol-free graduation celebrations.

For the fifth consecutive year, the Henderson, Nevada, high school Marine Corps Junior ROTC squad has won the National Male Armed Drill Team championship. The Female Unarmed Drill Team has come in first six out of the past eight years. In Loudoun County the local newspaper runs notices for various travel team tryouts. In one recent edition, I counted 55 teams announcing their tryouts, with names like The Loudoun Cyclones, the Herndon Surge, the Loudoun Volcanoes. (It's not socially acceptable to name your team after a group of people anymore, so most of the teams have nature names.) As you drive around a Sprinkler City you see SUVs everywhere with cheers scrawled in washable marker on the back windows: "Go Heat!" "#24 Kelly Jones!" "Regional Champs!"

The kids spend their days being chaperoned from one adult-supervised activity to another, and from one achievement activity to the next. They are well tested, well trophied, and well appreciated. They are not only carefully reared and nurtured, they are launched into a life of high expectations and presumed accomplishment.

The dominant ideology of Sprinkler Cities is a sort of utopian conservatism. On the one hand, the people who live here have made a startling leap into the unknown. They have, in great numbers and with great speed, moved from their old homes in California, Florida, Illinois, and elsewhere, to these brand new places that didn't really exist 10 years ago. These places have no pasts, no precedents, no settled institutions, very few longstanding groups you can join and settle into.

Their inhabitants have moved to towns where they have no family connections, no ethnic enclaves, and no friends. They are using their imaginations to draw pictures for themselves of what their lives will be like. They are imagining their golf club buddies even though the course they are moving near is only just being carved out of the desert. They are imagining their successful children's graduation from high school, even though the ground around the new school building is still rutted with the tracks of construction equipment. They are imagining outings with friends at restaurants that are now only investor grass, waiting to be built.

And when they do join groups, often the groups turn out to be still in the process of building themselves. The migrants join congregations that meet in school basements while raising the money to construct churches. They go to office parks at biotech companies that are still waiting to put a product on the market. They may vote, or episodically pay attention to national politics, but they don't get drawn into strong local party organizations because the local organizations haven't been built.

But the odd thing is that all this imaginative daring, these leaps into the future, are all in the service of an extremely conservative ideal. You get the impression that these people have fled their crowded and stratified old suburbs because they really want to live in Mayberry. They have this image of what home should be, a historical myth or memory, and they are going to build it, even if it means constructing an old fashioned place out of modern materials. It's going to be morally upstanding. It's going to be relaxed and neighborly. It's going to be neat and orderly. Sprinkler City people seem to have almost a moral revulsion at disorder or anything that threatens to bring chaos, including out-of-control immigration and terrorist attacks. They don't think about the war on terror much, let alone some alleged invasion of Iraq, but if it could be shown that Saddam Hussein presented a threat to the good order of the American homeland, then these people would support his ouster with a fervor that would take your breath away. "They have strong emotions when dealing with security," says Tom Tancredo, a congressman from suburban Denver. "Border security, the security of their families, the security of their neighborhoods."

Of course, from the moment they move in, they begin soiling their own nest. They move in order to get away from crowding, but as they and the tens of thousands like them move in, they bring crowding with them. They move to get away from stratification, snobbery, and inequality, but as the new towns grow they get more stratified. In Henderson, the $200,000 ranch homes are now being supplemented by gated $500,000-a-home golf communities. People move for stability and old fashioned values, but they are unwilling to accept limits to opportunity. They are achievement oriented. They are inherently dynamic.

For a time they do a dance about preserving the places they are changing by their presence. As soon as people move into a Sprinkler City, they start lobbying to control further growth. As Tancredo says, they have absolutely no shame about it. They want more roads built, but fewer houses. They want to freeze the peaceful hominess of the town that was growing when they moved there five minutes before.

But soon, one senses, they will get the urge to move again. The Hendersons and the Douglas Counties will be tomorrow what the Newport Beaches and the Los Altoses and the White Plainses are today, places where Patio Man no longer feels quite at home. And the suburban middle-class folks in these places will again strike out as the avant-garde toward new places, with new sorts of stores and a new vision of the innocent hometown.

So the dynamism and volatility will continue—always moving aggressively toward a daring future that looks like an imagined picture of the wholesome past, striving and charging toward that dream of the peaceful patio, the happy kids, the slender friends, and, towering over it all, the massive barbecue grill.

Discussion Questions

1. What is the "big" purchase that Patio Man makes at the local mega hardware complex? How does he get it home and where does he put it?
2. Describe Patio Man, his family, and what each of them does and wears.
3. In terms of national political parties and their values, why does Sprinkler City differ so much from the inner suburbs?
4. Describe a typical Sprinkler City.
5. Why do many people want to leave the suburbs to move to a Sprinkler City?
6. What is happening to the older suburbs as more of their residents leave for Sprinkler Cities?
7. What are the five goals that characterize Sprinkler Cities?
8. When people move to a Sprinkler City, what is usually the first thing they want to control?
9. Do you think this is an accurate portrayal of modern life in the United States? Would you want someone from another country and culture to think that all Americans believe and behave like Patio Man?
10. How do the lives of children in Sprinkler Cities differ from the lives of children in inner-city ghettos?

Additional Resources

For Internet links related to this chapter, please visit our website at www.mhhe.com/dettwyler

ABU-LUGHOD, JANET L. *Before European Hegemony: The World System A.D. 1250–1350.* New York: Oxford University Press, 1991.

BENTLEY, JERRY H. *Old World Encounters: Cross-Cultural Contacts and Exchanges in Pre-Modern Times.* New York: Oxford University Press, 1993.

BROOKS, DAVID. *Bobos In Paradise: The New Upper Class and How They Got There.* New York: Touchstone Books, 2001.

CHA, DIA. *Hmong American Concepts of Health.* New York: Routledge, 2003.

CRONK, LEE, and BETH LEECH. "Where's Koisa?" *The World & I,* January 1993, pp. 58–64.

CULHANE-PERA, KATHLEEN A., PHUA XIONG, and MARY M. SOLBERG, eds. *Healing by Heart: Clinical and Ethical Case Stories of Hmong Families and Western Providers.* Nashville, TN: Vanderbilt University Press, 2003.

FADERMAN, LILLIAN. *I Begin My Life All Over: The Hmong and the American Immigrant Experience.* Boston, MA: Beacon Press, 1999.

FADIMAN, ANNE. *The Spirit Catches You and You Fall Down: A Hmong Child, Her American Doctors, and the Collision of Two Cultures.* New York: Farrar, Straus & Giroux, 1997.

GREAVES, TOM. *Endangered Peoples of North America: Struggles to Survive and Thrive.* Westport, CT: Greenwood Publishing Group, 2002.

MOUA, MAI NENG, ed. *Bamboo Among the Oaks: Contemporary Writing by Hmong Americans.* St. Paul, MN: Minnesota Historical Press, 2002.

NUTTALL, MARK. *Protecting the Arctic: Indigenous Peoples and Cultural Survival.* New York: Routledge, 1998.

QUINCY, KEITH. *Hmong: History of a People.* 2nd ed. Spokane, WA: Eastern Washington University Press, 1997.

STEVENS, STAN, ed. *Conservation Through Cultural Survival: Indigenous Peoples and Protected Areas.* Washington, DC: Island Press, 1997.

Credits